# *Rick Steves*®

# AMSTERDAM
## & THE NETHERLANDS

Rick Steves & Gene Openshaw

# The Dutch Made Holland

The Dutch call their country *Nederland,* meaning "lowland." The Netherlands occupies the delta near the mouth of three of Europe's large rivers, including the Rhine. In medieval times, inhabitants built a system of earthen dikes to protect their land from flooding caused by tides and storm surges. The story of the little Dutch boy who saves the country—by sticking his finger in a leaking dike—summed up the country's precarious situation. (Many Americans know this story from the popular 19th-century novel *Hans Brinker or the Silver Skates*—but few Dutch people have ever heard of it.)

In 1953, severe floods breached the old dikes, killing 1,800 and requiring a major overhaul of the system. Today's 350 miles of dikes and levees are high-tech, with electronic sensors to monitor water levels. Dutch experts traveled to Louisiana after Hurricane Katrina to share their expertise with US officials after levee failure caused massive flooding. And after Hurricane Sandy, American hydrology experts began looking to the Netherlands for models of how to protect huge areas from flooding.

Much of the land of the Netherlands was reclaimed from the sea, rivers, and lakes, thanks to the country's iconic windmills. After diking off large tracts of land below sea level, the Dutch used windmills to harness wind energy to lift the water up out of the enclosed area, divert it into canals, and drain the land. They cultivated hardy plants that removed salt from the soil, slowly turning marshy estuaries into fertile farmland. The windmills later served a second purpose for farmers by turning stone wheels to grind their grain. ▶▶▶

*The powerful dikes, which can look as simple as a raised road, keep the land from being reclaimed by the sea. The story of the heroic Dutch boy who plugged a dike to save his country was invented in an 1865 book by the American author Mary Mapes Dodge.*

▶▶▶ The trifecta of Dutch reclamation technology is dikes, windmills...and canals. Picturesque waterways, big and small, course through both cities and the countryside. While we use the all-purpose term "canal," the Dutch recognize several variations, which can be helpful as you navigate place names: *singel* is a former moat, *gracht* is a dug-out waterway, *kanal* is for shipping, and *sloot* is a drainage canal (usually in the countryside).

The country's last major reclamation project created a new province, Flevoland, that was drained, dried, and populated within the last 100 years (see the Flevoland chapter for more info).

Today, Dutch reclamation projects are essentially finished. As the world's climate changes and sea levels rise, the Dutch are now focusing more on resources to upgrade their dikes and bulk up their beaches to hold back the sea. They also continue to innovate, building floatable homes and greenhouses (which rise with the tides) and relocating dikes farther back from the rivers to create wider floodplains.

All this technological tinkering with nature—past and present—has brought about a popular local saying: "God made the Earth, but the Dutch made Holland." ▪

*Spinning windmills (like this one at Enkhuizen) drain marshy lowlands. Boats dredge up silt to maintain the shoreline. The land is so flat, the Dutch like to joke that if you stand on a chair, you can see the whole country.*

first…then everyone else. Watch very carefully for bikes before crossing (or even stepping into) the street.

The Dutch generally speak English, pride themselves on their frankness, and like to split the bill. Thriftiness, efficiency, and a dislike of wastefulness are longstanding Dutch traits. Traditionally, Dutch cities have been open-minded, loose, and liberal (to attract sailors in the days of Henry Hudson). And today, Amsterdam is a capital of progressive policies—a city where they believe that society has to make a choice: tolerate alternative lifestyles or build more prisons. Coffeeshops sell marijuana (and sometimes cappuccinos), and prostitutes pose in government-licensed windows. The city is surprisingly diverse, housing many new immigrants—a trend that, unfortunately, has resulted in tension in recent years. The Netherlands in general, and Amsterdam in particular, is gay-friendly. Some of the biggest festivals and parades on the social calendar celebrate the LGBTQ community.

Although it expresses itself in a sometimes-jarring acceptance of drugs and sex, the Dutch passion for tolerance has deep historical roots: For generations, this part of Europe was a particularly fierce battleground between the Roman Catholic Church (backed primarily by Spain) and Reformation-era Protestants (Dutch nationalists). The Eighty Years' War and other conflicts flamed religious intolerance. But afterward, the reaction against the Spanish Inquisition and the wealth of the

*Prostitution (advertised in Amsterdam's Red Light District) and marijuana (sold in coffeeshops) are legal and regulated.*

*French fries (friets) are served with mayonnaise. The Begijnhof's courtyard is a peaceful oasis in downtown Amsterdam.*

golden age brought a new era of acceptance. Today—especially after the Nazi occupation's persecution of Jews and other minorities—the Dutch are determined to live and let live.

Another facet of this philosophy is Dutch humility. A popular saying here is, "The tree that grows the tallest gets blown by the strongest wind." While the Dutch have an affinity for Americans, they don't always quite know how to take our proud individualism.

This book presents the best of Amsterdam and the Netherlands—its great cities, small towns, fine food, rich history, and sensuous art. You'll experience both the quaintness of the countryside as well as the modern vibrancy of the Netherlands' forward-thinking urban centers.

Along the way, you'll meet intriguing people who will show you how to swallow a pickled herring, paddle a canoe through polder waterways, or slice off a hunk of cheese from a giant wheel. Rattling your bike over cobbles, past a line of gabled houses reflected in a mirror-smooth canal...it's just like you imagined it. It's as if the tourist clichés of the region—whirring windmills, Dutch Masters, canal rides, dike hikes, and tulips—all come to life in the Netherlands.

# The Netherlands' Top Destinations

*Wauw!* There's so much to see in the Netherlands. To help you decide where and how to spend your time, this overview categorizes the country's top destinations into home-base cities and day trips. I've ranked each and suggested a minimum amount of time to allow. Much of the country is an easy day trip from whichever home base you choose.

## BEST HOME BASES

If you intend to stay in one of these three cities for your whole trip, be sure to visit the other two on day trips.

### ▲▲▲Amsterdam (allow 2-4 days)

The dynamic capital, with golden age architecture lining shimmering canals, boasts magnificent museums, from the venerable Rijksmuseum (with Dutch Masters) to Van Gogh's colorful collection to the thought-provoking Anne Frank House. The city has a lively food scene, diverse nightlife, marijuana-selling "coffeshops," and an eye-opening Red Light District, along with bustling streets and markets...and bikes everywhere.

### ▲▲Haarlem (1 day)

The cozy town, with its grand market square, huge church, and stately architecture, was home to artist Frans Hals and author Corrie ten Boom (who hid Jews from the Nazis, as described in *The Hiding Place*). Just 20 minutes from Amsterdam and 10 minutes from the beach at Zandvoort, Haarlem is conveniently central yet invitingly small.

### ▲▲Delft (1 day)

The picturesque, canal-laced hometown of Vermeer (hosting a fine Vermeer Center but not his art) and Delft Blue porcelain (with a tourable factory) has a tranquil vibe. Delft makes a mellow home base for day-tripping to nearby cities: While one hour by train from Amsterdam, Delft is only 15-30 minutes from Leiden (a delightful university town), The Hague (which does have Vermeers), and Rotterdam (with avant-garde architecture).

*Photo fun inside (opposite) and outside the Rijksmuseum; Zandvoort's wide beach; bird's-eye view of Delft; Haarlem's sunny square*

## BEST DAY TRIPS

# North of Amsterdam

### ▲Alkmaar and Zaanse Schans (half-day each)

Little Alkmaar is hugely popular on Friday mornings for its cheese market, when big orange rounds of cheese are sampled and sold with flair (late March through Sept). Nearby Zaanse Schans is a touristy, re-created 17th-century Dutch town, with windmills and old-time shops. You can combine both destinations on a day trip, best on Fridays.

### ▲▲Edam, Volendam, and Marken (1 day)

The postcard-perfect region of Waterland harbors the adorable cheesemaking village of Edam, the tourist depot of Volendam (with a promenade and quirky museum), and the fascinating former fishing hamlet of Marken. You can see all three in a day, but with less time, focus on little Edam (market day is Wednesday, but it's cute anytime).

### ▲Hoorn and Enkhuizen (1 day)

This time-warp duo—the golden age merchant's town of Hoorn and the charming village of Enkhuizen, with an open-air museum on Zuiderzee culture—makes a good day trip. Take public transit or the slower, scenic Historic Triangle loop (including rides on a boat, steam train, and modern train).

### ▲Flevoland (1 day, worthwhile only for drivers)

The country's newest province, reclaimed from the sea, looks modern and plain except for Schokland. This former fishing village is now surrounded by dry land, with a museum describing the reclamation project, the region's history, and the villagers' lifestyle.

*Cheese for sale (opposite); re-created village at Zaanse Schans; barging past Edam; artisans at Enkhuizen's open-air museum; a café in Volendam*

## South of Amsterdam

### ▲Keukenhof and Aalsmeer (half-day each)

Holland has two flower-power destinations. The best is Keukenhof—a huge, beautifully landscaped garden park, blooming with millions of colorful tulips (open late March through late May). Near the airport, Aalsmeer Flower Auction fills a giant warehouse with fresh flowers, allowing you to observe the business behind the beauty year-round.

### ▲▲Leiden (half-day)

The historic, charming university town was Rembrandt's hometown before he moved to Amsterdam and the Pilgrims' last stop before they sailed to Plymouth Rock.

### ▲The Hague (half-day to 1 day)

The governmental town has an excellent art museum (Mauritshuis) showcasing the Dutch golden age, a Peace Palace with international courts, and the nearby beach resort of Scheveningen, with its amusement pier, boardwalk, and promenade.

### ▲▲Rotterdam (half-day to 1 day)

Europe's busiest port, Rotterdam, has soaring skyscrapers, pedestrian malls, a futuristic market hall, and a 21st-century buzz. Built new after being flattened by WWII bombs, this modern city is the opposite of quaint, offering a well-rounded look at the Netherlands today.

*Old-time bridge at Leiden; bicycle-truck at Arnhem's open-air museum; cube houses in Rotterdam*

## East of Amsterdam

### ▲Utrecht (half-day)

The bustling university city has the country's largest old town, best railway museum, and a fun musical museum, plus a climbable church tower for a view of it all. Utrecht can be done as a day trip, or it's an easy stop between Amsterdam and Arnhem.

### ▲▲Museums near Arnhem (1 day)

Near Arnhem are two Dutch treats—the worthwhile Netherlands Open-Air Museum and the excellent Kröller-Müller Museum, with a world-class collection of Van Gogh masterpieces, set in the middle of a lovely forested park. To avoid rushing your visit, consider overnighting in Otterlo, near the park.

*Balancing act at the Kröller–Müller Museum's sculpture park*

# Planning Your Trip

To plan your trip, you'll need to design your itinerary—choosing where and when to go, how you'll travel, and how many days to spend at each destination. For my best general advice on sightseeing, accommodations, restaurants, and more, see the Practicalities chapter.

## DESIGNING AN ITINERARY

As you read this book and learn your options...

### Choose your top destinations.

My recommended itinerary (on pages 20-21) gives you an idea of how much you can reasonably see in 12 days, but you can adapt it to fit your own interests and time frame.

Amsterdam is on everyone's list for good reason: museums, eclectic food, golden age architecture, street life, canal boats, markets, and entertainment. You could easily spend a week here. And if you like big cities, you'll enjoy Rotterdam and The Hague, too. Hobbits seek out quaint villages, such as Edam or Hoorn.

Historians focus on Amsterdam (Dutch golden age, Dutch Resistance during World War II, and more) and Leiden (pilgrim lore). To visit the Dutch past, head for one of the Netherlands' open-air museums: Zaanse Schans (touristy and closest to Amsterdam), the less touristy Enkhuizen, and the farthest but most authentic, near Arnhem.

Art lovers are drawn to Amsterdam and The Hague. For modern art (beyond Amsterdam's Van Gogh Museum), the country's best is the Stedelijk in Amsterdam, followed closely by the impressive Kröller-Müller Museum, set in a forest near Arnhem, where cyclists pedal free bikes through the woods.

If you like colorful markets, the Dutch won't disappoint, whether it's cheese (Alkmaar), flowers (Keukenhof and more), food and clothing (Haarlem), or everything (Amsterdam's street markets).

Photographers are happy wherever they go.

## Decide when to go.

Although Amsterdam can be plagued by crowds in summer (June-Aug), it's a great time to visit, given the long days, lively festivals, and sunny weather (rarely too hot for comfort, extremely long hours of daylight).

Amsterdam can also be busy—and hotel prices higher—in late March, April, and May, when the tulip fields are flowering in full glory. Fall comes with lighter crowds, though seasonal

*Golden age art by Frans Hals (opposite); costumed street performer; modern art at the Stedelijk; Rick in a windmill*

## 12 Days in the Netherlands

For an in-depth Netherlands experience, overnight in several places and use public transit. Start in small-town Haarlem (an ideal jet-lag pillow) and save big-city Amsterdam for your trip finale.

| Day | Plan | Sleep |
|---|---|---|
| 1 | Arrive in Amsterdam, head to Haarlem | Haarlem |
| 2 | Sightsee Haarlem | Haarlem |
| 3 | Day trip (e.g., Keukenhof in spring; Alkmaar if Friday; Aalsmeer, Leiden, or Zandvoort) | Haarlem |
| 4 | Head to Delft and sightsee | Delft |
| 5 | Day-trip to Rotterdam and/or The Hague (or add another day for more time in both) | Delft |
| 6 | From Delft, head to Arnhem, visit the Netherlands Open-Air Museum, end in Otterlo | Otterlo |
| 7 | Visit the Kröller-Müller Museum (near Arnhem), head to Utrecht to sightsee, end in Amsterdam | Amsterdam |
| 8 | Sightsee Amsterdam | Amsterdam |
| 9 | Amsterdam | Amsterdam |
| 10 | Amsterdam | Amsterdam |
| 11 | Day trip (e.g., Edam/Volendam/Marken) | Amsterdam |
| 12 | Day trip (Hoorn and Enkhuizen) | Amsterdam |
| 13 | Fly home or enjoy more of Europe | |

**With less time:** Focus on Amsterdam, Delft, and Haarlem (skipping Arnhem/Otterlo), plus another destination that interests you most. For simplicity, stay in one home base.

conferences can drive up prices in September. Both spring and fall have generally mild weather.

Winter (from late October through mid-March) is cold and wet. It's fine for visiting Amsterdam, but smaller towns and countryside sights feel dreary and lifeless. Some sights close for lunch, tourist information offices keep shorter hours, and some tourist activities vanish altogether.

For weather specifics, see the climate chart in the appendix.

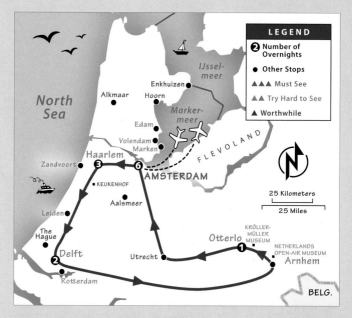

## Home Bases and Day Trips

If you'll be staying in two or three home bases, here are the most time-efficient day trips:

**From Amsterdam:** Edam/Volendam/Marken, Hoorn/Enkhuizen, Zaanse Schans, Utrecht, and museums near Arnhem

**From Haarlem:** Delft, Keukenhof, Leiden, and Zandvoort

**Similarly efficient from Amsterdam or Haarlem:** Alkmaar, Aalsmeer, Leiden, The Hague, and Rotterdam

**From Delft:** Leiden, Rotterdam, and The Hague

## Connect the dots.

Link your destinations into a logical route. Decide if you'll travel by car or public transportation, or a combination. Trains run at least hourly between major cities and are the easiest way to reach nearly any Dutch destination. A few destinations are best by bus. A car is useless in cities but essential to visit Flevoland and can be an efficient way to visit the Kröller-Müller Museum near Arnhem.

Begin your search for transatlantic flights (likely to Amsterdam) at Kayak.com. If you stick to the Netherlands, you're never farther than two hours from Amsterdam's Schiphol Airport.

For travel beyond the Netherlands, check train schedules at Bahn.com and budget flights within Europe at Skyscanner. com.

## Write out a day-by-day itinerary.

Figure out how many destinations you can comfortably fit in your time frame. Don't overdo it—few travelers wish they'd hurried more. Allow enough time per stop (see estimates in "The Netherlands' Top Destinations," earlier).

Choose a home base (or two or three): Amsterdam is liveliest and noisiest. Haarlem is small-town manageable, though noisy on weekends. Delft is the most tranquil but the least central.

The Netherlands is a day-tripper's dream. Nearly everything lies within an hour of Amsterdam, thanks to the country's excellent transportation system. That said, a few day-trip destinations are closer and quicker from Haarlem or Delft (generally saving 30-60 minutes round-trip; see suggestions on the previous page).

No matter where you're based, keep these tips in mind: When visiting market towns, it's worth braving the crowds to go on market day. Take sight closures into account; avoid visiting a town on the day your must-see sight is closed.

Check if any holidays or festivals fall during your trip— these attract crowds and can close sights (for the latest, visit www.holland.com). Note major sights where advance reservations are required, and consider whether you'll want to buy a museum pass.

Give yourself some slack. Every trip, and every traveler, needs downtime for doing laundry, picnic shopping, people-watching, and so on. Pace yourself. Assume you will return.

*Alkmaar's photogenic cheese market on Friday; Amsterdam's easy-to-navigate Schiphol Airport; Arnhem's futuristic train station; breakfast with friendly service*

*Amsterdam's Anne Frank House; herring with pickles; boat tour of the wetlands; Rotterdam's modern harbor*

## Trip Costs Per Person

Run a reality check on your dream trip. You'll have major transportation costs in addition to daily expenses.

**Flight:** A round-trip flight from the US to Amsterdam costs about $900-1,500, depending on where you fly from and when.

**Public Transportation:** For a 12-day trip, figure on spending about $150 for trams, buses, and trains.

**Car Rental:** Allow roughly $350-500 per week (booked well in advance), not including tolls, gas, parking, and insurance.

AVERAGE DAILY EXPENSES PER PERSON

**$200**
Applies to cities, figure on less for towns

**Lodging**
Based on two people splitting the cost of a $180 double room (includes breakfast).
$90

**Meals**
$20 for lunch and $40 for dinner
$60

**City Transit**
Trams and buses (or get a transit pass)
$10

**Sights and Entertainment**
This daily average works for most people.
$40

## Budget Tips

To cut your daily expenses, take advantage of the deals you'll find throughout the Netherlands and mentioned in this book.

If you'll use public transit frequently, a transit pass can be more economical than buying single-ride tickets.

Avid sightseers may save money by buying a sightseeing pass. If you don't get a pass, visit only the sights you most want to see and seek out free sights and experiences (people-watching counts).

Some businesses—especially hotels and walking tour companies—offer discounts to my readers (look for the RS% symbol in this book).

Reserve your rooms directly with the hotel or B&B. Some places offer a discount if you pay in cash and/or stay four ▶▶▶

## Rick Steves Amsterdam & the Netherlands

▶▶▶ or more nights (check online or ask). Rooms can cost less outside of spring and summer. And even seniors can sleep cheaply in hostels (most have private rooms) for about $40 per person. Or check Airbnb-type sites for deals.

It's no hardship to eat inexpensively in the Netherlands. You can get tasty, affordable meals at cafés, cafeterias, bars, food stands, delis, and bakeries (which often sell sandwiches). Cultivate the art of picnicking in atmospheric settings.

When you splurge, choose an experience you'll always remember, such as a memorable canalside meal, a food tour, or a guided canoe trip. Minimize souvenir shopping; focus instead on collecting wonderful memories. ▪

*Our Lord in the Attic's hidden Catholic church; cyclists in Amsterdam (where bikes often outnumber cars); cruising the canals*

## BEFORE YOU GO

You'll have a smoother trip if you tackle a few things ahead of time. For more details on these topics, see the Practicalities chapter and RickSteves.com, which has helpful travel-tip articles and videos.

**Make sure your travel documents are valid.** If your passport is due to expire within six months of your ticketed date of return, you need to renew it. Allow six weeks or more to renew or get a passport (www.travel.state.gov). Check for current Covid entry requirements, such as proof of vaccination or a negative Covid-19 test result.

**Arrange your transportation.** Book your international flights. Overall, Kayak.com is the best place to start searching for flights. Figure out your transportation options in the Netherlands: For most people, it makes sense to travel by train and get a transit pass that includes trains.

If traveling beyond the Netherlands, consider buying train tickets (often discounted if purchased in advance), getting a rail pass (normally must be purchased outside Europe), renting a car, or booking cheap European flights. (You can wing the car rental or European flights once you're in Europe, but it may cost more.)

**Book rooms well in advance,** especially if your trip falls during the peak season (summer) or any major holidays or festivals.

**Reserve ahead for key sights and meals.** At some Amsterdam sights—the Rijksmuseum, Van Gogh Museum, and Anne Frank House—advance reservations are required (even with a sightseeing pass). Because tickets often sell out for the Anne Frank House, buy them a month before your visit (when tickets go on sale). It's also smart to reserve ahead for fine dining restaurants—my favorites book up.

**Consider travel insurance.** Compare the cost of insurance to the cost of your potential loss. Check whether your existing insurance (health, homeowners, or renters) covers you and your possessions overseas.

**Call your bank.** Alert your bank that you'll be using your debit and credit cards in Europe. Ask about transaction fees, and, if you don't already have one, get a "contactless" credit card (request your card PIN too). You don't need to bring euros for your trip; you can withdraw euros from cash machines in Europe.

**Use your smartphone smartly.** Sign up for an international service plan to reduce your costs, or rely on Wi-Fi in Europe instead. Download any apps you'll want on the road, such as maps, translators, transit schedules, and Rick Steves Audio Europe (see sidebar).

**Pack light.** You'll walk with your luggage more than you think. I travel for weeks with a single carry-on bag and a day pack. Use the packing checklist in the appendix as a guide.

## Rick's Free Video Clips and Audio Tours

Travel smarter with these free, fun resources:

**Rick Steves Classroom Europe,** a powerful tool for teachers, is also useful for travelers. This video library contains about 500 short clips excerpted from my public television series. Enjoy these videos as you sort through options for your trip and  to better understand what you'll see in Europe. Check it out at Classroom.RickSteves.com (just enter a topic to find everything I've filmed on a subject).

**Rick Steves Audio Europe,** a free app, makes it easy to download my audio tours and listen to them offline as you travel. For this book (look for the 🎧), these audio tours include my Amsterdam  City Walk, Jordaan Walk, and Red Light District Walk. The app also offers interviews (organized by country) from my public radio show with experts from Europe and around the globe. Find it in your app store or at RickSteves.com/AudioEurope.

# Travel Smart

If you have a positive attitude, equip yourself with good information (this book), and expect to travel smart, you will.

**Read—and reread—this book.** To have an "A" trip, be an "A" student. Note opening hours of sights, closed days, crowd-beating tips, and whether reservations are required or advisable. Check the latest at RickSteves.com/update.

**Be your own tour guide.** As you travel, get up-to-date info on sights, reserve tickets and tours, reconfirm hotels and travel arrangements, and check transit connections. Visit local tourist information offices (TIs). Upon arrival in a new town, lay the groundwork for a smooth departure; confirm the train, bus, or road you'll take when you leave.

**Outsmart thieves.** Pickpockets abound in crowded places where tourists congregate. Treat commotions as smokescreens

## Tulip Mania

A Dutch icon since the 17th century, the colorful flowers are actually native to central Asia ("tulip" comes from a Turkish word for "turban"). When the Holy Roman Emperor's ambassador to Constantinople first sent some bulbs westward in the mid-1500s, a few eventually wound up in the hands of a Dutch botanist—and thus began one of the oddest chapters in the Netherlands' history.

The region's harsh conditions turned out to be ideal for the hardy bulbs, which also benefited from good timing: They arrived in the Netherlands in the middle of the Dutch golden age, delighting a relatively affluent populace who were fond of beauty and able to pay for it.

Within a generation the popularity of these then-exotic flowers—and for a few rare species in particular—grew from a trendy fad into an all-out frenzy. Prices shot skyward: Forty bulbs could fetch up to 100,000 florins (about $1.7 million

*Keukenhof's gardens bloom and are open only in spring, while Aalsmeer's flower auction runs year-round.*

in today's dollars); in the context of the times, an average laborer made around 150 florins a year. The most treasured variety was the Semper Augustus, with its distinctive red-and-white petals—just one bulb sold for 12 acres of land.

"Tulip mania" reached a fever pitch in late 1636, and for the next few months, frantic trading consumed the Dutch. Production of other goods declined as people dropped everything to get rich on the tulip exchange. Soon, instead of buying and selling actual bulbs, people began trading promissory vouchers—by that time, it wasn't really the flowers everyone was after, but the opportunity to resell them at a higher price. The number of potential buyers seemed endless...until it wasn't. In February 1637, one of history's most famous speculative bubbles burst, leaving many tulip investors with empty contracts or bulbs worth only a tiny fraction of what they'd cost. Investors were ruined, and the economic fallout helped contribute to the decline of the Dutch golden age. But the demand for tulips never died out—a love of the flowers had been firmly planted in the Dutch psyche, and they continue to be an integral part of the culture as well as a major export. ◼

for theft. Keep your cash, credit cards, and passport secure in a money belt tucked under your clothes; carry only a day's spending money in your front pocket or wallet. Don't set valuable items down on counters or café tabletops, where they can be quickly stolen or easily forgotten.

**Minimize potential loss.** Keep expensive gear to a minimum. Bring copies or take photos of important documents (passport and cards) to aid in replacement if they're lost or stolen. Back up photos and files frequently.

**Guard your time and energy.** Taking a tram across Amsterdam can be a good value if it saves you an exhausting walk. To avoid long lines, follow my crowd-beating tips, such as making advance reservations, or sightseeing early or late.

**Be flexible.** Even if you have a well-planned itinerary,

*Amsterdam lights up at night. The first-ever Dutch coffeeshop—the Bulldog—has sold marijuana since 1974 and is now the flagship branch of the high-profile chain.*

expect changes, strikes, closures, sore feet, bad weather, and so on. Your Plan B could turn out to be even better.

**Attempt the language.** Nearly all Dutch people speak English, but if you learn some Dutch, even just a few pleasantries, you'll get more smiles and make more friends. Apps such as Google Translate work for on-the-go translation help, but you can get a head start by practicing the survival phrases near the end of this book.

**Connect with the culture.** Interacting with locals carbonates your experience. Enjoy the friendliness of the Dutch people. Ask questions; most locals are happy to point you in their idea of the right direction. Set up your own quest for the best herring, coziest pub, tastiest *stroopwafel*, or the perfect "It's so Dutch!" sight. When an opportunity pops up, make it a habit to say "yes."

Your next stop... the Netherlands!

# AMSTERDAM

# ORIENTATION TO AMSTERDAM

If you fly a drone over Amsterdam, it still looks much like it did in the 1600s—the Dutch golden age—when it was the world's richest city, an international sea-trading port, and the cradle of capitalism. Wealthy, democratic burghers built a city upon millions of pilings, creating a wonderland of canals lined with trees and townhouses topped with fancy gables. Immigrants, Jews, outcasts, and political rebels were drawn here by its tolerant atmosphere, while painters such as young Rembrandt captured that atmosphere on canvas.

But, back on the ground, of course the city today is a world apart. Today's Amsterdam is a progressive place of 820,000 people and almost as many bikes. It's a city of good living, cozy cafés, great art, street-corner jazz, stately history, and a spirit of live and let live.

Amsterdam also offers the Netherlands' best people-watching. The Dutch are unique, and observing them is a sightseeing experience all in itself. They're a handsome and healthy people, and among the world's tallest. They're also open and honest—I think of them as refreshingly blunt—and they like to laugh. As connoisseurs of world culture, they appreciate Rembrandt paintings, Indonesian food, and the latest French film—but with an un-snooty, blue-jeans attitude.

Amsterdam, a bold experiment in freedom, may box your Puritan ears. For centuries, the city has taken a tolerant approach to things other places try to forbid. Traditionally, the city attracted sailors and businessmen away from home, so it was profitable to allow them to have a little fun. In the 1960s, Amsterdam became a magnet for Europe's hippies. Since then, it's become a world capital of alternative lifestyles. Stroll through any neighborhood and see things that are commonplace here but rarely found elsewhere. Prostitution is allowed in the Red Light District, while "smartshops" sell psychedelic drugs and marijuana is openly sold and smoked.

The Dutch aren't necessarily more tolerant or decadent than the rest of us—just pragmatic and looking for smart solutions.

Today, both citizens and city leaders are grappling with the right balance of freedom and sanity—to live for today yet be smart for tomorrow. And they're also struggling with too much tourism: Amsterdam attracts an amazing 20 million visitors each year. Sure, there's lots of money in being one of the world's most entertaining cities. But a little peace and quiet during the Covid pandemic made locals realize that maybe there's more to life than filling hotels.

Concerned that the flood of cheese shops, chocolate shops, and kitschy tourism are changing the city into a kind of amusement park, Amsterdam's leaders are working to protect the livability of the city for locals. A key tool is selective licensing: If a shop caters only to tourists and not locals, the city won't renew its license. If there are too many coffeeshops here and too many sex workers there, again, the city may simply allow their permits to expire. And to spread visitors around, the country's tourism board is promoting alternative Dutch destinations like Rotterdam and Delft.

I love Amsterdam even with its crowds. Approach Amsterdam as an ethnologist observing a strange culture. Raise your gaze above the commotion at street level. Walk away from the glitz. It's a place where carillons chime quaintly from spires towering above coffeeshops where young professionals go to smoke pot. Take it all in, then pause to watch the clouds blow past stately old gables—and see the golden age reflected in a quiet canal.

## AMSTERDAM: A VERBAL MAP

Amsterdam's Centraal station, on the north edge of the city, is your starting point, with the TI, bike rental, and trams branching out to all points. Damrak is the main north-south axis, connecting Centraal station with Dam Square (people-watching and hangout center) and its Royal Palace. From this main street, the city spreads out like a fan, with 90 islands, hundreds of bridges, and a series of concentric canals that were laid out in the 17th century, Holland's golden age. Amsterdam's major sights are all within walking distance of Dam Square.

To the east of Damrak is the oldest part of the city (today's Red Light District), and to the west is the newer part, where you'll find the Anne Frank House and the peaceful Jordaan neighborhood. Museums and Leidseplein nightlife cluster at the southern edge of the city center.

## AMSTERDAM BY NEIGHBORHOOD

Amsterdam can feel like a big, sprawling city, but its major sights cluster in convenient zones. Grouping your sightseeing, walks, dining, and shopping thoughtfully can save you time.

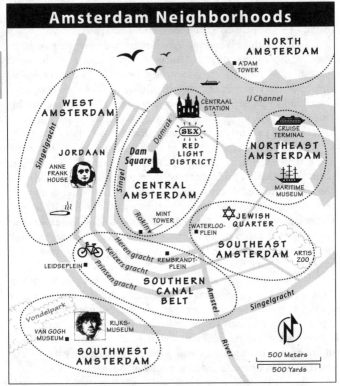

# Amsterdam Neighborhoods

**Central Amsterdam**—the historic core—runs from Centraal station south along Damrak, passing through two major city squares (Dam and Spui) and ending at the Mint Tower. The central spine of streets (Damrak, Kalverstraat, Rokin) has some of the city's main department, chain, and tourist stores. Underfoot, the new North-South Metro line serves as a kind of underground Damrak, extending many miles in both directions. Flanking Damrak to the east is the **Red Light District** and the revitalized waterfront around the train station.

**West Amsterdam** lies west of Damrak—from Dam Square to the Anne Frank House. This pleasant area is famous for its four grand canals—named Singel (the original moat), Herengracht (Gentleman's Canal), Keizersgracht (Emperor's Canal), and Prinsengracht (Prince's Canal)—that circle the historic core. West Amsterdam has tree-lined canals fronted by old, gabled mansions, as well as many of my recommended accommodations and restaurants. Within West Amsterdam is the boutique shopping district known as the Nine Little Streets. Farther west is the quieter, cozier Jordaan neighborhood, which is good for a stroll, though it's mostly

## Amsterdam Landmarks

| | |
|---|---|
| **Dam** (dahm) | Amsterdam's main square |
| **Damrak** (DAHM-rock) | main street between Centraal station and Dam Square |
| **Spui** (spow, rhymes with now) | both a street and square |
| **Rokin** (roh-KEEN) | street connecting Dam Square and Spui |
| **Kalverstraat** (KAL-ver-straht) | pedestrian street |
| **Leidseplein** (LIDE-zuh-pline) | lively square |
| **Jordaan** (yor-DAHN) | neighborhood in West Amsterdam |
| **Museumplein** (moo-ZAY-oom-pline) | square with top art museums |
| **gracht** (*hroht*, pronounce *h* gutturally) | canal |
| **straat** (straht) | street |
| **plein** (pline) | public square |
| **huis** (house) | house |
| **kerk** (kerk) | church |

residential. And to the north is the old "Haarlem dike"—Haarlem-merstraat and Haarlemmerdijk—which is emerging as a trendy, youthful zone for shopping and eating.

The **Southern Canal Belt**—the next ring of canals south of the historic core—is spacious and dotted sparsely with a few intimate museums, art galleries, and antique shops along Nieuwe Spiegelstraat. Rowdy Leidseplein anchors the lower corner.

**Southwest Amsterdam** is defined by two main features: museums and a city park. The city's major art museums (Rijksmuseum, Van Gogh, and Stedelijk) and other sights cluster together on an expansive square, Museumplein. The museums are just a short walk from Vondelpark, Amsterdam's "central park." While it's less central to stay in Southwest Amsterdam, I've recommended accommodations that are a quick, convenient walk to the area's tram lines.

**Southeast Amsterdam** contains the former Jewish Quarter and the Jewish Museum. Several sights can be found around the square known as Waterlooplein (Rembrandt's House and a flea market). Additional sights are gathered in a park-dotted area called the Plantage (Dutch Resistance Museum, a theater-turned-Holocaust-memorial, a zoo, and a botanical garden). Rembrandtplein, another nightlife center, is a five-minute walk away. The short but appealing street called Staalstraat, which connects this area with Rokin in the center, is a delightful place to browse trendy shops.

**Northeast Amsterdam** has the Netherlands Maritime Museum, Amsterdam's Central Library, and a children's science museum (NEMO).

**North Amsterdam** sits across the very wide IJ (pronounced "eye") waterway. Long neglected as a sleepy residential zone, recently it has sprouted interesting restaurant and nightlife options, thanks to the construction of the EYE Filmmuseum, the A'DAM Tower, and a new North-South subway connection to the center. Bikers and pedestrians can also get here on a free public ferry from just behind Centraal station.

## PLANNING YOUR TIME

Amsterdam is worth a full day of sightseeing on even the busiest itinerary. And though the city has a couple of must-see museums, its best attraction is its own carefree ambience. The city's a joy on foot—and a breezier and faster delight by bike. For a good walking overview, lace together my three walking tours, all of which can be connected by Dam Square (available as free audio tours—see page 28). They can be done in rapid succession—Amsterdam City Walk, Red Light District Walk, and Jordaan Walk—in as little as four hours...or take your time.

Note that tickets for the Van Gogh Museum, the Rijksmuseum, and the Anne Frank House must all be reserved online in advance (see those chapters for details).

### Amsterdam in One Day

9:00   Follow my self-guided Amsterdam City Walk, which takes you from the train station to Spui, with stops at Dam Square, the peaceful Begijnhof, and the flower market. Break up the walk with a relaxing hour-long canal cruise (departs from opposite Centraal station or Damrak Pier 5).

14:00   Visit Amsterdam's two great art museums, located side by side: the Van Gogh Museum and the Rijksmuseum.

19:00   Wander the Jordaan neighborhood, enjoying dinner by a canal or on a cobbled, quiet street.

21:30   Stroll the Red Light District for some of Europe's most fascinating window-shopping.

## Amsterdam in Two or More Days

### Day 1

| | |
|---|---|
| 9:00 | Follow my self-guided Amsterdam City Walk, leading from the train station to Spui, via the quiet Begijnhof and the flower market. |
| 12:00 | Visit Amsterdam's two outstanding art museums, located next to each other: the Van Gogh Museum and the Rijksmuseum. |
| 18:00 | Dinner. |
| 20:00 | Stroll the Red Light District for some memorable window-shopping. |

### Day 2

| | |
|---|---|
| 10:00 | Start your day with a one-hour canal boat tour. |
| 11:00 | Visit the sights of your choice around Rembrandtplein (Rembrandt's House, Waterlooplein flea market, Gassan Diamonds polishing demo, Dutch Resistance Museum). |
| 17:00 | Tour the Anne Frank House. |
| 18:30 | Take my self-guided Jordaan Walk. |
| 20:00 | Dinner in the Jordaan neighborhood. |

### Day 3

Use this day to browse your choice of Amsterdam's more than 50 museums, such as Our Lord in the Attic, Royal Palace, Stedelijk, Pipe, and Houseboat (see the Sights in Amsterdam chapter for more ideas). Or visit the nearby town of Haarlem, only 20 minutes away by train.

### Day 4

Visit Delft. Or side-trip by train to an open-air museum; choose among folk museums at Enkhuizen and Zaandijk (Zaanse Schans Museum), or Arnhem's Netherlands Open-Air Museum.

### With More Time

Plenty more destinations await you in the Netherlands.

# Amsterdam Overview

## TOURIST INFORMATION

Amsterdam's TI, located on Centraal station's IJ side (follow signs for *IJ-zijde*), is called the "I Amsterdam Store"—but it's an official TI. It's generally crowded and sometimes inefficient, but staff are helpful. You can buy a good city map (skip the free version) and the *I Amsterdam* entertainment guide here (Mon-Fri 10:00-19:00, Sat-Sun 9:00-18:00, +31 20 702 6000). There's also a TI at Schiphol Airport (daily 7:00-22:00).

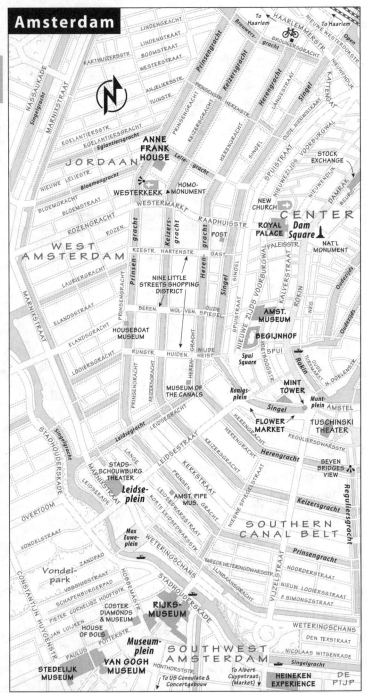

# Amsterdam

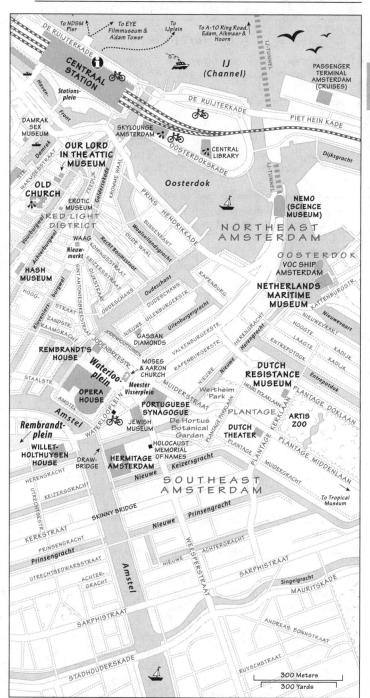

# Daily Reminder

The biggest Amsterdam sights—the Rijksmuseum, the Van Gogh Museum, and the Anne Frank House—are open daily year-round.

**Sunday:** These sights have limited, afternoon-only hours today: Our Lord in the Attic Museum (13:00-18:00) and Old Church (13:00-17:30). The Westerkerk church and the Old Church tower are closed, as is the Waterlooplein flea market.

**Monday:** The Museum of the Canals is closed. The Houseboat Museum is closed today off-season (Sept-June). Many businesses are closed Monday morning.

**Tuesday:** All recommended sights are open.

**Wednesday:** All recommended sights are open. Westerkerk hosts a free organ concert most Wednesdays at 13:00 (May-Oct).

**Thursday:** All recommended sights are open.

**Friday:** All recommended sights are open.

**Saturday:** The Portuguese Synagogue is closed today. All other recommended sights are open.

**Sights Open Late:** Most major sights close by 17:00, but the Anne Frank House is open daily until 22:00. The city's naughty sights, as you might expect, stay open later every day (Damrak Sex Museum until 18:00, Erotic and Red Light Secrets museums until 22:00 or 23:00, and Hash, Marijuana, and Hemp Museum until 22:00).

On Fridays and Saturdays year-round, the House of Bols is open until 21:00. In summer, the Van Gogh Museum may stay open late.

**Sights Open Early:** Most sights open at 10:00 or 11:00. Early birds will find the doors open at 9:00 for the Rijksmuseum, Van Gogh Museum, Anne Frank House, and diamond tours.

## ARRIVAL IN AMSTERDAM
## By Train

The portal connecting Amsterdam to the world is its aptly named Centraal station (Amsterdam Centraal). The Dutch spent a lot of money renovating this station—the north side looks more like a modern airport terminal than a century-old train station, and there are two shopping areas down the middle called IJ Passage and Amstel Passage.

Trains arrive on a level above the station. Go down the stairs or the escalator (at the "A" end of the platform) and follow signs to *Centrum* to reach the city center. (Those wanting buses and river ferries or the TI should head in the opposite direction, to the north/*Noord* exit.)

The station is fully equipped. International train-ticket offices are near the *Centrum* exits. Luggage lockers are in the east corridor, under the "B" end of the platforms (open 5:00-00:45, can fill up on busy summer weekends). You'll also find plenty of shops, eateries, and "to go" supermarkets. The Service Point store in the northern section is a handy place to buy phone accessories, mail a package, or print a ticket (daily 7:00-22:00). Platform 2 (at train level) is lined with eateries, including the tall, venerable, 1920s-style First Class Grand Café.

You can buy tickets for Amsterdam's public-transport system from machines labeled *Tram Bus Metro Tickets*. (Before buying that first tram or Metro ticket, consider your various pass options, described under "Getting Around Amsterdam," later.)

**Getting into Town:** To get from the station to your hotel, you can walk, take a tram, hop on a rental bike, or catch a taxi. For more specifics on each option, see the "Getting Around Amsterdam" section, later.

Exiting the station, you're in the heart of the city. Straight ahead is Damrak street, leading to Dam Square (a 10-minute walk away).

To the right of the station lie the postcard-perfect neighborhoods of West Amsterdam; some of my recommended hotels are within walking distance. Taxis are behind the station on the northwest side. They're pricey but can be worth it when dealing with baggage, jet lag, and trying to find your hotel.

Trams are easy (see the "Amsterdam by Tram" sidebar for a route rundown). You can buy tickets from machines inside the station (coins or credit cards). Or simply hop on, buy your ticket on board (ticket booth is usually in the back, credit cards only), and you're on your way.

## By Plane
For details on getting from Schiphol Airport to downtown Amsterdam, see the Amsterdam Connections chapter.

## HELPFUL HINTS
**Theft Alert:** Tourists are considered green and rich, and the city has more than its share of hungry thieves—especially in the train station, on trams, in and near crowded museums, at places of drunkenness, and at many hostels. Wear your money belt. If you'll be out late high or drunk, leave all valuables in your hotel. Blitzed tourists are easy targets for petty theft. Sadly, it's best to be suspect of anyone who's weirdly helpful.

**Street Smarts:** Beware of silent transportation—trams, electric mopeds, and bicycles—when walking around town. Don't walk on tram tracks or pink/maroon bicycle paths. Before you step off a sidewalk, double-check both directions to make sure all's clear.

**Sightseeing Strategies:** Amsterdam's huge tourist crowds all want to see three museums: the Anne Frank House, Van Gogh Museum, and Rijksmuseum. You must buy tickets for these sights online in advance (you'll pick an entry time for each; for details, see each museum's chapter in this book). Other than that, you should have no problems with lines at the city's other museums.

**Festivals:** Every year, **King's Day** (Koningsdag, April 27) and **Pride in Amsterdam** (celebrating equality for LGBTI folks, late July-early Aug) bring big crowds, fuller hotels, and inflated room prices. **SAIL Amsterdam,** a festival featuring tall ships and other historic boats, is held every five years (next in 2025).

**Resources for LGBTQ Travelers:** A short walk from Centraal station down Spuistraat is **GAYtic,** a TI and shop with clubwear and accessories (daily 12:00-19:00, Spuistraat 44, +31 20 330 1461, www.gaytic.nl). **Pink Point,** in a kiosk outside Westerkerk and next to the Homomonument, is less of a resource but has advice about nightlife (usually daily 10:00-18:00, +31 20 428 1070).

**Language Barrier:** It's safe to say most young or well-educated Dutch people will speak English. This is one of the easiest places in the non-English-speaking world for an English speaker. Nearly all signs and services are offered in two languages: Dutch and "non-Dutch" (i.e., English).

**Money:** Most ATMs in heavily touristed areas are operated by Travelex and other for-profit companies and should be avoided. You'll get better rates at a bank ATM; major Dutch banks include ABN AMRO, ING, and Rabobank. Yellow Geldmaat ATMs also offer good rates (to find the nearest one, go to www.geldmaat.nl and use the "Locate" feature).

**English Bookstores:** For fiction and guidebooks, try the **American Book Center** at Spui 12, right on the square (+31 20 625 5537). The huge and helpful **Scheltema,** with lots of English novels, guidebooks, and maps, is near Dam Square at Rokin 9 (+31 20 523 1481). **Waterstone's Booksellers,** a UK chain, also sells British newspapers (near Spui at 152 Kalverstraat, +31 20 638 3821).

**Maps:** Given the city's maze of streets and canals, you'll want a good city map. I like the ***Carto Studio Centrumkaart Amsterdam.*** You can download offline searchable maps from **City Maps 2Go.**

**Pharmacy:** The shop named **DA** (Dienstdoende Apotheek) sells basic toiletries and has a pharmacy counter in the back (Leidsestraat 74 near where it meets Prinsengracht, +31 20 627 5351). Near Dam Square, there's **BENU Apotheek** (Damstraat 2, +31 20 624 4331).

**Laundry:** Try **Clean Brothers Wasserette** in the Jordaan (self-service daily 8:00-20:00; drop-off available Mon-Fri 9:00-17:00, Sat until 18:00, ready in an hour, no drop-off Sun; Westerstraat 26, one block from Prinsengracht, +31 20 627 9888) or **Powders,** near Leidseplein (self-service daily 8:00-22:00; drop-off available Mon-Fri 10:00-17:00, no drop-off Sat-Sun; Kerkstraat 56, one block south of Leidsestraat, +31 6 1080 1859).

**Best Views:** Although sea-level Amsterdam is notoriously horizontal, there are a few high points where you can get the big picture. My favorite is the rooftop **SkyLounge Amsterdam,** on the 11th floor of the DoubleTree by Hilton Hotel (daily until very late, 5-minute walk east of train station; see page 218). Other good choices are from the top-floor view restaurant at the **Central Library** (Openbare Bibliotheek Amsterdam, Oosterdokskade 143), or nearby, the rooftop terrace—generally open to the public—at the **NEMO science museum.** It's pricey, but the **A'DAM Tower** has a sky deck, bar, and even a swing about 20 stories above the city (see page 80). Another option is the tower of the **Old Church** (Oude Kerk) in the Red Light District.

**Scamming Stoners:** Around town, delis and bakeries sell marijuana "space cakes" to tourists hoping to get high. But they're just CBD cakes with no psychoactive THC—and if you get high on that, it's all in your mind.

## GETTING AROUND AMSTERDAM

Amsterdam is big, and you'll find the trams handy. The longest walk a tourist would take is an hour from Centraal station to the Rijksmuseum. When you're on foot, be extremely vigilant for silent but potentially painful bikes, trams, and crotch-high bollards.

### By Tram, Bus, and Metro

Amsterdam's public-transit system (GVB) includes trams, buses, and an underground Metro. Of these, trams are most useful for most tourists. For a map of the system, see the color section at the back of this book.

**Information:** Bring your transit questions to the **OV Service and Tickets** office, a few doors to the left of the I Amsterdam store at Centraal station. Here you can use travel-planning kiosks, buy and print train tickets, and pick up a paper tram/bus/Metro/ferry

# Amsterdam by Tram

Amsterdam becomes much easier to wrap your brain around when you master the two main tram corridors—north-south and south-east. Here's a quick overview:

As if made for the sightseer, trams #2 and #12 travel **north-south,** connecting Centraal station, the Jordaan neighborhood, many of my recommended hotels, and Leidseplein. Both trams then continue beyond Leidseplein to Museumplein (the stop for the Rijksmuseum and Van Gogh Museum). The entire ride takes about 15 minutes, with trams zipping by every few minutes.

Tram #14 runs **south-east,** connecting Centraal station to Rembrandtplein, Waterlooplein, and Alexanderplein, and recommended Southeast Amsterdam sights.

To get to the **Anne Frank House** and the **Jordaan,** take tram #17 from Centraal station or the west side of Dam Square (or tram #13 from Paleisstraat) to Westermarkt, a block from the museum and the Jordaan neighborhood.

Use these trams to lace together your sightseeing—see the transportation map in the back of this book for a visual aid. Most trams pass through Dam Square. At any time you can simply hop out, cross the street, and catch a tram heading back to your starting point.

## North-South: Trams #2 and #12

Starting at the train station and heading south, here are the stops and landmarks you'll pass:

**Centraal Station:** As this is the beginning of both lines, any tram #2 or #12 that you catch here is headed in the right direction. This tram stop puts you near the Red Light District, Damrak (the beginning of my self-guided Amsterdam City Walk), and all your transportation options (trains, airport connections, city buses, other trams, Metro, bike rental, ferry across the IJ).

**Nieuwezijds Kolk:** There is nothing of interest nearby.

**Dam:** You'll roll by the back side of the towering New Church and Royal Palace (on your left). Nearby: Dam Square, Anne Frank House, and starting point for two of my self-guided walks—Jordaan and Red Light District.

**Spui:** Pronounced spow (rhymes with cow), this word means "spew," where water was once pushed away over a dike. Nearby:

Amsterdam Museum, Begijnhof, and the Nine Little Streets shopping zone.

**Koningsplein:** From here, the tram crosses four canals: Singel, Heren, Keizers, and Prinsen. To keep them straight, think "a Single Hairy Kaiser's Prince really knows his canals." Nearby: Mint Tower, flower market.

**Keizersgracht:** Here the street fills with people and gets so narrow that trams share one set of rails, and bikers are required to walk their bikes. This is the vibrant shopping district of modern Amsterdam.

**Prinsengracht:** You'll roll past more shops and more pedestrians.

**Leidseplein:** This is the tourists' nightlife center, with edgy nightclubs, the famous Bulldog Coffeeshop (marijuana), and the venerable city theater (Stadsschouwburg).

**Museumplein:** Here is the popular Museumplein park, Rijksmuseum, Van Gogh Museum, Stedelijk Museum, House of Bols, and Coster Diamonds.

## South-East: Tram #14

Leaving Centraal station you'll go south and then east, passing:

**Dam Square:** At this major hub, you'll roll past the front of the Royal Palace and through Dam Square itself. Nearby: the New Church, Anne Frank House, and starting point for my Jordaan and Red Light District self-guided walks.

**Rokin** (Spui): There's lots to do nearby; see "Spui," earlier, for a description.

**Rembrandtplein:** One of the city's top nightlife spots, this is a good place to hop off for the Tuschinski Theater and the Willet-Holthuysen Museum.

**Waterlooplein:** This large square perched on the edge of the historic Jewish Quarter is close to Rembrandt's House, Gassan Diamonds, Blawbrug ("Blue Bridge"), and the Waterlooplein Flea Market.

**Mr. Visserplein:** This busy intersection, named after Louis Ernst Visser, a president of the Dutch Supreme Court who protested Jewish oppression during WWII German occupation, is a handy stop for the Jewish Museum and Portuguese Synagogue.

**Artis:** Hop out here for the Dutch Theater (National Holocaust Museum), Dutch Resistance Museum, Artis Royal Zoo, and De Hortus Botanical Garden.

**Alexanderplein:** A grand gate that was part of the old city wall graces this intersection, convenient to the Tropical Museum.

map for Amsterdam (Mon-Fri 7:00-21:00, Sat-Sun 8:00-18:00, +31 307 515 155).

The **GVB** website has a journey planner and route map (www.gvb.nl; the app version isn't as useful). **Google Maps** or the **Citymapper** app both show your transit options (Citymapper comes with offline public-transit maps). For destinations outside Amsterdam, **NS**—the Dutch national railway—has a good website and app (www.ns.nl). And many readers swear by the **9292** app, offering a journey planner and online tickets.

**Tickets and Passes:** Consider your options before you buy that first ticket. Within Amsterdam, a **one-hour ticket** costs €3.20 and is good on the tram, bus, and Metro, including transfers. For short visits, paying for rides as you go is the simplest choice.

A **pass** is more economical if you're staying in Amsterdam for a few days and riding a lot of trams. Passes good for unlimited city transit are available for 24 hours (€8.50), 48 hours (€14.50), 72 hours (€20), and 96 hours (€25.50). There are also passes that cover both the tram-bus-Metro system and train rides in the Netherlands (discussed below).

You can buy tickets and day passes from ticket machines at most tram stops, or on board all buses and most trams (credit card only, usually at the rear of the tram or bus; if there's no conductor, pay driver). The full range of tickets and passes is also available at Metro-station vending machines and TIs.

The **I Amsterdam City Card,** a sightseeing pass, also covers all tram, bus, and Metro travel within Amsterdam (see "Sightseeing Passes" on page 58).

The **Amsterdam Travel Ticket** covers trams, buses, and the Metro, plus the train ride to and from Schiphol Airport (€17/1 day, €22.50/2 days, €28/3 days, http://en.gvb.nl/amsterdam-travel-ticket). If you plan to make day trips outside Amsterdam, consider the **Amsterdam & Region Travel Ticket.** This covers in-city trams and buses, as well as trains to nearby destinations such as Haarlem, Zaanse Schans, Edam, Volendam, Marken (by bus), Aalsmeer, and Schiphol Airport. If you do two or more day trips, the 2- or 3-day passes can save you a little money and the hassle of buying individual tickets (€28/2 days, €36.50/3 days; one-day pass not worth it); sold at TIs and at ticket machines at Schiphol Airport and Centraal station (on the IJ-Hall/north side; www.iamsterdam.com).

**Riding Trams:** Board the tram at any door not marked with a red/white "do not enter" sticker. Once aboard, you must immediately "check in" by touching your pass or ticket to one of the pink-and-gray scanners. (If you buy your ticket from the conductor at the back of the tram, you must still "check in" with your ticket once you have it.) The scanner will beep and flash a green light after a successful scan. Be careful not to accidentally scan your ticket or pass twice while boarding, or it becomes invalid. Just before exiting, you must "check out" by scanning it again. Occasionally, controllers fine people who don't check in and out. To open the rear door when you reach your stop, press a button on one of the poles near the exit. Don't try to exit through the front door—it's not allowed.

If you get lost in Amsterdam, remember that most of the city's trams eventually take you back to Centraal station, and nearly all drivers speak English.

**Buses and Metro:** Tickets and passes work on buses and the Metro as they do on the trams—pay with a credit card and scan your ticket or pass as you enter and again when you leave. The Metro system is limited and used mostly for commuting to the suburbs—but it does loosely connect Centraal station with some sights to the south (Rokin-Vijzelgracht-De Pijp) and east (Nieuwmarkt-Waterlooplein-Weesperplein) of Damrak.

## By Bike

Everyone—bank managers, students, pizza-delivery boys, and police—uses bikes to get around. It's by far the smartest way to travel in a city where 40 percent  of all traffic rolls on two wheels. You'll get around town by bike faster than you can by taxi. On my last visit, I rented a bike for five days, chained it to the rack outside my hotel at night, and enjoyed wonderful mobility. I highly encourage this for anyone who wants to get maximum fun per hour in Amsterdam. One-speed bikes, with *"brrringing"* bells and foot brakes, rent for about €10 per day (cheaper for longer periods) at any number of places—hotels can send you to the nearest spot. If you don't like the bike you're given, it's fine to ask for a better one.

**Rental Shops: Star Bikes Rental** has cheap rates, long hours, and inconspicuous black bikes. They're happy to arrange an after-hours drop-off if you give them your credit-card number and pre-pay (e-bikes-€20/day; Mon-Fri 8:00-19:00, Sat-Sun from 9:00; requires ID but no monetary deposit, walk east from behind Cen-

## Bike Theft

Bike thieves are bold and brazen in Amsterdam. Bikes come with two locks and stern instructions to use both. The wimpy ones go through the spokes, whereas the industrial-strength chains are meant to be wrapped around the actual body of the bike and through the front wheel, then connected to something stronger than any human. (Note the steel bike-hitching racks sticking up all around town, called "staples.") Follow your rental agency's locking directions diligently. Once, I used both locks, but my chain wasn't around the main bar of my bike's body. In the morning, I found only my front tire (still safely chained to the metal fence). If you're sloppy, it's an expensive mistake and one that any "included" theft insurance won't cover.

traal station along De Ruijterkade to #143, +31 20 620 3215, www. starbikesrental.com).

**MacBike** has an efficient outlet at Centraal station; cheaper foot-brake bikes are available at its Oosterdok, Vondelpark, and Waterlooplein locations (e-bikes-€35/day, free rental with I Amsterdam City Card; €50 deposit plus a copy of your passport, or provide credit-card number; free helmets, daily 9:00-18:00, at east end of station—on the left as you exit; +31 20 624 8391, www. macbike.nl). MacBike sells several cheap pamphlets outlining bike tours with a variety of themes in and around Amsterdam.

**Frédéric Rent-a-Bike,** a 10-minute walk from Centraal station, has quality bikes and a helpful staff (e-bikes-€27/day, RS%-10 percent discount; daily 9:00-17:30, after-hours drop-off available; no deposit but must leave credit-card number, Binnen Wieringerstraat 23, +31 20 624 5509, www.frederic.nl, Marne).

**Biking Tips:** As the Dutch believe in fashion over safety, no one here wears a helmet. They do, however, ride cautiously, and so should you: Use arm signals, follow the bike-only traffic signals, stay in the obvious and omnipresent bike lanes, and yield to traffic on the right. Fear oncoming trams and tram tracks. Carefully cross tram tracks at a perpendicular angle to avoid catching your tire in the rut. Police ticket cyclists just as they do drivers: Obey all traffic signals and walk your bike through pedestrian zones (fines are reportedly €80). Texting while biking can get you an expensive ticket...if you're not in an accident first. Google Maps helpfully includes bicycles as a mode of transportation for the Netherlands. For bike tours, see "Guided Bike Tours," later.

## By Boat

Though Amsterdam's **hop-on, hop-off** boats ceased operations during the Covid-19 pandemic, they may be underway again by the time you visit. For the latest, check locally and on the websites for Stromma and Lovers. If you're simply looking for a floating, nonstop tour, the regular canal tour boats (without stops) give more information, cover more ground, and cost less than hop-on, hop-off boats (see "Tours in Amsterdam," later).

If you're a confident boater, consider renting a serious vessel. **Sloep Delen Boat Rental** has a fleet of 12-seater boats with silent electric motors. Locals book online and use a smartphone to unlock their boat; for tourists it's smart to call and pay an attendant who will meet you at the dock, give you a little map and suggestions, and set you free (€65/hour for up to 12 people, minimum 2 hours, €150 deposit, pick up at Elandsgracht 150 or Mauritskade 3, +31 20 419 1007, www.sloepdelen.nl).

## By Taxi and Uber

For short rides, Amsterdam is a bad town for taxis. They're expensive and have to take circuitous routes through winding, traffic-filled streets. Given the good tram system and ease of biking, I use taxis less in Amsterdam than in just about any other city in Europe. The city's taxis have a drop charge (about €3), after which it's €2.19 per kilometer. You can wave them down, find a rare taxi stand, call one (+31 20 777 7777), or download their app (Taxi Amsterdam "TaxiTCA"). Legally, all taxis are required to have meters, and accept cash or credit cards.

Uber works in Amsterdam like in the US (pricing based on demand; about €30 from the airport into downtown).

## By Car

If you've got a car, park it—all you'll find are frustrating one-way streets, terrible parking, and meter readers with a passion for booting cars parked incorrectly. You'll pay €70 a day to park safely in a central garage. If you must bring a car to Amsterdam, it's best to leave it at one of the city's supervised suburban park-and-ride lots (follow *P&R* signs from freeway, €8/24 hours, includes round-trip transit into city center for up to five people, 4-day maximum).

# Tours in Amsterdam

🎧 To sightsee on your own, download my free audio tours that complement my self-guided Amsterdam City, Red Light District, and Jordaan walks (see sidebar on page 28 for details). Some companies offer a discount when you show this book (indicated in these listings with the abbreviation "RS%").

## BY BOAT
### ▲▲Traditional Canal Boat Tours

These long, low, tourist-laden boats leave continually from several docks around town for a relaxing, if uninspiring, one-hour intro-

duction to the city (with recorded headphone commentary). Some people prefer to cruise at night, when the bridges are illuminated. Select a boat tour based on your proximity to its starting point. The I Amsterdam City Card covers one cruise from any of these three outfits.

**Blue Boat Company**'s boats depart from two locations: opposite the Heineken Experience at Stadhouderskade 550 and opposite the Hard Rock Café at Stadhouderskade 501 (€20, cheaper online; daily, every half-hour 10:00-18:00, fewer off-season; 1.25 hours, +31 20 679 1370, www.blueboat.nl). Their evening cruise includes the Red Light District (€21, nightly at 20:00, 1.5 hours, March-Oct also at 21:00 and 22:00, reservations required).

**Lovers** boat lines offers basic one-hour canal cruises with narration, as well as dinner cruises. Boats depart right in front of Centraal station (€15; daily, every half-hour 10:00-21:00, fewer off-season; Prins Hendrikkade 25, +31 20 530 1090, www.lovers.nl).

**Stromma** offers similar one-hour cruises with three departure points: Centraal station and Rijksmuseum departures have timed tickets, while cruises from Damrak (running between Centraal station and Dam Square) are open tickets that you can use at any time. All boats run from about 11:00-17:30 and all tickets are cheaper online (Centraal station—€17.50, runs April-Dec; Damrak Pier 5—€19.50, runs April-Dec; Rijksmuseum—€18.50, runs year-round; +31 20 217 0500, www.stromma.nl).

### Smaller, Quirkier Canal Boat Tours

Small boat companies with impromptu offerings seem to pop up all over. They are youthful, come with hip narration, encourage drinking, and are simply lots of fun. Most charge about €20-25 per hour-long tour. Get tips on which tours recent visitors enjoyed by searching "boat tour" on a travel review website, talk to your hotelier, or try one of these more established options:

**Those Dam Boat Guys** gives 1.5-hour tours with entertaining and knowledgeable guides (generally ex-pats who ask for tips) and no set route. They encourage participants to bring a picnic (or drinks, or joints) and make a party of it. There are plenty of rude jokes, so younger kids aren't their best audience (€29.50, private tours-€230/up to 10 people, meet at their office at Prinsengracht 13, several departures daily, +31 202 101 669, reserve times at www.thosedamboatguys.com).

**Friendship Amsterdam Boat Tours** offers more standard one-hour tours in open boats seating about 40 (€19, generally 3/ hour—check website for times, Oudezijds Voorburgwal 230 in Red Light District, +31 20 334 4774, www.friendshipamsterdam.com).

### Canoe Tours near Amsterdam

For some exercise and a dose of the polder country and village life, consider the **Wetlands Safari** five-hour tour. Majel Tromp, a friendly villager who speaks great English, takes from 2 to 15 people per tour. The program: Meet Majel at the Noord Metro station at 10:00. From there, you'll catch a 5-minute public bus, stop for coffee, then embark on a 3.5-hour canoe trip with several stops, tour a village by canoe, munch an included canalside picnic lunch, then canoe and bus back to Amsterdam's Noord station by 15:00. In summer, a four-hour sunset tour is also available (€68, €35 for kids 7-16, RS%-€5 off—use the discount code "RICK" when reserving online, 2-3 people per canoe, daily April-mid-Sept, reservations required, +31 6 5355 2669, www.wetlandssafari.nl, info@ wetlandssafari.nl).

## ON FOOT
### Food Tours

Amsterdam has many competing food tours. A typical food tour will make six or eight stops in 3-4 hours and costs €80-100. They hit all the edible clichés (like pancakes, cheese, herring, Indonesian, apple pie, and Dutch gin) and come with fun commentary and the chance to meet local merchants. Tours generally focus on one neighborhood. The most popular neighborhoods are De Pijp (for a more authentic and trendy experience and an international market scene) and the Jordaan (which fits the typical visitor's image of Amsterdam).

I enjoyed **Amsterdam Food Tours** (€87.50, 8 people max, +31 615 428 120, www.amsterdamfoodtours.com, Thijs van Royen). You can comparison shop online: Check out **Hungry Birds** (www. hungrybirds.nl) or **Secret Food Tours** (www.secretfoodtours.com), or customize a tour with **Dennis Gerrits** (see "Private Guides," later).

## Free City Walk

**New Europe Tours** "employs" native English-speaking students to give irreverent and entertaining two-hour walks (using the same "free tour, ask for tips, sell their other tours" formula popular in so many great European cities). While most guides lack a local's deep understanding of Dutch culture, not to mention professional training, they're certainly high-energy. This long walk covers a lot of the city with an enthusiasm for the contemporary pot-and-prostitution scene (€1.50 charged to pay city's entertainment tax, tips expected, check schedule online, www.neweuropetours.eu). All tours leave from the National Monument on Dam Square.

## Private Guides

**Mark Law,** a knowledgeable guide who has clearly found his niche, offers three-hour small-group city walks for €35/person (up to 8 people). He also offers private tours (€60/hour, minimum 3 hours) and offers an array of creative programs both in Amsterdam and in the countryside (+31 627 269 604, www.thatdamguide.com, mark@thatdamguide.com).

**Dennis Gerrits** is like a personal host who wants you to get the most out of your visit. His customized tours of Amsterdam and its surrounding cities and countryside can be by foot, bike, private boat, or car. He's happy to help with reservations and planning and enjoys booking a video call in advance to design the right plan (from €50/hour, +31 6 3840 2919, www.lovemycitytours.com, dennis@lovemycitytours.com).

**Albert Walet** enjoys personalizing tours for Americans interested in getting to know his city. Al specializes in history, architecture, and water management, and exudes a passion for Amsterdam (€70/2 hours, €120/4 hours, up to 4 people, on foot or by bike, +31 6 2069 7882, abwalet2@yahoo.nl). Al also takes travelers to nearby Haarlem, Leiden, and Delft, or through rural villages by bike.

**Larae Malooly** will tailor a private tour to your interests, weaving in themes such as Renaissance architecture, Jewish heritage, and even local food, and will pick you up from your hotel or a convenient spot in town (€185/up to 4 people for 4-hour Amsterdam tour, optional add-ons include a private cruise or Rijksmuseum tour, book at www.amsterdamsel.com).

**Toms Travel Tours** offers custom-designed private tours. Tom van der Leij has assembled 20+ local, multilingual, and specialized guides who lead tours in Amsterdam, the Dutch countryside, and Belgium (€290/3 hours, +31 626 534 331, www.tomstraveltours.com, bookings@tomstraveltours.com).

# BY BIKE

## Guided Bike Tours

**Yellow Bike Guided Tours** offers city bike tours of either two hours (€26, daily at 11:00, in winter at 13:30) or three hours (€31, daily at 13:30), which both include a 20-minute break. They also offer a four-hour, 15-mile tour of the dikes and green pastures of the countryside (€36, lunch extra, includes 45-minute break, April-Oct daily at 10:00). All tours leave from Nieuwezijds Kolk 29, three blocks from Centraal station (reservations smart, +31 20 620 6940, www.yellowbike.nl).

## Do-It-Yourself Bike Tour of Amsterdam

A day enjoying the bridges, bike lanes, and sleepy, off-the-beat-en-path canals on your own bike is an essential Amsterdam experience. The real joys of Europe's best-preserved 17th-century city are the countless intimate glimpses it offers: the laid-back locals sunning on their porches under elegant gables, rusted bikes that look as if they've been lashed to the same lamppost since the 1960s, wasted hedonists planted on canalside benches, and happy sailors permanently moored but still manning the deck.

For a good day trip, rent a bike at or near Centraal station (see "Getting Around—By Bike," earlier). Head west down Haar-lemmerstraat, working your wide-eyed way down Prinsengracht and detouring through the small, gentrified streets of the Jordaan neighborhood before popping out at the Westerkerk under the tallest spire in the city.

Pedal south to the lush and peaceful Vondelpark, then cut back through the center of town (Leidseplein to the Mint Tower, along Rokin street to Dam Square). From there, cruise the Red Light District, following Oudezijds Voorburgwal past the Old Church (Oude Kerk) to Zeedijk street, and return to the train station.

Then, you can escape into the countryside by hopping on the free ferry behind Centraal station (described next). In five minutes, Amsterdam is gone, and you're rolling through your very own Dutch painting.

## Taking Bikes Across the Harbor on a Free Ferry

Behind Centraal station is a little commuter port where ferries come and go constantly (free, bikes welcome, signs count down minutes until next departure). Hopping on a ferry offers an easy escape from the frenzied bike paths of Amsterdam's core. Try these two excursions.

**North Amsterdam:** The middle two ferries (labeled *Buiksloterweg*) run immediately across the harbor (3-minute ride). The striking EYE Filmmuseum complex and A'dam Tower are just to the left of the north ferry landing. There's a handy bike-rental shop next to the restaurant just across from the ferry landing; they have bike-trail maps available (The Amsterdam North, IJpromenade 2, +31 613 998 675, www.bikerentalamsterdamnorth.nl). A bike path leads from the ferry landing directly ahead for a mile along the tree-lined North Holland Canal to a little windmill—biking there takes about 10 minutes—and eventually into the wide-open polder land and villages.

**Industrial Port and Hipster Zone:** Ferries leaving from Centraal station's far-left wharf (labeled *NDSM*) cruise 15 minutes across the North Sea Canal (2/hour, generally departing at :15 and :45). This little trip offers a fun peek at the fifth-biggest harbor in Europe (nearby Rotterdam is number one), old wheat silos now renovated into upscale condos, and the shoreline of north Amsterdam, where the new Metro connection to the center is bringing growth, with lots of new apartments under construction. The ferry deposits you in an industrial wasteland (a vacant old warehouse just past the modern MTV headquarters building is filled with artist studios and wacky ventures). **IJ-Kantine** is a fine modern restaurant/café 30 yards from the ferry landing (daily from 9:00, +31 20 633 7162). MacBike offers good bike-route maps for this area (see "Getting Around—By Bike," earlier).

# SIGHTS IN AMSTERDAM

One of Amsterdam's delights is that it has perhaps more small specialty museums than any other city its size. While all the commotion is over its top three museums (the Anne Frank House, Van Gogh Museum, and Rijksmuseum), don't underestimate the more than 50 others. From houseboats to sex, from marijuana to Old Masters, you can find a museum to suit your interests.

The following sights are arranged by neighborhood for handy sightseeing. In this chapter, some of Amsterdam's most important sights have the shortest listings and are marked with a 📖. That's because they are covered in much more depth in one of the self-guided walks or tours in this book. A 🎧 means the walk or tour is available as a free audio tour (via my Rick Steves Audio Europe app—see page 28).

## Sightseeing Strategies

### ADVANCE TICKETS

Buy timed-entry tickets online in advance for Amsterdam's three most popular museums: the **Anne Frank House** (tickets released on the first Tuesday of the month one month in advance), **Van Gogh Museum** (reserve at least a week in advance), and **Rijksmuseum.** In peak season, it's also smart to buy tickets online in advance for the **Stedelijk Museum.**

Always book directly on the sight's official website. You'll select your preferred date and entry time (usually with a 30-minute window to enter), then make the purchase with your credit card. Once you've booked, you'll receive an email—usually with a QR code—that acts as your digital ticket. (If you don't get the email, check your junk folder.) When you get to the sight at your designated time, pull up the digital ticket on your phone, let the attendant scan it, and walk right in.

You'll need to book a timed entry even if you're buying a sightseeing pass; you can make a reservation online before you receive your pass, but you'll need to present the pass with your reservation at the sight.

## SIGHTSEEING PASSES

Tally the cost of the covered sights you plan visit to determine if these passes are worthwhile for you. Note that even with a pass, you still must make an online reservation for sights that require them.

**I Amsterdam City Card:** If you'll use public transportation and plan to pack in a lot of sights, this pass can save you some cash. It provides free or discounted entry to many sights in and around Amsterdam (but not the Anne Frank House or Van Gogh Museum). It also includes a canal cruise, bike rental, and transit pass (€65/24 hours, €90/48 hours, €110/72 hours, buy at the I Amsterdam store in Centraal station or download the app to purchase (www.iamsterdamcard.com).

**Museumkaart:** This sightseeing pass might save you a little money, but you can only use it at five sights—of your choosing—out of the 450 sights it covers (€65, valid 31 days, full details and list of covered sights at www.museumkaart.nl).

## SOUTHWEST AMSTERDAM

The following sights are centered around the square called Museumplein and a short walk from Amsterdam's urban oasis, Vondelpark.

### ▲Museumplein

Bordered by the Rijks, Van Gogh, and Stedelijk museums, and the Concertgebouw (classical music hall), this park-like square is interesting even to art haters.  Amsterdam's best acoustics are found underneath the Rijksmuseum, where street musicians perform everything from chamber music to Mongolian throat singing. Locals enjoy a park bench or a coffee at the Cobra Café (playground nearby). The gardens *(tuinen)* by the Rijksmuseum are free to enter and a peaceful place to enjoy a coffee.

Nearby is **Coster Diamonds,** a handy place to see a diamond-cutting and -polishing demo (free, frequent, and interesting 30-minute tours followed by sales pitch, popular with tour groups,

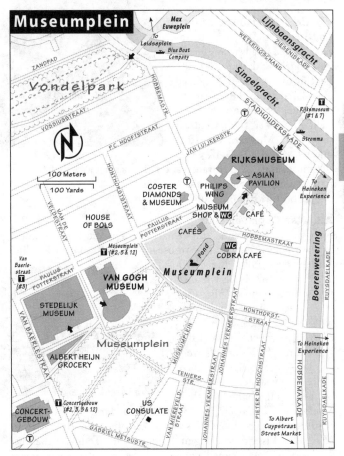

prices marked up to include tour-guide kickbacks, daily 9:00-17:00, Paulus Potterstraat 2, +31 20 305 5555, https://royalcoster.com). The end of the tour leads you straight into their Diamond Museum, which is worthwhile only for those who feel the need to see even more diamonds (€11, daily 9:00-17:00, +31 20 305 5300, www.diamondmuseum.com). The tour at **Gassan Diamonds** is free and better (see page 83), but Coster is convenient to the Museumplein scene.

### ▲▲▲Rijksmuseum

Built to house the nation's great art, the Rijksmuseum (RIKES-moo-zay-oom) owns several thousand paintings, including an incomparable collection of 17th-century Dutch Masters: Rembrandt, Vermeer, Hals, and Steen. Its vast collection also includes interesting artifacts—such as furniture—that help bring the golden age to life.

**Cost and Hours:** €20 for timed-entry ticket—best to reserve online in advance, free for kids under 18; daily 9:00-17:00; multimedia guide-€5, guided tour-€5, download free smartphone app (bring headphones); tram #2 or #12 from Centraal station to Museumplein stop; info tel. +31 20 674 7047, www.  rijksmuseum.nl. The entrance is off the passageway that tunnels right through the center of the building.

📖 See the Rijksmuseum Tour chapter.

## ▲▲▲Van Gogh Museum

Near the Rijksmuseum, this remarkable museum features works by the troubled Dutch artist whose art seemed to mirror his life. Vincent, who killed himself in 1890 at age 37, is best known for sunny, Impressionist canvases that vibrate and pulse with vitality. The museum's 200 paintings—which offer a virtual stroll through the artist's work and life—were owned by Theo, Vincent's younger, art-dealer brother. Highlights include  *Sunflowers, The Bedroom, The Potato Eaters,* and many brooding self-portraits. The third floor shows works that influenced Vincent, from Monet and Pissarro to Gauguin, Cézanne, and Toulouse-Lautrec. The worthwhile multimedia guide includes insightful commentaries and quotes from Vincent himself. Temporary exhibits fill the exhibition wing down the escalator from the ground-floor lobby.

**Cost and Hours:** €20 for timed-entry ticket—must reserve online at least one week in advance, free for kids under 18; daily 9:00-17:00, may stay open later in summer, shorter hours off-season; multimedia guide-€3.50, kids' multimedia guide-€2; Paulus Potterstraat 7, tram #2 or #12 from Centraal station to Museumplein stop, +31 20 570 5200, www.vangoghmuseum.com.

📖 See the Van Gogh Museum Tour chapter.

## ▲▲Stedelijk Museum

The Netherlands' top modern-art museum is filled with a permanent collection of 20th-century classics as well as far-out, refreshing, cutting-edge temporary exhibits.

**Cost and Hours:** €20, daily 10:00-18:00, top-notch gift shop, Museumplein 10, tram #2 or #12 from Centraal station to the Mu-

## Planning a Three-Museum Day

To see the art at the Rijksmuseum, Van Gogh Museum, and Stedelijk Museum in a single day, there are two good strategies to keep in mind when buying timed-entry tickets in advance.

One approach is to see the museums chronologically, in historical order: First, take in the Old Masters at the Rijks, then Impressionism at the Van Gogh, and finish with modern art at the Stedelijk.

But if you're in town during the busy season, you can avoid crowds by following this plan: See the Van Gogh Museum right when it opens at 9:00, then visit the less-congested Stedelijk. From there, you could have lunch and take in some other nearby sights—such as Coster Diamonds (see page 58) and the House of Bols (see page 64). Finally, hit the Rijksmuseum after 14:00, when crowds there begin to subside.

seumplein stop, +31 20 573 2911, www.stedelijk.nl. The fine included audioguide covers both permanent and temporary exhibits.

**Advance Tickets Recommended:** During peak season, reserve tickets online in advance to avoid the ticket-buying line. You'll pre-select the date you want to visit but are free to enter at any time during open hours.

**Eating:** Try the **$** simple first-floor café (sandwich, salad, pastries) or the **$$** full-service ground-floor restaurant with outdoor seating. Or visit the supermarket next door and picnic in the park.

**Visiting the Museum:** Before entering, notice the architecture of the modern entrance—aptly nicknamed "the bathtub." Once in-side, use your smartphone to scan the QR code near the ticket desk to access a map. The layout is always changing. There are always temporary exhibits, and even the "permanent" collection changes frequently. Pick up the good audioguide. Don't try to  do a painting-by-painting tour—this is a museum for exploring, so let yourself go.

The museum's permanent collection covers all the biggies of modern art—Picasso, Chagall, Kandinsky, etc.—but only a few are on display at any one time. It's easy to tour the displays roughly chronologically, starting with works from 1880-1950, then head-

AMSTERDAM SIGHTS

## Amsterdam at a Glance

▲▲▲**Rijksmuseum** Best collection anywhere of the Dutch Masters—Rembrandt, Hals, Vermeer, and Steen—in a spectacular setting. **Hours:** Daily 9:00-17:00. See page 59.

▲▲▲**Van Gogh Museum** More than 200 paintings by the angst-ridden artist. **Hours:** Daily 9:00-17:00, may stay open later in summer, shorter hours off-season. See page 60.

▲▲▲**Anne Frank House** Young Anne's hideaway during the Nazi occupation. **Hours:** Daily 9:00-22:00. See page 69.

▲▲**Stedelijk Museum** The Netherlands' top modern-art museum. **Hours:** Daily 10:00-18:00. See page 60.

▲▲**Amsterdam Museum** City's growth from fishing village to trading capital to today, including some Rembrandts and a playable carillon. **Hours:** Closed for renovation. See page 74.

▲▲**Red Light District** The world's oldest profession in the city's oldest neighborhood. **Hours:** Best from noon into the evening; avoid late at night. See page 75.

▲▲**Our Lord in the Attic Museum** Catholic church hidden in the attic of a 17th-century merchant's house. **Hours:** Mon-Fri 10:00-17:00, Sat until 18:00, Sun 13:00-18:00. See page 76.

▲▲**Netherlands Maritime Museum** Rich seafaring story of the Netherlands, told with vivid artifacts. **Hours:** Daily 10:00-17:00, closed Mon off-season. See page 77.

▲▲**Dutch Resistance Museum** History of the Dutch struggle against the Nazis. **Hours:** Mon-Fri 10:00-17:00, Sat-Sun from 11:00. See page 89.

ing to the top floor for works from 1950 to the present. Each room comes with thoughtful English descriptions.

Pay special attention to the museum's strength—Dutch artists. The Dutch have put their mark on modern art, starting with the man who may have been the first "modern" artist—Vincent van Gogh. Van Gogh's thick paint, messy brushwork, clashing colors, and strong emotions would inspire the later work of the Expressionists and Fauves. Later, Dutch artists such as Piet Mondrian and Theo van Doesburg helped define what we call abstract art by reducing painting to its basics: straight black lines, rectangular shapes, and the three primary colors. Amsterdam's Karel Appel

▲**Royal Palace** Lavish City Hall that takes you back to the golden age of the 17th century. **Hours:** Daily 10:00-17:00 when not closed for official ceremonies. See page 71.

▲**Begijnhof** Quiet courtyard lined with picturesque houses. **Hours:** Daily 10:00-18:00. See page 74.

▲**Hash, Marijuana, and Hemp Museum** All the dope, from history and science to memorabilia. **Hours:** Daily 10:00-22:00. See page 76.

▲▲**A'dam Tower** Entertainment complex with panoramic views over Amsterdam. **Hours:** Daily 10:00-22:00. See page 80.

▲**Rembrandt's House** The master's reconstructed house, displaying his etchings. **Hours:** Tue-Sun 10:00-18:00, closed Mon. See page 82.

▲**Willet-Holthuysen House** Elegant 17th-century house. **Hours:** Daily 10:00-17:00. See page 68.

▲**Jewish Museum and Portuguese Synagogue** Exhibits on Judaism and culture and beloved synagogue that serves today's Jewish community. **Hours:** Museum daily 10:00-17:00; synagogue Sun-Fri 10:00-17:00, closes earlier Dec-Jan and Fri off-season, closed Sat year-round. See page 85.

▲**Dutch Theater** Moving memorial in former Jewish detention center. **Hours:** Daily 11:00-17:00. See page 88.

▲**Tropical Museum** Large ethnographic collection exploring Dutch colonialism. **Hours:** Daily 10:00-17:00, closed Mon off-season. See page 90.

put the two trends together to pioneer Abstract Expressionism. He was a member of the CoBrA group of artists (from Copenhagen, Brussels, and Amsterdam), who created dense canvases of swirling ultra-bright colors and ultra-thick paints. Netherlands-born Willem de Kooning often included glimpses of the human figure amid his densely patterned canvases.

The Dutch have always been masters of creating everyday objects—tables, chairs, lamps, vases, tableware—for the prosperous middle class. Their style is both functional and beautiful. The Amsterdam School (Holland's Art Deco) took the flowery Art Nouveau style and squared it off to create objects that are both decorative and geometric. You may see sleek chairs by Rietveld or minimalist designs by the De Stijl group.

Besides the museum's paintings, enjoy other forms of art: everyday "found" objects presented as high art, installations, and interactive technology (lights, video, gizmos) to dazzle the eye and tickle your wonderbone.

## House of Bols: Cocktail & Genever Experience

This leading Dutch distillery runs a slick, pricey little museum/marketing opportunity across the street from the Van Gogh Museum. If you feel like a good stiff drink after your museum-going, it's ideal. The "experience" is a self-guided walk through what is essentially an ad for Bols—"four hundred years of working on the art of mixing and blending...a celebration of gin"—with some fun sniffing opportunities and a drink at a modern, mirrored-out cocktail bar for a finale. The line of bottles with 36 different scents (with the answers identifying each odor hidden until you guess) is fascinating. Your ticket includes one gin tasting with a talkative expert (pricier tickets include more tastings). It's fun to watch your barista mix up the cocktail of your dreams based on what you learned during your sniffing.

**Cost and Hours:** €16; daily 13:00-18:30, Fri-Sat until 21:00, last entry one hour before closing; must be 18, Paulus Potterstraat 14, +31 20 570 8575, www.houseofbols.com.

## Heineken Experience

This famous brewery, having moved its operations to the suburbs, has converted its old headquarters into a slick-yet-cheesy beer-fest—complete with a video-surround beer-making simulation in which visitors are brewed and bottled. The self-guided "experience" also includes photo ops that put you inside Heineken logos and labels, and no small amount of hype about the Heineken family and the quality of their beer. It can be a fun trip—like visiting a beer lover's amusement park—if you can ignore the fact that you're essentially paying for 90 minutes of advertising. Note that this place is a huge hit with twentysomething travelers and is especially busy on Saturdays.

**Cost and Hours:** €21 for timed-entry ticket—buy online or at kiosk in lobby, includes two drinks; daily 10:30-19:30, Fri-Sun until 21:00, longer hours July-Aug, last entry 2 hours before closing; tram #24 to Stadhouderskade or an easy walk from Rijksmuseum,

Stadhouderskade 78; +31 20 721 5300, www.heinekenexperience.com.

### De Pijp District

This former working-class industrial and residential zone (behind the Heineken Experience, near the Rijksmuseum)—once notorious as a slum—is gentrified now and has emerged as a colorful, vibrant district popular with food-tour groups. Its spine is Albert Cuypstraat, a street taken over by a long, sprawling produce/flea market packed with interesting people. With its many inviting cafés and edgy intellectual/artsy/working-class heritage, it's nicknamed the Latin Quarter of Amsterdam. Don't look for actual sights here. The charm is the fun, creative vibe.

### ▲Vondelpark

This huge, lively city park is popular with the Dutch—families with little kids, romantic couples, strolling seniors, and hipsters sharing blankets and beers. It's a favored venue for free summer concerts. On a sunny afternoon, it's a hedonistic scene that seems to say, "Parents... relax." The park's 'T Blauwe Theehuis ("The Blue Teahouse") is a delightful and recommended spot to  nurse a drink and take in the scene.

## SOUTHERN CANAL BELT

The ring of canals south of the historic core hosts a few small museums and some of the city's best nightlife.

### ▲Leidseplein

Brimming with cafés, this people-watching mecca is an impromptu stage for street artists, accordionists, jugglers, and unicyclists. It's particularly bustling on sunny afternoons. After dark, it's a vibrant tourists' nightclub center. Stroll nearby Lange Leidsedwarsstraat (one block north) for a taste-bud tour of multicultural eateries, from Greek to Indonesian.

### Amsterdam Pipe Museum

This small and unusual-yet-classy museum holds 300 years of pipes in a 17th-century canal house. (It's almost worth the admission price just to see the inside of one of these elegant homes.) You enter through the street-level shop, which is almost interesting enough to be a museum itself. It sells new and antique pipes, various smoking curiosities, and scholarly books written by the shop's owner. If you

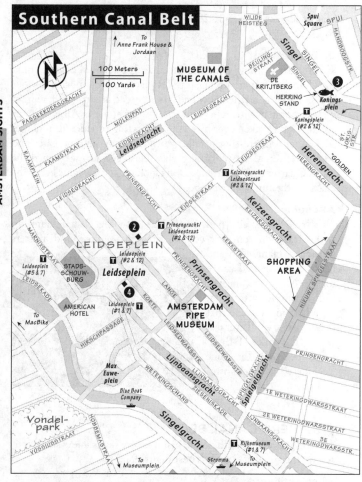

# Southern Canal Belt

want more, pay to enter the museum and a volunteer docent will accompany you upstairs through a tour of smoking history. You begin with some pre-Columbian terra-cotta pipes (from the discoverers of tobacco, dating from around 500 BC), followed by plenty of intricately carved Victorian smoking paraphernalia—long-stemmed Dutch pipes (the Dutch were the first importers of tobacco), meerschaum pipes (made from a soft white mineral), pipes carved into portraits, and so on. Ask questions—your guide is happy to explain why the opium pipes have their bowls in the center of the stem, or why some white clay pipes are a foot long.

**Cost and Hours:** €12.50, Mon-Sat 12:00-18:00, closed Sun, +31 20 421 1779, just off Leidsestraat at Prinsengracht 488, www.pijpenkabinet.nl.

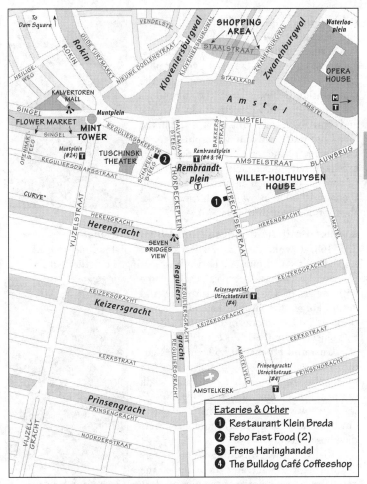

**Eateries & Other**
1. Restaurant Klein Breda
2. Febo Fast Food (2)
3. Frens Haringhandel
4. The Bulldog Café Coffeeshop

## Rembrandtplein and Tuschinski Theater

One of the city's premier nightlife spots is the leafy Rembrandt-plein (and the adjoining Thorbeckeplein). Several late-night dance clubs keep the area lively into the wee hours. Utrechtsestraat is lined with upscale shops and restaurants. Nearby Reguliersdwarsstraat (a street one block south of Rembrandtplein) is a center for gay and lesbian nightclubs.

The **Tuschinski Theater,** a movie palace from the 1920s (a half-block from Rembrandtplein down Reguliersbreestraat), glitters inside and out. Still a working theater, it's a delightful old place to see first-run movies (always in their original language—usually English—with Dutch subtitles). The exterior is an interesting hybrid of styles, forcing the round peg of Art Nouveau into the square hole of Art Deco. The stone-and-tile facade features stripped-down, functional Art Deco squares and rectangles, but is ornamented with Art Nouveau elements—Tiffany-style windows, garlands, curvy iron lamps, Egyptian pharaohs, and exotic gold lettering over the door. Inside (lobby is free), the sumptuous decor features fancy carpets, slinky fixtures, and semi-abstract designs. Grab a seat in the lobby and watch the ceiling morph, or, to see much more of the interior, take one of their excellent self-guided audio tours (€10, 30 minutes; theater open daily 9:30-11:00—get there by 10:00 to allow enough time to take the tour; Reguliersbreestraat 26).

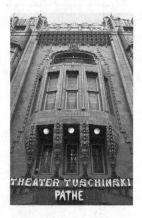

### ▲Willet-Holthuysen House (Huis Willet-Holthuisen)

This 1687 townhouse is a must for devotees of Hummel-topped sugar bowls and Louis XVI-style wainscoting. For others, it's a pleasant look inside a typical (rich) home with much of the original furniture and decor. Forget the history and just browse through a dozen rooms of beautiful saccharine objects from the 19th century.

**Cost and Hours:** €12.50, includes audioguide, daily 10:00-17:00; tram #4 or #14 to Rembrandtplein—it's a 2-minute walk southeast to Herengracht 605, +31 20 523 1822, www.willetholthuysen.nl. The museum also hands out a free brochure that covers the house's history.

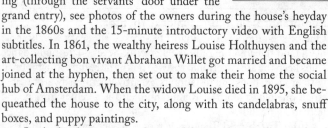

**Visiting the Museum:** Upon entering (through the servants' door under the grand entry), see photos of the owners during the house's heyday in the 1860s and the 15-minute introductory video with English subtitles. In 1861, the wealthy heiress Louise Holthuysen and the art-collecting bon vivant Abraham Willet got married and became joined at the hyphen, then set out to make their home the social hub of Amsterdam. When the widow Louise died in 1895, she bequeathed the house to the city, along with its candelabras, snuff boxes, and puppy paintings.

In the kitchen, picture the couple's servants—before electricity and running water—turning meat on the spit at the fireplace or filtering rainwater.

Continue to the **first floor,** where the Willet-Holthuysens entertained. Several rooms are decorated in the Louis XVI style, featuring chairs with straight, tapering legs (not the heavy, curving, animal-claw feet of earlier styles). You'll see blue, yellow, and purple-themed rooms; wainscoting ("wallpaper" covering only part of walls); and mythological paintings on the ceiling. Paintings introduce you to Abraham and Louise's artistic tastes, from still lifes to scenes of happy French peasants and nobles frolicking in the countryside.

The gilded ballroom—the house's most impressive space—displays a painting showing the room in its prime (and how little it's changed). Imagine Abraham, Louise, and 22 guests mingling here. Then they'd retire to the dining room laid out with its 275-piece Meissen porcelain tableware set, or chat in the blue "men's parlor" by the canal. In the conservatory they sipped tea while gazing out at symmetrically curved hedges and classical statues.

The **top-floor** bedroom is furnished with a canopy bed, matching oak washstand, makeup table, and elegant-yet-functional chamber pot. In other rooms, you can see Louise's favorite art and Abraham's book and antique collections, and trace the couple's travels.

## WEST AMSTERDAM

The mostly residential neighborhood around many of these sights is described in the ▢ Jordaan Walk chapter and ∩ audio tour.

### ▲▲▲Anne Frank House

A pilgrimage for many, this house offers a fascinating look at the hideaway of young Anne during the Nazi occupation of the Netherlands. Anne, her parents, an older sister, and four others spent a little more than two years in a "Secret Annex" behind her father's business. While in hiding, 13-year-old Anne kept a diary chronicling her extraordinary experience. Acting on a tip, the Nazis arrested the group in August 1944 and sent them to concentration camps in Poland and Germany. Anne and her sister died of typhus in March 1945, only weeks before their camp was liberated. Of the eight inhabitants of the Secret Annex, only Anne's father, Otto Frank, survived. He returned to Amsterdam and arranged for his daughter's diary to be published in 1947. It was followed by many translations, a play, and a movie.

The thoughtfully designed exhibit offers thorough coverage of the Frank family, the diary, the stories of others who hid, and the Holocaust.

**Cost and Hours:** €14 for timed-entry ticket—must reserve online in advance, includes excellent audioguide; €21 with 30-minute introduction in English; daily 9:00-22:00; no tickets sold onsite—tickets for following month released online on first Tue of each month; cloakroom for coats and small bags, no large bags allowed inside; tram #17 from Centraal station (or #13 from Paleisstraat) to

Westermarkt, then a one-block walk to Prinsengracht 267; +31 20 556 7105, www.annefrank.org.

📖 See the Anne Frank House Tour chapter.

### Houseboat Museum (Woonbootmuseum)

In the 1930s, modern cargo ships came into widespread use—making small, sail-powered cargo boats obsolete. In danger of extinction, these little vessels found new life as houseboats lining the canals of Amsterdam. Today, 2,500 such boats—their cargo holds turned into classy, comfortable living rooms—are called home. For a peek into this *gezellig* (cozy) world, visit this tiny museum aboard the *Hendrika Maria,* a former cargo ship built in 1914. Captain Vincent enjoys showing visitors around his houseboat, which feels lived-in because, until 1997, it was.

**Cost and Hours:** €4.50; daily 10:00-17:00 except closed Mon Sept-June; on Prinsengracht, opposite #296 facing Elandsgracht, +31 20 427 0750, www.houseboatmuseum.nl.

### Westerkerk

Located near the Anne Frank House, this landmark Protestant church has an appropriately barren interior, Rembrandt's body buried somewhere under the pews, and Amsterdam's tallest steeple. Built in the early 1600s, after the Reformation, it's very Dutch Reformed—plain, white walls, no statues, no stained glass—with the focus on the pulpit. The only ostentations: the church organ and the fancy gravestones of big-shot families. But even the organ (one of the top three in Amsterdam) had "modesty covers." The fine family tombstones lie on top of a chamber that held a coffin and six to eight bone boxes. When a leading family member would die, they'd pull up the tombstone, move the bones laying in the latest coffin into a bone box, and lay the body of the recently deceased family member to rest. This is the church that Anne Frank would gaze at out of her hiding-place window...the church bells reminded her of the world outside.

The Westerkerk tower is climbable only with a guided tour and rewards you with a look at the carillon and grand city views (185 steps, currently closed for restoration).

**Cost and Hours:** Free, donation requested; generally Mon-Sat 11:00-15:00, closed Sun, Prinsengracht 281, +31 20 624 7766, www.westerkerk.nl. You can hear the organ played during free concerts most Wednesdays at 13:00 (summer only, check website for schedule).

## Museum of the Canals (Grachtenmuseum)

Located in what once was once a grand 17th-century canal house, this museum tells the story of Amsterdam's evolution of canals, streets, and buildings, creatively using video projections and 3-D displays. Originally built for the director of the Dutch West India Company, the house has two rooms restored in Empire style. A model of the house echoes the transformation of the city with interior room details that illustrate the building's various incarnations: Peer through its windows to see scenes from its time as a wealthy family home through its use as a museum today. The back garden is a quiet oasis.

**Cost and Hours:** €15, includes audioguide, Tue-Sun 10:00-17:00, closed Mon, Herrengracht 386, +31 20 4211 656, www.hetgrachtenhuis.nl.

## CENTRAL AMSTERDAM, NEAR DAM SQUARE

Connect the following sights with my ⌂ Amsterdam City Walk chapter and ∩ audio tour.

### ▲Royal Palace (Koninklijk Huis)

This palace was built as a lavish City Hall (1648-1655), when Holland was a proud new republic and Amsterdam was the richest city on the planet—awash in profit from trade. The building became a "Royal Palace" when Napoleon installed his brother Louis as king (1806). After Napoleon's fall, it continued as a royal residence for the Dutch royal family, the House of Orange. Today, it's one of King Willem-Alexander's official residences, with a single impressive floor open to the public. Visitors can gawk at a grand hall and stroll about 20 lavishly decorated rooms full of chandeliers, paintings, statues, and furniture that reflect Amsterdam's former status as the center of global trade. Use my following mini-tour to see the highlights; supplement it with the multimedia guide.

**Cost and Hours:** €12.50, includes good multimedia guide, daily 10:00-17:00 but hours can vary for official ceremonies—check website, +31 20 522 6161, www.paleisamsterdam.nl.

**➌ Self-Guided Tour:** Start in the vast, white **Citizens' Hall.** It's the palace's highlight—120 feet by 60 feet by 90 feet, and lit by eight big chandeliers. At the far end, a statue of Atlas holds the globe of the world, and the ceiling painting shows Lady Amsterdam triumphant amid the clouds of heaven. On the floor, inlaid maps show the known world circa 1750 (back when the West Coast of the US was still being explored). The hall is used today to host foreign dignitaries and for royal family wedding receptions. From this central hall, you tour the palace counterclockwise.

Directly ahead (under Atlas) is the opulently draped-and-chandeliered **Throne Room.** Like all of the palace's rooms, this has

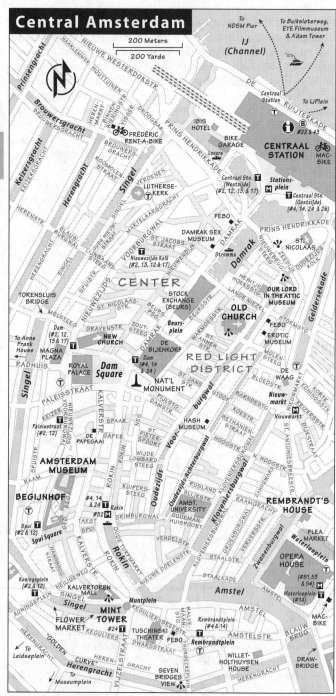

**AMSTERDAM SIGHTS**

# Central Amsterdam

elements from the three layers of the palace's history. Originally, it was the courthouse where self-governing citizens doled out justice (and couples were wed in the arcaded area to the right). In the early 1800s, Louis Bonaparte issued dictates from his throne in front of the fireplace to the left. (The painting over the mantle shows the original law-giver, Moses, with the Ten Commandments.) These days the chamber is a reception room for the ruling-as-entertainment Orange family.

Continue into the **Small Reception Room.** Get acquainted with the interior decor Louis introduced to the entire building—the so-called Empire Style. The curtains are heavy, the carpet has geometric patterns, and each room has a color-coordinated theme. The furniture is high-polished mahogany with upholstery featuring laurel wreaths and torches, and brass highlights. Chairs have arched backs, armrests, and tapered legs.

Exit into the South Gallery and take your first right into the **Chamber of the Mistress of the Robes of the Royal Household.** Originally the place where bureaucrats administered the city budget, this space was later a tax office, then a lavish bedroom for Louis' court, and more recently the childhood bedroom of the beloved Queen Beatrix.

Cross the gallery (past the Royal Apartment) to the **Treasury Ordinary Room,** which was Louis' personal bedroom. (We'll see his actual bed later.)

You pass through a couple of **Burgomasters' Chambers** where the city council met. Paintings (by Rembrandt's pupils) show righteous Romans after whom golden age Amsterdammers modeled themselves.

Pause in the narrow **Balcony Chamber** and take in the view outside, overlooking Dam Square. In olden times, the town crier or mayor made big pronouncements from here (note the trumpeting angels overhead), and the execution scaffold was set up nearby. These days, the small balcony outside is where today's royals give speeches, wave to TV cameras, and blow kisses to the adoring crowds.

Next is the **Execution Chamber,** with a portrait of WWII-era Queen Wilhelmina. The **Mozes Hall** (where the council once met) has appropriate decoration: the 36 coats-of-arms of the Netherlands' nobles and a huge painting of Moses with his council of 70 elders.

Farther along, gaze into the **Orphans' Chamber,** which now displays Louis' canopied bed. The **Salon of the English Quarter** is where Rembrandt officially went bankrupt. Back in the spacious Citizens' Hall—a testament to Amsterdam's greatness through the ages—head down the stairs to find one final room: the **Tribunal.** Here judges announced the type of death sentence handed down to the condemned: broken on the wheel, strangulation, or the most honorable—beheading.

### New Church (Nieuwe Kerk)

Barely newer than the Red Light District's "Old" Church, this 15th-century sanctuary has an intentionally spare interior, its decoration removed by 16th-century iconoclastic Protestants seeking to unclutter their communion with God. This is where many Dutch royal weddings and all inaugurations take place. The church hosts periodic organ concerts and a religious music festival in June.

**Cost and Hours:** Interior with special exhibits-€9-16, daily 10:00-18:00, audioguide-€4 or free depending on exhibit, on Dam Square, +31 20 626 8168, www.nieuwekerk.nl

See page 101 of the Amsterdam City Walk chapter.

### ▲▲Amsterdam Museum

Amsterdam's city history museum is closed while its permanent building undergoes renovation until 2025; you can visit a temporary display at the Hermitage Amsterdam (see page 85). Also closed is the Amsterdam Gallery (formerly known as the "Civic Guards Gallery"), the museum's public corridor lined with group portraits of Amsterdam citizens from the golden age to now.

### ▲Begijnhof

Stepping into this tiny, idyllic courtyard in the city center, you escape into the charm of old Amsterdam. (Please be considerate of the people who live around the courtyard, and don't photograph the residents or their homes.) Notice house #34, a 500-year-old wooden structure (rare, since repeated fires taught city fathers a trick called brick). Peek into the hidden Catholic church (Mass daily at 9:00), dating from the time when post-Reformation Dutch Catholics couldn't worship in public. It's opposite the English Reformed church, where the Pilgrims may have worshipped while waiting for their voyage to the New World—marked by a plaque near the door.

**Cost and Hours:** Free, only 50 people allowed in at a time, daily 10:00-18:00; on Begijnensteeg lane, just off Kalverstraat between #130 and #132; read the info board at the entrance for the Begijnhof's history.

See page 105 of the Amsterdam City Walk chapter.

# RED LIGHT DISTRICT

Between Damrak and Nieuwmarkt, this neighborhood is one of Amsterdam's oldest and has hosted prostitutes since 1200. While the main sight here is the neighborhood itself—peopled by sex workers, clients, revelers, and looky-loos—there are also two historic churches and a handful of museums dedicated to sex and other vices.

## ▲▲Red Light District Walk

Europe's most popular ladies of the night tease and tempt here, as they have for centuries, in about 200 display-case windows around Oudezijds Achterburgwal and Oudezijds Voorburgwal, surrounding the Old Church (Oude Kerk). Prostitution is entirely legal in the Netherlands, and the sex workers here are generally entrepreneurs who rent space and run their own businesses (and fill out tax returns). Drunks and druggies make the streets uncomfortable late at night after the gawking tour groups leave (about 22:30), but it's a fascinating walk earlier in the evening.

    📖 See the Red Light District Walk chapter and download my free 🎧 Red Light District audio tour.

## Sex Museums

Amsterdam has three sex museums: two in the Red Light District and another one nearby, a block in front of Centraal station on Damrak street. While visiting one can be called sightseeing, visiting more than that is harder to explain. The one on Damrak is the cheapest and most interesting. Here's a comparison:

    The **Damrak Sex Museum** tells the story of pornography from Roman times through 1960. Every sexual deviation is revealed in various displays. The museum includes early French pornographic photos; memorabilia from Europe, India, and Asia; a Marilyn Monroe tribute; and some S&M displays (€5, daily 10:00-18:00, Damrak 18, a block in front of Centraal station, +31 20 622 8376).

    The **Erotic Museum** in the Red Light District is five floors of uninspired paintings, videos, old photos, and sculpture (€7, daily 11:00-24:00, along the canal at Oudezijds Achterburgwal 54, +31 20 624 7303, www.erotisch-museum.nl; see the Red Light District Walk chapter).

    **Red Light Secrets Museum of Prostitution** is a pricey look at the world's oldest profession. If you're wondering what it's like to sit in those red booths, watch the video taken from a sex worker's perspective as "johns" check you out. The exhibit is much smaller than the others (€14.50; Sun-Thu 11:00-22:00, Fri-Sat until 23:00, last entry 45 minutes before closing; Oudezijds Achterburgwal 60, +31 20 846 7020, www.redlightsecrets.com; see the Red Light District Walk chapter).

### Old Church (Oude Kerk)

This 14th-century landmark—Amsterdam's oldest building and the needle around which the Red Light District spins—has served as a reassuring welcome-home symbol to sailors, a refuge to the downtrodden, an ideological battlefield of the Counter-Reformation, and, today, a tourist sight with a dull interior that serves as a space for temporary contemporary art exhibits.

**Cost and Hours:** €12, includes audioguide, Mon-Sat 10:00-18:00, Sun 13:00-17:30, +31 20 625 8284, www.oudekerk.nl. To climb the 167 steps to the top of the church tower, take a 30-minute tour in English (€9, April-Oct departs on the half hour Mon-Sat 12:00-18:00, none Sun or off-season). See the Red Light District Walk chapter.

### Marijuana Sights

Three related establishments cluster together along a canal in the Red Light District. The **Hash, Marijuana, and Hemp Museum,** worth ▲, is the most worthwhile of the three; it shares a ticket with the less substantial **Hemp Gallery.** Right nearby is **Cannabis College,** a free nonprofit center that's "dedicated to ending the global war against the cannabis plant through public education."

**Cost and Hours:** Museum and gallery—€10, includes audioguide, daily 10:00-22:00, Oudezijds Achterburgwal 148, +31 20 624 8926, www.hashmuseum.com. College—free to enter, daily 11:00-18:00, Oudezijds Achterburgwal 124, +31 20 423 4420, www.cannabiscollege.com.

For more on these sights, see the Red Light District Walk chapter. For the dope on Dutch dope, see the Smoking chapter.

### ▲▲Our Lord in the Attic Museum

Although Amsterdam has long been known for its tolerant attitudes, 16th-century politics forced Dutch Catholics to worship discreetly for a few hundred years.
At this museum at the north edge of the Red Light District you'll find a fascinating, hidden Catholic church filling the attic of three 17th-century merchants' houses. Seek out the silver collection and other exhibits of daily life from 300 years ago.

**Cost and Hours:** €15.50, includes audioguide; Mon-Fri 10:00-17:00, Sat until 18:00, Sun 13:00-18:00; near Centraal station at Oudezijds Voorburgwal 38, +31 20 624 6604, www.opsolder.nl.

📖 See the Our Lord in the Attic Museum Tour chapter.

## NORTHEAST AMSTERDAM
### NEMO (National Center for Science and Technology)
This kid-friendly science museum is a city landmark. Its distinctive copper-green building, jutting up from the water like a sinking ship, has prompted critics to nickname it the *Titanic*.

Designed by Italian architect Renzo Piano (known for Paris' Pompidou Center and Berlin's Sony Center complex on Potsdamer Platz), the building's shape reflects its nautical surroundings as well as the curve of the underwater tunnel it straddles.

Several floors feature permanent and rotating exhibits that allow kids (and adults) to explore topics such as light, sound, and gravity, and play with bubbles or topple giant dominoes. Head to their laboratory to do simple experiments, or check out the "Life in the Universe" exhibit.

Up top is a restaurant with a great city view, as well as a sloping terrace that becomes a popular "beach" in summer, complete with lounge chairs and a lively bar. On the second floor is a café with drinks and pastries.

**Cost and Hours:** €17.50, free for kids 3 and under, daily 10:00-17:30, closed Mon off-season, +31 20 531 3233, www.nemosciencemuseum.nl. The roof terrace—open until 20:00 in the summer—is generally free.

**Getting There:** It's above the entrance to the IJ tunnel at Oosterdok 2. From Centraal station, you can walk there in 15 minutes, or take bus #22 or #43 to the Kadijksplein stop.

### ▲▲Netherlands Maritime Museum (Nederlands Scheepvaartmuseum)
This huge, slick, and kid-friendly collection of model ships, maps, and sea-battle paintings fills the 300-year-old Dutch Navy Arsenal (cleverly located a little way from the city center, as this was where they stored the gunpowder). A highlight is a chance to explore below the decks of an old tall-masted ship and gaze at a royal barge. Given the Dutch seafaring heritage, this is an appropriately important and impressive place.

**Cost and Hours:** €17.50, €8.50 for kids 4-17, includes audioguide; credit card only, no cash; daily 10:00-17:00, closed Mon off-season; bus #22 or #43 from Centraal station to Kattenburgerplein 1, +31 20 523 2222, www.hetscheepvaartmuseum.com.

**Visiting the Museum:** Start your tour in the central court-

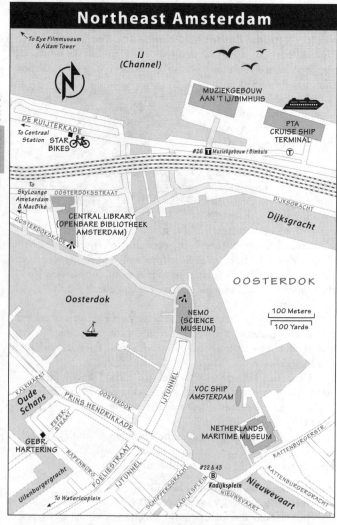

## Northeast Amsterdam

To Eye Filmmuseum
& A'dam Tower

IJ
(Channel)

MUZIEKGEBOUW
AAN 'T IJ/BIMHUIS

PTA
CRUISE SHIP
TERMINAL

DE RUIJTERKADE
To Centraal
Station  STAR
BIKES

#26  Muziekgebouw / Bimhuis

To
SkyLounge
Amsterdam
& MacBike

OOSTERDOKSSTRAAT

OOSTERDOKSKADE

DIJKSGRACHT

Dijksgracht

CENTRAL LIBRARY
(OPENBARE BIBLIOTHEEK
AMSTERDAM)

OOSTERDOK

Oosterdok

NEMO
(SCIENCE
MUSEUM)

100 Meters
100 Yards

KALKMARKT

Oude
Schans

PRINS HENDRIKKADE

OOSTERDOK

IJTUNNEL

VOC SHIP
AMSTERDAM

NETHERLANDS
MARITIME MUSEUM

KATTENBURGERSTR.

PIEPER-
STRAAT

GEBR.
HARTERING

RAPENBURG

FOELIESTRAAT

IJTUNNEL

SCHIPPERSGRACHT

#22 & 45
B
Kadijksplein

KADIJKSPLEIN

KATTENBURGERGRACHT

Uilenburgergracht

To Waterlooplein

NIEUWEVAART

Nieuwevaart

yard. From here, you can explore the buildings in any order you choose.

The **east** *(oost)* wing's level 1 holds a gallery of navigational instruments. A huge variety of tools for measuring latitude and longitude includes everything from astrolabes—cross-shaped devices used to measure the angle between the horizon and the sun—to steering compasses from the 19th century. In the ornamentation gallery, admire the busty gals that adorned the prows of ships and learn of their symbolic meaning for superstitious sailors.

Downstairs on level 0, see yacht models through the ages,

from early warships to today's luxury vessels. Note that the display case groups the boats by type—round-bottomed, square-sterned, keel, etc. The section on maps begins with Amsterdam from the mid-1500s and shows the territories and "discoveries" made by Amsterdam's sailors, from Brazil to Indonesia.

The **west wing** is kid-oriented, interactive, and less meaty, with an exhibit on whales and a debate-style look at the dichotomy of Amsterdam, serving as both an industrial port and as a livable city.

In the **north** *(noord)* wing, begin in the main gallery on the ground level. Pause at the first big painting—*The Battle of Gibraltar, 1607*—which shows the Dutch navy's crowning moment. In this battle, 26 Dutch ships routed the seemingly invincible Spanish force. Notice that virtually all the ships in the painting fly the three-color Dutch flag. That's because the Spanish fleet has already been sunk, killing thousands. The painting depicts the infamous mopping-up procedure. The Dutch are lowering their lifeboats to save the Spaniards—or, as other historians say, to finish them off. The rest of this gallery illustrates Netherlands' maritime history through paintings.

Upstairs on level 1, you'll learn about the Battle of Solebay via video and see two of the six Solebay tapestries (1685-1688). Temporary exhibits fill level 2.

Before exiting the north wing, head through the back door down to the colorful replica ship *Amsterdam* moored behind the building. This type of ship (called an East Indiaman) had its heyday during the 17th and 18th centuries, sailing for the Dutch East India Company (see the abbreviation *VOC*—for Vereenigde Oost-Indische Compagnie—on insignias throughout the boat). Wander the decks, then duck your head and check out the captain and surgeon's quarters. Don't forget to climb down into the hold to see the ship's essentials: bread, cheese, and gunpowder. On the main deck, don a heavy virtual-reality headset and get a 15-minute shipside view of 17th-century Amsterdam based on a painting by Reiner Nooms (VR experience open 11:00-16:00). The ship is light on historical information, but it's still fun to get a hands-on look at old-time life at sea.

The **Royal Barge**—in the building signed *De Koningssloep*—is no replica. Built for King William I in the early 19th century, this gaudy boat was a symbol of the might of the House of Orange after the chaos of the French Revolution and Napoleonic Wars. Last used in 1962 by Queen Juliana and Prince Bernhard for their silver wedding anniversary, the Royal Barge was renovated in 2014 and is still seaworthy.

## NORTH AMSTERDAM

These sights are across the IJ waterway, just a few minutes from Centraal station. From the docks behind the station, catch the free ferry (labeled *Buiksloterweg*) across the river (see page 55).

### EYE Filmmuseum

The most striking feature of the Amsterdam skyline is EYE, a film museum and cinema housed in an übersleek modern building immediately across the water from

Centraal station. Heralding the gentrification of the north side of the IJ waterway, EYE (a play on the Dutch pronunciation of "IJ") is a complex of museum spaces and four theaters playing mostly art films (shown in their original language, with selections organized around various themes). Its other offerings include a gallery of film posters, a shop, and a trendy terrace café with waterside seating (daily 10:00-late). Helpful attendants at the reception desk can get you oriented.

**Cost and Hours:** General entry and main-floor exhibit are free, films cost €11.50, and seasonal exhibits are around €12.50 (credit cards only, no cash), exhibits open 10:00-19:00, cinemas open daily at 10:00 until last screening (ticket office usually closes at 22:00 or 23:00), +31 20 589 1400, www.eyefilm.nl.

### ▲A'dam Tower

This mega entertainment complex offers 360-degree views of the city, with display panels pointing out landmarks and providing fun tidbits of history, along with a cocktail bar and plenty of comfy spots to relax and take in the view. For more thrills, try "Europe's highest swing" over the IJ, a virtual-reality rollercoaster ride over Amsterdam, or the virtual-reality game room. There's also a revolving restaurant, and, in the basement, the Shelter nightclub.

**Cost and Hours:** Observation deck-€16.50, kids 4-12-€8.50; swing or VR ride-€6, family and combo-tickets available; daily 10:00-22:00, last entry one hour before closing, Overhoeksplein 1, www.adamtoren.nl.

### This Is Holland

Hosted in a modern, cylindrical building, this immersive exhibit includes several video presentations about Dutch history and the contemporary Netherlands. You'll take flight around the country in a nine-minute Disney-esque simulation, complete with sights, smells, wind, and mist, before learning about the locations you saw in your "flight."

**Cost and Hours:** €17, daily 10:00-22:00, next to A'dam Tower at Overhoeksplein 51, +31 20 215 3008, www.thisisholland.com.

### Biking

Biking in North Amsterdam is much more mellow than anywhere in the city core. See page 55 for details.

## SOUTHEAST AMSTERDAM

The following sights (except the Tropical Museum) are close enough together that you could see them in a single day, connecting the dots by tram, bike, or even on foot. From Centraal station, take tram #14 to Waterlooplein. On foot from the Mint Tower, it's a 10-minute stroll along the pleasant shopping street called Staalstraat.

Waterlooplein, a large square with tram and Metro stops, is a good place to get oriented to the neighborhood. Survey the scene from the lamp-lined Blauwbrug ("Blue Bridge")—a modest, modern version of Paris' Pont Alexandre III. The bridge crosses the Amstel River. From this point, the river is channeled to form the city's canals.

Scan clockwise. The big, curved, modern facade belongs to the opera house, commonly called the "Stopera," as it's the combo City Hall *(stadhuis)* and opera. Behind the Stopera are these sights (not visible from here, but described next): the Waterlooplein flea market, Rembrandt's House, and Gassan Diamonds. To the right of the Stopera are the twin gray steeples of the Moses and  Aaron Church, which sits roughly in the center of the former Jewish Quarter. Nearby are the Jewish Museum and Portuguese Synagogue.

Continue panning. That cute little drawbridge, while not famous, is certainly photogenic. (Its traditional counterbalance design is so effective that even a child can lift the bridge.) Crossing the Amstel upstream is one of the city's romantic spots, the Magere Brug ("Skinny Bridge"). A block away is the city's best look at a Dutch golden age mansion, the Willet-Holthuysen House (described on page 68).

**AMSTERDAM SIGHTS**

### Waterlooplein Flea Market

For more than a hundred years, the Jewish Quarter flea market has raged daily except Sunday (at the Waterlooplein Metro station, behind Rembrandt's House). The long, narrow park is filled with stalls selling cheap clothes, hippie stuff, old records, tourist knick-knacks, and garage-sale junk (see photo on previous page).

### ▲Rembrandt's House (Museum Het Rembrandthuis)

A middle-aged Rembrandt lived here from 1639 to 1658 after his wife's death, as his popularity and wealth dwindled down to obscurity and bankruptcy. As you enter, ask when the next etching or painting demonstration is scheduled and pick up the excellent audioguide.

**Cost and Hours:** €15, includes audioguide; Tue-Sun 10:00-18:00, closed Mon; etching and paint-making demonstrations almost hourly between 11:00 and 15:00, fewer crowds (but fewer demos) early and late in the day, Jodenbreestraat 4, +31 20 520 0400, www.rembrandthuis.nl.

**Visiting Rembrandt's House:** The house is reconstructed and filled with period objects (not his actual belongings) that re-create what Rembrandt's bankruptcy inventory of 1656 said he owned. Tight spiral stairs make your visit a one-way circuit—if you want to go back to any room you have to go to the end and start over again. You'll start with his well-equipped kitchen. The former entrance hall and ante-room are covered floor-to-ceiling with old paintings. None of them are by Rembrandt (some are by pupils), but they re-create how Rembrandt used these rooms to display art to potential buyers. The salon (Rembrandt's bedroom) has a reconstructed box bed like Rembrandt would have slept in. The Art Cabinet room is filled with odd  curios collected by this eccentric genius—shells, books, classical busts, stuffed crocodiles, and a Baroque-era jackalope.

In the large studio, imagine Rembrandt at work here in the well-lighted room where he created *The Night Watch*, *The Portrait of Maria Trip*, and numerous self-portraits (seen at the Rijksmuseum). You can attend an etching demonstration and ask the printer to explain the etching process (drawing in soft wax on a metal plate that's then dipped in acid, inked up, and printed). For the finale, enjoy several rooms dedicated (generally) to original Rembrandt etchings. You're not likely to see a single Rembrandt painting in the whole house, but this interesting museum may make you come away wanting to know more about the man and his art.

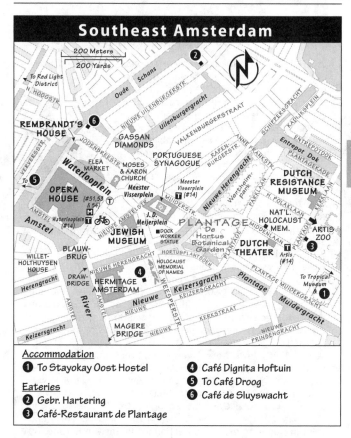

## Southeast Amsterdam

200 Meters
200 Yards

To Red Light District
N. HOOGSTR

Oude Schans
NIEUWE UILENBURGERSTR
Uilenburgergracht
NIEUWE UILENBURGERSTR
VALKENBURGERSTRAAT
SCHIPPERSGRACHT
KADIJKSPLEIN

**REMBRANDT'S HOUSE** ⑥
VERVERSSTR
JODENBREESTR
**GASSAN DIAMONDS**
FLEA MARKET
MOSES & AARON CHURCH
**PORTUGUESE SYNAGOGUE**
RAPEN BURGERSTR
ANNE FRANKSTR
ENTREPOTDOK
Entrepot Dok
PLANTAGEKADE

Waterlooplein
**OPERA HOUSE** (#51,53 & 54) Ⓣ
Meester Visserplein
Meester Visserplein Ⓣ (#14)
Nieuwe Herengracht
Wertheim-park
**DUTCH RESISTANCE MUSEUM**
H. POLAKLAAN
KERKLAAN

To ⑤
M
Waterlooplein Ⓜ (#14)
NIEUWE AMSTELSTR
MUIDERSTR
J.D. Meijerplein
**PLANTAGE**
De Hortus Botanical Garden
HORTUSPLANTSOEN
**DUTCH THEATER** Ⓣ (#14)
**NAT'L. HOLOCAUST MEM.**
MIDDENLAAN
PLANTAGE
Artis Ⓣ (#14)
**ARTIS ZOO** ③

Amstel
**JEWISH MUSEUM** Ⓣ
■ DOCK WORKER STATUE

BLAUW-BRUG
NIEUWE HERENGRACHT
Keizersgracht
KEIZERSGRACHT
Plantage
PLANTAGE MUIDERGRACHT

WILLET-HOLTHUYSEN HOUSE
Herengracht
DRAW-BRIDGE
**HERMITAGE AMSTERDAM** ④
HOLOCAUST MEMORIAL OF NAMES
WEESPERSTR
Nieuwe Keizersgracht
KEIZERSGRACHT

To Tropical Museum & ①
Muidergracht

AMSTEL River
NIEUWE
**MAGERE BRIDGE**
NIEUWE
KERKSTRAAT
NIEUWE PRINSENGRACHT

Keizersgracht

---

Accommodation
① To Stayokay Oost Hostel

Eateries
② Gebr. Hartering
③ Café-Restaurant de Plantage

④ Café Dignita Hoftuin
⑤ To Café Droog
⑥ Café de Sluyswacht

**Nearby:** Enjoy a scenic drink or snack at the historic black-brick **Café de Sluyswacht,** across the street (see page 223).

### Gassan Diamonds

Many shops in this "city of diamonds" offer tours. These tours come with two parts: a chance to see experts behind magnifying glasses polishing the facets of precious diamonds, followed by a visit to an intimate sales room to see (and perhaps buy) a mighty shiny yet very tiny souvenir.

The handy and professional **Gassan Diamonds** facility fills a huge warehouse one block from Rembrandt's House. A visit here plops you into the big-tour-group fray (notice how each tour group has a color-coded

## Jews in Amsterdam

In 1940, one in ten Amsterdammers was Jewish, and most lived in the neighborhood behind Waterlooplein. Jewish traders had long been welcome in a city that cared more about business than religion. In the late 1500s, many Sephardic Jews from Spain and Portugal immigrated, fleeing persecution. (The philosopher Baruch Spinoza's ancestors were among them.) In the 1630s, Yiddish-speaking Eastern European Jews (Ashkenazi) poured in. By 1700, the Jewish Quarter was a bustling, exotic, multicultural world, with more people speaking Portuguese, German, and Yiddish than Dutch.

Despite their large numbers, for several centuries Jews were not first-class citizens. They needed the city's permission to settle here, and they couldn't hold public office (but then, neither could Catholics under Calvinist rule). Still, the Jewish Quarter was not a ghetto per se, as the segregation wasn't forced and Jews faced no special taxes. Cosmopolitan Amsterdam was well acquainted with all types of beliefs and customs.

In 1796, Jews were given full citizenship. In exchange, they were required to learn the Dutch language and submit to the city's legal system. Over the next century or so, the Jewish culture began assimilating into the Dutch.

In 1940, Nazi Germany occupied the Netherlands. On February 22, 1941, the Nazis began rounding up Jews and shipping them to extermination camps in Eastern Europe. By war's end, more than 100,000 of the country's 140,000 Jews had died.

Today, about 15,000 Jews live in Amsterdam, and the Jewish Quarter has blended with the modern city. For more information on Amsterdam's many Jewish sights, see www.jck.nl.

sticker so they know which guide gets the commission on what they buy). You'll get a sticker, join a free 15-minute tour to see a polisher at work, and hear a general explanation of the process. Then you'll have an opportunity to sit down and have color and clarity described and illustrated with diamonds ranging in value from €100 to €50,000 (daily 9:00-17:30, Nieuwe Uilenburgerstraat 173, +31 20 622 5333, www.gassan.com, handy WC). Another company, **Coster,** also offers diamond demos. They're not as good as Gassan's, but Coster is convenient if you're near the Rijksmuseum (described on page 58).

## Hermitage Amsterdam

Though it cut ties with the famed Russian Hermitage in 2022, the Hermitage Amsterdam is hosting several collections while it considers its long-term plan. Visitors can see an exhibit on loan from the Amsterdam Museum, exploring the story of Amsterdam (until 2025); the Museum of Mind, with avant-garde "outsider" art; a second outsider art gallery; and other temporary exhibits.

**Cost and Hours:** Temporary exhibits-around €15, Amsterdam Museum exhibit-€18, Museum of the Mind-€17.50, combo-ticket for all three-€25, outsider art gallery-free; daily 10:00-17:00, mandatory free bag check, café, Amstel 51, tram #14 from Centraal station, recorded info +31 20 530 7488, www.hermitage.nl.

## De Hortus Botanical Garden

This is a unique oasis of tranquility within the city (no mobile phones are allowed, because "our collection of plants is a precious community—treat it with respect"). One of the oldest botanical gardens in the world, it dates from 1638, when medicinal herbs were grown here. Today, among its 6,000 different kinds of plants—most of which were collected by the Dutch East India Company in the 17th and 18th centuries—you'll find medicinal herbs, cacti, several greenhouses (one with a fluttery butterfly house—a hit with kids of all ages), and a tropical palm house. Much of it is described in English: "A Dutch merchant snuck a coffee plant out of Ethiopia, which ended up in this garden in 1706. This first coffee plant in Europe was the literal granddaddy of the coffee cultures of Brazil—long the world's biggest coffee producer."

**Cost and Hours:** €12, daily 10:00-17:00, tram #14 to Mr. Visserplein, Plantage Middenlaan 2A, +31 20 625 9021, www. dehortus.nl. The inviting Orangery Café serves tapas.

## ▲Jewish Museum (Joods Museum) and Portuguese Synagogue

A single ticket admits you to these two sights, located a half-block apart. The Jewish Museum tells the story of the Netherlands' Jews through three centuries, serving as a good introduction to Judaism and Jewish customs and religious traditions. Nearby, the 17th-century Portuguese Synagogue is again in use by a Jewish congregation.

**Cost and Hours:** €17, includes museum and Portuguese Synagogue; museum open daily 10:00-17:00; Portuguese Synagogue open Sun-Fri 10:00-17:00, closes earlier Dec-Jan and Fri off-season, closed Sat year-round; free audioguide, children's museum, tram #14 to Mr. Visserplein, Jonas Daniel Meijerplein 2, +31 20 531 0310, www.jhm.nl. The museum's modern, minimalist, kosher $$ café serves Jewish specialties.

**Visiting the Museum:** Originally opened in 1932, the Jewish Museum was forced to close during the Nazi years. It reopened after the war, and recent renovations have joined four historic former synagogues together to form the museum's single modern complex.

Go downstairs, follow signs for *Religion,* and you'll enter the impressive **Great Synagogue.** Have a seat, surrounded by religious objects, and picture it during its prime (1671-1943). The vast hall would be full for a service—men downstairs, women above in the gallery. On the east wall (the symbolic direction of Jerusalem) is the ark—the alcove where they keep the scrolls of the Torah (the Jewish scriptures, comprising the first five books of the Old Testament of the Bible). The rabbi and other men, wearing thigh-length prayer shawls, would approach the ark and carry the Torah to the raised platform in the center of the room. After unwrapping it from its drapery and silver cap, a man would use a *yad* (ceremonial pointer) to follow along while singing the text aloud.

Displays (well described in English) around the room explain Jewish customs, from birth (circumcision) to puberty (the bar/bat mitzvah, celebrating the entry into adulthood) to Passover celebrations to marriage—culminating in the groom stomping on a glass while everyone shouts "Mazel tov!"

Next, head up the spiral staircase to the **women's gallery,** with exhibits tracing the history of Amsterdam's Jews from 1600 to 1900. This was a golden age when Amsterdam and its Jewish population both thrived in relative harmony.

Exhibits about Jews in the 20th century are housed in the former **New Synagogue.** Circle the room clockwise to see it chronologically: first, the thriving community of 60,000—businessmen, intellectuals, civic leaders, and entertainers. Then comes the grim era of the Nazi occupation, when Jews were rounded up and deported. Everyone had to decide whether to stay, to hide, or to flee. The community was decimated. Personal artifacts—chairs, clothes—tell the devastating history in a very real way.

• *From here, you can continue your visit by heading to the nearby Portuguese Synagogue. (As you exit the Jewish Museum, it's the big brick building directly ahead of you, across busy Weesperstraat.)*

**Visiting the Portuguese Synagogue:** This grand structure brings together both old and new—a historic synagogue that today serves a revived Jewish community. It was built in the 1670s (when Catholics were worshipping underground) to house a community of Sephardic (Iberian) Jews who fled persecution. At the time,

# The Synagogue

A synagogue is a place of public worship, where Jews gather to pray, sing, and read from the Torah. Most synagogues have similar features, though they vary depending on the congregation.

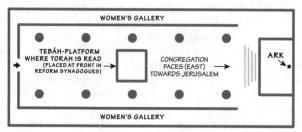

The synagogue generally faces toward Jerusalem. At the east end is an alcove called the **ark,** which holds the Torah. These scriptures (the first five books of the Old Testament) are written in Hebrew on scrolls wrapped in luxuriant cloth. The other main element of the synagogue is the **bema** (or a tebáh), a platform from which the Torah is read aloud. In traditional Orthodox synagogues, the bema is near the center of the hall, and the reader stands facing the same direction as the congregation. (In other branches of Judaism, the bema is at the front, and the reader faces the worshippers.) Orthodox synagogues have separate worship areas for men and women, usually with women in the balcony.

The synagogue walls might be decorated with elaborate patterns of vines or geometric designs, but never statues of people (as that might be considered idol worship). A lamp above the ark is always kept lit, as it was in the ancient temple of Jerusalem. Candelabras called menorahs also recall the temple. Other common symbols are the two tablets of the Ten Commandments given to Moses, or a Star of David, representing the Jewish king's shield.

At a typical service, the congregation arrives at the start of Sabbath (Friday evening). As a sign of respect toward God, men don yarmulkes (small round caps). As the cantor leads songs and prayers, worshippers follow along in a book of weekly readings. At the heart of the service, everyone stands as the Torah is ceremoniously paraded, unwrapped, and placed on the bema. Someone—the rabbi, the cantor, or a congregant—reads the words aloud. The rabbi ("teacher") might give a commentary on the Torah passage.

it was the world's largest. The building survived World War II, though its congregation barely did.

Inside, the synagogue is majestic in its simplicity—a spacious place of worship with four Ionic columns supporting a wooden roof. There's no electric lighting, only candles and windows. Find the main features: the platform (near the back) where the cantor presides, the wood-columned niche at the far end for the Torah, the two ceremonial sofas for VIPs, the special pew (middle of left wall) for important visitors, the upstairs balconies for women, and the wood canopy (far right corner) where weddings take place—there might even be sand under your feet, which (may) symbolize the Israelites' sojourn through the desert.

Explore the rest of the synagogue complex. (Any unlocked door is yours for the visiting.) You can see the Ladies Gallery, the candle-storage room, and the ritual bath, where women purify after menstruation. Don't miss the downstairs Treasury, containing precious Torah scrolls, ceremonial objects, textiles, and rare books, plus a narrated slideshow on the history of this beloved synagogue, known as the *Esnoga*.

## Holocaust Memorial of Names

Opened in 2021, this somber labyrinth of walls is designed in the shape of four Hebrew letters that mean "In memory of." It's made of 102,000 bricks, each with the name, date of birth, and age at death of a Dutch victim who was killed by the Nazis. About 140,000 Jews lived in the Netherlands before World War II—and by the end of the war, more than 70 percent had become victims of the Holocaust. To remember and give dignity to these people—as well as 220 Sinti and Roma victims—this memorial encourages visitors to walk thoughtfully through and ponder the humanity of this tragic time. Look up Anne Frank *(Annelies Frank 12.6.1929-15 jaar),* and when you do, notice how many Franks were lost with her. Any name on a brick here would have known hundreds of others on other bricks (free, daily 8:00-20:00, behind the Jewish Museum on Weesperstraat; the recommended Café Dignita is adjacent in the peaceful park).

## ▲Dutch Theater (Hollandsche Schouwburg), a.k.a. National Holocaust Memorial

Once a lively theater in the Jewish neighborhood and today a moving memorial, this building was used as an assembly hall for local Jews destined for Nazi concentration camps.

**Cost and Hours:** Donation requested, free with Jewish Museum/Portuguese Synagogue ticket, open daily 11:00-17:00, tram #14 to Artis, Plantage Middenlaan 24, +31 20 531 0380, www.hollandscheschouwburg. nl.

**Visiting the Theater:** As you enter, you'll see a wall covered with 6,700 family names, paying tribute to the more than 100,000 Jews deported and killed by the Nazis. Some 70,000 victims spent time here, awaiting transfer to concentration camps.

Upstairs (after passing a few costumes from the building's theater days), you reach a dated-but-evocative history exhibit. There's a model of the ghetto, where you can push a button to light up locations where important events happened. Grainy film footage shows a happy Jewish wedding. Other photos show smiling Jews living ordinary lives. Then came the Nazi occupation—the roundups, mandatory ID cards, deportation papers, and (as seen in film footage) Nazis loading Jews onto trains to the transit camp at Westerbork. A few reminders of the victims (such as their shoes and letters) puts a human face on the staggering numbers. Back downstairs in the ground-floor courtyard, notice the hopeful messages that visiting school groups attach to the wooden tulips.

**Nearby:** Across the street, in a former Jewish daycare, is the **National Holocaust Museum,** with a modest exhibit and plans to expand. A block away in Wertheim Park is the **Auschwitz Memorial,** inspired by a victim's poem referring to the broken sky of his world and declaring the motto "Never Again." A plaque explains that of the 140,000 Jews who lived in the Netherlands, 107,000 were deported, and of those, only 5,000 survived.

### ▲▲Dutch Resistance Museum (Verzetsmuseum)

This is an impressive look at how the Dutch resisted (or collaborated with) their Nazi occupiers from 1940 to 1945. You'll see propaganda movie clips, study forged ID cards under a magnifying glass, and read about ingenious and courageous efforts—big and small—to hide local Jews from the Germans and undermine the Nazi regime. While the masses crowd the Anne Frank House, this museum (which I find at least as impactful) is never busy. Take full advantage of the included audioguide for maximum understanding.

**Cost and Hours:** €12, includes audioguide; Mon-Fri 10:00-17:00, Sat-Sun from 11:00, children's section, mandatory and free bag check, tram #14 from the train station or Dam Square, Plantage Kerklaan 61, +31 20 620 2535, www.verzetsmuseum.org.

**Visiting the Museum:** The museum presents a timeless moral dilemma: Is it better to collaborate with a wicked system to effect small-scale change—or to resist outright, even if your efforts are doomed to fail? You'll learn why some parts of Dutch society opted for the former, and others for the latter. It doesn't shy away from the less heroic side of the story (for example, the fact that most of the population only became actively anti-Nazi after Dutch gentiles—not just Jews—were deported to forced-labor camps). You'll hear riveting first-person accounts of what it was like to go under-ground, strike, starve, or return from the camps.

The collection may be reorganized by the time you visit, but in general, the museum experience is broken into six periods—each with a short introductory video. There are plenty of screens and interactive exhibits, including personal stories from survivors.

You'll get a sense of life in the Netherlands before the Nazis—rich and poor, living peaceful and upright lives, ignoring the rise of fascism around them. Then—bam—it's May 1940 and the Germans invade the Netherlands, destroy Rotterdam, drive Queen Wilhelmina into exile, and—in four short days of fighting—hammer home the message that resistance is futile. The Germans install local Dutch Nazis in power. But for most Dutch people, life goes on as before.

In February 1941, Nazis start rounding up Jews from the neighborhood, killing nine protesters. Amsterdammers respond by shutting down the trams, schools, and businesses in a massive two-day strike.

You'll see many examples of Nazi oppression. People were forced to have ID cards. Nazi propaganda posters hung everywhere. Goods were rationed. Movies had Aryan-race themes.

The Dutch fought back, in small ways and big. Vandals turned Nazi V-for-Victory posters into W-for-Wilhelmina. Preachers gave pointed anti-Nazi sermons and schoolkids told "Kraut" jokes. Farmers organized a milk strike. Brave resisters forged documents. They hid forbidden radios under floorboards and Jewish people inside closets. Printers secretly cranked out underground newspapers (such as *Het Parool,* which became a major daily paper). As the war progressed, the armed Dutch Resistance became bolder and more violent, killing German occupiers and Dutch collaborators.

In September 1944, the Allies liberated Antwerp and the Netherlands started celebrating...too soon. The Nazis dug in and punished the country by cutting off rations, plunging West Holland into the "Hunger Winter" of 1944 to 1945, during which 20,000 died. Finally, it's springtime. The Allies liberate the country, and at war's end, the Dutch flag flies again, and Nazi helmets are turned into Dutch bedpans.

### ▲Tropical Museum (Tropenmuseum)

This imaginative museum focuses on Dutch colonialism in Suriname, the Caribbean, and Indonesia, exploring themes including expansion and trade, slavery and racism, and language and religion. The grand building was purpose-built by the Royal Tropen Institute a century ago to house and better understand colony culture. Ride the elevator near the ticket desk to the top floor and circle your way down through this immense collection, opened in 1926 to give the Dutch people a peek at their vast colonial holdings. Don't miss the rare *bisj* poles from New Guinea standing in the center.

**Cost and Hours:** €16, €8 for kids 4-18; daily 10:00-17:00, closed Mon off-season; tram #14 to Linnaeusstraat 2, +31 20 568 8200, www.tropenmuseum.nl.

**Eating:** The **$ Café de Tropen** is a delight overlooking a park in back.

# AMSTERDAM CITY WALK

*From Centraal Station
to Spui Square*

Amsterdam today looks much as it did in its golden age, the 1600s. It's a retired sea captain of a city, still in love with life, with a broad outlook and a salty story to tell.

Take a Dutch sampler walk from one end of the old center to the other, tasting all that Amsterdam has to offer along the way. It's your best single stroll through quintessentially Dutch scenes, hidden churches, surprising shops, thriving happy-hour hangouts, and eight centuries of history.

## Orientation

**Length of This Walk:** Allow about two hours.

**When to Go:** The walk is best during the day, when churches and sights are open. After about 17:00 you'll find three major stops (the hidden church, the Begijnhof, and the herring stand) closed.

**Alert:** Beware of silent transport—trams and bikes. Walkers should stay off the tram tracks and bike paths, and yield to bell-ringing bikers.

**Royal Palace:** €12.50, daily 10:00-17:00 but hours can vary for official business.

**New Church:** €9-16 to enter interior (depending on special exhibits), daily 10:00-18:00.

**De Papegaai Hidden Church:** Free, Mon-Sat 10:00-16:00, Sun until 13:30.

**Amsterdam Museum:** Typically a highlight of this walk, this wonderful museum is now closed for a major renovation.

**Begijnhof:** Free, daily 10:00-18:00.

**Tours:** ∩ Download my free Amsterdam City Walk audio tour.

**Services:** You can find WCs at fast-food places and in the Kalvertoren shopping mall.

## OVERVIEW

This walk starts at the central-as-can-be Centraal station and ends
at Spui Square. You'll head down Damrak to Dam Square, continuing south down Kalverstraat to the Mint Tower (Munttoren), then
waft through the flower market (Bloemenmarkt) before dropping
by the herring stand on Koningsplein and circling back to Spui.
The route basically follows the central tramline, so to zip from any
spot to anywhere else, simply hop on tram #2 or #12. Trams #2 and
#12 also continue to the Rijksmuseum (and Van Gogh Museum).

# The Walk Begins

### ❶ Centraal Station

Here, where today's train travelers enter the city, sailors of yore
disembarked from seagoing ships. They were met by street musicians, pickpockets, hotel
runners, and ladies carrying red lanterns. Centraal
station, built in the late
1800s, sits on reclaimed
land at what was once
the harbor mouth. With
warm red brick and prick-
ly spires, the station is the
first of several Neo-Goth-
ic buildings we'll see from the late 19th century, the era of Amsterdam's economic revival. One of the station's towers has a clock dial;
the other tower's dial is a weather vane. Watch the hand twitch as
the wind gusts in every direction—N, Z, O, and W.

Let's get oriented: *nord, zuid, ost,* and *vest.* Facing the station,
you're facing north. Farther north, on the other side of the station,
is the IJ (pronounced "eye"), the body of water that gives Amsterdam access to the open sea.

Now turn your back to the station and face the city, looking
south. The city spreads out before you like a fan, in a series of concentric canals. Ahead of you stretches the street called Damrak,
which leads—like a red carpet for guests entering Amsterdam—to
Dam Square a half-mile away. That's where we're headed.

To the left of Damrak is the city's old *(oude)* town. The crown-
topped steeple of the Old Church (Oude Kerk) marks the center
of that neighborhood. That historic quarter has long been the Red
Light District (☐ see the Red Light District Walk chapter). Closer to you, towering above the old part of town, is the domed St.

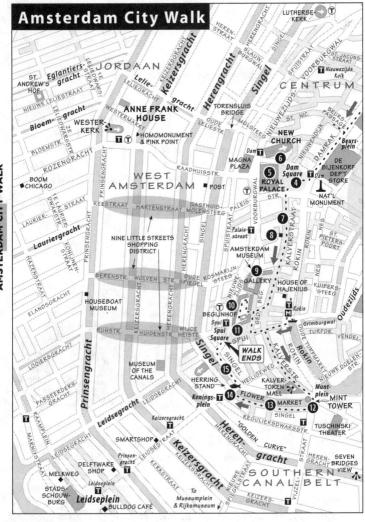

Amsterdam City Walk

Nicholas Church. It was built in the 1880s, when Catholics—after about three centuries of oppression—were finally free to worship in public. To your far left is the DoubleTree by Hilton Hotel, with its 11th-floor SkyLounge Amsterdam offering perhaps the city's best viewpoint.

To the right of Damrak is the new *(nieuwe)* part of town, where you'll find the Anne Frank House and the peaceful Jordaan neighborhood.

The train station is the city's transportation center. Many trams leave from out front. Beneath your feet is a new Metro line. In the "Golden 1990s" when the economy was booming, Am-

On the map:

To Central Station / To Ibis Hotel & Bike Garage — CENTRAAL STATION — Stations-plein — WALK BEGINS — To IJ (Channel) — To Cruise Terminal — DE RUIJTERKADE

DAMRAK SEX MUSEUM — ST. NICHOLAS — WEEPERS' TOWER — SKYLOUNGE AMST. — OSTERDOKSSTR. — CENTRAL LIBRARY

STOCK EXCHANGE (BEURS) — OUR LORD IN THE ATTIC MUSEUM — KROMME WAAL — PRINS HENDRIKKADE — Oosterdok — NEMO (SCIENCE MUSEUM)

OLD CHURCH — EROTIC MUSEUM

RED LIGHT DISTRICT — DE WAAG — Nieuwmarkt

HASH MUSEUM — BARNDESTEEG — ST. ANTONIESBREESTR.

**Amsterdam City Walk route:**

1. Centraal Station
2. Damrak
3. Stock Exchange
4. Dam Square
5. Royal Palace
6. New Church
7. Kalverstraat
8. De Papegaai Hidden Church
9. Amsterdam Museum
10. Begijnhof
11. Spui Square
12. Mint Tower
13. Flower Market
14. Konigsplein and a Herring Stand
15. Koningsplein to Spui

Heart of Red Light District

AMST. UNIVERSITY — GASSAN DIAMONDS — REMBRANDT'S HOUSE — FLEA MARKET — MOSES & AARON CHURCH — Waterlooplein — PORTUGUESE SYNAGOGUE — SOUTHEAST AMSTERDAM — OPERA HOUSE — Meester Visserplein — Jonas Daniel Meijerplein — Amstel — Waterlooplein — JEWISH HIST. MUSEUM — DOCK WORKER STATUE — De Hortus Botanical Garden — DUTCH THEATER — Rembrandtplein — WILLET-HOLTHUYSEN HOUSE — BLAUW BRUG — DRAW-BRIDGE — HERMITAGE AMSTERDAM — HOLOCAUST MEMORIAL OF NAMES — Nieuwe Keizersgracht — Keizersgracht

200 Meters / 200 Yards

sterdam committed the city to a grand infrastructure expansion to accommodate the tens of thousands of people living in North Amsterdam, the fast-growing suburb beyond the IJ. Today that investment is paying off, and this plaza, while providing a people-friendly welcome to the city, also works as an efficient transit hub.

On your far right, in front of Ibis Hotel, is a huge, multistory parking garage—for bikes only. Biking in Holland is the way to go—the land is flat, distances are short, and there are designated bike paths everywhere. The bike parking garage is free, courtesy of the government, and intended to encourage this green and ultra-efficient mode of transportation.

• *Let's head out. With your back to the station, start walking south into the city to the head of Damrak. Be aware of trams and bikes as you cross the street. Keep going south straight along the right side of the street, following the crowds on...*

## ❷ Damrak

This street was once a riverbank. It's where the Amstel River flowed north into the IJ, which led to a vast inlet of the North Sea called the Zuiderzee. It's this unique geography that turned Amsterdam into a center of trade. Visualize the physical layout of this man-made city: built on trees, protected by dikes, and laced with canals. Location, location, location. Boats could sail up the Amstel into the interior of Europe, or out to the North Sea, to reach the rest of the world. No wonder that St. Nicholas, protector of water travelers, was the city's patron saint.

As you stroll along Damrak, look left. There's a marina, lined with old brick buildings. Though they aren't terribly historic, the scene still captures a bit of golden age Amsterdam. Think of it: Back in the 1600s, this area was the harbor, and those buildings warehoused exotic goods from all over the world.

All along Damrak, you'll pass a veritable gauntlet of touristy shops. These seem to cover every Dutch cliché. You'll see wooden shoes, which the Dutch used to wear to get around easily in the marshy soil, and all manner of tulips; the real ones come from Holland's famed fresh-flower industry. Heineken fridge magnets advertise one of the world's most popular pilsner beers. There are wheels of cheese, marijuana-leaf hats, team jerseys for the Ajax football (soccer) club, and memorabilia with the city's "XXX" logo. You'll likely hear a hand-cranked barrel organ and see windmill-shaped saltshakers. And everything seems to be available in bright orange—because that's the official color of the Dutch royal family.

At the **Damrak Sex Museum** at Damrak 18, you'll find the city's most notorious commodity on display (museum described on page 75). As a port town catering to sailors and businessmen away from home, Amsterdam has always accommodated the sex trade.

Continue up Damrak (noting the **canal boats** on your left) for more touristy delectables. You'll pass places selling the popular local fast food: french fries. Here they're called *Vlaamse friets*—Flemish fries—since they were invented in the Low Countries. The stand at Damrak 41 is a favorite, where plenty of locals stop to dip their fries in mayonnaise (not ketchup).

Farther up Damrak, you'll pass many restaurants. It quickly becomes obvious that, here, international cuisine is almost like going local. Restaurants serving rijsttafel, a sampler of assorted Indonesian dishes, are especially popular, thanks to the days when the Dutch East Indies were a colony. Amsterdammers on the go often grab a simple sandwich *(broodje)* or a pita-bread wrap *(shoarma)* from a Middle Eastern takeout joint.

Remember, we're walking along what was once the Amstel River. Today, the Amstel is channeled into canals and its former mouth is covered by Centraal station. But Amsterdam still remains a major seaport. That's because, in the 19th century, the Dutch dug the North Sea Canal to create a shorter route to the open sea. These days, more than 100,000 ships a year dock on the outskirts of Amsterdam, making it Europe's fourth-busiest seaport (giant cruise ships stop here as well). For all of Amsterdam's existence, it's been a trading center.

• *The long brick building with the square clock tower, along the left side of Damrak, is the...*

### ❸ Stock Exchange (Beurs van Berlage)

This impressive structure, a symbol of the city's long tradition as a trading town, was built with nine million bricks. Like so many buildings in this once-marshy city, it was constructed on a foundation of pilings—some 5,000 tree trunks hammered vertically into the soil. When the Beurs opened in 1903, it was one of the world's first modernist buildings, with a geometric, minimal, no-frills style. Emphasizing function over looks, it helped set the architectural tone for many 20th-century buildings. Note how the reliefs celebrate the worker—it was a time of "capitalism with a heart" (free trade but with a greater respect for workers).

Make your way to the end of the long, century-old building. Amsterdammers have gathered in this neighborhood to trade since medieval times. Back then, "trading stock" meant buying and selling any kind of goods that could be loaded and unloaded onto a boat—goats, chickens, or kegs of beer. Over time, they began exchanging slips of paper, or "futures," rather than actual goods. Traders needed moneychangers, who needed bankers, who made money by lending money. By the 1600s, Amsterdam had become

# Amsterdam's Story

**Beginnings:** Situated at the mouth of the Amstel River, Amsterdam was where Rhine riverboats met sea-going vessels—trade flourished. Around 1250, locals built a dam on the Amstel, creating "Amstel-dam." They drained the marshy delta, channeled the water into canals, sank pilings, and built a city from scratch.

**1300s Charter:** Amsterdam was already an international trade center for German beer, locally caught herring, cloth, bacon, salt, and wine. When the region's leading bishop granted the town a charter (1300), Amsterdammers could then set up law courts, judge their own matters, and be essentially autonomous.

**1500s Growth:** Amsterdam became a bustling trade-and-banking center of 12,000 people crammed within the Singel canal. The walled city was ruled from afar by Catholic Habsburgs in Spain. Angry Protestants rose up, vandalizing Catholic churches and starting a war of independence (officially granted in 1648).

**1600s Golden Age:** Meanwhile, Holland was inventing the global economy. In 1602, hardy Dutch sailors (and Henry Hudson, an Englishman in Dutch service) tried their hand at trade with the Far East. When they returned, they brought with them valuable spices, diamonds, rijsttafel recipes...and the golden age. The Dutch East India Company (abbreviated "VOC" in Dutch), a state-subsidized import/export business, combined nautical skills with capitalist investing. With 500 or so 150-foot ships cruising in and out of Amsterdam's harbor, it was the first great multinational corporation.

Golden age Amsterdam (pop. 100,000) was perhaps the wealthiest city on earth—the "warehouse of the world." Goods came from everywhere. The VOC's specialties were spices (pepper and cinnamon), coffee and tea, Chinese porcelain, and silk. Meanwhile, the competing Dutch West India Company concentrated on the New World, trading enslaved African people for

one of the world's first great capitalist cities, loaning money to free-spending kings, dukes, and bishops.

When you reach the end of the building, look across the square called **Beursplein,** which houses the stock exchange. In 1984, the Beurs building was turned into a cultural center, and the stock exchange moved next door to the Euronext complex—a joint attempt by France, Belgium, and the Netherlands to compete with

South American sugar. With its wealth, the city expanded west and south, adding new canals lined with gabled mansions. Rembrandt, Vermeer, and Hals captured the can-do spirit on canvas.

At the peak of the golden age, Amsterdam was gripped by "tulip mania." Investors drove the value of tulip bulbs to insane heights. Then in 1637, the market crashed, symbolically marking the end of an era. Soon, Holland was eclipsed by new superpowers England and France, who took over the overseas trade and scuttled their fleet in demoralizing wars.

**1700s Decline:** Amsterdam became a city of backwater bankers and small manufacturers—still a cultural center but befitting Holland's small size. The city hit rock bottom in 1795: French troops invaded, and proud Holland was soon saddled with a monarchy.

**1800s Revival:** The tech-minded Dutch built a canal to the North Sea, rejuvenating Amsterdam's port. Railroads laced the country, and Amsterdam expanded southward by draining new land. The Rijksmuseum, Centraal station, and Magna Plaza (formerly the main post office) date from this economic upswing.

**1900s:** The 1930s Depression hit hard, followed by five years of occupation under the Nazis, aided by pro-Nazi Dutch. The city's large Jewish population was decimated by Nazi deportations and extermination (falling from about 75,000 Jews in 1940 to just 15,000 in 1945). With postwar prosperity, 1960s Amsterdam became a global center for Europe's hippies, promoting legal marijuana, free sex, and free bikes.

**Today:** Amsterdam is now a city of 820,000 people jammed into small apartments (often with the same floor plan as their neighbors'). Since the 1970s, many immigrants have become locals. One in 10 Amsterdammers is Surinamese, and one in 10 prays toward Mecca.

the power of Britain's stock exchange. See the stock price readout board. How's your Heineken stock doing? Green means it's going up, and red means it's losing value. Amsterdam still thrives as the center of Dutch business and, besides Heineken, is home to Shell Oil, Philips Electronics, and ING Bank.

Directly opposite Beursplein on Damrak (at #68) is **Beurspassage,** a fancy, faux Art Nouveau shopping passageway. Use the crosswalk and enter the passage. Wander down and back to notice the symbols of the city. Fill your water bottle in the mouth of a fish. Enjoy the marble floor, the chandeliers and Tiffany lanterns, and the mosaic ceiling depicting a primordial soup with all the stuff you'd find tossed into a canal, from old bike tires to Van Gogh's ear.

• *Continue south up Damrak until it opens into Dam Square. Make your way—carefully—across the street to the cobblestone pavement. Now, stand in the middle of the square and take it all in.*

### ❹ Dam Square

This is the historic heart of Amsterdam. The city got its start right here in about the year 1250, when fishermen in this marshy delta settled along the built-up banks of the Amstel River. They built a *damme*, blocking the Amstel River, and creating a small village called "Amstel-damme." To the north was the *damrak* (meaning "outer harbor"), a waterway that eventually led to the sea. That's the street we just walked. To the south was the *rokin* ("inner harbor"), for river traffic inland—and nowadays another busy street. With access to the sea, fishermen were soon trading with German riverboats traveling downstream and with seafaring boats from Stockholm, Hamburg, and London. Land-trade routes converged here as well, and a customs house stood in this spot. Dam Square was the center of it all.

Today, Dam Square is still the center of Dutch life, at least symbolically. The Royal Palace and major department stores face the square. Mimes, jugglers, and human statues mingle with locals and tourists. As Holland's most recognizable square, this is where political demonstrations begin and end.

**Circling the Square:** Pan the square clockwise and take in the sights, starting with the Royal Palace—the large domed building on the west side. To its right stands the New Church (Nieuwe Kerk); it's located on the pedestrian-only shopping street called Nieuwendijk, which runs parallel to Damrak and stretches all the way to Centraal station. Panning past Damrak, see the proud old De Bijenkorf ("The Beehive") department store. (The store's cafeteria on the top floor is a great place to rise above it all for a light meal; see page 242.)

Farther right, the Grand Hotel Krasnapolsky has a lovely circa-1900 glass-roofed "winter garden." The white obelisk is the National Monument, built in 1956 to honor WWII casualties. When the Nazis occupied Holland from 1940 to 1945, they deported some

60,000 Jewish Amsterdammers, driving many—including young Anne Frank and her family—into hiding. The "Hunger Winter" of 1944-1945 killed thousands of Dutch and forced many to survive on little more than tulip bulbs. This obelisk—with its carvings of the crucified Christ, men in chains, and howling dogs—remembers the suffering of that grim time and is also considered a monument for peace.

A few blocks behind the hotel is the edge of the Red Light District. To the right of the hotel stretches the street called the Nes, lined with some of Amsterdam's edgy live-theater venues. Panning farther right, find Rokin street—Damrak's southern counterpart, continuing past the square. Next, just to the right of the touristy Madame Tussauds, is Kalverstraat, a busy pedestrian-only shoppers mall.

## ❺ Royal Palace (Koninklijk Huis)

Despite the name, this is really the former City Hall. In medieval times, this was where the city council and mayor met. Amster-

dam was a self-governing community that prided itself on its independence and thumbed its nose at royalty. In about 1650, the old medieval Town Hall was replaced with this one. Its style is appropriately Classical, recalling the democratic Greeks. (That's a nice message, but the government was really more like an oligarchy, ruled by rich and powerful trading families.) The triangular pediment features denizens of the sea cavorting with Neptune and his gilded copper trident—all appropriate imagery for sea-trading Amsterdam. The small balcony (just above the entry doors) is where city leaders have long appeared for major speeches, pronouncements, executions, and (these days) for newly married royalty to blow kisses to the crowds.

Today, the palace remains one of the four official residences of King Willem-Alexander and is usually open to visitors (see page 71).

• *A few paces away, to the right as you're facing the Royal Palace, is the...*

## ❻ New Church (Nieuwe Kerk)

Though called the "New" Church, this building is actually 600 years old—a mere 100 years newer than the "Old" Church (in the Red Light District). The sundial above the entrance once served as the city's official timepiece.

This church is where many of the Netherlands' monarchs are married, and all are "inaugurated." (Dutch royals are not crowned, as they never actually wear the official crown.) If you pay the expensive fee to go inside, you'll see a spacious, well-lit, yet bare interior (occupied by a new art exhibit every three months) that looks quite different from the Baroque-encrusted churches found in the rest of Europe.

In 1566, clear-eyed Protestant extremists throughout Holland marched into Catholic churches (including this one), lopped off the heads of holy statues, stripped gold-leaf angels from the walls, urinated on Virgin Marys, and shattered stained-glass windows in a wave of anti-Catholic vandalism.

This iconoclasm (icon-breaking) of 1566 started an 80-year war against Spain and the Habsburgs, leading finally to Dutch independence in 1648. Catholic churches like this one were converted to the new dominant religion, Calvinist Protestantism (today's Dutch Reformed Church). From then on, Dutch churches downplayed the "graven images" and "idols" of ornate religious art.

• *From Dam Square, head south (going down the pedestrian mall just to the right of Madame Tussaud's).*

### ❼ Kalverstraat

Kalverstraat (strictly pedestrian-only—even bikers need to dismount and walk) has been a traditional shopping street for centuries. But today it's notorious among locals as a noisy, soulless string of chain stores. Along with familiar US and international brands, you'll see a few unfamiliar franchises from European countries. For smaller and more elegant stores, try the adjacent district called De Negen Straatjes ("The Nine Little Streets"). Only about four blocks west of Kalverstraat, it's where 200 or so shops and cafés mingle along tranquil canals.

• *About 100 yards along, keep a sharp eye out for the next sight (it's fairly easy to miss): On the right, just before and across from the McDonald's, at #58, is...*

AMSTERDAM CITY WALK

## City on a Sandbar

Amsterdam sits in the marshy delta at the mouth of the Amstel River—a completely man-made city, built on millions of wooden pilings. The city was founded on unstable mud, which sits on stable sand. In the Middle Ages, buildings were made of wood, which rests lightly and easily on mud. But devastating fires repeatedly wiped out entire neighborhoods, so stone became the building material of choice. But fire-resistant brick was too heavy to rest on mud, so for more support, pilings were driven 30 feet through the soggy soil and into the sand. The Royal Palace sits upon 13,000 such pilings—still solid after 350 years. (The wood survives if kept wet and out of the air.)

Since World War II, concrete has been used for the pilings, with foundations driven 60 feet deep through the first layer of sand, through more mud, and into a second layer of sand. Today's biggest buildings have foundations that go down as far as 120 feet deep.

Many of the city's buildings, however, tend to lean this way and that as their pilings settle—and local landowners were concerned that the tunneling for the new Metro line would cause their buildings to tilt even more. The snoopy-looking white cameras mounted on various building corners (such as on the Beurs) monitor buildings for settling.

## ❽ De Papegaai Hidden Church (Petrus en Paulus Kerk)

This Catholic church—with a simple white interior, nice carved wood, and Stations of the Cross paintings (try reading the Dutch captions)—is an oasis of peace amid crass 21st-century commercialism. It's not exactly a hidden church (after all, you've found it), but it still keeps a low profile. That's because it dates from an era when Catholics in Amsterdam were forced to worship in secret.

In the 1500s, Protestants were fighting Catholics all over Europe. As a center for trade, Amsterdam has long made an effort to put business above ideological differences, doing business with all parties. But by 1578 the division had become too wide to straddle, and Protestant extremists took political control of the city. They expelled Catholic leaders and bishops and outlawed the religion. Catholic churches were stripped of their lavish decoration and converted into Dutch Reformed churches. Simultaneously, the Dutch were rising up politically against their (Catholic) Spanish overlords, and eventually threw them out.

For the next two centuries, Amsterdam's Catholics were driven underground. While technically illegal here, Catholicism was tolerated (kind of like marijuana is, these days). Catholics could worship so long as they practiced in humble, unadvertised places, like this church. The church gets its nickname from a parrot *(papegaai)* carved over the entrance of the house that formerly stood on this site. Now, a stuffed parrot hangs in the nave to remember that original *papegaai*.

Today, the church asks visitors for a mere "15 minutes for God" (so says the sign: *een kwartier voor God*)—an indication of how religion has long been a marginal part of highly commercial and secular Amsterdam.

• *Return to Kalverstraat and continue south for about 100 yards. At #92, where Kalverstraat crosses Wijde Kapel Steeg, look to the right to find an archway that leads to the entrance and courtyard of the Amsterdam Museum.*

## ❾ Amsterdam Museum

The ▲▲ Amsterdam Museum—the city's history museum—is just through this door, but it's closed for several years for a major renovation. Also closed is the museum's public corridor, the Amsterdam Gallery (formerly known as the "Civic Guards Gallery"), lined with group portraits of Amsterdam's citizens from the golden age to modern times.

Pause at the entrance to the museum complex to view the archway. On the slumping arch is Amsterdam's coat of arms—a red shield with three Xs and a crown. The X-shaped crosses represent the crucifixion of St. Andrew, the patron saint of fishermen. (And here you thought the three Xs referred to the city's sex trade.) They also represent the three virtues of heroism, determination, and mercy—symbolism that was declared by the queen after the Dutch experience in World War II. (Before that, they likely symbolized the three great medieval threats: fire, flood, and plague.) The crown dates from 1489, when Maximilian I—a Habsburg emperor—also ruled the Low Countries. He paid off a big loan with help from Amsterdam's city bankers and, as thanks for the cash, gave the city permission to use his prestigious trademark, the Habsburg crown, atop its shield.

Below that is a relief (dated 1581) showing boys around a dove, asking for charity, reminding all who pass that this building was once an orphanage.

• *Continue down Kalverstraat to #128 from where a small lane on the right, Begijnensteeg, leads directly to the old door of the Begijnhof. (Admission into this sweet little haven is free but limited to 50 people at a time.)*

## ⓾ Begijnhof

This quiet courtyard, lined with houses around a church, has sheltered women since 1346 (and is quite a contrast with the noisy Kalverstraat just steps away).

For centuries this was the home of a community of Beguines—pious and simple women who removed themselves from the world at large to dedicate their lives to God. When it was first established, it literally was a "woman's island"—a circle of houses facing a peaceful courtyard, surrounded by water.

As you enter, keep in mind that this spot isn't just a tourist attraction; it's also a place where people live. Be considerate: Don't photograph the residents or their homes, be quiet, and stick to the area near the churches.

Begin your visit by walking to the far end and find the **statue** of one of these charitable sisters. You'll find it just beyond the church. The Beguines' ranks swelled during the Crusades, when so many men took off, never to return, leaving society with an abundance of single women. Later, women widowed by the hazards of overseas trade lived out their days as Beguines. Poor and rich women alike turned their backs on materialism and marriage to

live here in Christian poverty. And though obedient to a mother superior, the members of the lay order of Beguines were not nuns. The Beguines were very popular in their communities for the unpretentious lives they led, with a Christ-like dedication to serving others. They spent their days deep in prayer and busy with daily tasks—spinning wool, making lace, teaching, and caring for the sick. In quiet seclusion, they provided a striking contrast to the more decadent and corrupt Roman Church, inspiring one another as well as their neighbors.

The statue of the Beguine faces a black

**wooden house,** at #34 (see photo on previous page). This structure dates from 1528 and is the city's oldest. Originally, the whole city consisted of wooden houses like this one. They were eventually replaced with brick houses to minimize the fire danger of so many homes packed together.

Now turn your attention to the brick-faced **English Reformed church** (Engelse Kerk). The church was built in 1420 to serve the Beguine community. But then, in 1578, Catholicism was outlawed and the Dutch Reformed Church took over many Catholic monasteries. Still, the Begijnhof survived; in 1607, this church became Anglican. The church served as a refuge for English traders and religious separatists fleeing persecution in England. Strict Protestants such as the famous Pilgrims found sanctuary in tolerant Amsterdam and may have worshipped in this church. They later moved to Leiden, where they lived for a decade before sailing to religious freedom in America (see sidebar).

If the church is open, step inside, grab an English info sheet, and head to the far end, toward the stained-glass window. It shows the Pilgrims praying before boarding the *Mayflower*. Along the right-hand wall is an old pew (with columns and clock) they may have sat on, and on the altar is a Bible from 1763, with lotſof old-ſtyleſ's. Also of note is the front pulpit, carved of wood. It's by Piet Mondrian, the famous Dutch abstract artist, and was one of his first professional gigs. As you exit, look to the left of the door for a 1607 proclamation about a sermon preached here that the Pilgrims may have heard.

Back outside, find the **Catholic church,** which faces the English Reformed Church. Because Catholics were being persecuted when it was built, this had to be a low-profile, "hidden" church—notice the painted-out windows on the second and third floors. Step inside, through the low-profile doorway; you can pick up an English brochure near the entry. This church served Amsterdam's oppressed 17th-century Catholics, who refused to worship as Protestants. It's decorated lovingly, if on the cheap (try tapping softly on a "marble" column). Amsterdam's Catholics must have eagerly awaited the day when they were legally allowed to say Mass (that day finally came in the 19th century).

Today, Holland still has something of a religious divide, but not a bitter one. Amsterdam itself is, like many big cities in the West, pretty un-churched. But the Dutch countryside is much more religious, including a "Bible Belt" region where 98 percent of the population is Protestant. Overall, in the Netherlands, the

# The Pilgrims in Holland

The Pilgrims—a group of English Protestants—split from England's Anglican Church in the early 1600s. They believed the Church hadn't gone far enough in its break from medieval Catholicism. These "Separatists" (as they were called) were persecuted and fined.

In 1609, the Separatists decided to flee increasingly hostile England for the relatively tolerant Holland. But emigrating without permission was illegal. On their first attempt (in 1607), several were arrested, including the young William Bradford (who later became governor of Plymouth Colony). Trying again (1608), they were betrayed by the ship's captain.

Finally, in 1609, they succeeded, landing in **Amsterdam.** The Separatists lived in Amsterdam for a year, worshipping with fellow English ex-pats in (today's) English Reformed Church in the Begijnhof. Then they relocated south to **Leiden,** where they lived for more than a decade, making their homes near St. Peter's Church.

While in Leiden, Separatist leader William Brewster (who later wrote the Mayflower Compact—the document that governed Plymouth Colony and a forerunner to the US Constitution) began publishing religious tracts and smuggling them back to England. Under pressure from England, the Dutch authorities arrested Brewster. Holland was no longer safe. Compounding things, the Separatists were having trouble finding work in Leiden's textile trade. They decided they needed a fresh start—in America.

The cash-poor Separatists borrowed money from English investors, in return for whatever furs, timber, or other goods they could send back. Only the young and strong from the congregation would make the first journey, with the rest to follow once a colony was established. In the summer of 1620, they traveled to **Delfshaven** (near Rotterdam). There they said their goodbyes to loved ones, boarded a small ship called the *Speedwell,* and sailed to England. Once there, they met up with other colonists recruited by the investors. So it was that on September 16, 1620, 102 passengers set sail from Plymouth (on England's south coast) and traveled across the Atlantic on a new, larger ship—the *Mayflower.*

After an arduous crossing, the *Mayflower* arrived in what is now Plymouth Harbor, Massachusetts, on December 16, 1620. The rest is (grade-school) history: the Mayflower Compact, hardships and the first Thanksgiving, and the eventual success of Plymouth Colony.

Governor William Bradford remembered the group's sad departure from Holland and gave them the name we know them by today: "With mutual embraces and many tears, they took their leaves of one another, which proved to be the last leave to many of them...But they knew they were pilgrims."

country is divided fairly evenly between Catholics, Protestants, and those who see Sunday as a day to sleep in and enjoy a lazy brunch.

Step back outside. The last Beguine died in 1971, but this Begijnhof still thrives, providing subsidized housing to about 100 single women (mostly Catholic seniors). The Begijnhof is just one of a few dozen *hofjes* (little housing projects surrounding courtyards) that dot Amsterdam.

• *Leave the way you entered, turn right and head for a leafy, cobbled square.*

AMSTERDAM CITY WALK

## ⓫ Spui Square

Lined with cafés and bars, this square is one of the city's more popular spots for nightlife and sunny afternoon people-watching. Its name, Spui (rhymes with "now" and means "spew"), recalls the days when water was moved over dikes to keep the place dry.

We'll finish our tour at the far-right end of this square. But for now, head two blocks to the left, crossing busy Kalverstraat, to the bustling street called the **Rokin.** Across Rokin you can see the entry to the new North-South Metro line and a small black statue of Queen Wilhelmina daintily riding sidesaddle. Remember that in real life, she was the iron-willed inspiration for the Dutch resistance against the Nazis.

**Canal cruises** depart from the Rondvaart Kooij dock across the water, in the yellow canal house (see "Traditional Canal Boat Tours" on page 52).

Turn left on the Rokin and walk up 50 yards to the **House of Hajenius** (at Rokin 92). This temple of cigars is a "paradise for the connoisseur" showing "175 years of tradition and good taste." To enter this sumptuous Art Deco building with painted leather ceilings is to step back into 1910. Don't be shy—the place is as much a free museum for visitors as it is a store for paying customers. It's a world of pipes, cigars, a classy smoking lounge, and—farther back—tins of pipe tobacco that they proudly blend (lift the lid, take a whiff, and compare several). The personal humidifiers allow locals (some famous) to call in an order and have their cigars waiting for them at just the right humidity. Above the street entry door, humidifier pipes pump moisture into the room.

From Hajenius, backtrack to the busy pedestrian mall, Kalverstraat, and continue south. Just before the end of this shopping boulevard (at #206, on the right), you'll see the modern Kalverpassage and the **Kalvertoren** shopping mall. Enter and go deeper within to find a slanting glass elevator. You can ride this to the rec-ommended top-floor **Blue Amsterdam Restaurant,** where a coffee or light lunch buys you something that's rare in altitude-challenged Amsterdam—a nice view.

• *Back out on the street, at the end of Kalverstraat, stands the...*

## ⓬ Mint Tower (Munttoren)

This tower marked the limit of the medieval walled city and served as one of its original gates. In the Middle Ages, the city walls were

girdled by a moat—the Singel canal. Until about 1500, the area beyond here was noth-ing but marshy fields and a few farms on re-claimed land. The Mint Tower's steeple was added later—in the year 1620, as you can see written below the clock face.

Today, the tower is a favorite within Amsterdam's marijuana culture. Stoners love to take a photo of the clock and its 1620 sign at exactly 4:20 p.m.—the traditional time to quit work and light one up. (On the 24-hour clock, 4:20 p.m. is 16:20...Du-u-u-ude!)

Before moving on, look left (at about 10 o'clock) down Reguliersbreestraat. Midway down the block, the twin green domes mark the exotic **Tuschinski Theater.** Here you can see current movies (subtitled in Dutch) in a sumptuous Art Deco setting. If you like, take a quick detour to check out its lobby, and imagine this place in the Roaring '20s. Wa-a-ay at the end of the long block (where you see trees) is **Rembrandtplein,** another major center for nightlife.

• *Continue past the Mint Tower, first walking a few yards south along busy Vijzelstraat (keep an eye out for trams). Then turn right and walk west along the south bank of the Singel canal. It's lined with the greenhouse shops of the...*

## ⓭ Flower Market (Bloemenmarkt)

The stands along this busy block sell cut flowers, plants, bulbs, seeds, garden supplies, and flower-oriented souvenirs and knick-

knacks. Browse your way along while heading for the end of the block.

The Flower Market is a testament to Holland's longtime love affair with flowers. The Netherlands is by far the largest flower exporter in Europe and

a major flower power worldwide. If you're looking for a souvenir, note that certain seeds are marked as OK to bring back through customs into the US.

For more on the history of tulips in Holland, see page 30.

• *The long Flower Market ends at the next bridge, where you'll enter a square named* **Koningsplein** *(King's Square), with a characteristic herring shop.*

## ⓮ Koningsplein and a Herring Stand

Pleasant Koningsplein square hosts the popular and recommended **Frens Haringhandel** outdoor *haringhandel* (herring stand). This is a great place to choke down a raw herring—a fish that has a special place in every Dutch heart. After all, herring was the commodity that first put Amsterdam on the trading map. It's also what Dutch sailors ate for protein on those long cross-global voyages.

Throughout the Netherlands, old-fashioned fish stands like this one sell herring sandwiches and other fishy treats. Herring thrive in the shallow North Sea waters surrounding the Netherlands, and they're a delicacy here. While it seems the Dutch eat herring "raw," the fish is actually cured in salt (soaked for five days in an oak cask filled with a mild brine solution). Herring is caught fresh during the May/June fishing season and immediately preserved. Before the days of deep freezing, this curing process was a big deal. But these days, even Dutch herring connoisseurs admit that they can't tell what's fresh or frozen—and you get great herring all year.

Step up to the shop and see what's on ice. While herring is the star, you'll also see *garnalen* (little shrimp), *zalm* (salmon), *makreel* (mackerel), *paling* (eel), and *krabsalade* (crab salad). Most are available as a *broodje*. And every Dutch kid's favorite is *kibbeling* (deep-fried breaded cod) with a tasty sauce.

When ordering herring, you have choices. The easiest and most practical for novices is the sandwich (**broodje,** tucked into a soft roll with pickles and raw onions), while purists prefer their herring unadulterated. If you go with straight herring, your big decision is **Rotterdam-style** (pick it up by the tail, dredge it in chopped raw onions,

## Amsterdam's Canals

Amsterdam's canals are as pretty as they are practical. When the city's founders dammed the Amstel River, they used windmills to pump the excess water safely away into canals, creating pockets of dry land to build on. The canals became part of the transportation infrastructure, helping merchants move their goods efficiently.

Today, the city has about 100 canals, most of which are about 10 feet deep. They're crossed by some 1,200 bridges, fringed with 100,000 Dutch elm and lime trees, and bedecked with 2,500 houseboats. A system of locks (near Centraal station) controls the flow and periodically flushes out the system.

The word *gracht* (pronounced, roughly, "hroht," with guttural flair) can refer to a canal itself, or to the ensemble of a canal and the lanes that border it. A *straat* is a street without a canal, though a few paved-over canals, such as Elandsgracht, retain their old name.

Learn the general order of the watery semicircles radiating out from Centraal station. These four will matter most in your navigating: Singel (innermost, originally the medieval town's defensive moat), Herengracht (named for the aristocrats, or *heren,* who built the Dutch East India Company and with their profits, the fancy mansions along here), Keizersgracht (named for the Holy Roman Emperor), and lively Prinsengracht (less swanky, lined with old warehouses and smaller homes). Memorize this sentence to help you remember: A **S**ingle **H**airy **K**aiser's **P**rince really knows his canals.

and lower it into your mouth, all in one go) or **Amsterdam-style** (cut up in toothpick-friendly hunks, also with onions). Between the fish and the onion, herring ought to come with breath mints.

• *Lick your fingers—it's time to finish our walk.*

*From Koningsplein you have several options. The noisy and congested* **Leidsestraat** *leads straight to the museum zone; for a more pleasant walk to the museums, follow Leidsestraat just across the next canal (Herengracht), then go left along the canal and take the first right at Nieuwe Spiegelstraat. This long street, much of it lined with art galleries and inviting shops, leads directly to the Rijksmuseum (you'll see the grand museum in the distance). Or, from near Koningsplein, you could catch* **tram #2 or #5** *either to the museums or back to Centraal station.*

*But we'll finish off by following the Singel canal back to Spui Square.*

## ⑮ From Koningsplein to Spui

With your back to the flower market, walk along the canal (with the water on your left). Follow the tram tracks as they bend around to the right and lead you to Spui.

As you walk, consider that the Singel is wide today because it was the moat and wall of the city back in the Middle Ages. In about 1620, during the golden age period of building and expansion, the wall was torn down and the city expanded with the new town across the canal to your left.

The canalside street you're enjoying was, until recently, congested with cars. Today the lanes are for bikes, trams, and people. In a few years there'll be no more fossil fuel-powered traffic in the city—the trams are already electric, all the boats will be electric... and bikes will rule.

And notice, for a minute, the bikes. For the Dutch, biking is taken very seriously. They may not wear helmets, yet they place great importance on road safety: Bikes are considered equal to cars and must follow the same rules. Stiff fines are given to those biking in pedestrian zones or looking at their phones while pedaling. Little Dutch kids grow up on bikes. At about age 10, they take a biking exam. When a fifth grader passes this exam, it's like a coming of age...their world just got bigger and more real. (The most dangerous thing on an Amsterdam road is a tourist on a bike.)

When you finally get back to **Spui**, listen to the sounds of the city: people talking over drinks at the café, bike gears changing, the *brrring* of the bells, the chatter of the birds. Does the square seem spacious? Rather than 200 cars, within view are 200 bikes. At least for the Dutch, this is the urban environment of the future.

# RED LIGHT DISTRICT WALK

Amsterdam's oldest neighborhood has hosted the world's oldest profession since the Middle Ages. Today, prostitution and public marijuana use thrive here, creating a spectacle that's unique in all of Europe.

The Red Light District lies between Damrak and Nieuwmarkt. On our walk, we'll see history, sleaze, and cheese: prostitutes in windows, drunks in doorways, cruising packs of foreign twenty-somethings, cannabis being enjoyed, and sex for sale.

The sex trade runs the gamut from sex shops selling porn and accessories to blue video arcades, from glitzy nightclub sex shows featuring strippers and sex acts to the real deal—prostitutes in bras, thongs, and high heels, standing in window displays, offering their bodies—and it's all legal.

**Not for Everyone:** The Red Light District seems to have something to offend everyone. Whether it's in-your-face images of graphic sex, exploited immigrant women, whips and chains, passed-out drug addicts, the pungent smells of pot smoke and urine, or just the shameless commercialism of it all, it's not everyone's cup of tea. And though I encourage people to expand their horizons—that's a great thing about travel—it's also perfectly OK to say, "No, thank you."

## Orientation

**Length of This Walk:** Allow two hours.

**Photography:** Consider leaving your phone or camera in your bag. Don't take photos of women in windows—even with an inconspicuous phone camera—or a snarly bouncer may appear from out of nowhere to forcibly rip it from your hands. In this district, taking even seemingly harmless photos of ordinary people is frowned upon by privacy-loving locals. On the other hand, taking photos of landmarks like the Old Church and wide shots of distant red lights from the bridges is certainly OK. Remember that a camera or phone makes a prime target in this high-theft area.

**When to Go:** The best times to visit are afternoons and early evenings. Mornings are dead, but are also when you see more passed-out-drunk-in-a-doorway scenes. Avoid late nights (after about 22:30), when the tourists disappear and the area gets creepy. Earlier in the evening, the streets start filling with tourists, and the atmosphere feels safe, even festive.

**Safety:** The neighborhood is slowly gentrifying, with trendy restaurants and boutiques, and there are plenty of police on horseback keeping things orderly and plenty of other out-of-town tourists. But there are also plenty of rowdy drunks, drug-pushing lowlifes, con artists, and pickpockets. Assume any fight or commotion is a ploy to distract innocent victims who are about to lose their wallets. As always, wear your money belt, zip up your valuables, and keep a low profile.

**Old Church** (Oude Kerk): Church—€12, Mon-Sat 10:00-18:00, Sun 13:00-17:30; tower climb—€9 with 30-minute tour in English, April-Oct departs on the half-hour Mon-Sat 12:00-18:00, none Sun or off-season.

**Prostitution Information Center** (PIC): Wed-Sat 12:00-17:00, closed Sun-Tue, +31 20 420 7328, www.pic-amsterdam.com.

**Tours:** While guided tours are not allowed in the Red Light District, the Prostitution Information Center gives educational **"Walk & Talk"** tours several times a week (€25, Wed-Sat at 17:00, +31 20 420 7328, for details and to sign up visit www.pic-amsterdam.com). The "tour" begins with a talk in their shop. Next, they give you a proposed self-guided walking route. Afterward, there's a follow-up meeting for Q&A with a sex worker back in their office.

🎧 To listen to this chapter's self-guided walk, download my free Red Light District **audio tour.**

**Our Lord in the Attic Museum:** €15.50, Mon-Fri 10:00-17:00, Sat until 18:00, Sun 13:00-18:00.

**Erotic Museum:** €7, daily 11:00-24:00.

**Red Light Secrets Museum of Prostitution:** €14.50; Sun-Thu 11:00-22:00, Fri-Sat until 23:00, last entry 45 minutes before closing; www.redlightsecrets.com.

**Cannabis College:** Free, daily 11:00-18:00.
**Hemp Gallery and Hash, Marijuana, and Hemp Museum:** €10, includes audioguide, daily 10:00-22:00.

## OVERVIEW

You'll walk a big, long loop through the heart of De Wallen (the official name of the district): north on Warmoesstraat, past the Old Church, up Oudezijds Voorburgwal street; hook around on Zeedijk street; and return south on Oudezijds Achterburgwal street, ending two blocks from Dam Square.

# The Walk Begins

• *Start on Dam Square. Face the big, fancy Grand Hotel Krasnapolsky. To the left of the hotel stretches the long street called...*

## ❶ Warmoesstraat

You're walking along one of the city's oldest streets. It's the traditional border of the neighborhood tourists call the Red Light District.
• *Our first stop is the small shop with the large, yellow triangle sign, about 100 yards down on the right at #141.*

## ❷ Condomerie

Located at the entrance to the Red Light District, this is the perfect place to get prepared. Besides selling an amazing variety of condoms, this shop has a knack for entertainment, working to make their front-window display appropriate to the season. Pop in and look around.

• *From here, pass the two little street barricades with cute red lights around them and enter the traffic-free world of...*

## ❸ De Wallen

Amsterdammers call this area De Wallen ("The Walls"), after the old retaining walls that once stood here. It's the oldest part of town, with the oldest church. It grew up between the harbor and Dam Square, where the city was born. Amsterdam was a port town, located where the river met the sea. The city traded in all kinds of goods, including things popular with sailors and businessmen away from home—like sex and drugs.

RED LIGHT WALK

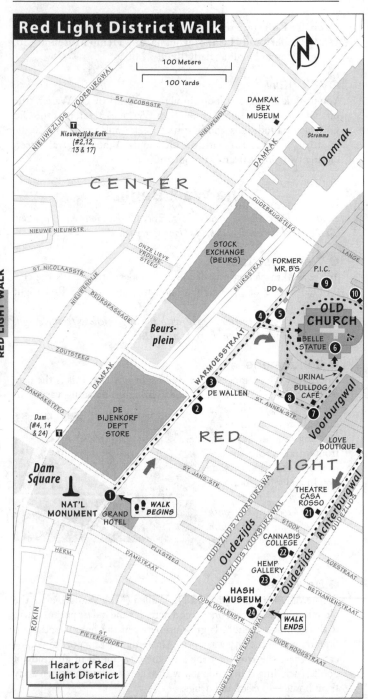

# Red Light District Walk

100 Meters
100 Yards

DAMRAK SEX MUSEUM

Stromma

Nieuwezijds Kolk (#2,12, 13 & 17)

CENTER

STOCK EXCHANGE (BEURS)

FORMER MR. B'S

P.I.C.
DD
9
10

OLD CHURCH

Beurs-plein

4  5

BELLE STATUE
6

De Wallen
3
2

URINAL
BULLDOG CAFÉ
8
7

Voorburgwal

Dam (#4, 14 & 24)

DE BIJENKORF DEP'T STORE

RED

LIGHT

LOVE BOUTIQUE

Dam Square

NAT'L MONUMENT  GRAND HOTEL

1  WALK BEGINS

THEATRE CASA ROSSO
21

Oudezijds Voorburgwal

CANNABIS COLLEGE
22

Achterburgwal

HEMP GALLERY
23

HASH MUSEUM
24

WALK ENDS

Oudezijds Achterburgwal

Heart of Red Light District

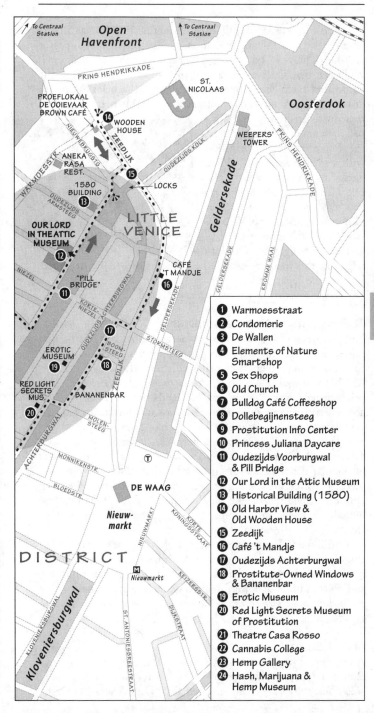

To Centraal Station

Open Havenfront

To Centraal Station

PRINS HENDRIKKADE

ST. NICOLAAS

Oosterdok

PROEFLOKAAL DE OOIEVAAR BROWN CAFÉ

WOODEN HOUSE

WEEPERS' TOWER

PRINS HENDRIKKADE

ANEKA RASA REST.

ZEEDIJK

OUDEZIJDS KOLK

Geldersekade

1580 BUILDING

LOCKS

OUR LORD IN THE ATTIC MUSEUM

LITTLE VENICE

CAFÉ 'T MANDJE

GELDERSEKADE

KROMME WAAL

"PILL BRIDGE"

KORTE-NIEZEL ACHTERBURGWAL

NIEZEL

OUDEZIJDS ARMSTEEG

WARMOESSTR

NIEUWEBRUGSTG

STORMSTEEG

BOOMSTEEG

EROTIC MUSEUM

OUDEZIJDS ACHTERBURGWAL

ZEEDIJK

RED LIGHT SECRETS MUS.

BANANENBAR

MOLENSTEEG

ACHTERBURGWAL

MONNIKENSTR.

BLOEDSTR.

DE WAAG

Nieuwmarkt

NIEUWMARKT

KORTE KONINGSSTRAAT

KEIZERSSTR.

DISTRICT

Nieuwmarkt

DIJKSTRAAT

KLOVENIERSBURGWAL

ST. ANTONIESBREESTRAAT

1. Warmoesstraat
2. Condomerie
3. De Wallen
4. Elements of Nature Smartshop
5. Sex Shops
6. Old Church
7. Bulldog Café Coffeeshop
8. Dollebegijnensteeg
9. Prostitution Info Center
10. Princess Juliana Daycare
11. Oudezijds Voorburgwal & Pill Bridge
12. Our Lord in the Attic Museum
13. Historical Building (1580)
14. Old Harbor View & Old Wooden House
15. Zeedijk
16. Café 't Mandje
17. Oudezijds Achterburgwal
18. Prostitute-Owned Windows & Bananenbar
19. Erotic Museum
20. Red Light Secrets Museum of Prostitution
21. Theatre Casa Rosso
22. Cannabis College
23. Hemp Gallery
24. Hash, Marijuana & Hemp Museum

According to legend, Quentin Tarantino holed up at a hotel here for three months in 1993 to write *Pulp Fiction* (you'll pass it on your right, at #129). As you get deeper into the neighborhood, you'll see that the area attracts many out-of-towners, especially Brits. They catch cheap flights here for "stag" (bachelor) parties or just a wild weekend—and the money-savvy Dutch accommodate them with Irish pubs and foot-ball matches on TVs in the bars.

Pause at the intersection with a small street called Wijde Kerksteeg, which leads to the Old Church. Standing here, you may see gay-pride flags in rainbow colors or S&M bars. Also notice the security cameras and modern lighting. Freedom reigns in this quarter—under the watchful eye of the neighbor-hood police department.

• *Continue down Warmoesstraat a few more steps. At #97 is the...*

### ❹ Elements of Nature Smartshop

This "smartshop" is a little grocery store of mind-bending natural ingredients. Like the city's other smartshops, it's a clean, well-lit, fully professional retail outlet that sells powerful drugs, many of which are illegal in America. Products are clearly marked with prices, brief descriptions, ingredients, and effects. The knowledge-able salespeople can give you more information on their "100 per-cent natural products that play with the human senses."

Their "natural" drugs include harmless nutrition boosters (such as royal jelly), harmful but familiar tobacco, and herbal versions of popular dance-club drugs (such as herbal Ecstasy). Marijuana seeds, however, are the big sellers. You'll also see mind-bending truffles, a trend that caught on after the EU forbade the retailing of hallucinogenic mushrooms. (Truffles grow underground—so they're technically not mushrooms.)

Still, my fellow travelers, *caveat emptor!* We've grown used to thinking, "If it's legal, it must be safe. If it's not, I'll sue." Though perfectly legal and aboveboard in the Netherlands, some of these substances can cause powerful, often unpleasant reactions.

• *Continue a bit farther down Warmoesstraat, to an area filled with so-called...*

### ❺ Sex Shops

A few steps down Warmoesstraat, at #89, was **Mr. B**'s Leather and Rubber Land, proudly flying an S&M flag. It's now Jamin, a candy store. Yes, things are changing—but **DD** (Dirty Dicks) across the

# The History of Prostitution in Amsterdam

Today nearly a thousand prostitutes work in the Red Light District, sharing about 200 windows...and a very long history. The tolerance of this sex industry swings with the times. But, as usual, Amsterdam finds a way for tolerance to win out. Sex has always been for sale in De Wallen.

Historically a port city, Amsterdam always had sailors in need of entertainment—and as far back as the 1400s, there were prostitutes walking with red lanterns and working mostly in the inns of De Wallen, the oldest surviving residential neighborhood in town. With the piety of the Reformation (late 1500s), there was a brief attempt to suppress the sex trade. But by the 1600s, a thousand prostitutes were working here, and sexually transmitted disease ran rampant—many customers enjoyed brief encounters, then paid with their lives.

With the age of Napoleon (early 1800s) came a pragmatic form of legal prostitution in an attempt to fight STDs. Sex workers were required to have permits and submit to twice-weekly check-ups to certify they were disease-free. By mid-century, effective (rubber) condoms were readily available. Prostitution boomed, with an estimated 3,000 sex workers here.

Widespread prostitution was targeted by the more moralistic Victorian Age. But creative tolerance prevailed again, and by about 1900, the streetwalkers were gone, replaced by the "window prostitution" we see today, limited to specific districts.

In recent times, prostitution has been seen more as a practical threat than a moral one—bringing disease, human trafficking, and organized crime. Many sex workers are forced to work by pimps who use their children back home as hostages. To fight these threats, prostitution was officially legalized in 2000, and is now considered just another profession, with rules, regulations, and taxes. In 2007, city leaders introduced Project 1012 (named for De Wallen's postal code), an attempt to normalize the trade while removing the criminal element.

With a vision of "gentrification by design," Amsterdam's city government is splicing in other "legitimate" businesses into a district that for centuries has relied on only one product. A major Red Light District landlord was essentially given the option either to lease many of his booths to the city or be zoned out of business. The city picked up the leases, and windows that once showcased "girls for rent" now showcase mannequins wearing the latest fashions—lit by lights that aren't red.

RED LIGHT WALK

street at #86 is still in business. Notice the very low-profile entrances to several men-only leather bars, with their black doors and windows. These places come with a bar, a dance floor, and a dark back room. (I guess that's one reason to get a glow-in-the-dark condom at Condomerie.)

Throughout the district, various sex-shop retail outlets deal in erotic paraphernalia (dildos, S&M starter kits, kinky magazines) and offer video booths with porn films, charging by the minute. While Amsterdam is notorious for its Red Light District, even small Dutch towns often have a sex shop and a brothel to satisfy their citizens' needs.

• *Backtrack a few steps to the intersection and head down Wijde Kerksteeg to the Old Church. Pause at the base of the impressive tower.*

## ❻ Old Church (Oude Kerk)

As the name implies, this was the medieval city's original church. Returning from a long sea voyage, sailors of yore would spy the steeple of the Old Church on the horizon and know they were home. Having returned safely, they'd come here to give thanks to St. Nicholas—the patron saint of this church, of seafarers, of Christmas, and of the city of Amsterdam.

Church construction began in the early 1200s—starting with a humble wooden chapel that expanded into a stone structure by the time it was consecrated in 1306. It was added onto in fits and starts for the next 200 years—as is apparent in the building's many gangly parts. Then, in the 15th century, Amsterdam built the New Church (Nieuwe Kerk) on Dam Square. But the Old Church still had the tallest spire, the biggest organ, and the most side-altars, and remained the city's center of activity, bustling inside and out with merchants and street markets.

The **tower** is 290 feet high, with an octagonal steeple atop a bell tower (you can pay to climb to the top). This tower served as the model for many other Dutch steeples. The carillon has 47 bells, which can chime mechanically or be played by one of Amsterdam's three official carillonneurs.

Circle to the right to the church entrance. While the church is historic, the **interior** doesn't offer much to see other than hundreds of gravestones in the floor (the most famous is for Rembrandt's wife, Saskia). Its stark plainness stems from the religious wars of the 16th century: Protestants gutted this Catholic church, smashing windows and removing politically incorrect statues they considered "graven images." (Strict Calvinists at one point even removed the organ as a senseless luxury, until they found they couldn't stay on key singing hymns without it.) Atop the brass choir screen, an inscription *('t misbruyk in Godes...)* commemorates the iconoclasm: "The false practices introduced into God's church were undone here in 1578."

The church, permanently stripped of "pope-ish" decoration, was transformed from Catholic to Dutch Reformed, "St. Nicholas" was dropped from the name, and it became known by the nickname everyone called it anyway—the Old Church. Nowadays, the church is the holy needle around which the unholy Red Light District spins.

Back outside, explore around the right side of the church. You'll see a **statue** dedicated to the Unknown Prostitute. She's nicknamed Belle, and the statue honors "sex workers around the world." Also nearby, you might trip over a bronze breast sculpted into the pavement being groped by bronze hands.

Attached to the church like barnacles are **small buildings.** These were originally used as homes for priests, church offices, or rental units. The house to the right of the entrance is now a delightful café (de Koffie Schenkerij).

The green metal structure over by the canal is a public **urinal.** It offers just enough privacy. This one gets a lot of use. City trucks circulate around town on a regular basis, suds-ing them down.

Consider that, on average, about 12 people drown in Amsterdam every year. When found, most of them turn out to be men with their zippers down. It's not hard to imagine the scene: Some

guy is drunk as a skunk at 3 a.m., goes to the edge of the canal to take a pee...and falls in.
• *From the urinal, go a half-block south along the canal toward the...*

### ❼ Bulldog Café Coffeeshop

The Bulldog claims to be Amsterdam's very first marijuana coffeeshop, established here in 1975. Now there's a chain of Bulldogs around the city.

As coffeeshops go, the Bulldog is considered pretty touristy, catering to a young crowd. (Older connoisseurs often seek out smaller places with better-quality pot.) The staff is unintimidating, though, and timid first-timers are guided through the process. Step in and snoop around. As long as you don't take photos, you're welcome. Check out the menu. Ask the budtender any questions. Climb down the stairs to the basement coffeeshop where a door leads back out into the street.

The political winds regarding cannabis are always shifting. Some Dutch leaders propose forbidding sales to nonresidents, hoping to discourage European drug dealers from driving over the Dutch border to buy large quantities of pot to sell illegally in their home countries. However, such a law would be devastating for Dutch businesses, which depend on out-of-towners. Many Amsterdam politicians favor keeping pot legal—for the sake of business and to prevent legal cannabis sales from moving back to the black market. For more on the pragmatic Dutch approach to pot and how coffeeshops work, see the Smoking chapter.

• *Time to dive into the heart of the Red Light District. We're right around the corner from what was once one of the neighborhood's main streets for legal prostitution. On either side of the Bulldog are long skinny lanes with big windows. Walk down the one to the left called...*

## ❽ Dollebegijnensteeg

This was once the thick of Amsterdam's high-density prostitution scene. What was until recently a can-can of sex workers flirting in their windows is now pretty empty as the city works to strategically contain and limit the sex trade. (The action that was once here is now farther along on our tour route.) Imagine how it appeared until a couple years ago: Window after window of women in panties and bras would wink at prospective customers, rap on the window to attract attention, text their friends, or look disdainfully at sightseers.

• *At the cross street, turn right to return to the Old Church. Circle the church clockwise. Around the side, at Enge Kerksteeg 3, is the...*

## ❾ Prostitution Information Center (PIC)

This center (a nonprofit run by donations) exists to demystify prostitution, giving visitors matter-of-fact information on how the trade works and what it's like to be a sex worker. It doles out pamphlets, books, condoms, T-shirts, and other offbeat souvenirs, and offers self-guided "Walk & Talk" tours (see "Orientation," earlier, for details). They have a map showing exactly where prostitution is legal, and sell a small, frank booklet answering the most common questions tourists have about Amsterdam's Red

Light District. The center also offers a one-to-one workshop, for women only, on what it's like to be a sex worker in Amsterdam (book in advance).

Next door is a room-rental office (#3, *Kamerverhuurbedrijf*). Prostitutes come here to rent window space and bedrooms to use for their work. The office also sells work supplies—condoms by the case, toilet tissue, and lubricants. This office does not arrange sex. The women who rent space from this business are self-employed and negotiate directly with their customers.

In return for their rental fees, prostitutes get security. The rental office provides constant video surveillance. (You may see small cameras and orange alarm lights above many windows.) If prostitutes have any trouble, they press a buzzer that swiftly calls a burly bouncer or the police. While the area may look rough, aside from tricky pickpockets these streets are actually pretty safe.

• *Continue circling clockwise around the church and find the brick building on the left at Oudekerksplein 8. This is the...*

## ⑩ Princess Juliana Daycare

De Wallen is also a residential neighborhood, where ordinary citizens go about their daily lives. Of course, locals need someplace to send their kids. The Princess Juliana Daycare is for newborns to four-year-olds. It was built in the 1970s, when the idea was to mix all dimensions of society together, absorbing the seedy into the decent. I don't know about you, but this location would be a tough sell where I come from.

• *Turn left at the canal and continue north along...*

## ⑪ Oudezijds Voorburgwal and Pill Bridge

Pause at "Pill Bridge" and enjoy the canal and all the old buildings with their charming gables. Back in the 1970s, this bridge was nicknamed for the retail items sold by the seedy guys who used to hang out here. Thanks to smart and pragmatic public policy, the Dutch have made great gains in fighting hard-drug addiction. And now this neighborhood is a pleasant place for a photo op.

• *Just past the bridge, at Oudezijds Voorburgwal 38, is one of the city's most worthwhile museums.*

## ⑫ Our Lord in the Attic Museum

With its triangular gable, this building looks like just another townhouse. But inside, it holds a secret—a small, lavishly decor-

# Prostitution 101

The system is simple. A customer browses around. A prostitute catches his eye. If the prostitute is interested in his business (prostitutes are selective for their own safety), she winks him over. They talk at the door as she explains her price and what she has to offer. A price is agreed on and paid in advance. A typical visit costs €50 for a promised 20 minutes. The customer goes in. The prostitute draws the curtain. Where do they actually do it? The rooms look tiny from the street, but these are just display windows. There's a bigger room behind or upstairs that comes with a bed, a sink, and not much else (or so I've heard). The average time for a visit: about 10 minutes.

Are there male prostitutes? Well—anything you might want is available somewhere in the Red Light District. But a 1990s experiment to put male prostitutes in windows didn't stand up. Today male prostitutes solicit work mostly online and in clubs. The district does, however, have some transgender prostitutes working in windows.

The prostitutes here are self-employed—renting space and running their own business. They usually work a four- to eight-hour shift. A good spot costs about €100 for a day shift and €180 for an evening. Prostitutes are required to keep their premises hygienic, make sure their clients use condoms, and avoid minors.

While the hope here is that sex workers are smartly regulated small-businesspeople, in reality the line between victim and entrepreneur is not always clear. Although some women choose sex work as a lucrative career, others (some say most) are forced into it by circumstance—poverty, drug addiction, abusive men, and immigration scams. After the fall of the Iron Curtain, many Eastern Europeans flocked here, and Russian and East European crime syndicates muscled in. A recent trend is women from Bulgaria and Romania coming to the Netherlands with the same goal as guest workers in other countries: to work hard long enough to return home and set up their family financially.

Popular sex workers can make about €1,000 a day. The law, not pimps, protects them, and they fill out tax returns. As shocking as legalized prostitution may seem to some, it's a good example of a pragmatic Dutch solution to an age-old dilemma.

ated place of worship hidden in the attic. Although Amsterdam has long been known for its tolerance, back in the 16th and 17th centuries there was one group they kept in the closet—Catholics. (For more, 📖 see the Our Lord in the Attic Museum Tour chapter.)

As we stroll up the canal, remember that this neighborhood is Amsterdam's oldest. It sits on formerly marshy land that was reclaimed by diking off the sea's tidal surge. That location gave Amsterdam's merchants easy access to both river trade and the North Sea. By the 1500s, Amsterdam was booming.

• *Beyond the next bridge, on your left at #14, is an old brick building with red shutters.*

## ⓭ Historical Building

This building dates from that very era—around 1580. At the time of

its construction, Amsterdam's citizens were rising up in revolt to throw out their Spanish rulers. Now free to govern themselves, a group of energetic businessmen turned the city into a sea-trading hub. By 1600, brave Dutch sailors were traveling as far as Africa, America, and Asia. They returned with shiploads of exotic goods to sell to the rest of Europe.

Next to the red door, notice the label: *"Leger des Heils"*—that's "Salvation Army." There was a time when this was a bastion of compassion and hope for the desperate people who littered these streets. By the canal is a statue of Major Alida Bosshardt—a Salvation Army officer who worked tirelessly in the Red Light District in the mid-20th century.

The part of the canal we're walking along now is known as **"Little Venice"** (a term used Europe-wide for any charming neighborhood with canalside houses). Houses rise directly from the water here, with no quays or streets. Like Venice, the city was built in a marshy delta area on millions of pilings. And, like Venice, it grew rich on sea trade.

Notice the handsome gable stones embedded in a wall at the end of the canal. There are hundreds of these still in place around town. They served one of several functions: to make a religious statement, act as an ad for a business, show off a noble family seal, or give an address a nickname so people could find your house before there were street numbers.

• *Continue straight up a small inclined lane called Sint Olofssteeg. You're ascending the protective sea dike (Zeedijk), which, until the 1930s when the broader sea was tamed, prevented this neighborhood from being in-*

RED LIGHT WALK

*undated by North Sea tidal surges. At the top, turn left and walk along the street called Zeedijk. Go about 100 yards to the end of the block, where it opens up to an...*

## ⓮ Old Harbor View and Old Wooden House

As you survey the urban scene of today's Damrak and Centraal station, imagine the scene as it looked in the 1600s. What today is mostly concrete was once the city's harbor. Ocean-going ships sailed in and out of the harbor through an opening located where the train station sits now (on reclaimed land).

The **old wooden house** near here (at Zeedijk 1, now a café) was once a tavern, sitting right at what was then the water's edge.

This was a bustling port. Amsterdam became home to the Dutch East India Company, the world's first multinational corporation. Goods from all over the world flowed into the harbor, where cargo was then transferred to smaller river-trade boats that sailed up the Amstel to Europe's interior. The city grew wealthier and larger, expanding beyond De Wallen to new neighborhoods to the west and south. In its golden age, this blend of overseas trade and canal-borne commerce helped Amsterdam become known as the "warehouse of the world" and perhaps the wealthiest city on Earth.

Picture a ship tying up in the harbor. The crew has just returned home from a two-year voyage to Bali. They're bringing home fabulous riches—crates and crates of spices, coffee, and silk. Sailors are celebrating their homecoming, spilling onto Zeedijk. Here they'll be greeted by swinging ladies swinging red lanterns. Their first stop might be nearby St. Olaf's chapel to say a prayer of thanks—or perhaps they'll head straight to this tavern at Zeedijk 1 and drop anchor for a good Dutch beer. *Ahh–hh!*

• *But our journey continues. Backtrack along the same street, to the crest of a bridge, on...*

## ⓯ Zeedijk

You're standing atop the historic dike, at about sea level. From here you can look down at the canal-side lanes and see how Amsterdam is below sea level. The waterway

below you is part of the city's system of **locks:** Once upon a time, each day a worker would open up the locks and the tide would flush out the city's canals.

In the early 1600s, this neighborhood was thriving with overseas trade. But Amsterdam would soon lose its maritime su-

---

## Social Control

De Wallen has pioneered the Dutch concept of "social control." In Holland, neighborhood security doesn't come from just the police, but from neighbors looking out for each other. If Geert doesn't buy bread for two days, the baker asks around if anyone's seen him. An elderly man feels safe in his home, knowing he's being watched over by the prostitutes next door. Unlike many big cities, there's no chance that anyone here could die or be in trouble and go unnoticed. Video-surveillance cameras keep an eye on the streets. So do prostitutes, who buzz for help if they spot trouble. As you stroll, watch the men who watch the women who watch out for their neighbors—"social control."

---

premacy to England and France, and by midcentury, its trading ships and economy had been destroyed by wars with these rivals. The city remained culturally vibrant, and banking flourished. But with less shipping, De Wallen never really recovered.

As you continue down Zeedijk and around the bend, you can see that the area has maintained its colorful character. Residents enjoy a mix of international restaurants—Thai and Portuguese, for example—and bars like the Queen's Head (at #20, on the right, with its various rainbow flags) that draw a gay clientele.

Back in the 1960s, Amsterdam was the world capital of experimental lifestyles, a wide-open city of sex and drugs. By the 1970s, Zeedijk had become unbelievably sleazy. When I made my first trip here, this street was nicknamed "Heroin Alley." Thousands of hard-drug addicts wandered the neighborhood and squatted in old buildings. "Pill Bridge" (which we passed earlier) became "Needle Bridge." It was a scene with little else besides sex, hard drugs, and wandering lonely souls. The area was a no-man's-land of junkies fighting among themselves, and the police just kept their distance.

But locals longed to take back this historic corner of their city and got to work. First, they legalized marijuana and allowed "coffeeshops" to sell small quantities. Then they cracked down on hard drugs—heroin, cocaine, and pills. Almost overnight, the illicit-drug trade dropped dramatically. Dealers got stiff sentences. Addicts got treatment. Decades later, the policy seems to have worked. Pot smoking has not gone up, hard-drug use is down, and for a time, Zeedijk belonged to the people of Amsterdam once again—only to be taken over by tourists. Today there's a push to remind visitors that, yes, real people live here.

• *Pause at #63, on the left.*

## ⓰ Café 't Mandje

This is one of Europe's first gay bars. It opened in 1927, closed in 1985, and is now a working bar once again. It stands as a memorial to the woman who ran it during its heyday in the 1950s and '60s: Bet van Beeren, "Queen of Zeedijk." Bet was a lesbian, and her bar became a hangout for gay people. It still is, though all are welcome. If you go inside for a drink, you'll enjoy a tiny interior crammed with photos and memorabilia. Bet was the original Zee-dyke—you might see a picture of her decked out in leather, cruising the streets on her motorcycle. Neckties hang from the ceiling, a reminder of Bet's tradition of scissoring off customers' ties.

• *This tour veers right at the next intersection (near #80), back into the heart of the Red Light District. For a quick detour, however, you could continue straight ahead for a peek into the local Chinatown. Otherwise, make the next right and head a few steps down narrow Korte Stormsteeg street, back to the canalside red lights. Then go left, walking along the left side of the canal.*

## ⓱ Oudezijds Achterburgwal

We're back in the quirky glow of the Red Light District. This beautiful, tree-lined canal is the heart of this neighborhood's nightlife, playing host to most of the main nightclubs. Stand here for a second and take it all in. The street is lined with ladies in windows, sex shops, sex museums, strip clubs, and theaters where sex acts are performed before live audiences.

• *Remember: Don't take any pictures, and watch for pickpockets if crowds jostle together. Start making your way down the street's left-hand side. After about 30 yards, pause at the small alleyway called Boomsteeg.*

## ⓲ Prostitute-Owned Windows and Bananenbar

Many of the prostitution windows near here (such as at Oudezijds #17, #19, and #27, and along Boomsteeg) are run by a cooperative of entrepreneurial prostitutes called Red Light Offices Boomsteeg. You may see their for-rent signs, seeking prostitutes who want to rent a window space. These women have banded together to create nice rooms for their clients and good working conditions for themselves, such as a lounge for sex workers between shifts.

Continue a few yards ahead, to #37. This popular nightclub ("Banana Bar") is a strip club with a-peel: For €60 you get admission for an hour, drinks included. Undressed ladies perch on the bar and serve the drinks. Touching is not allowed, but you can order a banana and the lady will serve it to you, any way you like. For a full description, step into the lobby.

• *A few yards farther along, at Molensteeg, cross the bridge to head to the other side of Oudezijds Achterburgwal. Once across the bridge, we'll turn left. But first, pause and look to the right. At #54 is the...*

## ⓲ Erotic Museum

"Wot a rip-off!" said a drunk British lout to his mates as he emerged from the Erotic Museum. If it's graphic sex you seek, this is not the place. To put it bluntly, this museum is not very good (the Damrak Sex Museum described on page 75 is better).

This museum, however, does offer a peek at some of the sex services found in the Red Light District. Besides the self-pleasuring bicycle girl in the lobby, displays include reconstructions of a prostitute's chambers, sex-shop windows, and videos of nightclub sex shows (on the third floor). There's also the S&M room, where S-mannequins torment M-mannequins for their mutual pleasure.

• *From the bridge, turn left and walk south along Oudezijds Achterburgwal. At #60H is the...*

## ⓴ Red Light Secrets Museum of Prostitution

Though overpriced, this museum is an earnest and mildly educational behind-the-scenes look at those women in the window. You'll walk through a typical (tiny) room where prostitutes stand at the window, and a typical (tiny) back room with a bed and sink where the dirty deed takes place. There's a cheesy hot-tub room for the high rollers, a display of S&M paraphernalia, and several videos about daily life for prostitutes. Perhaps most thought provoking: a video giving you the point of view of a sex worker as browsers check you out. The place is small, and a visit takes about as long as a typical session with a prostitute.

Farther down Oudezijds Achterburgwal (at #78) is **The Love Boutique.** Part lingerie store, part soft-core sex shop, this place caters to all of your sensual needs.

• *Continuing south, you'll pass two Casa Rosso franchises a block apart. The larger, lined by pink elephants, is...*

## ㉑ Theatre Casa Rosso

This is the Red Light District's best-known nightclub for live sex shows. Unlike some strip clubs that draw you in to rip you off with hidden charges, the Casa Rosso is a legitimate operation. Audience members pay a single price that includes drinks and a show. Eve-

**RED LIGHT WALK**

ning performances feature strippers, but the main event is naked people on stage engaging in sex acts—some simulated, some completely real (€50 includes drinks, nightly until 2:00 in the morning).

As you continue south along the canal, you gotta wonder, "Why does Amsterdam embrace prostitution and drugs?" It's not that the Dutch are any more liberal in their attitudes—they aren't. They're simply more pragmatic. They've found that when the sex trade goes underground, you get pimps, mobsters, and the spread of STDs. When marijuana is illegal, you get drug dealers, gangs, and violent turf wars. Their solution is to keep these markets legal and minimize problems through strict regulation.

• *But enough about sex. Let's talk about drugs. (Don't worry, our walk is nearly over.) Along the right side of the next block, you'll find several cannabis-related establishments, starting with the Cannabis College, at #124.*

## ㉒ Cannabis College

This free, nonprofit public study center aims to explain the pros and cons (but mostly pros) of the industrial, medicinal, and recreational uses of the green stuff. You can read about practical hemp prod-

ucts, the medical uses of marijuana, and police prosecution/persecution of cannabis users. The pride and joy of the college is downstairs. For a €3 donation, you can visit the organic flowering cannabis garden. The garden is small—it fits the Dutch legal limit of five plants per household.

• *Continue up the street to #130, the...*

## ㉓ Hemp Gallery

One ticket admits you to both the Hemp Gallery and the Hash, Marijuana, and Hemp Museum (described next). The gallery focuses mainly on extolling the wonders of industrial hemp, and isn't as meaty as the small, earnestly educational museum. If you have the patience to read its thorough displays, you'll learn plenty about how valuable cannabis was to Holland during its golden age. The leafy green plant was grown on large plantations. The fibrous stalks (hemp) were made into rope and canvas for ships, and even used to make clothing and lace. Without hemp, Henry Hudson would never have made it out of the harbor.

• *Next is our last stop at #148, the...*

## daan Walk

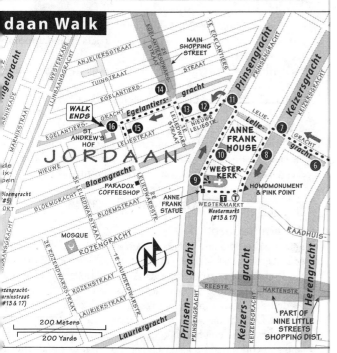

tramodern, symbolizing the city's economic revival after two
ies of decline. The North Sea Canal had just opened, indus-
ation was on the rise, and a World's Fair in 1883 capped it all
e building's decorative facade kicks off a theme we'll return
quently in this walk—Amsterdam's many varieties of archi-
e. (In the 1980s the post office was converted into a fashion-
opping mall.)

ng Magna Plaza, head right, walking 50 yards down the busy
o the corner of a tiny street called Molsteeg. Stand for a minute and
this slice of Amsterdam.

## lsteeg

the higgledy-piggledy fa-
along the busy street. Are
unk, high...or just in Am-
m, where the houses were
on mud? Check out the
ne of gables in this row of
. We'll see more like this
walk.

efore moving on, notice the T-shirt gallery on the corner.
es ago, I bought a Mark Raven T-shirt from a street ven-
ow this Amsterdam original has his own upscale shop, sell-

## ⓔ Hash, Marijuana, and Hemp Museum

This museum treats marijuana like it deserves scholarly study. The
exhibits are quite extensive and interesting.

Certain strains of the cannabis plant—particularly mature
females of the species *sativa* and
*indica*—contain the psychoactive
alkaloid tetrahydrocannabinol
(THC) that makes you high. The
buds, flowers, and leaves (marijuana) can be dried and smoked.
The brown sap/resin/pitch that
oozes out of the leaves (hash-
ish, a.k.a. hash) can also be dried and smoked. Both produce effects
ranging from euphoria to paranoia to the munchies.

Throughout history, various peoples have used cannabis as a
sacred ritual drug—from ancient Scythians and Hindus to modern
Nepalis and Afghans. Modern Rastafarians, following a Bible-
based religion centered in Jamaica, smoke cannabis. To worship,
they get high, bob to reggae music, and praise God. They love the
Bible verse (Genesis 1:11-12) that says God created "every herb"
and called them all "good." All over Amsterdam, you'll see the
Rastafarian colors: green, gold, and
red, mon.

The museum's highlight is the
flowering room, where you look
through windows at live cannabis
plants in bloom. At a certain stage
they're "sexed" to weed out the boring
males and "selected" to produce the
most powerful strains.

At the museum's exit you'll pass
through the **Sensi Seed Bank Store,**
which sells weed seeds, how-to books,
and knickknacks geared to growers.

• *We've reached the end of our tour. Dam
Square is just two blocks away. Continue a few steps farther up the canal
to the big and busy Oude Doelen street. Look right, and you'll see the
Royal Palace on Dam Square.*

## Congratulations

We've seen a lot. We've peeked at locals—from sex workers to drug
pushers to the ghosts of pioneer lesbians to politically active heads
with green thumbs. We've talked a bit of history, a little politics,
and a lot of sleaze. Congratulations. You've survived. Now, go back
to your hotel and take a shower.

# JORDAAN WALK

This walk takes you from Dam Square—the bustling center of Amsterdam—through what's called the "Western Canal Belt" to the Anne Frank House, and then deep into the characteristic Jordaan neighborhood. Cafés, boutiques, bookstores, and art galleries have gentrified the area. On this cultural scavenger hunt, you'll experience the laid-back Dutch lifestyle and catch a few intimate details that most busy tourists never appreciate. You'll see things in the Jordaan (yor-DAHN) that are commonplace in no other city in the world.

This is a short and easygoing walk—nice in the sleepy morning or en route to a Jordaan dinner in the evening. Be prepared to take lots of photos as you enjoy some of Amsterdam's most charming canal scenes.

## Orientation

**Length of This Walk:** Allow 1.5 hours.

**When to Go:** For the best views, and to hit a few minor sights while they're open, do this walk in daylight (and before 18:00, when some minor sights along the way close). Sundays aren't ideal, as many shops (and St. Andrew's Courtyard, our last stop) are closed.

**Westerkerk:** Church—free, donation requested, generally open Mon-Sat 11:00-15:00, closed Sun; tower—closed for renovation.

**Anne Frank House:** €14, must book timed-entry ticket online in advance, open daily 9:00-22:00, www.annefrank.org. No tickets are sold onsite. Tickets for the following month are released online on the first Tuesday of each month.

**Electric Ladyland:** €5; required 45-minute guided tours run Thu-

Sat at 14:00, 15:00, 16:00, and 17:00; closed S[un] appointment only via www.electricladyland.ap[ ] www.electric-lady-land.com.

**St. Andrew's Courtyard:** Free, generally open to the [ ] Sat 10:00-17:00, closed Sun.

**Tours:** ⌒ Download my free Jordaan Walk audio tou[r]

## OVERVIEW

The walk begins at Dam Square and ends at the [ ] Jordaan, along the Egelantiersgracht canal. From th[ ] short, scenic walk back to your starting point.

## The Walk Begins

### ❶ Dam Square

Start in Dam Square, where the city was born. The [ ] dents settled east of here, in the De Wallen neigh[ ] the Red Light District). But as Amsterdam grew [ ] trading village to a worldwide seagoing empire—[ ] needed new places to live. Citizens started reclaim[ing] west of Dam Square and built a "new church" (N[ ] serve these new neighborhoods. Over time they ne[ ] land and continued to push westward. Canal by can[al] waterways lined with merchants' townhouses.

By the 1600s—Amsterdam's golden age—[ ] moved even farther west, building an even newe[r] the Westerkerk (Western Church). The residentia[l] around it is what we'll explore on this walk—the J[ ]

Let's get going. From Dam Square, leave the f[ ] mimes, and tourists behind, and head to the p[ ] Amsterdammers live. Facing the Royal Palace, sl[ ] between the palace and New Church, toward a f[ ] white brick building. Approach the building by crossing the busy street called Nieuwezijds Voorburgwal. If it seems like this wide, traffic-filled street doesn't really fit the city, that's because it's new—built over what was a canal up until the 1880s.

Check out the red-and-white brick building—the **Magna Plaza mall.** When it was built in 1899, it was Amsterdam's main post office. Like so many buildings in this soggy city, it was constructed atop a foundation of thousands of pilings. In its day, it

JORDAAN WALK

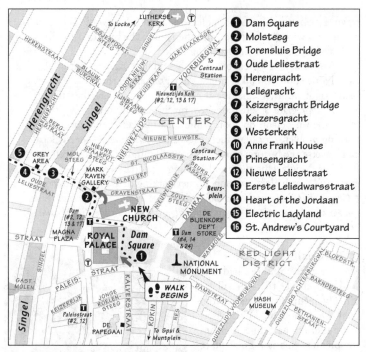

❶ Dam Square
❷ Molsteeg
❸ Torensluis Bridge
❹ Oude Leliestraat
❺ Herengracht
❻ Leliegracht
❼ Keizersgracht Bridge
❽ Keizersgracht
❾ Westerkerk
❿ Anne Frank House
⓫ Prinsengracht
⓬ Nieuwe Leliestraat
⓭ Eerste Leliedwarsstraat
⓮ Heart of the Jordaan
⓯ Electric Ladyland
⓰ St. Andrew's Courtyard

ing T-shirts and paintings featuring spindly lined, semi-abstract cityscapes. Raven works primarily with small etchings—as Rembrandt often did.

• *Now head left down tiny Molsteeg street—but don't walk on the reddish pavement in the middle; that's for bikes. From here this tour's essentially a straight shot west, though the street changes names along the way.*

A few steps along, on the left, find house #5: It's from 1644. Just one window wide, it's typical of the city's narrow old merchants' houses, with a shop on the ground floor, living space in the middle, and storage in the attic. Look up to see the hooks above warehouse doors. Houses like this lean out toward the street on purpose: Attach a pulley to the hook, and you can hoist cargo without banging it against the house (or, these days, lift up a sofa and send it through a big upper-story window).

Across the street, the building at #6 leans off-center; wooden support beams wedged into the side keep it from encroaching on its neighbor.

At the intersection with Spuistraat, you'll likely see rows of **bicycles** parked along the street. Amsterdam's 850,000 residents own nearly that many bikes. The Netherlands' 17 million people own 17 million bikes, with many people owning two—a long-distance racing bike and an in-city bike, often deliberately kept in poor maintenance so it's less enticing to the many bike thieves in town. Locals are diligent about locking their bikes twice: They lock the spokes with the first lock and then chain the bike to something immovable, such as a city hitching rack.

Amsterdam is a great bike town—and indeed, bikes outnumber cars. Notice how 100 bikes might be parked along the road, yet they blend right in. Then imagine if each bike were a car. The efficient Dutch appreciate a self-propelled machine that travels five times faster than a person on foot, while creating zero pollution, noise, parking problems, or high fuel costs. On a *fiets* (bike), a speedy local can traverse the historic center in about 10 minutes. Biking seems to keep the populace fit and good-looking—people here say that Amsterdam's health clubs are more for networking than for working out.
• *Cross what was another canal. After one more block, the street opens onto a small space that's actually a bridge, straddling the Singel canal. It's called...*

### ❸ Torensluis Bridge

We haven't quite reached the Jordaan yet, but the atmosphere already seems miles away from busy Dam Square. With cafés, art galleries, and fine benches for picnics, this is a great place to relax and take in a golden age atmosphere.

Find a place to enjoy the scene. Belly up to the railing, take a seat on a bench, or even pause the tour for a drink at one of the recommended **characteristic bars** that spill out onto the bridge. Café van Zuylen is famous for its variety of beers. Take in your surroundings.

The Singel canal was the original moat running around the old walled city. This bridge is so wide because it was the road that led to one of the original city gates. The area still looks much as it might have during the Dutch golden age of the 1600s. This was when Amsterdam's seagoing merchants ruled the waves, establishing trading colonies as far away as modern Indonesia. Fueled with this wealth, the city quickly became a major urban center, filled

with impressive homes. Each proud merchant tried to outdo his neighbor. Pan 360 degrees and take in the variety of buildings.

The houses crowd together, shoulder-to-shoulder. They're built on top of thousands of logs hammered vertically into the

# Gables

Along the rooftops, Amsterdam's famous gables are false fronts to enhance roofs that are, generally, sharply pitched.

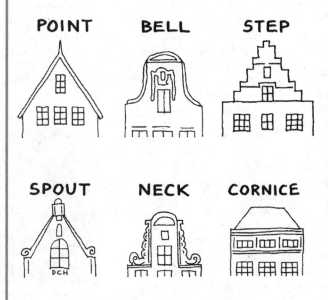

Gables come in all shapes and sizes. They might be ornamented with animal and human heads, garlands, urns, scrolls, and curlicues. Despite their infinite variety, most belong to a few distinct types. See how many of these you can spot.

A simple "point" gable just follows the triangular shape of a normal pitched roof. A "bell" gable is shaped like...well, guess. "Step" gables are triangular in shape and lined with steps. The one with a rectangular protrusion at the peak is called a "spout" gable. "Neck" gables rise up vertically from a pair of sloping "shoulders." "Cornice" gables make pointed roofs look classically horizontal. (There's probably even a "clark" gable, but frankly, I don't give a damn.)

marshy soil to provide a foundation. Over the years, they've shifted with the tides, leaving some leaning this way and that. Notice that some of the brick houses have iron rods strapped onto the sides. These act like braces, binding the bricks to an inner skeleton of wood. Almost all Amsterdam houses have big, tall windows to let in as much light as possible.

Although some houses look quite narrow, most of them extend far back. The rear of the building—called the *achterhuis*—is

JORDAAN WALK

often much more spacious than you might expect, judging from a skinny facade.

Mingled among the old houses are a few modern buildings. These sleek, gray-metal ones are part of the university. Built in the less affluent 1970s, architecture like this wouldn't be allowed today. Though these buildings try to match the humble, functional spirit of the older ones, they're still pretty ugly. But the students they house inject life into the neighborhood.

The "big head" statue honors a writer known by his pen name: **Multatuli.** Born in Amsterdam in 1820, Multatuli (a.k.a. Edu-

ard Douwes Dekker) did what many young Dutchmen did back then: He sought his fortune in the East Indies, then a colony of the Netherlands. While working as a bureaucrat in the colonial system, he witnessed firsthand the hard life of Javanese natives slaving away on Dutch-owned plantations. His semi-autobiographical novel, *Max Havelaar* (1860), follows a progressive civil servant fighting to reform colonial abuses. He was the first author to criticize Dutch colonial practices—a very bold position back then. For his talent and subject matter, Multatuli has been dubbed "the Dutch Rudyard Kipling."

The Singel is just one of Amsterdam's many canals—all told, there are roughly 50 miles of them. In the distance, way down at the north end of the Singel, beyond the dome, you can glimpse one of the canal's **locks.** Those white-flagpole thingies, sprouting at 45-degree angles, are part of the apparatus that opens and shuts the gates. While the canals originated as a way to drain diked-off marshland, they eventually became part of the city's sewer system. They were flushed daily: Just open the locks and let the North Sea tides come in and out.

The Dutch are credited with inventing locks in the 1300s. (Let's not ask the Chinese.) Locks are the single greatest innovation in canal-building. Besides controlling water flow in the city, they allow ships to pass from higher to lower water levels, and vice versa. It's because of locks that you can ship something by boat from here inland. Thanks to an extensive system of locks, from this very spot, you could hop a boat and go upriver, connect to the Rhine, and eventually—over the continental divide in Germany—connect to the Danube and then sail downstream, finally reaching Romania and the Black Sea.

The copper dome in the distance marks the Lutheran church. To the left of the church is the new city—reclaimed in the 1600s and destined to be the high-rent district. To the right is the old town.

• *Continue west on...*

## ❹ Oude Leliestraat

"Old Lily Street" is the well-worn path for tourists going to the Anne Frank House and is therefore lined with shops catering not to locals but to tourists. And one of those shops sells marijuana.

The **Grey Area** is a thriving coffeeshop; like Holland's other "coffeeshops," it sells pot. The green-and-white decal in the window identifies it as #092 in the city's licensing program. While smoking marijuana is essentially legal here, the café's name refers to the murky back side of the marijuana business— how coffeeshops get their supply from wholesalers. That's the "gray area" that

Dutch laws have yet to sort out. (The great accomplishment of Washington state and Colorado back in 2012 is that we tackled the gray area...and sorted it out. Now the Dutch are learning from us. For more on this and other coffeeshops, see the Smoking chapter.)

This esteemed coffeeshop, which works with the best boutique growers in Holland, regularly wins big at Amsterdam's annual Cannabis Cup Awards—a "high" honor, to be sure.

• *On the next bridge notice the work on the canals. While America may have crumbling bridges, the infrastructure challenge confronting Amsterdam is countless miles of aging canal embankments. To repair collapsing canals, temporary embankments are built in the canals with "sheet piling." The space behind them is then excavated to allow workers to rebuild the original embankments, making them stronger. It'll be a very long and very expensive process.*

## ❺ Herengracht

Amsterdam added this canal during its golden age boom in the 1600s. It's named for the *heren*, the wealthy city merchants who lined it with their mansions. Because the city was antiroyalty, there was no blue-blooded class; these *heren* functioned as

the town's aristocracy. Even today, Herengracht runs through a high-rent district. (Zoning here forbids houseboats.)

Check out the house that's kitty-corner across the bridge, at Herengracht 150. It has features you'll find on many old Amsterdam buildings. On the roof, rods support the false-front gable (which originally supported only a rich merchant's ego). From this side view, you can see that, though a townhouse might have a narrow entrance, it can stretch far back from the street.

• *Continue west, walking along...*

## ❻ Leliegracht

This is one of the city's prettiest small canals (at least when its embankments aren't being rebuilt), lined with trees and lanterns,

and crossed by a series of arched bridges. There are some 400 such bridges in Amsterdam. It's a pleasant street of eccentric boutiques, trendy furniture shops, and bookstores. Notice that some buildings have staircases leading down below the street level to residences. Looking up, you'll see the characteristic beams jutting out from the top with a cargo-hoisting hook on the end. The view from a bay window here must be exceptional.

• *Continue on to the next canal, and pause on the...*

## ❼ Keizersgracht Bridge

Take in another fine row of gables. Kitty-corner across the bridge is the gray Astoria building from 1905, an example of the architectural style known as Amsterdam School: geometrical windows and minimal ornamentation, brightened with a few mosaics, bay windows, and flowery reliefs. Rising behind it is the colorfully crowned tower of the Westerkerk—where we're headed.

• *After the bridge, we'll take a detour off our westward route and veer left along...*

## ❽ Keizersgracht

Walk south about 100 yards along the canal. You'll reach a set of steps leading down to the water, where a triangular pink stone juts into the canal. This is part of the so-called **Homomonument**—a memorial to homosexuals who lost their lives in

World War II, and a commemoration of all those persecuted for their sexuality. If you survey the square, you'll see that the pink triangle is just one corner of a larger triangle that comprises the entire Homomonument. (The pink-triangle design reclaims the symbol that the Nazis used to mark homosexuals.) You may see flowers or cards left here by friends and loved ones.

From here, walk through the square called Westermarkt, between the church and busy Raadhuisstraat. You'll pass several very Dutch kiosks. The first, called Pink Point, gives out information on gay and lesbian Amsterdam, especially nightlife. The next sells french fries; when it's closed, the shutters feature funny paintings putting *friet*s into great masterpieces of Western art. Then, before the flower kiosk, is one that sells fresh herring. If you've yet to try a delicious Dutch herring, this is the perfect opportunity (for pointers on how to eat one, see page 110).

• *Keep walking toward the entrance to...*

## ❾ Westerkerk (Western Church)

Near the western end of the church, look for a cute little statue. It's of Anne Frank, who holed up with her family in a house just down the block from here (we'll pass it in a minute).

For now, look up at the towering spire of the impressive Westerkerk. The crown shape was a gift of the Habsburg emperor, Maximilian I. In thanks for a big loan, the city got permission to use the Habsburg royal symbol. The tower also displays the symbol of Amsterdam, with its three Xs. The Westerkerk was built in 1631, as the city was expanding out from Dam Square. Rembrandt's buried inside...but no one knows where. You can pop into the church for free (see page 70).

The church tower has a carillon that chimes every 15 minutes. At other times, it plays full songs. Invented by Dutch bellmakers in the 1400s, a carillon is a set of bells of different sizes and pitches. There's a live musician inside the tower who plays a keyboard to make the music. Mozart, Vivaldi, and Bach—all of whom lived during the heyday of the carillon—wrote music that sounds great on this unique instrument. During World War II, the Westerkerk's carillon played every day. This hopeful sound reminded Anne Frank that there was, indeed, an outside world.

• *Continue around the church and walk north along the Prinsengracht canal to the Anne Frank House. Bypass the tourists entering through the modern annex and keep going a few steps more to #263. This doorway was the original entrance to the...*

## ⓾ Anne Frank House

This was where the Frank family hid from the Nazis for 25 months. With actual artifacts, the museum gives the cold, mind-boggling statistics of fascism the all-important intimacy of a young girl who lived through it and died from it. Even bah-humbug types find themselves caught up in Anne's story.

📖 See the Anne Frank House Tour chapter.

• *At the next bridge turn left. Stop at its high point, mid-canal, for a view of...*

## ⓫ Prinsengracht

The "Princes' Canal" runs through what's considered one of the most livable areas in town. It's lined with houseboats, some of the city's estimated 2,500. These small vessels were once cargo ships— but by the 1930s, they had become obsolete. They found a new use as houseboats lining the canals of Amsterdam, where dry land is so limited and pricey. Today, former cargo holds are fashioned into elegant, cozy living rooms. The once-powerful engines have generally been removed to make more room for living space. Moorage spots are prized and grandfathered in, making some of the junky old boats worth more than you'd think. Houseboaters can plug hoses and cables into outlets along the canals to get water, sewer, and electricity. (To learn more about houseboats, visit the charming Houseboat Museum, described on page 70.)

Notice the canal traffic. The official speed limit is about four miles per hour. At night, boats must have running lights on the top, the side, and the stern.  Most boats are small and low, designed to glide under the city's bridges. The Prinsengracht bridge is average height, with less than seven feet of headroom (it varies with the water level); some bridges have less than six feet. Boaters need good charts to tell them the height, which is crucial for navigating. Police boats roam on the lookout for anyone CUI (cruising under the influence).

Just across the bridge are some typical Jordaan cafés. The relaxed (and recommended) **Café de Prins** serves food and drink day and night. And the recommended **Café 't Smalle** (not visible from here, but a block to the right) has a deck where you can drink outside along a quiet canal.

JORDAAN WALK

• *Once you cross Prinsengracht, you enter what's officially considered the Jordaan neighborhood. Facing west (toward Café de Prins), cross the bridge and veer left down...*

## ⑫ Nieuwe Leliestraat

Welcome to the quiet Jordaan. Built in the 1600s as a working-class housing area, it's now home to artists and yuppies. The name Jordaan probably was not derived from the French *jardin*—but given the neighborhood's garden-like ambience, it seems like it should have been. Lush vegetation lines this street, as residents greenify their neighborhood with potted plants.

Train your ultra-sharp "traveler's eyes" on all the tiny details of Amsterdam life. Notice how the pragmatic Dutch deal with junk mail. On the doors, stick-ers next to mail slots say *Nee* or *Ja* (no or yes), tell-ing the postman if they'll accept or refuse junk mail. (A practical recent law made *Nee* the default, and residents now must re-quest junk mail to get it... that's so Dutch.) Residents

are allowed a "front-yard garden" as long as it's no more than one sidewalk tile wide. A speed bump in the road keeps things peace-ful. The red metal bollards known as *Amsterdammertjes* ("little Am-sterdammers") have been bashing balls since the 1970s, when they were put in to stop people from parking on the sidewalks. Though many apartments have windows right on the street, the neighbors don't stare and the residents don't care.

• *At the first intersection, turn right onto...*

## ⑬ Eerste Leliedwarsstraat

Pause and linger awhile on this tiny lane. Imagine the frustrations of home ownership here. If your house is considered "historic," you need special permission and lots of money to renovate.

On this street, you can see three different examples of reno-vation. At house #9, it was done cheap and dirty: A historic (but run-down) home was simply torn down and replaced with an in-expensive, functional building with modern heating and plumb-ing. This was done before the 1980s, when the city started writing more restrictive building codes to preserve the vintage ambience. At #5, there's no renovation at all. The owners were too poor (stuck with rent-control tenants), and they missed the window of time when a cheap rebuild was allowed. At #2A (across the street), the owners obviously had the cash to do a first-class sprucing up—it

JORDAAN WALK

looks historic but is fully modern inside. (In this case, it's the work of Yvonne—who loves plants and lives upstairs while making and selling her art on the ground-floor level.) Even newly renovated homes like this must preserve their funky leaning angles and original wooden beams. They're certainly nice to look at, but absolutely maddening for owners who don't have a lot of money to meet city standards.

• *Just ahead, walk out to the middle of the bridge over the next canal (Egelantiersgracht). This is what I think of as...*

## ❶ The Heart of the Jordaan

For me, this bridge and its surroundings capture the essence of the Jordaan. Take it all in: the bookstores, art galleries, working artists' studios, and small cafés full of

rickety tables. The quiet canal is lined with trees and old, narrow buildings with gables—classic Amsterdam.

Looking south toward the Westerkerk, you'll see a completely different view of the church than tourists get as they wait in line at the Anne Frank House. Framed by narrow streets, crossed with streetlamp wires, and looming over shoppers on bicycles—to me, this is the church in its best light.

Turning around and looking north, you'll see the street called Tweede Egelantiersdwarsstraat—the laid-back Jordaan neighborhood's main shopping-and-people street. If you venture down there, you'll find boutiques, galleries, antique stores, hair salons, and an enticing array of restaurants. You'll notice there are no chain stores in the Jordaan. Locals say that's because the buildings are protected and just pint-sized-big enough for a mom-and-pop shop but not some corporate venture. So, the neighborhood just stays cute...it fits that great Dutch word for cozy, *gezellig*.

Looking west down the canal, check out the junky old boats that litter the sides. Some aren't worth maintaining and are left abandoned. As these dinghies fill with rainwater and start to rot, the city confiscates them and stores them in a big lot. Unclaimed boats are auctioned off three times a year.

But most boats are well used. When the sun goes down and the lights come on, people cruise the sparkling canals with an on-board hibachi and a bottle of wine, and even the funkiest scows can become party magnets.

• *Now head west along the canal (Egelantiersgracht) to the next bridge, where you'll turn left onto Tweede Leliedwarsstraat, and walk a few steps to #5.*

## ⓰ Electric Ladyland

This small shop, with a flowery window display, calls itself "The First Museum of Fluorescent Art." Its funky facade hides an illu-

minated wonderland within, with a tiny exhibit of black-light art (under the shop, down a very steep set of stairs, visits by appointment only). It's the creation of Nick Padalino—one cool cat who really found his niche in life. He enjoys personally demonstrat-

ing the fluorescence found in unexpected places—everything from minerals to stamps to candy to the tattoo on his arm. Nick seems to get an even bigger kick out of it than his customers. You can see the historic first fluorescent crayon from San Francisco in the 1950s. Wow. Its label says, "Use with black light for church groups." Wow.

(After this tour, you might be interested in this little side trip: About 100 yards farther down the street and across the canal is the **Paradox Coffeeshop.** It's the perfect coffeeshop for the nervous American who wants a friendly, mellow place to go local—see listing in the Smoking chapter.)

• *To reach our last stop, backtrack 20 paces from Electric Ladyland to the canal and turn left, then walk 20 yards to Egelantiersgracht #107, the entrance to...*

## ⓰ St. Andrew's Courtyard (Sint-Andrieshof)

The black door is marked *Sint-Andrieshof 107 t/m 145.* The doorway

looks private, but it's the public entrance to a set of residences. It's generally open during daytime hours, except
on Sundays. Enter quietly; you may
have to push hard on the door. Go inside and continue through a blue-tile-
lined passageway into a tiny garden
courtyard *(hof)* surrounded by a dozen
or so homes. This is one of the city's
scores of similar *hofjes*—subsidized
residences built around a courtyard
and funded by churches, charities, and
the city for low-income widows and
pensioners. This one, from 1613, is one

of the oldest in Amsterdam. Three centuries ago, 60 people lived here. Today it's home to 20. Enjoy the greenery, the stone fountain, the colorful gable stones embedded in the walls...and the peace and quiet.

• *And this is where our walk ends—in a tranquil world that seems right out of a painting by Vermeer. You're just blocks from the bustle of Amsterdam, but it feels like another world. You're immersed in the Jordaan, where everything's in its place, where people—like Yvonne and Nick— find their place in life, and where life seems very good.*

# RIJKSMUSEUM TOUR

At Amsterdam's Rijksmuseum ("Rijks" rhymes with "bikes"), Holland's golden age shines with the best collection anywhere of the Dutch Masters—from Vermeer's quiet domestic scenes and Steen's raucous family meals to Hals' snapshot portraits and Rembrandt's moody brilliance.

The 17th century saw the Netherlands at the pinnacle of its power. The Dutch had won their independence from Spain, trade and shipping boomed, wealth poured in, the people were understandably proud, and the arts flourished. This era was later dubbed the Dutch golden age. With no church bigwigs or royalty around to commission big canvases in the Protestant Dutch Republic, artists had to find different patrons—and they discovered the upper-middle-class businessmen who fueled Holland's capitalist economy. Artists painted their portraits and decorated their homes with pretty still lifes and unpreachy, slice-of-life art.

This delightful museum—much improved after a long renovation—offers one of the most exciting and enjoyable art experiences in Europe. As if in homage to Dutch art and history, the Rijksmuseum lets you linger over a vast array of objects and paintings, appreciating the beauty of everyday things.

# Orientation

**Cost:** €20 timed-entry ticket, free for kids under 18.

**Hours:** Daily 9:00-17:00.

**Information:** Info tel. +31 20 674 7047, www.rijksmuseum.nl.

**Advance Tickets Recommended:** Purchase timed-entry tickets online in advance at www.rijksmuseum.nl. You must book an entry time even with a museum pass. Although limited walk-up tickets may be available, I recommend buying ahead.

**Avoiding Crowds/Lines:** Even with timed tickets, the museum is always crowded. Plan your visit for either first thing in the morning or later in the day to avoid tour groups.

**Getting There:** From Centraal station, catch tram #2 or #12 to the Museumplein stop. The museum entrance is inside the arched passage that cuts under the building at its center (watch out for bikes).

**Tours:** The museum's free **app** offers tours, maps, and other useful info (download in advance or use the museum's free Wi-Fi; bring your own headphones). A **multimedia guide** (€5) provides both a 45-minute highlights tour and an in-depth version. **Guided tours** are available on weekends—book at least a month in advance; pop-up guided tours are often offered on weekdays (€5).

**Length of This Tour:** Allow 1.5 hours.

**Baggage Check:** Leave your bag at the free checkroom in the Atrium.

**Cuisine Art:** The Rijksmuseum Café is in the Atrium. On the south side of the building, there's a restaurant in the Philips

Wing and a pleasant coffee-and-pastry café in the garden to the right. You'll also find an espresso bar in the garden in the summer.

Nearby on Museumplein, you'll find the Cobra Café, several take-out stands, and (at the far end, near the Stedelijk Museum), an Albert Heijn grocery. Museumplein and nearby Vondelpark are both perfect for a picnic. For locations, see the map on page 59.

**Starring:** Rembrandt van Rijn, Frans Hals, Johannes Vermeer, Jan Steen, and many interesting artifacts of the golden age.

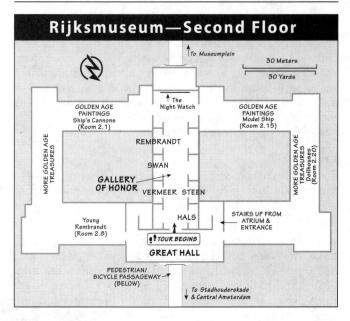

# Rijksmuseum—Second Floor

## OVERVIEW

Dutch art is meant to be enjoyed, not studied. It's straightforward, meat-and-potatoes art for the common man. The Dutch love the beauty of mundane things painted realistically and with exquisite detail. So set your cerebral cortex on "low" and let this art pass straight from the eyes to the heart, with minimal detours.

# The Tour Begins

Entering the building, you'll descend into the lower-level Atrium, which houses all the visitor services: info desk, baggage check, café, gift shop, and WCs.

• *After showing your ticket (and perhaps downloading the museum app or renting a multimedia guide), follow the crowds up the stairway to the top (second) floor, where you emerge into the...*

## GREAT HALL

With its stained-glass windows depicting great artists and thinkers, vaulted ceiling, and murals of golden age explorers, it feels like a cathedral to Holland's middle-class merchants. Gaze down the long adjoining hall to the far end, with the "altarpiece" of this cathedral—Rembrandt's *The Night Watch*.

• *Now, follow the flow of the crowds toward it, into the...*

**RIJKSMUSEUM**

## GALLERY OF HONOR

This grand space was purpose-built to hold the Greatest Hits of the Golden Age by the era's biggest rock stars: Hals, Vermeer, Steen, and Rembrandt. The best of the era's portraits, still lifes, landscapes, and slice-of-life "genre scenes" give us a close-up look at daily life in this happy, affluent era. The smaller rooms surrounding the gallery hold more treasures of the golden age.

• *In the first alcove to the right is the work of...*

## Frans Hals

Frans Hals (c. 1582-1666) was the premier golden age portrait painter. Merchants hired him the way we'd hire a wedding photographer. With a few quick strokes, Hals captured not only the features, but also the personality.

### *A Militiaman Holding a Berkemeyer,*
### a.k.a. *The Merry Drinker,* c. 1628-1630

You're greeted by a jovial man in a black hat, capturing the earthy, exuberant spirit of the Dutch golden age. Notice the details—the

happy red face of the man offering us a *berkemeyer* drinking glass, the sparkle in his eyes, the lacy collar, the decorative belt buckle, and so on.

Now move in closer. All these meticulous details are accomplished with a few thick, messy brushstrokes. The beard is a tangle of brown worms, the belt buckle a yellow blur. His hand is a study in smudges. Even the expressive face is created with a few well-chosen patches of color. Unlike Dutch still-life scenes, this canvas is meant to be viewed from a distance, where the colors and brushstrokes blend together.

Rather than posing his subjects, making them stand for hours saying "cheese," Hals tried to catch them at a candid moment. He often painted common people, fishermen, and barflies such as this one. He had to work quickly to capture the serendipity of the moment. Hals used a stop-action technique, freezing the man in mid-gesture, with the rough brushwork creating a blur that suggests the man is still moving.

Two centuries later, the Impressionists learned from Hals' scruffy brushwork. In the Van Gogh Museum, you'll see how Van Gogh painted, say, a brown beard by using thick dabs of green, yellow, and red that blend at a distance to make brown.

# The Dutch Golden Age (1600s)

Who bought this art? Look around at the Rijksmuseum's many portraits and you'll see ordinary middle-class people, merchants, and traders. Even in their Sunday best, you can tell that these are hardworking, businesslike, friendly, simple people (with a penchant for ruffled lace collars).

Dutch fishermen sold their surplus catch in distant areas of Europe, importing goods from these far lands. In time, fishermen became traders, and by 1600, Holland's merchant fleets ruled the waves with colonies as far away as India, the East Indies, and America (remember—New York was originally "New Amsterdam"). The Dutch slave trade—selling Africans to Americans—generated a lot of profit for luxuries such as the art you're viewing. Back home, these traders were financed by shrewd Amsterdam businessmen on the new frontiers of capitalism.

Look around again. Is there even one crucifixion? One saint? One Madonna? This art is made for the people, not for the church. In most countries, Catholic bishops and rich kings supported the arts. But the Dutch Republic, recently free of Spanish rule and Vatican domination, was independent, democratic, and largely Protestant, with no taste for saints and Madonnas.

Instead, Dutch burghers bought portraits of themselves and pretty, unpreachy, unpretentious works for their homes. Even poor people bought art—usually on smaller canvases, painted by no-name artists, and designed to fit their budgets and lifestyles. We'll see examples of their four favorite subjects—landscapes, portraits (often of groups), scenes from everyday life, and still lifes of food and mundane objects.

Pick a still life and get so close that the guard joins you. Savor the fruits of Holland's rich overseas trade—lemons from the south, pewterware from Germany, and spices from Asia. You'll swear you can see yourself reflected in the pewter vessels. Linger over the little things—the closer you get, the better they look. These carefully composed, photorealistic paintings capture the pride the Dutch had for their homes, which they cultivated like gardens to be immaculate, decorative, and in perfect order.

RIJKSMUSEUM

### Portrait of a Couple, Probably Isaac Abrahamsz Massa and Beatrix van der Laen, c. 1622

This likely wedding portrait of a chubby, pleasant merchant and his bride sums up the story of the Dutch golden age. Because this overseas trader was away from home for years at a time on business, Hals makes a special effort to point out his patron's commitment to marriage. Isaac pledges allegiance to his wife, putting his hand on his heart. Beatrix's wedding ring is prominently displayed dead

center between them (on her right-hand forefinger, Protestant-style). The vine clinging to a tree is a symbol of man's support and woman's dependence. And in the distance at right, in the classical love garden, are other happy couples strolling arm-in-arm amid peacocks, a symbol of fertility.

In earlier times, marriage portraits put the man and wife in separate canvases, staring out grimly. Hals' jolly side-by-side couple reflects a societal shift from marriage as business partnership to an arrangement that's more friendly and intimate.

Hals didn't need symbolism to tell us that these two are prepared for their long-distance relationship—they seem relaxed together, but each looks at us directly, with a strong, individual identity. Good as gold, these are the type of people who propelled this soggy little country into its glorious golden age.

• *A little farther along are the small-scale canvases of...*

## Johannes Vermeer

Vermeer (1632-1675) is the master of tranquility and stillness. He creates a clear and silent pool that is a world in itself. Most of his canvases show interiors of Dutch homes, where Dutch women engage in everyday activities, lit by a side window.

Vermeer's father, an art dealer, gave Johannes a passion for painting. Late in the artist's career, with Holland drained by wars against England, the demand for art and luxuries went sour, forcing Vermeer to downsize—he sold his big home, packed up his wife and 14 children, and moved in with his mother-in-law. He died two years later, and his works fell into centuries of obscurity.

The Rijksmuseum has the best collection of Vermeers in the world—four of them. (There are only some 34 in captivity.) But each is a small jewel worth lingering over.

### *The Milkmaid,* c. 1660

It's so quiet you can practically hear the milk pouring into the bowl.

Vermeer brings out the beauty in everyday things. The subject is ordinary—a kitchen maid—but you could look for hours at the tiny details and rich color tones. These are everyday objects, but they glow in a diffused light: the crunchy crust, the hanging basket,

## Shhh...Dutch Art

You're sitting at home late one night, and it's perfectly calm. Not a sound, very peaceful. And then...the refrigerator motor turns off, and it's really quiet.

Dutch art is really quiet art. It silences our busy world, so that every sound, every motion is noticeable. You can hear cows tearing off grass 50 yards away. Dutch art is still. It slows our fast-lane world, so we notice the motion of birds. We notice how the cold night air makes the stars sharp. We notice that the undersides of leaves and cats are always a lighter shade than the tops. Dutch art stills the world so we can hear our own heartbeat and reflect upon that most noble muscle that, without thinking, gives us life.

To see how subtle Dutch art is, realize that one of the museum's most exciting, dramatic, emotional, and extravagant Dutch paintings is probably *The Threatened Swan* (in the Gallery of Honor). It's quite a contrast to the rape scenes and visions of heaven of Italian Baroque paintings from the same time period.

even the rusty nail in the wall with its tiny shadow. Vermeer had a unique ability with surface texture, to show how things feel when you touch them.

The maid is alive with Vermeer's distinctive yellow and blue—the colors of many traditional Dutch homes—against a white backdrop. She is content, solid, and sturdy, performing this simple task as if it's the most important thing in the world. Her full arms are built with patches of reflected light. Vermeer squares off a little world in itself (framed by the table in the foreground, the wall in back, the window to the left, and the footstool at right), then fills this space with objects for our perusal.

### Woman Reading a Letter, c. 1663

Notice how Vermeer's placid scenes often have an air of mystery. The woman is reading a letter. From whom? A lover? A father on a two-year business trip to the East Indies? Not even taking time to sit down, she reads intently, with parted lips and a bowed head. It must be important. (She looks pregnant, adding to the mystery, but that may just be the cut of her clothes.)

Again, Vermeer has framed a moment of everyday life. But within this small world are hints of a wider, wilder world—the light coming from the left is obviously from a large window, giving us a whiff of the life going on outside. The map hangs prominently, reminding us of travel, and perhaps of where the letter is from.

### The Love Letter, c. 1669-1670

There's a similar theme here. The curtain parts, and we see through the doorway into a dollhouse world, then through the seascape on the back wall to the wide ocean. A woman is playing a lute when she's interrupted by a servant bringing a letter. The mysterious letter stops the music, intruding like a pebble dropped into the pool of Vermeer's quiet world. The floor tiles create a strong 3-D perspective that sucks us straight into the center of the painting—the woman's heart.

### View of Houses in Delft, a.k.a. The Little Street, c. 1658

Vermeer was born in the picturesque town of Delft, grew up near its Market Square, and set a number of his paintings there. This may be the view from his front door.

The details in the painting actually aren't very detailed—the cobblestone street doesn't have a single individual stone in it. But Vermeer shows us the beautiful interplay of colored rectangles on the buildings. Our eye moves back and forth from shutter to gable to window...and then from front to back, as we notice the woman deep in the alleyway.

• *In an alcove nearby are some rollicking paintings by...*

### Jan Steen

Not everyone could afford a masterpiece, but even poorer people wanted works of art for their homes (like a landscape from Sears for over the sofa). Jan Steen (c. 1625-1679, pronounced "yahn stain"), the Norman Rockwell of his day, painted humorous scenes from the lives of the lower classes. As a tavern owner, he observed society firsthand.

### The Feast of St. Nicholas, 1665-1668

It's Christmas time, and the kids have been given their gifts, including a little girl who got a doll. The mother says, "Let me see it," but the girl turns away playfully. Everyone is happy except the boy, who's crying. His Christmas present is only a branch in his shoe—like coal in your stocking, the gift for bad boys. His sister gloats and passes it around. The kids laugh at him. But wait—it turns out the family is just playing a trick. In the background, the grandmother beckons to him, saying, "Look, I have your real present in here." Out of the limelight, but smack in the middle, sits the father providing ballast to this family scene and clearly enjoying his children's pleasure.

Steen has frozen the moment, sliced off a piece, and laid it on a canvas. He's told a story with a past, a present, and a future. These are real people in a real scene.

Steen's fun art reminds us that museums aren't mausoleums.

### The Merry Family, 1668

This family—three generations living happily under one roof—is eating, drinking, and singing like there's no tomorrow. The broken eggshells and scattered cookware symbolize waste and extravagance. The neglected proverb tacked to the fireplace reminds us that children will follow in the footsteps of their parents. The father in this jolly scene is very drunk—ready to topple over—

while in the foreground his mischievous daughter is feeding her brother wine straight from the flask. Mom and Grandma join the artist himself (playing the bagpipes) in a lively sing-along, but the child learning to smoke would rather follow Dad's lead.

Dutch golden age families were notoriously lenient with their kids. Even today, the Dutch describe a rowdy family as a "Jan Steen household."

# Female Masters in the Gallery of Honors

Though not as well-known as Vermeer, Hals, or Rembrandt, several women master painters are worth seeking out.

The most celebrated female Dutch golden age painter is **Judith Leyster** (b. 1609), the first female master painter in the Netherlands and one of the two women admitted in the 17th century to Haarlem's prestigious Guild of St. Luke. Centuries before "equal work for equal pay" became a slogan, Leyster commanded the same rates for her work as male guildmembers and had her own workshop and pupils.

Next to Jan Steen's *The Merry Family,* you'll see Leyster's *The Serenade* (1629), depicting a lute player in a furry black hat. Sharp contrasts of light and dark echo Rembrandt's technique. This painting was formerly attributed to Frans Hals—perhaps understandably, since like Hals, Leyster used loose, rough brushstrokes and painted ordinary people in midaction doing everyday things. The similarities continue in Leyster's *The Merry Drinker* (1629), displayed next to Hals' *A Militiaman Holding a Berkemeyer*—also known as *The Merry Drinker.*

**Rachel Ruysch** (b. 1664), daughter of a botany professor, was famous for her detailed floral still lifes (look for *Still Life with Flowers in a Glass Vase*), while Flemish painter **Clara Peeters** (b. 1594) gained acclaim for the exquisite textures of her still-lifes (as seen in *Still Life with Fish, Sea, Food and Flowers*).

## Adolf and Catharina Croeser, a.k.a. *The Burgomaster of Delft and His Daughter,* 1655

Steen's well-dressed burgher sits on his front porch, when a poor woman and child approach to beg, putting him squarely between the horns of a moral dilemma. On the one hand, we see his rich home, well-dressed daughter, and a vase of flowers—a symbol that his money came from morally suspect capitalism (the kind that produced the folly of 1637's "tulip mania"). On the other hand, there are his poor fellow citizens and the church steeple, reminding him of his Christian duty. The man's daughter avoids the confrontation. Will the burgher set the right Christian example? This moral dilemma perplexed many nouveau-riche Dutch Calvinists of Steen's day.

This early painting by Steen demonstrates his mastery of several popular genres: portrait, still life (the flowers and fabrics), cityscape, and moral instruction.

• *You're getting closer to the iconic* Night Watch, *but first you'll find other works by...*

## Rembrandt van Rijn

Rembrandt van Rijn (1606-1669) is the greatest of all Dutch painters. Whereas most painters specialized in one field—portraits, landscapes, still lifes—Rembrandt excelled in them all.

The son of a Leiden miller who owned a waterwheel on the Rhine ("van Rijn"), Rembrandt took Amsterdam by storm with his famous painting *The Anatomy Lesson of Dr. Nicolaes Tulp* (1632, currently in The Hague's Mauritshuis Royal Picture Gallery). The commissions poured in for official portraits, and he was soon wealthy and married (1634) to Saskia van Uylenburgh. They moved to an expensive home in the Jewish Quarter (today's Rembrandt House Museum) and decorated it with their collection of art and exotic furniture. His portraits were dutifully detailed, but other paintings explored strong contrasts of light and dark, with dramatic composition.

In 1642, Saskia died, and Rembrandt's fortunes changed, as the public's taste shifted and commissions dried up. In 1649, he hired an 18-year-old model named Hendrickje Stoffels, and she soon moved in with him and gave birth to their daughter.

Holland's war with England (1652-1654) devastated the art market, and Rembrandt's free-spending ways forced him to declare bankruptcy (1656)—the ultimate humiliation in success-oriented Amsterdam. The commissions came more slowly. The money ran out. His mother died. He had to auction off his paintings and furniture to pay debts. He moved out of his fine house to a cheaper place on Rozengracht. His bitter losses added a new wisdom to his work.

In his last years, Rembrandt's greatest works were his self-portraits, showing a tired, wrinkled man stoically enduring life's misfortunes. Rembrandt piled on layers of paint and glaze to capture increasingly subtle effects. In 1668, his lone surviving son, Titus, died, and Rembrandt passed away the next year. His death effectively marked the end of the Dutch golden age.

### Isaac and Rebecca, a.k.a. *The Jewish Bride,* c. 1665-1669

The man gently draws the woman toward him. She's comfortable enough with him to sink into thought, and she reaches up unconsciously to return the

gentle touch. They're young but wizened. This uncommissioned portrait (its subjects remain unknown) is a truly human look at the relationship between two people in love. They form a protective pyramid of love amid a gloomy background. The touching hands form the center of this somewhat sad but peaceful work. Van Gogh said that "Rembrandt alone has that tenderness—the heartbroken tenderness."

Rembrandt was a master of oil painting. In his later years, he rendered details with a messier, more Impressionistic style. The red-brown-gold of the couple's clothes is a patchwork of oil laid on thick with a palette knife.

### The Wardens of the Amsterdam Drapers Guild, a.k.a. *The Syndics,* 1662

Rembrandt could paint an official group portrait better than anyone. In the painting made famous by Dutch Masters cigars, he

catches the Drapers Guild in a natural but dignified pose (dignified, at least, until the guy on the left sits on his friend's lap).

It's a business meeting, and they're all dressed in black with black hats—the standard power suit of the Dutch golden age. They gather around a table examining the company's books. Suddenly, someone (us) walks in, and they look up. It's as natural as a snapshot, though X-rays show Rembrandt made many changes in posing them perfectly.

The figures are "framed" by the table beneath them and the top of the wood paneling above their heads, making a three-part composition that brings this band of colleagues together. Even in this simple portrait, we feel we can read the guild members' personalities in their faces. (If the table in the painting looks like it's sloping a bit unnaturally, lie on the floor to view it at Rembrandt's intended angle.)

• At the far end of the Gallery of Honor is the museum's star masterpiece.

*The best viewing spot is to the right of center—the angle Rembrandt had in mind when he designed it.*

### The Night Watch, a.k.a. *The Militia Company of Captain Frans Banninck Cocq,* 1642

This is Rembrandt's most famous—though not necessarily greatest—painting. It's displayed behind glass and is being carefully studied by conservators as they determine the best way to combat deterioration.

Created in 1642, when Rembrandt was 36, *The Night Watch* was one of his most important commissions: a group portrait of a company of Amsterdam's Civic Guards to hang in their meeting hall.

It's an action shot. With flags waving and drums beating, the guardsmen (who, by the 1640s, were really only an honorary militia of rich bigwigs) spill onto the street from under an arch in the back. It's "all for one and one for all" as they rush to Amsterdam's rescue. The soldiers grab lances and load their muskets. In the center, the commander (in black, with a red sash) strides forward energetically with a hand gesture that seems to say, "What are we waiting for? Let's move out!" His lieutenant focuses on his every order.

Rembrandt caught the optimistic spirit of Holland in the 1600s. Its war of independence from Spain was heading to victory and the economy was booming. These guardsmen on the move epitomize the proud, independent, upwardly mobile Dutch.

Why is *The Night Watch* so famous? Compare it with other, less famous group portraits nearby, where every face is visible and everyone is well-lit, flat, and flashbulb-perfect. These people paid good money to have their mugs preserved for posterity, and they wanted it right up front. Other group portraits may be colorful, dignified works by a master...but not quite masterpieces.

## Ruffs

I cannot tell you why men and women of the Dutch golden age found these fanlike collars attractive, but they certainly were all the rage here and elsewhere in Europe. It started in Spain in the 1540s, but the style really took off with a marvelous discovery in 1565: starch. Within decades, Europe's wealthy merchant class was wearing nine-inch collars made from 18 yards of material.

The ruffs were detachable and made from a long, pleated strip of linen set into a neck (or wrist) band. You tied it in front with strings. Big ones required that you wear a wire frame underneath for support. There were various types—the "cartwheel" was the biggest, a "double ruff" had two layers of pleats, and a "cabbage" was somewhat asymmetrical.

Ruffs required elaborate maintenance. First, you washed and starched the linen. While the cloth was still wet, hot metal pokers were painstakingly inserted into the folds to form the characteristic figure-eight pattern. The ruffs were stored in special round boxes to hold their shape.

For about a century, Europeans loved the ruff, but by 1630, Holland had come to its senses, and the fad faded.

RIJKSMUSEUM

By contrast, Rembrandt rousted the Civic Guards off their fat duffs. By adding movement and depth to an otherwise static scene, he took posers and turned them into warriors. He turned a simple portrait into great art.

OK, some *Night Watch* scuttlebutt: First off, "night watch" is a misnomer. It's a daytime scene, but over the years, as the preserving varnish darkened and layers of dirt built up, the sun set on this painting, and it got its popular title. When the painting was moved to a smaller room, the sides were lopped off (and the pieces lost), putting the two main characters in the center and causing the work to become more static than intended. During World War II, the painting was rolled up and hidden for five years. In 1975, a madman attacked the painting, slicing the captain's legs, and in 1990, it was sprayed with acid (it was skillfully restored after both incidents).

*The Night Watch*, contrary to popular myth, was a smashing success in its day. However, there are elements in it that show why Rembrandt fell out of favor as a portrait painter. He seemed to spend as much time painting the dwarf and the mysterious glowing girl with a chicken (the very appropriate mascot of this "militia" of shopkeepers) as he did the faces of his employers.

Rembrandt's life darkened long before his *Night Watch* did. This work marks the peak of Rembrandt's popularity...and the beginning of his fall from grace. He continued to paint master-pieces. Free from the dictates of employers whose taste was in their mouths, he painted what he wanted, how he wanted it. Rembrandt goes beyond mere craftsmanship to probe into, and draw life from, the deepest wells of the human soul.

• *Backtrack a few steps to the Gallery of Honor's last alcove to find Rembrandt's...*

### Self-Portrait as the Apostle Paul, 1661

Rembrandt's many self-portraits show us the evolution of a great painter's style, as well as the progress of a genius's life. For Rembrandt, the two were intertwined.

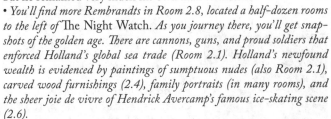

In this somber, late self-portrait, the man is 55 but he looks 70. With a lined forehead, a bulbous nose, and messy hair, he peers out from under several coats of glazing, holding old, wrinkled pages. His look is...skeptical? Weary? Resigned to life's misfortunes? Or amused? (He's looking at us, but not *just* at us—remember that a self-portrait is done staring into a mirror.)

This man has seen it all—success, love, money, fatherhood, loss, poverty, death. He took these experiences and wove them into his art. Rembrandt died poor and misunderstood, but he remained very much his own man to the end.

• *You'll find more Rembrandts in Room 2.8, located a half-dozen rooms to the left of* The Night Watch. *As you journey there, you'll get snap-shots of the golden age. There are cannons, guns, and proud soldiers that enforced Holland's global sea trade (Room 2.1). Holland's newfound wealth is evidenced by paintings of sumptuous nudes (also Room 2.1), carved wood furnishings (2.4), family portraits (in many rooms), and the sheer joie de vivre of Hendrick Avercamp's famous ice-skating scene (2.6).*

*Room 2.8 is dedicated to a promising artist who arrived in Amster-dam at the peak of the golden age...*

### The Young Rembrandt
#### Self-Portrait, c. 1628

Here we see the young small-town boy about to launch himself into whatever life has to offer. Rembrandt was a precocious kid. His

father, a miller, insisted that he become a lawyer. His mother hoped he'd be a preacher (you may see a portrait of her reading the Bible). Rembrandt combined the secular and religious worlds by becoming an artist, someone who can hint at the spiritual by showing us the beauty of the created world.

He moved to Amsterdam and entered the highly competitive art world. Amsterdam was a booming town and, like today, a hip and cosmopolitan city. Rembrandt portrays himself at age 22 as being divided—half in light, half hidden by hair and shadows—open-eyed, but wary of an uncertain future. Rembrandt's paintings are often light and dark, both in color and in subject, exploring the "darker" side of human experience.

### Portrait of a Woman, Possibly Maria Trip, 1639

This debutante daughter of a wealthy citizen is shy and reserved—maybe a bit awkward in her new dress and adult role, but still self-assured. When he chose to, Rembrandt could dash off a commissioned portrait like nobody's business. The details are immaculate—the lace and shiny satin, the pearls behind the veil, the subtle face and hands. Rembrandt gives us not just a person, but a personality.

Look at the red rings around her eyes, a detail a lesser painter would have airbrushed out. Rembrandt takes this feature, unique to her, and uses it as a setting for her luminous, jewel-like eyes. Without being prettified, she's beautiful.

### Young Woman in Fantasy Costume, Possibly Saskia, 1633

It didn't take long for Amsterdam to recognize Rembrandt's great talent. Everyone wanted a portrait done by the young master, and he became wealthy and famous. He fell in love with and married the rich, beautiful, and cultured Saskia, who is thought to be the sitter for this painting. (It's con-

## Other "Rembrandts"

The Rijksmuseum displays real Rembrandts, paintings by others that look like his, portraits of Rembrandt by his students, and one or two "Rembrandts" that may not be his. A century ago, there were 1,000 so-called Rembrandt paintings in existence. Since then, a panel of five art scholars has declared most of those to be by someone else, winnowing the number of authentic Rembrandts to 300, with some 50 more that may one day be "audited" by the Internal Rembrandt Service. Most of the fakes are not out-and-out forgeries, but works by admirers of his distinctive style. The lesson? Be careful the next time you plunk down $15 million for a "Rembrandt."

sidered a "fantasy" because she's dressed in clothing from centuries before her day.)

By all accounts, the two were enormously happy, entertaining friends, decorating their house with fine furniture, raising a family, and living the high life. In this painting, Saskia's face literally glows, and a dash of white paint puts a sparkle in her eye. Barely 30 years old, Rembrandt was the most successful painter in Holland. He had it all.

### *Jeremiah Lamenting the Destruction of Jerusalem,* 1630

The Babylonians have sacked and burned Jerusalem, but Rembrandt leaves the pyrotechnics (in the murky background at left) to Spielberg and the big screen. Instead, he tells the story of Israel's destruction in the face of the prophet who predicted the disaster. Jeremiah slumps in defeat, deep in thought, confused and despondent, trying to understand why this evil had to happen. Rembrandt turns his floodlight of truth on the prophet's deeply lined forehead.

Rembrandt wasn't satisfied to crank out portraits of fat merchants in frilly bibs, no matter what they paid him. He wanted to experiment, trying new techniques and more probing subjects. Many of his paintings weren't commissioned and were never even intended for sale. His subjects could be brooding and melancholy, a bit dark for the public's taste. His technique set him apart—you can recognize a Rembrandt canvas by his play of light and dark. Most of his paintings are a deep brown tone, with only a few bright spots glowing from the darkness. This allowed Rem-

RIJKSMUSEUM

brandt to highlight the details he thought most important and to express moody emotions.

Light has a primal appeal to humans. (Dig deep into your DNA and remember the time when fire was not tamed. Light! In the middle of the night! This miracle separated us from our fellow animals.) Rembrandt strikes at that instinctive level.

• *Finish your tour with another painting here in Room 2.8. It's a large group portrait by Bartholomeus van der Helst, called...*

### The Banquet at the Crossbowmen's Guild, 1648

This colorful portrait of several dozen Amsterdammers was painted to celebrate Holland's new era of peace after its war with Spain. Though shown in military uniforms, these men were really captains of industry—shipbuilders, seamen, salesmen, spice tasters, bankers, and venture capitalists—all part of the complex economic web that planned and financed overseas trade. With bright colors and down-to-earth realism, this group portrait captures the prosperity and can-do spirit of the Dutch golden age.

## THE REST OF THE RIJKS

The museum is most famous for the paintings you've just seen. But with a collection of 8,000 works—detailing Dutch history from 1200 to the present—the Rijks offers much, much more.

**Level 2:** The second floor is home to more **golden age artifacts.** Keep circling the floor counterclockwise (through Rooms 2.9, 2.10, and so on) to return to the stained-glass Great Hall. Pass through Rooms 2.28, 2.27, etc., keeping an eye out for a stunning collection of blue-and-white Delftware (in Room 2.22). There are dollhouses (*poppenhuizen,* Room 2.20) and a big wooden model of a 74-gun Dutch man-of-war that would have escorted convoys of merchant ships loaded with wealth (Room 2.15). Complete your circuit at *The Night Watch* and a stroll back through the Gallery of Honor.

**Level 1:** There's a **Van Gogh self-portrait** in Room 1.18 (from the Great Hall, go back downstairs the way you came to floor 1 and turn left). Vincent had just arrived in Paris, bought himself a new felt hat, and portrayed himself with the bright thick brushstrokes that would become his signature. A few rooms farther on, fans of Napoleon will enjoy the epic-scale painting of the **Battle of Waterloo** (Room 1.12).

**Level 0:** This has everything from **women's fashion** (Room 0.9) to more Delftware (0.7). The **Asian Art** Pavilion shows off objects from the East Indies—a former Dutch colony—as well as items from India, Japan, Korea, and China. The bronze dancing Shiva (*Shiva Nataraja*, in Room 1 of the pavilion) is considered one of the best in the world. Nearby, the Philips Wing hosts temporary exhibits and photography.

**Level 3:** Finally, you could ride the elevator up to the top floor for exhibits from the **20th century,** including an airplane. This brings you right up to the present—with prosperous Amsterdam enjoying yet another golden age.

RIJKSMUSEUM

# VAN GOGH MUSEUM TOUR

The Van Gogh Museum (we say "van GO," the Dutch say "van hock") is a cultural high even for those not into art. Located near the Rijksmuseum, the museum houses the 200 paintings owned by Vincent's younger brother, Theo. It's a user-friendly stroll through the work and life of one enigmatic man. If you like brightly colored landscapes in the Impressionist style, you'll like this museum. If you enjoy finding deeper meaning in works of art, you'll really love it. The mix of Van Gogh's creative genius, his tumultuous life, and the traveler's perspective makes this museum as much a walk with Vincent as with his art.

## Orientation

**Cost:** €20 timed-entry ticket, free for kids under 18, not covered by I Amsterdam City Card.

**Hours:** Daily 9:00-17:00, may stay open later in summer, shorter hours off-season.

**Information:** +31 20 570 5200, www.vangoghmuseum.com.

**Advance Tickets Required:** To assure you'll get in (and avoid a wait), buy timed-entry tickets online at least a week in advance at www.vangoghmuseum.com. Even with a museum pass, you must reserve a time slot in advance.

    Ticket and tour shops on Museumplein and elsewhere may sell in-person tickets, but it's better to buy in advance: Same-day tickets are usually unavailable.

**When to Go:** To avoid crowds, aim for the earliest entry time slot you can. Midmornings are the most crowded.

**Getting There:** It's the big, modern, gray-and-beige place a few blocks behind the Rijksmuseum; visitors enter via a glass pavilion on Museumplein. From Centraal station, catch tram #2 or #12 to the Museumplein stop.

**Getting In:** Pass through security into the glass-pavilion entrance hall. Here you'll find an info desk (pick up a free floor plan), bag check, multimedia-guide rental, and WCs. There's also a gift shop (a second, less-crowded gift shop is on level 0). A bookstore with several good, basic "Vincent" guidebooks is on level 3. Don't overlook the doorway leading to an excellent temporary exhibit gallery (generally free).

**Tours:** The 45-minute multimedia guide (€3.50) provides insightful commentary on Van Gogh's paintings and his technique, along with related quotes from Vincent himself. There's also a kids' multimedia guide (€2). The line to rent multimedia guides is shorter on level 0, just up the escalator from the entrance hall.

**Length of This Tour:** Allow one hour.

**Baggage Check:** Free and mandatory.

**Cuisine Art:** The museum has a cafeteria-style café on level 0 and a coffee/pastry stand in the entrance hall. For more recommendations in the Museumplein area, see the Eating in Amsterdam chapter.

## OVERVIEW

The collection is laid out roughly chronologically, tracing the changes in Vincent van Gogh's life and styles. You'll start on level 0, where self-portraits introduce you to the artist. Level 1 has his early paintings, level 2 focuses on the man and his contemporaries, and level 3 has his final works. But be flexible: Curators move the paintings around to illustrate various themes.

The paintings span five periods of Van Gogh's life—spent in the Netherlands, Paris, Arles, St-Rémy, and Auvers-sur-Oise. Some background on Vincent's star-crossed life makes the museum even better, so I've included doses of biographical material. (The unattributed quotations in this chapter are all Vincent's own words.) I've highlighted specific paintings that give a snapshot of a particular period in the artist's life. But, as you tour, don't bother so much about finding exact paintings. Read Van Gogh's story, and watch his style unfold.

**Art Beyond Van Gogh:** While this tour describes only paintings by Van Gogh, scattered throughout the museum are works by

VAN GOGH MUSEUM

fellow painters— those who influenced Van Gogh and those who were influenced by him: Academy painters and their smooth-sur-faced canvases, Impressionists Claude Monet and Camille Pissar-ro, and fellow Post-Impressionists Paul Gauguin, Paul Cézanne, and Henri de Toulouse-Lautrec.

## The Tour Begins

• *From the entrance hall, make your way up an escalator to the perma-nent collection, arriving on* **level 0.**

*Your tour starts by introducing you to Van Gogh with a series of* **self-portraits** *(see "Impressionism," later, for descriptions of some of these works). The various depictions show him with his distinctive red beard, wearing his painter's straw hat, standing at his easel, and smok-ing a pipe—always with intense-looking eyes. He was in his mid-30s, a working artist in his prime. But he hadn't always been a painter. Peruse the timeline and historical photographs in this room to see how Van Gogh got to this point.*

### VINCENT VAN GOGH, 1853-1890

*I am a man of passions...*

You could see Vincent van Gogh's canvases as a series of suicide notes—or as the record of a life full of beauty...perhaps too full of beauty. He attacked life with a passion, experiencing highs and lows more intensely than the average person. The beauty of the world overwhelmed him; its ugliness struck him as only another dimension of beauty. He tried to absorb the full spectrum of expe-rience, good and bad, and channel it onto a canvas. The frustration of this overwhelming task drove him to madness. If all this is a bit overstated—and I guess it is—it's an attempt to show the emo-tional impact that Van Gogh's works have had on many people, me included.

Vincent, a pastor's son from a small Dutch town, started work-ing at age 16 as a clerk for an art dealer. But his two interests, art and religion, distracted him from his dreary work, and after several years, he was fired.

The next 10 years were a collage of dead ends as he traveled northern Europe pursuing one path after another. He launched into each project with incredible energy, then became disillusioned and moved on to something else: teacher at a boarding school, assistant preacher, bookstore apprentice, preacher again, theol-ogy student, English student, literature student, art student. He bounced around England, France, Belgium, and the Netherlands. He fell in love but was rejected for someone more respectable. He quarreled with his family and was estranged. He lived with a pros-titute and her daughter, offending the few friends he had. Finally, in his late 20s, worn out, flat broke, and in poor health, he returned to his family in Nuenen and made peace. He then started to paint.

• *Ascend to **level 1**. Start with a display showing the kind of art Van Gogh was drawn to—paintings of hardscrabble workers with their simple dignity. Then work clockwise around the floor and follow the stages of Vincent's life, from roughly 1880 to 1889. The first room shows his stark, dark early work.*

*Just a reminder: Don't stress over finding the specific paintings I mention. Let the room's paintings capture the overall mood of Van Gogh's life at the time.*

## THE NETHERLANDS, 1880-1885
## Peasants, Poverty, and Religion

These dark, gray-brown canvases show us the hard, plain existence of the people and town of Nuenen in the rural southern Nether-lands. Van Gogh painted these during the years when he was living with his parents while struggling to make it as an artist. He painted the town's simple buildings, bare or autumnal trees, and overcast skies—a world where it seems spring will never arrive. What warmth there is comes from the sturdy, gentle people themselves.

The style is crude—Van Gogh couldn't draw very well and would never become a great technician. The paint is laid on thick, as though painted with Nuenen mud. The main subject is almost always dead center, with little or no background, so there's a claustrophobic feeling. We are unable to see anything but the immediate surroundings.

### *The Potato Eaters,* 1885

*Those that prefer to see the peasants in their Sunday-best may do as they like. I personally am convinced I get better results by painting them in their roughness... If a peasant picture smells of bacon, smoke, potato steam—all right, that's healthy.*

In a dark, cramped room lit only by a dim lamp, poor workers help themselves to a steaming plate of potatoes. They've earned it. Their hands are gnarly, their faces kind. Vincent deliberately wanted the canvas to be potato-colored.

Vincent had dabbled as an artist during his wandering years, sketching things around him and taking a few art classes, but it wasn't until age 29 that he painted his first oil canvas. He soon threw himself into it with abandon.

He painted the poor working peasants. He knew them well, having worked as a lay minister among peasants and miners. He joined them at work in the mines, taught their children, and even gave away his own few possessions to help them. The church authorities finally dismissed him for "excessive zeal," but he came away understanding the poor's harsh existence and the dignity with which they bore it.

### Still Life with Bible, 1885

*I have a terrible need of—shall I say the word?—religion. Then I go out and paint the stars.*

The Bible and Émile Zola's *La Joie de Vivre*—these two books dominated Van Gogh's life. In his art he tried to fuse his religious upbringing with his love of the world's beauty. He lusted after life with a religious fervor. The burned-out candle tells us of the recent death of his father. The Bible is open to Isaiah 53: "He was despised and rejected of men, a man of sorrows..."

### The Old Church Tower at Nuenen, a.k.a. The Peasants' Churchyard, 1885

The crows circle above the local cemetery of Nuenen. Soon after his father's death, Vincent—in poor health and depressed—moved briefly to Antwerp. He then decided to visit his younger brother Theo, an art dealer living in Paris, the art capital of the world. Theo's support—financial and emotional—allowed Vincent to spend the rest of his short life painting.

Vincent moved from rural, religious, poor Holland to Paris, the City of Light. Vincent van Gone.

• *Continue to the room with work he did in Paris. You'll likely see paintings by Impressionist masters like Monet and Gauguin hanging alongside Van Gogh's own Impressionist-style works.*

## PARIS, MARCH 1886-FEBRUARY 1888
### Impressionism

The sun begins to break through, lighting up everything he paints. His canvases are more colorful and the landscapes more spacious, with plenty of open sky, giving a feeling of exhilaration after the closed, dark world of Nuenen.

Paris of the 1880s was the world's cultural capital. He moved in with Theo in the bohemian neighborhood of Montmartre, just up the hill from the Moulin Rouge. In the cafés and bars, Vincent met the revolutionary Impressionists. He became friends with other struggling young painters, such as Paul Gauguin and Henri de Toulouse-Lautrec. His health improved. He became more sociable, had an affair with an older woman, and was generally happy. He signed up to study under a well-known classical teacher but quit after only a few classes. He couldn't afford to hire models, so he roamed the streets, sketch pad in hand, and learned from his Impressionist friends.

The Impressionists emphasized getting out of the stuffy studio and setting up canvases outside on the street or in the countryside to paint the play of sunlight off the trees, buildings, and water.

As you see in this room, at first, Vincent copied from the Impressionist masters. He painted garden scenes like Claude Monet, café snapshots like Edgar Degas, "block prints" like the Japanese masters, and self-portraits like...nobody else.

### Self-Portrait as a Painter, 1887-1888

*I am now living with my brother Vincent, who is studying the art of painting with indefatigable zeal.*
    —Theo van Gogh to a friend

Here, the budding young artist proudly displays his new palette full of bright colors, trying his hand at the Impressionist technique of building a scene using dabs of different-colored paint. A whole new world of art—and life— opened up to him in Paris. Inspired by his fellow Dutchman Rembrandt, Vincent would explore himself through self-portraits for the rest of his life.

### Self-Portrait with Straw Hat, 1887

*You wouldn't recognize Vincent, he has changed so much... The doctor says that he is now perfectly fit again. He is making tremendous strides with his work... He is also far livelier than he used to be and is popular with people.*

　　　　　—Theo van Gogh to their mother

In Paris, Vincent learned the Impressionist painting technique. The shimmering effect comes from placing dabs of different colors side by side on the canvas. At a distance, the two colors blend in the eye of the viewer to become a single color. Here, Vincent uses separate strokes of blue, yellow, green, and red to create a brown beard—but a brown that throbs with excitement.

### Red Cabbages and Onions, 1887

Vincent quickly developed his own style: thicker paint; broad, swirling brushstrokes; and brighter, clashing colors that make even inanimate objects seem to pulsate with life. The many different colors are supposed to blend together, but you'd have to back up to Belgium to make these colors resolve into focus.

### Self-Portrait with Gray Felt Hat, 1887

*He has painted one or two portraits which have turned out well, but he insists on working for nothing. It is a pity that he shows no desire to earn some money because he could easily do so here. But you can't change people.*

　　　　　—Theo van Gogh to their mother

Despite his new sociability, Vincent never quite fit in with his Impressionist friends. As he developed into a good painter, he became anxious to strike out on his own. He thought the social life of the big city was distracting him from serious work. And he'd been drinking too much absinthe, which alienated him from Theo. In this painting, his face screams out from a swirling background of molecular activity. He wanted peace and quiet, a place where he could throw himself into his work completely. He headed for the sunny south of France.

• *Travel to the far end of the room, where you finally reach...*

## ARLES, FEBRUARY 1888-MAY 1889
### Sunlight, Beauty, and Madness

Winter was just turning to spring when Vincent arrived in Arles, near the French Riviera. After the dreary Paris winter, the colors of springtime overwhelmed him. The blossoming trees and colorful fields inspired him to paint canvas after canvas, drenched in sunlight. He was drawn to the ordinary people in Arles—old women, his postman—and painted their portraits.

### The Yellow House, a.k.a. The Street, 1888

*It is my intention...to go temporarily to the South, where there is even more color, even more sun.*

Vincent rented this house with the green shutters. (He ate at the pink café next door.) Look at that blue sky! He painted in a frenzy, working feverishly to try and take it all in. For the next nine months, he produced an explosion of canvases, working very quickly when the mood possessed him. His unique style evolved beyond Impressionism—thicker paint, stronger outlines, brighter colors (often applied right from the paint tube), and swirling brushwork that makes inanimate objects pulse and vibrate with life.

### The Bedroom, 1888

*I am a man of passions, capable of and subject to doing more or less foolish things—which I happen to regret, more or less, afterwards.*

Vincent was alone, a Dutchman in Provence. And that had its downside. Vincent swung from flurries of ecstatic activity to bouts of great loneliness. Like anyone traveling alone, he experienced those high highs and low lows. This narrow, trapezoid-shaped, single-room apartment (less than 200 square feet) must have seemed like a prison cell at times. (Psychologists have pointed out that most everything in this painting comes in pairs—two chairs, two paintings, a double bed squeezed down to a single—indicating his desire for a mate. Hmm.)

He invited his friend Paul Gauguin to join him, envisioning a sort of artists' colony in Arles. He spent months preparing a room upstairs for Gauguin's arrival. He painted *Sunflowers* to brighten up the place.

### Sunflowers, 1889

*The worse I get along with people, the more I learn to have faith in Nature and concentrate on her.*

Vincent saw sunflowers as his signature subject, and he painted a half-dozen versions of them, each a study in intense yellow. He said he wanted the colors to shine "like stained glass." If he signed the work (look on the vase), it means he was proud of it.

Even a simple work like these sunflowers bursts with life. Different people see different things in *Sunflowers*. Is it a happy painting, or is it a melancholy one? Take your own emotional temperature and see.

### The Sower, 1888

A dark, silhouetted figure sows seeds in the burning sun. It's late in the day. The heat from the sun, the source of all life, radiates

out in thick swirls of paint. The sower must be a hopeful man, because the field looks slanted and barren. Someday, he thinks, the seeds he's planting will grow into something great, like the tree that slashes diagonally across the scene—tough and craggy, but with small, optimistic blossoms.

In his younger years, Vincent had worked in Belgium sowing the Christian gospel in a harsh environment (see Mark 4:1-9). Now in Arles, ignited by the sun, he cast his artistic seeds to the wind, hoping.

### Gauguin's Chair, 1888

*Empty chairs—there are many of them, there will be even more, and sooner or later, there will be nothing but empty chairs.*

Gauguin arrived. At first, he and Vincent got along great. They journeyed to the countryside and set up their easels, working side by side and critiquing each other's paintings. At night, they hit the bars, carousing and talking into the night.

But then things went sour. They clashed over art, life, and their prickly personalities.

On Christmas Eve 1888, Vincent went ballistic. Enraged during an alcohol-fueled argument, he pulled out a razor and waved it in Gauguin's face. Gauguin took the hint and quickly left town. Vincent was horrified at himself. In a fit of remorse and madness, he mutilated his own ear and presented it to a prostitute.

The people of Arles realized they had a madman on their hands. A doctor diagnosed "acute mania with hallucinations," and the local vicar talked Vincent into admitting himself to a peaceful mental hospital in the countryside around the quiet town of St-Remy. Vincent wrote to Theo: "Temporarily I wish to remain shut up, as much for my own peace of mind as for other people's."

• *Ascend to **level 2**. This floor is less about Van Gogh's paintings than about his relationships with family and friends, and his artistic process. The displays help deepen your understanding of the man as he approached the last, tumultuous years of his life.*

*To see his final paintings, continue up to **level 3**.*

## ST-REMY, MAY 1889-MAY 1890
## The Mental Hospital

In the mental hospital, Vincent kept painting whenever he was well enough. He often couldn't go out, so he copied from books, making his own distinctive versions of works by Rembrandt, Delacroix, Millet, and others.

At first, the peace and quiet of the asylum did Vincent good, and his health improved. Occasionally, he was allowed outside to paint the gardens and landscapes. Meanwhile, the paintings he had been sending to Theo began to attract attention in Paris for the first time. A woman in Brussels bought one of his canvases—the only painting he ever sold during his lifetime. In 1987, one of his *Sunflowers* sold for $40 million. Three years later a portrait of Vincent's doctor went for more than $80 million.

At St-Remy, we see a change from bright, happy landscapes to more introspective subjects. The colors are less bright and more surreal, the brushwork even more furious. The neat dots of paint characteristic of the Impressionist style now become bigger and thicker. The strong outlines of figures are twisted and tortured.

### *The Garden of Saint Paul's Hospital, a.k.a. Leaf Fall*, 1889

*A traveler going to a destination that does not exist...*

The stark brown trees are blown by the wind. A solitary figure (Vincent?)

VAN GOGH MUSEUM

winds along a narrow, snaky path as the wind blows leaves on him. The colors are surreal—blue, green, and red tree trunks with heavy black outlines. A road runs away from us, heading nowhere.

### The Sheaf Binder, after Millet, 1889

*I want to paint men and women with that something of the eternal which the halo used to symbolize...*

Vincent's compassion for honest laborers remained constant following his work with Belgian miners. These sturdy folk, with their curving bodies, wrestle as one with their curving wheat. The world Vincent sees is charged from within by spiritual fires, twisting and turning matter into energy, and vice versa.

### Wheat Field with a Reaper, 1889

*I have been working hard and fast in the last few days. This is how I try to express how desperately fast things pass in modern life.*

The harvest is here. The time is short. There's much work to be done. A lone reaper works uphill, scything through a swirling wheat field, cutting slender paths of calm. Vincent saw the reaper—a figure of impending death—as the flip side of the sower.

### Pietà, after Delacroix, 1889

It's evening after a thunderstorm. Jesus has been crucified, and the corpse lies at the mouth of a tomb. Mary, whipped by the cold wind, holds her empty arms out in despair and confusion. She is the tender mother who receives us all in death, as though saying, "My child, you've been away so long—rest in my arms." Christ has a Vincent-esque red beard.

• *Your visit concludes with Vincent's final paintings.*

VAN GOGH MUSEUM

## AUVERS-SUR-OISE, MAY-JULY 1890

*The bird looks through the bars at the overcast sky where a thunderstorm is gathering, and inwardly he rebels against his fate. 'I am caged, I am caged, and you tell me I have everything I need! Oh! I beg you, give me liberty, that I may be a bird like other birds.' A certain idle man resembles this idle bird...*

Though Van Gogh wished to be free of the mental hospital, his fits of madness would not relent. During these spells, he lost all sense of his own actions. He couldn't paint, the one thing he felt driven to do. He wrote to Theo, "My surroundings here begin to weigh on me more than I can say—I need air. I feel overwhelmed by boredom and grief."

### *Almond Blossom,* 1890

Vincent moved north to Auvers, a small town near Paris where he could stay under a doctor-friend's supervision. On the way there, he

visited Theo. Theo's wife had just had a baby, whom they named Vincent. Brother Vincent showed up with this painting under his arm as a birthday gift. Theo's wife later recalled, "I had expected a sick man, but here was a sturdy, broad-shouldered man with a healthy color, a smile on his face, and a very resolute appearance."

In his new surroundings, he continued painting, averaging a canvas a day, but was interrupted by spells that swung from boredom to madness. His letters to Theo were generally optimistic, but he worried that he'd soon succumb completely to insanity and never paint again.

• *Vincent's final landscapes are walls of bright, thick paint. Nature is charged from within with a swirling energy.*

### *Wheat Field with Crows,* 1890

*Since my illness, loneliness takes hold of me in the fields... This new attack...came on me in the fields, on a windy day, when I was busy painting.*

On July 27, 1890, Vincent left his room, walked out to a nearby field, and put a bullet through his chest. He stumbled back to his room, where he died two days later, with Theo by his side.

This is one of the last paintings Vincent finished. We can try to search the wreckage of his life for the black box explaining what happened, but there's not much there. His life was sad and tragic,

but the record he left is one not of sadness, but of beauty—intense beauty.

The windblown wheat field is a nest of restless energy. Scenes like this must have overwhelmed Vincent with their incredible beauty—too much, too fast, with no release. The sky is stormy and dark blue, almost nighttime, barely lit by two suns boiling through the deep ocean of blue. The road starts nowhere, leads nowhere, disappearing into the burning wheat field. Above all of this swirling beauty fly the crows, the dark ghosts that had hovered over his life since the cemetery in Nuenen.

# ANNE FRANK HOUSE TOUR

*Anne Frank Huis*

ANNE FRANK
TAGEBUCH

On May 10, 1940, Germany's Luftwaffe began bombing Schiphol Airport, preparing to invade the Netherlands. The Dutch army fought back, and the Nazis responded by leveling Rotterdam. Within a week, the Netherlands surrendered, Queen Wilhelmina fled to Britain, and Nazi soldiers goose-stepped past the Westerkerk and into Dam Square, where they draped huge swastikas on the Royal Palace. A five-year occupation began. The Netherlands had been neutral in World War I, and Amsterdam—progressive and modern, but a bit naive—was in for a rude awakening.

The Anne Frank House immerses you, in a very immediate way, in the struggles and pains of the war years. Walk through rooms where, for two years, eight Amsterdam Jews hid from Nazi persecution. You'll see actual artifacts: the secret bookcase entry, Anne's movie-star cutouts on the wall, and her diaries.

Though the eight Jews were eventually discovered and all but one died in concentration camps, their story has an uplifting twist—the diary of Anne Frank, an affirmation of the human spirit that cannot be crushed.

## Orientation

**Cost:** €14, must book timed-entry ticket online in advance, includes excellent audioguide; €21 with 30-minute introduction in English; €7 for ages 10-17, €1 for kids under 10.

**Hours:** Daily 9:00-22:00. Open every day except Yom Kippur (Sept 24 in 2023, Oct 11 in 2024).

**Information:** +31 20 556 7105, www.annefrank.org.

**Advance Reservations Required:** The Anne Frank House is both very popular and very small—and tickets sell out quickly. Tickets are only sold online. There are no tickets sold at the museum.

**Plan to buy tickets two months before your trip:** Tickets are released online on the first Tuesday of each month for visits the following month. You'll choose between a stand-alone museum visit or a visit with a 30-minute introduction in English (the intro program tickets are easier to get).

**With a Sightseeing Pass:** The Museumkaart sightseeing pass grants free entry, but you still must reserve an entry time online for €1. You can make this reservation even if you haven't purchased the pass yet—just be sure to buy the pass at another sight before your Anne Frank House visit.

**Scam Alert:** Don't buy tickets from scalpers. Tickets are only available at www.annefrank.org. Beware of third-party companies offering "Anne Frank House tours"—these do not include access to the house.

**Getting There:** It's at Prinsengracht 267, near Westerkerk and about a 20-minute walk from Centraal station. The museum entrance is around the corner, in the modern building at Westermarkt 20. You can also take tram #13 or #17 to the Westermarkt stop, about a block south of the museum's entrance.

**Visitor Information:** The museum includes an excellent audioguide and posted descriptions in English, with excerpts from Anne's diary throughout.

**What to Expect:** You'll snake your way through the museum and point your audioguide at an activation point in each room. The house has many steep, narrow stairways that can be difficult for mobility-impaired visitors or the very young.

**Length of This Tour:** Allow one hour.

**Baggage Check:** Cloakroom for coats and small bags. No large bags are allowed.

**Eating:** The $$ museum café serves simple fare and has good views.

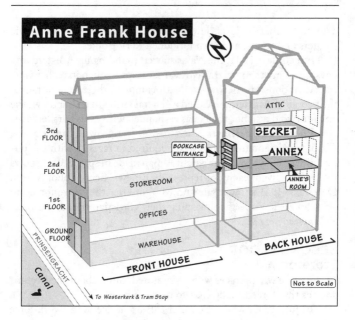

Anne Frank House

ATTIC

3rd FLOOR

SECRET

BOOKCASE ENTRANCE

ANNEX

2nd FLOOR

STOREROOM

ANNE'S ROOM

1st FLOOR

OFFICES

GROUND FLOOR

WAREHOUSE

PRINSENGRACHT

Canal

FRONT HOUSE

BACK HOUSE

Not to Scale

To Westerkerk & Tram Stop

## The Tour Begins

We'll walk through the rooms where Anne Frank, her parents Otto and Edith, her sister Margot, and four other Jews hid for 25 months. The front half of the building, facing the canal, remained the offices and warehouses of an operating business. The back half, where the Franks and others lived in a tiny apartment, was the Secret Annex, its entrance concealed by a swinging bookcase.

• *After scanning your ticket, enter the ground-floor exhibit. Start with the important five-minute video (or 30-minute introduction). Then continue through a few more ground-floor rooms, which set the stage for how the Franks arrived in Amsterdam from Germany and established their business on these premises. In each of the following rooms, graphics and photos recreate the furnishings of the now-bare spaces. Now go upstairs to the offices of the Franks' business.*

### FIRST FLOOR
### Offices

From these rooms, Otto Frank ran a successful business called Opekta, selling spices and pectin for making jelly. When the Nazis gained power in Germany in 1933, Otto moved his family from Frankfurt to tolerant Amsterdam, hoping for a better life.

As the Nazis swarmed over the Netherlands, they were at first lenient toward, even friendly with, the vanquished Dutch. But soon they began imposing restrictions that affected one in ten Amsterdammers—that is, Jews. Jewish people were banned from movie theaters and trams, and even forbidden to ride bikes.

In February 1941, the Nazis started rounding up Amsterdam's Jews, shipping them by train to "work camps," which in reality were transit stations on the way to death camps in the east. Outraged, the people of Amsterdam called a general strike that shut down the city for two days...but the Nazis responded with even harsher laws.

**Photos and artifacts** bring to life the growing anxiety the Frank family endured. Jews were required to register with the police and wear a yellow-star patch. A map made in spring 1941 shows where Jews lived; each dot represents 10 Jews. School photos from December 1941 show Anne and Margot after they were forced to go to an all-Jewish school, leaving their Christian friends behind.

• *Go upstairs to the...*

## SECOND FLOOR
### Storeroom

In the space where spices were once stored, think about the circumstances that forced the Franks to move in here.

In July 1942, Margot got her call-up notice for a "work-force project." Otto could see where this was headed. He handed over the keys to the business to his "Aryan" colleagues, sent a final postcard to relatives, gave the family cat to a neighbor, spread rumors that they were fleeing to Switzerland, and prepared his family to "dive under" (*onderduik*, as it was called) into hiding.

**Photos** put faces on the brave people who kept Otto's business running while the Frank family hid in the back of the building. Johannes Kleiman helped Otto set up the annex hiding place. During the Nazi occupation, Miep Gies, Otto's secretary, brought food to the Frank family every few days, while bookkeeper Victor Kugler cheered up Anne with the latest movie magazines.

**Videos** show interviews with Otto, Miep, and Victor from the 1960s and '70s, describing how they organized the concealment, got supplies, and set up the Secret Annex.

• *It's now time to enter the hiding place. At the back of the second-floor storeroom is the clever hidden passageway into the Secret Annex.*

## SECRET ANNEX

The Secret Annex hid eight people in a tiny apartment smaller than 1,000 square feet. First were the Frank family—Otto and Edith and their daughters, 13-year-old Anne and 16-year-old Margot. A week later, they were joined by the Van Pels (called the "Van Daans" in her diary), with their teenage son, Peter. A few months later, Fritz Pfeffer (called "Mr. Dussel" in the diary) was invited in. Though its furniture was ransacked during the arrest, the

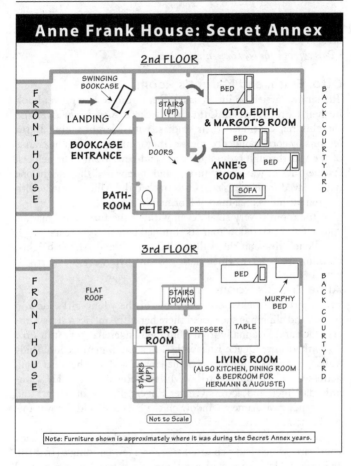

# Anne Frank House: Secret Annex

### 2nd FLOOR

SWINGING BOOKCASE

BED

STAIRS (UP)

OTTO, EDITH & MARGOT'S ROOM

LANDING

BED

BOOKCASE ENTRANCE

DOORS

BED

ANNE'S ROOM

SOFA

BATH-ROOM

FRONT HOUSE

BACK COURTYARD

### 3rd FLOOR

FLAT ROOF

BED

STAIRS (DOWN)

MURPHY BED

PETER'S ROOM

DRESSER

TABLE

STAIRS (UP)

LIVING ROOM
(ALSO KITCHEN, DINING ROOM & BEDROOM FOR HERMANN & AUGUSTE)

FRONT HOUSE

BACK COURTYARD

Not to Scale

Note: Furniture shown is approximately where it was during the Secret Annex years.

rooms of the annex remained virtually untouched, and we see them today much as they were.

## The Bookcase Entrance

On a rainy Monday morning, July 6, 1942, the Frank family—wearing extra clothes to avoid carrying suspicious suitcases—breathed their last fresh air, took a long look at the Prinsengracht canal, and disappeared into the back part of the building, where they spent the next two years. Victor Kugler concealed the entrance to the annex with this swinging bookcase, stacked with business files.

Though not exactly a secret (since it's hard to hide an entire building), the annex was a typical back-house *(achterhuis)*, a common feature in Amsterdam buildings, and the Nazis had no reason to suspect anything on the premises of the legitimate Opekta business.

• *Pass through the bookcase entrance into...*

## Otto, Edith, and Margot's Room

The family carried on life as usual. Edith read from a **prayer book** in their native German, Otto read Dickens' ***Sketches by Boz***, and the children continued their studies, with Margot taking **Latin lessons** by correspondence course. They avidly followed the course of the war through radio broadcasts and news from their helpers. As the tides of war slowly turned and it appeared they might one day be saved from the Nazis, Otto tracked the Allied advance with colored pushpins on a **map** of Normandy.

The room is very small, even without the furniture. Imagine yourself and two fellow tourists confined here for two years.

**Pencil lines** on the wall track Margot's and Anne's heights, marking the point at which these growing lives were cut short.

## Anne Frank's Room

Pan the room clockwise to see some of the young girl's idols in photos and clippings she pasted there herself: American stars Robert Stack and Deanna Durbin from the Cinderella-story film *First Love,* the future Queen Elizabeth II as a child, matinee idol Rudy Vallee, figure-skating actress Sonja Henie, and, on the other wall, actress Greta Garbo, actor Ray Milland, Renaissance man Leonardo da Vinci, and actress Ginger Rogers. Photos of flowers and landscapes gave Anne a window on the outside world she was forbidden to see.

Out the window (which had to be blacked out) is the back courtyard, which had a chestnut tree and a few buildings. (In 2010, the tree, which Anne had greatly enjoyed, toppled in a storm.) These things, along with the Westerkerk bell chiming every 15 minutes, represented the borders of Anne's "outside world." Imagine Anne sitting here at a small desk, writing in her diary.

In November 1942, the Franks invited a Jewish neighbor to join them, and Anne was forced to share the tiny room with Fritz Pfeffer, a middle-aged dentist. Pfeffer wrote a farewell letter to his German fiancée, who lived nearby and continued to receive news of him from Miep Gies without knowing his whereabouts.

## The Bathroom

The eight inhabitants shared this bathroom. During the day, they didn't dare flush the toilet.

• *Ascend the steep staircase—silently—to the...*

## Life in the Annex

By day, it's enforced silence, so no one can hear them in the offices. They whisper, tiptoe, and step around squeaky places in the floor. The windows are blacked out, so they can't even look outside. They read or study, and Anne writes in her diary.

At night and on weekends, when the offices close, one or two might sneak downstairs to listen to Winston Churchill's BBC broadcasts on the office radio. Everyone's spirits rise and sink with news of Allied victories and setbacks.

Anne's diaries make clear the tensions, petty quarrels, and domestic politics of eight people living under intense pressure. Mr. Van Pels annoys Anne, but he gets along well with Margot. Anne never gets used to Mr. Pfeffer, who is literally invading her space. Most troublesome of all, pubescent Anne often strikes sparks with her mom. (Anne's angriest comments about her mother were deleted from early editions of the published diary.)

Despite their hardships, the group feels guilty: They have shelter, while so many other Jews are being rounded up and sent off. As the war progresses, they endure long nights when the house shakes from Allied air raids, and Anne cuddles up in her dad's bed.

Boredom tinged with fear—the existentialist hell of living in hiding is captured so well in Anne's journal.

## Common Living Room

This was the kitchen (note the remains of the stove and sink) and dining room. Otto Frank was well off, and early on, the annex was well stocked with food. Miep Gies would dutifully take their shopping list, buy food for her "family" of eight, and secretly lug it up to them. Buying such large quantities in a coupon-rationed economy was highly suspect, but she knew a sympathetic grocer (a block away on Leliegracht) who was part of a ring of Amsterdammers risking their lives to help the Jews.

The **menu** for a special dinner lists soup, roast beef, salad, potatoes, rice, dessert, and coffee. Later, as war and German restrictions plunged Holland into poverty and famine, they survived on canned foods and dried kidney beans.

The inhabitants spent their days reading and studying in this room. At night, it became sleeping quarters for Hermann and Auguste van Pels.

## Peter van Pels' Room

On Peter's 16th birthday, he got a Monopoly-like board game called "The Broker" as a present. Initially, Anne was cool toward Peter, but after two years together, a courtship developed, and their flirtation culminated in a kiss.

The **staircase** (no visitor access) leads up to where the inhabitants stored their food. Anne loved to steal away here for a bit of privacy. At night they'd open a hatch to let in fresh air.

One hot August day, Otto was in this room helping Peter learn English, when they looked up to see a man with a gun. The hiding was over.

• *From here we leave the Secret Annex, returning to the Opekta storeroom and offices in the front house. As you work your way downstairs, you'll see a number of exhibits—photos, video testimonials, and memorabilia—on the aftermath of this story.*

## AFTERMATH
## Arrest, Deportation, and Auschwitz Exhibits

On August 4, 1944, a German policeman accompanied by three Dutch Nazis pulled up in a car, politely entered the Opekta office, and went straight to the bookcase entrance. No one knows who tipped them off. The police gave the surprised hiders time to pack. They demanded their valuables and stuffed them into Anne's briefcase...after dumping her diaries onto the floor.

Taken in a van to Gestapo headquarters, the eight were processed in an efficient, bureaucratic manner, then placed on a train to Westerbork, a concentration camp northeast of the city. You'll see the **transport list,** which includes "Anneliese Frank," and their 3-by-5-inch **registration cards.**

From there they were locked in a car on a normal passenger train and sent to Auschwitz, a Nazi extermination camp in Poland. On the platform at Auschwitz, they were "forcibly separated from each other" (as Otto later reported) and sent to different camps. Anne and Margot were sent to Bergen-Belsen.

If it's playing, don't miss the **video** of one of Anne's former neighbors, Hannah Goslar, who, by chance, ended up at Bergen-Belsen with Anne. In English she describes their reunion as they talked through a barbed-wire fence shortly before Anne died. She says of Anne, "She didn't have any more tears."

Anne and Margot both died of typhus in March 1945, only weeks before the camp was liberated. The other Secret Annex residents—except Otto—were gassed or died of disease.

The Franks' story was that of Holland's Jews. The seven who

died were among the more than 100,000 Dutch Jews killed during the war years. (Before the war, 140,000 Jews lived in the Netherlands.) Of Anne's school class of 87 Jews, only 20 survived.

• *The next room is devoted to...*

## The Diaries

Anne wrote three different diaries. (You may see one, two, or all three of them, as well as individual pages.) She received the first

diary (with a red-plaid binding) as a birthday present when she turned 13, shortly before the family went into hiding. The other two were written in school-exercise books. Anne wrote the diaries in the form of a letter to an imaginary friend named Kitty.

As she wrote more and more, Anne began to recognize the uniqueness of her situation. She set about improving and revising the diaries, hoping that one day she'd see them published. You may see some loose-leaf pages on which she reworked parts of her diary. You may also see a book of Anne's short stories and a notebook in which she compiled "beautiful sentences" from books she'd read.

When the diaries were published, the book quickly became a best-seller. *De Achterhuis,* "The Back House" in Dutch, soon became *The Diary of a Young Girl* in English (1952), followed by translations in many other languages. The book became a popular play, *The Diary of Anne Frank,* and then a Hollywood movie.

• *Downstairs you come to...*

## The Otto Frank Room

After the war, Otto returned to Amsterdam. The displayed newspaper notice he placed in August 1945 seeking information about his daughters is heartbreaking. In November of that year he received confirmation that they had died in Bergen-Belsen.

Miep Gies gave him Anne's diaries, which she had found on the floor of the annex after the arrest. Listen to a 1967 **video,** in which Anne's father talks about his reaction as he read the diaries. He was struck by the enormous power of Anne's ideas and emotions—a secret world he'd never known inside his daughter. Determined to make her writings available to a wider audience, he set about contacting publishers (you may see his letters or notebooks or early typed-up drafts of the diaries). In 1947, the diaries were first published in Dutch as *De Achterhuis.*

• *Continue downstairs to the ground-floor exhibits.*

## Anne's Legacy

These displays (which change often) capture the Anne Frank legacy.

You may see video interviews of people who knew Anne, such as childhood friends or Miep Gies (who passed away in 2010 at the age of 100). You may see memorabilia of the Franks and their friends (or even the Oscar statuette won by Shelley Winters for the 1959 movie). Scale models of the annex with furniture created in the early 1960s were based on details from Otto and used as a source for multiple film sets. You may learn about Otto's struggles to save the house from demolition and turn it into a museum.

Everyone attests to what a radiant spirit Anne was. Otto wanted the Anne Frank House to be, in his words, "more than a museum." Its displays do not try to sum up "the moral" of the story. Instead, they recognize that World War II presented many gray areas and ethical dilemmas, and different people had different responses. The point? To keep visitors from leaving the museum with pat feelings of easy moral clarity.

The Anne Frank Foundation is obviously concerned that we learn from Europe's Nazi nightmare. The thinking that made the Holocaust possible still survives. Even today, some groups promote the notion that the Holocaust never occurred and contend that stories like Anne Frank's are only a hoax. It was Otto Frank's dream that visitors come away from the Anne Frank House with hope for a better world. He wrote: "The task that Anne entrusted to me continually gives me new strength to strive for reconciliation and for human rights all over the world."

# OUR LORD IN THE ATTIC MUSEUM TOUR

*Ons' Lieve Heer op Solder*

For two centuries (1578-1795), Catholicism in Amsterdam was illegal but tolerated (kind of like marijuana is today). When hardline Protestants took power in 1578, Catholic churches were vandalized and shut down, priests and monks were rounded up and kicked out of town, and Catholic kids were razzed on their way to school. The city's Catholics were forbidden to worship openly, so they gathered secretly to say Mass in homes and offices. In 1663, a wealthy merchant built Our Lord in the Attic (Ons' Lieve Heer op Solder), one of a handful of places in Amsterdam that served as a secret parish church until Catholics were once again allowed to worship in public.

The church was hidden within the businessman's own home. From the outside, it's a typical townhouse on a historic canal. But within lies a 150-seat, three-story church that's the size of a four-lane bowling alley. On this tour we'll get to see a bit of both—the one-of-a-kind church, and a rare glimpse inside a historic Amsterdam home straight out of a Vermeer painting.

## Orientation

**Cost:** €15.50, includes audioguide.

**Hours:** Mon-Fri 10:00-17:00, Sat until 18:00, Sun 13:00-18:00.

**Information:** +31 20 624 6604, www.opsolder.nl.

**Getting There:** It's at Oudezijds Voorburgwal 38, a seven-minute walk from either Centraal station or Dam Square.

**Length of This Tour:** Allow one hour.

**What to Expect:** The museum has several steep, narrow staircases.

**Baggage Check:** There are free lockers for compulsory bag check.

## OVERVIEW

Before entering, stand back and notice that, from the street, you can't actually see the church you're about to visit. The museum's one-way route (and this chapter's tour) will take you through living spaces in the front of the townhouse, then the secret church, and finally the "back house" (*achterhuis*, a common feature in historic townhouses).

## The Tour Begins

• *Enter through the modern building (to the right of the old townhouse), where you'll find the ticket desk, gift shop, lockers, and WC. Go downstairs, where you can pick up a free audioguide, enjoy a short slideshow with background about religious conflicts and the man who built the church, and see a cutaway model of the house with the church inside. Then head upstairs.*

*As you pass through a few nondescript rooms and hallways, pause in the* **19th-century kitchen.** *How Dutch! With its blue-and-white-tiled walls, cozy stove, and diffuse Vermeer lighting, it calls up everyday life in this quaint townhouse. Continue on, climbing up one flight of stairs, to our first stop—a room with corkscrew columns, paintings, and a big fireplace. This is the...*

### Parlour *(Sael)*

By humble Dutch standards, this is an enormous, very ornate room. Here, in the largest room of the house, the family received guests and hosted parties. The decor is the Dutch version of classical, where everything comes in symmetrical pairs—corkscrew columns flank the fireplace, the coffered ceiling mirrors the patterned black-and-white marble floor, and a fake exit door balances the real entrance door.

Over the fireplace is the coat of arms of Jan Hartman (1619-1668), the rich Catholic businessman who built this house for his family and the church for his fellow Catholics in the neighborhood. Look closely at the coat of arms to find the family symbol, the crouching hart (deer), which became the nickname of the church—*Het Hert.*

The painting over the fireplace *(The Presentation in the Temple)* has hung here since Hartman's time and shows his taste for Italian, Catholic, Baroque-style beauty. On the wall opposite the windows (above the mirror), the family portrait is right out of the Dutch golden age, showing a rich merchant and his family of four (though it's not Hartman).

A black ebony knickknack cabinet is painted with a Bible scene portrayed by inhabitants of the 1600s Red Light District. On the right door, the Prodigal Son spends his inheritance, making merry with bare-breasted, scarlet-clothed courtesans—high-rent prostitutes who could entertain educated, cello-loving clients. On the left door, the Prodigal Son has spent it all. He can't pay his bill and is kicked out of a cheap tavern—still half-dressed—by a pair of short-changed prostitutes.

• *Now continue up eight curved steps, leading to the...*

## Drawing Room

Unlike the rather formal parlor, this was where the family hung out, warming themselves at the stove or gazing out the windows at the canal and the gabled homes across the way—a scene that's remained unchanged for centuries. The furnishings are typical of a wealthy merchant's home at the time. The wood stove and the textiles on the walls are re-creations but look like the originals. In the Dutch custom (still occasionally seen today), the family covered tables with exotic Turkish rugs imported by traders of the Dutch East India Company.

Check out the room's cabinet bed. Despite the family's wealth, space was tight. In the 1600s, entire families would often sleep together in small bed cabinets. They sat up to sleep because they believed reclining would cause blood to pool in their heads and kill them.

• *Climb more creaky stairs to a landing where a window lets you peek in on a servant's room, which has another cabinet bed and some personal items. Then continue up the staircase and into the actual hidden church.*

## Our Lord in the Attic Church

The church is long and narrow, with an altar at one end, an organ at the other, and two balconies overhead to maximize the seating in this relatively small space. While Amsterdam's Protestant churches were whitewashed and austere, this Catholic church has touches of elaborate Baroque decor, with statues of saints, garlands, and baby angels. Note how, to create the open space for worship, the building was gutted and the floors cut

## Anti-Catholic = Anti-Spanish

Protestants imposed anti-Catholic laws in the 16th century partly as retribution for the Catholics' own oppressive rule and partly from a desire to reform what was seen as a corrupted religion...but mostly they did it for political reasons.

By a quirk of royal marriage, Holland was ruled from afar by Spain, Europe's most militantly Catholic country and home of the Inquisition, the Jesuits, and the pope's own Counter-Reformation army. In 1578, Amsterdam's hard-line Protestants staged the "Alteration"—a coup kicking out their Spanish oppressors and allying the city with the Prince of Orange's rebels.

Catholics in the city—probably a majority of the population—were considered guilty by association. Viewed as potential enemies, they were suspected to be puppets of the pope, spies for Spanish kings, or subverters of the social order. In addition, Catholics were considered immoral worshippers of false idols, bowing down to graven images of saints and the Virgin Mary.

In Amsterdam, Catholic churches were seized and looted, and prominent Catholics were dragged to Dam Square by a lynch mob, before being freed, unharmed, outside the city gates. Protestant extremists gave Catholics a taste of their own repressive medicine, passing laws that prohibited open Catholic worship (although few were actually arrested or prosecuted). Still, many families over many generations were torn apart by the religious and political strife of the Reformation.

away. That left the balconies (with their beams cut) needing the support provided by metal rods.

This attic church certainly is hidden, but everyone knew it was here. In tolerant (and largely Catholic) Amsterdam, Protestant authorities rarely made an issue of Catholic worship as long as it was kept from public view. Hartman was a respected businessman who used his wealth and influence to convince the city fathers to look the other way as the church was built. Imagine the jubilation when the church opened its doors in 1663 and Catholics could gather together and worship (if secretly) in this fine space.

The **altar** is flanked by classical columns and topped with an arch featuring a stucco God the Father, a dove of the Holy Spirit, and trumpeting angels.

The **altarpiece painting** (Jacob de Wit's *Baptism of Jesus*) is one of four (three survive) that could be rotated with the feast days. (Other surviving paintings are on display in the room behind the altar.)

The **base of the left column**—made of wood painted to look like marble—is hollow. Inside was a foldout wooden pulpit that could be pulled out for the priest to preach from. A video shows how it could swing out like a door.

• *Climb the stairs to the church's...*

## Lower Balcony (First Gallery)

The 1749 **organ** is small, but more than adequate. By pulling on its 12 knobs, the organist can make it sound like a flute, cornet, or a mixture of instruments. These days, music lovers flock here on special evenings for a *Vondelkonzert* (wandering concert). They listen to a few tunes here, have a drink, then move on to hear more music at, say, the Old Church or the Royal Palace.

The window to the left of the altar (as you face it) looks south across ramshackle rooftops (note the complex townhouse-with-back-house design of so many Amsterdam buildings) to the steeple of the Old Church (Oude Kerk). The Old Church was the main Catholic church until 1578, when it was rededicated as Dutch Reformed (Protestant), the new official religion of the Netherlands. For the next hundred years, Catholics had no large venue to gather in until Our Lord in the Attic opened in 1663.

Make your way to the window just to the right of the altar and look out. Gaze north across the rooftops to the impressive dome and twin steeples of St. Nicholas Church, near Centraal station. This is the third Amsterdam church to be dedicated to the patron saint of seafarers and of the city. The first was the Old Church (until 1578), then Our Lord in the Attic (1663).

When St. Nicholas Church was dedicated in 1887, Our Lord in the Attic closed up shop. The next year, wealthy Catholics saved it from the wrecking ball, turning it into one of Amsterdam's first museums.

Here on the lower balcony (behind the altar), you can also check out the sacristy—the religious green room where priests could dress and prepare for the service.

• *Now head upstairs to the...*

## Upper Balcony

Looking down from this angle, the small church really looks small. It can accommodate 150 seated worshippers. From here the tapering roofline creates the "attic" feel that gives the church its nickname.

At the back of the upper balcony is a canalside room. Looking out the window, you can see that you're literally in the attic.

## Calvinism

Holland's Protestant movement followed the stern French reformer John Calvin more than the beer-drinking German reformer Martin Luther. Calvin's French followers, called Huguenots, fled religious persecution in the 1500s, finding refuge in tolerant Amsterdam. When Catholic Spain began persecuting them in Holland, they entered politics and fought back.

Calvin wanted to reform the Catholic faith by condemning corruption, simplifying rituals, and returning the faith to its biblical roots. Like other Protestants, Calvinists emphasized that only God's grace—and not our good works—can get us to heaven. Today, the Dutch Reformed Church, as well as some other Reformed and Presbyterian churches, carry on Calvin's brand of Christianity.

Straight across the canal is a house with an ornate gable featuring dolphins. This street was once the city's best address.

• *Head back downstairs to the church's ground floor. Step behind the altar, into the...*

## Maria Chapel

The **statue** of the Virgin Mary, holding Baby Jesus and trampling an evil snake, is probably one of the church's original objects. Catholics have tradition-

ally honored Mary, addressing prayers to her or to other saints, asking them to intercede with God on their behalf. To Calvinist extremists, this was like bowing down to a false goddess. They considered statues of the Virgin to be among the "graven images" forbidden by the Ten Commandments (Exodus 20:4).

A **cabinet** in the chapel holds objects used during Mass: a censer, incense boat, chalice, Communion-wafer holder, and the altar bells that are rung during the Eucharist.

The **collection box** (*voor St. Pieter,* on the wall by the staircase down) was for donations sent to fund that most Catholic of monuments, the pope's own church, the Basilica of St. Peter in Rome—to Calvinists, the center of corruption, the "whore of Babylon."

• *Go downstairs (past the offering box). At this point, we're entering the back part* (achterhuis) *of the townhouse. Ahead on the left is a...*

## Confessional

The confessional dates from 1740. The priest sat in the left half, while parishioners knelt on the right to confess their sins through a grilled window. Catholic priests have authority to forgive sins, whereas Protestants take their troubles directly to God.

The sociologist Max Weber theorized that frequently forgiven Catholics more easily accept the status quo, whereas guilt-ridden Protestants are driven to prove their worth by making money. Hence, northern Protestant countries—like the Netherlands—became capitalist powerhouses, while southern Catholic countries remained feudal and backward. Hmm.

Just past the top of the stairs, in a nearby room, is some of the religious hardware used in Catholic church services—elaborate gilded silver monstrances (ornamental holders in which the Communion wafer is displayed), chalices (for the Communion wine), and ciboria (chalices with lids for holding consecrated wafers). "Holy earth boxes" were used for Catholics denied burial in consecrated ground. Instead, they put a little consecrated dirt in the box and placed it in the coffin.

While you admire these beautiful pieces, remember that it was this kind of luxury, ostentation, and Catholic mumbo-jumbo that drove thrifty Calvinists nuts.

• *Go down another flight and turn right, into the...*

## Priest's House

The *achterhuis* was often rented out to other families, but in this case it was given to the hidden church's priest. It's fitted with a cupboard bed. The room's colors are those seen in countless old homes—white walls, ocher-yellow beamed ceiling, oxblood-red landing, and black floor tiles. The simple colors, lit here by a light shaft, make small rooms seem bright and spacious.

Jan Hartman intended for the priest to have lifetime rights to this dwelling. But when Hartman died, he had so many debts that the family was forced to sell the property—and the priest was forced to move.

• *Some very steep stairs (use that rope!) lead down to the...*

## 17th-Century Kitchen

This reconstructed room was inhabited as is until 1952. The blue tiles on the wall show tiny playful scenes of kids and animals. Step into the small pantry, then open a door to see the toilet.

Notice the portrait of the small girl in her white communion dress who could have worshipped in this hidden church. Think of how her age overlaps our age...of all the change since she was born. Consider the contrast of this serene space with the wild world that waits just outside the door of this hidden church.

• *To reach the exit, climb the rope back up the stairs, turn left, then go back downstairs to a modern room displaying monstrances, priests' robes, and other items. A statue of St. Peter points the way to the exit—or you can take a look at...*

## The Rest of the Museum

Upstairs in the new building, you'll find a temporary exhibit and a window from where you can view the broad side of the hidden church.

• *When you're ready, plunge back into today's Amsterdam.*

# SLEEPING IN AMSTERDAM

Greeting a new day by descending steep stairs and stepping into a leafy canalside scene—graceful bridges, historic gables, and bikes clattering on cobbles—is a fun part of experiencing Amsterdam. But Amsterdam is a tough city for budget accommodations, and any hotel room under €200 (or B&B room under €150) will have rough edges. Still, you can sleep well and safely in a great location for around €140 per double.

I've grouped my hotel listings into several neighborhoods, each of which has its own character.

**West Amsterdam** (which includes the Jordaan) has Old World ambience, with quiet canals, traditional Dutch architecture, and candlelit restaurants. It's also just minutes on foot to Dam Square. Many of my hotels are charming, friendly gabled mansions (albeit with small rooms). The downside here is that you'll pay more and likely have lots of stairs to climb.

Staying in **Central Amsterdam** is ideal for people who like shopping, tourist sights, and easy access to public transportation (including Centraal station). On the downside, the area has traffic noise, concrete, and urban grittiness, and the hotels can lack character.

**Southwest Amsterdam,** farther afield in the quieter semi-suburban neighborhood around Vondelpark and Museumplein, is close to the Rijks and Van Gogh museums, and you'll find good hotel values. However, it's a half-hour walk (or 10-minute tram ride) to Dam Square. Just north of bustling Leidseplein, the charming Southern Canal Belt is walkable (or an easy tram ride) to the center of town.

**Hotel Tips:** Some national holidays merit making reservations far in advance (see "Holidays and Festivals" in the appendix). Amsterdam is jammed during tulip season (late March-mid-May), conventions, festivals, and on summer weekends. During peak season, prices are higher and some places won't take weekend bookings for those staying fewer than two or three nights.

Downtown Amsterdam is a sea of construction: cranes for big transportation projects and small crews of bricklayers repairing the wobbly, cobbled streets that line the canals. Canalside rooms can come with great views—and early-morning construction-crew noise. Light sleepers should ask for a quiet room in the back. Parking in Amsterdam is even worse than driving—if you must park a car, ask your hotelier for advice. If you'd rather trade away big-city action for small-town coziness, consider sleeping in Haarlem, 20 minutes away by train.

Canal houses were built tight. They have steep stairs with narrow treads, and only some have elevators. If that's a problem, look for a hotel with an elevator—and confirm that it reaches your room. Hotels that don't have air-conditioning almost always have good fans.

For some travelers, traditional B&Bs or short-term, Airbnb-type rentals can be a good alternative; search for places in my recommended hotel neighborhoods. Unfortunately, B&Bs may be an endangered species in Amsterdam, where Airbnb is controversial and the city has placed limits on short-term rentals. Some Amsterdam residents see vacation rentals as damaging to the fabric of traditionally residential neighborhoods. I like to counterbalance this trend by treating my temporary Amsterdam home—and neighbors—with a little extra courtesy.

I rank accommodations from $ budget to $$$$ splurge. For the best deal, contact my family-run places directly by phone or email. When you book direct, the owner avoids a commission and may be able to offer a discount. For more details on reservations, short-term rentals, and more, see the "Sleeping" section in the Practicalities chapter.

# West Amsterdam

## STATELY CANALSIDE HOTELS

These hotels face historic canals, and their rooms can feel like they're from another century. The first two come with lovely lobbies; the last listing is smaller and has a quaint tearoom. This area oozes elegance and class, and is fairly quiet at night.

**$$$$ The Toren** is a smartly renovated, chandeliered mansion with a pleasant canalside setting and a peaceful backyard garden. This romantic hotel is classy yet friendly, with 40 rooms in a great location on a quiet street two blocks northeast of the Anne Frank House. The capable staff is a good source of local advice. The gilt-frame, velvet-curtained rooms are an opulent splurge (RS%—use code "RSSTEVES", breakfast extra, air-con, elevator, some stairs, laundry service, valet parking, Keizersgracht 164, +31 20 622 6033, www.thetoren.nl, info@thetoren.nl).

**$$$$ Hotel Ambassade** is elegant, traditional, and modern all at once, lacing together 55 rooms in a maze of connected houses. The staff is top-notch, and the library of books signed by authors who've slept here was designed by Rijksmuseum architects (RS%, breakfast extra, air-con, elevator, some stairs, Herengracht 341, +31 20 555 0222, www.ambassade-hotel.nl, info@ambassade-hotel.nl).

**$$$$ Hotel The Craftsmen** is a memorable splurge hotel run by the Zandbergen family. Each of its 14 rooms is beautifully decorated with reclaimed industrial items: For example, the Cartographer room's reading lights are made from sextants and the Clockmaker room features art created from antique clock pieces (family rooms, air-con in most rooms, elevator, located between Centraal station and Dam Square, Singel 83—entrance on Lijnbaanssteeg, +31 20 210 1218, http://hotelthecraftsmen.com, info@hotelthecraftsmen.nl).

**$$$$ 't Hotel** is cozy with eight small, fresh rooms, each delicately decorated with handmade wallpaper designed by the owner's daughter. The 17th-century house offers garden and canal views and a tearoom (family room, air-con, Leliegracht 18, +31 20 422 2741, www.thotel.nl, amsterdam@thotel.nl).

## CANALSIDE HOTELS & B&BS

Some of these hotels have basic, downright spare rooms; others offer tight-spaced boutique comfort—but all of them have romantic canalside charm. And if you enjoy getting to know the Dutch and appreciate a personal touch, consider the last listing—one of the few traditional B&Bs remaining in Amsterdam.

**$$$$ Mr. Jordaan Hotel,** graciously managed by Patrick in the heart of this Greenwich Village-like neighborhood, offers 34 rooms with funky-but-stylish touches. Some are very snug, but they warn you in advance it's a "cozy" double (RS%—use code "enjoyjordaan" when booking, breakfast extra, family rooms available, air-con, elevator, staff can arrange local guides and canal boat rides, Bloemgracht 102, +31 20 626 5801, www.mrjordaan.nl, stay@mrjordaan.nl).

**$$$ Linden Hotel** is Mr. Jordaan's sister hotel, with tight teal-and-brown rooms, friendly staff, and slightly cheaper rates. While it's on the edge of the Jordaan neighborhood, some of its

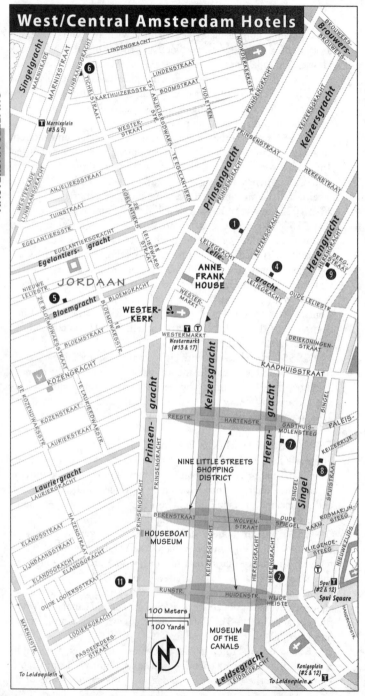

# West/Central Amsterdam Hotels

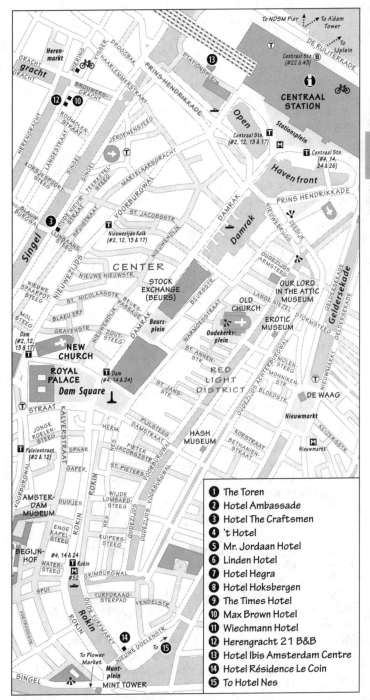

**AMSTERDAM SLEEPING**

1 The Toren
2 Hotel Ambassade
3 Hotel The Craftsmen
4 't Hotel
5 Mr. Jordaan Hotel
6 Linden Hotel
7 Hotel Hegra
8 Hotel Hoksbergen
9 The Times Hotel
10 Max Brown Hotel
11 Wiechmann Hotel
12 Herengracht 21 B&B
13 Hotel Ibis Amsterdam Centre
14 Hotel Résidence Le Coin
15 To Hotel Nes

25 rooms have canal views (RS%—use code "enjoylinden" when booking, breakfast extra, family rooms, air-con, Lindengracht 251, 020 622 1460, www.lindenhotel.nl, info@lindenhotel.nl).

**$$$ Hotel Hegra** is cozy, with nine rooms filling a 17th-century merchant's house overlooking the canal. While some rooms are small, everything is clean, modern, and functional (no breakfast, family room, some canal views, part of the Stanley Hotels group, just north of Wolvenstraat at Herengracht 269, +31 20 623 7877, www.hotelhegra.be, info@hotelhegra.nl).

**$$$ Hotel Hoksbergen** is a slightly lower-priced option for a canalside setting, with no-frills cramped rooms and a decidedly lived-in feel. The owners promise to renovate all 14 rooms eventually—and the bathrooms are already up to snuff—but there are lots of steep stairs and ho-hum hallways. Avoid Room 4, which is sold as a double but should be a single (family rooms, hotel bar and free drink, Singel 301, +31 20 626 6043, www.hotelhoksbergen.com, info@hotelhoksbergen.nl).

**$$ The Times Hotel** is a business-comfort hotel in a scenic canal setting. The 33 modern rooms are tight, and a handful have a real bathtub instead of just a shower. Rooms are spare yet elegant, decorated in muted tones (breakfast extra, family room, air-con, elevator, some stairs, valet parking, Herengracht 135, +31 20 330 6030, www.thetimeshotel.com, info@thetimeshotel.com, Sharif and Glenn at the front desk).

**$$ Max Brown Hotel,** the flagship hotel of a boutique-style chain, has a trendy urban design geared toward a hipster clientele. Located in a quiet neighborhood near Centraal station, it offers 34 modern rooms and public areas with funky-chic details. Rooms with canal views are pricier and breezier (spread over three canalside buildings, guest happy hour, Herengracht 13, +31 20 522 2345, www.maxbrownhotels.com, hello.cd@maxbrownamsterdam.com). Another location is near Vondelpark and the Rijksmuseum.

**$$ Wiechmann Hotel**'s 37 rooms are worn and sparsely furnished with just the dark-wood essentials, but they're spacious, and the *gezellig* (cozy) public areas are chock-full of Old World charm. Expect lots of stairs and no elevator in this historic building (family rooms, some canal views, back rooms are quiet, nicely located at Prinsengracht 328, +31 20 626 3321, www.hotelwiechmann.nl, info@hotelwiechmann.nl, John).

**$$ Herengracht 21 B&B** is on the same quiet street as the Max Brown Hotel, near Centraal station and offering two stylish, intimate rooms in a canal house filled with art. This traditional B&B is run with care by lovely Loes Olden, who also offers private tours in her family's 1920s-era canal boat (Herengracht 21; tours—€150/4 people, 1.5 hours, weather permitting; +31 20 625

6305, mobile +31 6 2812 0962, www.herengracht21.nl, loes@herengracht21.nl).

# Central Amsterdam

You won't get an especially warm welcome at these places, but if you're looking for a no-nonsense room that's convenient to plenty of tram lines, these fit the bill. For locations see the "West/Central Amsterdam Hotels" map earlier in this chapter.

**$$$ Hotel Ibis Amsterdam Centre,** next door to Centraal station, is a modern, efficient, 363-room place. It offers a handy location, comfort, and good value, without a hint of charm (pricier Sept-Oct, breakfast extra, book long in advance—especially for Sept-Oct, air-con, elevators; facing Centraal station, go left toward the multistory bicycle garage to Stationsplein 49; +31 20 721 9172, www.ibishotel.com, h1556@accor.com).

**$$$ Hotel Résidence Le Coin** has 42 larger-than-average rooms complete with small kitchenettes. The bathrooms have been updated, while the rooms have a slightly dated look. Located near the Mint Tower, this hotel is a two-minute walk to the Flower Market and a five-minute walk to Rembrandtplein (breakfast extra, elevator, by the university at Nieuwe Doelenstraat 5, +31 20 524 6800, www.lecoin.nl, hotel@lecoin.nl).

**$$ Hotel Nes** is a well-located, functional-but-bland hotel that often books up six months in advance. The 36 rooms are tight but have modern fixtures; some come with canal views (breakfast extra, family room, elevator, some stairs, Kloveniersburgwal 137, +31 20 624 4773, www.hotelnes.com, info@hotelnes.nl).

# Southwest Amsterdam

## NEAR VONDELPARK AND MUSEUMPLEIN

These options cluster around Vondelpark in a safe neighborhood. Though they don't have romantic Old Dutch flavor, they're reasonable values and only a short walk from the action. Many are in a pleasant nook between rollicking Leidseplein and the park, and most are a 5- to 15-minute walk to the Rijks and Van Gogh museums. They easily connect with Centraal station by tram #2 or #12.

**$$$ Hotel Fita** has 21 bright, spacious rooms in a great location—100 yards from the Van Gogh Museum, an even shorter hop from the tram stop, and on a pleasant corner with a grade school's lively recess yard filling a traffic-free street. The style is modern yet rustic, with minimalist furniture and nice extras, including espresso machines in every room. It's well run by Pieter, who offers a friendly welcome (free breakfast when you book direct, air-con on upper floors, elevator, free laundry service, bike

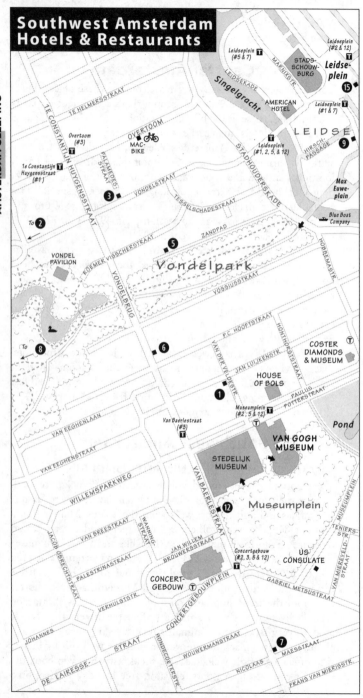

# Southwest Amsterdam Hotels & Restaurants

Leidseplein (#5 & 7)

Leidseplein (#2 & 12)

STADS-SCHOUW-BURG

Leidse-plein

MARNIXSTR.

LEIDSEKADE

Singelgracht

AMERICAN HOTEL

Leidseplein (#1 & 7)

STADHOUDERSKADE

LEIDSE

Leidseplein (#1, 2, 5, & 12)

HIRSCH-PASSAGE

1e Constantijn Huygensstraat (#1)

1e CONSTANTIJN HUYGENSSTRAAT

Overtoom (#3)

OVERTOOM

MAC-BIKE

Max Euwe-plein

PALAMEDESSTRAAT

VONDELSTRAAT

Blue Boat Company

TESSELSCHADESTRAAT

ROEMER VISSCHERSTRAAT

ZANDPAD

VONDELBRUG

Vondelpark

HOBBEMASTR.

VONDEL PAVILION

VONDELPARK

VOSSIUSSTRAAT

To 8

P.C. HOOFTSTRAAT

VAN DER VELDESTR.

JAN LUIJKENSTR.

HONTHORSTSTRAAT

COSTER DIAMONDS & MUSEUM

HOUSE OF BOLS

PAULUS POTTERSTRAAT

Museumplein (#2, 5 & 12)

Van Baerlestraat (#5)

VAN GOGH MUSEUM

Pond

VAN EEGHENLAAN

STEDELIJK MUSEUM

VAN EEGHENSTRAAT

VAN BAERLESTRAAT

Museumplein

MUSEUMPLEIN

WILLEMSPARKWEG

TENIERS-STR.

JACOB OBRECHTSTRAAT

VAN BREESTRAAT

WANNING STRAAT

JAN WILLEM BROUWERSSTRAAT

Concertgebouw (#2, 3, 5 & 12)

US CONSULATE

VAN MIEREVELD-STRAAT

PALESTRINASTRAAT

GABRIEL METSUSTRAAT

CONCERT-GEBOUW

VERHULSTSTR.

CONCERTGEBOUWPLEIN

JOHANNES

STRAAT

HONDECOETERSTR.

WOUWERMANSTRAAT

MAESSTRAAT

DE LAIRESSE-

NICOLAAS

FRANS VAN MIERISSTR.

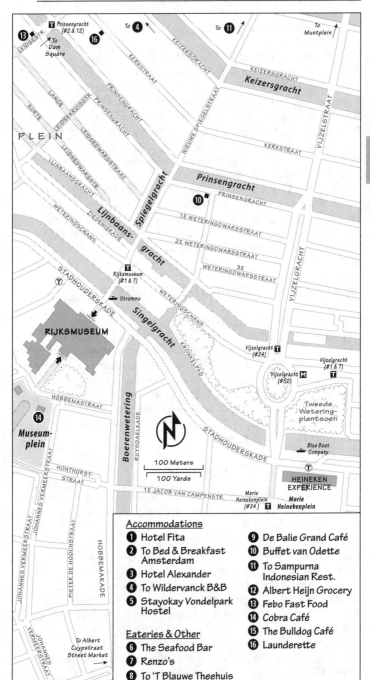

## Accommodations

1 Hotel Fita
2 To Bed & Breakfast Amsterdam
3 Hotel Alexander
4 To Wildervanck B&B
5 Stayokay Vondelpark Hostel

## Eateries & Other

6 The Seafood Bar
7 Renzo's
8 To 'T Blauwe Theehuis & Restaurant Blauw
9 De Balie Grand Café
10 Buffet van Odette
11 To Sampurna Indonesian Rest.
12 Albert Heijn Grocery
13 Febo Fast Food
14 Cobra Café
15 The Bulldog Café
16 Launderette

AMSTERDAM SLEEPING

rental, honesty bar, Jan Luijkenstraat 37, +31 20 679 0976, www.fita.nl, info@fita.nl).

**$$$ Bed & Breakfast Amsterdam,** a suite that sleeps up to four people, is run by a friendly Englishwoman, Karen, and her Dutch husband, Paul. It's clean, white, and bright, with wood floors, a full kitchen, a balcony, and canal views (cash, bank transfer, or PayPal only; fridge can be stocked with breakfast foods for a fee, no shoes, no elevator but not many stairs; south end of Vondelpark at Sloterkade 65, 7-minute walk from tram stop, +31 20 679 2753, www.bedandbreakfastamsterdam.net, rooms@bedandbreakfastamsterdam.net).

**$$ Hotel Alexander** is a modern 35-room hotel on a quiet street. Some of the rooms overlook the garden patio out back. If you're looking for a smart, clean, relaxed place, this is it (breakfast extra, elevator, some stairs, family room, +31 20 589 4020, Vondelstraat 44, www.hotelalexander.nl, info@hotelalexander.nl).

## NEAR LEIDSEPLEIN, IN THE SOUTHERN CANAL BELT

**$$ Wildervanck B&B,** run by Helene and Sjoerd Wildervanck, offers two tastefully decorated rooms in an elegant 17th-century canal house. If you want to meet a friendly Dutch family, this is the place. The location has a lot to offer, since it's near the lively Leidseplein, within walking distance of major museums, and steps off the tram line (2-night minimum, cash or bank transfer only, breakfast in their pleasant dining room, just west of Leidsestraat at Keizersgracht 498, +31 20 623 3846, www.wildervanck.com, info@wildervanck.com).

# Hostels

Amsterdam has a world of good, cheap hostels located throughout the city. Most are designed for the party crowd, but here are two quieter options, both ¢.

**In Vondelpark:** Although it's one of Amsterdam's top hostels for the under-25 set, **Stayokay Vondelpark (IYHF)** feels comfortable for all ages (some doubles, family rooms, lots of school groups, bike rental; right on Vondelpark at Zandpad 5—see the "Southwest Amsterdam Hotels and Restaurants" map; +31 20 589 8996, www.stayokay.com, vondelpark@stayokay.com). Though Stayokay Vondelpark is generally booked long in advance, a few beds occasionally open up each day at 11:00.

**Farther East:** While it's away from the center, at **Stayokay Oost (IYHF)** you have all the modern services, and you're just

15 minutes from Damrak street by tram or bike. Oldsters fit in here with the youngsters (games, restaurant, bike rental; from Amsterdam Centraal station take bus #22, direction: de Indische Buurt, to the Javaplein stop and walk to Timorplein 21, see the map on page 83, +31 20 551 3190, www.stayokay.com, amsterdamoost@stayokay.com).

# EATING IN
# AMSTERDAM

Amsterdam has a thriving and ever-changing restaurant scene. In this international city, there's something for every taste. While I've listed many options, I've only scratched the surface.

In this extremely touristy city with its cruise groups, English stag parties, and masses of low-end travelers, it's important to avoid sloppy tourist ghettos. With a bike or a willingness to walk 10 minutes, you can easily leave the tourist zone and find more rewarding dining experiences. If you eat in the Leidseplein area or along Damrak, it's your own fault.

Most hoteliers keep a list of reliable neighborhood eateries and know which places keep their travelers happy. For a local take on restaurants, check out food blogs like DutchGrub.com.

Note that many of my listings are lunch-only (usually termed "café" rather than "restaurant")—good for a handy bite near major sights. Similarly, many top restaurants serve only dinner. Before trekking across town to any of my listings, check the hours. And if you're serious about enjoying a serious restaurant, make a reservation.

While in Amsterdam, three characteristic food experiences

are worth having on your list: an Indonesian rijsttafel dinner, a herring snack at a fish stand, and a drink or light meal at a characteristic brown café.

I rank eateries from $ budget to $$$$ splurge. For more advice on eating in Holland, including ordering, tipping, and Dutch cuisine and beverages, see the "Eating" section of the Practicalities chapter.

## Fine Dining with a Chef's Choice *Menu*

If you want to eat very well and for a good value, try a fine restaurant offering a "chef's choice" surprise *menu*. My three favorite choices have the same formula: multicourse tasting *menus*, often with smart wine pairing options; no à la carte dishes; and always booked up in advance.

Unless otherwise noted, each of these places serves dinner daily from about 18:00-22:00. Expect to pay about €40 for a three-course meal without wine (€60 for a six-course meal). You'll choose either a meat or a vegetarian fixed-price *menu* and leave it up to the chef to cook what they're inspired to serve that day. It's always fresh and seasonal, fusing local ingredients with an international twist; the plates are beautifully presented—and served by young, enthusiastic waitstaff; and you'll be dining with smart locals rather than noisy tourists.

Expect a sleek, modern, dressy atmosphere (with mostly indoor seating) that's romantic without being stuffy and pretentious. Given the mystery of what you'll eat paired with the certainty that it'll be fine dining, your meal promises to be a gourmet adventure in creative Dutch cuisine.

**$$$$ Restaurant Hemelse Modder** is beautifully situated on Waalseilands canal with a spacious dining area, fine wine list, and a subdued vibe (closed Sun, just beyond the Red Light District at Oude Waal 11—see the "West/Central Amsterdam Restaurants" map on the next page, +31 20 624 3203, www.hemelsemodder.nl).

**$$$$ Restaurant Klein Breda,** three doors off Rembrandtplein, feels like the hottest place in town. The tight, trendy interior has an exciting energy, and a few bustling tables are out front (also quick "businessman's lunch" from 12:00, Utrechtsestraat 6—see the "Southern Canal Belt" map on page 66, +31 20 362 0030, www.bredagroup-amsterdam.com).

**$$$$ Gebr. Hartering,** named for brothers Paul and Niek Hartering, applies the trendy "nose-to-tail" philosophy to Dutch cooking. It's a bit more expensive than the other two, with a tight rustic-chic dining room that surrounds the open kitchen (Peperstraat 10—see the "Southeast Amsterdam" map on page 83, +31 20 421 0699, www.gebr-hartering.nl).

AMSTERDAM EATING

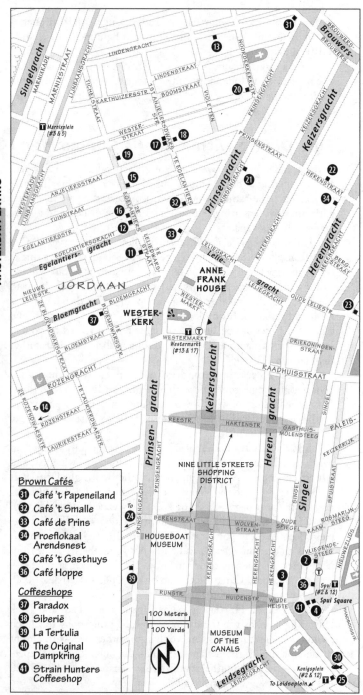

Brown Cafés
- **31** Café 't Papeneiland
- **32** Café 't Smalle
- **33** Café de Prins
- **34** Proeflokaal Arendsnest
- **35** Café 't Gasthuys
- **36** Café Hoppe

Coffeeshops
- **37** Paradox
- **38** Siberië
- **39** La Tertulia
- **40** The Original Dampkring
- **41** Strain Hunters Coffeeshop

100 Meters

100 Yards

# West/Central Amsterdam Restaurants

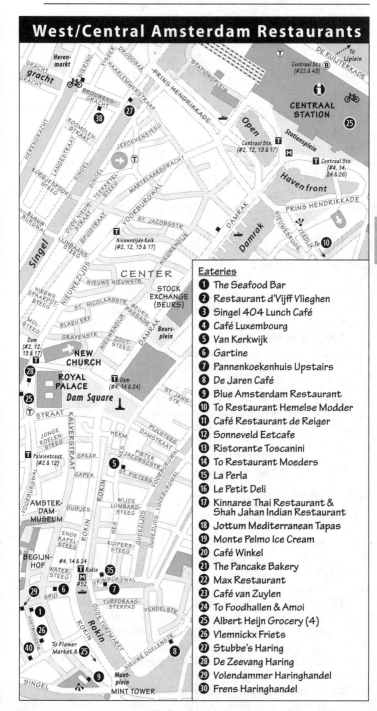

## Eateries

1. The Seafood Bar
2. Restaurant d'Vijff Vlieghen
3. Singel 404 Lunch Café
4. Café Luxembourg
5. Van Kerkwijk
6. Gartine
7. Pannenkoekenhuis Upstairs
8. De Jaren Café
9. Blue Amsterdam Restaurant
10. To Restaurant Hemelse Modder
11. Café Restaurant de Reiger
12. Sonneveld Eetcafe
13. Ristorante Toscanini
14. To Restaurant Moeders
15. La Perla
16. Le Petit Deli
17. Kinnaree Thai Restaurant & Shah Jahan Indian Restaurant
18. Jottum Mediterranean Tapas
19. Monte Pelmo Ice Cream
20. Café Winkel
21. The Pancake Bakery
22. Max Restaurant
23. Café van Zuylen
24. To Foodhallen & Amoi
25. Albert Heijn Grocery (4)
26. Vlemnickx Friets
27. Stubbe's Haring
28. De Zeevang Haring
29. Volendammer Haringhandel
30. Frens Haringhandel

AMSTERDAM EATING

# Central Amsterdam

You'll likely have a meal at some point in the city's core for a break from your sightseeing. Here are a few good spots near the big landmarks.

## ON AND NEAR SPUI

$$$ **The Seafood Bar** focuses on fresh and fishy, with an appetizingly briny menu. From the white subway-tile walls to the modern decor, it's understandably popular—reserve ahead for lunch or dinner. Their fish-and-chips are cheap and their mixed platters are popular for sharing (daily 12:00-22:00, Spui 15, +31 20 233 7452, www.theseafoodbar.nl). Another branch is near the Rijksmuseum (listed later).

$$$$ **Restaurant d'Vijff Vlieghen,** in spite of its name ("The Five Flies"), is a dressy museum of a restaurant with an interior right out of a Rembrandt painting. It's a romantic splurge, offering Dutch and international cuisine, professional service, and a multi-course tasting menu with matching wines. Although it's huge, its 300 seats are mixed into a candlelit labyrinth (Wed-Sun 18:00-22:00, closed Mon-Tue; Spuistraat 294, +31 20 530 4060).

$ **Singel 404 Lunch Café,** just across the Singel canal from Spui and near the Nine Little Streets, is a sweet little café serving burgers, bagel sandwiches, and more (daily 10:00-18:00, Singel 404, +31 20 428 0154).

$$$ **Café Luxembourg** is a venerable old bistro with a tired "grand café" interior and tables (some in a heated veranda) looking right out on Spui Square. The food's basic, but the relaxed atmosphere mixes well with nice Belgian beer on tap. They're famous for their croquettes. If it's a burger you want, try their Luxemburger (daily 9:00-23:00, Spui 24, +31 20 620 6264).

## NEAR ROKIN

$$ **Van Kerkwijk** is tucked away on the narrow, relatively quiet street called Nes, running south from Dam Square. This popular, unpretentious but quirky eatery has a loyal following. There's no written menu—your server explains the day's offerings of freshly prepared international dishes. They don't take reservations and there's often a line (daily 11:00-23:00, Nes 41, +31 20 620 3316).

$$ **Gartine** is a hidden gem, filling a rustic and relaxed little space tucked just off the tourist-thronged Spui and Rokin zones that serves brunch until noon and then lunch after that. It's a calm and classy spot for a light meal or high tea (Wed-Sun 9:00-17:00, high tea served from 14:00, closed Mon-Tue, Taksteeg 7, +31 20 320 4132).

$$ **Pannenkoekenhuis Upstairs** is a tight, tiny (just four

tables), characteristic perch up some extremely steep stairs, where Arno, Ali, and Toto cook and serve delicious pancakes. They'll tell you that I discovered this place long before Anthony Bourdain did (daily 12:00-18:00, Grimburgwal 2, +31 20 626 5603).

**$$ Café 't Gasthuys** is a simple quiet spot just off the busy boulevard with good canalside seating (Grimburgwal 7; see "Characteristic Brown Cafés," later in this chapter.

## NEAR THE MINT TOWER

**$$$ De Jaren Café** ("The Years") is a big, modern local favorite with a prime terrace overlooking a bend in the canal. It's handy for light lunches (soups, salads, and sandwiches served all day and evening) or just coffee. On a sunny day or a balmy evening, the café's canalside patio is a fine spot to savor a drink (daily 9:30-23:00, a long block up from Muntplein at Nieuwe Doelenstraat 20, +31 20 625 5771).

**$$ Blue Amsterdam Restaurant** may be a shopping-mall diner, but it has one of the best views in town and a menu that includes light lunches, soups, salads, and vegetarian dishes (in the Kalver Passage Mall at #206 Kalverstraat, just ride up the slanted elevator, daily 11:00-18:30, +31 20 427 3901).

# West Amsterdam, in the Jordaan District

Nearly all these places are within a few scenic blocks of the Anne Frank House, providing handy lunches and atmospheric dinners in the city's most charming neighborhood—perfect after taking my Jordaan Walk or while browsing the shops.

## FINER DINING IN THE JORDAAN

**$$$ Café Restaurant de Reiger** must serve up the best cooking of any *eetcafé* in the Jordaan. Famous for its fresh fish, ribs, good beer on tap, and delightful bistro ambience, it's part of the classic Jordaan scene. People leave with a smile (daily 17:00-24:00, closed Sun-Mon, Nieuwe Leliestraat 34, +31 20 624 7426).

**$$ Sonneveld Eetcafe,** named after the Dutch cabaret legend Wim Sonneveld (who lived in the Jordaan), has a warm staff who offer traditional fare (ribs and *stamppot*—mashed potatoes and sausage) plus good salads. In the spirit of Sonneveld, they crank up the music on Friday and Saturday. Whether you choose a cozy indoor table or sidewalk seating in good weather, you'll feel right at home (daily 11:00-23:00, Tweede Egelantiersdwarsstraat 72, +31 20 423 4287, Cora with Aimee and Bryan).

**$$$ Ristorante Toscanini** is an upmarket Italian place (no pizza here) that's always packed. With a lively, spacious ambience,

AMSTERDAM EATING

# Rijsttafel and Other Indonesian Dishes in Amsterdam

Today's Indonesia (the East Indies) was a Dutch colony for over 300 years, until World War II. In those days, trade was all about

spices, which made the East Indies hugely important—in fact, the Dutch called the archipelago "the Spice Islands." And today, Indonesian cuisine still has an important place at the Dutch table.

The essential Indonesian dining experience is the rijsttafel ("rice table")—a spread of 14 or so different dishes and sauces (always available with a vegetarian option). Rijsttafel is not really an Indonesian dish, but a Dutch creation to showcase an extravagant array of food and spices from their colony.

You'll begin with a mound of rice, then take a bit of chicken, beef, lamb, or vegetable with the accompanying sauce. Start with mild and work up to spicy. Try to keep your rice clean—to cleanse your palate between each dish as you savor the variety of flavors and textures.

A rijsttafel is huge—generally more food than you can comfortably eat. Many restaurants require a two-person minimum

order; budget diners can try asking to share one (with the partner ordering something lighter), but don't count on it. More commonly, a single traveler dining alone may be able to order just one portion of rijsttafel—ask.

The rijsttafel is a memorable experience. But if you have a smaller appetite, you can order many of the dishes à la carte (see the menu decoder on page 486), or ask for *nasi rames*—a cheaper, one-plate version of a rijsttafel. Or try *bami goreng*, a plate of stir-fried noodles (or *nasi goreng*, fried rice) served with rijsttafel items.

Experiment with the different sauces. *Sambal* is a chutney-like hot peppery paste that comes in hundreds of varieties. *Atjar tjampoer* are sweet-and-sour mixed pickles that help cool down your tongue. Other common sauces and flavors are peanut *(kacang)*, dark soy *(kecap)*, sour tamarind *(asam)*, and coconut *(lodeh)*. You'll wash it down with a Dutch beer and finish up with *spekkoek,* a cake with thin layers of pungent spices.

## Where to Try Indonesian Food

It's a challenge—especially in the touristy center—to get an authentic Indonesian rijsttafel, as many mix it up with Chinese cuisine. Here are some solid, truly Indonesian options: The first one
is away from the center, beyond Vondelpark, but it's also the best
choice for serious diners. The others are scattered around the
city center. For a rijsttafel, the first two are more formal and finer
(€35/person, reservations smart) and the third is cheaper and
cheerier (€25/person, reservations not possible). The last two
feel trendy rather than traditional, but serve good food.

**In Southwest Amsterdam** (see map on page 204): The local
choice for upmarket Indonesian cuisine, **$$$$ Restaurant Blauw** is
bright and modern with none of the touristy bling. If you're biking,
just pedal through Vondelpark and out the back end—it's across
the street and to the left (daily 17:00-23:00, Amstelveenseweg
158, +31 20 675 50 00).

**$$$$ Sampurna Indonesian Restaurant,** while a bit dark,
with more tourists and tighter seating, is great for the true Indonesian experience (daily 12:00-22:00, facing the Mint Tower and
flower market at Singel 498, +31 20 625 3264).

**Near the Red Light District** (see map on page 116):
**$$$ Aneka Rasa Indonesian Restaurant** is a weirdly bright, spa-
cious, and peaceful place at the edge of the otherwise unappetiz-
ing Red Light District. Jerry takes your order at the counter, then
you grab a seat and prepare to feast (daily 17:00-20:00, closed
Sun, Warmoesstraat 25, +31 20 626 1560).

**In West and Central Amsterdam** (see map in this chapter):
Happy eaters fill the colorful, upscale, modern bar at **$$$ Amoi**
("Little Sister"). It feels hip, but the dishes—inspired by Tante
(Aunt) Uddie—are traditional and delicious. They don't serve a
full rijsttafel, but their à la carte menu and creative cocktails make
for a memorable meal (reservations smart, Wed-Sun 17:00-22:30,
closed Mon-Tue, Kinkerstraat 53a, +31 20 846 2755). You'll find
it along trendy Kinkerstraat, just west of the Jordaan near the
Foodhallen (described later).

**$$$$ Max Restaurant,** a short walk from the Anne Frank
House, offers an intriguing menu of upscale Indonesian food
fused with French influences. Their formula is to let you choose
from a short list to assemble a two-course or three-course meal.
They also offer a fine rijsttafel tasting menu (dinner Wed-Sat
17:00-22:00, closed Sun-Tue, reservations recommended—pref-
erably by email: info@maxrestaurant.nl, Herenstraat 14, +31 20
420 0222, www.maxrestaurant.nl).

nice acoustics, and great cuisine, this place is a treat—if you can get a seat. Reservations are essential. Eating with the dressy, local, in-the-know crowd and the busy open kitchen adds to the fun energy (Tue-Sun 18:00-22:30, closed Mon, deep in the Jordaan at Lindengracht 75, +31 20 623 2813, http://restauranttoscanini.nl).

**$$$ Restaurant Moeders** is a celebration of motherhood with a homey menu and a mismatched world of tables, chairs, plates, and silverware—all donated by neighbors at the grand opening. The tight interior feels like a family rec room, and tables spill out onto the street overlooking a canal. The fun, accessible menu features Dutch and international home cooking. Make a reservation before taking the long walk out here (Mon-Fri 17:00-24:00, Sat-Sun from 12:00, food served until 22:30, Rozengracht 251, +31 20 626 7957, www.moeders.com).

## JORDAAN'S "RESTAURANT ROW"

The Jordaan's trendiest area is home to a variety of tempting places to eat. This is a youthful and exuberant scene, with high-energy eateries that spill out into lively brick-sidewalk seating. Stroll Tweede ("2nd") Egelantiersdwarsstraat along its length from Egelantiers Canal to Westerstraat to survey your options: Japanese pancakes, Italian trattoria, top-end Spanish/Basque, fancy burgers, and more. Many of these places are popular; as you explore, consider reserving a spot for a return dinner visit. Along with Sonneveld Eetcafe (listed earlier under finer dining), here are my favorites:

**$$ La Perla** has a big, busy wood-fired pizza oven surrounded by a few humble tables, with a more casual and jumbled dining room across the street and—best of all—sidewalk tables on one of the liveliest intersections in the Jordaan (daily 12:00-24:00, locations face each other at Tweede Tuindwarsstraat 14 and 53, reserve online, www.pizzaperla.nl).

**$ Le Petit Deli,** a quaint little spot with takeaway fare, also has a few seats to enjoy pastries, coffee, tea, salads, and sandwiches. While the sandwiches are freshly made, the service can be slow (Wed-Mon 10:30-18:00, closed Tue, Tweede Egelantiersdwarsstraat 16, +31 20 337 3228).

**Eerste ("1st") Anjeliersdwarsstraat:** This smaller street, one block parallel to "Restaurant Row," has a few more **$$** fun choices within steps of each other. **Kinnaree Thai Restaurant,** with a modern ambience, features delicious, freshly prepared Thai cuisine served by an attentive waitstaff (daily 17:30-22:00, at #14, +31 20 627 7153). **Shah Jahan Indian Restaurant** at #18 is steamy and real, with tasty €20 plates (daily 17:00-24:00, +31 20 624 0122). **Jottum Mediterranean Tapas** offers a fun, mostly Spanish mix-it-up-with-small-plates menu (across from the Thai place at #17, 17:30-22:00, closed Mon, +31 20 420 5262).

Dessert: **Monte Pelmo Ice Cream** has delightful ice cream and often a long line (daily 13:00-22:00, Tweede Anjeliersdwarsstraat 17).

## NEAR PRINSENGRACHT

Two recommended **$$** brown cafés are set along Prinsengracht. See the "Characteristic Brown Cafés" section later in this chapter for lengthier descriptions of **Café 't Smalle,** a good place for a light lunch with canalside seating (Egelantiersgracht 12), and **Café de Prins,** just across the canal from the Anne Frank House, with delightful canalside tables and a longer menu than most.

**$$ Café Winkel,** the North Jordaan's hangout, is a sloppy and youthful favorite serving hearty plates. The rustic interior and great casual tables on the big open square give it a borderline-hipster vibe. It's particularly busy on market mornings (Monday's flea market, Saturday's farmer's market). But Amsterdammers come from across town all week for the *appeltaart.* Rather than having a meal here, I'd come to enjoy the square and a slice of pie. They have no dessert menu...just apple pie (daily 8:00-late, Noordermarkt 43, +31 20 623 0223).

## BETWEEN DAM SQUARE AND THE JORDAAN

Also in this area is **Max Restaurant** (see the "Rijsttafel and Other Indonesian Dishes in Amsterdam," sidebar, earlier).

**$$ The Pancake Bakery** has long been a favorite of backpackers, youth hostelers, and people who just want a pancake for dinner. They offer a fun and creative menu with lots of hearty savory pancakes (including a rainbow of international-themed options— kind of like a pizza place, but with pancakes) and dessert pancakes. The sloppy scene feels like a bar, with a quieter zone upstairs (daily 9:00-21:30, American breakfasts until noon, two blocks north of the Anne Frank House at Prinsengracht 191, +31 20 625 1333).

**$$ Café van Zuylen** on Torensluis Bridge (a.k.a. "Big Head Square") is great in nice weather for a scenic meal and perfect for people watching. In bad weather you can sit in the glassed-in front room or the cozier and classier back room (farther down Torensteeg). They serve salads, burgers, local standards, and Dutch and Belgian beers on tap (open long hours daily, Torensteeg 4, +31 20 639 1055).

## SOUTHWEST OF THE JORDAAN

**Foodhallen,** a quick tram ride or 10-minute walk southwest of the Jordaan, is an international food festival. This lively, trendy food circus jams two dozen food and drink vendors and lots of communal seating into an atmospheric old tram depot. It's lively and rollicking, and diners can take their pick: Basque tapas, Chinese dim

## Dining with a View

This low-slung, flat city doesn't offer many high-altitude dining options, but here are a few.

**SkyLounge Amsterdam** crowns the DoubleTree by Hilton Hotel, a five-minute walk east of Centraal station. Ride the elevator to the 11th floor, where you'll find a chic indoor bar (best views) and an amazing open roof terrace with a trendy crowd enjoying the scene. Scan the horizon to see how Amsterdam's building code protects the downtown core, where spires still stand high (lunch plates—burgers, salads, and so on—served 11:00-18:00, dinner menu features small international plates designed to be shared, open daily 11:00 until late, DJ from 21:00 nightly, no reservations, Oosterdoksstraat 4, +31 20 530 0875).

**Central Library**'s restaurant is on the top floor of Amsterdam's slick library with a commanding view terrace (daily 10:00-21:00, Oosterdokskade 143, +31 20 523 0900).

**Across the River:** Directly across the water from Centraal station, the **Eye Bar and Restaurant** serves upscale Dutch and international fare on their sprawling view terrace or in their spacious modern interior (daily 10:00-23:00, IJpromenade 1, +31 20 589 1402). From the back side of the train station, ride the free ferry across the IJ and walk to the far-out white building to the left of the landing.

**Near the Mint Tower:** The **Blue Amsterdam Restaurant** in the Kalvertoren shopping mall at the end of Kalverstraat offers a 360-degree view of the city from right in the center. It's popular for a coffee or a light lunch (see listing earlier in this chapter).

sum, Hawaiian poke, Mexican tacos, Dutch *bitterballen,* and much more (daily 12:00-22:00, weekends until 23:00, Bellamyplein 51, take tram #7 to Bilderdijkstraat, www.foodhallen.nl).

**Kinkerstraat**—the street between the Foodhallen and the heart of the Jordaan—is emerging as a foodie hotspot, lined with a variety of intriguing places (including the recommended **Amoi** restaurant; see the "Rijsttafel and Other Indonesian Dishes in Amsterdam" sidebar, earlier in this chapter).

## Southwest Amsterdam: Near the Rijksmuseum

The area surrounding Amsterdam's museum quarter is one of the city's most upscale, with swanky broad boulevards, the top-of-the-line fashion street (P. C. Hooftstraat), and exclusive homes. While a few eateries are just a few steps from the big museums, my picks are within a 10-minute walk and have better food and service.

These restaurants are good for a lunch or early dinner combined with museum-going. For locations, see the "Southwest Amsterdam Hotels and Restaurants" map on page 204.

**$$$ The Seafood Bar**—modern, slick, and popular—features a tasty array of seafood. The menu focuses on fresh and sustainable dishes with a Burgundian flair (reservations essential, daily 12:00-22:00, Van Baerlestraat 5, between the Rijksmuseum and Vondel-park, +31 20 670 8355, www.theseafoodbar.nl). Another branch is in the city center, on Spui (listed earlier).

**$$ Renzo's** is a tempting Italian delicatessen where you can buy good sandwiches or prepared pasta dishes and antipasti (priced by weight, can be heated up). Get your food to go, or pay a bit more to sit at one of the tables in the tiny interior, with more seating upstairs (house wine by the glass, or buy a bottle for the takeaway price to enjoy with your meal, daily 10:00-20:00, Van Baerlestraat 67, +31 20 763 1673).

**$$ 'T Blauwe Theehuis** ("The Blue Tea House"), deep in Von-delpark, has been a popular meeting place for a century, welcoming all generations for drinks and light meals. The leafy setting is like a Monet painting. Sit at tables outside, inside, and on the rooftop. Sandwiches are served until 17:00, then pizza until 21:00; craft beer is poured out all day (daily 9:00-22:00 in summer, Vondelpark 5, +31 20 662 0254).

**$$$ De Balie Grand Café** is a ground-floor eatery in a for-mer prison complex that's now home to galleries and concert ven-ues. While just a block off the touristy Leidseplein, you'll feel as if you're in a parallel, tourist-free world. They serve salads, sand-wiches, and simple plates, and your bill helps support culture and progressive thinking—peruse the program of events at your table (open daily for lunch and dinner, dinner served 17:00-21:00, local beers, Kleine-Gartmanplantsoen 10, +31 20 553 5130).

**$$$ Buffet van Odette,** an elegant little restaurant with a feminine twinkle, serves Mediterranean and Italian cuisine with lots of farm-fresh, seasonal vegetables. Select from three €20 main dishes—meat, fish, or vegetarian. It seems just perfect: healthy, unpretentious, romantic, and peaceful, with a good wine list. A few tables outside face a picturesque canal (Wed-Sat 12:00-22:00, closed Sun-Tue, two blocks past the Amsterdam Pipe Museum at Prinsengracht 598, +31 20 423 6034).

## Southeast Amsterdam

If you're sightseeing in the southeast past Rembrandt's house, these places—also near the Jewish Memorials and the Dutch Resistance Museum—are worth considering. For locations, see the "Southeast Amsterdam" map on page 83.

**$$ Café-Restaurant de Plantage** was built in the late 1800s in the Art Nouveau style as part of the venerable Artis Zoo (it was the original zoo patrons' club). It opens up on a prize-winning public square with spoonbills and flamingos and a lively children's fountain. A great scene both inside and out, it serves European and Mediterranean plates for lunch from 11:00 and dinner from 17:30 (closed Mon, across the street from the Dutch Resistance Museum at Plantage Kerklaan 36, +31 20 760 6800).

**$$$ Café Dignita Hoftuin,** in the park behind the Holocaust Memorial of Names, is a fine place for a drink or meal (brunchy menu, €15 plates, daily 9:00-18:00, reservations smart, Nieuwe Herengracht 18a, +31 20 370 2723).

**$$ Café Droog,** despite a name that evokes controlled substances, is a bright and airy eatery above a gallery with cutting-edge installations. They serve healthy and delectable breakfasts and soups, salads, and sandwiches (Staalstraat 7b, Wed-Sun 9:00-15:00, closed Mon-Tue, +31 20 217 0100).

## Cheap and Fast Eats

To dine cheaply yet memorably, grab a meal to go, then find a bench on a lively neighborhood square or along a canal. Sandwiches *(broodjes)* of delicious cheese on fresh bread are cheap at snack bars, delis, and *broodje* shops. International restaurants—many of them Indonesian or Surinamese, and seemingly all named with varying puns on "Wok"—serve inexpensive, splittable carryout meals. Middle Eastern fast-food stands and diners abound, offering a variety of meats wrapped in pita bread. Supermarkets and grocery stores are handy for anyone seeking picnic fare.

**Supermarkets:** The big name in Holland is **Albert Heijn,** a handy chain with long hours, picnic-friendly deli sections with take-away salads and sandwiches, and good prices (daily 8:00-22:00). Helpful locations are on Museumplein (Van Baerlestraat 33), near Dam Square behind the Royal Palace (Nieuwezijds Voorburgwal 226), near the Mint Tower (Koningsplein 4), on Leidsestraat (at Koningsplein, on the corner of Leidsestraat and Singel), and inside Centraal station (at the far end of the passage under the tracks).

**Dutch Fried Fast Food:** An Amsterdam junk-food institution, **Febo** caters mainly to late-night drinkers looking for greasy fried foods to soak up the booze. A wall of self-service, coin-op windows provides warmed-up fried cheese, burgers, croquettes, and so on. While many diners turn up their noses, a certain breed of locals swears by their slogan—*De lekkerste!* (The tastiest!) You'll find branches all over town, including at Leidsestraat 94, just north of Leidseplein; in the Red Light District (facing the Old Church across the canal); and near Rembrandtplein and the Tuschinski Theater.

**Not French Fries:** Resist the inclination to call your fries French here in the land of their origin. Amsterdam has countless *Vlaamse friets* ("Flemish fries") stands serving fries (with a selection of dips from mayonnaise to curry) and often an arsenal of wicked deep-fried gut bombs referred to as "snacks." Locals and in-the-know visitors head for **$ Vlemnickx,** an unpretentious hole-in-the-wall *friets* counter hiding just off the main Kalverstraat shopping street. They sell only fries, with a wide variety of sauces—they call themselves "*de sausmeesters*" (daily 11:00-19:00, Voetboogstraat 31).

# Amsterdam Experiences

## TRADITIONAL HERRING STANDS

Amsterdam's old-fashioned fish stands *(haringhandel)* sell herring sandwiches and other salty seafood concoctions, usually from easy photo menus. Most stands are generally open 10:00-18:00 (often closed Sun and Mon). For more on this fishy tradition—including what and how to order—see page 110.

Like a local hotdog stand, these are designed to accommodate cyclists swooping through to pick up a quick bite. You'll see herring stands on convenient corners and bridges all over the country. Here are a few with handy locations and good reputations in Amsterdam.

**Near Centraal Station:** A few blocks from Centraal station on the Singel canal, the well-established **Stubbe's Haring** is where the Stubbe family has been selling herring for 100 years.

**Near Dam Square:** Just behind the Royal Palace, **De Zeevang** sits at a busy tram-and-traffic intersection (corner of Nieuwezijds Voorburgwal and Raadhuisstraat).

**On Spui Square:** Central **Volendammer Haringhandel** is at the Rokin end of Spui Square.

**On Koningsplein** (King's Square): The especially handy **Frens Haringhandel** is right along my Amsterdam City Walk, between the Flower Market and Spui.

## CHARACTERISTIC BROWN CAFÉS
### *Gezellig* Places for a Drink or Light Bar-Snack Meal
Be sure to experience the Dutch institution of the *bruin* café (brown café)—so called for the typically hardwood decor and nicotine-

stained walls. (While cigarette smoking was banned several years ago—making these places even more inviting to nonsmokers—the traditional color survives.) Akin to a British pub, the corner brown café is the neighborhood's living room. Exemplifying the *gezellig* (cozy) quality that the Dutch hold dear, these are convivial hangouts, where you can focus on conversation while slowly nursing a drink (nondrinkers can enjoy a soft drink or coffee).

Some brown cafés specialize in beer, while others focus on the Dutch gin, *jenever;* most also serve wine (for more on drinks, see page 485). Some offer light meals, but any food menu is usually very short—often limited to bar snacks called *hapjes* (mostly deep-fried goodies; common options are listed on page 481).

Admittedly, the line separating a brown café from a plain old bar is blurry, but here are my favorites. While some brown cafés are jammed with noisy drinkers, others are a bit more sleepy and mellow.

**In the North Jordaan:** A classic brown café, **$ Café 't Papeneiland** has Delft tiles, an evocative old stove, and a stay-awhile perch overlooking a canal with welcoming benches. It's been the neighborhood hangout since the 17th century. It feels a little exclusive; patrons who come here to drink and chat aren't eager to see it overrun by tourists (daily 10:00-24:00, drinks but almost no food—cheese or liverwurst sandwiches plus famous apple pie, overlooking northwest end of Prinsengracht at #2, +31 20 624 1989).

**Buried Deep in the Jordaan:** Extremely charming **$ Café 't Smalle** has three zones where you can enjoy a light lunch or a drink: canalside (on a little barge in the canal), inside around the bar, and up some steep stairs in a quaint little back room. The café is open late, and serves simple meals of soups, salads, and sandwiches from 11:00-17:00 (bar snacks only after 17:00, plenty of fine Dutch beers on tap, interesting wines by the glass; at Egelantiersgracht 12—where it hits Prinsengracht, +31 20 623 9617).

**$$ Café de Prins,** with pleasant outdoor seating on the canal across from the Anne Frank House, is a fine spot for *poffertjes*—those beloved tiny Dutch pancakes—as well as simple bar food (daily 10:00-late, Prinsengracht 124, +31 20 624 9382).

**Other Jordaan Brown Cafés:** Earlier in this chapter, I recommend some places that aren't quite "brown cafés" but offer similar ambience. These include **Café Winkel** (at the north end of the Jordaan) and **Café van Zuylen** (with a longer menu than most and a sterling location right on "Big Head Square").

**Between Centraal Station and the Jordaan:** Beer lovers will find the ideal brown-café experience at **$ Proeflokaal Arendsnest.** Awash in wonderful old-fashioned decor, it displays 52 rotating Dutch beers (not a single Belgian one) "on tap/on draft" on a big chalkboard. They also have more than a hundred bottled beers, as well as *jenever*. The only food is Dutch bar snacks—local meats and cheeses with crackers—but the place is so inviting (with seating inside and on the canal) that it's tempting to make them into a meal (daily 12:00-24:00, Herengracht 90, +31 20 421 2057).

**Between Centraal Station and the Red Lights:** Fittingly for this neighborhood, **$ Proeflokaal de Ooievaar** ("Pelican") feels like a grubby sailors' tavern—which is exactly what it was. Although it dates from the golden age of Dutch seafarers (1782), today its tight nautical-themed interior is crammed with tourists coming up for air from the crowded Red Light District streets (open long hours daily, on the edge of the Red Light District at Sint Olofspoort 1—see the map on page 116, look for the pelican on the sign, +31 20 420 9004).

**Near Rokin:** With a lovely secluded back room and peaceful canalside seating, **$$ Café 't Gasthuys** offers a long bar and some-times slow service. I'd come here to eat outside on a quiet canal in the city center. The busy dumbwaiter cranks out light lunches, sandwiches, and reasonably priced basic dinners (cheeseburgers are a favorite, daily 12:00-16:30 & 17:30-22:00, Grimburgwal 7—from the Rondvaart Kooij boat dock, head down Langebrugsteeg, and it's one block down on the left, +31 20 624 8230).

**On Spui Square:** A classic drinking bar, **$ Café Hoppe** is as brown as can be. This is a good choice if you want to hang out with locals and drink hard. "Hoppe" is their house brew, but there are many beers on tap, a good selection of traditional drinks, and big wooden casks of *jenever*. They have sandwiches until 18:00, very simple bar food, a packed interior, and fun stools outside to oversee the action on Spui (daily 12:00-24:00, Spui 18, +31 20 420 4420). Mr. Heineken drank wine here.

**Near Waterlooplein:** Great for drinks and snacks with a view, **$ Café de Sluyswacht** is just across the street from Rembrandt's House. This "Lockkeeper's House" dates from 1695. Their out-door terrace, idyllically looking out over wide canals, has one of Amsterdam's best views. If the weather's bad, head upstairs and hunker down in the cozy painted-wood room. While mostly about the drinks, they serve bar snacks that you could turn into a light—and very scenic—meal (Dutch and Belgian beers on tap, Mon-Sat 13:00-24:00, Sun until 19:00, Jodenbreestraat 1—for location, see the map on page 83, +31 20 625 7611).

# SMOKING

The Dutch have a long (and complicated) relationship with smoking, whether marijuana or tobacco. This chapter considers Dutch tobacco habits, explains current Dutch laws regarding marijuana, and offers advice both on how marijuana-selling "coffeeshops" work and which ones in Amsterdam may be worth a visit.

## TOBACCO

More than a quarter of Dutch people smoke tobacco. Holland has a long tradition as a smoking culture, being among the first to import the tobacco plant from the New World. (For a history of smoking, visit the fascinating Amsterdam Pipe Museum.)

Tobacco shops, such as the House of Hajenius (described on page 108), glorify the habit, yet the Dutch people are among the healthiest in the world. Tanned, trim, firm, sixty-something Dutch people sip their beer, take a drag, and ask me why Americans murder themselves with Big Macs.

Still, the Dutch version of the Surgeon General is speaking out loud and clear about the health risks of smoking. Warning stickers bigger than America's are required on cigarette packs, and some of them are almost comically blunt—for example, "Smoking will make you impotent...and then you die."

Since 2008, a Dutch law has outlawed smoking tobacco almost everywhere indoors: trains, hotel rooms, restaurants, bars... and even marijuana-dealing coffeeshops.

## MARIJUANA (A.K.A. CANNABIS)

For tourists from lands where you can do hard time for lighting up, the open use of marijuana here can feel either somewhat disturbing, or exhilaratingly liberating...or maybe just normal. Several decades after being decriminalized in the Netherlands, marijuana causes about as much excitement here as a bottle of beer. The Dutch experiment in legalizing pot—while cracking down on hard drugs—has inspired several US states to follow suit with their own policies.

## Marijuana Laws and "Coffeeshops"

Throughout the Netherlands, you'll see "coffeeshops"—cafés selling marijuana, with display cases showing various joints or baggies for sale.

**Rules and Regulations:** The retail sale of marijuana is strictly regulated, and proceeds are taxed. The minimum age for purchase is 18, and coffeeshops can sell up to five grams of marijuana per person per day. It's also illegal for these shops (or anyone) to advertise marijuana. In fact, in many places, the prospective customer must take the initiative and ask to see the menu of products for sale. In some coffeeshops, you have to push and hold down a button to see an illuminated menu.

Shops sell marijuana and hashish both in pre-rolled joints and in little baggies. Joints are generally sold individually (€4-5, depending on whether it's hash with tobacco, marijuana with tobacco, or pure marijuana), though some places sell only small packs of three or four joints. Baggies generally contain a gram and go for €8-15. The better pot, though costlier, can be a better value, as it takes a smaller quantity to get high—and it's a better high. But if you want to take it easy, as a general rule, cheaper is milder.

Each coffeeshop is allowed to keep an inventory of about a pound of pot in stock: The tax authorities don't want to see more than this on the books at the end of each accounting cycle, and a shop can lose its license if its inventory exceeds this amount. A popular shop—whose supply must be replenished five or six times a day—simply must put up with the hassle of constantly taking small deliveries. A shop can sell a ton of pot with no legal problems, as long as it maintains that tiny stock and just refills it as needed. The reason? Authorities want shops to stay small and not become export bases (to neighboring countries with stricter laws).

**Smoking Tips:** Shops have loaner bongs and inhalers, and dispense rolling papers like toothpicks. While it's good style to ask first, if you're a paying customer (e.g., you buy a cup of coffee), you can generally pop into any coffeeshop and light up a joint, even if you didn't buy your pot there.

Tourists who haven't smoked pot since their college days are famous for overindulging in Amsterdam. Coffeeshop baristas nickname tourists about to pass out "Whitey"—the color their faces turn just before they hit the floor. They warn Americans (who aren't used to the strength of the local stuff) to try a lighter leaf. If you do overdo it, the key is to eat or drink something sweet to avoid getting sick. Cola is a good fast fix, and coffeeshop staff keep sugar tablets handy. They also recommend trying to walk it off.

Don't ever buy pot on the street in Amsterdam. Well-established coffeeshops are considered much safer, and coffeeshop owners have an interest in keeping their trade safe and healthy. They're also generally very patient in explaining the varieties available.

**Types of Cannabis:** The Dutch sell several forms of cannabis: They smoke both hashish (an extract of the cannabis plant) and the leaf of the plant (which they call "marihuana" or "grass"). While each shop has different brands, it's all derived from two types of marijuana plant: *Cannabis indica* and *Cannabis sativa. Indica* gets you a stoned, heavy, mellow, "couch-weed" high—more often used for medical purposes. *Sativa* is light, fun, uplifting, and more psychedelic. *Sativa* makes you giggle.

While the hash is mostly imported from Morocco, most of the marijuana sold in Dutch coffeeshops is grown locally, as coffeeshops find it's safer to deal with Dutch-grown plants than to import marijuana (the EU prohibits any international drug trade). Technological advances have made it easier to cultivate exotic strains. You may see joints described as if they'd come from overseas, e.g. "Thai"—and indeed the strain in that joint may have originated elsewhere—but it's still Dutch-grown. "Netherlands weed" is refined, like wine. Most shops get their inventory from the pot equivalent of local home- or microbrewers. Shops with better "boutique suppliers" develop a reputation for having better-quality weed. (These are the places that proudly display a decal announcing them as winners at Amsterdam's annual Cannabis Cup Awards.)

**Tobacco and Marijuana:** While most American pot-smokers like their joints made purely of marijuana, the Dutch (like most Europeans) are accustomed to mixing tobacco with marijuana. Pre-rolled marijuana joints are sold either pure, with tobacco, or with a nontobacco "hamburger helper" herb mix. Any place that caters to Americans will have joints without tobacco, but you have to ask specifically for a "pure" joint.

Back in the 1970s, most "pot-smokers" here smoked hash, which needs to be mixed with something else (like tobacco) to light up. Today, more Dutch prefer "herbal cannabis"—the marijuana bud common in the US—but they still keep the familiar tobacco in their joints. Tobacco-mixed joints also go back to hippie days, when pot was expensive and it was simply wasteful to pass around a pure marijuana joint. Mixing in tobacco allowed poor hippies to be generous without going broke. And since the Dutch don't dry and cure their marijuana, it's simply hard to smoke without tobacco.

The Netherlands' indoor-smoking ban pertains to tobacco smoke, not pot smoke. It might seem strange to an American, but these days, if a coffeeshop is busted, it can be for tobacco. Coffeeshops with a few outdoor seats have a huge advantage, as their customers can light up outside. Shops without the outdoor option are in for an extra challenge, as many local smokers would rather get their weed to go than smoke it without tobacco at their neighborhood coffeeshop.

## The Dutch Approach to Marijuana

To some visitors, the Netherlands can seem frighteningly comfortable with—even nonchalant about—drug use. But the Dutch are well aware of the problems associated with drugs, especially the more addictive hard drugs. (The Dutch word for addiction is "enslavement.") Most also believe that the concept of a "victimless crime" is a contradiction in terms: Any drug-related behavior that affects others is taken seriously. Drive under the influence of anything and you're toast. Because of their wide-reaching social costs, heroin and cocaine are strictly illegal in the Netherlands, and the police stringently enforce laws prohibiting their sale and use.

The Dutch are not even necessarily pro-marijuana; most people here simply believe that outlawing marijuana creates more problems than it solves—and statistics indicate they may be right. No one here would say that smoking pot was healthy. It's a drug. It can be dangerous, and it can be abused. But the Dutch have chosen to allow marijuana's responsible adult use as a civil liberty, and treat its abuse as a health-care and education challenge rather than a crime.

Most Dutch believe that America's long-standing "War on Drugs" is based on fear, misinformation, and electoral politics. After several decades of not arresting pot-smokers, the Dutch can point to studies showing that they smoke less than the European average—and fewer than half as many Dutch smoke pot, per capita, as Americans do. (My Dutch friends also enjoy pointing out that, while three of our most recent US presidents admitted or implied that they had smoked marijuana, no Dutch prime minister ever has.) The Dutch have found that strict regulation of the soft-drug trade has helped minimize many of the problems associated with it, such as street crime, gang warfare, and hard-drug use.

So what am I? Pro-marijuana? Let's put it this way: I agree with the Dutch people, who remind me that a society either must allow some room for drug use on the less-harmful end of the spectrum...or build more prisons. About 575,000 Americans are arrested every year for simple possession of marijuana. While a wide

# New Pressure to Recriminalize Marijuana

Dutch pot-smokers complain that the generation that ran naked on acid around Amsterdam's Vondelpark during the '60s is now threatening the Netherlands' well-established, regulated marijuana trade. Responding to international pressure and conservatives in rural and small-town Holland, the federal government has cracked down on coffeeshops. While they're still allowed to sell marijuana, many aspects of these businesses' operations exist in a legal limbo, with certain restrictions usually going unenforced—until now.

Neighboring countries (France and Germany) complain that it's too easy for citizens to make drug runs across the border, returning home with lots of pot. In response, some Dutch border towns implemented a "weed pass" system, allowing pot sales only to ID-toting Dutch citizens. But the independent-minded Dutch (especially young people) don't want to be registered as pot users, so in those towns they're buying it on the street—rekindling the black market and, many fear, the crime and social problems associated with it.

In 2012, marijuana tourists—and the businesses that rely on them—panicked when it was announced that a similar "weed pass" would be instituted nationwide. But the plan was shelved, and Amsterdam's coffeeshops remain open to the public.

In general, Amsterdam city leaders recognize that legalized marijuana and the Red Light District's prostitution are part of the city's edgy appeal; the city wants to keep both, but get rid of the accompanying sleaze. Amsterdam values the pragmatic wisdom of its progressive policies and is bucking the federal shift to the right. Locals don't want shady people pushing drugs in dark alleys; they'd rather see marijuana sold in regulated shops.

The future is uncertain. Coffeeshop licenses are not being renewed in some neighborhoods—the number of coffeeshops in Amsterdam has fallen from a peak of more than 700 (in the mid-1990s) to about 150 today. With all this talk of new restrictions, coffeeshops are on their best behavior and are being very careful to nurture good relations with their neighbors.

The Netherlands (along with the rest of Europe) is watching carefully and learning from the US as more and more states legalize, tax, and regulate the otherwise black-market marijuana trade.

SMOKING

variety of Americans smoke pot, the people prosecuted for possessing it are disproportionately poor and/or black or Latino.

If you'd like to learn more about marijuana (and don't feel like Googling "Rick Steves marijuana" or watching my talk on YouTube—search "Rick Steves Spokane"), drop by Amsterdam's Cannabis College or the Hash, Marijuana, and Hemp Museum (both located on Oudezijds Achterburgwal street—see pages 130-131). Back home, if you'd like to support an outfit dedicated to taking the crime out of pot, read up on the National Organization for the Reform of Marijuana Laws (www.norml.org).

## COFFEESHOPS IN AMSTERDAM

Most of downtown Amsterdam's coffeeshops feel grungy and foreboding to American travelers who aren't part of the youth-hostel crowd. The neighborhood

places (and those in small towns around the countryside) feel more inviting to people without piercings, tattoos, and favorite techno artists. I've listed a few places with a more pub-like ambience for Americans wanting to go local, but within reason. Most purchases are in cash. For locations, see the "West/Central Amsterdam Restaurants" map on page 210 in the Eating in Amsterdam chapter.

**Paradox** is the most *gezellig* (cozy) coffeeshop I've found—a mellow, graceful place. Wiljan and Sieb are patient with descriptions

and happy to walk you through all your options. The music is easy and the neighborhood is charming (daily 11:00-20:00, loaner bongs, games, Wi-Fi, two blocks from Anne Frank House at Eerste Bloemdwarsstraat 2, +31 20 623 5639).

**Siberië Coffeeshop** is a short walk from Centraal station but feels cozy, with a friendly canalside ambience. Clean, big, and bright, it has the vibe of a mellow Starbucks, hosts the occasional astrology reading, and is proud that all their pot is "lab tested" (daily 10:00-23:00, Fri-Sat until 24:00, helpful staff, English menu, Brouwersgracht 11, +31 20 623 5909).

**La Tertulia** is a sweet little mother-and-daughter-run coffeeshop with pastel decor and a cheery terrarium atmosphere. You can sit at outdoor tables, and they also serve light food and fresh juices (Tue-Sat 11:00-19:00, closed Sun-Mon, sandwiches, brownies, games, Prinsengracht 312).

The **Bulldog Café** is Amsterdam's high-profile, leading tour-
isty chain of coffeeshops. These establishments are young but welcoming, with reliable selec-tions. They're pretty comfortable for green tourists wanting to just hang out for a while. The flag-ship branch, in a former police station right on Leidseplein, is very handy, offering alcohol up-stairs, pot downstairs, and fun

outdoor seating on a heated patio. It's the rare place where you can have a beer while you smoke and watch the world skateboard by (daily 10:00-24:00, later on weekends, Leidseplein 17—see map on page 66, +31 20 625 6278). Their original café still sits on the canal near the Old Church in the Red Light District (and is a stop on my self-guided walk through that neighborhood—see page 116).

The **Original Dampkring** is a rough-and-ready constant party where whoever picks the tunes believes music from the 1960s and '70s is still hip. It's a high-profile, busy place, filled with a young clientele, but the owners still take the time to explain what they offer. Scenes in the movie *Ocean's Twelve* were filmed here (daily 10:00-24:00, close to Spui at Handboogstraat 29, +31 20 638 0705).

**Strain Hunters Coffeeshop,** conveniently located near Spui Square on Singel canal, has an inviting and friendly vibe with a couple of tables overlooking the canal that are perfect for enjoying the late-afternoon sunshine (daily 10:00-24:00, on the corner of Heisteeg and Singel at Singel 387, +31 20 624 7624). Their walls are entertaining: decorated with photos of the celebrities who've smoked here, videos about how they scour the world for natural strains to import and grow in the Netherlands, and their many Cannabis Cup trophies.

SMOKING

# AMSTERDAM WITH CHILDREN

Amsterdam is a great destination for families. From vibrant street life to peaceful pond-filled parks, engaging and interactive museums to sit-back-and-relax canal cruises, Amsterdam (and the Netherlands in general) has something fun for every age.

## Trip Tips

### PLAN AHEAD

Involve your kids in trip planning. Have them read about the places you may include in your itinerary (even the hotels you're considering) and let them help with your decisions.

#### Where to Stay

- Choose hotels in a kid-friendly area near a park. The neighborhoods near Vondelpark and Museumplein are both good.
- Minimize hotel changes by planning three-day stays or consider renting an apartment (for more on short-term rentals, see the Practicalities chapter).

#### What to Bring

- If traveling with infants, plan on bringing a light stroller for neighborhood walks and a child backpack for tram rides.
- Bring drawing supplies and English-language books, as these supplies can be harder to find and pricey in the Netherlands.
- For a touch of home at the hotel, download some favorite movies onto your electronic devices.

### EATING

Try these tips to keep your kids content throughout the day.

- Be sure to start with a good breakfast (at hotels and B&Bs, breakfast is nearly always included).

## Books for Kids

Get your kids into the Dutch spirit with these books about the Netherlands. (Also see my recommended books and films, including additional good choices for teenagers, in the appendix.)

*Anne Frank: The Diary of a Young Girl* (Anne Frank, 1947). Kids' can read this book or watch the 1959 film to learn a little bit about the Netherlands during World War II. If you're visiting Haarlem, consider a similar account of the Nazi occupation, Corrie ten Boom's *The Hiding Place*.

*The Fault in Our Stars* (John Green, 2012). Two teens diagnosed with cancer make it their dying wish to travel to Amsterdam and meet their favorite author. Read the book or see the 2014 film adaptation, which includes beautiful shots of the city.

*Girl with a Pearl Earring* (Tracy Chevalier, 1999). This fictional story is based on Vermeer's famous painting, which is exhibited in the Mauritshuis Royal Picture Gallery in The Hague.

*Knuffle Bunny Free: An Unexpected Diversion* (Mo Willems, 2010). Trixie visits her grandparents in the Netherlands with her stuffed bunny in tow. Mo Willems charmingly juxtaposes drawings and photography in the third book of his Caldecott Honor-winning series.

*Mission Amsterdam: A Scavenger Hunt Adventure* (Catherine Aragon, 2014). Young travelers will have hands-on fun discovering the city's landmarks and museums in this spy-themed scavenger hunt.

Any art book on Van Gogh. Many young people (and adults) find his swirling, colorful art compelling.

- Picnic lunches or dinners work well. Try large grocery stores, like the popular Albert Heijn supermarket chain. Having snacks on hand can avoid meltdowns.
- As a treat, stop for *friets* (fries), *pannenkoeken* (pancakes), or *stroopwafels* (a delicious cookie-waffle hybrid). You can typically find any of these Dutch specialties at street stands around the city.
- Kids will have fun choosing their meal from a Febo. This wall of coin-op windows features rows upon rows of warmed-up (though not necessarily healthy) food, such as burgers and fried chicken sticks (see page 220). Also, department-store cafeterias are centrally located and a safe bet for kid-friendly food.
- For older kids, be aware that the legal drinking age is 18.

CHILDREN

## SIGHTSEEING

The key to a successful Dutch family vacation is to slow down.

### Planning Your Time

- Involve your children in the trip. Let them help choose daily activities, lead you on the tram, and so on.
- Older kids and teens can help plan the details of a museum visit, such as what to see, how to get there, and ticketing details.
- Balance your museum-going with fun and energetic activities, like biking or playing in a park. Tackle one or two key sights each day, mix in a healthy dose of pure fun, and take extended breaks when needed.

### Successful Sightseeing

- Follow this book's crowd-beating tips. Kids despise long lines even more than you do.
- Seek out museums with kid appeal and interactive exhibits, such as the NEMO science museum or Tropical Museum Junior. Ask at TIs about kid-friendly activities. For other museums, limit visits to 45 minutes—period! Kids will tolerate a little culture if it's short and focused, with plenty of breaks.
- Deputize your child to lead you on my self-guided walks and museum tours.
- Museum audioguides are great for older children. For younger children, hit the gift shop first so you can buy postcards; then hold a scavenger hunt to find the pictured artwork (or give them this book with its photos). If boredom sets in, try "I spy" games or have them count how many babies or dogs they can spot in all the paintings in the room.
- Bring a sketchbook to a museum and encourage kids to select a painting to draw. It's a great way for them to slow down and observe.
- Public WCs are hard to find: Try museums, bars, and fast-food restaurants.
- Take a bike tour with the family.

### Making or Finding Quality Souvenirs

- Buy your kids a trip journal and encourage them to write down their observations, thoughts, and favorite memories. It could end up being their favorite souvenir.
- For a group project, keep a family journal. Pack a small diary and a glue stick. While relaxing at a café, take turns writing or drawing about the day's events and include mementos such as ticket stubs from museums and postcards.
- Teens might love shopping (or even window-shopping). See the Shopping in Amsterdam chapter for fun areas.

## MONEY AND SAFETY

Before your trip gets under way, talk to your kids about safety and money.

- Give your child a money belt and an expanded allowance; you are on vacation, after all. Let your children budget their funds by comparing and contrasting the dollar and euro.
- If you allow kids to explore a museum or neighborhood on their own, be sure to establish a clear meeting time and place.
- It's good to have a "what if" procedure in place in case something goes wrong. If your child has a mobile phone, enable the "Find My Phone" feature in case you get separated. Give your kids your hotel's business card, your mobile-phone number, and emergency taxi fare. Show them how to make calls in the Netherlands, or tell them to ask to use the phone at a hotel if they are lost.

## STAYING CONNECTED AND TRANSPORTATION

- Readily available Wi-Fi (at hotels, some cafés, and all Starbucks and McDonald's) makes bringing a mobile device worthwhile.
- Most parents find it worth the peace of mind to buy a supplemental messaging plan for the whole family: Adults can stay connected to teenagers while allowing them maximum independence, and teens can keep in touch with friends both old and new via apps such as FaceTime, WhatsApp, Facebook Messenger, Snapchat, Google Chat, or Skype.
- Children under age four ride for free and kids 4-11 get a discounted rate on public transportation. Light strollers usually work fine on the tram (enter through the large central doors near the conductor; there are designated stroller areas, look for a stroller icon on the floor), but backpacks are easier.
- If you're taking the train to another city, check for family and youth discounts; see the Practicalities chapter for details.

# Sights and Activities

### NEMO (National Center for Science and Technology)
This waterfront science museum for children offers a world of hands-on explorations, from building a bridge to conducting scientific experiments. See listing on page 77.

### Netherlands Maritime Museum (Nederlands Scheepvaartmuseum)
This comprehensive collection of model ships and instruments includes several exhibitions geared toward children. At the museum's dock is the *Amsterdam,* a replica of an 18th-century sailing ship with an onboard virtual-reality experience, and a royal barge. See page 77 for details.

### Dutch Resistance Museum (Verzetsmuseum)
Both educational and interactive, the excellent junior section of this WWII museum lets kids follow the stories of four children who lived through the war. Kids can wander through different homes, exploring hidden rooms and playing games where they make decisions based on wartime scenarios. This section makes a great introduction to some of the heavier content in the museum. See listing on page 89.

### Tropical Museum Junior (Tropenmuseum Junior)
Part of the Tropenmuseum, this interactive section for children focuses on a different country every three years. Open only on weekends, the rotating 1.5-hour programs let kids participate in dance, music, and arts and crafts (usually in Dutch, programs in English must be reserved in advance at reserveren@tropenmuseum.nl or +31 88 004 2840, www.tropenmuseumjunior.nl). See listing on page 90.

### Van Gogh Museum
The artist's swirling, colorful, emotional work can be easier for kids to appreciate than dark Rembrandts. Van Gogh's relatively simple subjects (self-portraits, bedroom furniture, sunflowers, sowers in fields) can be taken in at a glance. His work is childlike in a way—his broad, vibrant strokes resemble children's drawings with color crayons. For older, more discerning children, it's a good experience to be in a museum focused on one artist's work, allowing them to see the evolution in an artist's style over time. The museum offers various hands-on activities for children, including a treasure hunt and painting workshops (available with instruction in English).
     &#x1F4D6; See the Van Gogh Museum Tour chapter.

### Rijksmuseum
The Rijksmuseum is a must-see destination in Amsterdam, but it can be challenging to keep kids' interest here. To make things

a little more interactive, the museum offers a one-hour Family Quest tour for kids 7-12. For kids 13-18 with smartphones and earbuds, there's a Snapguide, a free tour with challenges incorporating the phone's camera. The museum's outdoor gallery features a kids' area with playground equipment and a playful water fountain.

📖 See the Rijksmuseum Tour chapter.

### Anne Frank House

A visit to the place where Anne Frank and her family hid for two years can be a powerful experience, especially for children who have read her journal or watched the movie. The museum recommends the visit for children ages 10 and up, and its website supplies supplementary in-depth information about Anne and World War II.

📖 See the Anne Frank House Tour chapter.

### Mouse Mansion (Het Muizenhuis)

In the Jordaan area, this mini museum of mice figures and their dwellings, shops, carnival rides, and even a room-size harbor is exquisitely detailed and fascinating for kids (free to visit, closed Mon-Tue, Eeste Tuindwarsstraat 1—see map on page 244, www.themousemansion.com).

### A'dam Tower and This Is Holland

Take the free ferry over to North Amsterdam and enjoy some *poffertjes* and soft drinks while you admire 360-degree views of the city at A'dam Tower, then take a thrill ride on the Tower's sky-high swing over the IJ or virtual rollercoaster, or "fly" over the Netherlands at the This Is Holland attraction next door (both described on page 80).

## PARKS AND PLAYGROUNDS

Amsterdam is filled with great parks that are fun for kids, especially Vondelpark, Amstelpark, and Woeste Westen. Other good outdoor spaces include:

- Museumplein, with a playground adjacent to the Cobra Café and a big grassy area for running and picnicking.
- Oosterpark, south of the zoo, with a pond, wading pool, and free Wi-Fi.
- The waterfront park next to the EYE Filmmuseum (see page 80).
- Outdoor markets, for kids who enjoy browsing: Check out the

Waterlooplein flea market (see page 82), or explore the Albert Cuyp street market (see page 242) and head to Sarphatipark for a picnic afterward.

## Vondelpark

Vondelpark is the largest and most famous park in Amsterdam. It's great for people-watching and has plenty of space for kids to run free, including several

fun playground areas (such as the delightful treehouse structure nearly hidden in the woods, about mid-park). Cycling through Vondelpark on one of its many bike paths is great for a family outing (see page 65).

## Amstelpark

Located at the southern edge of the city, Amstelpark has plenty of gardens and green space, along with extra entertainment for kids, including a train ride, small amusement park, petting zoo, playground, and miniature golf.

**Cost and Hours:** Free to enter but fee for some of the activities; attractions have different hours but generally open daily between 10:00 and 11:00 and close between 16:00 and 18:00; take tram #4 or the Metro to RAI station, then walk 10 minutes; +31 20 644 1744, www.speeltuin-amstelpark.nl.

## Woeste Westen

At this "adventurous nature playground," located in the northwest corner of Westerpark, kids 13 and under are welcome to climb logs, wade across streams, paddle rafts, play with sand, and tread through the tall grass and trees. Just make sure to bring a change of clothes, as this place can get messy.

**Cost and Hours:** Free; always open but playground supervisor and main building are accessible during certain hours, starting daily between 11:00 and 13:00 and closing at 18:00; Overbrakerpad 3, www.woestewesten.nl.

## OTHER KID-CENTRIC ATTRACTIONS

### Canal Cruises

A canal boat ride is a great way to view the city from a new perspective, especially after a long day of walking on little feet. Cruises last about an hour and leave from various docks around the city (see "Tours in Amsterdam" in the Orientation to Amsterdam chapter).

For a longer outing, join **Wetlands Safari** for a canoe trip through the beautiful Dutch countryside. See listing on page 53.

The **Pancake Cruise** (De Pannenkoekenboot) takes a 1.25-hour glide through the canals of Amsterdam while families indulge in an all-you-can-eat pancake buffet (€16.50 for kids 3-11, €21.50 for adults, generally 3-4/day, +31 20 636 8817, www.pannenkoekenboot.nl).

### Artis Royal Zoo (Natura Artis Magistra)

The Artis is a convenient escape from the bustle of Amsterdam. Besides legions of plants and animals, these historical grounds also feature a planetarium, aquarium, insectarium, and butterfly pavilion. Kids can wander through the petting zoo or learn about animal training and care in one of the daily programs.

**Cost and Hours:** €21 for kids 3-12, free for kids under 3; daily 9:00-18:00, Nov-Feb until 17:00; Plantage Kerklaan 38—take tram #14 (from Centraal station or from Dam Square) and get off at Artis stop; +31 20 523 3670, www.artis.nl.

**Nearby:** The **botanical gardens** (Hortus Botanicus) are a couple of blocks away, offering a lovely butterfly greenhouse (see page 85). **Oosterpark,** with a pond and wading pool, is south of the zoo. Take tram #14 to Alexanderplein and transfer to tram #19 (direction: Diemen Sniep) for the short ride to the park.

### Amsterdam Marionette Theatre

Beautiful wooden marionettes come to life in shows based on classics from opera and musical theater. Though performances are in Dutch, kids should still find the visuals and music entertaining regardless of the language barrier. Bonus: A playground is just outside the theater.

**Cost and Hours:** Typically €8 for kids 7-14 and €17 for adults, performances generally on weekends at 15:00 with occasional shows Fri at 20:15, Nieuwe Jonkerstraat 8, +31 20 620 8027, www.marionettentheater.nl.

### Wind n' Wheels

Try land sailing on a go-cart. Each person sits in his or her own "land yacht" (like a sailboat on wheels), but two-seaters are also available for parents with younger kids or those who prefer to ride with an instructor (must be at least 11 years old to drive). If there's not enough wind to keep these vehicles sailing (check wind speeds on their website), you can try other adrenaline-pumping activi-

CHILDREN

ties, such as electric skateboarding, trampolining, and acro bungee (jumping on a trampoline while tethered to a bungee).

**Cost and Hours:** €32.50 for 1.5-hour sailing clinic; Mon-Tue by appointment, Wed from 12:00, Sat-Sun from 10:00, closed Thu-Fri; Zuiderzeeweg 1—take tram #26 from Centraal station (direction: IJburg) to the Zuiderzeeweg stop; +31 20 752 1790, www.windnwheels.nl.

## SIGHTS OUTSIDE AMSTERDAM
### Railway Museum (Spoorwegmuseum)
Just 30 minutes by train from Amsterdam, Utrecht's Railway Museum is a fun mix of exhibits, historic locomotives, and rides, including a roller coaster and miniature train. See listing on page 435.

### Scheveningen
What kid doesn't like a beach? This popular spot, near The Hague and Delft, is great on a sunny day. Expect cafés, shops, a boardwalk, bungee-jumping fun, a wide beach, and sun worshippers. See listing on page 399.

### Madurodam
With replicas of ships, canals, windmills, and the airport, this miniature theme park in The Hague makes even the smallest kids feel like giants. See page 399.

**Cost and Hours:** €17, free for kids 2 and under, family tickets and discounts available online; open daily 10:00-17:00 but check website for possible longer hours, last entry one hour before closing; George Maduroplein 1, +31 70 416 2400, www.madurodam. nl.

### Open-Air Museums
With old structures to explore (farmhouses, schools, windmills), fun interactive activities, and workers dressed up in period cos-

tumes, open-air museums are great for kids of all ages. The excellent **Enkhuizen Zuiderzee,** an hour north of Amsterdam, is a re-creation of an early-1900s fishing village, where kids can try out chores that Zuiderzee children used to do and craft a ship out of old wooden shoes (see page 352); if you have extra time, spend it in the pleasant town of Enkhuizen. Holland's first folk museum (and one of its finest) is found in **Arnhem,** an hour southwest from Amsterdam (see page 439); although the museum is great, the town has little to offer tourists. If you prefer a museum closer to Amsterdam, **Zaanse Schans** is handy, though also more touristy and commercial (charging separate prices for most exhibits rather than one overall admission fee). Its main attractions include a clock museum, a cookie factory, and an abundance of windmills (about 15 minutes by train from Amsterdam, plus a 15-minute walk; see page 334).

### De Adriaan Windmill

For kids, a trip to the Netherlands would not be complete without visiting a windmill. Haarlem's town windmill offers nice views from the top, along with exhibits, videos, and demonstrations on how it all works. See listing on page 290.

### Zandvoort

The coastal town of Zandvoort is a fun family outing, with its large sandy beach, pedestrian promenade, and abundance of ice-cream

shops. It's easy to reach by train (about 10 minutes from Haarlem and 30 minutes from Amsterdam), and the beach is only 150 yards from the station. If you're staying in Haarlem, consider renting bikes and cycling to the shore—it's a flat ride that takes less than an hour (but consider the wind factor). See listing on page 291.

# SHOPPING IN AMSTERDAM

Amsterdam brings out the browser even in those who were not born to shop. The city has lots of one-of-a-kind specialty stores, street markets, and specific streets and neighborhoods worthy of a browse. Poke around and see what you can find.

Ten general markets, open six days a week (generally 9:30-17:00, closed Sun), keep folks who brake for garage sales pulling U-turns. Markets include Waterlooplein (the flea market), the huge Albert Cuyp street market, and various flower markets (such as the Singel canal Flower Market near the Mint Tower).

**Store Hours:** Most shops in the center are open 9:00-17:30 (later on Thu—typically until 20:00 or 21:00). The businesslike Dutch know no siesta, but many shopkeepers take Sundays and Monday mornings off. Supermarkets are generally open Monday-Saturday 8:00-20:00, with shorter hours on Sunday; Albert Heijn grocery stores are open until 22:00 every day.

**Tax Refunds, Shipping, and Red Tape:** To find out how to get a VAT (Value-Added Tax) refund on merchandise, see page 468. While the Netherlands has closed most of its post offices, you can still mail your purchases home (ask your hotelier for the nearest ersatz post office, or use Service Point, a shipping service at Centraal station and Schiphol Airport). If you want to bring home edibles and drinkables, see page 468 for restrictions.

**Souvenir Ideas:** Good consumable souvenirs include **cheese** (many travel well), **chocolates,** or a bottle of *jenever* (traditional Dutch gin, sold in traditional stone bottles and carefully wrapped in your checked luggage). Art lovers enjoy packing home a postcard or print of their favorite **artwork** from the Van Gogh or other museums. For something higher end, consider **Delftware** or **diamonds.** The city's many small shops are fun for browsing for items of unique **design** (both clothes and housewares) and **vintage.** If you're seeking Dutch clichés (**wooden shoes, flower seeds,** or **bulbs,** and so on), make a surgical strike at any souvenir stand, or at the shops at the airport. Just make sure bulbs are certified to bring into the United States. Look for a paper certificate in the package.

**Bad Idea:** Don't try to bring home anything drug-related—smartshop herbal supplements, marijuana, or even bongs or marijuana pipes (yes, even to states where it's legal). American laws are written so that—technically—even importing an unused pipe could get you arrested. If you want to take that chance, make sure the pipe is clean and unused, because even a little residue can get you busted at US Customs.

## SHOPS
### Department Stores

**Hema** is handy for everything from inexpensive clothes and notebooks to cosmetics. Stores are in the Kalvertoren shopping mall at Kalverstraat 212 and at Centraal station.

The **De Bijenkorf** department store, towering high above Dam Square, is Amsterdam's top-end option and worth a look even if you're not shopping. It sparkles with name brands, which are actually independent stores operating under the Bijenkorf roof. The entire fifth floor is a ritzy self-service cafeteria with a rooftop terrace.

### Dutch Design

Like their Belgian neighbors, the Dutch have a knack for practical and eye-pleasing design. Think Piet Hein, the 20th-century jack-of-all-trades known for everything from scientific theory to designing housewares to creating beloved games. Amsterdam has a variety of worth-a-detour shops that showcase both established and emerging designers in the Dutch tradition. **The Frozen Fountain** is an extremely fun warehouse of innovative creations, from kitchen gadgets and furniture to textiles and bold wallpaper. Drop in here to explore, and don't miss the upstairs (closed Sun-Mon, just south of the Nine Little Streets shopping zone—described later—at Prinsengracht 645, +31 20 622 9375, www.frozenfountain.nl).

### Albert Cuyp Market

Amsterdam's biggest open-air market, stretching for several blocks along Albert Cuypstraat, bustles daily (roughly 9:00-17:00) except Sunday. You'll find fish, exotic vegetables, bolts of fabric, bargain clothes, native Dutch and international food stands (especially *stroopwafels* and Surinamese *rotis*), and great people-watching. It's located a 10-minute walk east of Museumplein and a block south of the Heineken Experience (tram #24).

## Flower Market (Bloemenmarkt)

While flower shops are scattered around the city, the most enjoyable browsing is at the **Flower Market,** which stretches luxuriously along the Singel canal be-

tween the Mint Tower and Koningsplein. Situated on a row of barges, this floating market boasts a well-stocked cornucopia of pretty petals tucked under tents. Buy a bouquet for your hotel room, or stock up on seeds and bulbs to bring home—look for ones packed with a seal or certificate that promises they are US Customs-friendly.

## Delftware Galleries

Ceramic plates, vases, and tiles decorated with a fake Chinese blue-and-white design were all the rage in the 1600s. Only a few licensed places sell the real stuff (expensive) and antiques (very expensive). You can find fireplace tiles (cheap) at most gift shops.

Pricey, authentic Delftware shouldn't be an impulse buy, so do your homework be-

fore committing. Ideally, you'd hop on the train to the town of Delft (an hour away), where you can tour the official Royal Dutch Delftware Manufactory and buy directly from its shop (see the Delft chapter). In Amsterdam, reputable vendors include **Heinen Delfts Blauw,** with locations between the museum neighborhood and Rokin (at Prinsengracht 440); at the Mint Tower (Muntplein 12); near the Old Church (Damrak 65); in the IJpassage at Centraal station (www.heinendelftsblauw.nl); and **Galleria D'Arte Rinascimento,** in the Jordaan (Prinsengracht 170, www.delft-art-gallery.com).

## Oudemanhuispoort Book Market

Book lovers will want to seek out this rustic book market, tucked down a hidden corridor between two big university buildings (Mon-Sat 9:00-17:00, closed Sun). On the canalside Oudezijds Achterburgwal, just east of Rokin, find the stone gate marking a passage next to #229. (You can also enter through the other end, next to Kloveniersburgwal 82.) The gallery is lined with stalls and

# Shopping in Amsterdam

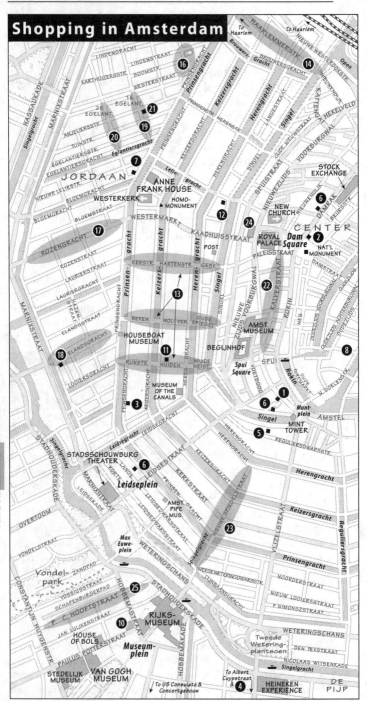

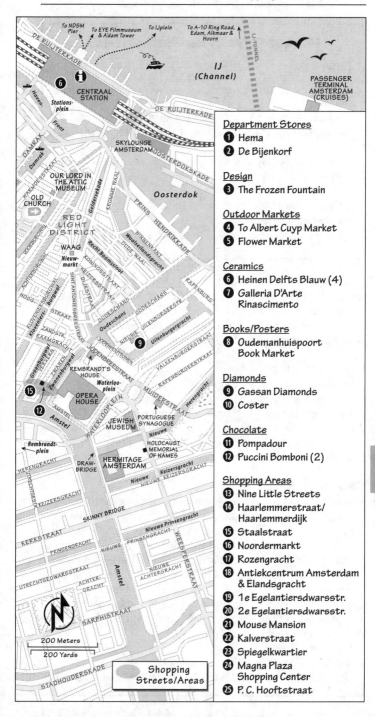

## Market Days in the Netherlands

If you're day-tripping, keep in mind that most open-air markets are held only in the morning (e.g., 10:00-12:30), though in bigger cities such as Rotterdam, markets bustle throughout the day.

**Alkmaar:** Friday (cheese, late March-late Sept).

**Delft:** Thursday (general & flower) and Saturday (general & flea).

**Edam:** Wednesday (general year-round, plus cheese July-Aug).

**Haarlem:** Monday and Saturday.

**Leiden:** Wednesday and Saturday (bigger).

**Rotterdam:** Daily.

**Utrecht:** Wednesday, Friday, and Saturday.

tables stacked high with secondhand books (many in English), all surrounded by university bustle. Vendors at the Kloveniersburgwal end specialize in prints and posters. The tranquil courtyards just off this hallway are jammed with students enjoying a sunny escape from the classrooms and clogged streets.

### Diamond Shops

Diamonds have been a big Dutch commodity ever since golden age traders first exploited the mines of Africa. In Amsterdam, you can get them cut or uncut, expensive or really expensive. Diamond dealers offer free cutting and polishing demos at their shops. **Gassan Diamonds,** near Rembrandt's House, is best (page 83); **Coster** is on Potterstraat, behind the Rijksmuseum (page 58).

### Chocolate Shops

While neighboring Belgium is famous for its chocolates, the Dutch dabble as well. Dutch Verkade and Droste cocoa are sold in tins. **Pompadour** chocolate-and-pastry shop is elegant and decadent (Huidenstraat 12 in the Nine Little Streets). Or you can stop by a branch of the premium Dutch chocolatier **Puccini Bomboni,** which sells an enticing array of pralines in various flavors, all made on the premises. This can be a tasty souvenir or a splurgy gift—especially if you're not also going to Belgium (locations at Staalstraat 17 and between Dam Square and the Jordaan at Singel 184; open daily, www.puccinibomboni.com).

### Museum Shops

Shops at major museums (such as the **Rijksmuseum** and **Van Gogh Museum**) are well stocked with posters, postcards, and gorgeous glossy books showing off masterpieces. They also sell protective mailing tubes for carrying or shipping your posters home.

## AMSTERDAM'S TOP SHOPPING ZONES

This section focuses on four of the city's top shopping areas—all equally good, but each with a different flavor: the **Nine Little Streets** (touristy, tidy, and central), **Haarlemmerstraat/Haarlemmerdijk** (emerging, borderline-edgy neighborhood of creative, unpretentious shops), **Staalstraat** (postcard-cute, short-and-sweet street tucked just away from the tourist crowds), and the **Jordaan** (mellow residential zone with a smattering of fine shops).

### The Nine Little Streets (De Negen Straatjes)

This handy central zone—hemmed in by a grid plan between Dam Square and the Jordaan—is home to a diverse array of shops mixing festive, inventive, nostalgic, practical, and artistic items. Trendy cafés dot the area. While ubiquitous chain stores are sneaking in and it's not quite as artsy or funky as it once was, this zone remains a very convenient place to browse. Walking west from the Amsterdam Museum/Spui Square or south from the Anne Frank House puts you right in the thick of things. For a preview, see https://de9straatjes.nl.

The cross streets make a tic-tac-toe with a couple of canals and bicycle-friendly canalside streets just west of Kalverstraat. Because each street changes names when it crosses a canal, this small area really does include nine separate little streets (hence the name). Here are a few pointers on what you can expect to find on each street, from south to north (but visit them in any order you like):

**South Strip:** Starting from Spui and heading west, **Wijde Heisteeg** is the shortest of the little streets, with a deli, a cheese store, and some clothes shops. **Huidenstraat** is more clothes-oriented, from fancy and vintage-fashion boutiques to bags, jewelry, and shoes, as well as the recommended Pompadour chocolate/pastry shop. **Runstraat** has a line down the block for Fabel Friet (at #1), which serves Dutch fries topped with Parmesan or cheddar cheese and a variety of sauces. You'll also find yet more clothes and an excellent, well-stocked cheese shop (De Kaaskamer van Amsterdam, ideal for stocking a memorable picnic, at #7). From where Runstraat hits the Prinsengracht canal, it's a short stroll south to The Frozen Fountain design shop, described earlier.

**Center Strip:** In general, this zone feels a bit more yuppie/posh than the others. From east to west, first you'll come to **Oude Spiegelstraat,** a short stretch with some fashion boutiques. **Wolvenstraat** has some upscale clothing shops and several eateries, plus an upscale supermarket called Jumbo. **Berenstraat** is a bit younger and more dynamic, with a large vintage-clothes store.

**North Strip:** The funkiest of the nine streets, **Gasthuismolensteeg** has vintage shops and a hole-in-the-wall selling world folk art. **Hartenstraat** is loaded with upscale clothes, shoes, and accessories shops, as well as a game shop and hip home decor (at DR Wonen, #27). **Reestraat** has yet more clothing stores, as well as a bit more variety—including vintage shops.

**North of the Nine Little Streets:** The area just north of the Nine Little Streets and Anne Frank House—particularly the Herenstraat/Prinsenstraat corridor between Damrak and the Jordaan—is another fine place to browse. If you're looking for jewelry, accessories, trendy clothing, and fancy delicatessens, this may be an expensive but rewarding stroll. **Herenstraat** feels relatively local-oriented, with upscale clothes, home decor, and shops that ooze creativity and charm. **Prinsenstraat** is a bit more youthful, with more fashion galleries and eateries.

## Haarlemmerstraat/Haarlemmerdijk

The area just west of Centraal station has morphed from a bit grotty into a thriving and trendy string of shops, cafés, and restaurants.

It's edgier and more in-your-face than the sleepy Jordaan, but still more accessible than the Red Light District. It's the kind of place where you'll see "coffeeshops" (selling green "coffee," a.k.a. marijuana, to tourists) mixed in with coffee shops (selling gourmet black coffee to residents). And it has arguably the most inspired and eclectic assortment of shops in Amsterdam—a browse here is a fun chance to spot new trends, and maybe to pick up some local clothes and goods (vintage and casual young fashions abound). The former dike along what was Amsterdam's harborfront provides the high spine of this neighborhood. From the Singel canal near Centraal station, this lively drag leads a half-mile west along a colorful string of lanes all the way to Haarlem Gate, a triumphal arch built in the 1840s.

From the train station, follow the canal west, then use the underpass to go beneath the busy traffic bridge. Emerging, turn right across the smaller bridge (passing my favorite herring stand—Stubbe's Haring, on the bridge—then a cluster of coffeeshops on the left) and continue straight down **Haarlemmerstraat.** Near the start of the street, on the left, is Wini Vintage (at #29), with well-curated finds that may tempt even those turned off by their hometown Salvation Army. This boutique sets the tone for the street, which features secondhand shops, ironic T-shirts, young and casual fashion, international takeaway joints, internationals taking away joints, hair salons, nail parlors, launderettes, and more, all under leaning gables.

After crossing the canal, you'll continue on **Haarlemmerdijk.** Things get even more artsy and eclectic along here, and it feels a bit less seedy (more urbane/Jordaan, less touristy/Red Light District). As you browse, keep an eye out for some beautiful Art Nouveau facades (on the left, at #39, #43, and #51) shuffled among the brick gables. The street ends at The Movies, an art-house cinema with a built-in *eetcafé.* You'll pop out at the relaxing Haarlemmerplein, with its wannabe-Brandenburg Gate.

## Staalstraat

This lively street, just east of the university zone, boasts an array of creative design shops, whimsical doodads, and vintage shops. It's a quick walk from the bustling Rokin zone. From where the canal hits Rokin (by the boat-tour kiosk), head east (with the canal at your back, turn right) down Langebrugsteeg/Grimburgwal. At the second canal you cross, when you dead-end at the university buildings, jog left and go through the stone arch of the **Oudemanhuis- poort Book Market** (described earlier in this chapter). Halfway through the market, duck through the student-filled courtyard on the right; when you pop out onto Vendelstraat, turn left, then jog right to go over the bridge. This marks the start of Staalstraat.

Keep an eye out for **Mario Shop** (at #5), a smartshop selling intense, sometimes mind-bending herbal supplements (for more on smartshops, see page 118). **Puccini Bomboni** (#17) is an outpost of the top-of-the-line local chain selling varied and expensive Belgian-style pralines (described earlier in this chapter).

The street ends at yet another bridge (with Frenzi Café). Crossing this and turning left (at the "Stopera" music center), you'll follow the canal up to the bustling **Waterlooplein flea market.** The somewhat sketchy-feeling streets just north of Waterlooplein—past the colorful tattoo parlors—are fertile breeding grounds for smart young designers; poking around here you'll discover some shops on the cutting edge of Amsterdam's young fashion scene.

## The Jordaan

Once a working-class district, this colorful old neighborhood is now upscale—a veritable wonderland of funky shops. But they're not as concentrated in the Jordaan as they are along Staalstraat, Haarlemmerdijk, or the Nine Little Streets (described earlier). Here are a few areas to focus on:

On Mondays, you'll find the busy **Noordermarkt** market at the end of Westerstraat and spilling onto the neighboring street, Lindengracht.

**Rozengracht,** the wide street just southwest of the Anne Frank House, has several eclectic shops (though the busy traffic makes lingering in the area less enticing). Kitsch Kitchen, near the big canal, has a fun, colorful collection of mostly Latin American-themed kitsch (at #8).

**Antiekcentrum Amsterdam** isn't just an antique mall—it's a sprawling warren of display cases crammed with historic bric-a-brac (including lots of smaller items, easily packed home), and all of it for sale. You'll find everything from old helmets and medals to vintage blue tiles (Mon and Wed-Fri 11:00-18:00, Sat-Sun until 17:00, closed Tue, Elandsgracht 109, +31 20 624 9038). While you're in the neighborhood, browse **Elandsgracht**'s many specialty food stores (high-end butcher, bakery, and so on). The cross street **Hazenstraat** has a fine assortment of art galleries and other shops.

**Eerste** and **Tweede Egelantiersdwarsstraat,** both lined with great restaurants and recommended in the Eating in Amsterdam chapter, also have some fun shops mixed in. For unique kids' gifts, head to the **Mouse Mansion** (Het Muizenhuis, at Eerste Tuindwarsstraat 1), a family-run shop with books (available in English) and toys featuring the creations of Karina Schaapman. Using recycled materials, she started building the original mouse house in 2008 to photograph for a children's book and has been expanding the mouse world since. The shop is crammed with mice at work and play in intricately detailed displays—and you can buy books, puzzles, mice, and DIY house kits as well (closed Mon-Tue, www.themousemansion.com).

## Other Shopping Areas
### Kalverstraat-Heiligeweg-Spui

This is the busiest shopping corridor in town. Kalverstraat, a pedestrian street, is a human traffic jam of low-end shoppers. It's clogged with cheap and midrange international chains—Forever 21, Pull and Bear, Desigual, Pimkie, Urban Outfitters, Mango, Claire's, Zara, Bershka, and so on, along with the big Hema department store (described earlier). It feels soulless, but if you explore the fringes, there are some interesting places.

### Spiegelkwartier

Located between the Rijksmuseum and the city center, this is *the* place for art and antiques. You'll find 70 dealers offering 17th-century furniture, old Delftware, Oriental art, clocks, jewelry, and Art Nouveau doodads. Wander down Spiegelgracht and Nieuwe Spiegelstraat. **Leidsestraat,** just to the west, is a tourist artery clogged with pedestrians, bikes, trams, and some trendy international shops.

## Magna Plaza Shopping Center

Formerly the main post office, this grand 19th-century building has been transformed into a stylish mall with 40 boutiques. You'll find fashion, luxury goods, and gift shops galore. It's just behind the Royal Palace a block off Dam Square.

## P. C. Hooftstraat

The city's most expensive shopping street, with a storefront for nearly every top-name designer, is between Museumplein and Vondelpark.

# ENTERTAINMENT IN AMSTERDAM

Many Amsterdam hotels serve breakfast until 11:00 because so many people—visitors and locals—live for nighttime in this city.

On summer evenings, people flock to the main squares for drinks at outdoor tables. Leidseplein is the liveliest square, surrounded by theaters, restaurants, and nightclubs. The slightly quieter Rembrandtplein (with adjoining Thorbeckeplein and nearby Reguliersdwarsstraat) is the center of gay clubs and nightlife. Spui features a full city block of bars. And Nieuwmarkt, on the east edge of the Red Light District, is a bit rough but probably the least touristy.

The Red Light District (particularly Oudezijds Achterburgwal) is less sleazy in the early evening, and almost carnival-like as the neon lights come on and the streets fill with tourists. But it starts to feel scuzzy after about 22:30 (☐ see the Red Light District Walk chapter).

The **brown cafés** recommended on page 221 are ideal after-hours hangouts. Peruse those listings for pre- or post-dinner drink ideas.

## INFORMATION

The TI's website, www.iamsterdam.com, has good English listings for upcoming events (select "See and do," then "What's on"). Newsstands sell the *I Amsterdam* entertainment guide and Dutch newspapers (Thu editions generally list events). *Uitkrant* is in Dutch, but it's just a calendar of events, and anyone can figure out the name of the event and its date, time, and location (available at TIs, bars, and bookstores).

## MUSIC

You'll find classical music at the **Concertgebouw** (free 12:30 lunch concerts on Wed except in July and Aug; arrive at 12:00 for best first-come, first-served seating; at far south end of Museumplein, +31 900 671 8345, www.concertgebouw.nl). For chamber music and contemporary works, visit the **Muziekgebouw aan 't IJ,** a mod concert hall on the waterfront, near the train station (Piet Heinkade 1, +31 20 788 2000, www.muziekgebouw.nl). For opera and dance, try the **opera house** in the Stopera building (Amstel 3, +31 20 625 5455, www.operaballet.nl). In the summer, Vondelpark hosts open-air concerts.

Three of Amsterdam's historic churches have extensive music programs. In summer, the **Westerkerk** has free lunchtime concerts most Wednesdays at 13:00 (summer only—check their website for schedule), plus an annual Bach organ-concert cycle in August (Prinsengracht 281, +31 20 624 7766, www.westerkerk.nl). The **New Church** offers periodic organ concerts and a religious-music festival in June (included in €9-16 church entry, Dam Square, +31 20 626 8168, www.nieuwekerk.nl). The Red Light District's **Old Church** (Oude Kerk) hosts occasional concerts, listed on their website (Oudekerksplein 23, +31 20 625 8284, https://oudekerk.nl).

Jazz has a long tradition at the **Bimhuis** nightclub, now housed in a black box jutting out from the Muziekgebouw performance hall, right on the waterfront. Its great bar has citywide views and is open to the public after concerts (Piet Heinkade 3, +31 20 788 2188, www.bimhuis.com).

The nearby town of Haarlem offers free pipe-organ concerts on Tuesday evenings in summer at its 15th-century church, the **Grote Kerk** (at 20:15 mid-May-mid-Oct, additional concerts Thu at 16:00 July-Aug).

## COUNTERCULTURE HISTORY

If you're a child of the 1970s, you may have a warm spot for Melkweg and Paradiso—the granddaddies of Amsterdam clubs. Today, the beat goes on at these two rock-music (and hip-hop) clubs, just off Leidseplein.

**Paradiso** was once the church of a former prison complex that was taken by squatters (artists and musicians) in the 1960s. The city allowed it because of the creative work the squatters contributed to local culture. But, not surprisingly, the scene attracted drug users. The first pot-selling coffeeshops were here at Paradiso, which was also the venue for rising (and falling) counterculture stars. Today they still present big-name acts you might recognize... if you're younger than me (Weteringschans 6, +31 20 626 4521, www.paradiso.nl).

**Melkweg** has a similar history going back to the 1960s and offers a comparable lineup to Paradiso's (Lijnbaansgracht 234a, +31 20 531 8181, www.melkweg.nl).

## COMEDY

**Boom Chicago,** an R-rated comedy improv act, was started more than 25 years ago by a group of Americans on a graduation tour. They have been entertaining tourists and locals ever since, and some of their alumni (Seth Meyers, Jason Sudeikis, Jordan Peele) have gone on to great fame among stateside comedy fans. The two-hour English-only show is a series of rude, clever, and high-energy sketches mixed with improv games, all offering a raucous look at both Dutch culture and local tourism. The big, boxy, 300-seat Rozentheater has small tables for drinks—you can text your order to the bar. If you need a break from museums and canal boat tours, this might be the ticket (€22-29, evening shows Tue-Sun—check schedule at their website, no shows Mon, ticket office open daily from 15:00 until 15 minutes after curtain time, in the Jordaan a couple of long blocks past Westerkerk at Rozengracht 117, +31 20 217 0400, www.boomchicago.nl).

## THEATER

Amsterdam is one of the world centers for experimental live theater (much of it in English). Many theaters cluster around the street called the Nes, which stretches south from Dam Square, parallel-ing the wide street named Rokin. Along here you'll find theaters big and small, as well as cafés and eateries catering to the pre- and post-theater crowd. Most of the shows are oriented to Dutch audi-ences, but some are in English (or work in any language). You can browse the offerings on the theaters' websites: **Vlaams Cultuurhuis de Brakke Grond** (at #45, creative and artistic performances from cutting-edge Flanders/Belgium, options suitable for an "interna-tional audience" listed on their website, www.brakkegrond.nl), **Frascati** (at #63, off-Broadway-style experimental theater by most-ly Dutch artists, www.frascatitheater.nl), and **Tobacco Theater** (at #75, concerts and shows in an industrial space, www.tobacco.nl).

## MOVIES

In the Netherlands, most movies are subtitled, rather than dubbed, so English-only speakers have plenty of cinematic options. It's not unusual for movies at many cinemas to be sold out—consider buy-ing tickets during the day. Catch modern movies in the 1920s set-ting of the classic **Tuschinski Theater** (between Muntplein and Rembrandtplein, described on page 67). Seats are pricey, but the experience is more than a movie.

The splashy **EYE Filmmuseum Netherlands,** across the

water from Centraal station, is another memorable place to see a movie (described on page 80).

## MUSEUMS

Several museums stay open late. The **Anne Frank House** is open until 22:00 (requires timed-entry ticket purchased in advance).

The **Hash, Marijuana, and Hemp Museum** is open daily until 22:00. And the **Erotic Museum** and **Red Light Secrets Museum of Prostitution** stay open until at least 22:00.

## SKATING AFTER DARK

Amsterdammers get their skating fix every Friday night in Vondelpark. Huge groups don in-line skates and meet at the round bench near the Vondel Pavilion (around 20:15, www.fridaynightskate. com). Anyone can join in. Ask your hotelier about the nearest place to rent skates, or try SkateDoktor, though it's 1.5 miles north of the park (€10/day, valid ID for deposit; Tue-Sat 10:00-17:30, closed Sun-Mon; Jan van Galenstraat 161, +31 20 260 0055, www. skatedokter.nl).

# AMSTERDAM CONNECTIONS

The Netherlands is so small, level, and well covered by trains and buses that transportation is a snap. Buses take you where trains don't go, and bicycles take you where buses don't go. Bus stations and bike-rental shops cluster around train stations. Easy-to-navigate Schiphol Airport is well connected to Amsterdam and other destinations by bus and train. Use the comprehensive transit website www.9292.nl to plan connections inside the Netherlands by train, bus, or both. For more tips on how to buy train tickets and information on tickets, deals, and rail passes, see the Transportation section of the Practicalities chapter.

## By Train

Amsterdam is the country's hub, but all major cities are linked by speedy trains that come and go every 15 minutes or so. Dutch rail schedules are online at www.ns.nl (domestic) and www.nshispeed.nl (international). Google Maps also does a good job of giving you real-time schedules, including departures, transfers, and which track *(spoor)* your train will use.

If you have a rail pass, it's quicker to validate it via app or in person when you arrive at Schiphol Airport than at Amsterdam's Centraal station, but keep in mind that you don't need to start using your rail pass that day; you could buy an inexpensive point-to-point ticket into Amsterdam and save your rail-pass travel days for a longer journey.

The train-information center at Amsterdam's Centraal station can require a long wait. Save lots of time by getting international train tickets and information at a small-town station (such as Haarlem), the airport upon arrival, or online.

Budget travelers and rail-pass holders heading to Brussels or

# Amsterdam Connections

25 Kilometers
25 Miles

Leeuwarden

Harlingen

To Amsterdam

Texel

Den
Helder

Hindeloopen

AFSLUITDIJK (A-7)

Stavoren

IJsselmeer

Medemblik

ZUIDERZEE
MUSEUM

NORTH

North
Sea

Alkmaar

Enkhuizen

Urk

SCHOKLAND

HOUTRIBDIJK (N-302)

Hoorn

Markermeer

ZAANSE
SCHANS

Edam

To Newcastle,
England

Zaandijk
Zaanse Schans

Volendam

Lelystad

FLEVOLAND

Sloter-
dijk

Zaandam

Marken

IJmuiden

Haarlem

Amsterdam

Zandvoort

Lisse
(KEUKENHOF)

Schiphol

EAST

To Hanover
& Berlin

Leiden

Aalsmeer
(AUCTION)

Amersfoort

KRÖLLER-
MÜLLER
MUSEUM

Scheveningen

SOUTH

The
Hague

Tram

Utrecht

Otterlo

NETH.
OPEN-AIR
MUSEUM

Delft

Hoek

To
Harwich,
England

Ede-Wageningen

Gouda

Arnhem

To Cologne
& Rhine

Rotterdam

| | Rail |
| | Bus |
| | Tram |
| | Boat |

To Brussels
& Paris

Antwerp should avoid the pricey Thalys train and take an InterCity (IC) train instead. For details, see page 494.

Thalys has a monopoly on direct trains between Amsterdam and Paris. Rail-pass holders need to buy a seat reservation (these can sell out quite early), and the pass must cover both ends of the trip.

## AMSTERDAM CENTRAAL STATION
See "Arrival in Amsterdam" on page 42 for more details on station services.

## By Train to Domestic Destinations
**Schiphol Airport** (8/hour, 20 minutes), **Haarlem** (8/hour, 20

AMSTERDAM CONNECTIONS

minutes; see page 292 for a train-window tour of the countryside), **Keukenhof** (catch train to Leiden—4/hour, 45 minutes; then bus #854, called Keukenhof Express, to garden—4/hour, 30 minutes), **Aalsmeer** (take the bus; see "By Bus," later), **Zandvoort** (2/hour, 30 minutes), **Leiden** (9/hour, 45 minutes, some with transfer), **Delft** (2/hour, 1 hour, more with transfer), **The Hague/Den Haag** (4/hour, 50 minutes, more with change in Leiden), **Rotterdam** (4/hour on express ICD train, 45 minutes), **Arnhem** (3/hour, 1 hour, more with transfer in Utrecht), **Kröller-Müller Museum/Hoge Veluwe National Park** (get off at Ede-Wageningen—hourly, 1 hour, half with transfer in Utrecht; from Ede-Wageningen, take bus to Otterlo near park entrance—1-2/hour, 20 minutes), **Utrecht** (6/hour, 30 minutes), **Edam/Volendam/Marken** (take the bus; see "By Bus," later), **Hoorn** (2/hour, 30 minutes), **Enkhuizen/Zuiderzee Museum** (2/hour, 1 hour), **Alkmaar** (4/hour, 40 minutes), **Zaanse Schans Open-Air Museum** (get off at Zaandijk Zaanse Schans station; train direction: Uitgeest; 4/hour, 15 minutes, then 15-minute walk).

## By Train to International Destinations

**Bruges** (hourly, 3-4 hours; fastest connection changes in Brussels; otherwise change in Antwerp and Ghent, if possible avoid costly Thalys trains), **Brussels** (hourly, 2 hours direct by pricey Thalys to Midi/Zuid station; otherwise hourly, 3 hours direct on cheaper IC train to all three Brussels stations), **Antwerp** (every 1-2 hours, 1.25 hours by pricey Thalys; otherwise hourly, 1.75 hours by cheaper IC trains), **Copenhagen** (3/day, 12 hours, multiple transfers), **Bacharach/St. Goar** (roughly every 2 hours, 5.5 hours), **Frankfurt** (every 2 hours, 5 hours direct), **Berlin** (5/day, 6.5 hours, transfer in Hannover), **Munich** (roughly hourly, 9 hours with 1-2 transfers), **Bern** (5/day, 8-10 hours, fastest trains change once in Frankfurt), **Paris** (nearly hourly, 3.25 hours direct on fast Thalys train or 4.75 hours with change to Thalys train in Brussels, www.thalys.com). Save money by taking a bus to Paris—see "By Bus," later.

## By Eurostar Train to London

The Eurostar zips from Amsterdam to **London** at 190 mph in 4 hours (3/day, more with transfer in Brussels, also stops at Rotterdam). The tunnel crossing under the English Channel is a 20-minute, silent, 100 mph nonevent. Your ears won't even pop.

**Eurostar Tickets and Fares:** One-way tickets between Amsterdam and London vary widely in price; for instance, $45-235 (Standard class), $105-265 (Standard Premier), and $345 (Business Premier). Fares depend on how far ahead you reserve and whether you're eligible for any discounts—available for children (under 12), youths (under 26), and adults booking months ahead or purchasing round-trip. You can book tickets up to six months in advance. Tickets can be exchanged before the scheduled departure for a fee (about $55, may be waived for early exchanges) plus the cost of any

**Rail Routes**

price increase, but only Business Premier class allows any refund.

Buy tickets ahead at www. ricksteves.com/rail or at www. eurostar.com (Dutch +31 20 716 8325, with €14 phone-handling fee). In continental Europe, you can buy tickets at any major train station in any country or at any travel agency that handles train tickets (expect a booking fee). In Britain, tickets are issued only at the Eurostar office in the St. Pancras train station.

If you have a Eurail Global Pass, seat reservations are available at Eurostar departure stations, www.eurail.com, or by phone with Eurostar (generally harder to get at other train stations and travel agencies; $35 in Standard, $45 in Standard Premier, can sell out).

**Taking the Eurostar:** Trains depart from and arrive at Amsterdam Centraal, on the north side of the station near track 15B. Arrive early to go through security and passport control (must be completed at least 45 minutes before departure) and locate your departure track (shown on a TV monitor).

# By Bus

The biggest companies serving towns near Amsterdam are Arriva (www.arriva.nl) and Connexxion (www.connexxion.nl).

**From Amsterdam by Bus to: Edam/Volendam** (EBS bus #312, #314, or #316; 3/hour, fewer after 18:30 and on weekends, 30 minutes), **Marken** (bus #315, 2/hour, 30 minutes), **Aalsmeer Flower Auction** (Connexxion bus #357, 2/hour, 1 hour). Buses depart from just north of Amsterdam's Centraal station (exit station through the back of the west passageway and head up the escalator). Bus #391 departs from Centraal station Platform E to **Zaanse Schans** (3/hour, 40 minutes).

**To Paris by Bus:** Without a rail pass, the cheapest way to get to Paris is on a Eurolines or FlixBus bus (about 12/day including night buses, 8 hours, about €46 one-way, €80 round-trip; price depends on demand—nonrefundable, advance-purchase one-way tickets as cheap as €17 and round-trip as cheap as €28, check online for deals; Eurolines leaves from Amsterdam Duivendrecht station,

8 stops by Metro from Centraal station, French +33 141 862 421, www.eurolines.eu; FlixBus leaves from Amsterdam Sloterdijk station, UK +44 178 829 8784, www.flixbus.com).

# By Plane

## SCHIPHOL AIRPORT

Schiphol (SKIP-pol) Airport is located about 10 miles southwest of Amsterdam's city center. Like most of Holland, it is user-friendly and below sea level. With an appealing array of shops, eateries, and other time-killing opportunities, Schiphol is a fine place to arrive, depart, or change planes. A truly international airport, Schiphol has done away with Dutch—signs are in English only.

**Information:** Find Schiphol flight times and airline contact info at their website or on their free app (code: AMS, +31 20 794 0800, www.schiphol.nl).

**Orientation:** Though Schiphol officially has four terminals, it's really just one big building. You could walk it end to end in about 20 minutes (but allow plenty of time to pass through security checkpoints between terminals). Interactive info kiosks and the Schiphol app have handy maps to find nearby services and eateries. All terminals have free Wi-Fi. An inviting shopping and eating zone called Holland Boulevard runs between Terminals 2 and 3.

**Arrival at Schiphol:** Baggage-claim areas for all terminals empty into the same central zone, officially called Schiphol Plaza but generally signed *Arrivals Hall*. It's a big atrium of shops, tourist services, a busy **TI** (near Terminal 2, daily 7:00-22:00), and transportation options for getting into the city: train, bus, taxi, and Uber.

**Services:** Avoid the Travelex **ATMs** around the airport that charge high exchange rates, and hold out for a bank ATM. **Service Point,** in Schiphol Plaza at the end of the shopping mall near Terminal 4, is a useful all-purpose service counter that sells SIM cards, prints tickets, and ships packages (daily 7:00-22:00). Convenient **luggage lockers** are at various points—allowing you to leave your bag here on a lengthy layover (both short- and long-term lockers, cash and cards accepted; biggest bank of lockers near the train station at Schiphol Plaza). If you're leaving from Schiphol and need to get VAT forms stamped, the customs office is next to gate F2.

If you'll be traveling by rail, take advantage of the **"Train Tickets and Services" counter** (Schiphol Plaza ground level, across from Burger King). They have an easy info desk and generally short lines—so transactions here tend to be much quicker than at Amsterdam's Centraal station ticket desks. While you're here, consider validating your rail pass, booking future international train tickets, and making seat reservations for later in your trip.

**Time-Killing Tips:** If you have extra time at Schiphol, check out the **Rijksmuseum Amsterdam Schiphol,** a little art gallery and museum store on Holland Boulevard, the lively shopping/eating zone between Lounges 2 and 3. The Rijksmuseum loans a dozen or so of its minor masterpieces from the Dutch golden age to this unique airport museum, including actual Dutch Masters (free, always open, gift shop good for last-minute gifts). Or, to escape the airport crowds, follow signs for the **Panorama Terrace** to the third floor of Terminal 2, where you'll find a quieter, full-of-locals cafeteria, a kids' play area, and a view terrace where you can watch planes come and go while you nurse a coffee. If you plan to visit the terrace on arrival, stop there before you pass through customs.

## From Schiphol Airport to Amsterdam

To get between Schiphol and downtown Amsterdam, you have several options, all leaving from Schiphol Plaza:

**By Train:** This is your fastest and cheapest option. Direct trains to Amsterdam's Centraal station run frequently from Schiphol Plaza (4-6/hour, 20 minutes, €5.70, shortest lines at ticket machines near baggage claim). Ticket machines accept coins and contactless credit cards (start the no-brainer transaction by pressing "I want to go to Amsterdam Centraal"). Schiphol's train station also serves other destinations (see next section). When traveling *from* Amsterdam Centraal to Schiphol, trains generally leave every 15 minutes from track 14a.

Before buying your train ticket into Amsterdam, consider various passes and options that include both the train ride from the airport and the tram-bus-Metro system in the city. If you're only going to Amsterdam and you're also leaving from the airport, consider the **Amsterdam Travel Ticket.** It covers all city trams and buses, as well as the train ride to and from Schiphol (€17/1 day, €22.50/2 days, €28/3 days, http://en.gvb.nl/amsterdam-travel-ticket).

**By Public Bus to Leidseplein:** Connexxion #397 is handy for those going to the Leidseplein district (€6.50, buy ticket from driver—credit card only, departs from lane B17 in front of the airport).

**By Taxi:** Allow about €50 to downtown Amsterdam by regular **taxi.** Hotels may have cabs offering a fixed-price airport deal; ask your hotelier for details. **Uber** serves the airport for about €36. The pickup spot is just outside the car-rental offices in Schiphol Plaza.

## From Schiphol Airport to Other Destinations

**To Haarlem:** The big red #300 **bus** is direct, stopping at Haarlem's train station and near the Grote Markt/Market Square (every 10 minutes, 40 minutes, €6.50, buy ticket from driver—credit card only, departs from lane B4 in front of airport). The **train** is just as quick, but you'll have to transfer at Amsterdam Sloterdijk station (6/hour, 30-40 minutes). Figure about €40 to Haarlem by **taxi.**

**By Train to: Delft** (7/hour, 45 minutes, some with transfer in Leiden), **The Hague/Den Haag** (4/hour, 30-40 minutes, more with change in Leiden), **Rotterdam** (5/hour, 30 minutes), **Bruges** (hourly, 3-3.5 hours, change in Antwerp or Brussels), **Brussels** (hourly, 3 hours on IC to Brussels' three main stations; hourly, 1.5 hours on pricey Thalys to Midi/Zuid station).

**By Bus to: Keukenhof** (bus #858, Keukenhof Express, 8/hour, 40 minutes).

## By Cruise Ship

Most ships arrive at **Passenger Terminal Amsterdam** (PTA), a short tram ride or walk along the water to Centraal station. From the cruise terminal, cross the busy portside street to the stop for tram #26 and ride it one stop to Centraal station. To walk, turn right as you exit the terminal and stroll with the water on your right for about 15 minutes toward the station's glass-and-steel arch. From the station, you can follow my self-guided walk, or hop a train to other nearby destinations (connections listed earlier).

To go directly from the cruise terminal to the Rijksmuseum or Van Gogh Museum, take a taxi or the tram (see "Getting Around Amsterdam" on page 45). The nearest bike rental is AmsterBike, just to the right of the PTA exit (www.amsterbike.eu); more bike-rental options are near Centraal station.

A few ships dock at **Felison Terminal** in IJmuiden. Connexxion buses run to Amsterdam Sloterdijk station (bus #82) and Haarlem (bus #385); see www.felisonterminal.nl.

For more details, see my *Rick Steves Scandinavian & Northern European Cruise Ports* book.

# HAARLEM

# HAARLEM

A golden age kind of town, cute and cozy Haarlem is quintessentially Dutch. With small-town warmth and easy access to Amsterdam or Schiphol Airport (20-30 minutes by train), it makes a good home base. It's a bit less romantic than Amsterdam (lacking the many canals and footbridges)—but it's also much more user-friendly, making it a good choice as a "soft landing" after a long flight or simply as a break from intense Amsterdam.

In the heart of Haarlem, the Gothic Grote Kerk, or Great Church, towers over the market square (Grote Markt). To uncover more of Haarlem's sights, dodge bikes down the narrow, characteristic lanes. The top museum in town features the work of its most famous son, portrait-artist Frans Hals. The Corrie ten Boom House relates the inspirational story of a family that courageously hid Jews from the Nazis. And the Teylers Museum is like a museum of museums—a time-warp to an authentic 18th-century collection of science and art treasures. There's even a windmill that you can clamber around inside. And if it's a sunny day, head to the beach at nearby Zandvoort or just go for a pedal through the polderland.

## Orientation to Haarlem

Haarlem, with about 160,000 inhabitants, feels like a small town. At its eastern edge, the city gate—no longer needed as fortification—welcomes all into Haarlem's old center. Bustling Haarlem gave America's Harlem its name back when New York was New Amsterdam, a Dutch colony. For centuries, Haarlem has been a market town, buzzing with shoppers heading home with fresh bouquets.

Enjoy the smaller market on Monday (clothing) or the big one on Saturday (general), when the town's atmospheric main square bustles like a Brueghel painting, with cheese, fish, flowers, and families. Make yourself at home; buy some flowers to brighten your hotel room.

## TOURIST INFORMATION

Haarlem's **TI** (VVV), in the Town Hall building on Grote Markt, is friendlier, more helpful, and less crowded than Amsterdam's, so ask your Amsterdam questions here (Mon-Sat 10:00-17:00, Sun 11:00-15:00 except closed Sun Oct-March, shorter hours off-season and when it's quiet, +31 23 531 7325, www.visithaarlem.com).

Next door to the TI is the free **Anno Haarlem** exhibit, a humble yet thoughtful introduction to Haarlem with a short film about the evolution of local industry, art, and architecture. Sincere volunteers are eager to answer your questions about the town's history (limited hours, likely Thu-Sat 10:00-16:00, closed Sun-Wed).

## ARRIVAL IN HAARLEM

**By Train:** Lockers are available at the station at the very end of platform 3A (the far-left end of the middle platform, as you face the main hall; pay by card only). Two parallel streets flank the train station: Kruisweg and Jansweg. Head up either one and you'll reach the town square and church in about 10 minutes. If you need help, ask someone to point you toward Grote Markt (Market Square). If you're arriving by train from Amsterdam, see the "Amsterdam to Haarlem Train Tour" later in this chapter for a description of sights you'll see along the way.

**By Bus:** Buses from Schiphol Airport stop at the train station and in the center (Centrum/Verwulft stop, a short walk south of Grote Markt).

**By Car:** Street parking is expensive (€5/hour). Several central garages are more affordable (most are €3.50/hour, then €3.50 overnight—19:00-8:00, www.parkeren-haarlem.nl): Try Parkeergarage Kamp at the southern end of Gedempte Oude Gracht (the main thoroughfare), Parkeergarage Raaks at the western edge of town (just inside the canal), and Parkeergarage Houtplein near the Frans Hals Museum's main building (Hof). The most central is the Parkeergarage Appelaar, near the Teylers Museum; it's also the most expensive. The Interparking garage near the train station is operated by a different company and cheaper if you prebook online (www.parkerencentrumhaarlem.nl).

**By Plane:** For details on getting from Schiphol Airport to Haarlem, see the end of this chapter.

## HELPFUL HINTS

**Blue Monday and Early Closures:** Most sights are closed on Monday, except the Grote Kerk, De Adriaan Windmill, and

Verwey Museum Haarlem. The Corrie ten Boom House is closed on Sunday and Monday, and closes early the rest of the week (15:30).

**Sightseeing Tips:** The Museumkaart discount card covers entry to Haarlem's Frans Hals Museum, Museum Haarlem, and Teylers Museum (potentially worthwhile for those also visiting Amsterdam, www.museumkaart.nl).

**Laundry:** Handy and fairly central, **My Beautiful Launderette** is on a quiet square a short walk south of Grote Markt (self-service wash and dry daily 8:30-20:30, full service available Mon-Fri 9:00-17:00, Botermarkt 20). For location see the "Haarlem Hotels and Restaurants" map, later.

**Bike Rental:** Two good bike-rental options are near the train station. Both charge similar rates, have a range of bikes, and are open long hours daily (more in good weather, less in bad weather): **Green Bikes,** on the right as you exit into the big plaza in front of the station (Kruisweg 30, +31 23 751 6512, www.greenbikes.nl), and **Rent a Bike Haarlem,** tucked around behind the big parking garage in front of the station (Lange Herenstraat 36, +31 23 542 1195, www.rentabikehaarlem.nl).

**Taxi:** Taxis are pricey; figure no less than €10 for even a short ride in town. Uber also operates here and may be marginally cheaper.

**Canal Cruise:** Two companies do lazy cruises on Haarlem's canal; in both cases, it's smart to prebook online in nice weather to ensure a seat. Both depart from across the canal from Teylers Museum. **Smidtje Cruise,** the bigger outfit, does a scenic 50-minute loop through and around Haarlem; the captain may provide some commentary in Dutch and a bit of English, or you may be given an audioguide, but either way the trip is more relaxing than informative (€16, departs at the top of the hour daily 11:00-16:00, no cruises Nov-March, Spaarne 11a, +31 23 535 7723, www.smidtjecanalcruises.nl). **Haarlem Canal Tours,** run by Jeroen, is a smaller, friendlier, more intimate option, using an open 12-person boat (€16, 1.25 hours, generally departs every 1.5 hours daily 11:00-17:30, may not run in bad weather or off-season, Spaarne 17, www.haarlemcanaltours.com).

## Grote Markt Spin Tour

Haarlem's ▲▲ Grote Markt (Market Square), where 10 streets converge, is the town's delightful centerpiece...as it has been for 700 years. To enjoy a coffee or beer here, simmering in Dutch good living, is a quintessential European experience. Observe. Sit and gaze at the church, appreciating essentially the same scene that

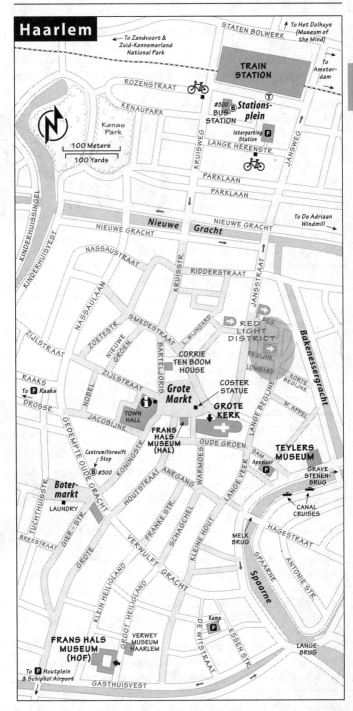

# Haarlem

STATEN BOLWERK

To Het Dolhuys (Museum of the Mind)

To Zandvoort & Zuid-Kennemerland National Park

TRAIN STATION

To Amster-dam

ROZENSTRAAT

KENAUPARK

#300 BUS STATION

Stations-plein

Kenau Park

Interparking Station

100 Meters

100 Yards

LANGE HERENSTR.

JANSWEG

KRUISWEG

PARKLAAN

PARKLAAN

KINDERHUISSINGEL

Nieuwe Gracht

NIEUWE GRACHT

To De Adriaan Windmill

NIEUWE GRACHT

NASSAUSTRAAT

KINDERHUISVEST

KRUISSTR.

RIDDERSTRAAT

JANSSTRAAT

NASSAULAAN

ZIJLSTRAAT

ZOETESTR.

SMEDESTRAAT

NIEUWE GROEN.

L. WIJNGARD

RED LIGHT DISTRICT

D. BEG

BAKENESSERGRACHT

BARTELJORIS

CORRIE TEN BOOM HOUSE

BEGIJNE

ZIJLSTRAAT

NOBEL

Grote Markt

COSTER STATUE

LOMBARD

KORTE BEGIJNE

RAAKS

To Raaks

DROSSE.

TOWN HALL

GROTE KERK

LANGE BEGIJNE

W. APPEL

JACOBIJNE

FRANS HALS MUSEUM (HAL)

OUDE GROEN.

TEYLERS MUSEUM

GEDEMPTE OUDE GRACHT

Centrum/Verwulft Stop

#300

KONINGSTR.

WARMOES

DAM

Appelaar

GRAVE STENEN-BRUG

Botermarkt

HOUTSTRAAT

ANEGANG

LANGE VEER

CANAL CRUISES

TUCHTHUISSTR.

LAUNDRY

GIER-STR.

FRANKE STR.

SCHAGCHEL

KLEINE HOUT

HAGESTRAAT

BREESTRAAT

GROTE

VERWULFT

MELK BRUG

ANTONIE STR.

VERWULFT GRACHT

SPAARNE

KLEIN HEILIGLAND

FRANS HALS MUSEUM (HOF)

GROOT HEILIGLAND

VERWEY MUSEUM HAARLEM

DE WITSTRAAT

Kamp

ESSEN STR.

LANGE-BRUG

To Houtplein & Schiphol Airport

GASTHUISVEST

Dutch artists captured centuries ago in oil paintings that now hang in museums.

Until the 1990s, trolleys ran through the square and cars were parked everywhere. But now it's a pedestrian zone, with market stalls filling the square on Mondays and Saturdays and café tables dominating on other days.

This is a fun place to build a picnic with Haarlem finger foods and enjoy great seating on the square. Look for pickled herring (takeaway stand on the square in good weather), local cheese (Gouda and Edam—tasty shop a block away on Grote Houtstraat), french fries with mayonnaise (there's a decent fries place behind the church on Warmoesstraat), and, in the summer, *stroopwafels* (waffles with built-in syrup, best when warmed up) and *poffertjes* (puffy mini-doughnuts, cooked on the spot and sprinkled with powdered sugar). As you enjoy a snack, take this simple spin tour.

• *Overseeing the square is the...*

**L. J. Coster Statue:** Forty years before Gutenberg invented movable type, this man carved the letter *A* out of wood, dropped it into some wet sand, and saw the imprint it left. He got the idea of making movable type out of wood (and later, he may have tried using lead). For Haarlemmers, that was good enough, and they credit their man Coster with inventing modern printing. In the statue, Coster (c. 1370-1440) holds up a block of movable type and points to himself, saying, "I made this." How much Coster did is uncertain, but Gutenberg trumped him by building a printing press, casting type in metal, and pounding out the Bible.

• *Coster is facing the...*

**Town Hall:** Whereas most of medieval Europe was ruled by kings, dukes, and barons, Haarlem has been largely self-governing since 1425. This building—built from a royal hunting lodge in the mid-1200s, then rebuilt after a 1351 fire—has served as Haarlem's Town Hall since about 1400. The facade dates from 1630.

The town drunk used to hang out on the bench in front of the Town Hall, where he'd expose himself to newlyweds coming down the stairs. Rather than arresting the man, the townspeople simply

# Haarlem of the Golden Age

Parts of Haarlem still look like they did four centuries ago, when the city was a bustling commercial center rivaling Amsterdam. It's easy to imagine local merchants and their wives dressed in black with ruff collars, promenading on Grote Markt.

Back then, the town was a port on the large Haarlemmer Lake, with the North Sea only about five miles away. As well as being the tulip capital of the country, Haarlem was a manu-facturing center, producing wool, silk, lace, damask cloth, furniture, smoking pipes (along with cheap, locally grown tobacco), and mass quantities of beer. Haarlemmers were notorious consumers of beer—it was a popular breakfast drink, and the average person drank six pints a day.

In 1585, the city got an influx of wealthy merchants when Spanish troops invaded the culturally rich city of Antwerp, driving Protestants and Jews north. Even when hardline, mor-alistic Calvinists dominated Haarlem's politics, the city re-mained culturally and religiously diverse.

In the 1700s, Haarlem's economy declined, along with that of the rest of the Netherlands. In the succeeding cen-turies, industry—printing, textiles, ship building—once again made the city an economic force.

moved the bench. This is a characteristically Dutch solution: prag-matic, deceptively simple, and effective.

• *Spin to the left. The fancy-gabled building just to the right of the church is the...*

**Meat Market** (Vleeshal): This fine Flemish Renaissance building is the old meat hall (1603), built by the rich butchers' and leatherworkers' guilds. The meat market was on the ground floor, the leather was upstairs, and the cellar was filled with ice to pre-serve the meat. It's decorated with carved bits of early advertis-ing—sheep and cows for sale. Today, rather than meat, the hall displays modern art as part of the Frans Hals Museum's secondary "Hal" location (described later, under "Sights in Haarlem") and bits of the town's past in its cellar-level Archaeology Museum (closed Mon-Tue, www.archeologischmuseumhaarlem.nl).

# Sights in Haarlem

## ON GROTE MARKT

### ▲▲St. Bavo Church (Grote Kerk)

Haarlem's impressive St. Bavo Church is better known here as the Grote Kerk—the Great Church. One of the best-known landmarks in the Netherlands, it's visible from miles around, rising above the flat plain that surrounds it. This 15th-century Gothic church is worth a look, if only to see Holland's greatest pipe organ (from 1738, 100 feet high). The organ, which fills the west end, seems to steal the show from the altar; its more than 5,000 pipes impressed both Handel and Mozart. But the interior is also packed with other details that speak volumes about Haarlem history, making it a delight to explore. Allow about 45 minutes for this self-guided tour.

**Cost and Hours:** €3; Mon-Sat 10:00-17:00, closed Sun to tourists; Sun service at 10:00 (May-Oct) and 19:00 (June-Sept); Grote Markt 22, +31 23 553 2040, www.bavo.nl. WCs are inside, just past the ticket desk.

**Tours:** English tours are offered Sat at 14:00 and possibly more often with demand (€7, includes church entry).

**Concerts:** Consider attending even just part of a concert to hear Holland's greatest pipe organ (€3.50; mid-May-mid-Oct Tue at 20:15, plus July-Aug Thu at 16:00; bring a sweater—the church isn't heated). They also do brief "lunch concerts" on summer Saturdays (at 13:15, 30 minutes, free with cathedral entry).

**Background:** After a fire destroyed the old church, the Grote Kerk was built over a 150-year period (c. 1390-1540) in the late-Gothic style of red-and-gray brick, topped with a slate-covered wood roof and a stacked tower bearing a golden crown and a rooster weathervane.

Originally Catholic, the church was named after St. Bavo (Baaf in Dutch)—a nobleman from Ghent who frequented seventh-century red-light districts during his youth. After his wife's death, Bavo converted to Christianity, became a monk, moved out of his castle, and took up residence in a hollow tree, where he spent his days fasting and praying. In the late 1500s, St. Bavo Church became Protestant (Dutch Reformed) along with much of the country. From then on, the anti-saint Protestants simply called it Grote Kerk. (Much later, starting in 1895, local Catholics built the huge Cathedral of St. Bavo, often called the **KoepelKathedraal,** on the outskirts of downtown—giving this small town two gigantic churches with similar names.)

## Grote Kerk

Grote Markt

ENTRY (TICKETS, SHOP & WC INSIDE)

N

ⓐ

⓭

ⓘ

ⓐ ⓑ ⓚ

ORGAN   NAVE   ❶   CHOIR   ⓐ ❸   ⓛ ALTAR

PULPIT   ❻

⓮   ❽ ❺   ❾

⓯   ⓰

❼

30 Meters

30 Yards

❶ Center of Church Viewpoint
❷ Poor Peasant Bending
❸ Grave of Frans Hals
❹ "Pillar Biter" (2)
❺ Three Little Ships
❻ Memorial to Hydraulic Engineers
❼ Brewers' Chapel & Café
❽ Black Marks

❾ Old Map of "Harlemum"
⓾ Church Rosters
⓫ Pelican Lectern
⓬ Foucault's Pendulum
⓭ Dog-Whipper's Chapel
⓮ Model of the Church
⓯ Wood-and-Iron Chest
⓰ Cannonball

### ❯ Self-Guided Tour

Before entering, take a few minutes to walk around the **exterior** of this incredible building. Notice the rough buttress anchors, which were never needed. Money ran out, and the planned stone ceiling (which would have required these buttresses) was replaced by a lighter wooden one. Some windows are bricked up because the organ fills the wall.

The original stone tower crowned the church from 1522 until 1530, when the church began sinking under its weight. The tower was removed and replaced by the lighter, lead-covered wood version you see today. (The frugal Dutch recycled the old tower, using it to cap the Bakenesser church, a short walk away.)

Because the tower was used as a lookout by Napoleon, it was classified as part of the town's defense. As a result, the tower (but not the rest of the church) became city property; since Haarlem's citizens own it, they must help pay to maintain it.

The base of the church is encrusted, barnacle-like, with shops—selling jewelry, souvenirs, haircuts, gelato, and artwork in the colonnaded former fish market—hearkening back to medieval times, when religion and commerce were more intertwined. The little shops here have long been church-owned, rented out to bring in a little cash.

During the day, a machine plays music on the bells of the Grote Kerk's carillon (live carillonneurs play occasionally). If you're in Haarlem at night, you'll hear the carillon chiming a simple "de dong, de dong" ("Don't worry, be happy") at 21:00. In days gone by, this warned citizens that the city gates would soon close for the night.

• *Enter the church on the Grote Markt side, near the north transept (look for the small* Entrée *sign). Walk to the* **center of the church**—*where the nave crosses the transept—and take it all in.*

### ❶ Center of Church Viewpoint

Simple white walls, a black floor, a brown ceiling, and a mahogany-colored organ make this spacious church feel vast, light, and airy. Considering it was built over a span of 150 years, its architecture is surprisingly homogenous. Originally, much of the interior was painted in bright patterns, similar to the carpet-like frescoes on some columns near the center of the church. But in 1566, Protestant extremists stripped the church of its graven images and ornate Catholic trappings, leaving it relatively stark, with minimal decoration. They whitewashed everything. The few frescoes you see today were restored in the 1980s.

Look up to see the fan-vaulted cedar ceiling from 1530. Look down to see tombstones paving the floor. And look midway up the walls to catch squatting characters supporting the pilasters. The three-story organ fills the west wall.

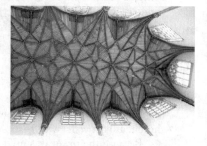

• *Turn left and walk to the candle-lined, fence–like brass barrier. Look into an enclosed area of wooden benches and the altar, known as...*

## The Choir

After the church's foundation was laid, the choir was built first and used for worship for more than a century while the rest of the building was completed.

Today, the brass-and-wood barrier keeps tourists from entering the most sacred area, just as peasants were kept out in medieval times. While the commoners had to stand during services, local big shots got to perch their heinies on the little ledges (called misericords, carved in 1512) of the **wooden stalls** that line the choir; the eighth stall along the left side shows a ❷ **poor peasant bending** over to bear a rich guy's bum on his back. The stalls are also decorated with the coats of arms

of noble families, whose second sons traditionally became priests.

The choir's floor holds a simple slab marked with a lantern—the ❸ **grave of Frans Hals** (just right of center, marked *Graf van Frans Hals*), Haarlem's own master artist of the golden age. When he was a child, Hals' family moved to Haarlem, and he lived and worked here all his life, worshipping in the Grote Kerk. A friend of mayors and preachers, he chronicled middle-class citizens and tavern life, producing hundreds of masterpieces...and 10 kids.

At both ends of the brass barrier, look for the knee-level carvings of the ❹ **"pillar biter."** The man, on the right, wears pointy Dutch over-shoes, while the woman, on the left, is draped in a dress and a fashionable turban; both wear rosary beads from their belts. The message of these carvings, aimed at those who were "more Catholic than even the pope," was this: Don't go overboard on devotion.

More than a thousand wealthy people are buried under the church's pavement stones. Only those with piles of money to give to the church could be buried in a way that gave them an advantage in the salvation derby. But even though the dead bodies were embalmed, they stunk. Imagine being a peasant sitting here, trying to think about God...and thinking only of the stench of well-fed bodies rotting below. This is where the phrase "stinking rich" was born.

• *To your right (as you face the choir), are three huge columns. Suspended between two of them are...*

## ❺ Three Little Ships

Sailing under the red-white-and-blue Dutch flag and the flag of a rearing lion, ships like these helped make Holland the world's number-one sea-trading nation in the 1600s.

The biggest model ship of the three is a frigate. These fast, heavily armed, three-masted, fully rigged ships rode shotgun for merchant vessels, protecting them from pirates in their two-year journey to the Far East and back. This one has a flat-bottomed hull, necessary to ply Amsterdam's shallow harbor. It could fire a 21-gun salute from each side, and extra cannons on the poop deck and forecastle made it more powerful than the average frigate. The keel has an iron saw, a Dutch military specialty for slicing through the chains that commonly blocked harbors (see the chain between two towers near the bow).

At the base of the next column down, just to the right, is a ❻ **memorial to hydraulic engineers** Christiaan Brunings and Frederik Willem Conrad. The marble relief shows Neptune in his water chariot. In the low-lying Holland of the 1800s, when flooding could mean life or death, hydraulic engineers were heroes, specifically the two commemorated here.

• *Behind the columns, set into the wall of the church, is the...*

## ❼ Brewers' Chapel (Brouwerskapel)

This chapel, with its humble café, marks the long and short of the city's 750-year history—literally. ❽ **Black marks** on the right side of the chapel's central pillar show the height of Haarlem's shortest citizen, 33-inch-high Simon Paap, who supposedly died in a dwarf-tossing incident, and—wow!—8-foot-8-inch-tall Daniel Cajanus.

On the wall to the left of the café—facing the nave, and farther toward the apse—hangs an ❾ **old map of "Harlemum."** It shows the walled city in 1688, with ramparts and a moat. Surrounding panels showcase Haarlem's 750-year history. The lower-left panel shows the 1572-1573 Siege of Haarlem, as brave Haarlem women join their menfolk in battle—bombs exploding around them—to fight off invading Spanish troops.

The lower-right panel shows knights kneeling before a king in the 12th century, while in the distance, ships sail right along the city walls. Up until the 1840s, when it was drained and reclaimed, there was a large lake (the Haarlemmermeer) standing between Haarlem and Amsterdam. The Grote Kerk, when viewed by distant travelers, seemed to float like a stately ship on the lake, as seen in the landscape along the bottom of the map.

• *From here, turn left and circle the church counterclockwise, heading around the altar. Just after rounding the bend, on the outer wall, you'll see the first of many lists of prominent church members. The fifth* **⓾ roster** *on the right, from 1736, has mesmerizingly ornate calligraphy. Opposite this list, inside the choir, is the...*

## ⓫ Pelican Lectern

According to medieval lore, pelicans are so attentive to their chicks that mothers, when necessary, feed their young with their own blood. Because of this myth, the pelican became a symbol of Christ's self-sacrifice. This lectern from 1499 has a brass bird that looks just like other symbolic pelicans—shown stabbing itself with its own beak—except for one important difference: It looks like an eagle. Apparently, its creator had never come across an actual pelican.

• *Carry on past the end of the choir. In the right (north) transept, look for...*

## ⓬ Foucault's Pendulum

A ball on a wire hangs from the ceiling (see the brass sphere pulled to the right side). When set in motion (by a church tour guide, mostly on Saturdays), it swings across a dial on the floor, re-creating physicist Léon Foucault's pendulum experiment in Paris in 1851. If it's swinging, stand here patiently and watch the earth rotate on its axis.

As the pendulum swings steadily back and forth, the earth rotates counterclockwise underneath it, making the pendulum appear to rotate clockwise around the dial. The earth rotates once every 24 hours, of course, but at Haarlem's latitude of 52 degrees, it makes the pendulum (appear to) sweep 360 degrees every 30 hours, 27 minutes (to knock over the bowling pin). If you happen to catch it swinging, stand here for five minutes and you'll see the earth move one degree.

As the world turns, find several small relief statues (in a niche on the right-hand wall to the right of a white bust) with beheaded bodies and defaced faces—victims of the 1566 Iconoclastic Fury, when angry Protestant extremists vandalized Dutch Catholic churches (as this once was).

About 40 yards farther on, past the entrance, the shallow niche on the right is the ⓭ **Dog-Whipper's Chapel.** In a sculpted relief (top of column at left end of chapel, above eye level), an angry man whips an angry dog while striding over another angry dog's head. Back when churches served as rainy-day marketplaces, this man's responsibility was to keep Haarlem's dogs out of the church.

• *Next up, you can't miss...*

## The Organ

Even when silent, this organ impresses. Finished in 1738 by Amsterdam's Christian Muller, it features a mahogany-colored casing with tin pipes and gold trim, studded with statues of musicians and an eight-piece combo of angels. Lions on the top hold Haarlem's coat of arms—a sword, surrounded by stars, over a banner reading *Vicit Vim Virtus* ("Virtue Conquers Violence"). There are larger pipe organs in the world, but this is one of the best.

With three keyboards, a forest of pedals, and 65 stops (the knobs on either side of the keyboards), this magnificent organ produces an awesome majesty of sound. Picture  10-year-old Mozart at the controls of this sound machine. In 1766, he played Haarlem at the tail end of his triumphant, three-year whirlwind tour of Europe. He'd just returned from London, where he met J. C. Bach, the youngest son of Johann Sebastian Bach (1685-1750), the grandfather of organ music. Mozart had recently written several pieces inspired by Bach, and he may have tried them out here.

"Hal-le-lu-jah!" That famous four-note riff may have echoed around the church when Handel played here in 1740, the year before his famous *Messiah* oratorio debuted. The 20th-century organist/humanitarian Albert Schweitzer also performed here.

The organist sits unseen amid the pipes, behind the section that juts out at the bottom. While the bellows generate pressurized air, the organist presses a key, which opens a valve, admitting forced air through a pipe and out its narrow opening, producing a tone. An eight-foot-long pipe plays middle C. A four-foot-long pipe plays C exactly one octave up. A 20-foot pipe rumbles the rafters. With 5,068 pipes ranging from more than 20 feet tall to just a few inches, this organ can cover eight octaves (a piano plays seven), and each key can play a variety of sounds. By pulling one of the stops (such as "flute" or "trumpet"), the organist can channel the air into certain sets of pipes tuned to play together to mimic other instruments. For maximum power, you "pull out all the stops."

• *Cross in front of the organ and look left to find the glass box holding a...*

## ⓮ Model of the Church

A hundred times smaller than the church itself, this model still took a thousand work-hours to build. See if you can spot the matchsticks, washers, screens, glue, wire, and paper clips used to make it.

Turn around and look to the right to find a ⓯ **wood-and-iron chest** that served as a safe for the church's cash and precious documents—such as those papers granting the power to sell forgiveness. See the board of keys for the many doors in this huge complex.

Now head back up the nave. On the far side of the green-gated chapel, on your right, look for the ⓰ **cannonball** in the wall: Duck! Placed here in 1573, this cannonball commemorates the city's finest hour: the Siege of Haarlem.

In the winter of 1572-1573, Holland rebelled against its Spanish oppressors. Haarlem proclaimed its alliance with William of Orange (and thus, independence from Spain). In response, the angry Spanish governor—camped in Amsterdam—laid siege to Haarlem. The winter was cold, food ran low, and the city was bombarded by Spanish cannons. Inside huddled 4,000 cold, hungry Calvinists. At one point, the city's women even joined the men on the barricades, brandishing kitchen knives.

But Spain had blockaded Haarlem's lake, and by June 12, 1573, the city had to surrender. The Spanish rounded up 1,500 men (three-quarters of Haarlem's able-bodied male population) and executed them.

Still, Haarlem's brave seven-month stand against overwhelming odds became a kind of Dutch Alamo, inspiring their countrymen to fight on. Following Haarlem's valiant lead, other Dutch towns rebelled, including Amsterdam. Though Holland and Spain would skirmish for another five decades, the battles soon moved southward, and Spanish troops would never again seriously penetrate the country's borders.

• *Circle back to the transept, then turn left across the wood floor into the nave, approaching the organ. On your left, look for the impressive wooden...*

### Pulpit

Elaborately carved from oak in 1679, the pulpit is topped with a tower-shaped roof. Brass handrails snake down the staircase—serpents fleeing the word of God. In this simply decorated Protestant church, the pulpit is perhaps the most ornate element, directing worshippers' eyes to the speaker. During the Reformation, Protestants changed the worship service. As teaching became more important than ritual, the pulpit was given a higher profile.

• *Our tour is complete. Go in peace.*

## NEAR GROTE MARKT
### ▲▲Corrie ten Boom House

Haarlem was home to the Ten Boom family, who, from this house, created a safe haven for Jews during World War II. This museum gives the other half of the Anne Frank story—the point of view of those who risked their lives to hide Dutch Jews during the Nazi occupation. The family's story was popularized by Corrie ten Boom's inspirational 1971 book (and 1975 movie), *The Hiding Place.*

Access to the Ten Boom House is by tour only and reservations can be smart. The gentle and loving one-hour tour comes with evangelizing that some may find uncomfortable.

**Cost and Hours:** Free, but donations accepted; Tue-Sat first English tour at 10:00, last at 15:00; Nov-March first English tour at 11:00, last at 14:30; closed Sun-Mon year-round; 50 yards north of Grote Markt at Barteljorisstraat 19; the clock-shop people get all wound up if you go inside—wait in the little side street at the door, where tour times are posted; +31 23 531 0823, www.corrietenboom. com.

**Reservations:** Tours are limited to 20 people and often fill up. You can reserve a spot only on morning tours—sign up at least 10 days in advance on their website or via email at tours@corrietenboom.com. A donation of €2.50/person is requested if you reserve in advance. Without a reservation, go in the morning to check the sign on the door for openings, then line up about 30-60 minutes before the tour begins. Tuesdays tend to be busiest.

**Background:** The clock shop was the Ten Boom family business. The elderly father and his two daughters—Corrie and Betsie, both in their 50s—lived above the store and in the brick building attached in back (along Schoutensteeg alley). Corrie's bedroom was on the top floor at the back. This room was tiny to start with, but then the family built a second, secret room (less than a yard deep) at the very back—"the hiding place," where they could hide six Jews at a time. Devoutly Christian, the family had a long tradition of tolerance, having hosted prayer meetings here in their home for both Jews and Christians for generations.

The Gestapo, tipped off that the family was harboring Jews, burst into the Ten Boom house on February 28, 1944. Finding a suspicious number of ration coupons, the Nazis arrested the family but failed to find the four Jews and two resistance fighters in the hiding place. The six fugitives hid for 47 hours in the cramped space before they were set free by police officers who were secretly members of the Dutch underground. Corrie's father and sister died while in prison, but Corrie survived the Ravensbrück concentration camp to tell her story in her memoir.

**Visiting the Museum:** Your tour starts with a compelling account of Corrie's life as you sit surrounded by family photos in the Ten Boom living room. Next you visit Corrie's bedroom, site of the hiding place. Ten tour members get to stand inside as the guide explains what happened on the night the Gestapo came—and why they never discovered the fugitives. In all, the family saved about 800 Jews and resistance fighters. The tour ends with exhibits on the Nazi occupation and Corrie's postwar work, and a talk about the Christian faith.

## ▲Teylers Museum

Famous as the oldest museum in the Netherlands, Teylers is a time-warp experience, filled with all sorts of fun curios for science buffs—fossils, minerals, primitive electronic gadgetry, and examples of 18th- and 19th-century technology—plus two painting galleries. It also hosts good temporary exhibits. This unique sight feels like a "museum of a museum." They're serious about authenticity: The presentation is perfectly preserved, right down to the original labels. Since there was no electricity in the olden days, you'll find little electric lighting...if it's dark outside, it's dark inside.

**Cost and Hours:** €15, includes excellent audioguide; Tue-Sun 10:00-17:00, closed Mon; Spaarne 16, +31 23 516 0960, www.teylersmuseum.eu. The museum's modern **$ café** has good prices and faces a delightful garden.

**Background:** The museum's benefactor, Pieter Teyler van der Hulst, was a wealthy merchant who willed his estate (worth the equivalent of €80 million today) to a foundation whose mission was to "create and maintain a museum to stimulate art and science." The museum opened in 1784, six years after Teyler's death. The last of his bequest was finally spent in 1983—and now it's a national museum.

**Visiting the Museum:** Pick up the essential audioguide and the helpful map, which illustrates an efficient route through the collection. From the entrance, you'll carry on straight ahead through **three galleries** with dusty wood-and-glass display cases (the first two with fossils, the third with early scientific instruments). From here you step into the museum's centerpiece, the **Oval Room**—a temple of science and learning. Peruse the displays in here; look for the "highest point in Europe" (the very top of Mont Blanc, Europe's highest peak in the French Alps, hacked off and brought here to Europe's lowest country).

To the left sprawls the **home of Pieter Teyler,** a string of rooms decorated as they were when he lived here. And to the right from the Oval Room are the coin collection and two lovely **painting galleries,** where works are hung above and below each other, floor-to-ceiling, in the old style. While there are no world-famous works in here, the curators are especially proud of *The Garden* by Jacobus van Looy (an Impressionist-inspired field of red flowers) and *The Drummer Girl* by Isaac Israels.

Just beyond is a modern extension featuring typically good **temporary exhibits** and the fine **café**. On your way out, see how even the toilets—a long row of wood-doored individual stalls—carry on the museum's unique mix of classy and slightly bizarre. Add your name to the guest book, which goes back to before Napoleon's visit here.

## SOUTH OF GROTE MARKT
## ▲▲Frans Hals Museum (Frans Halsmuseum)

Haarlem is the hometown of Frans Hals (c. 1582-1666), the foremost portrait painter of the 17th-century Dutch golden age. This

bold humanist painted everyday people in their warts-and-all glory. He was a forerunner of Impressionist brushwork, a master of composition, and an articulate visual spokesman for his generation.

Your ticket covers the museum's two locations: the main building ("Hof") described here and the smaller building ("Hal") a short walk away. The refreshing main museum displays many of Hals' greatest paintings and works by other Dutch masters. You'll stand eye-to-eye with life-size, lifelike portraits of Haarlem's citizens: brewers, preachers, workers, bureaucrats, and housewives. Take a close look at the people who built Holland in its heyday and then watched it start to fade.

**Cost and Hours:** €16 covers both Frans Hals buildings; both open Tue-Sun 11:00-17:00 (may open later on Sun), closed Mon; main building ("Hof") is a five-minute walk from Grote Markt at Groot Heiligland 62, secondary building ("Hal") is at Grote Markt 16; +31 23 511 5775, www.franshalsmuseum.nl.

**Hof Versus Hal:** While this tour focuses on the museum's main "Hof" exhibit, the museum's secondary location, **Frans Hals "Hal,"** is worth a look for its collection of modern art influenced by Hals' themes and techniques. It presents art inspired by (and sometimes presented alongside) pieces by Frans Hals.

**Cuisine Art:** In the main building, the **$ Frans Hals Museum Café** serves sandwiches and other simple food (daily 9:30-16:00).

HAARLEM

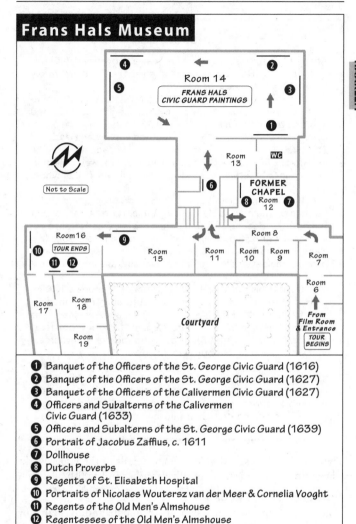

# Frans Hals Museum

Room 14

**FRANS HALS
CIVIC GUARD PAINTINGS**

Room 13

WC

**FORMER
CHAPEL**
Room 12

Room 16
**TOUR ENDS**

Room 8

Room 15

Room 11

Room 10

Room 9

Room 7

Not to Scale

Room 17

Room 18

*Courtyard*

Room 6

From
**Film Room
& Entrance**

**TOUR
BEGINS**

Room 19

❶ Banquet of the Officers of the St. George Civic Guard (1616)
❷ Banquet of the Officers of the St. George Civic Guard (1627)
❸ Banquet of the Officers of the Calivermen Civic Guard (1627)
❹ Officers and Subalterns of the Calivermen
   Civic Guard (1633)
❺ Officers and Subalterns of the St. George Civic Guard (1639)
❻ Portrait of Jacobus Zaffius, c. 1611
❼ Dollhouse
❽ Dutch Proverbs
❾ Regents of St. Elisabeth Hospital
❿ Portraits of Nicolaes Woutersz van der Meer & Cornelia Vooght
⓫ Regents of the Old Men's Almshouse
⓬ Regentesses of the Old Men's Almshouse

## ❯ Self-Guided Tour of Frans Hals Hof

My one-hour tour covers the main Frans Hals building ("Hof"). Here, Frans Hals' paintings are just one part of the collection. The museum fancies itself as *the* museum of the Dutch golden age, offering you the rare opportunity to enjoy 17th-century art in a 17th-century building.

Frans Hals' masterpieces are usually in Room 14 (and nearby rooms), but the other paintings rotate, so the order of artworks on my self-guided tour may vary. Ask a guard if you can't locate them easily. If you're using this book to navigate the collection, note that

HAARLEM

## Frans Hals, c. 1582-1666

At age 10, Frans Hals, the son of a weaver, moved with his family to Haarlem. He would spend the rest of his life there, rarely traveling even to nearby Amsterdam.

His early years are known to us only through his paintings of taverns and of drunks, musicians, and actors, crafted in a free and colorful style (like the Rijksmuseum's *The Merry Drinker* on page 150). In 1610, he married and joined Haarlem's St. Luke's Guild of painters. In 1612, he was admitted to the prestigious St. George Civic Guard. In 1617, widowed Hals married again; altogether, he produced ten children, five of whom took up painting.

Hals' group portrait of the St. George Civic Guard (1616) put him on the map as Haarlem's premier portrait painter. For the next five decades, he abandoned the lighthearted slice-of-life scenes of his youth and dedicated himself to chronicling Haarlem's prosperous, middle-class world of businessmen and professionals—people he knew personally, as well as professionally.

Despite his success, Hals had trouble with money. In 1654, he had to sell his belongings to pay debts, and he fought poverty for the rest of his life. Commissions became scarce, as the public now preferred more elegant, flattering portraits. His final works (1650-1666) are dark and somber, with increasingly rough and simple brushwork.

In 1664, the city granted him a pension for his years of service. When he died two years later, his work quickly passed out of fashion, dismissed as mere portraiture. In the 1800s, the Impressionists rediscovered him, and today he's recognized for his innovations, craftsmanship, and unique style.

many of the photos in this section are details of the larger works. The entire museum is thoughtfully described in English.

### Introduction and Rooms 1-11

Your visit begins with an insightful 15-minute **audiovisual show** introducing the artist and his works. From here, you'll circle around to the core of the collection, which is roughly on the opposite side of the complex. Well-described exhibits unfold as the rectangular museum wraps around a peaceful central courtyard. The building's layout makes sense when you realize it was built as subsidized housing for poor old men (in 1610).

• *Exiting the film, go straight ahead to enter the main exhibit. Turn right and begin to circle darkened rooms 1-11, around the courtyard, in a counterclockwise order. Don't be shy about opening a door to the next wing; because of the climate-control system, there are lots of closed doors here.*

*When you reach the far end of the complex, you should see a big sign pointing you to the right, into Room 14—labeled* **Frans Hals: All Civic Guard Pieces.** *You'll know you've arrived in the right place when you find yourself well-guarded by canvases full of companies of uniformed men. We'll start with the men in the bright-red sashes, which is over your right shoulder as you enter this room.*

❶ *Banquet of the Officers of the* *St. George Civic Guard,* 1616

In 1616, tiny Holland was the richest country on earth, and these Haarlem men are enjoying the fruits of their labor. The bright-red sashes, the jaunty poses, the smiles, the rich food, the sweeping tilt of the flags...the exuberant spirit of the Dutch golden age. These weekend warriors have finished their ceremonial parade through town and hung their weapons on the wall, and now they sit down for a relaxed, post-show party.

The man in the middle (next to the flag bearer, facing us) is about to carve the chicken when the meal is interrupted. It's us, arriving late through the back door, and heads turn to greet us. Rosy-cheeked Nicolaes Woutersz van der Meer (see his portrait later on this tour), hand on hip, turns around with a friendly look, while the man to the right, the colonel in charge, waves us in. Frans Hals knew these men well as friends and colleagues, since he himself was a lifelong member of this Civic Guard company.

This band of brothers is united by common gestures—two men have hands on hips, three turn their palms up, two plant their hands downward, three clutch wine glasses. But mostly, they're joined by the uniform sashes. The red sashes slant both left and right, perfectly forming opposing diagonals.

With this painting, Frans Hals broke the mold of stuffy group portraits. He relegates the traditional symbolic weapons to the shelf (upper right) and breaks up the traditional chorus line of soldiers by placing the men naturally around a table. Van der Meer sticks his elbow in our faces (another Hals trademark) to define a distinct

## Civic Guard Portraits

The fathers of the men pictured in this room fought, suffered imprisonment, and died in the great Siege of Haarlem (1572-1573), which helped turn the tide against Spanish oppression. But their sons were bankers, merchants, traders, and sailors, boldly conquering Europe on the new frontier of capitalism. The Civic Guards became less of a militia and more a social club for upwardly mobile men. Their feasts—huge eating-and-drinking binges, punctuated by endless toasts, poems, skits, readings, dirty limericks, and ceremonial courses—could last for days on end.

Standard Civic Guard portraits (like many of those in the Rijksmuseum in Amsterdam) always showed the soldiers in the same way—two neat rows of men, with everyone looking straight out, holding medieval weapons that tell us their ranks. It took master artists like Hals and Rembrandt to turn these boring visual documents into art.

foreground, while the flag bearer stakes out the middle ground, and a window at the back opens up to a distant, airy background.

Then Hals sets the scene in motion. One guy (third from the left) leans over to tell a joke to his friend. The dashing young flag-bearer in the middle turns back to listen to the bald-headed man. An ensign (standing, right side) enters and doffs his cap to Captain Van der Meer. And then we barge in, interrupting the banquet, but welcomed as one of the boys.

• *On the facing wall, look for...*

### ❷ Banquet of the Officers of the St. George Civic Guard, 1627

A decade later, Hals painted the same militia again. Familiar faces appear (Captain Van der Meer is in the upper left), but most of the old men have been replaced by a crop of younger, battle-tested officers. These men had recently seen action in the Battle of Breda (1625), fighting for Dutch independence from Spain. The man in the center—facing us and turning his empty glass down to show he needs a refill—was a well-known Haarlem pub owner. (Find him again, in the same tan coat with blue sash, in the 1639 painting described later.)

The banquet looks spontaneous, but the men's poses were carefully planned. Hals painted the bodies first, then brought in the men one by one for their portraits. As colorful as these Civic Guard paintings appear, much of the canvas is black, white, or gray. Van Gogh marveled at Hals' ability to capture "27 shades of black."

• *On the wall between these two canvases is...*

### ❸ Banquet of the Officers of the Calivermen Civic Guard, 1627

The men are bunched into two symmetrical groups, left and right, with a window in the back. The figures form a Y, with a tilted

flag marking the right diagonal (echoed by several tilted ruffs), and a slanting row of heads forming the left diagonal (echoed by several slanting sashes). The diagonals meet at the back of the table, marking the center of the composition, where the two groups of men exchange food, drink, and meaningful eye contact.

• *Now move on to the wall on the left (straight ahead from where you came in). The canvas to the far left is...*

### ❹ The Officers and Subalterns of the Calivermen Civic Guard, 1633

Six years later, Hals painted many of these same men gathered

around an outdoor table. The horizontal row of faces is punctuated by three men standing sideways, elbows out. Again, the men are united by sashes that slant in (generally) the same direction and by repeated gestures—hands on hips, hands on hearts, and so on.

• *On the wall to the left, look for...*

### ❺ The Officers and Subalterns of the St. George Civic Guard, 1639

When 57-year-old Frans Hals painted this, his last Civic Guard portrait, he included himself among his St. George buddies. (Find Frans in the upper left, second from left, under the faint gray number 19.)

As he got older, Hals refined and simplified his group-portrait style, using quieter colors, the classic two horizontal rows of soldiers, and the traditional symbolic weapons.

A decade after this was painted, Holland officially ended its war with Spain (Treaty of Munster, 1648), the Civic Guards lost their military purpose, businessmen preferred portraits showing themselves as elegant gentlemen rather than crusty soldiers, and the tradition of Civic Guard group portraits quickly died.

• *Now head out of Room 14. As you exit, immediately to your right is the small...*

### ❻ *Portrait of Jacobus Zaffius,* c. 1611

*Arr-r-r-r-rh!* This fierce, intense, rough-hewn man is not a pirate, but a priest, the rogue leader of an outlawed religion in Haarlem—Catholicism. In the 1600s, Haarlem was a Protestant town in the midst of a war against Catholic Spain, and local Catholics were guilty by association. But Zaffius refused to be silenced. He turns to glare and snarl at the Protestant town fathers. He was so personally imposing that the city tolerated his outspokenness.

The face jumps out from a background of neutral gray-brown-black. His features are alive—head turning, mouth twisting, face wrinkling up, beard bristling. Hals captures him in action, using a slow shutter speed. The rough brushstrokes of the fur coat and beard suggest the blur of motion of this agitated individual. This is Frans Hals' first known portrait, painted when he—a late starter in the art world—was nearly 30.

• *Proceed a few steps, then go up the short staircase on your left into a...*

### Former Chapel

At the far end of this room is a fancy ❼ **dollhouse** *(poppenhuis),* the hobby of the lady of the house. Handmade by the finest local craftsmen, this delicately crafted dollhouse offers a glimpse of wealthy 18th-century living.

The real treasure of this room is on the facing wall: It's Pieter Brueghel the Younger's ❽ *Dutch Proverbs (Nederlandse Spreekwoorden).* Dating from 1625, this fun painting contains more than 90 charming Dutch scenes representing different folk sayings; 25 of these are labeled in English on the panel in front. True to form, this piece of Dutch art isn't preachy religious art or political propaganda; rather, it shares the simple, decent morals of these hardworking people.

• *From here, head back out into the series of room that rings the courtyard. Turn right into Room 15. On the right wall, at the far end (near the next door), look for...*

### ❾ *Regents of St. Elisabeth Hospital,* 1641

These aren't the Dutch Masters cigar boys, though it looks like Rembrandt's famous (and later) *Wardens of the Amsterdam Drapers Guild* (described in the Amsterdam Rijksmuseum Tour chapter). It's a board meeting, where five men in black hats and black suits with lace collars and cuffs—the Dutch power suit of the day—sit around a table in a brown room.

Pretty boring stuff, but Hals was hired to paint their portraits, and he does his best. Behind the suits, he captures five distinct men. The man on the far left is pondering the universe or raising a belch. The man on the right looks like the classic Dutch poster boy, with moustache, goatee, ruddy cheeks, and long hair. The guy second from left is nearly clean-shaven. Hals links these unique faces with one of his trademark techniques—similar poses and gestures. The burping man and the goateed man are a mirror image of the same pose—leaning on the table, hand on chest. Several have cupped hands; several have hands laid flat, or on their chests, or on the table. And the one guy keeps working on that burp.

• *Proceed into Room 16, with the rest of the paintings on our tour. Begin with the two matching canvases straight ahead, at the far end of the hall as you enter.*

### ❿ Portraits of Nicolaes Woutersz van der Meer and His Wife, Cornelia Vooght, 1631

Hals knew Nicolaes van der Meer, a fellow Civic Guard lodge member, personally. Van der Meer was a brewer, an important post in a city where average beer con-sumption was six pints a day per person (man, woman, and child). He was also the mayor, so his pose is official and dignified, larger than life-size. But the face is pure Dutch golden age—red-cheeked and healthy, confident and intelligent, his even gaze tinged with wisdom. This mayor kept a steady hand on the tiller of Haarlem's ship of state.

The face is the focus of this otherwise messy painting. The ruffled collar is a tangle of simple, figure-eight swirls of white paint; the brocaded coat is a patchwork of white lines; and the lace cuffs are a few broad outlines. But out of the rough brushwork and somber background, Van der Meer's crystal-clear eyes meet ours. The finely etched crow's-feet around his eyes suggest that Hals had seen this imposing man break into a warm smile. Hey, I'd vote for him as my mayor.

The companion painting shows Van der Meer's companion,

his wife, **Cornelia.** Husband-and-wife portraits were hung together—notice that they share the same background, and the two figures turn in toward each other. Married couples in 17th-century Holland divvied up the work—men ran the business, women ran the home—and prided themselves on their mutual independence. (Even today, in the progressive Netherlands, fewer women join the workforce than in many other industrial nations.) Cornelia's body is as imposing as her husband's, with big, manly hands and a practical, slightly suspicious look. The intricate work in her ruff collar tells us that Hals

certainly could sweat the details when it suited his purpose.

• *Now turn to face the wall on your left. Of these paintings, the one on the right (next to the door) shows...*

## ⓫ *Regents of the Old Men's Almshouse,* 1664

These men look tired. So was Holland. So was Hals. At 82, Hals, despite years of success, was poor and dependent on the charity of the city, which granted him a small pension.

He was hired to paint the board of directors of the Old Men's Almshouse, located here in the building that now houses the Frans Hals Museum. Though Hals himself never lived in the almshouse, he fully understood what it was to be penniless.

The portrait is unflattering, drained of color. Somber men dressed in black peer out of a shadowy room. These men were trying to administer a dwindling budget to house and feed an aging population. Holland's golden age was losing its luster.

The style is nearly Impressionistic—collars, cuffs, and gloves rendered with a few messy brushstrokes of paint. Hands and faces are a patchwork of light and dark splotches. Despite the sketchiness, each face captures the man's essence.

Historians speculate that this unflattering portrait was Hals' revenge on tightwad benefactors, but the fact is that the regents were satisfied with their portrait. By the way, the man just to the right of center isn't drunk, but suffering from facial paralysis. To the end, Hals respected unvarnished reality.

• *The painting immediately to the right is...*

# Frans Hals' Style

- Hals' forte is portraits. Of his 240 paintings, 195 are individual or group portraits, mostly of Haarlem's citizens.

- His paintings are life-size and realistic, capturing everyday people—even downright ugly people—without airbrushing out their blemishes or character flaws.

- Hals uses rough, Impressionistic brushwork, where a few thick, simple strokes blend at a distance to create details. He works quickly, often making the rough sketch the final, oil version.

- His stop-action technique captures the sitter in mid-motion. Aided by his rough brushwork, this creates a blur that suggests the person is still moving.

- Hals adds 3-D depth to otherwise horizontal, widescreen canvases. (Men with their elbows sticking out sometimes serve to define the foreground.)

- His canvases are unified by people wearing matching colors, using similar poses and gestures, and gathered in symmetrical groups.

- His paintings have a relaxed, lighthearted, even comical atmosphere. In group portraits, the subjects interact with one another. Individual portraits meet your eyes as if meeting an old friend.

- His works show nothing religious—no Madonnas, Crucifixions, angels, or Bible scenes. If anything, he imbues everyday objects with heavenly beauty and grants ordinary people the status of saints.

### ⑫ *Regentesses of the Old Men's Almshouse,* 1664

These women ran the women's wing of the almshouse, located across the street. Except for a little rouge on the women's pale faces, this canvas is almost a study in gray and black, as Hals pared his palette down to the bare essentials. The faces are subtle variations on old age. Only the woman on the right resolutely returns our gaze.

The man who painted this was old, poor, out of fashion, in failing health, perhaps bitter, and dying. In contrast with the lively group scenes of Hals' youth, these individuals stand forever isolated. They don't look at one another, each lost in her own thoughts, perhaps contemplating mortality (or stifling belches). Their only link is the tenuous, slanting line formed by their hands, leading to the servant who enters the room with a mysterious message.

Could that message be...death? Or just that this tour is over?

HAARLEM

## MORE MUSEUMS AND SIGHTS
### Verwey Museum Haarlem
This small museum, across the street from the Frans Hals Museum's main building, offers a glimpse of old Haarlem. It begins with a large-scale model of Haarlem in 1822, when its fortifications were still intact, explained by a 10-minute sound-and-light show (narrated in English on the audioguide). From there, you can wander through rooms that tell the history of this little town.

**Cost and Hours:** Overpriced at €10.50, includes audioguide; Sun-Mon 12:00-17:00, Tue-Sat from 11:00; Groot Heiligland 47, +31 23 542 2427, www.museumhaarlem.nl.

### ▲Red Light District
Wander through a little red light district that's as precious as a Barbie doll—and legal since the 1980s (2 blocks northeast of Grote Markt, off Lange Begijnestraat, no senior or student discounts). Don't miss the mall on Begijnesteg marked by the red neon sign reading 't Steegje ("free"). Just beyond that, the nearby 't Poortje ("office park") charges admission to enter. Jog to the right to pop into the much more inviting "Red Lantern" (window-shopping welcome, at Korte Begijnestraat 27). As you wander through this area, remember that the people here probably have the same reservations about sex work that your own community back home does; they just find it practical not to criminalize it and drive it underground, but instead to regulate it and keep the practice as safe as possible.

### ▲De Adriaan Windmill
Haarlem's windmill, located just a 10-minute walk from the train station or Teylers Museum, welcomes visitors with a short video, a little museum, and fine town views. The windmill may look old, but it's a replica from 2002 (the original windmill burned down in 1932). Be prepared for steep stairs that are more like ladders—if you get vertigo, skip it.

**Cost and Hours:** €7.50, €3.50 for ages 5-12; Mon-Fri 13:00-17:00, Sat-Sun from 10:30, until 16:30 Nov-Feb; Papentorenvest 1, +31 23 545 0259, www.molenadriaan.nl.

### More Sights in Haarlem
This city has more than its share of things to see. In addition to the items listed above, those with a special interest may enjoy some of these options:

**Almshouses (Hofje):** These small courtyards, dotted around the town center (and marked on local maps), were places where widowed women could live affordably. Consider ducking into a few.

**Catholic Cathedral:** Haarlem's Grote Kerk began as a Catholic church before it was taken over by Protestants. Not forgetting this fact, Catholics built an even bigger church just southwest of the town center. The huge **KoepelKathedraal** (a.k.a. Basilica of St. Bavo) is one of the largest churches built in the 20th century (consecrated in 1898, completed in 1930). Its eclectic, historicist style ranges from Neo-Romanesque and Neo-Gothic, to the Jugendstil dome, to Moorish-inspired flourishes. You can climb the nearly 200-foot-tall tower, visit the vast interior (featuring works from more than 60 artists), and tour the church museum (Leidsevaart 146, www.koepelkathedraal.nl).

**Het Dolhuys:** Hiding in a park behind Haarlem's train station is this former mental asylum and quarantine facility. After the asylum closed, it housed a conventional museum of psychiatric history. It was recently transformed into a "Museum of the Mind" (Museum van de Geest), with conceptual and provocative exhibits probing the hard-to-define notion of the "mind" (www.museumvandegeest.nl).

## Near Haarlem
### Zandvoort

For a quick and easy look at the windy coastline in a shell lover's Shangri-la, visit the beach burg of Zandvoort, just 10 minutes away from Haarlem. This pret-ty, manicured resort has plenty of cafés, ice-cream parlors, *Vlaamse friet* stands, restaurants, and boutiques. Just beyond the town is the vast and sandy beach, lined with cafés and rentable chairs. Above it all is a pedestrian promenade and a line of high-rise hotels. South of the main beach, sunbathers work on all-over tans. Come to Zandvoort if the weather's hot and you want a taste of the sea and sun, if you want to see how Dutch and German holidaymakers have fun, or if you just want an excuse for a long bike ride from Haarlem (www.vvvzandvoort.nl).

**Getting There:** It's easy to reach by train, and the station is just around the corner from the beach (2/hour from Haarlem, 10 minutes; 2/hour from Amsterdam, 30 minutes). By bike, it's a breezy 45-minute ride from Haarlem, heading west and following road signs for *Bloemendaal,* then *Zandvoort.*

### Zuid-Kennemerland National Park

This wild, 15-square-mile polderland—with forests and sand dunes—sprawls just northwest of Haarlem all the way to the North Sea. On a nice day, it's a popular place for a bike ride, long walk,

## The Haarlemmermeer

The land between Haarlem and Amsterdam—where trains speed through, cattle graze, and big jets touch down—was once a lake the size of Washington, DC, called the Haarlemmermeer.

In the 1500s, a series of high tides and storms caused the IJ River to breach its banks, flooding this sub-sea-level area and turning a bunch of shallow lakes into a single one nearly 15 feet deep, covering 70 square miles. By the 1800s, floods were licking at the borders of Haarlem and Amsterdam, and the residents needed to act. First, they dug a ring canal to channel away water (and preserve the lake's shipping business). Then, using steam engines, they pumped the lake dry, turning marshy soil into fertile ground. The Amsterdam-Haarlem train line that soon crossed the former lakebed was the country's first.

or even a dip in a pond. If you'd like to get out of town, ask at the Haarlem TI for ideas on how to enjoy this natural zone that's right at the city's doorstep.

### Amsterdam to Haarlem Train Tour

Since you'll probably take the train from Amsterdam to Haarlem, here's an out-the-window tour to keep you entertained while you travel. Departing from Amsterdam, grab a seat on the right (with your back to Amsterdam, top deck if possible). Everything is on the right unless I say it's on the left.

You're riding the oldest train line in Holland. Leaving Amsterdam, you'll see the cranes and ships of its harbor—sizable, but nothing like Europe's biggest in nearby Rotterdam.

On your left, a few minutes out of Amsterdam, you should be able to see an old **windmill** (you can visit a similar one in Haarlem). In front of it, the little garden plots and cottages are escapes for big-city people who probably don't even have a balcony.

Coming into the **Sloterdijk station** (where trains connect for Amsterdam's Schiphol Airport), you'll see huge office buildings, such as Dutch telecom giant KPN. These sprouted after the station made commuting easy. On the horizon, sleek and modern windmills whirl.

Passing through a forest and by some houseboats, you enter a **polder**—an area of land reclaimed from the sea. This is part of an ecologically sound farm zone, run without chemicals. Cows, pigs, and chickens run free—they're not raised in cages.

At the little train station in **Halfweg-Zwanenburg**—so named because it's halfway between Amsterdam and Haarlem—

you'll pass a gigantic red-brick building on the left. This mammoth former sugar factory, including two giant sugar silos, has been re-developed into a futuristic complex called Sugar City, with events space and an outlet mall.

Continuing past Halfweg, notice that the terrain flattens out even more and the train tracks run along a dike—providing a raised foundation less susceptible to flooding. The transportation system generally keeps running even in bad weather. Looking out at another dike in the distance (visible on clear days), consider that you're in the most densely populated country in mainland Europe.

The big telecom tower marks the next train station, Haarlem-Spaarnwoude, in front of a giant IKEA. Just after that, on the right, find a big beige-and-white building. This is the **mint,** where currency is printed (top security, no advertising). This has long been a family business—see the name: Joh. Enschedé.

As the train slows down, you pass a giant, silvery structure on the left (the Netherlands' biggest train-car maintenance facility) and enter Haarlem. Keep looking left. The domed building is a **prison,** built in 1901 and still in use. The **De Adriaan Windmill** you see was rebuilt in 2002, after the original burned down (the windmill is open for visits—see listing earlier).

When you cross the Spaarne River, you'll see the great **church spire** of the Grote Kerk towering over Haarlem, as it has since medieval times, back when a fortified wall circled the town. Notice the white version of the same spire capping the smaller church (between the prison and the big church): This was the original sandstone steeple that stood atop the big church. However, structural problems forced its move to another church, and a new spire was built for the big church.

Exit the train into one of Holland's oldest stations, adorned with Art Nouveau decor from 1908. Welcome to Haarlem.

# Sleeping in Haarlem

Haarlem is most crowded in April (particularly on Easter weekend, during the annual flower parade, and on King's Day), and in May, July, and August (especially during Haarlem's jazz festival in August). For dates, see the list of holidays in the appendix.

## IN THE CENTER
### Hotels and B&Bs

$$$$ **ML Hotel** faces the back of the Grote Kerk. Modern yet elegant, it's located in a renovated 300-year-old building with a grand staircase. With bare floors, comfy high-quality beds, and minimalist touches in its 17 rooms, what it lacks in warmth it makes up for in style. Many rooms have church views, and the double-paned

windows help keep down the noise. There's also a bustling bistro and bar and the recommended ML Restaurant (family rooms, aircon, breakfast extra, elevator, Klokhuisplein 9, +31 23 512 3910, www.mlinhaarlem.nl, welkom@mlinhaarlem.nl).

**$$$ Hotel Lion D'Or** is a 55-room business hotel with all the professional comforts and pleasingly posh decor. While classy, it's across from the train station and a bit farther from the town center (RS%, air-con, elevator, Kruisweg 34, +31 23 532 1750, www.hotelliondor.nl, reservations@hotelliondor.nl, friendly Dirk Pauw).

**$$ Brasss Haarlem** rents 14 upscale suites in a turn-of-the-century building once home to Haarlem's first department store. Each cushy room is named after a fish and has an open-floor plan with a see-through bathroom (in-room espresso machine, room-service breakfast is extra, air-con, elevator, lavish honeymoon suites, Korte Veerstraat 40, +31 23 542 7804, www.brassshaarlem.nl, info@brassshaarlem.nl).

**$$ Haarlem Hotelsuites,** run by Brasss Haarlem, offers 20 cozy, apartment-style units with kitchens (check-in at Brasss Haarlem, www.haarlem-hotelsuites.nl, haarlemhotelsuites@gmail.com).

**$$ Hotel Malts** rents 14 modern, bright, and fresh rooms in a central location for a good price. Owners Henk and Annemarie have a wealth of Haarlem knowledge and share the town's secrets with each guest. Free coffee, tea, and fruit is available all day, and breakfast in the cozy lounge is an education in Dutch ways (stairs and no elevator, Zijlstraat 58, +31 23 551 2385, www.maltshotel.nl, info@maltshotel.nl).

**$$ Ambassador City Centre Hotel,** with 104 dated, straightforward rooms, is located just behind the Grote Kerk. It has swanky-feeling public spaces and a sprawling restaurant out front. If you're willing to trade some street noise for church views, ask for a room in the front (family rooms, breakfast extra, elevator plus some stairs, Oude Groenmarkt 20, +31 23 512 5300, www.ambassadorcitycentrehotel.nl, info@haarlem.com).

**$ The Niu Dairy** is a sleek, slick hotel (part of a German chain) just outside the western edge of the old center, a 10-minute walk from Grote Markt. It's affordable and efficient, with milk-themed decor, 84 rooms, and all the modern amenities (elevator, Zijlsingel 1, +31 23 206 2230, the.niu.de, dairy@the.niu.de).

**$ Hotel Amadeus,** on Grote Markt, is charming and has 15 small, bright, and basic rooms. Front rooms with views of the square are noisy, while the back rooms are relatively quiet. Breakfast is served in a trendy restaurant overlooking the main square—a great place to watch the town greet a new day. Mike and Inez take good care of their guests (RS%, use code "RS," Grote Markt 10—from the square it's a steep climb to the lounge, check-in at ground-floor restaurant where there's an elevator accessible during open hours, otherwise expect lots of stairs, +31 23 532 4530, www. amadeus-hotel.com, info@amadeus-hotel.com).

## NEAR HAARLEM

**$ Van der Valk Hotel Haarlem,** with 315 modern rooms, is sterile but a good value for drivers. It sits in an industrial zone a 20-minute walk from the center, on the road to the airport (breakfast extra, elevator, free parking, restaurant, Toekanweg 2, +31 23 536 7500, www.hotelhaarlem.nl, haarlem@valk.com). Bus #300 conveniently connects the hotel with the train station, Grote Markt, and the airport (every 10 minutes, stop: Europaweg).

¢ **Stayokay Haarlem Hostel,** with all the youth-hostel comforts, also has some simple doubles (Jan Gijzenpad 3, two miles from Haarlem station—take bus #2 from station, direction: Haarlem-Noord; or a 10-minute walk from Santpoort Zuid train station, +31 23 537 3793, www.stayokay.com/haarlem, haarlem@stayokay.com).

# Eating in Haarlem

Haarlem is a surprise culinary hotspot. Several eateries in town are starred or recommended by Michelin, and competition is fierce. This means simple, old-fashioned, affordable Dutch-style eateries are on the outs, prices tend to be high, and style all too often trumps substance. (Locals explain that, outside of the popular summer season, high-end restaurants help attract Dutch day trippers—and their much-needed money.) Assuming you're not coming to Haarlem for fine dining, I've focused my listing on midrange places offering variety and good value, with a few nicer and simpler options mixed in, too.

**$$ Jacobus Pieck Eetlokaal** is popular with locals for its fine-value "global cuisine," good salads, and unpretentious flair. Sit in the peaceful garden courtyard, at a sidewalk table, or in the romantically cozy interior. The Oriental Peak Salad is a perennial favorite, and the dish of the day *(dagschotel)* always sells out (great sandwiches at lunch, Tue-Sat 11:00-16:00 & 17:30-22:00, closed Sun-Mon, cash only, Warmoesstraat 18, behind church, +31 23 532 6144).

**$$$ Metzo,** across the street, is a bit more upscale, with a short menu of Dutch/Mediterranean/international plates. The outdoor seating is appealing, and the interior—under stylish wicker chandeliers—is cozy when the weather's bad (daily 11:30-16:00 & 17:30-21:00, Warmoesstraat 21, +31 23 532 2398). .

**$$$ De Lachende Javaan** ("The Laughing Javanese") is a long-established Indonesian place on a quiet back street not far from the main square. There's no outdoor seating, but the interior

HAARLEM

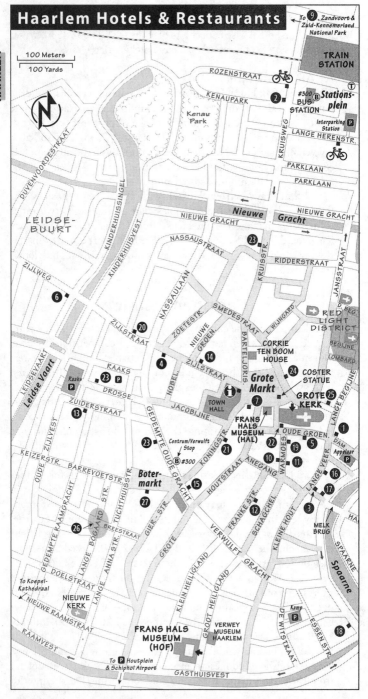

# Haarlem Hotels & Restaurants

To ⑨ Zandvoort & Zuid-Kennemerland National Park

TRAIN STATION

100 Meters
100 Yards

ROZENSTRAAT

KENAUPARK

② #300 BUS STATION

Ⓑ Stations-plein

Ⓣ

Kenau Park

KRUISWEG

Interparking Station

LANGE HERENSTR.

DUYVENVOORDESTRAAT

PARKLAAN

PARKLAAN

KINDERHUISSINGEL

LEIDSE-BUURT

Nieuwe Gracht

NIEUWE GRACHT

ZIJLWEG

NIEUWE GRACHT

NASSAUSTRAAT

② ㉓

KRUISSTR.

RIDDERSTRAAT

⑥

JAN.STRAAT

NASSAULAAN

ZIJLSTRAAT

⑳

SMEDESTRAAT

NIEUWE GROEN

L. WIJNGARD

BARTELJORIS

D. BEG.

RED LIGHT DISTRICT

ZOETESTR.

④

⑭

ZIJLSTRAAT

CORRIE TEN BOOM HOUSE

BEGIJNE

LOMBARD

LEIDSEVAART

Leide Vaart

RAAKS

Raaks Ⓟ

㉓ Ⓟ

NOBEL

Grote Markt

㉔ COSTER STATUE

LANGE BEGIJNE

ZUIDERSTRAAT

DROSSE

ⓘ ⑦

GROTE KERK

㉕

⑬

KEIZERSTR.

ZIJLVEST

OUDE ESTR.

BARREVOETESTR.

JACOBIJNE

TOWN HALL

FRANS HALS MUSEUM (HAL)

OUDE GROEN.

① DAM

⑤ Appelaar Ⓟ

GEDEMPTE OUDE GRACHT

Centrum/Verwulft Stop

KONINGSTR.

㉒ ⑲

㉓ Ⓑ #300

㉑

⑩ ⑪

ANEGANG

WARMOES

⑯

Botermarkt

⑮

HOUTSTRAAT

LANGE VEER

⑰

TUCHTHUISSTR.

㉗

GIER- STR.

FRANKE STR.

SCHAGCHEL

KLEINE HOUT

③

MELK BRUG

GEDEMPTE RAAMGRACHT

LANGE BOGAARD STR.

㉖

BREESTRAAT

LANGE ANNA STR.

GROTE

⑫

VERWULFT GRACHT

Spaarne

DOELSTRAAT

KLEIN HEILIGLAND

SPAARNE

To Koepel-Kathedraal

NIEUWE KERK

NIEUWE RAAMSTRAAT

GROOT HEILIGLAND

VERWEY MUSEUM HAARLEM

DE WITSTRAAT

Kamp Ⓟ

ESSEN STR.

⑱

RAAMVEST

FRANS HALS MUSEUM (HOF)

To Ⓟ Houtplein & Schiphol Airport

GASTHUISVEST

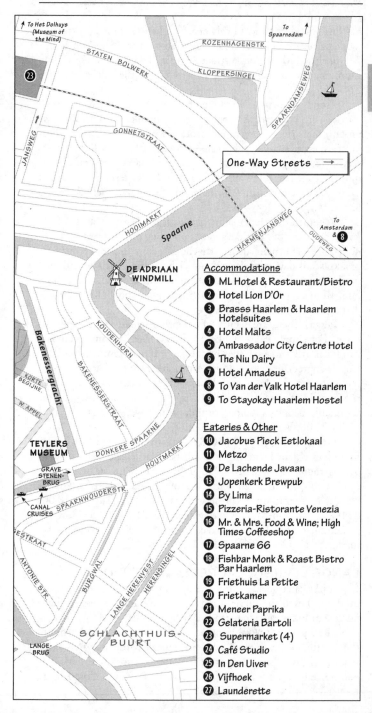

To Het Dolhuys (Museum of the Mind)

To Spaarndam

ROZENHAGENSTR.

STATEN BOLWERK

KLOPPERSINGEL

㉓

JANSWEG

GONNETSTRAAT

SPAARNDAMSEWEG

One-Way Streets

HOOIMARKT

Spaarne

HARMENJANSWEG

To Amsterdam & ⑧

OUDEWEG

DE ADRIAAN WINDMILL

KOUDENHORN

Bakenessergracht

BAKENESSERSTRAAT

KORTE BEGIJNE.

W. APPEL.

TEYLERS MUSEUM

DONKERE SPAARNE

HOUTMARKT

GRAVE-STENEN-BRUG

CANAL CRUISES

SPAARNWOUDERSTR.

STRAAT

ANTONIE STR.

BURGWAL

LANGE HERENVEST

HERENSINGEL

LANGE-BRUG

SCHLACHTHUIS-BUURT

## Accommodations

① ML Hotel & Restaurant/Bistro
② Hotel Lion D'Or
③ Brasss Haarlem & Haarlem Hotelsuites
④ Hotel Malts
⑤ Ambassador City Centre Hotel
⑥ The Niu Dairy
⑦ Hotel Amadeus
⑧ To Van der Valk Hotel Haarlem
⑨ To Stayokay Haarlem Hostel

## Eateries & Other

⑩ Jacobus Pieck Eetlokaal
⑪ Metzo
⑫ De Lachende Javaan
⑬ Jopenkerk Brewpub
⑭ By Lima
⑮ Pizzeria-Ristorante Venezia
⑯ Mr. & Mrs. Food & Wine; High Times Coffeeshop
⑰ Spaarne 66
⑱ Fishbar Monk & Roast Bistro Bar Haarlem
⑲ Friethuis La Petite
⑳ Frietkamer
㉑ Meneer Paprika
㉒ Gelateria Bartoli
㉓ Supermarket (4)
㉔ Café Studio
㉕ In Den Uiver
㉖ Vijfhoek
㉗ Launderette

has Javanese decor and a lively energy. The memorable rijsttafel—while pricey—can be ordered even by solo diners (Tue-Sun 17:00-22:00, closed Mon, Frankestraat 27, +31 23 532 8792). For tips on Indonesian food and enjoying a rijsttafel, see the sidebar on page 214.

**Trendy Brewpub:** The Jopen brewery has converted a church into a flashy, popular gastropub called **$ Jopenkerk.** With 18 brews on tap, including a *Hoppenbier* from a 1501 recipe, this is a beer lover's mecca. Budget pub grub—burgers, salads, and quiche—is served on the ground floor; the pricey upstairs restaurant offers more elegant fare (brewpub daily 12:00-24:00; restaurant Tue-Sat 17:30-22:00, closed Sun-Mon; Gedempte Voldersgracht 2, +31 23 533 4114).

**Vegetarian Café:** A short block off the Grote Markt, **$$ By Lima** has some of Haarlem's most appealing outdoor seating that's not right on the main square. This health-conscious eatery features breakfast all day, open-faced sandwiches (think variations on avocado toast), fresh juices, coffee drinks, desserts, and other tasty fare, all in a momentum-shattering location (daily 8:00-18:00, Zijlstraat 65, +31 23 785 3564).

**Pizza:** There are plenty of tempting, trendy pizza spots in town. For simple value, I like **$$ Pizzeria-Ristorante Venezia,** run for nearly three decades by the same Italian family from Bari. Locals appreciate its remote-ish location—facing a former department store a couple of long blocks off the main drag—to avoid the crowds of tourists and day trippers downtown. Sit outdoors for quality people-watching, or indoors at a well-worn table (daily 13:00-23:00, Verwulft 7, +31 23 531 7753).

**Dressy Splurge:** At **$$$$ Restaurant ML,** chef Mark Gratama serves chichi French-fusion cuisine in an elegant and modern dining room below the ML Hotel. This Michelin-starred restaurant offers five- to seven-course tasting *menus* starting at €85, as well as à la carte dining (reservations necessary, Tue-Sat 18:00-22:00, closed Sun-Mon, Klokhuisplein 9, +31 23 534 5343, www.restaurant-ml.nl). They also have a more affordable **$$ bistro** serving lunches, indoors or out, until 17:00.

## LANGE VEERSTRAAT RESTAURANT ROW

If you just can't decide, stroll the delightful Lange Veerstraat behind the church and survey a fun range of restaurants—from cheap falafels to Indonesian to pizza to Michelin-starred splurges. Along here, **$$$$ Mr. & Mrs. Food & Wine**—where Mark churns out thoughtful, locally sourced fixed-price meals while his wife Corina tends to the wine list—has a rustic-modern dining space and a few outdoor tables (no à la carte, Tue-Sun 17:00-22:00, closed Mon, Lange Veerstraat 4, +31 23 531 5935).

## ON THE SPAARNE RIVER CANAL

When the weather is fine, it's tempting to enjoy an outdoor table overlooking Haarlem's canal.

**$$ Spaarne 66** is close to the heart of town, just around the corner from the end of the Lange Veerstraat restaurant strip. It has good local dishes of meat and fish, a classy old-meets-modern interior accented in gold, and lots of outdoor tables sprawling along the prettiest stretch of canal (daily 9:30-23:00, closed Mon Oct-May, Spaarne 66, +31 23 551 3800).

Two more places, which share the same owners, sit side-by-side a few minutes' walk south along the canal. **$$$ Fishbar Monk** is the best place in town for seafood, with "snack," small, and large plates. It has a nicely tiled interior with an actual fish counter at the back, as well as ample outdoor seating (Mon-Fri 17:00-24:00, Sat-Sun from 12:00, Turfmarkt 20, +31 23 727 1266). Next door, **$$$ Roast Bistro Bar Haarlem** adds "turf" to the "surf" with grilled meats—specializing in rotisserie chicken (daily 16:00-24:00, Turfmarkt 26, +31 23 844 2271).

## BUDGET OPTIONS

**Fries:** A couple of places near Grote Markt sell old-fashioned, fresh Flemish-style fries with various sauces. The closest choice is **Friethuis La Petite,** behind the church (Tue-Sun 11:30-19:00, closed Mon, Warmoesstraat 3). The purist's choice, **Frietkamer,** is just a short walk to the west (Tue-Wed 16:00-20:00, Thu-Sun from 12:00, closed Mon, Zijlstraat 31).

**For Families:** Tucked in a fun toy-store setting, the little café at **$$ Meneer Paprika** ("Mr. Pepper") offers snacks and sandwiches, an inviting play area, and rental bikes with child seats available (café open Mon-Sat 9:00-17:00, Sun from 10:00, shop usually open one hour later than café, a block off Grote Markt at Koningstraat 19, +31 23 202 3268, www.meneerpaprika.nl).

**Ice Cream:** Local favorite **Gelateria Bartoli,** on the south side of the church, has both classic Italian and Dutch-inspired flavors (daily, often closed Mon off-season, closed entirely in Nov and Feb).

**Supermarkets:** With three handy locations, **Albert Heijn** is cash only and open daily. One is in the train station, another is at Kruisstraat 10, and their largest store is near the river and recommended Jopenkerk pub at Drossestraat 11. The **DekaMarkt** is a few blocks west of Grote Markt (daily, Gedempte Oudegracht 54).

## Marijuana in Haarlem

Haarlem is a laid-back place for observing the Dutch approach to recreational marijuana. The town is dotted with about a dozen coffeeshops, where pot is sold and smoked by relaxed, noncriminal types. These easygoing coffeeshops are more welcoming than they may initially seem—bartenders understand that Yankee travelers might feel a bit out of their element and are happy to answer questions.

If you don't like the smell of pot, avoid places sporting wildly painted walls; plants in the windows; or Rastafarian yellow, red, and green. **High Times,** with a living-room ambience and loaner bongs, is inviting and particularly friendly to American visitors. Smokers choose from 14 varieties of joints in racks behind the bar (neatly prepacked in trademarked "Joint Packs," Mon-Fri 8:00-23:00, Sat from 9:00, Sun from 11:00, Lange Veerstraat 47, www.coffeeshophightimes.nl). Across the street and just to the left, at Crackers Rock Café, you can see what too much alcohol does to people.

# Nightlife in Haarlem

Haarlem's evening scene is great. Consider four basic zones: Grote Markt, in the shadow of the Grote Kerk; Lange Veerstraat; Botermarkt; and Vijfhoek. If you want more high-powered nightlife, Amsterdam is just 20 minutes away by train.

**Grote Markt** is lined with trendy bars that seem made for nursing a drink—**Café Studio** is generally the hot spot for a drink here (at Grote Markt 25); I'd also duck into the dark interior of **In Den Uiver** (near the Grote Kerk entry at Riviervischmarkt 13, occasional live jazz).

**Lange Veerstraat** (behind the Grote Kerk) is colorful and bordered with lively spots.

**Botermarkt** (connected to Grote Markt by Koningstraat street) is more convivial and local, as it's less central and away from the tourists—or try the nearby **Jopenkerk** brewpub (described earlier).

Charming **Vijfhoek** (Five Corners, named for the five lanes that converge here) is the cutest corner in town. Although it has only one pub (with plenty of drinks, bar snacks, a relaxed crowd, and good indoor or outdoor seating), this quaint zone is fun to wander in the evening. Also worth exploring is the area from Vijf-hoek to the New Church (Nieuwe Kerk), a couple of blocks away.

# Haarlem Connections

If you take the train from Amsterdam to Haarlem, see the "Amsterdam to Haarlem Train Tour" (earlier, under "Sights in Haarlem") for a train-window tour of the countryside.

**From Haarlem by Train to: Zandvoort** (2/hour, 10 minutes), **Amsterdam** (8/hour, 20 minutes), **Leiden** (6/hour, 20 minutes), **The Hague/Den Haag** (4/hour, 40 minutes), **Delft** (2/hour, 40 minutes), **Rotterdam** (4/hour, 1 hour), **Utrecht** (7/hour, 50 minutes, transfer in Amsterdam), **Hoorn** (2/hour, 70 minutes, more with change in Amsterdam Sloterdijk), **Alkmaar** (2/hour, 40 minutes), **Brussels** (hourly, 3.25 hours, transfer in Rotterdam), **Bruges/Brugge** (hourly, 4 hours, 2-3 changes—avoid Thalys connections if traveling with a rail pass).

**By Bus to Aalsmeer:** Connexxion bus #340 connects Haarlem to Aalsmeer's town center, where you can take bus #357 to the flower auction (4/hour, 1 hour, see "Getting There" on page 370).

**To Keukenhof:** Bus #50 takes you to Lisse (4/hour, 1 hour), a 15-minute walk from the park entrance. Or take a train to Leiden, then bus #854 (Keukenhof Express) to the park entrance.

**To Schiphol Airport:** Your best option is **bus #300** (departs every 10 minutes or so, takes 40 minutes, €6.50—buy ticket from driver, card only). For most of the trip, this bus travels on its own limited-access roadway—what transit wonks call a "busway." To catch the bus from the middle of Haarlem, head to the Centrum/Verwulft stop, a few blocks south of the Grote Markt. Or, to catch this bus from Haarlem's train station, look for the "K" bus stop, where it pulls up to the curb in front of the station rather than out in the big lot. You can also get to the airport by **train** (6/hour, 30-40 minutes, transfer at Amsterdam-Sloterdijk station) or **taxi** (about €40).

# DELFT

# DELFT

Peaceful as a Vermeer painting and as lovely as its porcelain, Delft has a special soul. It feels like an idyllic mini-Amsterdam...urban Holland with training wheels. Enjoy this typically Dutch, "I could live here" town best by simply wandering around, munching *stroopwafels*, people-watching, and daydreaming on the canal bridges. If you're eager for some sightseeing, visit a pair of churches, learn more about favorite son Vermeer, or tour the famous porcelain factory.

Think of Delft as an alternative to Haarlem: a low-key, midsized city with fast and easy connections to big cities (Rotterdam or The Hague). Laced with tranquil and picturesque canals, Delft would easily win the cuteness contest. If you love Vermeer's quiet, exquisite paintings, you understand why it's said that the painter's muse was his hometown of Delft.

## PLANNING YOUR TIME

Delft works wonderfully as a side trip by train from Amsterdam (one hour) or Haarlem (40 minutes), or as an overnight stop. If you spend the night anywhere in the Netherlands outside the capital, make it Delft.

Strategically located along the train line between Amsterdam and Belgium, Delft is within very easy side-tripping distance of The Hague (30 minutes by tram or 15 minutes by train), Rotterdam (15 minutes by train), and Leiden (20 minutes by train)—and its canalside charm makes it a far more pleasant place to stay than the bustling cities.

Whether side-tripping or home-basing, for a busy day of contrasts, visit both Delft and one of its big neighboring cities. In the morning, take in The Hague's impressive Mauritshuis collection (with a world-famous Vermeer); Rotterdam's modern architecture, busy harbor, and urban vibrancy; or smaller Leiden's Rembrandt and Pilgrim sights. Then continue to Delft to visit its churches, Vermeer Center, and Royal Dutch Delftware Manufactory (closes at 17:00 and closed Sun in winter)...or to simply mellow out by a canal.

# Orientation to Delft

Delft feels much smaller than its population of 100,000. Squeezed between the two giant cities of Rotterdam and The Hague, locals describe Delft as a "small town."

Nearly everything of interest (except the porcelain factory) is contained within Delft's almost perfectly oval-shaped, canal-laced historic core. The vast Markt (Market Square), with the tall and skinny spire of the New Church, marks the center of the Old Town. A couple of blocks to the southeast is the lively, restaurant-lined Beestenmarkt. You could walk from one end of the Old Town to the other in about 15 minutes.

## TOURIST INFORMATION

This TI is very helpful and may be able to store day-trippers' bags for free if the lockers at the train station are closed or full (TI open Sun-Mon 10:00-16:00, Tue-Sat until 17:00, shorter hours Oct-March; next to the train station in the modern Huis van Delft complex on Houttuinen street, +31 15 215 4051, www.delft.com).

If you plan to visit the Royal Dutch Delftware Manufactory, pick up a €3 discount coupon at the TI (may also be available at your hotel; same discount with the Museumkaart) and confirm details on the various options for getting to the porcelain factory.

## ARRIVAL IN DELFT

**By Train:** Delft's oversized, futuristic train station opened in 2015. Track 1 typically serves northbound trains (toward The Hague, Leiden, Haarlem, and Amsterdam), while track 2 serves southbound trains (Rotterdam, Belgium). From the platform, follow signs to *Stationshal* to surface. As you emerge from the turnstiles,

DELFT

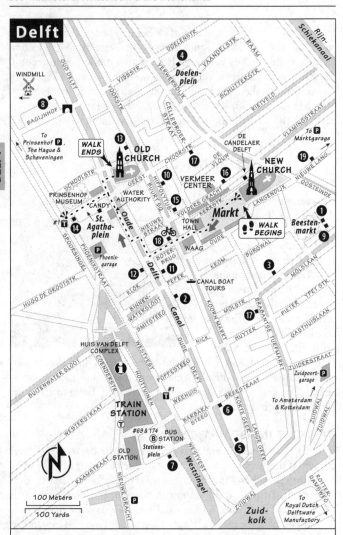

# Delft

WINDMILL

8 BAGIJNHOF

To Prinsenhof, The Hague & Scheveningen

PRINSENHOF MUSEUM

CANDY

#1 🔵 14 St. Agatha-plein

P Phoenix-garage

HUIS VAN DELFT COMPLEX

TRAIN STATION

#69 & 174 BUS STATION

OLD STATION

Stations-plein 7

100 Meters
100 Yards

OUD DELFT

VOORSTR.

VISSTR.

SCHOOLSTR.

SPOORSINGEL

HUGO DE GROOTSTR.

PHOENIXSTR.

BUITENWATER SLOOT

WESTERSTRAAT

RAAMSTRAAT

NIEUWE GRACHT

COENDERSTR.

HOUTTUINEN

WESTVEST

POPPESTEEG

#1 WEEHUIS

BAKARA STEEG

WESTVEST

Wesssingel

Zuid-kolk

DOELENSTR.

4 Doelen-plein

VERWERSDIJK

CELLEBROERSTRAAT

GEEST

WATER AUTHORITY

NIEUWE STRAAT

BOTER-BRUG

PEPER

KLOK.

BINNEN-WATERSLOOT

SMITSTEEG

Oude

Delft

Canal

OUDE DELFT

NICK.

SCHUTTERSTR.

VAANDELSTR.

RAAM

KIEVTVELD

CHOORSTR.

HIPOLYTUS BUURT SO.

13 OLD CHURCH

WALK ENDS

17

10 ⚫

15

TOWN HALL

18 🚲

WAAG

DE VLOUW

VERMEER CENTER

VOLDERS GRACHT

Markt

16

DE CANDELAER DELFT

NEW CHURCH

Langendijk

NIEUWELANG

OOSTEINDE

VLAMINGSTRAAT

To P Mārktgarage

19 ⚫

1 ⚫

Beesten-markt

9 ⚫

WALK BEGINS 👣

BURGWAL

3 ⚫

KROM.

KOORNMARKT

MOLSTR.

HUYTER

MOLSLAAN

BRABANTSE TURFMARKT

PIETER YPEI STR.

GASTHUISLAAN

ZUIDERSTRAAT

17 ⚫

Canal Boat Tours

2 ⚫

11 ⚫

12 ⚫

KORTE GEER

BREESTRAAT

6 ⚫

5 ⚫

LANGE GEER

ZUIDWAL

Zuidpoort-garage P

To Amsterdam & Rotterdam

ROTTER-DAMSEWEG

ZUIDWAL

To Royal Dutch Delftware Manufactory

Rijn-Schiekanaal

## Accommodations
1. Hotel de Koophandel
2. Bridges House Hotel & Hotel la Noire
3. Hotel Johannes Vermeer
4. Hotel de Plataan
5. Hotel Arsenaal
6. Hostel Grand Canal
7. The Student Hotel Delft

## Eateries & Other
8. Van der Dussen Restaurant
9. Spijshuis de Dis
10. 'T Postkantoor Restaurant
11. Restaurant Matties
12. Stads-Koffyhuis
13. De V Pub
14. Barbaar
15. Van der Eyk Visbanken
16. De Parel van Flores Indonesian Restaurant
17. Supermarket (2)
18. Bike Rental
19. Laundry

carry on straight ahead. Just inside the doors, on the left, are some lockers.

To reach the **Old Town**—about a 10- to 15-minute walk—exit through those doors and walk with the canal on your right, passing the slick, modern Huis van Delft complex (and the TI) on your left. When you reach the bridges, use them to turn right across the canal, then carry on straight along Binnenwatersloot, a pretty canal with streets on both sides that lead toward the tall, pointy tower of the New Church on the Markt. You'll run into the Oude Delft canal. Most recommended hotels are within a short walk of here.

To instead reach accommodations in the **southern part of town,** turn right at the top of the station's escalators, exit through those doors, cross the canal by the tram stop, and follow the map.

If you're in Delft just for the famous Royal Dutch Delftware **porcelain factory,** you can catch bus #69 or #174 straight there from the south side of the station (see the "Royal Dutch Delftware Manufactory" listing, later in this chapter, for details).

**By Car:** Drivers take Delft exit #9 off the A-13 expressway. Don't attempt to park within the Old Town; that's only allowed with a permit. Instead, use one of three parking garages that ring the Old Town—Marktgarage (east end, at Willem Naghelstraat 1), Prinsenhofgarage (northwest end, near the windmill at Kampveldweg 3), or Zuidpoortgarage (south end, at Zuidwal 14). They're each about equidistant from the Markt (€18/24 hours, higher per-hour rates for shorter time periods, https://parkerendelft.com). A fourth garage, Phoenixgarage (west end, at Phoenixstraat 29), is marginally closer but nearly double the cost.

## HELPFUL HINTS

**Sightseeing Tips:** The Museumkaart sightseeing pass covers entry to Delft's Prinsenhof Museum and offers discounts at the Vermeer Center and the Royal Dutch Delftware Manufactory (potentially worthwhile for those also visiting Amsterdam, www.museumkaart.nl).

**Markets:** Delft adds to its considerable charms with a selection of markets on Thursdays and Saturdays. On Thursdays, you'll find a huge general market with fish, cheese, fruits, and vegetables on the Markt, and flowers along Brabantse Turfmarkt and Burgwal. On Saturdays, look for a general market with flowers on Brabantse Turfmarkt and Burgwal (with frantic discounting of soon-to-be-worthless flowers at the end of the day), and antiques on and near Hippolytusbuurt, behind Town Hall.

**Laundry:** For fast and affordable full-service laundering, **Rein-Tex** is just off the Markt, beyond the New Church (self- and same-day service; Mon-Fri 9:30-17:30, Sat until 17:00, closed Sun; Nieuwe Langendijk 4a, +31 15 214 5439).

**Supermarkets:** Two well-stocked **Albert Heijn** supermarkets are in the city center. One is north of the Markt at Choorstraat 35; the other is a short walk south of the Markt, along a canal at Brabantse 41 (cash only, Mon-Sat 8:00-22:00, Sun 9:00-20:00).

**Bike Rental:** Delft—a low-impact mini-Amsterdam with pretty canals and very little car traffic—is an easy place to ride a bike, but you won't need one to reach most sights. Still, if you just enjoy biking, want to explore the countryside, or even pedal to The Hague or Rotterdam, it's an option. **Halfords** rents bikes behind the Town Hall at the bottom of the Markt (generally open Tue-Fri 9:30-18:00, Sat until 17:00, closed Sun-Mon, Wijnhaven 17, +31 15 213 8558).

## Tours in Delft

### Walking Tours
The TI offers occasional walking tours in Dutch and English (ask for details). They also sell self-guided walking-tour brochures to see Delft on your own—both a general one and a "Vermeer Trail" version. Or follow my Delft Old Town Walk detailed below.

### Canal Boat
**Rondvaart Delft** boats depart from along Koornmarkt canal—look for the sales kiosk. They offer a 50-minute boat tour of the Old Town (€10.50, April-Oct daily 11:00-17:00, boats depart hourly, +31 15 212 6385, www.rondvaartdelft.nl). The company also rents paddleboats (€15/hour) and provides transport to the Royal Dutch Delftware Manufactory (€20 includes admission, 4/day, 2.5-3 hours round-trip).

### Hop-On, Hop-Off Bus
The quirky **Delft City Shuttle** uses golf cart-like vehicles fitting about six people to connect the city center to suburban sights—most notably the Royal Dutch Delftware Manufactory (€5 day ticket, daily 10:30-17:00, runs with demand—the TI or factory desk can call one for you, www.delftcityshuttle.nl).

## Delft Old Town Walk

Lace together many of Delft's sights with this pleasant 30-minute stroll through the heart of town (allow more time if you go inside the sights along the way—all described in more detail under "Sights in Delft"). The proud churches, spires, and memorials attest to Delft's once-bustling economy during the golden age of the

1600s. But this walk also meanders past the placid canals, wind-mills, and pockets of greenery of the postcard village that Delft has become.

• *Stand in the center of Delft's market square—the Markt—and face the towering New Church.*

## The Markt

This is clearly a city with a rich history and a wealthy past. Its look today was defined in 1536, when lightning struck the spire of the **New Church** (Nieuwe Kerk; described in detail later in this chapter), starting a fire that destroyed two-thirds of the town. While all the buildings that ring the square have cellars dating from before the fire, what you see above ground made of brick was built after 1536.

Delft recovered well from the fire. In the 17th century, its golden age, this was a thriving market town, with an economy stoked by textiles and breweries. (With 200 breweries, the city exported 80 percent of its beer.) Then, in the 18th century, the economy collapsed. Without the infrastructure of a trading city—there's no river, local harbor, or major roads—Delft was left behind. It became a sleeping-beauty town, cocooned in an intact medieval structure, awaiting awakening.

The **square** has never really been renovated, perhaps because it must always be ready, on a day's notice, to host a royal funeral. In 1584, William I of Orange (b. 1533), leader of the Dutch revolt against Spain, was assassinated in Delft. Under normal circumstances, he would have been buried in his family's hometown of Breda, but the Spanish had occupied the city. So William was laid to rest in Delft, and to this day, the House of Orange—the Dutch royal family—buries its nobility in the New Church (if you pay to visit the interior, you'll see his elaborate tomb inside).

The statue dominating the square in front of the New Church honors **Hugo Grotius.** Born in Delft in 1583, Grotius was the first to establish international rules of the sea, putting forth the idea that all the oceans were free-trade territory, open to every nation. That didn't go over so well with the rival English, who claimed dominion over all the sea around Britain. The controversy went on for nearly a century, during which the two nations fought a two-year war over it. (The eventual agreement—the sea within the range of a cannonball fired from your shore is yours; any waters beyond that are open to all nations—forms the basis for today's maritime laws.)

Part of Delft's economic heritage is in printing. At #57 (above the Subway sandwich shop) a Bible on the building's upstairs corner recalls the first printed Dutch Bible, produced here in 1477.

Opposite the New Church stands the **Town Hall,** rebuilt in 1620 in the Renaissance style after a fire. It's a law court, with

Lady Justice and her scales prominently positioned on the facade. Of the 17 states in the Spanish Netherlands, seven seceded and created the Dutch Republic—the United Provinces of the Netherlands. Holland was one of these; above Lady J, look for the coat of arms with the red lion. The independent Netherlands were dominated by Holland (which contained Amsterdam and drove 85 percent of the country's economy). The lower banner (under the stone canopy, above the door) is Delft's—it features a canal, which is what "Delft" means.

• *Walk around behind the left side of the Town Hall. The building with the Greek-style pediment roof decorated with a set of scales, facing the back of the Town Hall, is known as...*

## The Waag

The city's medieval trading center, the Waag, was the weighing or **customs house,** with workspaces for goldsmiths and silversmiths

upstairs. Step inside (now a fun bar/restaurant) to see its huge timbers and part of the massive old scales. At the end of the street (far to the right of the Waag—marked *de centrale*) is the Vleeshal, or meat market—decorated with cow heads above its doors. Fish was traded in the Visbanken (left of the meat market).

The sturdy tower around which the Town Hall is built was originally a **prison.** For security, the prison needed to be built of weighty stone—a potential problem in this naturally marshy place. The builders chose this spot, on a clay foundation, as the best place for the structure. It just made sense that the county seat—Delft—would be here, too.

• *With your back to the Town Hall, walk down Waagsteeg lane, a narrow alley to the right of the Waag. Cross a small canal bridge and look back at...*

## Boterbrug

At the back side of the Waag, down below, is the **water gate** where produce was off-loaded from boats to be weighed and taxed.

Continue walking straight down **Boterbrug** (literally "Butter Bridge"), a wide street that once was the approach canal (now covered over) to the customs house. Merchants knew the drill for all their goods: Before you traded, first you weighed, then you paid. During Spanish rule, taxation got so out of hand that the Dutch revolted—much as high British taxes angered American colonists during the same period.

DELFT

Boterbrug leads one block to the 11th-century Oude Delft canal, the town's first and major trading canal. On the black iron fence on the corner, facing the canal, is a **memorial plaque** to Antonie van Leeuwenhoek (1632-1723), who invented an early microscope and then used it to discover bacteria. He's buried in the Old Church, visible in the distance (to the right; look for the tilting spire).

• *Turn right and walk toward the Old Church alongside the...*

## Oude Delft Canal

In the past, boats passing the town used this waterway. Barges are now allowed to line the canal from April through September. Historically, barges like these brought in the goods and produce that fueled Delft's economy—but today they provide the city's restaurants with sunny outdoor tables, fueling the *new* economy...tourism. For dining suggestions, see "Eating in Delft," later.

• *Walking toward the church, cross left over the first bridge (Nieuwstraat), turn right, and continue to the ornate facade at #167.*

This building is the headquarters of the **water authority** (Gee-meenlandshuis), responsible for keeping waterways dredged and

managing water levels in towns and polders (lowlands). The colorful coats of arms of the various 17th-century water-authority directors decorate the exterior wall.

Water levels are a big deal here. Turn around and look at the yardstick across the canal; the red *NAP* marking—"normal

Amsterdam point"—is the average sea level in Amsterdam. The wide-open Dutch countryside plots reclaimed from the sea, known as polders, are generally three yards below this point. According to the NAP, we're above sea level and the canal is below, so we're standing on what was an island.

• *Keep walking along this side of the canal. Across from the Old Church, under the trees, find the* **photo cube** *(rotate and learn) recalling the painter Vermeer, who's buried in the church. Turn left from the photo cube and church, and walk under a brick arch into a tiny, covered brick lane (look for the Museum* Prinsenhof Delft *sign above the arch). You'll pop out into a very long, wide courtyard called the...*

## Prinsenhof

This was once the convent of St. Agatha. William of Orange took refuge here after the king of Spain put a bounty on his head in 1580 for his role in the revolt of the Netherlands. Figuring the convent was a safe place in a safe city, William stayed here until 1584, when an assassin finally killed him (for more about William, see page 454). Today this building houses the **Prinsenhof Museum,** with exhibits on William of Orange—including the chance to see the bullet holes from his assassin's gun, still embedded in the wall—and other facets of Delft history (for details, see the "Prinsenhof Museum" listing later in this chapter).

• *In the middle of the square, on the right, step into the tranquil green* **park,** *an old monastic herb garden (free, daily 11:00-17:00).*

The statue here honors William, considered the founder of the Netherlands. When the provinces broke away from Spain, they also broke from the Roman Catholic Church. The Dutch became "reformed" and dissolved the Catholic convents and monasteries (like the complex of buildings surrounding you now). Although they had declared their freedom in 1579, a treaty ending the war for Dutch independence (which formally established their freedom) didn't come until 1648.

Back out in the main courtyard, notice the three blue-and-white **lampposts;** these were made in Delft's Chinese sister city and serve as reminders of the 400-year relationship between porcelain makers in China and Delft. The only color that could survive the extremely hot fire of the Chinese porcelain technique was blue, and that's the color of Delftware.

In the far-left corner, you'll see the **Winkeltje Kouwenhoven** old-timey candy shop, where sweets are still made the traditional way.

• *Leave the park opposite where you entered; this takes you to the noisy real world and...*

## Phoenixstraat

You've arrived at the edge of the Old Town. Far to the left is the glassy, modern train station; between here and there is the Huis van Delft, a futuristic housing development that's also home to the TI. And to the right you'll see a tower and windmill. Twenty such structures once stood on the 11th-century city wall. The **windmills,** which ground the city's grain, date back to the 13th century. Tram line #1 heads (right) along Phoenixstraat (past the windmill) to The Hague and the beach at Scheveningen.

• *Turn around and finish this walk by retracing your steps through the Prinsenhof to the Old Church (with the tilting spire).*

## Old Church (Oude Kerk)

The Old Church is smaller and less impressive (inside and out) than the New Church. For 150 years, its spire was the tallest in Delft; it leans because it's built on an unstable foundation, over a filled-in canal. (For details on the interior, see the Old Church listing under "Sights in Delft.")

At the end of the short canal bridge in front of the Old Church is a statue of **Geertruyt van Oosten** (1330-1358), a particularly devout nun whose deep faith is meant to inspire worshippers. Supposedly Geertruyt was so moved by the power of Christ that she began to lactate during the Christmas season, and the stigmata (Crucifixion wounds) appeared on her hands and feet during the Easter season.

While I've never been that moved by a mere town walk, taking a moment to enjoy the sheer beauty of Delft that surrounds you is mightily impressive in its own way.

# Sights in Delft

## IN THE OLD TOWN
### Markt (Market Square)

The historic center of Delft, the rectangular Markt is bookended by the 14th-century New Church at one end (with a statue of legal scholar Hugo Grotius out front) and the 15th-century Town Hall at the other. The Markt is bordered by characteristic buildings—a mix of shops, cafés, and homes. For more on the Markt, see its description in the "Delft Old Town Walk," earlier.

## ▲New Church (Nieuwe Kerk)

Delft has two grand churches that hold tombs of prominent local residents. The can't-miss-it New Church rockets up from the Markt: It's the needle around which Delft spins and has the most important tombs of Dutch royalty. The more modest Old Church (described later) sits along a canal a few blocks away. Both are covered by the same ticket; when you buy it, be sure to pick up the well-explained, illustrated brochure, which locates and describes points of interest in both churches.

**Cost and Hours:** €6.50 for both churches, €10 covers both churches and New Church tower, €5.50 tower only; both churches open Mon-Sat 10:00-17:00, shorter hours Nov-Jan, closed to tourists Sun year-round, last tower entrance one hour before closing, tower can close in bad weather; +31 15 212 3025, www.oudeennieuwekerkdelft.nl.

**Visiting the New Church:** The giant, Gothic New Church boldly presides over the town from its prominent position overlooking the Markt. Inside are buried the beloved Dutch ruler William I of Orange and the Dutch royalty that succeeded him.

Construction on the New Church, with its Late Gothic lines, began in 1393 and took 100 years to complete. The stone tower you see today houses a carillon, which locals proudly consider the Stradivarius of carillons. Its chimes, played on request by the town bell ringer, are in demand by couples getting married at Town Hall.

The church has been through a lot. It was devastated by a fire in 1536 and ransacked by iconoclasts in the 1560s. The first "reformed" service was held here in 1572. After a nearby gunpowder depot exploded and ruined its windows in 1654, the church was rebuilt, giving it the look you see today. Until 1829, city leaders were buried under the floor stones. Because of the "stinking rich" problem of the stench of decaying bodies wafting into the church, only royals have been buried here since then. The chandeliers, produced in 1981 in traditional 17th-century style, marked the 600th birthday of the church.

Head inside and walk all the way down the nave to the altar area. The church has rolled out the orange carpet to lead you past displays and videos to the ornate, canopied **tomb of William of Orange,** which dominates the choir area at the far end of the church. William I was the founder of the House of Orange, the dynasty that still (in name) rules the Netherlands. It was William who rallied the Dutch to begin their revolt against the Spanish Habsburg rulers: That's why he's considered the father of the country. This monument to his greatness features two representations of William: one of white marble, reclining peacefully, and a strong, armored king in bronze, sitting royally. The sweet dog reclining at William's feet symbolizes loyalty. Above the pooch, the angel of Fame blows a trumpet (notice that this whole bronze statue is supported by just one slender ankle). At the corners of his monument are female statues representing Liberty, Justice, Religion, and Fortitude. Unfortunately, all these fine virtues could not save William from  being gunned down by an assassin's bullet right here in Delft. The assassin had hoped to collect a reward offered by Spanish King Philip II for killing William of Orange (but instead the assassin was caught, tortured, and executed).

Most of William I's descendants of the House of Orange are also buried in this church. A few paces in front of William (near the transept), a large stone slab marks the entrance to the sprawling underground labyrinth that holds crates of Oranges. (The crypt is strictly off-limits for anyone unrelated.) In the transept, look for TV monitors showing the last few royal burials here.

Besides ruling Holland, the Orange family once owned the independent principality of Orange in the south of France. The royal family's official color is—what else?—orange, which is why today's Dutch wear orange to soccer matches and consider it their national color (despite having a flag that's red, white, and blue).

If you want to work off your *pannenkoeken,* you can climb the New Church's **tower** (three levels and 376 steps in a very narrow staircase). This is a particularly dizzying tower climb, one of Europe's more dramatic. On a clear day you can see the towers of The Hague and, in the other direction, Rotterdam.

• *From the New Church, walk a few blocks up pretty Hippolytusbuurt street (or follow my "Delft Old Town Walk") to find the smaller Old Church.*

### ▲Old Church (Oude Kerk)

The Old Church, with its leaning spire, is Dutch Reformed (English service Sun at 12:00). It has been around for a long time and feels more lived-in than the New Church.

**Cost and Hours:** Same as the New Church (see earlier).

**Visiting the Church:** The names of its ministers, going back to 1592, fill the wall on your right as you enter. Nearby, the wooden canopied pulpit—which dates from 1548—is considered one of the finest in the Netherlands, thanks to the fine carvings on its sides, which demonstrate a mastery of perspective.

The church interior is sober and clean because of iconoclastic riots, in 1566 and 1572, that made a violent point of destroying all hints of Roman Catholicism and its imagery. Follow the contemporary cube-shaped displays to learn about the town heroes buried underneath this church. The Old Church holds the tombs of three local boys done good: an admiral, Piet Hein (in the center nave at the front), who during the Eighty Years' War captured a Spanish silver fleet and became the subject of a popular children's song; microscope inventor Antonie van Leeuwenhoek (the tall, pyramid-shaped monument set into a wall at the very back of the left nave); and the painter Johannes Vermeer. Vermeer's actual tombstone is just a simple stone plaque in the floor (in the left transept, across from the pulpit). The grander Vermeer monument, installed in 2007 (and also in the floor), is a reflection of his greater popularity now than in previous generations.

### ▲Vermeer Center (Vermeercentrum)

Although it doesn't have any Vermeer originals, this intelligent exhibit does a good job of tracing the career and unique creative mind of Delft's favorite resident. Try to visit before you see the originals in The Hague.

**Cost and Hours:** €10, includes essential audioguide, daily 10:00-17:00, a block from the Markt—through the gap where Vermeer's house used to be—at Voldersgracht 21, +31 15 213 8588, www.vermeerdelft.nl.

**Visiting the Museum:** Begin in the basement, where a short movie orients you to Vermeer and his ties to Delft. Then view copies of all 37 known Vermeer paintings, arranged chronologically and accompanied by brief and interesting commentary. On the middle floor, a mock-up of Vermeer's studio thoughtfully analyzes and explains some of the painter's techniques, including his dazzling use of perspective and how he represented light. Finally, the top floor hosts an exhibit explaining the hidden symbols of love found in many of Vermeer's paintings and features a brief film about the restoration of *Woman in Blue Reading a Letter*.

### Prinsenhof Museum

This former convent where William of Orange sought refuge and was ultimately assassinated is now a museum focusing on the life of that great statesman. It also displays a fine collection of blue Delft-

DELFT

# Johannes Vermeer (1632-1675)

The great Dutch golden age painter Johannes Vermeer was born in Delft, grew up near the Markt, and set a number of his paintings here. His father, an art dealer, gave Johannes a passion for painting. Late in the artist's career, as Holland fought draining wars against England, the demand for art and luxuries went sour in the Netherlands, forcing Vermeer to downsize—he sold his big home, packed up his wife and 14 children, and moved in with his mother-in-law. He died two years later.

Vermeer painted some 37 surviving works (though experts debate whether all were actually his). Although Vermeer painted landscapes and scenes from mythology and the Bible, he specialized in depicting the everyday actions of regular people. And though his scenes are usually still and peaceful, he artfully conveys deep tension and suggests a complicated story with subtle body language (the subject glances at something out of view) or the inclusion of a small item (a letter that seems pregnant with significance). Vermeer also was a master of light, capturing it with an artistry that would make the Impressionists jealous two centuries later.

After centuries of relative obscurity—we still know very little about him—Vermeer and his paintings are now appreciated. Delft owns none of his works (you'll have to visit Amsterdam's Rijksmuseum, with four masterpieces, or The Hague's Mauritshuis museum). However, the town's Vermeer Center pays tribute to this great artist and his talent.

ware and a spirited exhibit about Dutch innovation. Interesting to historians, but overpriced and underwhelming for the layperson, it's a decent rainy-day activity. The included audioguide offers thorough—but dry—commentary. Note that this museum is slated to close temporarily for renovation in the near future.

**Cost and Hours:** €13.50; Tue-Sun 11:00-17:00, closed Mon; Sint Agathaplein 1, +31 15 260 2358, www.prinsenhof-delft.nl.

**Visiting the Museum:** The ground floor uses old paintings, video projections, and other displays to tell the story of William of Orange, including a room about his descendants all the way to today's king. At the base of the stairs, you'll see the two actual bullet holes from his assassination, embedded in the wall. (The shooting is continuously reenacted with silhouettes projected on the wall.)

Upstairs are more exhibits: on Dutch innovation (an important resource for this little country cursed with marshy land) and on blue Delftware pottery, with a small but impressive selection of fine pieces. If you don't want to make the trip out to the Royal Dutch Delftware Manufactory, this is a good chance to see examples of the town's most famous product. There's also a collection of Dutch Masters paintings.

Across the courtyard, the **Prinzenkwartier** building houses temporary exhibits, art galleries, and a café.

## DELFTWARE FACTORIES

The Markt is jammed with shops selling Delft's famous blue-hued pottery. Those with a passing interest in Delftware can peruse a few window displays on the main square and call it good. But to delve deeper, consider visiting the centrally located De Candelaer Delft workshop (easiest), or head to the edge of town to tour the famous Royal Dutch Delftware Manufactory.

### De Candelaer Delft Workshop

The workshop of fourth-generation Delftware potter Steffan Delfos faces the left side of the New Church. You're welcome to walk to

the back of the store to view the workshop where Steffan makes the ceramic biscuit; nearby are tables where painters create designs. Once painted, the pieces go back to Steffan for firing in a kiln, the final step of the process. Up front, browse the pieces on sale and find the display case of photos of all four generations working in the craft—Steffan's son may pick up the art one day (free, Mon-Sat 9:30-17:00, closed Sun except during April-May tulip season at Keukenhof, Kerkstraat 13A, +31 15 213 1848, www.candelaer.nl).

### Royal Dutch Delftware Manufactory

The Delft Blue earthenware made at this factory (known as the Koninklijke Porceleyne Fles in Dutch) is famous worldwide, mak-

ing this the biggest tourist attraction in town. The Dutch East India Company, partly headquartered in Delft, imported many exotic goods from the Far East, including Chinese porcelain. The Chinese designs (including flowers and peacocks) were copied by many local potters. Three centuries later, their descendants are still going strong, and you can see them at work in this factory—the only one left of an original 32. While some may think this is just an excuse to shop for Delftware, it's a worthwhile stop for those who enjoy porcelain. An ambitious expansion is underway, so some details may differ from what's described here.

# Delft Blue Manufacturing Process

Delft Blue earthenware is made from a soupy mix of clay and water. (The clay is mainly imported from England and Germany; below-sea-level Holland only has "dirty clay," used to make bricks.) To make plates, the glop is rotated on a spinning disk until it looks like a traditional Dutch pancake. This "pancake" is then placed in a plate mold, where a design is pressed into it.

To make vases, pitchers, cups, and figurines, the liquid clay is poured into hollow plaster molds. These porous molds work like a sponge, sucking the water out of the clay to leave a layer of dry clay along the mold walls. Once the interior walls have reached the correct thickness, the excess clay within is poured off and recycled.

After the clay object is removed from the mold and allowed to dry completely, it's fired in the kiln for several hours, turning from gray to white. The pottery removed from the kiln is called "biscuit." Next, painters trace or freehand traditional decorations with sable-hair pencils onto the biscuit pottery; these are then painted with a black paint containing cobalt and copper oxide. The biscuit immediately soaks up the paint, making it a very unforgiving medium for mistakes.

Finally, the objects are dipped into an opaque white glaze and then fired a second time. A chemical reaction transforms the black paint into the famous Delft Blue, and the white glaze melts into a translucent, glass-like outer layer.

**Cost and Hours:** €14, includes audioguide, €3 discount coupon available at TI and many hotels; daily 9:00-17:00 except closed Sun Nov-March; Rotterdamseweg 196, +31 15 251 2030, www.royaldelft.com.

**Getting There:** From the Old Town, the **Delft City Shuttle** (a golf cart) goes from the Markt to the factory several times a day, with demand; or, for a more scenic approach, you can take a Rondvaart Delft **canal boat** (for details on both, see "Tours in Delft," earlier). You can also take a **taxi** (about €10) or go on **foot** (25-minute walk). Ask the TI or your hotelier for directions or to call a taxi for you.

The **public bus** can get you close, but there's no stop right at the factory. To go this route, from the south side of the train station hop on bus #69 or #174 (€1.30, 2/hour, 5 minutes, pay by

DELFT

card only). Get off at the TU-Aula stop, near a giant flying saucer-looking structure. This puts you in the heart of Delft's technical university. Head back the way the bus came, turn left on Jaffalaan, and walk for a few minutes with the campus buildings on your left and a parklike canal strip on your right. When you reach Rotterdamsweg, turn left; the factory is ahead on your right.

**Visiting the Factory:** The visitors center and its recently expanded museum uses displays and videos to introduce you to the history of Royal Delft (with its ties to the rulers of Holland), as well as the production process. You'll also see the company's priceless collection. Along with tableware and vases, there are gorgeous pictures made from tiles (including a life-size replica of Rembrandt's *The Night Watch* that took two artists a year to paint) and outdoor architectural elements (such as chimneys).

But the real highlight is the chance to see the process in action. You'll walk through part of the factory, past work stations and racks upon racks of unfired and finished pieces. Take some time to watch artisans paint designs on the fired pottery "biscuit"—and feel free to stop and chat with them.

The tour ends in the gift shop. For bargain hunters, the factory store offers "seconds" with slight blemishes for 20-40 percent off. The clerks can also prepare VAT refund documents for you.

## Sleeping in Delft

Delft has a limited array of accommodations, and most are in creaky old canalside buildings rather than modern, cookie-cutter ones. That means more character and lower prices. If I don't mention an elevator, expect some steep stairs.

### NEAR THE MARKT

These options are the most centrally located, within a short walk of the main square.

**$$ Hotel de Koophandel** has 25 painting-over-the-bed rooms right on the charming, lively, tree-and-restaurant-lined Beestenmarkt. Request either a view room on the square (with reasonably well-soundproofed windows), or a quieter room in the back (reception closed 23:00-7:00, Beestenmarkt 30, +31 15 214 2302, www.hoteldekoophandel.nl, info@hoteldekoophandel.nl, helpful Irma).

**$ Bridges House Hotel,** with 21 rooms around the corner from the Markt, was once the home of painter Jan Steen and overlooks one of Delft's prettiest canal intersections. Rayn and his parents work hard to run this lovely accommodation (air-con, Oude Delft 74, +31 15 212 4036, www.bridges-house.com, info@bridges-house.com). Their next-door annex, **Hotel la Noire,** has five newer, slightly pricier rooms.

**$ Hotel Johannes Vermeer** owns a fine location in an old cigar factory facing a canal with a garden courtyard in the back. Some of the 30 nondescript rooms have canal views, and the public spaces are particularly inviting—from the stay-a-while lobby/bar/break-fast room, to the cozy inner courtyard, to the roof deck with views of neighboring church spires (family rooms, air-con, Molslaan 20, +31 15 212 6466, www.hotelvermeer.nl, info@hotelvermeer.nl).

**$ Hotel de Plataan** has an imaginative spirit and artistic flair. Its ground floor is a big, high-ceilinged-yet-rustic, inviting bar that faces a lively, leafy square that's filled with al fresco tables in good weather. About half of its 29 rooms are larger and dramatically themed, with outlandish decor—it's worth paying the extra charge to stay in these exotic settings (family rooms; the square can get noisy, especially on weekends—request a quieter back room; air-con in some rooms, elevator, limited parking, Doelenplein 10, +31 15 212 6046, www.hoteldeplataan.nl, info@hoteldeplataan.nl).

## SOUTH OF THE MARKT, CLOSER TO THE TRAIN STATION

These choices are at the southern edge of the old center (or, in the case of the final listing, just outside it). While a bit farther from the heart of town—figure a 10- or 15-minute stroll to the Markt—they are much handier for train travelers.

**$$$ Hotel Arsenaal** is the town splurge: a bold business-class hotel filling a grand old brick building. Originally a 17th-century warehouse for the Dutch East India Company, the building later became a prison for Dutch collaborators with the Nazis, and finally an Army Museum. Now it houses 63 crisp, comfortable, modern rooms and a sprawling, atmospheric ground-floor lounge with gi-gantic beams. The hotel does an admirable job of mixing its history with modern touches and comfort (air-con, elevator, limited pay parking—reserve ahead, Korte Geer 1, +31 15 205 2090, www.hotelarsenaal.com, receptie@hotelarsenaal.nl).

**$ Hotel Grand Canal** has 18 tidy, efficient rooms, all facing a canal in a sleepy part of town. It feels a bit more modern and unclut-tered compared to other Delft options (family rooms, Breestraat 1, +31 15 215 7133, www.grandcanal.nl, info@grandcanal.nl).

**$ The Student Hotel Delft,** part of an innovative Europe-wide chain, mostly houses students—but its ninth and tenth floors (plus others in summer) are dedicated to well-equipped hotel rooms for travelers. Because you're at the top of a high-rise, some rooms come with grand views over Delft's rooftops and steeples. Guests and residents alike share the big, sleek ground-floor lounge, plus a gym and laundry facilities. It's a good choice for the young or young-at-heart (air-con, elevator, Van Leeuwenhoekpark 1, +31 15 200 1323, www.thestudenthotel.com/delft, delft@thestudenthotel.com). The hotel sits just south of the train station, facing an Ibis Styles hotel (the other option for those seeking modern predictability in this ye olde town, www.ibisstylesdelftcity.nl).

# Eating in Delft

As Delft is a university town, lively, affordable, and quality eateries abound. Most places have outdoor seating, sometimes on an inviting square (try Beestenmarkt) or on a little barge floating in the canal out front.

Delft's giant Markt, under the looming tower of the New Church, is a scenic spot for a meal. Most of the places around here are interchangeable, but some good options with outdoor seating can be found behind the Town Hall, across the square from the church.

## FINE DINING

$$$$ **Van der Dussen Restaurant** feels tucked away on a quiet courtyard. It's pricey and a bit pretentious, but the food's good and the setting is delightful—with the chef busy in the showy open kitchen, and rustic elegance under huge beams. For a romantic and formal splurge, this is a good choice. The menu is a fun, borderline-gourmet selection of French, Dutch, and Mediterranean cuisine, with small plates designed for sharing and exploration, and a tempting tasting *menu* starting at €50 (inside seating only, Tue-Sat from 17:30, closed Sun-Mon, Bagijnhof 118, +31 15 214 7212).

$$$ **Spijshuis de Dis** is driven by the creative energy of chef Jan Boheemen, who cooks Dutch with attitude. With an open kitchen, inviting menu, friendly service, top-end beer (local craft or Belgian Westmalle), and great food, the entire experience is a joy. Choose between a characteristic interior or out on a lively square shared with other restaurants. Reservations are smart (Tue-Sat from 17:00, closed Sun-Mon, Beestenmarkt 36, +31 15 213 1782, www.spijshuisdedis.com).

$$$ **'T Postkantoor Restaurant** fills the big old post office with a rollicking energy. It has a fun and convivial vibe both in its spacious wood-and-brick living room—decked out with sofas and old carpets—and a big back courtyard, plus a few sidewalk tables. They have an eclectic international menu and local beer on tap. Consider the enticing prix-fixe dinner (daily 9:30-23:00, Hippolytusbuurt 14, +31 15 750 3243).

$$$ **Restaurant Matties**—with a tight, stylish, borderline-stuffy interior—serves modern Dutch dishes and has a few nice canalside tables (always a serious vegetarian dish, daily 17:00-22:00, Oude Delft 92, +31 15 215 9837).

## MIDRANGE AND BUDGET CHOICES

**$$ Stads-Koffyhuis** is a local institution that's won prizes for its sandwiches (see the trophies above the counter); they also serve panini and Dutch pancakes with various sweet and savory toppings. This is a great spot for an affordable bite, either in the country-cozy interior or out on a canal barge (Mon-Sat 9:00-17:00, closed Sun, may stay open later in busy times, just down the canal from the Old Church at Oude Delft 133, +31 15 212 4625).

**$$ De V** is a lively pub with a dark, cozy ambience and a local following loyal to its straightforward and well-priced food—from ribs and burgers to French and Asian. Sit in the crowded area near the bar, elbow your way up top to the glassed-in patio, or enjoy one of the few tables on a barge on the canal (daily 16:00-22:00, just past the Old Church along the canal at Voorstraat 9, +31 15 214 0916).

**$$ Barbaar** is a fresh, airy bar and café with tables through the courtyard outside the Prinsenhof Museum (in the same building as the Prinzenkwartier gallery). They serve soups, sandwiches, and salads for lunch and drinks and snacks in the evening; in busy times, they may also do dinners (Tue-Sun generally 10:00-20:00, closed Mon, Agathaplein 4, mobile +31 6 3391 8668).

**$ Van der Eyk Visbanken,** overlooking a canal a few steps from the bottom of the Markt (look for the long awning), is the handiest place in town to sample the Dutch delicacy of herring. The long display case shows off a variety of options: deep-fried, raw, smoked, or in a sandwich. This place is fun for its scenic setting and for the chance to see all your options spread out before you. Pick what you like, then choke it down at one of the stand-up counters (daily 9:00-18:00, Cameretten 2, +31 15 361 2014).

**$$ De Parel van Flores Indonesian Restaurant** is a humble, homey, and family-run little place serving pure Indonesian fare. They have rijsttafel in different sizes and prices so you can order according to hunger levels. The decor is super-basic wood paneling... come here for the food, not the ambience (Tue-Sat 17:30-22:00, closed Sun-Mon, just off main square at Voldersgracht 31, +31 15 213 0946).

# Delft Connections

## BY PUBLIC TRANSPORTATION

**From Delft to Rotterdam:** Trains run every 15 minutes for the 15-minute journey to Rotterdam Centraal station.

**From Delft to The Hague:** It's easy and cheap to travel to The Hague by train or tram. While the train may seem faster, the tram is more convenient.

**Tram #1** leaves from in front of the Delft train station—or, closer to the town center, in front of the Prinsenhof courtyard—and clatters through residential neighborhoods to The Hague (stopping at the center, the Peace Palace, and the beach). This connection is frequent, comes with nice urban scenery, and delivers you right into the center of The Hague's tourist zone (€4 for a single ride of up to 2 hours, €7.10 day pass covers the trip there and back, buy either ticket at machine on board). Trams run about 6/hour (direction: Scheveningen Noorderstrand; get off after about 30 minutes at The Hague's Centrum stop for the major sights including the Maurit-shuis). You can continue on this tram directly to the Peace Palace (Vredespaleis stop, about 5 minutes beyond Centrum stop) or go all the way to the beach at Scheveningen (Kurhaus stop, about 15 minutes beyond Centrum stop). Note that this tram does *not* stop at The Hague's Centraal station—for that, take the train (see next).

Regular **trains** depart from Delft's station for The Hague (4/hour, 15 minutes). Get off at The Hague's Centraal station (CS), not the Hollands Spoor station (HS). Note that The Hague's Centraal station is a 15-minute walk or a 5-minute tram ride to reach the tourist zone (for details, see "Arrival in The Hague" on page 391).

For more information on trams and buses, call toll +31 900 486 4636 or use the Netherlands' slick public-transit site, 9292.nl.

**From Delft by Train to: Amsterdam**'s Centraal station (2/hour, 1 hour, more with change in Leiden or The Hague), **Haarlem** (2/hour, 40 minutes), **Leiden** (4/hour, 20 minutes), **Utrecht** (4/hour, 1 hour, change in Rotterdam), **Arnhem** (4/hour, 2 hours, transfer in The Hague or Rotterdam, then Utrecht), **Antwerp** (2/hour, 1.5 hours, change in Rotterdam), **Brussels** (2/hour, 2.5 hours, change in Rotterdam), **Ghent** (hourly, 3 hours, change in Rotterdam and Antwerp), **Bruges** (hourly, 3 hours, change in Rotterdam, Antwerp, and Ghent).

# DAY TRIPS

# NORTH OF AMSTERDAM

While cities sprawl to the south, the idyllic area north of Amsterdam is wonderfully dotted with Dutch clichés: cutesy cobbled villages, gently spinning windmills, and locals whom you can imagine will actually wear wooden shoes from time to time. This region holds some of the quaintest easy day trips from the city. (While you could stay the night in some of these towns—Edam is the most tempting for its village cuteness—side-tripping from Amsterdam is so simple that I wouldn't bother.)

Some of these northern destinations once fronted the Zuiderzee ("South Sea"), but generations of land reclamation reshaped this part of the country, converting the stormy inlet into a pair of tame, freshwater lakes: the Markermeer and the IJsselmeer. To deepen your understanding of these places, read the "Taming the Zuiderzee" sidebar (see page 360).

## DESTINATIONS
Each of these is reachable from Amsterdam by public transportation: train, bus, or boat. But if you want to explore Flevoland, it's much easier by car.

### ▲Alkmaar and Zaanse Schans
Allow a half-day for either destination.

**Alkmaar:** This likeable town is jammed with gawking tour groups on Friday mornings (late March-Sept) and Tuesday evenings (July-Aug), when it holds ye olde traditional cheese market (worth ▲▲).

**Zaanse Schans Open-Air Museum:** Packed with windmills (and greedy shops), this museum is easy to reach from central Amsterdam (15-minute train ride plus 15-minute walk or 40-minute

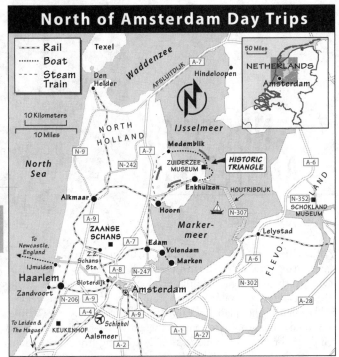

direct bus ride). Or you can visit it on your way back from Alkmaar (40 minutes by train, then a 15-minute walk).

### ▲▲Edam, Volendam, and Marken

Figure on a day (leaving Amsterdam by 10:00) to visit these picturesque villages in the region aptly called Waterland. If you have only a half-day, choose Edam.

**Edam:** Mellow out like a hunk of aging cheese in this quiet town. There are no real sights, but its tiny main square and peaceful canals may win you over. Edam's museum is closed Monday (shorter hours and closed Mon-Thu off-season) and its market is held Wednesday morning.

**Volendam:** A transit hub for the Waterland region, this workaday town has an extremely touristy seafront promenade and a boat across to Marken.

**Marken:** Once an island and now connected by a causeway to the mainland, this time-warp fishing village preserves traditional buildings and lifestyles.

### ▲Hoorn, Enkhuizen, and the Historic Triangle

The two towns of Hoorn and Enkhuizen, on the former Zuiderzee, combine for a day of fascinating sightseeing (leave Amsterdam in the morning for a train to Hoorn, explore that town and its museum, then train over to Enkhuizen for the Zuiderzee Museum).

**Hoorn:** This strollable town boasts the fascinating Westfries Museum—a creaky old house crammed with an engaging collection from the Dutch golden age (closed Mon).

**Enkhuizen:** This town is worth a visit for its excellent open-air Zuiderzee Museum (worth ▲▲▲, outdoor museum closed Nov-March), with an emphasis on seaside lifestyles.

**Historic Triangle:** To slow things down even more, you can connect Hoorn and Enkhuizen with this time-consuming but quaint loop trip via historic steam train and boat.

## Flevoland

Worthwhile only by car, the reclaimed polder land around the former Zuiderzee makes for a fun day of joyriding—cross the sea on the Houtribdijk road, get a dose of the youngest (1986) province of Flevoland (its capital, Lelystad, is home to some land-reclamation museums), and visit Schokland, an old fishing island left high and dry by the draining of the Zuiderzee.

# ALKMKAAR AND ZAANSE SCHANS

Two handy day trips line up north of Amsterdam: Alkmaar is a famous cheesemaking town with a charming square and a bustling cheese market; Zaanse Schans, while the least interesting of Holland's open-air museums, is also its most convenient—offering a taste of traditional life a stone's throw from the capital. Consider combining the two destinations for a full day of sightseeing, ideally on a day when Alkmaar's festive cheese market enlivens the town.

# Alkmaar

Alkmaar is Holland's cheese capital (and, perhaps, the unofficial capital of high cholesterol). In addition to being an all-around delightful city, Alkmaar has a rich history and a zesty cheese-loving spirit. And though it's enjoyable to visit any time, it's most colorful, lively, and crowded during its bustling Friday-morning cheese market (late March-Sept). On your train ride here, you can study up by reading the "Dutch Cheeses" sidebar on page 482.

## Orientation to Alkmaar

Once a stoutly walled city, Alkmaar (pop. 95,000) now has a tidy Old Town laced by canals. The main square, Waagplein, is named for Alkmaar's cheese weighing. The mighty Weigh House, containing the TI and Cheese Museum, is at one end of the square, and the Beer Museum is at the other. (Think of it as "Holland's Wisconsin.") From this area, the main pedestrian drag, Langestraat, leads visitors to the Grote Kerk and Stedelijk Museum.

**Tourist Information:** Alkmaar's TI, in the old Weigh House, sells a town walking-tour brochure (Mon-Sat 9:30-17:00, Sun from 12:00, Waagplein 2, +31 72 511 4284, www.visitalkmaar.com).

The Museumkaart **sightseeing pass** (a potentially worthwhile purchase for those visiting Amsterdam—see page 58) covers entry to Alkmaar's Cheese Museum, Beer Museum, and Stedelijk Museum.

**Arrival in Alkmaar:** From the train station, it's a 15-minute walk to the town center. The route is well marked (just follow signs for *Centrum*): Exit the station to the right and veer left with the arterial down Stationsweg, then turn left (onto Scharlo) when the street dead-ends. Soon you'll cross a canal and see the big church (Grote Kerk), with the modern library and Stedelijk Museum to the left. From the church, walk straight up the main pedestrian street (Langestraat). When you reach the next canal, turn left and walk one more block to the main square and TI.

## Sights in Alkmaar

### ▲▲Cheese Market (Kaasmarkt)

Tellingly, Alkmaar's biggest building isn't the church or the Town Hall, but the richly decorated **Weigh House** (Waaggebouw), used since the 16th century for weighing cheese. (It was converted from an old chapel.) The right to weigh, sell, and tax cheese is what put Alkmaar on the map in the Middle Ages, and it's still what the town is celebrated for today.

Think about the udder importance of cheese to this culture—wheying the fact that it has long kept the Dutch economy moo-ving. If you travel through the Dutch countryside, you'll pass endless fields filled with cows, which are more reliable producers than crops in this marshy landscape. Because cheese offers similar nutritional value to milk but lasts much longer without refrigeration, it was a staple on long sea voyages—and Holland was the first country to export it. Today the Netherlands remains among the world's biggest cheese exporters.

There's no better time to sample a sliver of this proud wedge of Dutch culture than during Alkmaar's **cheese market,** which takes place on Fridays in spring and summer (late March-Sept 10:00-13:00) and Tuesday evenings in July and August (19:00-21:00; www.kaasmarkt.nl).

To start the market, cheesemakers line up their giant orange wheels in neat rows on the square. Prospective buyers (mostly wholesalers) examine and sample the cheeses and make their selections. Then the cheese is sold off with much fanfare, as an emcee narrates the action (in Dutch and English). To close the deal, costumed cheese carriers run the giant wheels back and forth to the Weigh House just as they have for centuries: They load a wheel onto a "cheese-barrow"—kind of a wooden stretcher—then sling each end over their shoulders on ropes and run it to and fro. The cheese carriers' guild has four "fraternities" of seven carriers each: red, yellow, blue, and green (with color-coded hats, cheese-barrows, and scales). There is one "cheese father," who wears an orange hat, enforces the strict rules, and levies fines on carriers who show up late or drink beer before carrying cheese (which is strictly forbidden).

On cheese-market days, the town erupts in a carnival atmosphere, becoming one big street fair with festive entertainers and vendors selling souvenirs, snacks...and, of course, cheese. It can get crowded—especially midmorning—and even the Cheese Museum (described next) is packed, yet its windows allow great unobstructed views of the action below.

### ▲Cheese Museum (Het Hollands Kaasmuseum)

This is probably the Netherlands' best cheese museum...and in this country, that's saying something. With displays on two floors above the TI in the Weigh House, the museum explains both traditional and modern methods of cheesemaking. You'll learn that as the economy evolved, cheesemaking went from being the labor of farmers' wives to factory workers. The museum also has old equipment (much of it still used for today's cheese market), such as big scales, wagons, cheese-barrows, and (upstairs) old presses for squeezing the last bit of whey out of the cheese molds. Ask for an English showing of the eight-minute movie that traces the history and traditions of Alkmaar cheesemaking. (You'll find out what a "cheesehead" really is, and the technical difference between Gouda and Edam cheeses.) Smaller screens around the museum show informative videos—press the flag for English subtitles. There's a special area for kids, too.

**Cost and Hours:** €6; Mon-Sat 10:00-16:00, Sun from 13:00; winter closed Mon-Fri except open Dec 26-Jan 7; enter TI at Waagplein 2 and walk upstairs to museum, +31 72 515 5516, www.kaasmuseum.nl.

### Beer Museum (Nationaal Biermuseum De Boom)

This hokey old museum in a former brewery covers beer production across the centuries—from the days of barrels to the earliest bottling plants. The 1700s-era replica bar has sand on the floor, from a time when men were men and didn't have to aim into a spittoon. An exhibit highlights craft brewers from the Alkmaar area, and a map guides you on a historic brewery walk through the old city. If you're not a beer lover or a backyard brewer, I'd skip it.

**Cost and Hours:** €9.50; Mon-Sat 10:30-17:00, shorter hours off-season, closed Sun year-round; across Waagplein from Weigh House at Houttil 1, +31 72 511 3801, www.biermuseum.nl.

### Grote Kerk

Alkmaar's 500-year-old "Great Church" is similar to others in Holland (such as Haarlem's and Delft's). Visit if you want to see a typically austere Dutch interior.

**Cost and Hours:** Free; generally Tue-Sun 11:00-17:00, closed Mon; closed off-season to sightseers. The church hosts frequent concerts and other events (for schedules, call +31 72 514 0707 or see www.grotekerk-alkmaar.nl).

### Stedelijk Museum Alkmaar

The Stedelijk, which has its primary collection in Amsterdam, also runs this worthwhile branch in little Alkmaar (next to Grote Kerk). The museum has two parts: a permanent collection about the history of Alkmaar and the Dutch golden age, and a space for temporary exhibits. There are several excellent short movies in the town history section, enlivened by props and sound effects (ask to see it in English). But the rest of the history exhibit—with stiff group portraits, other paintings, and artifacts from the town's illustrious past—is only in Dutch and difficult for tourists to appreciate. You can also see works of the Bergen School, the Dutch version of Expressionism (1915-1925). Visit here only if the temporary exhibit intrigues you.

**Cost and Hours:** €13.50; Tue-Sun 11:00-17:00, closed Mon; Canadaplein 1, +31 72 548 9789, www.stedelijkmuseumalkmaar.nl.

## Alkmaar Connections

Alkmaar is connected by frequent fast trains to **Amsterdam** (4/hour, 40 minutes). However, these trains do not stop at the Zaanse Schans museum. To visit the **Zaanse Schans** museum on your way back to Amsterdam, take a train from Alkmaar to Uitgeest or Zaandam (2/hour), where you can transfer to a slower regional train (typically just across the platform) to Zaandijk Zaanse Schans (trip takes 40 minutes total). On busy days, the info desk in the tunnel of the Alkmaar train station hands out schedules for this connection.

# Zaanse Schans
# Open-Air Museum

This re-created 17th-century town puts Dutch culture—from cheesemaking to wooden-shoe carving—on a lazy Susan. Lo-

cated on the Zaan River in the town of Zaandijk, the museum is devoted to the traditional lifestyles along the Zaan—once lined with hundreds of wind-mills used for every imaginable purpose and today heavily in-dustrialized (including a giant corporate chocolate factory). In the 1960s, houses from around

the region were transplanted here to preserve traditional culture. Most of the exhibits are run by quirky locals who've found their niche in life and do it with gusto.

Zaanse Schans (ZAHN-zeh shahns), a hodgepodge of loosely related attractions in a pretty park with old houses, feels less like a museum than Arnhem's or Enkhuizen's open-air museums. And, since each attraction charges a separate entry fee (and those that are free are either selling or promoting something), it also feels more crassly commercial...you'll be nickel-and-dimed for your cultural education. But it's undeniably handy, just 15 minutes by train (plus a 15-minute walk) from downtown Amsterdam. Two of the attrac-tions here—the Zaanse Time Museum and the tourable, working windmills—are unique and genuinely interesting (and worth ▲). Because it's the easiest one-stop look at the Netherlands' traditional culture, Zaanse Schans can be flooded at midday by busloads of tour groups. To avoid the hordes, come early or late.

## GETTING THERE

**By Public Transportation:** From Amsterdam, catch a slow **train** going toward Uitgeest (4/hour), ride for about 15 minutes, then hop out at Zaandijk Zaanse Schans. Reaching Zaandijk Zaanse Schans from Alkmaar requires a change in Uitgeest or Zaandam (see "Alkmaar Connections," earlier).

Once at the Zaandijk Zaanse Schans station, it's a 15-minute walk to the museum (well-marked, just follow the signs...and the

*(vertical text in left margin)* ALKMAAR & ZAANSE SCHANS

other tourists). Go through the underpass and exit straight ahead, watching on your left for a TI machine where you can pull the crank to get a map or get one at the café on the station platform. Then continue straight until the road forks. (If this area seems surprisingly sweet-smelling for an industrial district, thank the chocolate factory.) From the fork, follow *Zaanse Schans* signs. Turn left, then right across the river, which puts you at the "back entrance" to the park, near the Time Museum.

**Bus #391,** the "Industrial Heritage Line," runs from Amsterdam Centraal station's platform E directly to Zaanse Schans, stopping next to the Zaans Museum (4/hour, 40 minutes).

**By Car:** From Amsterdam, take A-8 (direction: Zaanstad/Purmerend), turn off at *Purmerend A-7,* then follow signs to *Zaanse Schans* (€12 for parking, discount with the Zaanse Schans Card, explained below).

## ORIENTATION TO ZAANSE SCHANS

**Cost:** Entry is free, but you'll pay to visit some historical presentations (prices noted in each listing). If you'll be visiting the main Zaans Museum, the Weaver's House, the Zaanse Time Museum, and at least one windmill, you might save a little money with the €23.50 **Zaanse Schans Card** (also includes discounts on parking and at some shops and cafés). The Museumkaart covers every sight here except the windmills.

**Hours:** The grounds are open all the time because people actually live here. During the spring and summer (April-Sept), most building interiors are open daily 9:00-17:00 (though some are closed Mon, and individual opening and closing times can vary). After about 16:30, things get really quiet. In the off-season (Oct-March), only some of the buildings are open (roughly 9:00-17:00 Sat-Sun, shorter hours or closed entirely Mon-Fri; www.dezaanseschans.nl).

**Information and Services:** The visitors center, located in the Zaans Museum building, has a good, free map of the grounds. Ask if any events are scheduled for the day you visit (daily 9:00-17:00, lockers, free WCs in Zaans Museum, pay WCs in park, +31 75 681 0000, www.zaansmuseum.nl).

## SIGHTS AT ZAANSE SCHANS

I've arranged these sights in order from the train station. Drivers should park at the Zaans Museum and visit these in reverse order, or walk five minutes to the Time Museum and begin there.

### ▲Zaanse Time Museum (Museum Zaanse Tijd)

More interesting than it sounds, this collection is brought to life by its curator—clock enthusiast Pier van Leeuwen—and other vol-

ALKMAAR & ZAANSE SCHANS

unteers. If Pier is there and not too busy, he can show you around and will lovingly describe his favorite pieces. (Or pick up the free brochure and explore seven centuries' worth of timepieces on your own.) Upstairs is a big, bulky, crank-wound turret clock from around 1520. Back then, the length of an "hour" wasn't fixed—there were simply 12 of them between sunrise and sunset, so the clock's weights could be adjusted to modify the length of an hour at different times of year. Also up here are the museum's prized possessions: two of the world's four surviving, original 17th-century pendulum clocks, which allowed for more precision in timekeeping. Downstairs, appreciate the fine craftsmanship of the Zaans clocks (one clock is wound by being pushed up on a rack, rather than pulling a chain) and Amsterdam clocks.

**Cost and Hours:** €10; daily 11:00-16:00; +31 75 617 9769, www.mnuurwerk.nl.

• *Next door is the...*

### Albert Heijn Grocery "Museum" (Museumwinkel)

Little more than a thinly veiled advertisement for the Dutch supermarket chain, this replica grocery store from the 1880s re-creates the first shop run by Albert Heijn. The scant exhibits lead you to a room promoting Heijn coffee.

**Cost and Hours:** Free, get English description sheet; Tue-Sun 10:30-13:00 & 14:00-16:00, closed Mon; off-season Sat-Sun only 11:00-16:00; +31 75 670 5657, https://albertheijnerfgoed.nl.

• *A few doors up the street is the recommended **De Hoop op d'Swarte Walvis** restaurant. Just beyond is a boat-tour dock (see the Zaanse Schans website for more info on your choices). From here, enjoy a lovely view of the windmills. But before you visit them, poke into the little village area across from the boat landing. First you'll pass an adorable curiosity shop that's a pack rat's heaven. Then you'll encounter the...*

### Bakery Museum (Bakkerijmuseum)

This fragrant and very modest "museum" displays old bakery equipment (including cookie molds) and sells what it bakes. Borrow the English descriptions to navigate the slapdash exhibit.

**Cost and Hours:** Free to enter museum, various treats available—most around €3, cash only; Tue-Sun 9:00-18:00, closed Mon; off-season daily-9:30-17:00; +31 75 617 3522.

• *Now head for the...*

### ▲Windmill Museum (Molenmuseum) and Windmills (Molens)

The very industrious Zaan region is typified by hardworking windmills, which you'll see everywhere. Mills are built with sturdy oak-timber frames to withstand the constant tension of movement. To catch the desired amount of wind, millers—like expert sailors—know just how much to unfurl the sails. When the direction of the wind shifts, the miller turns the cap of the building, which weighs several tons, to face the breeze. The **Windmill Museum** immerses you in four centuries of social and economic context before

turning you loose to explore Zaanse Schans' old-fashioned windmills. From the museum's top floor you can orient yourself with an excellent view across the landscape. (If you don't have time for the museum, simply visit the mills that interest you.)

**Cost and Hours:** €18 museum ticket includes visit to two mills, otherwise €5 per mill; museum open daily 10:00-17:00, off-season Fri-Sun only; mill hours vary; Kalverringdijk 30, +31 75 621 5148, www.zaanschemolen.nl.

**Visiting the Windmills:** Each mill has its own purpose. **De Gekroonde Poelenburg** is a sawmill, where stout logs are turned

into building lumber. **De Kat** ("The Cat") grinds dyes. Watch its gigantic millstones rolling over the colored dust again and again, as wooden chutes keep it on its path. Climb the steep steps (practically a ladder) for a closer look at the wooden gears and the fine views out over the museum grounds. **De Zoeker** ("The Seeker") crushes oil from seeds and nuts, a drop at a time—up to an incredible 100 quarts per day. **De Huisman** ("The Houseman") grinds spices and fills the air with wonderful scents. Try to visit a mill that's spinning—you'll see more action inside. And though these structures appear graceful, and even whimsical from the outside, on a windy day you can experience their awesome power by getting up close to their grinding gears.

• *After exploring the windmills, cross the little canal to the big...*

## De Catharina Hoeve Cheese Farm (Kaasmakerij)

Essentially a giant cheese shop, this is worthwhile only if you catch one of their presentations. A movie shows how cheese is made, and periodically a costumed Dutch maiden explains the process in person and dispenses samples...followed by a confident sales pitch.

ALKMAAR & ZAANSE SCHANS

**Cost and Hours:** Free entry, daily 9:00-18:00, off-season until 17:00, +31 75 621 5820, https://henriwillig.com.
• *Walk past the mini-windmill to the...*

## Weaver's House (Wevershuis)

Inside this small house you will be taken through the weaving process by energetic volunteers who show you how families lived and worked among the looms in the 18th century (€2, April-Sept daily 9:00-17:00, off-season Fri-Sun only).
• *Then walk to a shopping zone, which includes the...*

## Wooden Shoe Workshop (Klompenmakerij)

More engaging than the park's other free attractions, this shoe store features a well-presented display of clogs from different regions of the Netherlands. You'll see how clogs were adapted for various purposes, including wooden clogs with boot-like leather to the knee, frilly decorative bridal clogs, high-heel clogs, roller-skate clogs, and spiky clogs for ice fishing. Watch the videos and try to catch the live demonstration that sends wood chips flying as a machine carves a shoe. Your visit ends—where else?—in the vast clog shop.

**Cost and Hours:** Free entry, daily 9:00-18:00, off-season until 17:00, +31 75 617 7121, www.woodenshoes.nl.
• *Nearby is the recommended* **De Kraai** *restaurant, and just across the big parking lot is our final stop, the...*

## ▲Zaans Museum and Verkade Pavilion

This museum, with a modern structure that evokes both the hull of a ship and the curved body of a whale, is the focal point of the complex.

**Cost and Hours:** €12.50, includes good audioguide; daily 10:00-17:00; +31 75 681 0000, https://zaansmuseum.nl.

**Visiting the Museum:** The museum houses the visitors center, as well as a fresh, modern multimedia presentation that explains Holland's industrial past and present. The exhibit, with some English descriptions, is thematically divided into four parts: life, work, wind, and water.

The other half of the building is given over to Verkade, a beloved Dutch brand of cookie (translations here use the British term "biscuit"). The pavilion is essentially a very slick version of several other "museums" around the park—thinly disguised branding opportunities for major Dutch companies. Nonetheless, this re-created cookie factory is a fun treat, especially if they are giving out free samples. Look for well-written explanations and clever computer-based games. Don't miss your chance to make like Lucy and Ethel and see how many virtual cookies you can pick off a speeding conveyor belt and pack into a box—my score: 1,253.

## EATING AT ZAANSE SCHANS

Walking from the train station into town, across from the windmill before crossing the bridge, you'll pass a handful of simple sandwich-and-coffee shops and a SPAR supermarket (picnic options; Mon-Sat 7:30-20:00, Sun 9:00-18:00, Guisweg 9). Once you cross the bridge into the sightseeing village you'll find these places:

**$$ Restaurant de Kraai,** across from the Wooden Shoe Workshop, is a cafeteria-style eatery offering traditional sweet and savory pancakes (daily 9:00-18:00, off-season until 17:00, on slow days may close earlier, indoor and outdoor seating, +31 75 615 6403).

**$$$$ De Hoop op d'Swarte Walvis** ("The Hope of the Black Whale") is the park's splurge, with a white-tablecloth interior, outdoor seating, and an ambitiously priced menu (Tue-Sun 11:00-22:00 except closed Sun in Feb; closed Mon year-round; dinner served 18:00-21:30, +31 75 616 5629, www.dewalvis.nl).

ALKMAAR & ZAANSE SCHANS

# EDAM, VOLENDAM & MARKEN

The aptly named region of Waterland (VAH-ter-lahnd), just north of Amsterdam on the west shore of the IJsselmeer, is laced with canals and sprinkled with picturesque red-brick villages. Two in particular—the homey cheesemaking village of Edam and the trapped-in-a-time-warp hamlet of Marken—offer visitors an enticing peek at rural Holland. To travel between the two towns, you'll pass through the touristy waterfront town of Volendam.

If choosing just one Waterland town, make it Edam—and consider spending the night. Because of its charm and its proximity to Amsterdam, this region is popular. But if you'd like to get a taste of traditional Dutch living, it's worth joining the crowds.

## PLANNING YOUR TIME

The most efficient way to see this area is as a one-day loop trip by public transportation from Amsterdam (or Haarlem); to have enough time for the whole loop, get started by 10:00. Begin with a bus from Amsterdam to Edam. Then, after enjoying Edam, continue by bus to Volendam for a stroll and to catch the passenger-only boat across to Marken. Leave Edam by around 14:00 to have sufficient time in Volendam (you'll want at least an hour there), and to be able to reach Marken before its museum and shops close (around 17:00). Poke around salty Marken before taking the bus back to Amsterdam.

All the bus rides in this loop are covered by a €12.50 Waterland/Go Dutch day ticket (covers everything between Amsterdam and Hoorn, sold by EBS bus company, located at rear of Centraal station, catch buses here, www.localbus.nl; routes not covered by Amsterdam transit passes). The Volendam-Marken boat costs extra and doesn't take cars. The drive from Volendam to Marken is a delight.

Sightseeing Tip: The Museumkaart sightseeing pass (a potentially worthwhile purchase for those visiting Amsterdam—see the
"Sights in Amsterdam" chapter) covers entry to Edam's Museum,
the Voldendams Museum, and Marken's Marker Museum.

# Edam

This adorable cheesemaking village, worth ▲▲, is sweet but not
saccharine, and is just 30 minutes by bus from Amsterdam. It's

mostly the terrain of day-trippers, who
can mob the place on summer weekends. For the ultimate in cuteness and
peace, make your home in tiny Edam
(ay-DAHM) and stay overnight.

Although Edam is known today
for cheese, it was once an industrious
shipyard and port. But having a canal
to the sea caused such severe flooding
in town—cracking walls and spilling
into homes—that one frustrated resident even built a floating cellar (which
you can visit in what's now Edam's
oldest house). To stop the flooding, the
harbor was closed off with locked gates (you'll see the gates at Dam
Square next to the TI). Eventually the harbor silted up, forcing the
decline of the shipbuilding trade.

Edam's Wednesday market is held year-round, but it's best in
July and August, when the focus is on cheese. You, along with piles
of other tourists, can meet the cheese traders and local farmers.

## Orientation to Edam

Edam is a very small town—you can see it all in a lazy 20-minute
stroll. It's so nice, though, that you may be tempted to stay longer.
Dam Square (Damplein), with the City Hall and its TI, is right
along the big canal called Spui (rhymes with "cow"); the town's
lone museum is just over the big bridge.

### TOURIST INFORMATION
The TI, often staffed by volunteers, is in City Hall on Dam Square.
Pick up a free simple map and consider buying the *Stroll Through
Edam* brochure outlining a self-guided walking tour (Wed-Sun
11:00-16:00, closed Mon-Tue; WC and ATM just outside, +31 299
315 125, www.vvvedamvolendam.nl).

EDAM, VOLENDAM & MARKEN

## ARRIVAL IN EDAM

The bus "station"—really just a line of bus stops with no ticket office—is a five-minute walk from Dam Square and the TI. At the canal by the bus lot, turn right (following the *Centrum* sign) and walk along the water (on Schepenmakersdijk). Cross the next bridge (Kwakelbrug; a white bridge just wide enough for two people) and head straight up the street toward the gray-and-gold bell tower. Hook right around the church, pass one bridge, and you'll wind up across the canal from Dam Square.

## HELPFUL HINTS

**Cheese Market:** From early July through August, farmers bring their cheese by boat and horse to the center of town on Wednesday mornings (10:30-12:30), where it's weighed and traded by Edamers in traditional garb (www.kaasmarktedam. nl).

**Bike Rental: Ronald Schot** is near the cheese market, between Dam Square and the Grote Kerk (€10/day, tandem-€22.50/ day; Tue-Fri 8:30-18:00, Sat until 16:00, closed Sun-Mon except by appointment; sells regional maps with bike routes, Grote Kerkstraat 7, +31 299 372 155, www.ronaldschot.nl).

# Sights in Edam

Edam has a handful of sights, but the best thing to do is to just wander its storybook lanes and canals—a stroll worth ▲.

## ▲Edam's Museum: Edam's Oldest House

This 400-year-old historical home, across the bridge from Dam Square, provides a fun peek at what all these old canal houses once looked like inside. The house is particularly interesting for its floating cellar, designed to accommodate changes in water level without destabilizing the building. A classic town map shows how Edam would have been a mighty sight in 1698. Exhibits on the town's history and how people lived are invigorated by the included and essential audioguide. A comprehensive collection of the locally produced Fris art pottery is displayed here and across the bridge in City Hall (covered by the same ticket).

**Cost and Hours:** €5; Tue-Sun 10:00-16:30, closed Mon; Nov-March Fri-Sun only; Dam Square 8, +31 299 372 644, www. edamsmuseum.nl.

### Grote Kerk

Perched on the edge of town, the "Great Church" feels surprisingly huge for tiny Edam. Like other fine churches in Holland, it was built around 1500, then gutted by iconoclasts during the

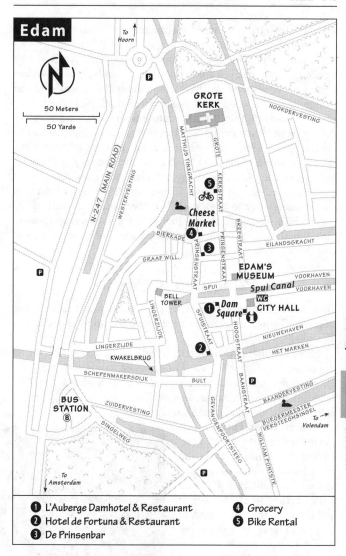

**Edam**

To Hoorn

N

50 Meters

50 Yards

N-247 (MAIN ROAD)

WESTERVESTING

GROTE KERK

NOORDERVESTING

MATTHIJS TINXGRACHT

GROTE

KERKSTRAAT

BREESTRAAT

EILANDSGRACHT

**⑤** 🚲

🦢 **Cheese Market**

BIERKADE

**④** ■

GRAAF WILL

**③**

PRINSENSTRAAT

PRINSENSTRAAT

SPUI

**EDAM'S MUSEUM**

*Spui Canal*

VOORHAVEN

VOORHAVEN

**BELL TOWER**

**①** ■ *Dam Square* ■

WC

**CITY HALL**

**①**

LINGERZIJDE

SPUISTRAAT

HOOGSTRAAT

NIEUWEHAVEN

LINGERZIJDE

**②**

HET MARKEN

KWAKELBRUG

BAANSTRAAT

SCHEPENMAKERSDIJK

BULT

BAANDERVESTING

**BUS STATION**
Ⓑ

ZUIDERVESTING

GEVANGENPOORTSTEEG

🦢

BURGERMEESTER VERSTEEGHSINGEL

To Volendam

SINGELWEG

WILLIAM FONISTR.

To Amsterdam

**EDAM, VOLENDAM & MARKEN**

**①** L'Auberge Damhotel & Restaurant

**②** Hotel de Fortuna & Restaurant

**③** De Prinsenbar

**④** Grocery

**⑤** Bike Rental

tumult that came with the Reformation; it's been Dutch Reform since 1566.

**Cost and Hours:** Free, daily 13:30-17:00, closed late Oct-March, www.grotekerkedam.nl.

**Getting There:** From Dam Square, walk over the bridge, turn left, then head right down Prinsenstraat to Nieuwenhuizen-plein, the traditional cheese-market square. Find the "cheese weigh house" on the left—the one with the cheese frieze—and peek in-

344 Rick Steves Amsterdam & the Netherlands

side if it's open (tasty samples). Continue through the square to the canal, which leads to the church.

**Visiting the Church:** The church's vast interior is covered by a ceiling constructed just like a stone vault—but built of wood, because heavier stone would have made the building sink into the wet ground. The wooden catwalks are original. Near the pulpit, find the massive "cabinet organ," dating from 1640, interesting for the big painted side panels that can swing around like shutters to cover it. Many 19th-century Dutch homes had one of these, cleverly disguised to evade a tax on organs. Buy the church's booklet for more on the church's interior, including some good background on the stained-glass windows. If you haven't landed in Edam on cheese-market day, look for the TV tucked in the side wall on the right, which plays a 12-minute loop video of scenes around town, including the cheese market. The church has a cute café corner and free WCs.

## Sleeping in Edam

These two hotels are both distinctive and classy. For cheaper rooms in private homes, check www.vvvedamvolendam.nl or ask at the TI.

**$$$ L'Auberge Damhotel,** centrally located on a canal across the street from City Hall, has 11 overpriced rooms with over-the-top plush decor that doesn't quite seem to fit (reception at the hotel restaurant bar, family rooms, air-con, Keizersgracht 1, +31 299 371 766, www.damhotel.nl, info@damhotel.nl).

**$$ Hotel de Fortuna** is a canalside wonderland with flowers and the sounds of ducks and other birds. It offers steep stairs and 23 low-ceilinged rooms in a cozy collection of five ancient buildings in the old center of Edam. A fine value, it's been run by the Dekker family for more than 30 years (family room,  Spuistraat 3, +31 299 371 671, www.fortuna-edam.nl, fortuna@fortuna-edam.nl).

## Eating in Edam

Considering how close it is to Amsterdam, coming to Edam for a romantic dinner in the countryside and then heading back to your hotel in the big city can be a fine plan. The **$$$$** restaurant at **L'Auberge Damhotel** (listed above) dominates the main square

EDAM, VOLENDAM & MARKEN

with outdoor seating and a dressy interior, and Edam's lanes are lined with tourist-friendly restaurants (within a block or two of Dam Square).

**$$$$ Hotel de Fortuna,** listed earlier, has a lovely restaurant, with a romantic dining room and seating in a gorgeous garden alongside a picturesque canal (three-course "Fortuna *menu*" is a good value, daily 12:00-15:00 & 18:00-21:30, shorter hours Jan-Feb).

**$$ De Prinsenbar** offers a variety of ways to taste Edam cheese (as well as other regional cheeses) in a pub setting with darts and stay-awhile stools. Their café and terrace are good for a light lunch or a midday snack (Mon-Thu 15:00-24:00, Fri from 14:00, Sat-Sun from 11:30, Prinsenstraat 8, +31 299 372 911).

**Picnics:** Stock up on the essentials at **Gerard Visser,** a simple grocery that also sells small, premade meals (Tue-Fri 9:00-18:30, Sat 8:30-17:00, closed Sun-Mon, Prinsenstraat 12, +31 299 371 753).

## Edam Connections

EBS runs frequent buses between Edam and **Amsterdam.** From Amsterdam, buses leave from the bus platforms behind Centraal station (exit from the station's west corridor and take escalators up to the bus stops). Buses #312, #314, and #316 are the most direct options (3/hour, fewer after 18:30 and on weekends, 40 minutes). For bus schedules, see www.9292ov.nl.

**By Bus to Volendam on the "Waterland Loop":** Buses #110 and #316 zip you from Edam to Volendam in about 10 minutes (2/hour, direction: Amsterdam CS). Hop off at the Zeestraat/Centrum stop (other buses also go to Volendam, but not to this handy town-center stop).

# Volendam

Less cute and more functional than the other two Waterland towns, Volendam enjoys some workaday charm of its own—including a lively dike-top walkway stretching along a shimmering bay and a fun town museum.

**Orientation to Volendam:** If arriving by bus from Edam, get off at the Zeestraat/Centrum stop. The museum and TI share a building within a block of the bus stop, in the modern part of town—look for the building with the miniature windmills out front. At the **TI** pick up a free Volendam/Marken map (Zeestraat 37, +31 299 363 747, www.vvvedamvolendam.nl). To reach the boat to Marken, walk straight from the bus stop toward the water, then turn left and walk along the dike.

**Visiting Volendam:** The town's lone sight is the **Volendams Museum** (in the same building as the TI). Its hokey but charming little collection oozes local pride, with displays of traditional costumes, replica house and shop interiors, scenes from village life, and nostalgic old grainy black-and-white movies that are worth watching even if you don't speak Dutch. The museum's highlight is the Cigar-band House, where a local artist glued 11 million cigar bands to big boards to create giant images—from Dutch windmills to Venice to a sour-looking Statue of Liberty (Zeestraat 41, +31 299 369 258, www.volendamsmuseum.nl).

To reach the **waterfront** from the museum, walk two blocks down Zeestraat to Europaplein, head left, cross the dark-green bridge, turn right, then zigzag back across the next bridge and follow the brick steps up to the harbor. Volendam's touristy **promenade** has a lively boardwalk appeal and is lined with souvenir shops, indoor/outdoor eateries, and Dutch clichés. The walls inside **Hotel Spaander** (eight houses down from the northern end of the harbor, on the right) are decorated with paintings by starving artists who slept or ate there. Don't miss the maze of sleepy residential courtyards below sea level just behind the promenade, with an adorable dollhouse charm and fewer crowds.

**Volendam Connections:** The **"Marken Express"** boat connects Volendam with Marken in 30 minutes (€8.75 one-way, €13.50 round-trip, cheaper online, bring your bike for €1.75 extra each way; summer—daily about 10:00-19:00, departures every 30-45 minutes; off-season—shorter hours, departs every 1.5 hours or by appointment only; check website for daily departure times, leaves from northern corner of harbor, no outside food allowed on board, +31 299 363 331, www.markenexpress.nl).

# Marken

Famous as one of the Netherlands' most traditional fishing communities, Marken is a time-passed hamlet in a bottle—once virtually abandoned, now revived but kept alive solely as a tourist attraction.

This island town once had a harbor for whaling and herring fishing, but when the Zuiderzee began to silt up in the late 17th century, it became more and more difficult to eke out a living here, and many people from Marken fled to easier conditions on the mainland. When the Zuiderzee was diked off in 1932 to become a giant freshwater lake (the IJsselmeer), it forced saltwater fishermen to adapt or find a new calling (which most did). Marken became a virtual ghost town. But in 1957, a long causeway was constructed from the mainland to the island hamlet, which allowed easy access for visitors—who today come in droves to walk its tiny lanes and marvel at its cuteness.

Marken has no TI; the nearest one is in Volendam. The museum is in the town center.

**Visiting Marken:** The village has two districts connected by counterweight bridges. The famously conservative village, which is historically both very religious and royalist, named its bridges after Dutch queens. Arriving by boat, first wander through the colorful Havenbuurt ("Harbor Neighborhood"), then head for the charming Kerkbuurt ("Church Neighborhood") to get a taste of Marken's old-time charm.

Land is tight on Marken and so are its lanes. They may appear private, but they actually are public and you're welcome to explore them. As you walk, notice the unique architecture, adapted to survive the challenging local conditions. Because the tides could be so temperamental, Marken's houses tend to huddle together on manmade hills called *werven*. Homes in lower locations were built on pilings to keep them high and dry. After the Zuiderzee was diked and tamed, the pilings were boxed in to create basements. Traditional Marken homes, while dull and black-tarred outside, are painted a cheerful yellow and blue inside.

The delightful harbor dates to 1837. At its peak in 1890, the fishing fleet here boasted about 200 vessels. But when the big flood of 1916 spurred construction of the massive dike 50 miles north of here, the saltwater fishing industry dried up. Enjoy some *kibbeling* (local fish-and-chips) at an idyllic eatery on the harbor.

The town's main attraction, located in the cute Kerkbuurt neighborhood, is the modest **Marker Museum,** celebrating the 16th-century costumes (hand-sewn and still worn for special events) and traditional lifestyles of the people of Marken. As you enter, ask for an English showing of the good eight-minute movie (+31 299 601 904, www.markermuseum.nl). The **church** is generally closed, but if it's open, peek in. In this very Protestant town (unlike Volendam, which is Catholic), the church posts a list of pastors next to the altar that goes back in an unbroken line to 1579, when the Reformation came.

Just outside town, on the way to the parking lot and the bus stop, you'll pass Marken's raised **cemetery.** Open the black iron gates and step in. Because of the very limited land (so high and dry), plots are shared. That's why the graves are marked with numbers rather than names. With more time, you can walk (about 40 minutes) out to the **lighthouse,** picturesquely situated at the far end of the island at the tip of a sandy spit.

At the far end of town is a parking lot where you'll find the bus stop, bike rental (summer only, from the ice-cream wagon), and a wooden-shoe factory that is just a touristy shop unless a bus tour stops by (when they demonstrate the traditional way to carve a set of shoes).

**Marken Connections:** Bus #315 connects Marken with **Amsterdam's** Centraal station (2/hour, 30 minutes). In Marken, catch the bus along the main road that skirts the town, a little past the south end of the harbor and just past the big parking lot. For info on the boat to Volendam, see "Volendam Connections," earlier.

Driving to and from Marken, you'll enjoy a scenic road taking you under majestic modern windmills along a four-mile spit. Bikers have their own lane running along the top of the dike. You'll notice lots of cows and sheep but no fences separating the farms. As the animals can't pole-vault, the canals keep them from roaming.

# HOORN, ENKHUIZEN & THE HISTORIC TRIANGLE

Two towns in North Holland, each conveniently located on the same speedy train line, make this side trip from Amsterdam a great day out: Hoorn, with its Westfries Museum, offers the best look I've seen at golden age Dutch East India Company heritage. And Enkhuizen has the Zuiderzee Museum, Holland's most complete and interactive open-air folk museum for traditional Dutch culture. For a lazier day out, take the Historic Triangle loop, which combines the two towns with countryside scenery via steam train, vintage boat, and modern-day train.

## PLANNING YOUR TIME

From Amsterdam, twice-hourly trains connect both towns easily (Amsterdam to Hoorn: 30 minutes, Hoorn to Enkhuizen: 25 minutes, Enkhuizen to Amsterdam: 1 hour). Each town is easy to explore on foot and can keep you busy for a good three to four hours of sightseeing. It's possible to see both Hoorn and the open-air museum in one long day on your own.

In **Hoorn,** spend 1.5 hours at the Westfries Museum and set aside 30 minutes to wander and enjoy the town and its harbor.

The **Enkhuizen Zuiderzee Museum** merits at least three hours, plus a little time in the sweet little town.

The **Historic Triangle** loop—a combination steam train, 1920s-era ship, and regular train circuit from Hoorn—gives you a fun and memorable look at the countryside. However, the loop trip doesn't leave you enough time to fully appreciate the sights in both Hoorn and the Enkhuizen Zuiderzee Museum (with more time, you could add an overnight stop and spread the trip over two days). If you're contemplating the Historic Triangle, read that section carefully and confirm schedules before committing, as it requires a bit more planning.

# Hoorn

Hoorn, with 72,000 people, is big enough that it has 21st-century urban problems and unsightly sprawl around the old core. But when you walk from the train station into the center, you go back in time and find yourself surrounded by the facades and cobbles of a day when New York City was called New Amsterdam and the Dutch really were masters. With a major harbor, Hoorn was a prosperous trade center during Holland's golden age in the 1600s. The town's merchant ships sailed to exotic corners of the globe to stuff their holds with precious commodities. Hoorn was the birthplace of Jan Pieterszoon Coen, an officer of the Dutch East India Company. Another local boy, Willem Schouten, sailed around South America's stormy southernmost point in 1616 and named it after his hometown—Kaap Hoorn (Cape Horn).

## Orientation to Hoorn

### TOURIST INFORMATION
The helpful TI is by the old tower at the harbor (Tue-Sun 11:00-17:00, closed Mon and Nov-March, Hoofd 2B, +31 654 791 816, www.hoorninformation.nl).

### ARRIVAL IN HOORN
The Hoorn **train station** is about a half-mile from the old center. The TI is about 20 minutes away in the main square, but there's a good town map right outside the station to help you get oriented.

To **walk** into town, head south down Veemarkt (the diagonal street with trees in the median), turn right on Gedempte Turfhaven, then take a left on Grote Noord—the big, bustling main commercial drag. Follow Grote Noord straight to Roode Steen, the main square (where you'll find the Westfries Museum). The TI is just a bit beyond that (well signed from the square).

## Sights in Hoorn

### Grote Noord
Stroll the bustling main drag of Hoorn just to feel the pulse of the city today. You'll pass Koepel Kerk on the right, with a big dome indicating that it's the Catholic church. Stepping inside you see a church filled with statues, colored glass, and decoration—definitely not Protestant.

### ▲De Roode Steen
Hoorn's small main square, literally "The Red Stone," is named for the blood that once flowed from the gallows here. It was a tough

heritage. The statue in the center is of Jan Pieterszoon Coen, an officer of the Dutch East India Company and the ruthless governor-general of the Dutch East Indies (present-day Indonesia) in the early 1600s. He was so cruel to people in lands the Dutch colonized that honoring the mean sonofabitch with this statue has become controversial. Read the plaque for all the gory details. The old building with the brightly colored facade is the Westfries Museum (described next). Opposite it is the delightful weigh house (Waag) sporting a unicorn, the symbol of the city. Dating from the 1600s, today this building houses a popular café and restaurant, d'Oude Waegh, serving traditional dishes and providing a great place to just sip a drink and enjoy the scene at the center of Hoorn.

## ▲▲▲Westfries Museum

This museum—with a curiosity cabinet, still lifes, devotional art, city-bigwig group portraits, and elegantly furnished living rooms and a kitchen—takes the art and heritage of the Rijksmuseum and the Dutch Masters and puts it in the context of a real town and golden age community. The building that houses the museum is perfectly suited for its task, dating from the 1630s, with a distinctive, ornate facade. In addition to standard displays, the museum uses 21st-century technology to celebrate its 17th-century heritage via a popular virtual-reality exhibit.

**Cost and Hours:** €10, Tue-Sun 11:00-17:00, closed Mon, Roode Steen 1, +31 229 280 022, www.wfm.nl.

**Visiting the Museum:** When you arrive, check the times and reserve the 40-minute **virtual-reality** walk through Hoorn during the golden age (generally 4/day).

Visit the rest of the **museum** while you await your virtual-reality time slot. You're engulfed in the 17th-century golden age, when the Dutch ruled the waves. From the cellar to the attic, via creaky spiral staircases and upon floorboards recycled from old ships, you'll explore lavish period rooms filled with actual artifacts of the age. The riches and painted canvases inside give a sense of the age when local tycoons divvied up their world. Don't miss the basement model of Hoorn in 1650, complete with high-tech theatrical videos featuring a cast of historical characters talking about Hoorn in their time. The audio is in Dutch, but between the English subtitles and dramatic gesturing, you'll get the gist.

## Hoorn Harbor

The town harbor, ringed by leaning golden age merchants' houses and still guarded by an ancient tower, is an evocative scene. The old locks, once they were shut, protected the fleet from changing tides. That was before the Zuiderzee was controlled and made into a vast lake with the 1932 completion of a big dike, the Afsluitdijk. The great merchant ships are gone, replaced by seaworthy recreational boats. But under the tower, the charming statues of three boys still gaze out to sea, dreaming of salty adventures back when the Zuiderzee really was a sea and great ships sailed from here for the East Indies.

### Museum Stoomtram

Train enthusiasts will enjoy the steam-train museum at the Hoorn station. Just across the tracks are an old-time station, a workshop where steam trains are maintained, and the departure point for a historical steam-train journey (14 miles each way to Medemblik and back; €14.70 one-way, 1.25-hour trip; €24.75 round-trip, www.stoomtram.nl). This ride is part of the Historic Triangle loop (described later). Note the museum is only open on days when the train is running.

## Hoorn Connections

From the main train station, trains zip back to **Amsterdam** (2/hour, 30 minutes) or on to **Enkhuizen** (2/hour, 25 minutes).

**To Enkhuizen:** The direct train is the quickest way to reach Enkhuizen if you're trying to squeeze maximum sightseeing into one day. But another option is via the sleepy loop trip called the **Historic Triangle:** Take a steam train to Medemblik, then a vintage boat to Enkhuizen. While this takes much longer than the direct train (and connections run far less frequently), it's a relaxing way to soak up the Dutch scenery.

# Enkhuizen Zuiderzee Museum

ENKHUIZEN

When the huge Zuiderzee (ZOW-der-zay) inlet was diked off and made into a lake in 1932, age-old Dutch lifestyles were in danger of disappearing. To preserve the traditional culture of the communities along the bay, the open-air Zuiderzee Museum, worth ▲▲▲, came into being. (For more on the Dutch land reclamation projects that closed off the Zuiderzee, see page 360.)

The museum's original buildings were collected from around the Zuiderzee. You'll meet people who do a convincing job of role-playing no-nonsense 1905 villagers. You're welcome to take their picture, but they won't smile—no one said, "Have a nice day," back then. Children enjoy trying out old-time games, playing at the dress-up chest, and making sailing ships out of old wooden shoes. Scattered throughout the grounds are historic images of Zuiderzee children and posts where kids can listen to audio of kids describing events in their day-to-day lives.

The museum is in Enkhuizen, a sleepy town of about 20,000 that was once a mighty harbor home to the Dutch merchant fleet. Towns like Enkhuizen were hit hard by the great reclamation projects that tamed the sea, landlocked once-vital ports, and destroyed hearty fishing traditions by turning the fertile sea into a big freshwater lake. The modern age left it behind, and today only holiday yachts and sailboats berth here. From Enkhuizen, a 17-mile dike, the Houtribdijk (route N-307), stretches east toward Lelystad in Flevoland, disappearing into the lake called IJsselmeer.

**Tourist Office:** In the small square to the right of the train station, a helpful TI sells tickets to the museum, allowing visitors to hop on the shuttle boat just next to the office and skip the 15-minute hike (daily 8:00-17:00, closed Nov-March, +31 228 313 164).

## GETTING THERE

Whether you're arriving by **train** from Amsterdam (2/hour, 1 hour) or Hoorn (2/hour, 25 minutes), it's a 15-minute walk from Enkhuizen's train station to the museum (follow signs for *Zuiderzeemuseum*), or you can buy a museum ticket and take the shuttle boat (details below).

If you're taking the **Historic Triangle** trip, you'll arrive by boat from Medemblik and dock directly at the museum.

**Drivers** can park for free at the train station and then take the shuttle boat or walk to the museum.

**Museum Shuttle Boat:** A shuttle boat circles counterclockwise between the train station and the museum (free with museum ticket, 3/hour, 20-minute circuit).

## ORIENTATION TO ZUIDERZEE MUSEUM

**Cost:** €18, €12 for kids 4-12, free for kids under 4, family ticket available. Tickets are sold online, at the town TI, at the east end of the outdoor museum, and in the indoor museum.

**Hours:** Daily 10:00-17:00, outdoor museum closed Nov-March.

**Information:** +31 228 351 111, www.zuiderzeemuseum.nl.

**Sightseeing Strategies:** The outdoor part of the museum has two entrances. To tour it from west to east (in the same direction as my self-guided tour), take the boat from the train station, exit at the museum's east end when you're done, then walk through the town back to the station. To start at the east end, walk from the station along the harbor, tour the museum from east to west, and catch the boat at the west end of the museum back to the Enkhuizen train station (last boat at 17:30).

## ❍ SELF-GUIDED TOUR (WEST TO EAST)

The Zuiderzee Museum is a delight to explore, with something for all the senses—smell the wood fires and tanning vats, savor a bite of aged cheese and old-fashioned licorice, watch a windmill turn, hold a lump of coal, and catch the sound of wooden clogs on a brick road. Follow this tour, but don't be afraid to poke into houses and backyards (the curious get a lot more out of this experience—any open door is open for you). While I've listed stops here going from west to east, you can easily turn this book upside down and do it from east to west. The museum has two sections: the outdoor part (Buitenmuseum) with more than 100 historic buildings from around the Zuiderzee relocated right here and, 200 yards away, the indoor museum (Binnenmuseum), filling a fine old merchant's home and warehouse. Regardless of which direction you go, the museum is laid out in a nice meandering flow with one section leading to the next.

**West Dock:** As you disembark the shuttle boat, a nature preserve lies to the right. Head to the left. The first building to the left (the brickmaker's place) functions as an information center where you can get oriented to the museum.

The museum is organized by section (e.g., the Church District). Every building has a little plaque with a brief English description and a map showing the building's original location in the Zuiderzee region.

**Fishing Village:** The first section is the fishing village. Fun-to-explore homes and locals in period costumes populate the ramshackle village street from Urk—once a remote island across the Zuiderzee, now high and dry with a seemingly over-sized fishing fleet.

**Polder Land:** Head to the polder area, near the windmill. Windmills harness the power of the wind to turn Archimedes' screws, which, by rotating in a tube, pump water up over a dike and into the sea—continuing to drain reclaimed polder land. (Try it.) Nearby are vats used to cure fish and a smokehouse where you can buy a tasty snack of smoked herring or eel.

**The Urban Canal:** Circle around to the urban canal zone (near the pavilion), lined with shops—such as a bakery and a cheese shop where 15,000 clumps of Gouda could be aged. Don't miss the pharmacy (marked *Apotheke De Groote Gaper,* under the queen with her mouth hanging open); ask if they stock any opium. Past the counter where the pharmacist weighs out little bottles of camphor, you'll find a room full of open-mouthed giant heads. Traditionally, Dutch pharmacies were marked by a head with a gaping mouth (opening wide to say "aaaah" for the doctor, or for taking a pill). Many of these original heads are dark-skinned—medicine, like people from the east or south of Europe, was considered mysterious and magical. A nearby theater may be showing a dramatic film that includes some grainy black-and-white footage of traditional Zuiderzee life. As you curl around along the little canal, you'll pop into a rich sailor's home from the 18th century and find other trades represented, such as a barber and a sailmaker.

**The Church District:** Next, head into the church district, surrounding a reconstructed church dating from the 15th century. Because local builders were more familiar with boats than buildings, standing inside this church feels like being under an overturned boat (a common feeling in many Dutch village churches). Around the church are more shops, including the blacksmith and the fascinating cooper shop, where you can watch barrels being made. Don't miss the schoolhouse, with two period classrooms: one from 1905 and another from 1930. Just across the canal from the church area is a big **$** cafeteria-style **restaurant,** with indoor and outdoor seating.

**Harbor:** Now walk toward the cute, enclosed harbor, filled with Zuiderzee watercraft from ages past (just beyond it is a modern harbor, filled with pleasure boats). The little cluster of houses just beyond the harbor (where you may be able to catch a rope-making demonstration) is based on the island village of Marken.

**Indoor Museum:** Finally, as you leave the park through the main entrance, head for the indoor museum (200 yards from the outdoor section). As you exit, turn left, cross the street and walk two blocks, watching for the museum on your right. This half of the museum puts a personal touch on the villages.

The impressive hall is filled with nine old Zuiderzee boats. Notice that many of the boats have big, flat fins on the sides. Because the Zuiderzee could be very shallow, these boats didn't have a keel; the fins could be extended down into the water to provide more stability. The rest of the museum focuses on the people of the Zuiderzee region, with clothing and home furnishing displays, as well as personal stories. You may see film footage from a feast of St. Nicholas, a funeral with a line of women in identical striped skirts and flippy hats, and weddings, christenings, and ice-skating fun—all fascinating faces of yesteryear.

**Returning to Amsterdam:** From the indoor museum, it's a scenic 15-minute walk, mostly along the water, through the bricks-and-canals town to the Enkhuizen train station: Exit the indoor museum to the right, follow the wall, and cross three canal bridges (watching for *Station* directional signs). If you finish the visit on the east end, hop on a shuttle boat to ride back to the train station (last boat at 17:30).

# The Historic Triangle

This three-part journey designed for tourists makes for an interesting trip out from Hoorn (or from Amsterdam, connecting via Hoorn). If you're more interested in steam trains, the pastoral countryside, and a little IJsselmeer cruise than the museums in Hoorn or Enkhuizen, it's a great way to spend a day.

De Historische Driehoek, as it's called in Dutch, consists of a steam train from Hoorn to Medemblik, followed by a cruise from Medemblik on the 1920s-era boat *MS Friesland* to Enkhuizen, stopping at the Zuiderzee Museum. There you can catch a regular train from Enkhuizen back to Hoorn or your accommodations in Haarlem, Amsterdam, or elsewhere.

The schedule can be frustrating, as most days there's just one steam-train departure from Hoorn connecting to one daily boat at Medemblik. This means you leave Hoorn without even seeing the Westfries Museum, and you arrive in Enkhuizen without enough time to do the Zuiderzee Museum properly before it closes. (With more time, you could overnight in Hoorn and/or Enkhuizen.) Note that the train and the boat occasionally don't run on Mondays.

**Cost:** €24.75 for combo-ticket covering stream train and vintage boat, www.stoomtram.nl; €4.30 for train from Enkhuizen to Hoorn, www.ns.nl.

**Sample Schedule:** 9:39—Train from Amsterdam to Hoorn; 10:15—Arrive in Hoorn; 10:40—Take steam train from Hoorn; 12:00—Arrive in Medemblik; 13:20—Boat sails from Medemblik; 14:50—Boat arrives at Zuiderzee Museum in Enkhuizen; 14:50-17:00—Enjoy Zuiderzee Museum; 17:00-18:00—Free time in Enkhuizen; 18:00—Catch the train to Amsterdam, arriving by 19:00. Confirm all times carefully before setting out.

## STEAM TRAIN FROM HOORN TO MEDEMBLIK

The train departs from the Museum Stoomtram historical depot behind the main train station (across the tracks from the main arrivals hall; described earlier, under "Sights in Hoorn").

After you choose a seat inside the train, you can get up and walk around. The best views are standing on the train balcony at the very back of the train. You'll feel like a whistle-stop presidential candidate as the train plods through the Dutch countryside.

Enjoy the purely Dutch scenery on this serene, old-fashioned joyride. Count sheep. Moo at cows. Watch horses playfully run alongside the train. Look for ducks in the canals and pheasants in the fields. Go ahead, order the *poffertjes* (puffy mini-pancakes). If you see Dutch kids waving to the train from their backyards, wave back. The modern white windmills in the distance jolt you back into the 21st century, just in time to arrive at...

## MEDEMBLIK

If connecting the steam train with the vintage boat ride, you'll have about an hour in this pleasant town before boarding the boat (confirm the exact departure time at station). One of the oldest ports in the area, it has a Hanseatic League heritage and characteristic lanes and fortified buildings huddled around its old harbor. Medemblik has three main sights (all closed Mon): a bakery museum, the Kasteel Radboud (former castle, now a fortified mansion), and the Stoommachine Museum (an old pump station turned steam-engine museum just outside of town). Exit the station and bear left, then right, to walk up the main drag—a pretty market street lined with cafés, bakeries, shops, and postcard stands. If you're hungry, you could grab a quick sandwich at an outdoor café, but you likely won't have time for a full meal. Basic food is available on the boat.

**Shortcut Back to Hoorn:** If you skip the boat trip, you can ride back to Hoorn on the steam train or catch the bus (bus #139, at least hourly, 40 minutes, around €5, buy ticket from driver). There's no direct overland connection from Medemblik to Enkhuizen—if you miss the boat, you'll have to take the bus back to Hoorn, then the train or bus from there to Enkhuizen.

HISTORIC TRIANGLE

## BOAT FROM MEDEMBLIK TO ENKHUIZEN

Catch the *MS Friesland* to Enkhuizen just over the dike from the Medemblik station (you'll see the boat moored there as your train pulls in, €12.10 one-way ticket, info-www.msfriesland.nl, tickets-www.stoomtram.nl). It's a 1.5-hour putter along the coast to the Zuiderzee Museum in Enkhuizen. You can grab a bite in the boat's surprisingly comfortable dining room. If you've brought a picnic, grab a wicker chair and enjoy the peaceful, windswept deck. Kids can safely run around on the open spaces of the top deck or play wooden board games in the lounge. In good weather, you'll pass small pleasure craft—little sailboats and windsurfers—close enough to shake hands.

HISTORIC TRIANGLE

# FLEVOLAND

About a sixth of the Netherlands is reclaimed land—much of it a short drive northeast of Amsterdam. To appreciate the Dutch quest to show the sea who's boss (and what the sea did to deserve it), visit the youngest Dutch province, Flevoland. The area is worthwhile only with a car, and far less charming than most other day-trip options. But it offers a fascinating drive for engineers or anyone else who wants to understand how the Dutch have confidently grabbed the reins from Mother Nature. It combines well with a visit to the town of Marken or Enkhuizen's Zuiderzee Museum.

## PLANNING YOUR TIME

On a day's drive out from Amsterdam, I'd start by heading north to Enkhuizen. (For insight into the traditional lifestyles laid high and dry by the diking of the Zuiderzee, consider detouring to Marken for a stroll, or tour Enkhuizen's Zuiderzee Museum.) Drive over the Houtribdijk (N-307) to Lelystad, and then—if time allows—continue up to the Schokland Museum. Figure about an hour from Amsterdam to Enkhuizen, a half-hour across the dike to Lelystad, a half-hour from Lelystad north to Schokland, and about an hour from Schokland back to Amsterdam (depending on traffic).

**Sightseeing Tip:** The Museumkaart sightseeing pass (see page 58) covers entry to Lelystad's Batavialand exhibit and the Schokland Museum.

## Sights in Flevoland

### DIKE ROAD (Houtribdijk, N-307)

This 17-mile dike, built in 1975 as part of the Markerwaard reclamation project, is a reminder of the audacity of the Dutch vision to block off and pump out the entire inland sea. While the plan to re-

## Taming the Zuiderzee

Look at a map of the Netherlands. The big expanse of water in the middle was once the Zuiderzee—literally the "South Sea." The Dutch have always had a love/hate relationship with this tempestuous sea. While it provided a convenient source of fish and trade—and an outlet to the Atlantic—the unpredictable bay also made life challenging. Over the centuries, entire towns were gradually eroded off the map.

But in 1918, the Dutch fought back and began to ingeniously tame the sea and reclaim their land with the Zuiderzee Works. The vision: to carve up what was the South Sea, bit by bit, drain it out, and turn it into dry and fertile land.

First, in 1932, they completed a sturdy dike (the Afsluitdijk) across the mouth of the sea—stretching 20 miles from Den Oever to Friesland and the northern Netherlands. This enclosed a body of water a bit smaller than Rhode Island, and succeeded in turning a dangerous, raging sea into a mild puddle.

After the Zuiderzee was diked off, the Dutch began to partition pieces of the sea floor, dike them off, and drain the water. The Noordoostpolder (185 square miles) and Flevopolder (375 square miles) were created; together, these became (in 1986) the 11th governmental province of Flevoland, with about 400,000 inhabitants—many of them older than the land they live on. An area that was once a merciless sea is now dotted with tranquil towns. The salty new seabed soil was treated organically and eventually became fertile farmland. The roads, commercial centers, and neighborhoods—made affordable to the masses—are all carefully planned and as tidy as can be.

Over time, the remaining salty water of the Zuiderzee became fresh, and in 1975, it was further divided in the middle with

claim all of the land south of the dike (the floor of the Markermeer, to your right) was abandoned, this road remains a handy transportation link connecting North Holland and Flevoland and the East. While there's little to actually see, driving over it is a novel experience. At the start (near Enkhuizen), ships float in a channel (hydroduct) above the road. The stone monument midway marks the joining of North Holland with Flevoland.

At the other end, a bridge deposits you in Flevoland, the only entirely reclaimed province in the Netherlands. It's filled with bedroom communities famous for being nondescript. But it allows the residents of a densely inhabited country the option of owning a freestanding home, big garage, and piece of yard. The commute to Amsterdam is long for working parents, so Flevoland kids are bored, and often have drug problems and need counseling. These planned communities create an almost "Stepford Wives"-style contentment, a community designed to make

the 17-mile-long Houtribdijk, connecting Enkhuizen and Lelystad. This created two bodies of water: the IJsselmeer in the north and the Markermeer in the south. The eventual plan was to drain almost the entire Markermeer to create a third big polder, called the

Markerwaard (160 square miles), to use for farming, residential zones, and a new airport. However, by this time, public opinion about the need for polder land had swayed. There were ecological concerns: Fishermen in villages like Urk and Marken reported that they could no longer harvest the increasingly unsalty lake, dismantling the local economy. (Nowadays, these old fishing towns host more pleasure craft than serious fishing boats.) Also, people enjoyed the Markermeer as a recreation zone and viewed it as a useful reservoir in case of drought. The Markerwaard was never built.

There are several places in the Netherlands to appreciate the greatness of the Zuiderzee Works. Driving over either of the big dikes—the Afsluitdijk (A-7) in the north, or the Houtribdijk (N-307), between Enkhuizen and Lelystad—gives you a sense of the scale of these projects. And actually driving around Flevoland drives home how a little country worked hard to create new land; Flevoland's Schokland Museum and the museums in Lelystad are particularly evocative.

Dutch suburban dreams come true—at the expense of the Dutch free spirit.

## LELYSTAD

The capital of Flevoland, Lelystad is named for the statesman who originally proposed the Zuiderzee Works. Driving around the town, it's clear that everything was planned. The residential neighborhoods feel computer-generated and were all built at the same time. There are speed bumps on all roads, and the layout is a winding maze, making it easy to get lost. The business district attempts to spice things up with wacky modern design elements.

### Batavialand

The *VOC Batavia* was a 17th-century sailing ship built for the Dutch East India Company. Here on the waterfront you can tour a replica and see how workers currently are building a sec-

FLEVOLAND

ond vessel—a replica of the 17th-century Dutch battleship *De 7 Provinciën,* one of the largest historical naval reconstructions in the world. You can also peek into a woodcarving workshop, a rigging workshop, and a blacksmith's foundry. The associated museum covers the largest reclamation project in history—the "taming" of the Zuiderzee (see sidebar on page 360). The story of the struggle against the water is told through historic films, sound bites, models, and interactive displays. Exhibits also explore the geological evolution of Flevoland and the prehistoric people—hunters, fishermen, and gatherers—who lived here 6,000 years ago. The unusual building consists of two superimposed blocks, symbolizing the region's interconnections between land and water.

**Cost and Hours:** €16; Mon-Sat 10:00-17:00, Sun from 11:00; closed Mon in winter; Oostvaardersdijk 1, +31 320 225 900, www.batavialand.nl.

## ▲▲Schokland Museum

Once a long, skinny island with a few scant villages, Schokland (about a half-hour drive northeast of Lelystad) was gradually enveloped by the sea, until the king condemned and evacuated it in 1859. But after the sea around it was tamed and drained, Schokland was turned into a museum of Dutch traditions...and engineering prowess.

**Cost and Hours:** €8; Tue-Sun 11:00-17:00, closed Mon except July-Aug; Middelbuurt 3, +31 527 760 630, www.museumschokland.nl.

**Getting There:** From Amsterdam, it's about an hour's **drive** north (assuming there's no traffic), but the trip offers travelers an insightful glimpse at Dutch land reclamation. Leave Amsterdam's ring freeway, following signs for *Almere*—first southeast on A-1, then northeast on A-6. You'll drive the length of the very flat reclaimed island of Flevoland—past the towns of Almere and Lelystad—and pass a striking line of power-generating windmills spinning like gigantic pinwheels as you cross out of Flevoland and into Noordoostpolder, the reclaimed "Northeast Polder" that includes Schokland. Take the Urk exit (#13), turn right, and follow blue signs for *Schokland.*

**Visiting the Museum:** After buying your ticket, you'll watch a 15-minute **film** (press button to start in English) about the history of the town, its loss to the sea, and its reclamation.

Then tour the exposition called **Schokland: An Island in Time,** which explains how Schokland was reclaimed as part of what would become the Northeast Polder, beginning in 1936. After being enclosed by a sturdy dike, a yearlong project drained this area of water in 1942 (while the Netherlands was occupied by the Nazis). Various Allied bombers were shot down and crashed into this area (including one whose mangled propeller is displayed just outside the museum), joining the dozens of shipwrecks that already littered the seafloor.

A model shows the full territory of the Northeast Polder, which is carefully planned in concentric circles around the central town of Emmeloord (with Schokland and another former island, Urk, creating a pair of oddball bulges in the otherwise tidy pattern).

The exhibit explains that this isn't the first time this area has been dry land. From prehistoric times through the Middle Ages, much of what is today the Northeast Polder was farmed (many old tools have been discovered). In 1100, medieval engineers even attempted a primitive (and ultimately unsuccessful) effort to reclaim the land. Other remains from former residents include bones from mammoths and other prehistoric mammals, and a primitive 2,450-year-old canoe.

Then you'll head into the **Schokkerhuisje** to learn about the people who lived here (called *Schokkers*) until they were evacuated in 1859. Up to 650 people at a time lived on Schokland, residing in settlements on hills called *terpen* while they farmed the often-flooded land below. Like the rest of the Netherlands, this little island was divided in half by religion: part Catholic, part Protestant. This museum holds artifacts from the former town of Middelbuurt. You'll see traditional *Schokker* costumes (abandoned when they left the island) and a map of the entire island.

Back outside, go into the former **town church,** with a ceiling like the hull of a ship, a pulpit like a crow's nest, and a model ship hanging from the ceiling—appropriate for the seafaring residents of a once nearly submerged island.

Finally, follow the path (below the church) to walk around the base of the former island—now surrounded by **farm fields.** When farmers first tilled their newly reclaimed soil a half-century ago, they uncovered more than just muck and mollusks.

You'll see a pair of rusty anchors and a giant buoy that used to bob in the harbor—now lying on its side and still tethered to the ground. Examine the stone dike and black wooden seawall built by residents in a futile attempt to stay above water. The post with the long blue measuring strip helped residents keep an eye on the ever-rising water level.

# SOUTH OF
# AMSTERDAM

Most of the Netherlands' most historic and interesting cities—as if purposefully arranged by the tourist board—line up along a single train line that runs south from Amsterdam.

With trains running at least every 15 minutes, it takes just over an hour to conveniently lace together Amsterdam, Haarlem, Leiden, The Hague, Delft, and Rotterdam. A couple of flowery destinations off the main train line—the Keukenhof garden show and the Aalsmeer flower auction—are also worth a visit.

As you travel through the countryside, make a point to look out the window for a glimpse of the Netherlands both past and present. Overstuffed cows moo contentedly in pastures, canals big and small turn pristine fields into graph paper, old-fashioned windmills spin, sleek modern bike paths trace canals and train tracks, idyllic pea patches burst with produce watched over by little potting sheds, and so on. The trip is a sightseeing treat in itself.

The towns themselves are so different, yet all unmistakably Dutch. Familiarize yourself with your options so you can hop out at whichever place intrigues you...and enjoy. In most cases, the train drops you right in the heart of town or just a short and scenic stroll away.

The towns in this section are neatly bookended by a pair of home-base cities: Haarlem (to the north, near Amsterdam) and Delft (to the south, near Rotterdam). From either of these bases—or from Amsterdam itself—you can reach any of these destinations in a quick hop.

Notice that sleepy, accessible Delft—with its mellow pace, postcard-perfect canals, and generous selection of hotels and restaurants—is sandwiched between the big cities of The Hague and Rotterdam (both interesting but less appealing to stay in). Delft is

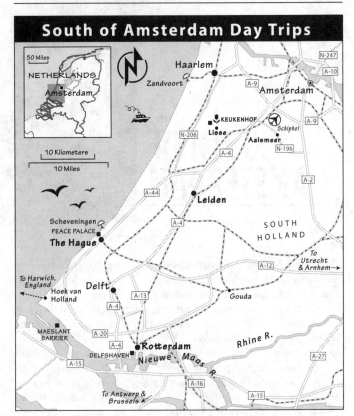

# South of Amsterdam Day Trips

basically a bedroom community for both cities—close enough that you could make the connection on bicycle rather than on rails.

If you need a beach fix, try Scheveningen (near The Hague, listed on page 399) or Zandvoort (near Haarlem, described on page 291).

## DESTINATIONS

One of the best destinations in this region—**Delft**—is covered earlier in this book.

### ▲Keukenhof and Aalsmeer

Flower lovers have two very different choices:

**Keukenhof:** The can't-miss-it garden show in the town of Lisse, rated ▲▲▲, is open from late March to late May.

**Royal FloraHolland Aalsmeer Flower Auction:** This vast warehouse near Schiphol Airport shows you the business side of the Netherlands' beautiful flower scene (weekday mornings year-round).

### ▲▲Leiden

With its prestigious university, this pleasant small city—which was also the birthplace of Rembrandt—is the Netherlands' answer to Cambridge or Oxford. It offers visitors a low-impact, fun-to-explore cityscape of canals and old ivy-covered university buildings, as well as more and better museums than other Dutch cities of its size (American Pilgrim Museum closed Sun-Wed; Windmill and Lakenhal Museums closed Mon).

### ▲The Hague

This big-city seat of Dutch government is a sleepy, modern-feeling town with the tourable parliament complex and a smattering of good museums. But the reason most visitors come is to tour the excellent Mauritshuis Royal Picture Gallery, with a remarkable collection of Dutch Masters art—including Vermeer's *Girl with a Pearl Earring.*

### ▲▲Rotterdam

Europe's largest port is built for trade much mightier than tourism, and its lack of cutesy wooden-shoe culture makes for a harsh contrast with most other Dutch towns. Still, it's a mighty city, bombed during World War II and rebuilt with a gleaming skyline. A bike ride through its towering skyscrapers and a sightseeing harbor cruise provide a dose of honest Holland you'll find nowhere else.

# KEUKENHOF AND AALSMEER

Of all the day trips mentioned in this book, these are all about flowers: a lovely garden show (open only in spring) and a business-like flower warehouse (open weekday mornings year-round). Both are an easy half-day trip from Amsterdam or Haarlem.

# Keukenhof

This ▲▲▲ garden is the greatest bulb-flower patch on earth, open for only two months in spring. Each year, seven million flowers, enjoying the sandy soil of the Dutch dunes and polder land, conspire to thrill even the most horticulturally challenged. Along with flowers, you'll enjoy all the Dutch icons, with a working windmill, gaily playing carillons, canal boat rides, warm-off-the-griddle syrup waffles, and wooden shoes galore. It's flat-out fun.

## ORIENTATION TO KEUKENHOF

**Cost:** €18.50 (purchase on Keukenhof website), €33.50 combo-ticket covers park entry and round-trip bus transport from Amsterdam; €29.50 from Haarlem, Leiden, or Schiphol Airport (available on website under "Plan your visit," then "Travel advice").

**Hours:** Late March-late May daily 8:00-19:30, last entry at 18:30.

**Information:** +31 252 465 555, www.keukenhof.nl.

**Avoiding Lines:** The park is packed with tour groups daily; for smaller crowds and the best light, go early or late in the day. If your heart is set on the optional canal boat ride, buy your ticket online in advance or get your time slot as soon as you arrive at Keukenhof—the 36-passenger boats fill quickly on busy days.

**Getting There:** Keukenhof is located at the northern tip of the town of Lisse, at the center of the "Dune and Bulb Region." From Amsterdam's Leidseplein, take bus #397 to Schiphol and change to bus #858 (Keukenhof Express, 2/hour, 75 minutes total). From Schiphol Airport, catch bus #858 (8/hour, 40 minutes). From Haarlem, take bus #50 to Lisse (4/hour, 1 hour). From Amsterdam or Haarlem you can also take a train to Leiden, then bus #854 (another Keukenhof Express). Drivers will find Lisse well marked from the A-4 expressway south of Amsterdam.

**Visitor Information:** To check the status of the blooms, use www.visitduinenbollenstreek.nl, which shows recent photographs of different areas around the gardens. Even in a late-blooming year, the gardens are impressive.

**Baggage Check:** It's free to store small suitcases and backpacks in lockers just outside the park's entrance.

**Eating:** Cafeterias and waffle stands are scattered within the gardens, along with areas for picnics.

## VISITING THE GARDENS

Get the map at the entrance and begin exploring the 80-acre park filled with pavilions linked by garden paths. Head first to the **Juliana Center,** where you can learn about the history of the tulip, understand how they grow, and see how the 40 gardeners here plant the bulbs in "lasagna" layers four deep so flowers bloom all spring. Friendly and helpful park employees and volunteers mingle around this pavilion to answer any questions about the 800 varieties of tulips.

Three other pavilions are full of greenhouse flowers. The largest and most impressive, **Willem-Alexander,** is dedicated to the perfection of the tulip and its surprising varieties. The **Beatrix** showcases another featured flower, with the focus changing yearly. The **Oranje Nassau,** with displays related to the festival's annual theme, also has a large cafeteria. Nearby is a children's area with a playground and small petting zoo.

You have two options to see the expansive **blooming fields** beyond the gardens. A 45-minute **canal boat ride** with a narrated audioguide quietly whisks visitors through the fields. Look for the "whisper" electric-boat dock and ticket office near the windmill just past the Willem-Alexander pavilion (€9; daily 9:30-17:00 on the hour and half-hour).

A second option is to **rent a bike.** As you exit the gardens, you'll spot bike parking and a rental hut across from the main parking lot (Rent-a-Bike Van Dam, €15/day, daily 9:30-19:00, +31 252 284 075, www.rentabikevandam-keukenhof.com). While you can't take bikes into the gardens themselves, Van Dam has mapped out four routes (3-15 miles) that circle alongside nearby flower fields; the farthest goes to a lake, the dunes, and the sea.

# Aalsmeer Flower Auction

Get a bird's-eye view of the huge Dutch flower industry at the Aalsmeer location of Royal FloraHolland, where the world's flower prices are set. You'll wander on elevated walkways (through what's claimed to be the biggest commercial building on earth) over literally trainloads of freshly cut flowers.

About half of all the flowers exported from Holland are auctioned off through this building. The flowers are shipped here overnight (for maximum freshness), auctioned at the crack of dawn, and distributed as quickly as possible. Historically buyers jammed into big auditoriums, watched a giant "Dutch auction" clock tick down prices, and placed their bids as carts of fresh flowers trundled through. Today, those auction halls are usually empty, and most of the buying is done online. While some travelers are disappointed that you can no longer watch a live flower auction, it's a reminder that FloraHolland isn't a tourist attraction: It's a busy industrial facility that also welcomes curious visitors. The big draw here is the gigantic space, the bustle of global commerce, and colorful flowers as far as the eye can see.

**Cost and Hours:** €10; Mon-Fri 7:00-11:00, Thu until 9:00, closed Sat-Sun and holidays—check website; gift shop, cafeteria.

**Tours:** Download the IZI Travel app to access the Royal FloraHolland audio tour, with a narrated 30-minute walking route along the elevated walkway.

**Information:** +31 297 398 050, www.royalfloraholland.com.

**Getting There:** You can reach the flower auction by bus from Amsterdam (Connexxion bus #357 from Centraal station, 2/hour, 1 hour, get off at Aalsmeer "FloraHolland-FloriWorld" stop) or from Haarlem (take bus #340 to the town of Aalsmeer, transfer to bus #357, 4/hour, 1 hour).

Aalsmeer, which is close to Schiphol Airport, makes a handy last fling for drivers before dropping off your car at the airport and catching a late-morning weekday flight out (bus #198 also runs between the auction and the airport; 4/hour, 20 minutes). From the A-4 expressway south of Amsterdam, drivers take the Aalsmeer exit (#3) and follow signs for *Aalsmeer,* then *FloraHolland.* Once you reach the complex, follow the *P Tourist* signs to park on top of the garage, then take the elevator downstairs and follow *Tourist* signs to the visitors center.

**Visiting the Flower Auction:** Things get rolling quickly after the 7:00 opening time; for peak floral variety, the earlier, the better (best before 9:30; things get much quieter later in the morning).

Standing above all those blooms, take a deep, fragrant breath and hold it in. Follow the audio tour on your mobile device to listen to information at two dozen different stops (marked with pink signs). You'll see the busy beehive of the distribution process as workers scurry to load carts of flowers onto little tractors to zip to awaiting buyers. Up along the ceiling, look for the suspended orange trams. This "Aalsmeer Shuttle" zips loads of flowers over the workers' heads to the distribution center across the street, far more quickly and efficiently than trucks.

Most of the flowers are purchased by wholesalers and exporters. You may see some big auction halls—likely empty these days, as most bidders log in remotely (or work from little cubicles). The auction here works in a unique way. Keep an eye out for big clock-like dials: This is a "Dutch auction," meaning that the price starts high and then ticks down, until buyers push the button at the price they're willing to pay. Think about the high stakes and the need for decisiveness...there's no time to think things over as the auctioneer calls, "Going once, going twice..."

Exhibits (which include an old auction clock) explain the process and let you try it out for yourself. You may also get to peek into the company's testing lab, where they create and test new varieties of flowers.

# LEIDEN

Leiden (LIE-den) is the Oxford of Holland. Its prestigious university imbues the town with an upscale aura—and with 20,000 students, who keep otherwise hoity-toity Leiden firmly rooted on the ground. As an academic center, the birthplace of Rembrandt, and the final European home of the Pilgrims before they set sail for America, Leiden has many claims to fame. But perhaps most enticing of all is that it's simply a pleasant, relatively low-key Dutch city that's easy to get to, fun to explore...and happens to have more than its fair share of great sights and museums.

## PLANNING YOUR TIME

Often-overlooked Leiden is tucked between Amsterdam and The Hague on Holland's busy north-south rail line. If you have only a few hours to spare, hop out at the station, throw your bag in a locker, and follow my self-guided walk in this chapter. The pretty and historic core can be appreciated in a two-hour stroll; with more time, you can dip into some of Leiden's fascinating museums. Note that the American Pilgrim Museum is closed Sunday through Wednesday, and Leiden's other museums are closed Monday. Market days are Wednesday and Saturday (bigger).

# Orientation to Leiden

With about 120,000 residents, Leiden is slightly smaller than Haarlem but bigger than Delft. The neatly oblong old center is lassoed by its former moat *(singel),* and the two branches of the Rhine River merge at its center—creating an inviting network of canals big and small. The train station sits at its north-western corner, a short walk from the town center.

**Tourist Information:** The TI is a block in front of the station (on the right; Mon-Fri 8:00-18:00, Sat 10:00-16:00, Sun 11:00-15:00; Stationsweg 26, +31 71 516 6000, www.visitleiden.nl).

**Arrival in Leiden:** Leiden's manageable **train station** has lockers (up the escalator just inside the main entrance, by tracks 1 and 2; credit card only). To rent a bike, exit out the main doors and turn immediately left (look for the Oldenburger shop, long hours daily; www.olden-burger.nl). To reach the center of town—narrated by my self-guided walk—exit out the main doors and proceed straight down Stationsweg for five minutes.

**Helpful Hints:** Marike Hoogduin-Berkhout is an art historian and excellent **local guide** who leads tours of Leiden, The Hague, and Amsterdam, plus bike tours through the tulip fields and Keukenhof (€175 up to 3 hours, mobile +31 6 5377 3808, www.marikeculturaltours.nl, info@marikeculturaltours.nl). Canal **boat tours** are available (see "Sights in Leiden"). The Museumkaart **sightseeing pass** (see page 58) covers entry to Leiden's Boerhaave Museum, Windmill Museum, and Lakenhal Museum.

# Leiden Walk

This two-mile self-guided walk begins at the train station, curls through the center of the city to reveal its university and Rembrandt connections, climbs up to Leiden's historic castle, then loops right back to where you started. I'd give it about two hours at a leisurely pace, not counting any sightseeing stops.

• *Walk out the front door of the train station. Pause in the plaza and take in today's Netherlands: bike garage on left (with taxi stand on top), Lego-style world of modern office buildings and condos all around, park-and-ride-lot buses on right, herring shack straight ahead.*

*Head down Stationsweg, which bends to the right. You'll pass the*

LEIDEN

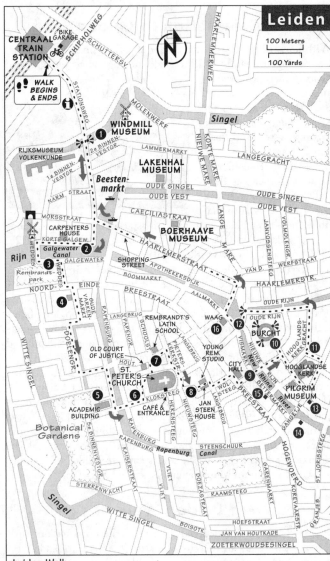

## Leiden Walk

1. Singel
2. Galgewater
3. Rembrandtplein
4. Loridanshofje
5. Leiden University
6. St. Peter's Church Square
7. Gerecht
8. Back-Streets Wander
9. Rhinefront Market & Corn Bridge
10. Burcht
11. Hooglandse Kerkgracht
12. Hoogstraat

## Eateries

13. Bar Lokaal
14. Mamie Gourmande
15. ROOS Taste & Smile
16. Waag

*TI on your right, and a block later, reach a bridge. Find a spot on the left side of the bridge and look out over the canal known as...*

# ❶ Singel

Like many Dutch towns, historically Leiden was surrounded by a *singel* (moat). But Leiden's is unusually well preserved. Much of the moat was built in the late 16th and early 17th centuries—after the Spanish siege, when Leiden was booming. The jagged zigzags of its serrated city wall and moat are still evident in the city's footprint (see map).

Originally the moat ran in front of a fortified wall. That wall is long gone, but the **windmill** in the distance suggests how tall it was. The higher a windmill is situated, the better it's able to capture the wind—so, logically, windmills were often built on top of the town walls. This one is a "platform mill" *(stellingmolen)*—the miller lived in the house below and could rotate only the windmill's head (with the wings) to face the wind. After our walk, you can climb up there to tour the fascinating Windmill Museum that fills its many funhouse floors (described later, under "Sights in Leiden").

Turn around to face the opposite direction. On the riverbank to your left is the **Rijksmuseum Volkenkunde** (Royal Museum of Ethnology), with exhibits on world cultures; their display of art from the former Dutch East Indies colony (present-day Indonesia) is especially good. This is one of several major museums in this small town. As the Netherlands' traditional seat of learning, Leiden seems to have more than its share of culture.

• *Continue straight across the bridge. After another block, you'll reach the market square called **Beestenmarkt** (where animals—beesten—were traditionally traded). Continue to the end of the square. The big bridge on the left leads to **Haarlemmerstraat**, the city's main shopping drag and a good place to browse for lunch (we'll return this way later, after our walk). In the opposite direction, the similarly shop-lined **Morsstraat** leads to the Morspoort gate. **Canal cruises** leave from the little house at the top of the bridge.*

*For now, pass up these temptations and keep going straight along the canal. When you hit the wider canal, turn right and walk toward the windmill along...*

# ❷ Galgewater

"Gallows Water" is (morbidly) named for the field at the far end of the canal, where the corpses of executed criminals were put on public display to bully people into compliance many centuries ago.

Stroll along the canal. On your left, notice the fine collection of historic **houseboats** from the 1880s through the 1920s. The older ships' big, pivoting fins, called swords, can be dropped from the sides when necessary to stabilize the boats and allow more nimble navigation of inland Holland's shallow waters. Locals still live in these, paying about €200,000 for their cramped, if waterfront, "property." Look for their mailboxes near the dock.

After one block, look for the tall **"Carpenters House"** building on the right (at #21, just after the little lane). Appreciate this

quintessentially Dutch house: stripes of red and white bricks, shutters with the town colors of red and white, and a classic stepped-gable design. Built in 1612 as Leiden was booming, this building housed architects, carpenters, and bricklayers who were hard at work expanding the city. Since 1988, it has been a subsidized housing complex for local seniors—who must navigate a very old building with no elevators. Walk a few steps past the front door and discreetly duck through the gate into the garden courtyard to see how the crenellated facade hides a much larger complex.

Continuing along the canal, you'll reach another **windmill.** A different style than the one we saw earlier, this 1987 replica of a 1619 original is a "post mill" *(standerdmolen)*, which means that the entire structure rotates on its base. On Saturdays, you may be able to go inside to see the gears.

Turn left at the windmill and cross the bridge (pedestrians on the left, bikes on the right). Notice the **poem** written high on the wall on your right—one of over a hundred such verses scrawled on buildings all over highly literate Leiden. While this one's in the local Frisian dialect, others are in English.

• *Once across the bridge, continue straight a few more steps down Weddesteeg and pause at the pebbled square.*

## ❸ Rembrandtplein

Leiden's favorite son was born in 1606 in a house that faced this square (find the plaque on the modern building that replaced that one). Rembrandt van Rijn was

the son of a miller who operated a windmill "on the Rhine" (as the name implies; you can faintly see the brick footprint of the rampart upon which the mill stood—it's by the boat-rental place on the right side of the square, now covered with plants). His family owned a lot of property and was well-to-do enough to send young Rembrandt to Latin school (like today's prep schools) and later to Leiden University. Rembrandt enrolled at Leiden U. but never actually attended any classes—even at age 14, he was only interested in painting. At age 17, he decided that he'd make more money in Amsterdam than here...and with that, he was gone. (For more on his life and career, see page 157.)

On the little mound in the pebbled park, a life-size statue of a young Rembrandt appreciates his later self-portrait. Leiden savors the idea that this world-famous artist spent his formative years right here. Exploring town today, imagine li'l Rembrandt poking his way through Leiden's tight courtyards and zipping across its tranquil canals, finding inspiration for his later artistic life.

• *Continue down Weddesteeg, then turn left at the cross-street (Noordeinde). After one block, turn right down the wide, tree-lined Oude Varkenmarkt ("Old Pig Market"). In the middle of the long, brick building near the start of this street (on the right, across from #10), check to see if the door under the yellow arch is unlocked. If it's open, go inside. (Don't be shy, but do be discreet.)*

## ➍ Loridanshofje

Leiden has 35 *hofjes*—residential courtyards—like this one. Similar to a *begijnhof,* this was a building funded by wealthy, churchgo-

ing donors to house poor people in exchange for prayer. Today, many *hofjes* are used for student housing. The layout of this one is typical: 12 houses (symbolic of the 12 Apostles) in a U-shape, ringing a central courtyard with a well in the middle and a covered gallery on the far side. We'll pass through another *hofje* later on this walk (a TI brochure locates all of them). These are public property, but remember that people do live in them (notice the mailboxes and bikes in the entryway)—so please keep a low profile.

• *Keep going down Oude Varkenmarkt. You'll pop out at a canal crossroads. Continue straight, under the **St. George Gate** (Sint Jorispoort, from 1645, marking the former headquarters of the local civic guard— like the gang in Rembrandt's* Night Watch*). The two red crossed keys on the gate are Leiden's city symbols (locals joke: "One key is St. Peter's, and the other is a spare.") Continue straight along the lily-padded canal, with a social-housing project on your right. Turn left over the next bridge (under the brick arch). You're surrounded by modern university facilities. Continue one block along Doelensteeg. At #9 on the left is a fancy door leading to another quaint and peaceful* hofje.

# Leiden History

The Romans built a settlement in the lowlands here along the Rhine River as early as the fifth century AD. Later, a medieval town sprouted where the two Rhine branches meet, marked by an artificial mound with a bailey on top (today's fortified Burcht). Leiden became part of the realm of the counts of Holland, achieving city rights in 1266. Throughout the Middle Ages, Leiden steadily produced cloth that was sold across Europe, as well as beer and pewter. By 1500, it was Holland's biggest and most important city.

With the arrival of the religious wars of the 1500s, Leiden's strategic location made it a target. Beginning in October 1573, during the Eighty Years' War, pro-Catholic Spanish troops invaded the rebellious, Protestant Netherlands. They laid siege to Leiden for the better part of a year, hoping to overtake the city. Completely surrounded and cut off from resources, Leiden's population was halved by starvation and the plague.

Finally, William of Orange raised an army to come to Leiden's aid. William's army breached the dikes near Rotterdam, flooding the low-lying territory all the way to Leiden. Then they waited for prevailing winds to push their flat-bottomed boats north, to advance on terrified Spanish troops and, eventually, to liberate Leiden. The boats also brought bread and herring to feed the starving townspeople. On October 3, 1574, the city gave thanks for "The Relief of Leiden" by feasting on foods that are still eaten ceremonially on that date each year: herring on white bread and *hutspot* (a pot of stew that the Spaniards left

*The lane continues to a wide canal called **Rapenburg**, with some of the finest homes in Leiden. Turn right and walk along the canal toward the next bridge. But before you reach that bridge, duck through the black iron gate of the big, stately, striped-brick building on your right.*

## ❺ Leiden University

William of Orange founded the Netherlands' first university in Leiden in 1575. Albert Einstein taught here, and its students have included philosopher René Descartes, painter Jan Steen, novelist Henry Fielding, US President John Quincy Adams, scientist Enrico Fermi, and filmmaker Paul Verhoeven, as well as multiple Dutch prime ministers and several Dutch monarchs (including Queen Beatrix and the current king, Willem-Alexander). Today, one in every six Leiden residents is a student. There's no unified campus; instead, students live scattered around the city center (including at *hofjes* like the ones we saw earlier). Because Delft is home to the technical university, and Leiden U. has more of a liberal-arts bent, locals half-joke that male students ride the train in from Delft to find a wife in Leiden.

simmering as they beat a hasty retreat).

Following the siege, Leiden boomed. Over the next 50 years, the town's population tripled, buoyed by immigrants from lands where Protestants were still persecuted (including Huguenots from France and Belgium). These new arrivals had know-how and a desire to work, and Leiden's textile trade again brought it wealth and fame. Its specialty was a flannel-like fabric called *laken,* coveted by bourgeois merchants and wealthy aristocrats. (In most famous Dutch portraits of stuffy-looking people from this time, the subjects wear suits of Leiden-made *laken.*) The material was so prized that outfits were passed down from parent to child.

During Leiden's post-siege golden age (late 16th and early 17th centuries), several other events helped put it on the map. As a sign of appreciation for the city's determined resistance, William of Orange founded Holland's first university in Leiden in 1575. In 1606, a Leiden miller's wife gave birth to a boy named Rembrandt, who would grow up, move to Amsterdam, and eventually become one of the world's greatest painters. And a small group of religious refugees from across the English Channel spent 12 years here before setting sail for the New World—the Pilgrims.

Leiden continues to be a center of learning, trade, and the arts...and a pleasant, low-impact place to stop off for an engaging visit between Amsterdam and the big Dutch and Belgian cities farther south.

As you stand in the entry courtyard, the big building on your left is the main **Academic Building** (Academiegebouw). This former nunnery was repurposed after the Reformation and now hosts university events (not open to visitors—but you can peek through the windows).

Straight ahead at the end of the corridor, step out into the impressive **botanical gardens.** This historic complex was founded in the 1590s—back when understanding plant life went hand-in-hand with the medical sciences. They say that a Flemish professor, recently returned from a trip to Turkey, planted the first tulip bulb in Dutch soil right here. Scientists like those at Leiden University found that tulips thrive in Holland, and before long...tulip mania. You can enjoy nice views for free from the entry, but those who pay admission can explore the sprawling grounds, with an extensive collection of Japanese plants, a fine rose garden, and a complex of restored old greenhouses (€8, buy ticket and enter on the right, daily 10:00-18:00, until 16:00 Nov-March; inviting café inside, www.hortusleiden.nl).

• *Head back out to the big Rapenburg canal, turn right, continue to the bridge at the corner, cross it, and head up charming Kloksteeg. In one block, you emerge at...*

## ❻ St. Peter's Church Square (Pieterskerkhof)

The huge church itself is worth a peek, though it isn't an active church—it's used mostly for events and concerts (€4, daily 11:00-18:00, entrance on the far end through a little café, pick up extensive English info sheets). For American visitors, this site is most significant for its role in Pilgrim history. In 1609, a large community of Pilgrims fled religious persecution in England, coming first to Amsterdam, then settling here in Leiden, concentrated in the square around this church.

The building on the right, at #21 (an almshouse marked *Anno 1683*), was the site of the home and church of John Robinson, the Pilgrims' minister. You can push open the door and pop in. Directly across the street, giant plaques embedded in the rounded corner of the church explain some Pilgrim history.

The Pilgrims were forced to thread a theological needle: While extremely rigid in their faith, they needed a relatively tolerant, progressive social context to thrive. When Holland's truce with Spain expired, the Pilgrims feared that the peace they found here wasn't to last. In the summer of 1620, they set out for the New World.

Leiden residents feel proud of their connection to American history. While at sea, the Pilgrims outlined rules for their planned society, the Mayflower Compact (which later influenced the US Constitution). Many of its tenets were inspired by the tolerant policies of William of Orange, which the Pilgrims became familiar with here. And the American Thanksgiving—celebrated in the autumn by the Pilgrims and their new Native American neighbors—seems partly inspired by the "Relief of Leiden" ceremonial meal that takes place here each October 3. For more about the Pilgrims, see page 107.

• *Circle clockwise around the left side of the church. About 20 steps after rounding the bend, take a left up the narrow lane called Muskadelsteeg to...*

## ❼ Gerecht

This tranquil, leafy square—whose name literally means "Justice"—is dominated by a large, turreted building that housed the 17th-century prison and court of justice. Parts of the building are much older—from the 12th century—and the justice meted out here was medieval in every sense. Prisoners would be put to work: men dyeing cloth, women spinning wool. Many were tortured and executed right on this square. They'd be drawn and quartered, or their bones crushed on a wheel. Then their corpses were taken out to display at the park at the end of the "Gallows Water" (Galgewater) we saw earlier.

At the opposite corner of the square from the justice tower, find the stepped-gabled house (with the tallest, fanciest, and most tilted facade) at the start of the tiny lane called Schoolsteeg. This building was the young **Rembrandt's Latin school** (so we've basically been retracing his daily walk from his home to school). The windows display bits of Rembrandt history. The first window also has a box painted on the glass and a camera inside; if you hold a pose with your face framed by the box for 10 seconds, you can go online later to find your portrait as a Rembrandt-style "etching."

• *Head past the house up Lokhorststraat, turning right down Pieterskerkstraat. This takes you past the apse of St. Peter's Church. Notice the houses that huddle up against the apse; the church rented out these houses as a source of income. Just around the back end is a café, which serves as the entrance to the church if you care to visit.*

*At the far end of the church, in the corner across from the café/entrance (on your left, just behind the single tree), is a small doorway leading into a tiny brick lane. Go there.*

## ❽ Leiden Back-Streets Wander

This lane leads into another adorable, whitewashed courtyard. Push the door and enter St. Peter's *hofje*. Rather than students, these four homes house seniors. Continue through the far end of the *hofje*, then angle left through the grass yard and up the lane. You'll end up at the street called **Langebrug.**

Just to your right, at #93, was a residence of the painter **Jan Steen.** Imagine this street when it was still a canal with broad and busy sidewalks on either side.

Now turn left—three doors down at #89—to the **Young Rembrandt Studio.** This is a classy gift shop with a free, well-produced film in the back that tells the story of the young artist and his friends. Well worth a restful and informative seven-minute sit, it's narrated by his (very proud) first teacher from the Latin school we saw earlier, Jacob van Swanenburgh, who lived in this building (free—ask for English showing as you enter; Tue-Sun 12:00-17:00, closed Mon).

Back where you entered this street, turn left to continue straight up the little lane called Wolsteeg. You'll emerge at the busy and aptly named Breestraat ("Broadway")—busy with buses, bikes, and taxis. You're face-to-face with Leiden's late-16th-century **City Hall,** whose carillon tower jangles happy tunes on the quarter hour.

• *Cross Breestraat (carefully) and jog a bit to the right to curl around the side of City Hall (following Koornbrugsteeg). You'll run into...*

LEIDEN

### ❾ Leiden's Rhinefront Market

This is the New Rhine (Nieuwe Rijn), which meets up with the Old Rhine (Oude Rijn) about a hundred yards to your left—we'll be there later. From here, the Rhine River heads to the North Sea. While we've passed a few smaller market squares (basically wide streets) on this walk, Leiden lacked the "Grote Markt" (Great Market) of some Dutch towns, like Haarlem or Delft. So merchants would simply unload their wares at the wide wharf along this river—today made even wider with restaurant-table-loaded barges.

**Koornbrug**—the covered "Corn Bridge"—was built in 1825 to provide grain merchants protection from the rain. Leiden still hosts a thriving market here: Saturday is the big market day, while Wednesday hosts a smaller assortment. This area is fun to explore and browse for a meal; I've recommended some options within a two-minute walk under "Eating in Leiden," later.

• *Head across the covered Koornbrug and proceed straight up Burgsteeg (lined with nice shops—kitchenware, home decor, and so on). You'll dead-end at Nieuwstraat. Turn left through the gate, cut through the café courtyard, and head up the steep stairs to the...*

### ❿ Burcht

Let me guess—huffing and puffing, are we? This hike is a rude awakening if you've gotten used to the near-total lack of hills here in the Netherlands. This artificial mound, built in the eighth or ninth century, is part of a system of castle construction called "motte and bailey"—that is, a fort (bailey) sitting upon a mound (motte). A castle has stood here since around 1150—first made of wood, later of stone. Climbing up into today's version, you enter what feels like an empty shell. But there was never a big fortress here—just a walled courtyard where residents could safely set up tents in times of siege. And their siege resistance relied upon the well you see in the middle of the courtyard, which is still attached via a network of pipes to a wellhead down on the market canal. Climb up to the top of the wall and stroll all the way around for 360-degree views over Leiden, with key land-

marks identified by orientation boards. Examining the wall you're standing on, notice the porous gray stone, which formed part of the original wall and was scavenged from Roman ruins.

• *From the top of the stairs, looking back the way you came up, note the towering Gothic **Hooglandse Kerk** (Highlands Church). Now get down from the wall, backtrack through the gate, and walk straight along Nieuwstraat toward the church. About halfway along the side of the church, on the corner of Beschuitsteeg, is the oldest house in town. This is home to the unique and excellent **American Pilgrim Museum** (highly recommended, but open only Thu-Sat afternoons; for details, see "Sights in Leiden," later). But any time of day you can peer into the windows to see a slice of 17th-century local life.*

*Consider stepping into the Hooglandse Kerk's vast, whitewashed interior (free) for a chance to walk over the tombstones of "the stinking rich" and see the clock mechanism from 1609 (just left of door).*

*Circle three-quarters of the way around the church. Turn right when you get to the wide, tree-lined, boulevard-like street called...*

## ⓫ Hooglandse Kerkgracht

This gracefully arcing strip passes (on the left) the beautiful building that once housed the **Holy Ghost Orphanage** (Heilige Geest of Arme Wees en Kinderhuis). Notice the colorful but wretched orphans topping the ceremonial gateway. Step into its courtyard to appreciate the enormous scale of this building, which—from the 16th century until 1961—housed up to 700 orphans at once. (While the locals provided these kids shelter, they also worked them hard in an age long before child-labor laws.)

Directly across the street from the orphanage is the stern 17th-century brick facade of a **Lutheran church,** which for 200 years hid behind a row of houses (now torn down to open up land for its front yard). Back then, Lutherans—like any nonconformist, non-Calvinist Christian denomination—were allowed to worship, but it had to be out of sight.

Leaving the orphanage, turn left and head to the canal, with its **green bridge** dating from 1867. It's a counterbalance bridge, calibrated so a single person could pull the chain and open it for tall boats heading up the Old Rhine.

At the canal, don't cross the bridge. Instead, head left about 100 yards up the Old Rhine—passing the footbridge—to the Fish Bridge (a wide brick bridge over the New Rhine). From the crest of the bridge, turn left, then cross another bridge and go to the right. You'll pass (on your left) a big department store. At its far end is the entrance to a **bike garage,** provided free by the city to lessen congestion. Look around and imagine, with this population density, if every bike were a car—chaos.

Just beyond that, the fancy gray Neoclassical **Waag** building dates from the mid-17th century. Once a customs house where merchants would weigh their goods (in the relief above the door, notice the burly stevedores doing some heavy lifting), it's now a café. Step inside to peek at surviving bits of the original business, such as the huge scales to weigh everything sold in the market. In back of the café, the fine arcade was once the butter market. It's tempting to celebrate the end of your town walk here with some coffee and apple pie, or, perhaps, some *bitterballen* with a beer.

### ⑫ Hoogstraat and Back to the Station

When you're ready to head back to the station, cross the modern Waaghoofdbrug footbridge. Continue up one block (to the Neo-classical Catholic church), where you can turn left and wander the lively **Haarlemmerstraat** pedestrian shopping zone. After just a few short blocks, you could detour a block to the right to visit the **Boerhaave Museum,** with its bizarre and fascinating collection of historical science exhibits. The **Lakenhal Museum** (master painters) is a few blocks farther north. Otherwise, continue straight ahead until you hit the canal. From here, you could turn right to walk up to the **Windmill Museum,** or you could continue over the bridge, turn right along the side of Beestenmarkt, and retrace your steps back to where you started: the station.

## Sights in Leiden

### ▲▲American Pilgrim Museum

Worth ▲▲▲ for historians, this quirky and engaging sight is Leiden's hidden treasure. Dr. Jeremy Bangs, an American historian, has filled the oldest house in Leiden (from the late 1360s, including the original fireplace and floors) with an eclectic collection of historical items. No Pilgrims actually lived here, but the collection offers an intriguing glimpse at early-17th-century lifestyles. This isn't just a "museum"—it's an experience.

If he's there, Dr. Bangs may tell you (with his entertainingly dry wit) the complete story behind any item that interests you. It's very hands-on (mostly *his* hands), as he demonstrates how various antique items were used. Be careful as you explore the house's two delightfully creaky rooms—many items are as fragile as they are priceless, and there are essentially no barriers between you and the collection.

**Cost and Hours:** €9.50; Thu-Sat 13:00-17:00, closed Sun-Wed; Beschuitsteeg 9, +31 6 2726 4651, www.leidenamerican-pilgrimmuseum.org.

## ▲Boerhaave Museum

Fun, fascinating, and appropriate for this very academic town, the modern, well-presented Boerhaave Museum traces the evolution of science with many interactive exhibits, and all of them well described in English.

**Cost and Hours:** €13, daily 10:00-17:00, Lange Sint Agnietenstraat 10, +31 71 521 4224, www.museumboerhaave.nl.

**Visiting the Museum:** You'll begin at the replica of an old operating theater—a reminder that Leiden's university was one of the first places where human corpses were dissected to understand how they functioned. A seven-minute audiovisual introduction plays on a loop (for the English soundtrack, make your way upstairs, put on the headphones, and look down toward the gurney).

Then follow the one-way, loosely chronological loop through the exhibit, focusing on medical science but also including astronomy and other disciplines. You'll learn how Holland's (and Leiden's) golden age was a time of enlightenment, learning, and study. The medical-science section is particularly engaging—with antique doctors' tools and the gruesome, larger-than-life anatomical models of Dr. Louis Auzoux. You'll also see some priceless collections of old scientific equipment; noticing the ornate decorations, you'll appreciate how these precious instruments offered credibility and prestige to scientific pursuits. Downstairs is a variety of hands-on areas, including a fun garden with a water playground for kids (and a café for their parents).

## ▲Windmill Museum (Molenmuseum De Valk)

Worth ▲▲ for fit engineers, this is a fun chance to climb—steeply and claustrophobically—through the guts of a huge, working windmill (named De Valk—"The Falcon"). You'll begin by walking through the miller's house on the ground floor, then climb up to view an excellent 10-minute film about Dutch windmills. As you work your way up, up, up through the cramped structure (with ladder-like stairs), you can browse exhibits at each level about the Netherlands' tradition for harnessing the wind's power, including lots of model windmills. At the top, you'll enjoy fine views over the rooftops of Leiden.

**Cost and Hours:** €5; Tue-Sat 10:00-17:00, Sun from 13:00, closed Mon; Tweede Binnenvestgracht 1, +31 71 516 5353, www.molenmuseumdevalk.nl.

### ▲Lakenhal Museum (Museum De Lakenhal)

Leiden's leading museum features art treasures from the 16th century to the present, as well as a fine collection of local history. The Dutch Masters collection excites art lovers, but the museum may be of less interest to casual museumgoers.

**Cost and Hours:** €12.50, Tue-Sun 10:00-17:00, closed Mon, Oude Singel 32, +31 71 581 8463, www.lakenhal.nl.

**Visiting the Museum:** The ground floor has temporary exhibits, as well as the museum's highlight—the Dutch Masters collection. Entering through the door marked *Hartereltzaal* into **Room 3,** you're surrounded by altarpieces. Straight ahead is an exquisitely detailed *Last Judgment* triptych (three-part altarpiece) by local engraver and painter Lucas van Leyden. Painted in 1527 and originally displayed in St. Peter's Church, its bright colors and energy-charged composition represent the arrival of the Renaissance in the Low Countries.

Turn right to continue into **Room 4** ("Leiden as the Cradle of Dutch Painting"). Here you'll find works by Rembrandt. On the left wall, see *Spectacles-Seller* (from 1623), one of his earliest compositions; with its poorly painted hands, awkward profile, and clashing colors, it lacks the mastery of his later Amsterdam heyday. Also in this room are works by Jan Lievens (Rembrandt-like portraits) and Jan van Goyen (Turner-esque seascapes).

Proceed into the long, narrow, darkened **Room 5.** Rembrandt's pupil Gerrit Dou kicked off a school called the Leiden Fijnschilders, which specialized in small, extremely detailed scenes with a strong light/dark contrast—a fine collection of which is displayed here.

Finally, in **Room 6** ("Public and Private"), look on the left wall as you enter for works by Jan Steen. *Merry Couple* (1650), depicting a man playfully throwing himself at a smiling woman, is loaded with sexually charged symbolism. (Next to that, as an antidote, is the far more sedate *A Couple Reading the Bible*.)

There's more to see upstairs. On the **first floor** are historical rooms, including an explanation of the prized *laken* cloth produced in Leiden that brought the city wealth and fame. This museum fills the cloth hall *(lakenhal)* used to store this precious cargo.

On the **second floor** is an exhibit about the Spanish Siege of Leiden. Here you can't miss the large painting illustrating how

Mayor Pieter van der Werf offered to sacrifice his left arm during the siege so the starving people of Leiden could eat (keeping his right arm intact to defend the town with his sword). They declined...but appreciated the gesture. Just to the left is Erwin Olaf's modern (2011), giant-scale photograph, using real models from Leiden, showing his interpretation of that gruesome era. An adjoining wing on this floor features modern art.

**Canal Boat Tours**

For a relaxing hour on the water with recorded narration and lovely views, hop on one of the canal tours that leaves regularly from the Beestenmarkt, a couple of blocks from the train station.

**Cost and Hours:** €12, both run daily, Bootjes en Broodjes uses open electric boats (www.bootjesenbroodjes.nl); Rederij Rembrandt uses more standard covered tour boats (www.rederijrembrandt.nl).

# Eating in Leiden

These listings are focused on lunch places in the center, mostly clustered around the New Rhine (Neiwe Rijn)—conveniently situated near the end of the self-guided walk.

**$$ Bar Lokaal,** kitty-corner from the giant Hooglandse Kerk (Highlands Church), feels like an idyllic neighborhood hangout, with inviting atmosphere inside and out. They offer a tempting menu of tasty dishes—flatbreads, croquettes, shakshuka, and so on—plus good coffee and treats (Hartesteeg 13, +31 71 888 4949).

**$ Mamie Gourmande** is a French bakery selling takeaway sandwiches, baguettes, and croissants; they also run a *traiteur* next door, with salads, charcuterie, and prepared meals (closed Sun, Gangetje 14, +31 71 532 6198).

**$$ ROOS Taste and Smile** is yet another hip, inviting café that serves sandwiches and salads, with cozy indoor seating or tables out on a river barge (Botermarkt 12, +31 71 785 1294).

**$$ Waag,** in the old customs house, feels bigger and less characteristic than the others listed here. It's industrial-sized and features a grand old interior, plus lots of prime tables out in the huge terrace overlooking the river. Their lunch menu includes burgers, sandwiches, and the like (Waag, +31 71 740 0300).

# Leiden Connections

Trains depart from Leiden at least every 15 minutes and head north to **Haarlem** (20 minutes) and **Amsterdam** (45 minutes), and south to **The Hague** (15 minutes), **Delft** (20 minutes), and

**Rotterdam** (35 minutes). There are also two direct trains each hour to **Utrecht** (45 minutes). With a change in Roosendaal or Rotterdam, you can also reach **Antwerp** (about 2 hours) and **Brussels** (3 hours, some require additional change in Antwerp; both are faster with transfer to pricey Thalys train in Rotterdam). For **Ghent** or **Bruges,** transfer in Antwerp.

Bus #854 (Keukenhof Express) links Leiden to Keukenhof (4/hour, 30 minutes).

# THE HAGUE

*Den Haag*

The Dutch constitution may identify Amsterdam as the official "capital," but The Hague has been the Netherlands' seat of government since 1588. It's home both to the country's parliament and to international organizations such as the International Court of Justice (at the tourable Peace Palace, where nations try to settle their disputes without bloodshed) and the UN International Criminal Tribunal for the Former Yugoslavia (not tourable).

From a sightseeing perspective, The Hague is a one-trick pony...and it's a fine trick. The excellent Mauritshuis Royal Picture Gallery boasts perhaps the Netherlands' best collection of homegrown art outside of the Rijksmuseum, including its masterpiece, Vermeer's *Girl with a Pearl Earring.* There's also a fine museum dedicated to the crowd-pleasing modern Dutch artist M.C. Escher, as well as a few other sights to fill out a day.

But beyond those attractions, The Hague's appeal diminishes quickly—given its sterile, upscale, businesslike vibe. I'd come for the museums, then head on to more purely enjoyable destinations. Fortunately, The Hague is a particularly easy half-day side trip from Delft—so close it's practically a neighborhood of this city.

THE HAGUE

## Orientation to The Hague

Though it has a half-million residents (the Netherlands' third-largest city), The Hague feels manageable for a sightseer. For a quick visit, focus on the center of town: the Mauritshuis art gallery and Binnenhof parliament complex, on the lovely lake called Hofvijver. The major sights in The Hague are well signed—just look for the black-and-gold directional arrows.

### TOURIST INFORMATION

The TI is inside The Hague's Centraal station—look for *VVV* signs behind the stairs in front of tracks 9-12. They hand out a free city map and sell some interesting self-guided walk brochures, but unless you arrive here, it's not worth a special trip (Mon-Fri 10:00-18:00, Sat-Sun until 17:00, Spui 68, www.denhaag.com).

**Sightseeing Pass:** The **Museumkaart** sightseeing pass (see page 58) covers entry to The Hague's Mauritshuis Royal Picture Gallery, Prison Gate Museum, Panorama Mesdag, and Historical Museum.

## ARRIVAL IN THE HAGUE

**By Tram:** Handy **tram #1** clatters in 30 minutes to the very heart of The Hague. Get off at the Centrum stop—right in the middle of The Hague's busy urban zone, on a wide street called Spui. Across the street to the left sprawls a bustling but charmless shopping zone. To find the Mauritshuis art gallery, walk a few steps straight ahead up Spui, turn right on Lange Poten, and follow it to the café-lined square called Plein. Exit the square at the far-left corner; the Mauritshuis and Binnenhof (parliament) are just around the bend.

**By Train:** If coming from other parts of the country, your train may stop either at Centraal station (also "CS" or "Den Haag CS") or Hollands Spoor ("HS" or "Den Haag HS," used by more international trains). If you have a choice, Centraal station has the TI and is closer to the tourist area, though it still requires a walk or tram ride to the main sights. (From Delft, the train to The Hague's Centraal station takes half as long, but requires more walking, so it's basically a wash.)

At **Centraal station,** stairs in front of tracks 9-12 lead downstairs to WCs and lockers; the TI is just beyond the stairs, on the main level. It takes about 15 minutes to walk to the Mauritshuis and other major sights: Exit straight out the door beyond the TI (marked *Centrum/Museumquartier*), turn left, and walk toward the big, hulking building labeled *Stadion*. Circle around the right side of this building and carry on across a canal as the street you're on becomes tree-lined Herengracht; follow this as it becomes Korte Poten and takes you to the lovely square called Plein, in the heart of the museum action. To shave a little time off the walk, you could take a tram from the train station's upper level (above the intercity tracks); ride tram #2, #3, #4, or #6 one stop to Spui.

If arriving at the **Hollands Spoor station,** it's easiest to walk out in front of the station and take tram #1 (direction: *Scheveningen Noorderstrand*) to the Centrum stop, described above.

## GETTING AROUND THE HAGUE

Most sights are within walking distance of the Centrum tram stop or Centraal station. For more distant sights or to avoid a walk, The Hague has an efficient public transit system. Trams and buses cost €4 (buy tickets from machines on board, www.htm.nl).

# Sights in The Hague

## MUSEUMS IN THE CITY CENTER

These attractions are all within a 10-minute walk of the Hofvijver—the pretty lake in the heart of town, anchored by the Binnenhof parliament complex.

THE HAGUE

## ▲▲Mauritshuis Royal Picture Gallery

One of the Netherlands' best art museums, the Mauritshuis features Dutch golden age art, including top-notch pieces by Vermeer

(his famous *Girl with a Pearl Earring* lives here), Rembrandt, Rubens, and many others. This so-called "mini-Rijksmuseum" is more intimate and less overwhelming than its bigger cousin in Amsterdam. It's well worth a visit.

**Cost and Hours:** €17.50, Tue-Sun 10:00-18:00, Mon from 13:00, free coat-and-small-bag check; Plein 29—to get here from the Centrum tram stop or Centraal station, see "Arrival in The Hague," earlier; +31 70 302 3456, www.mauritshuis.nl.

**Tours:** The museum has a good, free audioguide that must be used on your personal device; either download the Mauritshuis app in advance or use the museum's Wi-Fi when you arrive.

**Visitor Services:** In the entrance and ticketing area, you'll find a bag-and-coat-check desk; straight ahead is the shop and, up a flight of stairs, temporary exhibits and the museum's good **$$ brasserie,** with salads, sandwiches, and a few hot dishes.

**Visiting the Museum:** The entrance to the permanent collection is to the left as you enter the main door. From here, climb up two flights of stairs. The collection is displayed on two floors: "Floor 1" (actually the third floor) has just a few highlights and can be skipped if you're in a rush. "Floor 2" (actually the fourth) is packed with masterpieces.

• *On Floor 1, begin in Room 2, with portraits of wealthy patrons by Peter Paul Rubens and his protege, Anthony van Dyck. Continue into...*

**Room 3:** The touching scene in Peter Paul Rubens' **Old Woman and a Boy with Candles** (c. 1616-1617) features an elderly woman passing her light to the boy—encouraging him to enjoy life in a way that she perhaps hasn't. Her serene smile suggests her hope that he won't have the same regrets she does. Rubens was an early Dutch adopter of the ultrarealism practiced by the Italian painter Caravaggio.

• *Carry on through Rooms 4, 5, 6, and 7—where you'll find Hans Holbein the Younger's* **Portrait of Robert Cheseman** *(1533), the chief falconer of England's King Henry VIII. Complete your circuit in Room 8, then head up the stairs to Floor 2. Turn right into...*

**Room 9:** One of Rembrandt's most famous works, *The Anatomy Lesson of Dr. Nicolaes Tulp* (1632) made him a star in the Amsterdam art scene. This physician really did dissect a human cadaver, once each year, to better understand the miracle of our anatomy...

for example, how muscles and tendons allow a hand to open and close (as he's demonstrating here). Surgeons huddled close to learn, and the public was also invited—making this quite the spectacle. Notice the artist's uniquely engaging version of a (typically dull) group portrait—inquisitive faces lean in, hanging on the doctor's every word, and each surgeon's face carries a different expression. The cadaver resembles a notorious criminal of the day.

This room features many other, lesser Rembrandts, plus a pair of portraits by Haarlem native Frans Hals.

• *Continue into...*

**Room 10:** This room features two portraits of aging men, both painted by Rembrandt late in his own life. On the right is ***Portrait of an Elderly Man*** (1667), painted when Rembrandt was 61; on the left is ***Rembrandt Self-Portrait*** (1669)—the last of more than 80 self-portraits he painted throughout his life. Both are typical of his style: The clothes are painted lightly, but the face is caked on, built up by layer after layer of paint, carefully slathered on by the master. In the self-portrait, we see a man beaten down by life: The artist was bankrupt and had lost both loves of his life and his only child. Rembrandt would be dead within a year. (For more on Rembrandt, see page 157.)

• *Circle around through Room 11 to...*

**Room 12:** Would it surprise you to know that this giant bovine portrait was, at one time, one of the Mauritshuis' most beloved

works? Paulus Potter's ***The Bull*** (1647) elevates livestock to high art—celebrating this bull as if he's a ruff-collared aristocrat. Big, dreamy, brown eyes...mouth open as if to speak knowledgeably... legs spread, contrapposto, to balance his weight dynamically: This could be a member of the royal family, or a famous merchant. (Remember this pose: craning his neck slightly and glancing over his shoulder. We'll see a similar one soon.) The cow, goat, sheep—even the farmer—are an afterthought to the painting's star. And that's why this painting made such an impact: It was a revolutionary example of naturalism, elevating the mundane natural world into the realm of high art and beauty. There's even a perfectly formed patty of manure in the foreground.

• *Carry on through Room 13 until you reach...*

**Room 14:** This room displays two very small paintings that deserve special scrutiny.

First, on the left between the windows is Carel Fabritius' ***The***

THE HAGUE

*Goldfinch* (c. 1654), made famous by Donna Tartt's 2013 novel of the same title. This luminous, simple painting shows a pet goldfinch perched on its feeder, shackled by a slender chain. Fabritius was Rembrandt's pupil and Vermeer's teacher, and this painting shows traces of both masters' styles. Get close to see how the artist rendered the wing by painting bold yellow strokes over the black and then scratching the paint off with the back of his brush.

Next to the door into the next room, Jan Steen's *Girl Eating Oysters* (c. 1658-1660) displays a seemingly innocent scene. But this still life combined with a portrait—on the smallest canvas Steen ever painted—is loaded with 17th-century sexual innuendo. Oysters were considered a powerful aphrodisiac, and behind the subject, peeking through the curtains, we can see a bed. The girl's impish grin suggests that she's got more than shellfish on her mind.

• *Ready? For the museum's highlight, continue into...*

**Room 15:** Sometimes called "the Dutch *Mona Lisa*" for its enigmatic qualities, Vermeer's *Girl with a Pearl Earring* (c. 1665)

became a sensation in our times as the subject of a popular book and film. This is a "tronie"—a type of picture in which the painter's goal is not to depict an individual person, but to capture mood or character by focusing on the expression of the subject. In fact, we don't even know who this mysterious girl is. Wearing a blue turban and with a gigantic pearl dangling from her earlobe, she glances over her shoulder and catches the viewer's gaze expectantly, maybe even seductively. Vermeer's portrayal subtly implies a much more complicated story than we'll ever know. The artist was a master of color and at suggesting shape with light—look closely and you'll see that the famous pearl is essentially formed by two simple brushstrokes. (For more on Vermeer, see page 317.) By the way, does this pose seem familiar? It's Potter's *The Bull*.

On the opposite wall, find Vermeer's *View of Delft* (c. 1660-1661). If this were a photograph, it'd be a bad one—you'd want to wait for the clouds to pass to snap another one with the entire scene bathed in light. But Vermeer, an expert at capturing light effects on canvas, uses the cloudy/sunny contrast to his advantage, illuminating the foreground and the distant, inner part of town instead of the more predictable middle ground. This makes your eye probe deep into the canvas, subconsciously immersing you in Vermeer's world.

• *Finish up in...*

**Room 16:** In this large hall, which is also the top landing of the staircase, look on one of the partitions near the windows to find a small, circular masterpiece that you would not want to miss before leaving. Frans Hals' lovable *Laughing Boy* (c. 1625) depicts an exuberant scamp grinning widely despite his decaying teeth and rat's-nest hair. Like *Girl with a Pearl Earring*, this is another tronie, less about the subject than about what he's doing: laughing spontaneously. (For more on Hals, see page 282.)

After enjoying this concise but impactful museum, I must admit, I feel as giddy as this kid.

**And Lots More:** These paintings are just the beginning. Now that you've blitzed the highlights, dig in (perhaps using the audioguide) to find works by Jan Brueghel the Elder (a painting of the Garden of Eden, done jointly with Rubens), Hans Holbein the Younger (a portrait of one of Henry VIII's wives), Anthony van Dyck, Hans Memling, and many other famous painters.

**Nearby:** While the Mauritshuis is the big draw, while you're here you can check out some other important sights. Just beyond the Mauritshuis, you can step through the fancy gateway to explore the interlocking **courtyards** of the Binnenhof parliament complex (described next). Both structures sit alongside the lake called **Hofvijver;** if you have time and nice weather, it's enjoyable to stroll the nicely manicured, tree-lined trail all the way around. As you do the spin, you'll pass various other museums, described later in this section (and noted on "The Hague" map earlier in this chapter).

## Binnenhof Parliament Complex

The castle-like Binnenhof complex, overlooking the Hofvijver lake right in the center of The Hague, is the seat of Dutch political power. The prime minister's office is here, and it's also the meeting place of the two-house parliament, or Staten-Generaal. The power resides in the directly elected Second Chamber (a.k.a. House of Representatives), whereas the mostly figurehead  First Chamber (a.k.a. Senate, but more like the UK's House of Lords) meets once weekly to harrumph their approval.

The complex is undergoing an ambitious, multiyear renovation. Certain sections may still be open to visitors, and if so, it can be surprisingly easy to dip inside for a peek. (There's an entrance just past the Mauritshuis, and another one on the opposite side of the complex, facing the square called Buitenhof.) If you can get to the inner courtyard—surrounded by orange-and-white-striped awnings—you'll find a golden fountain depicting Queen Beatrix (who ruled until 2013), a reminder that the respectful Dutch parliamentarians govern with the monarch's symbolic approval. Dominating the middle of the complex is the historic Knights' Hall (Ridderzaal), where the two houses meet jointly on special occasions.

**Tours:** If you're curious to learn more, **ProDemos** runs tours of whatever parts of the Binnenhof are currently open—including, likely, the modern, temporary facility where the Dutch House of Representatives meets during renovation (for details and to book, see www.prodemos.nl; their visitors center is next to Café Brasserie Dudok at Hofweg 1, +31 70 757 0200).

### Prison Gate Museum (Gevangenpoort)

This torture museum, in a 13th-century gatehouse that once protected a castle on the site of today's parliament, shows you the medieval mind at its worst. You'll get the full story on crime and punishment from 1420 to 1823. You can wander around by yourself with an audioguide; live English tours may be offered on summer weekends—check ahead and reserve on the website.

**Cost and Hours:** €15, Tue-Fri 10:00-17:00, Sat-Sun from 12:00, closed Mon, across from parliament at Buitenhof 33, +31 70 346 0861, www.gevangenpoort.nl.

### Panorama Mesdag

For an overpriced look at the 19th century's attempt at virtual reality, stand in the center of this 360-degree painting of nearby Scheveningen in the 1880s, with a 3-D, sandy-beach foreground. As you experience this nostalgic attraction, ponder that this sort of "art immersion" experience was once mind-blowingly cutting-edge.

**Cost and Hours:** €15, Tue-Sun 10:00-17:00, closed Mon, a few blocks north of the parliament area at Zeestraat 65, +31 70 310 6665, www.panorama-mesdag.nl.

### ▲Escher in the Palace (Escher in Het Paleis)

Celebrating Dutch optical illusionist M. C. Escher (1898-1972), this thoughtful exhibit is crowd-pleasing, supremely engaging, and deeper than you might expect...much like the artist's works. While the many Escher woodcuts and other works are a delight to scrutinize, the building itself—the former winter palace of Queen

Mother Emma of the Dutch royal family, with far-out chandeliers by Dutch artist Hans van Bentem—is also worth a look.

**Cost and Hours:** €11, Tue-Sun 11:00-17:00, closed Mon, mandatory bag check in basement, Lange Voorhout 74, +31 70 427 7730, www.escherinhetpaleis.nl.

**Visiting the Museum:** Escher may not be considered a "serious artist" by art-world elites, but the exhibit does an admirable job of challenging that assumption. It traces both the artist's life and his artistic evolution.

As a young man, Escher fell in love with Italy, and his perspective-driven works of everything from jagged coastlines to St. Peter's Basilica built a foundation that served him well later in life. The rise of Mussolini's Fascism led to Escher's departure with his family and an itinerant period, as he moved from place to place before finally settling in the Dutch town of Baarn.

Here Escher synthesized his various artistic obsessions: perspective, reflections, metamorphoses, impossible architecture,

and tessellations (infinitely repeating patterns of tiles, which he became obsessed with after visiting the Alhambra in Granada). The exhibit covers each of these in turn, culminating in Escher's later works, which ambitiously mixed-and-matched his many artistic tricks. In this phase of his life, Escher transitioned from literal landscapes of his beloved Italy to what have been termed "mindscapes"—fantastical, impossible worlds. One of his "metamorphosis" works is mounted in a giant circle, allowing you to walk around it and see how it truly is an infinite loop. (It works in both directions.)

Along the way, you can watch a 20-minute film about the artist. The top floor features kid-friendly displays that let you step right into an Escher engraving—but Escher is one of those artists who encourages anyone to be a kid at heart.

**Nearby:** The delightful, restaurant-lined **Denneweg**—described later, under "Eating in The Hague"—begins just outside the museum's front door and is worth a wander: Just exit to the right and stroll.

## Historical Museum of The Hague (Haagshistorischmuseum)

This museum's eclectic collection includes landscapes of The Hague in its golden age, portraits of its movers and shakers, dollhouses,

THE HAGUE

tile panels, and the well-preserved tongue and finger of a 17th-century murderer.

**Cost and Hours:** €15, Tue-Fri 10:00-17:00, Sat-Sun from 12:00, closed Mon, across the lake from parliament at Korte Vijverberg 7, +31 70 364 6940, www.haagshistorischmuseum.nl.

## OUTSIDE THE CITY CENTER

The following sights lie north of the main tourist zone. Though worthwhile for the thorough sightseer, they take more effort to reach than the previous sights.

### ▲Peace Palace (Vredespaleis)

The palace houses the International Court of Justice and the Permanent Court of Arbitration. These two Peace Palace courts attempt

to reach amicable settlements for international disagreements, such as border disputes. While the judicial process is interesting, the building itself is the big draw. A gift from American industrialist Andrew Carnegie, it's filled with opulent decorations (donated by grateful nations who found diplomatic peace here), from exquisite Japanese tapestries, to a Hungarian tile fountain, to French inlay floors.

A free visitors center offers modest multimedia exhibits about the building and international courts. There's also a persuasive video about the history of the Peace Palace and the role of international law. You'll learn how modern nations attempt to resolve their disputes here instead of on the battlefield. Tours generally run on weekends only and primarily cover the grounds; interior tours are less frequent.

**Cost and Hours:** Visitors center—free, includes audioguide, Wed-Sun 12:00-17:00, closed Mon-Tue, Carnegieplein 2, +31 70 302 4242, www.vredespaleis.nl.

**Getting There:** Take tram #1 directly from Delft or bus #24 from The Hague's Centraal station (direction: *Westduin*) and get off at the Vredespaleis stop (right in front of the palace).

**Tours:** Because of the busy schedule of the Peace Palace's important work, tours are typically limited to weekends (Sat-Sun). Most tours focus on the gardens and grounds without entering the building itself ("Around the Palace"-€12.50). Occasional "In the Palace" tours include the judicial chambers and grandly decorated halls (€15). Check Vredespaleis.nl for the complete schedule and to book in advance. Be sure to bring your passport. It's also possible to attend a hearing (conducted in English or French) of the International Court of Justice; see icj-cij.org for details.

## Scheveningen

This Dutch Coney Island, with its broad sandy beach, is at its liveliest on sunny summer afternoons (but is dead when the weather cools). Its biggest appeal is watching urbanites from all over South Holland enjoy a day at the seashore. Dominating the scene is the long double-decker pleasure pier, with shops down below, a boardwalk up top, and a bungee-jumping pavilion at the far end. A café-lined promenade stretches along the sand.

By the way, if you can't pronounce this tongue-twisting name (roughly SK*H*EH-veh-ning-ehn), you're not alone. In World War II, Dutch soldiers would quiz suspicious-looking visitors on how to pronounce this name as a test to determine who was Dutch-born and ferret out potential German spies. (This is the textbook example of an insider passphrase, known as a "shibboleth.")

**Getting There:** Take northbound tram #1 from Delft or from Hofweg/Spui (the street in front of the Binnenhof), or tram #9 from The Hague's Centraal station. Get out at Kurhaus (one stop before the end of the line) and follow signs for *Boulevard/Strand* and *Pier*.

## Madurodam

This mini-Holland amusement park, with miniature city buildings that make you feel like Godzilla, is fun for kids.

**Cost and Hours:** €17-22, smart to prebook online; open daily in summer 9:00-18:00, shorter hours off-season, last entry one hour before closing; George Maduroplein 1, tram #9 or bus #22 from Centraal station, +31 70 416 2400, www.madurodam.nl.

# Eating in The Hague

Assuming that you're here for lunch, I've focused my listings on eateries close to the sights. Unless otherwise noted, these places are open every day for lunch.

**Plein and Nearby:** The delightful, convivial, leafy square called Plein—just in front of the Mauritshuis—is the no-brainer choice for an enjoyable lunch between sightseeing stops on a nice day. Survey menus and views and pick anywhere that appeals. If you'd like more options, follow the street called Korte Poten, which becomes Herengracht, as it exits the square and heads northeast.

Just a few steps off the square, **$$ Happy Tosti** serves tasty grilled sandwiches (and has a mission to employ people with occupational disabilities; Korte Poten 5). Carrying on a couple of blocks, you'll reach **$$ Café Bartine,** a trendy, upscale-feeling café with quality coffee and good lunches on a leafy street with outdoor tables (Herengracht 11).

**Denneweg:** Easily the most enjoyable street in The Hague for a stroll, this historic strip—just north of the Escher in the Palace museum—is the answer to the question, "Where did all of The Hague's charm go?" The street is lined with midrise brick buildings, cafés, pubs, global-cuisine restaurants, and intriguing shops. Near the end of the street, **$$ Walter Benedict** (at #69A) serves all-day breakfast plus some lunch dishes. Across the street, hip **$$ Dekxels** (at #130) and **$$$ Vincenzo's** (at #134, closed Mon-Tue)—revered for its Italian cuisine—are dinner-only.

**West of the Lake:** Two squares—one big, the other small— are just west across the busy street from the Hofvijver lake. Of the two, triangular-shaped Plaats has the most tempting eateries, including the French-style café **$$ Palmette** (at #27).

From here you can venture deeper into the congested streets of the city center. All roads seem to lead to the five-point intersection called Groenmarkt. Here you'll find **$$ 't Goude Hooft,** the city's oldest inn, which today has loads of al fresco tables positioned to catch the sun and watch The Hague's bustle (at Dagelijkse Groenmarkt 13).

Just to the south, **Foodhallen**—The Hague's much smaller version of Amsterdam's multicultural food circus—has about a dozen different food counters, ranging from Italian, Mexican, and Spanish to dim sum, sushi, and Vietnamese (daily 12:00-22:00, Haagsche Bluf).

## The Hague Connections

From **Centraal Station by Train: Delft** (4/hour, 15 minutes), **Leiden** (4/hour, 15 minutes), **Rotterdam** (6/hour, 30 minutes), **Amsterdam** (4/hour, 50 minutes, more with change in Leiden or Hoofddorp), **Haarlem** (4/hour, 40 minutes), **Arnhem** (4/hour, 1.5 hours, transfer in Utrecht). Note that many of these trains also stop at the Hollands Spoor station (see next).

From **Hollands Spoor Station by Train:** Trains leave approximately twice hourly for **Belgium.** The IC connections, which change in Breda, are much more affordable than those that transfer to Thalys in Rotterdam. From here it's about 1.5-2 hours to **Ant-**

**werp** and 2.5 hours to **Brussels;** with additional changes, it's about 3-4 hours to **Ghent** or **Bruges.**

**By Tram to Delft:** Take tram #1 from any stop (6/hour, direction: *Delft Tanthof,* about 30 minutes). To reach the Markt in Delft, get off at the Prinsenhof stop (just past the windmill a little north of the Markt). The tram also stops at Delft's train station.

# ROTTERDAM

The Dutch say that money is made in Rotterdam, divvied up in The Hague, and spent in Amsterdam. The country's second-biggest city (with 630,000 in the center and nearly a million in the metropolitan area), Rotterdam has a long history as the Netherlands' muscular moneymaker. Its strategic position at the delta of multiple major European rivers has made it a lucrative trading point for centuries. Today, it's home to Europe's busiest port (the ninth biggest in the world). They say that in Rotterdam, shirts are sold with the sleeves already rolled up.

The city had a particularly tumultuous 20th century. Its highly strategic port earned it complete destruction—down to its very foundations—during World War II. When the time came to rebuild, Rotterdammers decided to leave their salty old town as a memory and started from scratch to build a boldly modern city. Ever since, the city has been—and remains—a stimulating urban showcase of architectural experimentation, with buildings big and small designed by a Who's Who of contemporary architects. You'll see wildly creative and futuristic train stations, libraries, market halls, office towers, bridges, subway stations, and apartment complexes that push the envelope of science fiction. But the city also respects its past, with a few historic buildings mixed in and lots of stories to be told.

Strolling Rotterdam's sleek pedestrian malls, ogling its fantastical skyline, browsing for a meal on its eclectic shopping streets, or cruising its busy harbor, you'll experience another slice of the Netherlands. A visit to Rotterdam makes it clear: For Dutch urbanites, the days of milkmaids and wooden shoes are long gone.

## PLANNING YOUR TIME

Big, intense Rotterdam works well as a side-trip from Delft (or even from Amsterdam or Haarlem): Ride the train in and poke around for a few hours, following my self-guided walk (or bike ride). With more time, take a harbor cruise (to see the busy port) or an architectural bike tour (to appreciate its rich array of modern buildings). If you're desperate for cute canals, ride the Metro to the historic Delfshaven quarter. A half-day is enough for a good first look, but with additional time, there's certainly more to see.

# Orientation to Rotterdam

Rotterdam sprawls along both banks of the Maas River. But the central zone—on the north bank, with most of the important sights and architectural landmarks—is fairly compact. A loop from the train station to the river and back again is a long-but-doable walk or an easy bike ride.

## TOURIST INFORMATION

The handiest TI branch is in a small, blocky structure inside Rotterdam Centraal station's cavernous main hall (daily 9:00-18:00). The main branch is downtown at Coolsingel 114 (daily 9:30-18:00, +31 10 790 0185, www.rotterdam.info). Their inexpensive map is good enough to get you around for the day.

## ARRIVAL IN ROTTERDAM

In Rotterdam's cutting-edge **Centraal train station,** a wide concourse crosses beneath the train platforms. Safe, secure, pricey lockers are at the "back" end of the train station (they're on the right, tucked under track 16, behind a closed door—look for *Kluis*). To head into the city center, follow *Centrum* and *Stationsplein* signs. When you pop out into the main hall, the TI kiosk is on the left, beneath the huge video screen and just before the main doors. My self-guided walk begins inside this hall.

While I've designed this chapter in the order of a long loop walk through the city, public transit can help you zip directly to certain sights (such as the harbor cruise or Delfshaven). As you exit the station, look left for a row of **tram** platforms (#7 heads to the harbor cruise dock at Erasmus Bridge, direction: Willemsplein, ride to end of line; #4 goes to Delfshaven, direction: Marconiplein). There's also an entrance to the **Metro** in the plaza in front of the main entrance (the trip to Delfshaven requires a change at Beurs). Public transportation is covered by a paper ticket (€4 for up to a two-hour ride) or day pass (€9); see www.ret.nl.

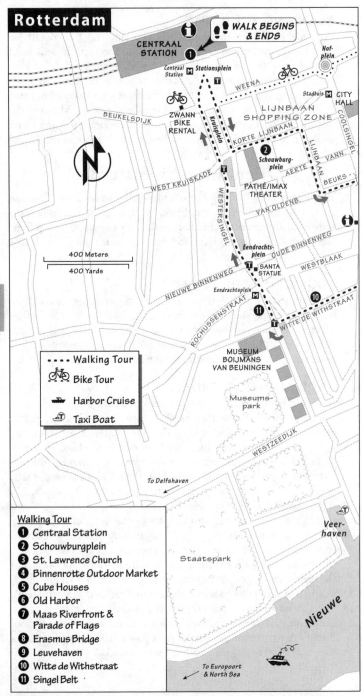

# Rotterdam

**WALK BEGINS & ENDS**

CENTRAAL STATION ❶

Hof-plein

Centraal Station Ⓜ Stationsplein

WEENA

Stadhuis Ⓜ CITY HALL

BEUKELSDIJK

ZWANN BIKE RENTAL

Kruisplein

LIJNBAAN SHOPPING ZONE

KORTE LIJNBAAN

COOLSINGEL

❷ Schouwburg-plein

LIJNBAAN

AERTE VANN.

WEST KRUISKADE

WESTERSINGEL

PATHÉ/IMAX THEATER

BEURS

VAN OLDENB.

**N**

400 Meters
400 Yards

Eendrachts-plein

SANTA STATUE

OUDE BINNENWEG

WESTBLAAK

NIEUWE BINNENWEG

Eendrachtsplein Ⓜ

❿

ROCHUSSENSTRAAT

⓫

WITTE DE WITHSTRAAT

MUSEUM BOIJMANS VAN BEUNINGEN

Museums-park

WESTZEEDIJK

To Delfshaven

Veer-haven

Staatspark

Nieuwe

To Europoort & North Sea

ROTTERDAM

---

**Legend:**

- ···· Walking Tour
- �🚲 Bike Tour
- ⛴ Harbor Cruise
- ⛴ Taxi Boat

---

## Walking Tour

❶ Centraal Station
❷ Schouwburgplein
❸ St. Lawrence Church
❹ Binnenrotte Outdoor Market
❺ Cube Houses
❻ Old Harbor
❼ Maas Riverfront & Parade of Flags
❽ Erasmus Bridge
❾ Leuvehaven
❿ Witte de Withstraat
⓫ Singel Belt

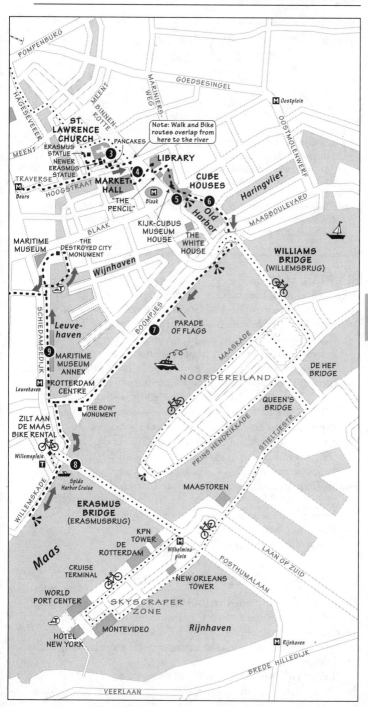

POMPENBURG

HAGESEVEER

GOEDSESINGEL

MARINIERS WEG

M *Oostplein*

MEENT

BINNEN ROTTE

MEENT

ST. LAWRENCE CHURCH

PANCAKES

ERASMUS STATUE

NEWER ERASMUS STATUE

**3**

Note: Walk and Bike routes overlap from here to the river

LIBRARY

OOSTMOLENWERF

TRAVERSE

HOOGSTRAAT

MARKET HALL

**4**

"THE PENCIL"

M *Blaak*

**5**

CUBE HOUSES

**6**

Old Harbor

Haringvliet

M *Beurs*

BLAAK

KIJK-CUBUS MUSEUM HOUSE

THE WHITE HOUSE

MAASBOULEVARD

MARITIME MUSEUM

THE DESTROYED CITY MONUMENT

Wijnhaven

WILLIAMS BRIDGE (WILLEMSBRUG)

SCHIEDAMSEDIJK

*Leuve- haven*

BOOMPJES

**7**

PARADE OF FLAGS

MAASKADE

DE HEF BRIDGE

**9**

MARITIME MUSEUM ANNEX

ROTTERDAM CENTRE

NOORDEREILAND

M *Leuvehaven*

"THE BOW" MONUMENT

QUEEN'S BRIDGE

ZILT AAN DE MAAS BIKE RENTAL

PRINS HENDRIKKADE

STIELTJESTR.

*Willemsplein*

T

**8**

*Spido Harbor Cruise*

MAASTOREN

WILLEMSKADE

ERASMUS BRIDGE (ERASMUSBRUG)

KPN TOWER

DE ROTTERDAM

M *Wilhelmina- plein*

LAAN OP ZUID

*Maas*

CRUISE TERMINAL

POSTHUMALAAN

NEW ORLEANS TOWER

WORLD PORT CENTER

SKYSCRAPER ZONE

*Rijnhaven*

HOTEL NEW YORK

MONTEVIDEO

M *Rijnhaven*

BREDE HILLEDIJK

VEERLAAN

**ROTTERDAM**

## Old City, New City:
## The Rotterdam Blitz

Hitler invaded the Netherlands on May 10, 1940. He quickly grew impatient at the resistance he encountered, so to get the Dutch on board, on May 14 he systematically bombed the country's heavily industrialized second city: Rotterdam. As Rotterdam had already been evacuated, fewer than 1,000 people were killed—but the city center was, quite literally, flattened. Following the bombing, a fire raged for three days, consuming what was left of the city. Photos of post-WWII Rotterdam are startling: A scant few historic buildings still stand—barely—and the outlines of the streets around them are barely visible. Hitler's methods proved successful. When the Nazis threatened to similarly destroy Utrecht the next day, the Dutch government surrendered immediately.

## HELPFUL HINTS

**Bike Rental and Tours:** In this spread-out city, getting around on two wheels can be a smart choice. Guided options change from year to year, and most are private tours; the TI can tell you the latest. For independent cycling, **Zwaan Bike Rentals** is a block from the train station, with a variety of bikes and e-bikes. From the main plaza directly in front of the station, turn right and go a block down the busy boulevard—called Weena—to #705 (Mon-Fri 8:30-18:00, Sat-Sun from 9:00, +31 10 412 6220, www.czwaan.nl). If you rent a bike, you can store your bag here for half the price of the train-station lockers. To rent a bike on the river, find **Zilt aan de Maas** under the Erasmus Bridge (daily 9:00-17:00, +31 10 210 5118, www.ziltaandemaas.nl).

**Water Taxi:** Rotterdam has a memorable and affordable water-taxi service. Fast taxi boats shuttle between Leuvehaven, Veerhaven, the skyscraper zone's Hotel New York, and several other points (€4.50 one-way, every 10 minutes, www.watertaxirotterdam.nl).

# Rotterdam Walk

This four-mile self-guided walk takes you through the shopping zone of Rotterdam and past some of its most dynamic architectural treasures to the river, then loops you back to the landmark Erasmus Bridge (where you can catch the harbor cruise) before heading back up to the station.

**Length of This Walk:** You could do it at a brisk pace in about four hours (without stops for sightseeing or taking the harbor cruise), but it's also a useful spine for spending the entire day in the city. If four miles is too much, I list several places where you can head back early—at the Maas Riverfront/Williams Bridge, Erasmus Bridge (tram stop), and Rotterdam Centre tower (Metro stop).

**Bike Variation:** Rotterdam is spread out, and this walk is lengthy. To speed things up, consider renting a bike near the station (see "Helpful Hints," earlier). You can link most of the stops on this walk by bike but will need to walk your bike through pedestrian-only zones. On two wheels, a brisk and even more scenic route to the Erasmus Bridge is to pedal across the red Williams Bridge (Willemsbrug), then head to the southwestern tip of Noordereiland for a great view of the bridge and skyscrapers. From here, loop back around and take the Queen's Bridge (Koninginnebrug) to the far side of the river, where you'll pedal south to the Erasmus Bridge (see map). Cross it and follow the rest of the walk from there.

• *We'll begin inside the grand main arrivals hall of Rotterdam's...*

## ❶ Centraal Station

The city's sleek, futuristic, gigantic (430,000-square-foot) train station—opened by King Willem-Alexander in 2014—is a marvel in itself. A quick and easy ride from The Hague, Delft, Dordrecht, and many fine little bedroom communities, Rotterdam's station accommodates more than 100,000 daily commuters (and a few tourists). Stand under its soaring roof—which makes travelers seem like ants—and take it all in. The enormous screen high on the wall—the size of a tennis court—plays video clips of Rotterdam life and its busy harbor; below that sits the TI.

Head straight out the main doors into the vast plaza in front of the station, called **Stationsplein.** Walk to the busy road and turn 180 degrees to appreciate the swoop of the station's roofline. Shaped like an arrow (or perhaps the Starfleet emblem), it marks Rotterdam as a city of the future—in strong contrast to Amsterdam, which revels in being a city of the past. (The sta-

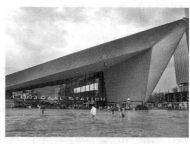

tion's futuristic signage only reinforces what sure seems like an intentional *Star Trek* homage.) The angled glass pavilion to your left leads to an underground park-and-ride garage...not for cars, but for 5,000 bicycles. You'll also see a yellow M marking an entrance to what was the first Metro stop in the country (from 1968). Tucked around the right side of the station are platforms for trams that fan out across the city.

Turn around (with the station at your back) and look left and right, up and down the busy cross-boulevard called **Weena.** After Rotterdam was leveled by Hitler's *Blitzkrieg,* postwar city officials sent architects to Washington, DC, for inspiration. This street (and others like it) feels more like an American-style "downtown" zone than a European street. Some are even laid out according to specific American dimensions and proportions. While skyscrapers seem to be popping up randomly all over Rotterdam, they're carefully zoned; this boulevard is one of four central axis streets where tall towers are permitted.

• *Cross Weena and head straight down Kruisplein (through the big, pedestrian-friendly median, with grassy parks on both sides) for two short blocks. Enjoy the architectural harmony. Even the landscaping plays along—notice how the trees are groomed to grow with a uniform V. After the second parking pavilion, turn left down the street in front of the red tower. You'll emerge into one of many bold Rotterdam public spaces.*

## ❼ Schouwburgplein and Rotterdam's Central Shopping Zone

Named for the giant theater building (Schouwburg) that sits at its far end, **Schouwburgplein** is also ringed by a giant Pathé/IMAX theater and other entertainment venues. The adjustable red crane-like lampposts evoke the busy port that made this city wealthy, and behind them are caged ventilation towers. (You can push buttons at the command center in the middle to make the lampposts move.) Like the features of Paris' Pompidou Center, these adhere to the "form follows function" aesthetic of celebrating—rather than hiding—the inner guts of a working building. At night, the lights embedded in the square simulate floating through the Milky Way. And on a sunny day, the big green plastic lounge chairs invite loitering.

Continue straight ahead and head down the pedestrian-only street called Korte Lijnbaan (under the big *Lijnbaan* sign, toward the copper-topped tower; cyclists must dismount and walk their bikes). This is just one leg of the **Lijnbaan,** a network of completely pedestrianized shopping streets that burrow through downtown Rotterdam. In the postwar boom of the 1960s and 1970s, several European cities pedestrianized downtown streets for shoppers—but Rotterdam's Lijnbaan was the first, created in 1953.

After one block, you reach a big intersection with a statue of rasslin' bears in the center. Our walk proceeds to the right from here (down Lijnbaan), but first, pause and look straight ahead at Rotterdam's **City Hall** (one block ahead and across the street).

Dating from 1917, it's one of a handful of old Rotterdam structures that wasn't destroyed in World War II. (The Germans, who knew they'd need a headquarters in the city, intentionally spared it—but if you get close, you can still see bullet holes from the fighting.) Today it's a popular place for weddings, and it houses the office of Rotterdam's mayor. In keeping with the city's global demographics and progressive politics, the current mayor is the son of a Moroccan immigrant and is a practicing Muslim. If you'd like to detour, you're welcome to step inside this civic palace and enjoy the Art Deco space under the cupola—so slathered in symbolism. Also in the lobby is a plaque honoring George Marshall (father of the Marshall Plan), placed there as a thank you for all the money the US gave the city to rebuild after World War II. It sums up the brilliant mission of the Marshall Plan with these simple words: "The only way to win a war is to prevent it."

Back at the bears, head south (right) down Lijnbaan. While not quite "charming," this zone is very user-friendly; daydream about doing your shop-ping here instead of at a suburban mall. After two blocks, at Van Olden-barneveltplaats (with the tram tracks), turn left and follow an even more entic-ing shopping zone called the **Beurstraverse,** where a swooping green canopy dips gracefully under a busy street.

Continuing straight up the stairs after the tunnel, you'll wind up on **Hoogstraat.** This is known as Rotterdam's "High Street": It's a major shopping thoroughfare, and it's literally high—it sits upon a dike. As you browse, keep in mind that this was the heart of Rotterdam's Old Town until 1940. Imagine that this area looked much like Amsterdam, with canals lined by old buildings before the bombs fell. The skinny green bell tower marks the Beurs-World Trade Center, a major office building and convention center.

• *After crossing the wide canal, you'll see a church steeple on your left. Head up little Wijde Kerkstraat to reach the square in front of the church.*

## ❸ St. Lawrence Church (Laurenskerk)

This is the oldest surviving structure in Rotterdam (completed in 1525)—a rare survivor of the 1940 Nazi bombing campaign. The church's nondescript exterior belies its vast, pristine interior with a huge organ. There's not much to see inside, but if you enter, be sure to look up to see a roof that was clearly built by a city of shipbuild-

ROTTERDAM

ers—it feels like you're huddled beneath an overturned boat (€3, Tue-Sat 10:00-17:00, closed Sun-Mon).

Grotekerkplein, the "Great Church Square" in front of St. Lawrence, has a statue of Rotterdam native **Desiderius Erasmus** (1466-1536), who was born in a house nearby (now gone). This humanist philosopher and satirist grew nervous when his like-minded friend, Thomas More, was beheaded by the English king. So, to evade a similar fate, Erasmus traveled far and wide—to Italy, England, Belgium, Switzerland, and beyond. He forged the notion of being a European— a citizen of the world, not tied to a single nationality. In this way, Erasmus is the intellectual forebear of the European Union, which named its highly successful foreign-study program after him. On the pedestal, in Dutch, a famous Erasmus quote is inscribed: "The entire world is your fatherland." (Several other major landmarks in this city are named for Erasmus, including Rotterdam's main university and its landmark bridge.)

Retracing your steps toward Hoogstraat, veer left along the side of the church into a peaceful little garden square with a newer **Erasmus Monument** (dedicated in 2016). It has the outline of a stepped-gable house and is covered with excerpts from his writings.

• *Continue past the garden square and turn right at the next opening between the buildings. You'll emerge back on Hoogstraat, across from a long, grassy square.*

*Turn left and continue down Hoogstraat. A few doors down, on the left, is **Poffertjessalon Seth**—a local favorite for their traditional tiny pancakes, made to order with powdered sugar and lots of butter before your very eyes. A small order (10 for €4) is plenty for two people and worth it for the cooking demo alone.*

*At the end of the grassy square, you reach a vast, empty concrete zone surrounded by striking architecture.*

## ❹ Binnenrotte Outdoor Market, the Market Hall, and Modern Architecture

On Tuesdays and Saturdays (and less so on Sundays), **Binnenrotte** street is lively with an outdoor market: food, clothing, housewares, flowers, and so on. This is a good chance to shop around for a snack or meal. The market sits upon the original "Rotter-dam"—the dam on the Rotte River, which runs underground perpendicular to the Hoogstraat axis. As you're browsing, tune into these buildings:

First, on your right is Rotterdam's strikingly modern **Market Hall** (Markthal, Mon-Sat 10:00-20:00, Fri until 21:00, Sun

12:00-18:00). Inside, beneath the grandiose arch, is a bustling food market (conveniently protected from the elements, a plus in this famously drizzly city). Arcing above and around that are 230 apartments—some with an ideal view of what's fresh today, and others with terraces overlooking the city. Step inside this cathedral for shoppers and look up at the wildly colorful ceiling tiles. The market itself is a foodie's festival with both local-traditional and fancy-international stalls.

Back outside, continue straight ahead to the **City Library** (the blocky white building with yellow tubes). The exterior is another example of Pompidou-like  "form follows function," while the interior reminds us that functionality is a very good thing for people using these buildings. Head inside (Mon 13:00-20:00, Tue-Fri 10:00-20:00, Sat 10:00-17:00, Sun 13:00-17:00, Hoog-straat 110, www.bibliotheek.rotterdam.nl). First, simply appreciate the space: Peering up into the atrium, see the many levels (with funky 1970s-style lampshades) that reach up through the structure, like a well-stocked warehouse of knowledge. But this is more than a library—it's a thriving and well-used community center. The information desk hands out brochures about local events, and you'll also find pay WCs, a handy café, and—behind the life-size chessboard busy with retirees and kids—a music library. Members get a world of benefits. Imagine funding a library like this with a levy in your hometown.

• *Exiting the library building, turn left and walk toward the unmistakably pointy-topped building that locals have dubbed "The Pencil." (There was really no other option.) The next stop on our walk is the blocks jutting out at its base.*

*The big industrial arch (which marks the busy Rotterdam Blaak tram-and-Metro hub) is nicknamed "The Manhole Cover" or "The UFO." Walk up the gap between the library and "The Pencil." Look back at the Market Hall (best view) and then follow the reddish ramp up into the...*

## ❺ Cube Houses (Kubuswoningen)

In the late 1970s, architect Piet Blom turned urban housing on its ear with this bold design: 39 identical yellow cubes, all tilted up on their corners, and each filled with the residence of a single family. Taken together, the Cube Houses look like dozens of dice in mid-toss. If Rotterdam has a single icon representing its bold approach to postwar architecture, this is it.

For a good look, follow the *museum* signs into the courtyard in the middle of the complex. Shops fill the gray boxes at the base, while people live in the yellow tops. The circle of angled cubes facing each other around this courtyard facilitates connections among neighbors. Inside each cube, the space is a bit awkward in places, but more functional than you might guess. Each cube has three floors: kitchen and living room downstairs, two bedrooms and one bathroom upstairs, and atop the ladderlike stairs in the summit, a cramped but relaxing sun lounge that feels made-to-order for reclining and gazing up at the stars. Everything is custom-designed to maximize efficient use of the odd space—cheap IKEA furniture just won't fit. To get a look inside one of the cubes, visit the **Kijk-Kubus Museum House** (at #70, €3, daily 10:00-18:00, www.kubuswoning.nl).

• *From the main courtyard, carry on over the busy street (find the long yellow cube corridor, beyond the entrance to the museum house). At the far end, just past the Stayokay hostel, take eight steps down on your right and enjoy a view of Rotterdam's...*

## ❻ Old Harbor (Oudehaven)

This mostly modern re-creation is what's left of the harbor that was the basis for Rotterdam's early prosperity. Today it's a bustling social zone, its embankments lined with inviting al fresco cafés and restaurants. You'll see a few houseboats and a shipyard used for repairing historic vessels.

Directly across the harbor is **The White House** (Het Witte Huis), another rare example of a surviving prewar building. When it was built in 1898, this structure was Europe's tallest building, at about 140 feet. It was inspired by American skyscrapers of the time...with the addition of frilly Jugendstil (Art Nouveau) turrets. In the 1970s, there were plans to build a superhighway right through the Old Harbor area, but local demonstrations kept this historic zone intact.

• *Follow the ramp down and curl around the left side of the Old Harbor, passing some enticing outdoor tables—handy if you're ready for a drink or snack. At the end of the harbor, pause at the little drawbridge to ap-*

*preciate the great view of the harbor and White House. (The towers just beyond mark another harbor, Leuvehaven, where we'll be later.)*

*Continue straight ahead, cross the busy street, and duck under the bridge's flyover, then bear right to the boardwalk, with a great viewpoint of the...*

## ❼ Maas Riverfront

The Maas River begins in France (where it's called the Meuse) and flows through Belgium, merging with several other rivers (including the Rhine) on its way to the sea. As you face the river, to the left (upstream) are Belgium, France, Germany, and Switzerland, and to the right (downstream)—past ever-larger harbors—is the North Sea.

You're standing next to the big, red **Williams Bridge** (Willemsbrug). In the distance, just to the right, is the green, industrial-style bridge called **De Hef.** Before 1992, this rail drawbridge was part of the only train line through the city—so passengers would have to wait patiently while it went up and down.

Across the river is the island neighborhood called **Noordereiland,** whose low-lying buildings were largely spared the bombs of World War II and retain a certain historic charm today. This evokes what much of Rotterdam's center might look like had Hitler not made an example of the city. In the near foreground is a curiously entertaining black-iron modern-art installation by Auke de Vries.

Panning right, you'll see several big towers surrounding the Erasmus Bridge—where we're headed next. If you're on a bike, now's the time for a long, scenic detour pedaling over this bridge and along Noordereiland. If you're tired and want to head back to the station, you can retrace your steps through the Cube Houses complex to the Blaak tram/Metro hub (where you can take tram #21 in direction: Schiedam Woudhoek or #24 in direction: Holy to get back to Centraal station).

But if you're on foot and ready to see more, turn right and head about a half-mile (15 minutes) south along the **Parade of Flags**—a line of about 200 flags representing the nationalities of the citizens who make up this city's multiethnic population. Much of the harborfront stroll is through a fine manicured park, with ever-changing views of the skyline across the river.

Nearing the Erasmus Bridge, you'll see a towering **monument.** From the land side, it looks like a nondescript gray tower with a hole in the top. But circling around to the riverfront park, its symbolism is more apparent: It resembles a ship's prow, cutting through the water. Officially the National Monument for the Merchant Marine, but nicknamed "The Bow" (De Boeg), this honors all seamen from Allied countries who were killed in World War II. If you find it a bit too abstract, you're not alone: The sailors lashed together at the bottom of the monument were added later to inject it with a bit more humanity.

• *At the monument, head inland to reach the drawbridge. Crossing it, turn left (toward the water) to head back down to the base of the bridge.*

### ❽ Erasmus Bridge (Erasmusbrug) and Rotterdam's Skyscraper Zone

Built in 1996, this icon of Rotterdam created an essential link between the north and south banks of the Maas River. Its huge, 450-foot-tall tower, at the south end, planted a flag for the then-underdeveloped part of the city—which has (thanks largely to the bridge) exploded into a new "downtown" zone of commerce.

Just past the base of the bridge, find the Spido boat dock, offering harbor cruises (see "More Sights in Rotterdam," later). From this point, take a visual tour of Rotterdam's modern skyline. (You can do this while waiting for your tour boat to depart, or in lieu of the cruise; if you're on foot, note that the views get better the farther down the embankment you go, with the best just before the Veerhaven harbor—a rare bit of Old World charm.)

At the far end of the bridge stands a lineup of creations—nicknamed "Manhattan on the Maas"—by the top architects working on this planet today. Many of these buildings were completed after 2000 and are engineered to sit upon pylons driven deep into the marshy riverfront soil. From left to right, find these buildings: First, behind the bridge (with the Deloitte logo), the **Maastoren** is the tallest building in Rotterdam (and in all of the Low Countries). It's also one of the greenest—it actually creates a surplus of energy by harnessing tidal power. The small cluster of buildings nearby are municipal and cultural institutions (court, customs, and theater)—placed here intentionally to spur development. Then comes the short, wavy **KPN Tower** by Renzo Piano (best known for Paris' Pompidou Center). The dots embedded in the side can illuminate and display patterns for a lightshow. Next is the **De Rotterdam** building—three independent towers with separate purposes (hotel, local government, and apartments) that share a unified base. This was designed by world-famous Rotterdam native Rem Koolhaas, who also created Rotterdam's Kunsthal, Porto's Casa de Música, and Seattle's Central Library. The tall, sandstone-colored **New Orleans** tower is by the Portuguese architect Álvaro Siza Vieira. In the next clump of two buildings, the gray, round **World Port Center** is by Lord Norman Foster (famous for Berlin's Reichstag dome; he also designed the plan for this entire peninsula and renovated the low-lying cruise terminal), while the multicolored **Montevideo** (look for the *M* on the roof) is by the Delft-based Mecanoo firm. As you might guess, the real estate on this peninsula is 100 percent committed for future projects; architects are already trying to figure out ways to build new structures on the water itself. Stay tuned.

The much lower-lying building at the tip of land (with the copper-domed turrets) is the jarringly old-fashioned **Hotel New York.** This was built in 1901 as the world headquarters of Holland America Line—which, back then, catered primarily to immigrants seeking a better life in the New World. Passengers would undergo rigorous health screenings in this building, and if found to be contagious, they'd be quarantined in the shipyards. To commemorate the place where so many soon-to-be-former Europeans last set foot on their home soil, today the grassy park in front of the hotel is decorated with street names from New York City. (If you'd like a closer look, you can catch a water taxi across the river from the nearby Veerhaven harbor, or from the Leuvehaven harbor, which we'll visit next.)

Looking far to the right, you can see the beginnings of Rotterdam's busy **port.** The "Europoort" was the largest in the world until 2004, when it was surpassed by both Singapore's and Shanghai's. From the Erasmus Bridge, it's more than 20 miles to the North Sea—and virtually every inch is lined with heavy industry. Each year, around 30,000 oceangoing ships stop here, hauling over 450 million tons of cargo. The plodding ships are weighted down with petroleum products, chemicals, and pharmaceuticals. This is also the biggest oil port on the planet, with five separate refineries.

• *If you're ready to return to the station from here, it's easiest to head for the Willemsplein tram stop, just above the Spido boat dock; as this is the end and start of the line, any tram from here will bring you back to the station.*

*Or, to continue our walk, head back the way you came and proceed straight past the drawbridge you crossed earlier, up Schiedamsedijk. You'll pass under the black, top-heavy **Rotterdam Centre tower** and the Leuvehaven Metro stop (another option for a quick return to the station). Just beyond, step down to dock level (at the 40,000-pound anchor) and walk alongside the historic port area called...*

ROTTERDAM

ROTTERDAM

### ❾ Leuvehaven

When Antwerp was taken over by fiercely pro-Catholic Spanish invaders in the late 16th century, Rotterdam welcomed Protestant

refugees seeking safe harbor. And those refugees built this harbor—named for Leuven, Belgium. Today it's a strangely picturesque mix of old and new, with a few historic harbor buildings and a rash of glittering towers that try to keep to the footprints of the original street plan.

Along the way, you'll pass a modern annex for the **Maritime Museum** (Maritiem Museum); the main building is a couple hundred yards up ahead, at the far end of the dock. Together, they offer an interesting look at Rotterdam's busy port, as well as some engaging children's exhibits (www.maritiemmuseum.nl). Stroll this embankment to peruse an open-air collection of historical ships and equipment that will be especially interesting to sailors.

Near the end (just before the red lighthouse), a **gangway** crosses the harbor. For a scenic detour, follow it. Along the way, you'll pass a water-taxi station—one of many stops in Rotterdam that lets you connect various waterfront areas (for example, from here—for €4.50—you can ride over to the Hotel New York for a closer look at the skyscraper zone).

At the end of the gangway, back on dry land, turn left and walk toward the giant main building of the Maritime Museum.

In the plaza between here and there is the poignant statue *De Verwoeste Stad (The Destroyed City),* commemorating Rotterdam's WWII destruction. An anguished figure—his heart pierced by a void—flails his arms, face frozen in a *Guernica* scream. This monument is an important symbol of this city, which is defined by the architecture built upon the blank canvas caused by that harrowing destruction.

• *Backtrack down the Leuvehaven embankment toward the tall cranes. Here you can use the crosswalk to cross the busy street and head up Schilderstraat; after two blocks, the street angles left a bit and becomes...*

### ❿ Witte de Withstraat

This lively, tree-lined street is an ideal place to browse boutiques,

window-shop, or restau-
rant-hunt. For all those
200 flags along the wa-
terfront, here we have the
actual people they repre-
sent. It's funky but still
accessible, with a rainbow
of eateries: *shoarma, döner
kebab,* Indonesian, burg-
ers, hipster cafés, spit-and-

sawdust pubs, and more. It also has several art galleries and fashion
boutiques. Relax, linger, and enjoy...our walk is almost finished. To
really kick back, you'll find two Dutch "coffeeshops" near the end
selling marijuana. The one just around the corner (Coffeeshop the
4 Floors at Eendrachtsweg 29A) is most inviting.

• *You'll pop out at a canal, which marks the...*

## ⓫ Singel Belt
*Singel* means "moat," and this north-south stretch of grassy canals
defines the edge of what was old Rotterdam. From here, you have
several options.

Directly across the street (through the canal belt), on the left,
is the city's top art collection at **Museum Boijmans Van Beuningen** (www.boijmans.nl)—with the big Picasso in front. From this
anchor, several additional museums sprawl south (back toward the
river), surrounding Museumpark. And modern artworks, starting
with a Rodin, line the canal all the way back to the train station.

To return to the **train station,** you can hop on a tram (#7;
the Museumpark stop is immediately to your left where Witte de
Withstraat hits the Singel belt). Or you can walk along these pleasant canals for about three-quarters of a mile to reach the station.

After one long block, you'll reach the Eendrachtsplein Metro
stop, where you can catch a train out
to the cute, cobbled Delfshaven zone
(described later, under "More Sights in
Rotterdam").

A couple of blocks farther along
the Singel belt, you enter a small
square called **Eendrachtsplein.** The
Oude/Nieuwe Binnenweg cross-street
(with some more buildings that survived the 1940 bombs) is another good
place to browse for restaurants and is
also known for its (sometimes outside-
the-box) modern art and sculpture. For
example, soon after the Metro stop, in

the square on the right, look for another Rotterdam landmark by American sculptor Paul McCarthy (see photo on previous page; the piece is officially named *Santa Claus*). But what is Santa Claus holding—a misshapen Christmas tree, a giant ice-cream cone, or a sex toy? (Locals call the statue "The Butt-Plug Gnome.") Originally designed for the Schouwburgplein—the square we saw near the start of this walk—the sculpture pushed the bounds even of Rotterdam residents' sense of tolerance and propriety. After hiding it away in a museum for a few years, they moved it here as a compromise.

• *With that image vivid in your mind, continue straight along the Singel belt. Before long, you'll see the unmistakable outline of Centraal station, straight ahead.*

## More Sights in Rotterdam

Most of the main sights in town are described along my self-guided walk. But here are some additional options.

### ▲Harbor Cruises

The **Spido** company runs 75-minute cruises that offer a good look at part of Rotterdam's vast port. These sleek boats—with indoor and outdoor areas, a fully stocked bar, and WCs—broadcast a quadrilingual recorded commentary over the loudspeakers. Cruises depart from near Rotterdam's landmark Erasmus Bridge. You'll see the sprawling Staatspark (marked by the Euromast tower), several innovative waterfront housing blocks, and  one small section of the bustling port, with stacks upon stacks of containers and a forest of busy cranes. While interesting, a little of this trip goes a long way, and the tour can get a bit boring. But if you view it as a nice chance to relax on a sunny boat deck while cruising through Europe's busiest port, it's fun and illuminating.

**Cost and Hours:** €16; April-Sept daily 9:30-17:00, departs about every 45 minutes, fewer departures off-season, confirm schedule at www.spido.nl; Willemsplein 85, +31 10 275 9988.

**Getting There:** From the train station, you can either zip there directly on tram #7 (get off at the Willemsplein stop, at the end of the line), or follow my self-guided walk for a look at Rotterdam old and new en route to Spido's departure point.

### ▲Delfshaven

One of the few well-preserved bits of Rotterdam's golden age wasn't even part of Rotterdam—it was the port for Delft. Lacking its own

outlet to the sea, Delft was given this harbor, which is still connected to Delft's town center by six miles of canals. Strolling along here, you can imagine the Pilgrims setting sail. You'd never know that modern Rotterdam is just around the corner.

**Getting There:** Delfshaven is on the outskirts of Rotterdam's center, but it's easy to reach on the Metro: Ride line A toward Schiedam Centrum or Vlaardingen West, line B toward Hoek van Holland Haven or C toward De Akkers, and get off at the Delfshaven stop. From Centraal station this requires a transfer at Beurs (on line D); for nicer scenery, you could ride tram #4, but it's less frequent.

**Visiting Delfshaven:** Exit the Metro following signs for *Uitgang—Historisch Delfshaven*. You'll pop out in the middle of a busy immigrant neighborhood. Walk east on Schiedamsweg for about three blocks and you'll emerge at the top of historic Delfshaven (on your right)—an idyllic canal pulled straight out of a Vermeer painting: old boats, a cantilevered drawbridge, and even a windmill still churning away in the distance. Wander and explore, going up and down Voorhaven canal and over the bridges. Next to the main drawbridge is the **Pilgrim Fathers Church** (Oude of Pelgrimvaderskerk), where the Pilgrims prayed the night before setting sail for the New World on August 1, 1620. (Their ship, the *Speedwell*, had to be swapped out for the *Mayflower* in England before continuing to Plymouth Rock.) If it's open, step inside to catch some history (www.pelgrimvaderskerk.nl). For more on the Pilgrims' time in Holland, see the sidebar on page 107. The parallel Achtershaven canal, one block east, is half charming, half more modern.

## Eating in Rotterdam

To grab a bite along the course of my self-guided walk, you have several great options to browse for a meal (in order):

The modern **Market Hall** (Markthal) is filled with tempting eateries, either for a quick stand-up bite or a sit-down meal. Around the **Old Harbor** (Oudehaven), just below the Cube Houses, you'll find an inviting array of restaurants with waterfront seating. **Witte de Withstraat** is simply a delight to browse, with a wide variety of places to eat and drink. If you've made it all the way through the walk, **Oude Binnenweg** is another pedestrianized street lined with places where you can grab a bite before heading back to the train station.

# Rotterdam Connections

## BY TRAIN
Trains depart from Rotterdam's Centraal station at least every 15 minutes and head north to **Delft** (15 minutes), **The Hague** (30 minutes), **Leiden** (35 minutes), **Haarlem** (1 hour), and **Amsterdam** (4/hour on express ICD train, 45 minutes; slower trains stop at all of the above, 75 minutes). Trains also head to **Utrecht** (4/hour, 40 minutes), where you can change to reach **Arnhem** (1.5 hours total). To reach **Antwerp**—where you can connect to other Belgian destinations—you can take the slower, cheaper IC train (hourly, 1 hour) or the speedy, expensive Thalys (hourly, 30 minutes—but reservations are required and the cost is about triple). To reach **London,** take the Eurostar (6/day, 4 hours for Thalys-Eurostar connection, slower but cheaper with IC-Eurostar connection, most transfer in Brussels, reservations required).

## BY CRUISE SHIP
Ships use the Cruise Terminal Rotterdam, centrally located along the Wilhelmina Pier—the skyscraper-studded strip that juts out from the southern end of the Erasmus Bridge. The historic building, home to the Holland America Line when Ellis Island-bound emigrants departed from here, is still used by Holland America (among others) as a starting point for many Northern European cruises (www.cruiseportrotterdam.com). For more details, see my *Rick Steves Scandinavian & Northern European Cruise Ports* book.

The Metro easily connects the cruise terminal to Rotterdam's Centraal station. From the cruise port, walk five minutes to Wilhelminaplein Metro station and ride to Rotterdam Centraal. You can also take tram #23 or #25 from Wilhelminaplein to Rotterdam Centraal. From the station, you can follow my self-guided walk, or hop on a train to Delft, The Hague, Leiden, or even Haarlem or Amsterdam (see connections listed earlier).

# EAST OF AMSTERDAM

Most of this book's coverage hugs the western part of Holland. But some interesting sights lie to the east of Amsterdam. Near the German border, on the outskirts of Arnhem, are two very different, but equally fascinating, museums: one devoted to Dutch culture, and one to 20th-century art and sculpture. And halfway between Amsterdam and Arnhem is the hub city of Utrecht, with beautiful canals, lively student bustle, and several good museums.

Utrecht and Arnhem are on the same train line and complement each other well. But because Arnhem's two big sights are time-consuming to reach by public transportation, it's not practical to combine everything in one day. So it's smart to choose: Do both museums near Arnhem in one very long day from Amsterdam; pick one Arnhem museum to focus on, then stop in Utrecht on your way back to Amsterdam; visit only Utrecht; or spend the night in Otterlo, near the Kröller-Müller Museum, to buy yourself more time for this area.

## DESTINATIONS
### ▲Utrecht
This medieval city located in the heart of the country is known for its lively downtown core, good museums (including the Netherlands' top railway museum), and double-decker canals with a particularly fun café scene.

### Museums near Arnhem
Allow an extremely long day to visit the open-air and modern-art museums (but not on Mon, when art museum is closed); you'll need to leave Amsterdam by 8:00. If you stay overnight near the art museum (in Otterlo), you'll have more time to fit in Utrecht's train museum on your return to Amsterdam.

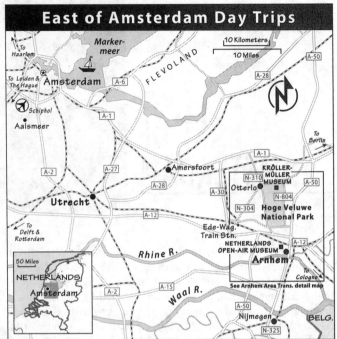

**▲▲Netherlands Open-Air Museum:** Holland's original and biggest open-air museum is also one of its best, sprinkling traditional buildings from around Holland across a delightful park and populating them with chatty docents who provide a flavor of old-time lifestyles.

**▲▲Kröller-Müller Museum:** This superb modern-art museum features the world's second-largest collection of Van Goghs and a sculpture garden. Located on the outskirts of Arnhem, it's set within the vast **Hoge Veluwe National Park**—a fun place to explore on a bike (available for free).

# UTRECHT

The Netherlands' crossroads city, Utrecht has a thriving old center with unique and inviting canalside embankments, the towering remains of a half-ruined church, a variety of fun museums (including the country's best railroad museum and a quirky collection of music-making machines), and a huge student population to keep things humming. Bigger and more bustling than Haarlem, Delft, or Leiden, but still exuding a small-town warmth along its gorgeous canalfront wharves, Utrecht feels at once packed with weighty history, and yet also fun to explore.

## PLANNING YOUR TIME

Utrecht is a quick side trip from Amsterdam (30 minutes by train). You can see the downtown highlights in an easy two-hour stroll, following my self-guided walk. With more time, dip into some museums or climb the cathedral tower. The excellent Railway Museum, a bit farther out (but still an easy walk or a train ride from Utrecht Centraal station), is also worth a visit and demands an extra three hours or more.

Because it's on the same train line as **Arnhem,** it's tempting to combine a peek at Utrecht with a visit to Arnhem—but to fit everything in takes careful planning (see the previous chapter for suggestions).

## Orientation to Utrecht

With about 330,000 inhabitants, Utrecht (OO-trekht) is the Netherlands' fourth-biggest city (after Amsterdam, Rotterdam, and The Hague). But it feels quite a bit smaller than those cities, thanks to its relatively compact central zone. Most of the sights are contained within or just outside the harp-shaped old town (Binnenstad)—

which takes about 15 minutes to traverse on foot from end to end. This central zone is ringed by a moat *(singel)*—much of it now covered over with a ring road—and crisscrossed by two main canals, the Oudegracht (old canal) and Nieuwegracht (new canal).

## TOURIST INFORMATION
The **main TI** is on Cathedral (Dom) Square, facing the cathedral tower. You can get tower tickets inside (TI open daily 10:00-17:00, Domplein 9, +31 30 236 0004, www.visit-utrecht.com). The **Utrecht Info Counter** within Hoog Catharijne—the train station shopping mall—is also helpful (Tue-Sat 10:00-18:00, Sun-Mon from 12:00).

## ARRIVAL IN UTRECHT
At Utrecht's Centraal **train station,** you'll find pay WCs above tracks 20-21 on the station's main level and lockers (credit cards only) on the second floor above tracks 18-19, next to Bar Beton. The train station and Hoog Catharijne shopping mall are basically one large building. My self-guided walk starts from your train platform and leads you into town.

# Utrecht Walk

This lazy, one-mile tour loops you from the train station into town, along Utrecht's most scenic canals, past a few of its worthwhile museums, and to its landmark cathedral tower. From there, you can head back to the station, or proceed across town to visit the excellent Railway Museum (adding about a half-mile of walking each way). The basic loop takes about 1.5 hours, not including sightseeing stops; to add the Railway Museum, figure another three hours (including two hours at the museum).

• *Step off your train into Utrecht. Find a quiet corner in the busy terminal to read the following before making your way into town.*

## ❶ Centraal Station
Situated in the middle of the Netherlands, Utrecht is the country's primary transportation hub—with its biggest and busiest train station, the headquarters of the Dutch Railway, and the national rail museum (across town).

Built in the 1970s, the train station was wrapped inside a gigantic American-style shopping mall called Hoog Catharijne. While the station/mall succeeded in jump-starting a flagging economy, it was the opposite of user-friendly: The maze of shops made arriving visitors feel like overwhelmed toddlers lost in a shopping mall in Anytown, USA. Inside and out, architecture like this earned its name: brutalist.

# Utrecht History

While most of Holland flourished during the 17th-century golden age after the Reformation wars (Amsterdam, Haarlem, Delft, Leiden) or during the second half of the 20th century (Rotterdam, The Hague), Utrecht feels older. That's because it is: Utrecht was the biggest city in the Netherlands from about 1100 until 1550 and has the country's largest surviving medieval old town.

The Romans—eager to fortify the Rhine River, which marked their boundary with barbarian lands—built a *castellum* (fort) on today's Cathedral (Dom) Square in AD 47. They called their settlement Trajectum ("crossing point"), which later became U-trecht.

At the end of the seventh century, an English missionary named Willibrord traveled to the wilds of Holland. He built a church in the center of town, near today's cathedral. Later, to help cement Utrecht's standing as a seat of Church power, four churches were built at the endpoints of an imaginary city-sized cross—symbolically making Utrecht one gigantic megacathedral, with the actual cathedral at its center. To this day, Utrecht's nickname is Domstad ("Cathedral Town").

Strategically situated Utrecht—midway between seaside Dutch settlements and big Germanic cities farther inland—flourished as a trade crossroads, attaining city status in 1122. At its peak in 1500, Utrecht had around 25,000 inhabitants—more than Amsterdam (which soon eclipsed it).

The city's location made it pivotal not only for trade, but also for defense. Looking at a map of Utrecht, you can still faintly see the outline of its moat and former star-shaped bastions ringing the Old Town. Utrecht was a critical fortress of the "Holland Waterline," a network of strategically linked canals and breakable dikes that served as a last-resort defense from the 17th through the 20th century. A band of low-lying land running through the middle of the country—from the Markermeer lake just east of Amsterdam, south through Utrecht, and all the way down to the broad river deltas near Belgium—could be quickly flooded at an ideal depth for thwarting would-be invaders: too deep to easily walk, but too shallow to maneuver large boats. Large, fortified cities like Utrecht anchored the defense as militarized, high-and-dry bastions ideal for keeping an eye on approaching armies. Meanwhile, large population centers farther west—Amsterdam, Rotterdam, The Hague—could be isolated on what was effectively a giant island.

Over the centuries, Utrecht has soldiered on with the same historical roles: transportation hub (with a sprawling train station), spiritual center (as the official seat of the Catholic Church in the predominantly Protestant Netherlands), and center of learning (with the biggest university in the country). This old and young city also looks to the future, with ambitious plans to reverse some of the grim architectural choices of the postwar period—and make welcoming Utrecht even more so.

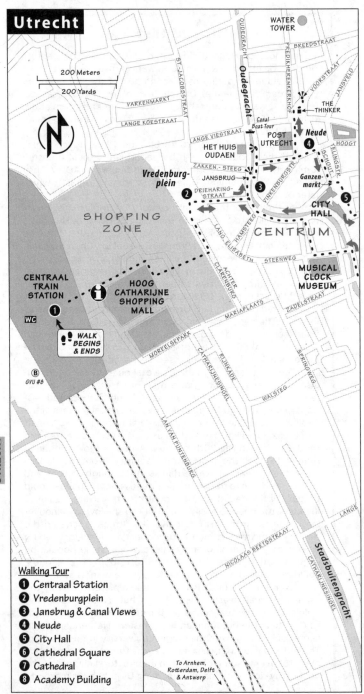

# Utrecht

WATER TOWER

BREEDSTRAAT

VOORSTRAAT

JANSVELD

ST. JACOBSSTRAAT

PREDIKHERENKERKHOF

OUDEGRACHT

200 Meters
200 Yards

VARKENMARKT

LANGE KOESTRAAT

Oudegracht

THE THINKER

HOOGT

Canal Boat Tour

LANGE VIESTRAAT

HET HUIS OUDAEN

POST UTRECHT

❹ Neude

Neude

TELINGSTR.

SCHOUT

Vredenburg-plein

ZAKKEN-STEEG

JANSBRUG

❷

DRIEHARING-STRAAT

❸

Ganzen-markt

❺

VINKENBURGSTR.

CITY HALL

SHOPPING ZONE

HAMSTEEG

LANG ELISABETH

CENTRUM

AGHTER CLARENBURG

STEENWEG

MUSICAL CLOCK MUSEUM

CENTRAAL TRAIN STATION

❶

WC

HOOG CATHARIJNE SHOPPING MALL

WALK BEGINS & ENDS

MARIAPLAATS

ZADELSTRAAT

Ⓑ GVU #8

MOREELSEPARK

CATHARIJNESINGEL

RIJNKADE

SPRINGWEG

WALSTEG

LANG VAN PUNTENBURG

NICOLAAS BEETSSTRAAT

CATHARIJNESINGEL

Stadsbuitengracht

LANGE

To Arnhem, Rotterdam, Delft & Antwerp

UTRECHT

## Walking Tour

❶ Centraal Station
❷ Vredenburgplein
❸ Jansbrug & Canal Views
❹ Neude
❺ City Hall
❻ Cathedral Square
❼ Cathedral
❽ Academy Building

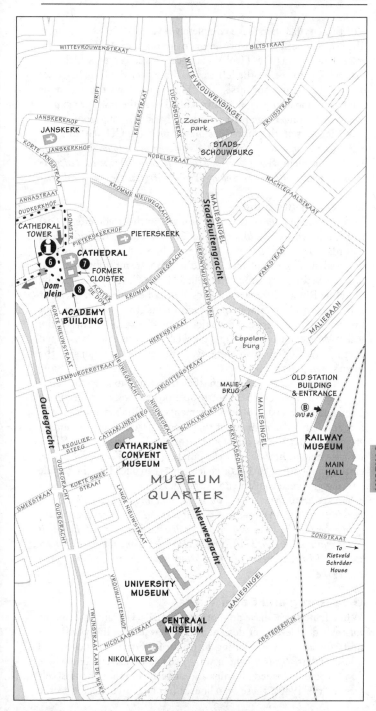

UTRECHT

But city planners have completely revamped the station area. They've also built a state-of-the-art convention center (behind the tracks), as well as the TivoliVredenburg music center, which you may be able to see on the left as you cross over the busy highway on the glassed-in concourse. That highway follows the course of the former moat *(singel)*, which was filled in as the town grew; part of Utrecht's long-range plan is to bring back that long-gone canal. (For the latest on this ambitious master plan, see CU2030.nl.)

• *Exit the train station through the shopping mall, following signs to* Vredenburgplein. *When you leave the mall, turn left onto the pedestrian street named Achter Clarenburg. You'll emerge at the square called...*

## ❷ Vredenburgplein

This historic market square (one of many in this trade crossroads) is still busy with an outdoor market every Wednesday, Friday, and Saturday. It's named for a long-gone-but-not-forgotten, deeply despised symbol of outsiders meddling in Utrecht's business. The original Vredenburg (ironically called "Peace Castle") was built by the Holy Roman Emperor Charles V after he annexed Utrecht. It kept the peace not by watching for invaders from the outside, but by keeping close tabs on the would-be enemies that lived inside the walls. Worse, during the Eighty Years' War, the castle was taken over by invading Spanish forces who trained their cannons on the town's own people.

After the siege was broken, the city wanted to keep the castle intact for its own defense...but people power took over. Trijn van Leemput led a cadre of local women who climbed up onto the fort and—in a dramatic event that looms large in local folklore—started pulling bricks off of the structure, inspiring their fellow townspeople to literally tear the building apart. (For a peek at the castle's foundation, curious archaeologists can duck into the bicycle parking garage at the left end of the square.)

• *Now cut across the middle of the square and find the lane called Drieharingstraat. This street—crammed with café tables—offers one of many good opportunities in Utrecht to have a drink, snack, or meal. Follow it to the main canal, called Oudegracht. Turn left along the embankment, then head halfway across the first bridge you come to (Jansbrug) and survey the scene.*

## ❸ Jansbrug and Canal Views

While Dutch cities have no shortage of canals, Utrecht's are unique for their double-decker design: an upper walkway, lively with pedestrians and cyclists jostling in front of pretty townhouses, and a lower wharf *(kaden)*, which was once the industrial zone where goods could be loaded off ships and directly into those houses' cellars. In the 1940s, these warehouses (no longer connected to the mansions above) were re-purposed as restaurants and cafés. Today the canal itself allows only leisure traffic (including touristy canal cruises and rental paddleboats), plus a few hardworking service barg-es: Look for the garbage-collection boat and the

red-and-white, city-operated "beer boats" that deliver kegs.

• *Let's head down for a better look. Continue the rest of the way across the bridge, turn left, and take the first set of steps down to the embank-ment. Notice how the leafy trees provide nice shade, but their burly roots also bully up the pavement. The fence and undulating barrier hopefully prevent people from stumbling into the canal.*

Look up across the canal, at the house marked ***Het Huis Ou-daen,*** dating from around 1300. This is a typical, ritzy canal house

(sometimes called "city castles") from Utrecht's trading heyday. Scanning the building from left to right, identify the four parts: The tallest, skinny, turreted structure on the far left is the stair house (used for reaching the upper stories); next is the main house (with huge windows to let in maximum light and to show off residents' wealth); then, tucked on the right side, comes the shorter "side house" (where the cheapskate owners lived in the win-ter, since it was smaller and cheaper to heat); and finally, on the embankment

down below, the warehouse cellars. This building was rebuilt after it was destroyed during the Spaniards' Vredenburg siege in 1577; the cannonballs embedded in the wall commemorate that dark his-tory. Later, in the 18th century, the building became a home for seniors—notice the elderly couple decorating the stone entryway of the side house.

Before heading back up, look around and enjoy the canal's-eye view. While the walls rising up from the canals are uniform, you can gauge at a glance how wide each house is by the distance be-tween the nose-high drainpipes that flank each foundation. Look-ing up to street level, notice the fine details carved into the square stone bases (called "corbels") of the wrought-iron lampposts. Each one of the 300-plus corbels in the city center is different, carved by local stonecutters. These whimsical sculptures may relate to the history of a nearby building or may simply be biblical or mythological scenes.

• *Retrace your steps back to street level. At the top of the stairs, notice that the big building at the start of Drakenburgstraat is another typical canal house (now a shop). Canal cruises depart from the bridge a block farther up the canal.*

*Now head up Drakenburgstraat. Emerging into the big square, wade through hundreds of café tables to the middle.*

## ❹ Neude

This square is one of Utrecht's main gathering points. The hulking building on your left as you entered the square is **Post Utrecht,** the former post office, now a sleek public library *(bibliotheek)* and café combo. The Dutch are extremely early adopters of new technology—and quick to abandon the old ways. In 2011, the Dutch mail system simply closed all its post offices. Home delivery still exists, but if you want to mail a package, you'll have to

do it from smaller postal counters located in bookstores, tobacco shops, and supermarkets. The closure of Dutch post offices left a big question mark for historic old buildings like this one, which is considered an important landmark of the architectural transition from the ornamented Jugendstil/Art Nouveau of the 1920s to the straightforward functionalism of the 1930s (a period collectively called the "Amsterdam School"). Step inside to peek at its far more impressive interior—with a swooping, parabolic roofline of shimmering yellow brick.

Past the end of the *bibliotheek,* just across the busy road, look for the sculpture of *The Thinker* as a hare, by Welsh sculptor Barry Flanagan. Behind the sculpture, walk up Voorstraat one block to Predikherenstraat. Between the buildings, look for a classic old **water tower.** These were built in cities throughout the Netherlands in the late 19th century, when scientists realized the importance of clean water in protecting public health.

• *Head back to Neude square and walk south down Schoutenstraat. You'll emerge into a square called Ganzenmarkt (also labeled* Korte Minrebroeder- *straat), dominated by the eclectic facade of...*

## ❺ City Hall

Utrecht's seat of government is an architectural hodgepodge. It started out as several linked townhouses; later, in the 19th century, they slapped the stern Neoclassical facade on the front. More recently, in the early 2000s, renowned Catalan architect Enric Miralles added the modern extension. Notice that he left a jarring gap (the glass corridor) for future growth. Miralles' choices have been controversial on aesthetic grounds—although this is the main entrance of the building, it feels unfinished.

• *Walk to the far end of the square and turn left, following the pleasant, shop-lined Oudkerkhof, with lots of youthful boutiques and creative stores. At the end of the street, turn right down Domstraat and head for those flying buttresses. Reaching the church, turn right and circle around to the square. Stand directly between the church and the tall tower. (If you're weary, rest at the base of the WWII monument.)*

## ❻ Cathedral Square (Domplein)

Standing right here a few hundred years ago, you'd be in the middle of a massive cathedral's nave.

Several churches have stood on this spot, each marked today by a faint footprint of gray stones in the pavement. In the late seventh century, the English missionary Willibrord built a chapel dedicated to St. Martin on this square. It was later replaced by a Romanesque version, then by a gigantic French-style Gothic structure, which was completed in the early 16th century. At the time of its completion, St. Martin's Cathedral was the biggest church in the Netherlands. But money ran out near the end of construction, causing the builders to skimp on the nave: Rather than weight-supporting flying buttresses (like the ones you just saw supporting the apse), it had a simple, flat wooden roof. On the hot summer evening of August 1, 1674, a violent tornado ripped through Utrecht, collapsing the nave of the church around where you're standing now. Trying to salvage what they could of the hulking building, the townspeople sealed off the transept—enclosing a new, much smaller church—and let the jumble of ruins sit here for a century and a half, finally clearing out the rubble to create this square in 1826. Noticing how the outline of the nave is still visible in the wall of the surviving church, mentally resurrect what a mighty house of worship this once was.

Look up at the cathedral tower—368 feet tall, with 465 steps to the top, it's still the tallest one in the Netherlands. The open-work structure allows stiff breezes to blow right through, creating less wind resistance—and, some believe, preventing it from being toppled with the rest of the church. The carillon halfway up plays cheery jingles every quarter-hour, all day (and night), every day.

## ❼ Cathedral (Domkerk)

You have three options for visiting the cathedral: Climb the tower, tour the interior of the modern-day church (entrance to the right as

you face the building), and descend under-ground to see the fragments of earlier church structures embedded below the square (buy tickets a few doors to the right of the TI).

**Cathedral Tower Climb:** You can climb the tower (Domtoren) with a one-hour escorted tour (€12.50, €20 combo-ticket in-cludes Musical Clock Museum, buy tickets at the TI across the square; daily 10:00-17:00; +31 30 236 0010, www.domtoren.nl; tours in Dutch and English).

Pick up your ticket and meet your guide at the TI, across the square from the tower (free lockers for day bags). Your guide will lead you over to the tower and up, up, up to the top (465 steps, no elevator). Each level has history exhibits. Just over halfway up, you'll get up close to the giant bells. It's another 80 feet to the view-point near the top. From here, more than 300 feet above the square, you can clearly see the outline of the once-massive cathedral—and pretty much everything else in Utrecht.

**Cathedral Interior:** The interior is free to visit but a €2 do-nation is suggested (Mon-Fri 10:00-17:00, Sat until 15:30, Sun 14:00-16:00, shorter hours off-season; audioguide-€3, www.domkerk.nl).

Step inside the truncated church. The organ marks the point from which the nave once stretched much farther—all the way to the tower, now outside. Buried at the main altar isn't a saint, but an admiral and war hero, Willem Joseph Baron van Gendt.

In the small chapel on the right as you face the main altar, find the poignant statues whose faces were ripped off from the 1560s through the 1580s. While originally Catholic, like many Dutch churches this became Protestant following the Reformation. But unlike in other churches, you can actually see the damaging effects of the iconoclasts that sought to destructively unclutter the worshippers' communion with God. The next chapel farther back has more such disfigured statues. These statues were later covered over by a wall and only rediscovered in the 20th century.

**DOMunder** (Underground Church Foundations): The DOMunder experience lets you wander among giant old pillars in a subterranean visitors center 15 feet below the square (€12.50; Tue-Wed and Sun 12:00-16:00, Thu-Sat from 11:00, closed Mon; check website for tour times, www. domunder.nl).

The tour starts in the TI (across from the cathedral) with a talk and video presentation as the guide explains the history of the many churches that have stood here. Afterward, you enter the underground space through the rusted entrance in the middle of the square, and then follow the one-way route through the interactive exhibition. Point your innovative audioguide flashlight at items scattered around the ruins to hear about them on your headphones. This is a fun tour for kids and a good rainy-day activity.

• *Facing the cathedral, head right, to the frilly building in the corner of the square.*

**❽ Academy Building (Academiegebouw)**

Originally the cathedral's chapterhouse, after the Reformation this gorgeous building became the center of Utrecht University. The Netherlands' biggest university—with an enrollment of about 30,000— U.U. is also one of its oldest (founded in 1636). These days, the science faculties are neatly segregated at a modern campus called De Uithof, which was built on reclaimed polder land just

east of town in the 1970s. But law and humanities are still in the city center, and students of all stripes still hang out downtown.

In the 19th century, architects celebrated the university's 250th birthday by dressing up this building with a stunning Neo-Renaissance facade. U.U.'s symbol is the shining sun, represented both by the vivid sculpture on the gable above the main door (with the red-and-white crest of Utrecht) and by the giant sphere in the pavement in front. The building is usually open; if so, peek inside.

Facing the building, look for the ornately carved stone Gothic gateway just to the left. Step inside to enjoy a harmonious and peaceful space—the **former cloister** of the church, today used for special events for students. The carved triangles over the arches depict scenes from the life of the cathedral's namesake, St. Martin.

Leaving the cloister, look left down Korte Nieuwstraat. This street leads several blocks south through town to Utrecht's **museum quarter**—worth exploring if you have extra time. Among the city's fine museums are the Centraal Museum (displaying art, design, fashion, and city-history exhibits in a former monastery), the Catharijne Convent Museum (filling a medieval convent with religious art), and the University Museum (with a fine botanical garden and hands-on exhibits for children; may be under renovation). Architecture students make a pilgrimage to the Rietveld Schröder House, a famous Piet Mondrian-style single-family house in the suburbs just outside the center. For more details on any of these, ask at the TI.

The **Nieuwegracht,** a peaceful and scenic canal with the same double-decker construction as the Oudegracht, parallels Korte Nieuwstraat one block to the left. The **Railway Museum** is a pleasant 15-minute walk from here: Head down Korte Nieuwstraat and, after a block, turn left down Hamburgerstraat, which becomes Herenstraat, and leads you to a park that traces the former city wall and moat. The museum is through the park and to the right.

• *Or, if you're ready to move on, you can head...*

## Back to the Train Station

From Cathedral Square, go through the big tunnel at the base of the tower. In one block, you'll emerge at the main canal, Oudegracht. Turn right and wander, simply enjoying the people-watching (but watch for cyclists, who recklessly

whiz along this embankment). After one short block, you'll reach a square covering the canal. At the far end of this, turn left up Hanengeschrei, which becomes Steenweg. The entrance for the **Musical Clock Museum** (described later) is on the left.

You can follow the busy Steenweg shopping street all the way back to the station (it becomes Lange Elisabethstraat partway along). Or, for a more scenic stroll, turn right up the street just after the clock museum (Massegast), then turn left along the canal to follow Oudegracht for a few short-but-scenic blocks; just turn left on Drieharingstraat to return to the station.

# Sights in Utrecht

### ▲▲Railway Museum (Spoorwegmuseum)

The most interesting sight in town is Holland's biggest and best display of all things locomotive. It's full of vintage engines and cars (including the Dutch

royal family's official train), model railways, and re-creations of historic scenes. Although primarily designed for Dutch families (with spotty English translations), it's easy for anyone to appreciate and particularly fun for kids. Even the most train-blasé will want to spend at least two hours here.

**Cost and Hours:** €17.50, free for kids 3 and under; Tue-Sun 10:00-17:00, closed Mon; at east edge of town in the old-fashioned Maliebaan train station, +31 30 230 6206, www.spoorwegmuseum.nl.

**Getting There:** From downtown (and the end of my self-guided walk), it's an easy 15-minute **walk**—see directions earlier. Another option is to take the **train** from Utrecht Centraal (runs about hourly on weekdays—confirm schedule for "Utrecht Maliebaan"; typically does not run Sat-Sun; 20 minutes, €2.20 one-way). While this sounds romantic, the train uses a boring, middle-of-nowhere spur line and takes about the same amount of time as the pleasant walk through town. (However, the train can be a nice option for a sweat-free return to Centraal station—and your connecting Amsterdam-bound train.) GVU **bus** #8 from Centraal station (direction: Stadsschouwburg) also runs to the museum (get off at the Maliebaan stop.

**Visiting the Museum:** The ambitious, well-presented museum combines a remarkable collection of old train cars with a modest, Disney-style amusement park. You'll enter the fully restored Maliebaan train station, which evokes the genteel early days of rail travel (c. 1874), and buy your ticket (which includes a map and high-quality booklet describing what you'll see). Cross the train tracks (passing the royal train, which is usually parked here) to reach the main hall and get oriented to the different areas.

The **main hall,** called World 4, is filled with historic locomotives and carriages. You'll experience an interactive exhibit combining the images and sounds of 10 iconic trains to tell the history of rail transport. Along the right side of the hall are several more engaging attractions: the Steel Monsters roller coaster for kids, an Orient Express exhibit with an original carriage from the train line that once connected Western Europe to Istanbul (as well as a small theater presenting a live show in Dutch several times a day—read the translations in your booklet beforehand), and a lavishly re-created mining village from 19th-century England (with a replica of the world's oldest passenger train car, from 1829).

**Outside** is a picnic area, a mini railroad that kids enjoy riding, and the prizewinning Trial by Fire ride—a jostling simulator of a harrowing steampunk train ride, narrated by Dutch actor Rutger Hauer (who is speaking Dutch—but the ride is still fun). Be sure to explore the sprawling grounds, which include a giant playground, an enormous turntable for locomotives, an old shunting yard (used to supply steam locomotives), a thought-provoking exhibit on the use of railway cars in World War II and the Holocaust, and temporary exhibits.

## Musical Clock Museum (Museum Speelklok)

This fun museum fills the cavernous hall of a former church with a fascinating array of self-playing instruments: musical clocks, calliopes, and street organs in all their clicking, clanking, and tooting glory. On the main floor, several soundproof rooms house hulking calliopes and player pianos, while upstairs in the gallery, smaller pieces overlook the former nave. Everything is explained in English and some items are hands-on. For the best experience, make a point to join the 40-minute included tour.

**Cost and Hours:** €14 includes tour, €20 combo-ticket includes cathedral tower (Domtoren); Tue-Sun 10:00-17:00, closed Mon, tours depart at :30 past each hour, last tour at 15:30; well-signed 10-minute walk from station, located on busy shopping street in city center at Steenweg 6, +31 30 231 2789, www.museumspeelklok.nl.

# Utrecht Connections

Utrecht is the crossroads of the Netherlands, with major lines running north to **Amsterdam** (6/hour, 30 minutes), where you can connect to **Haarlem** (7/hour, 50 minutes, transfer in Amsterdam); west to **The Hague** (4/hour, 40 minutes); northwest to **Leiden** (2/hour, 45 minutes); southeast to **Rotterdam** (4/hour, 40 minutes), where you can connect to **Delft** (1 hour total) and **Antwerp,** Belgium (2 hours total); and east to **Arnhem** (4/hour, 40 minutes).

# MUSEUMS NEAR ARNHEM

*Netherlands Open-Air Museum ·
Kröller-Müller Museum*

While the city of Arnhem itself is nothing special, it's close to a pair of fun and worthwhile side trips: the Netherlands Open-Air Museum and the exceptional Kröller-Müller Museum. Of all open-air folk museums in the Netherlands, Arnhem's—set just within the city limits—feels the most authentic. Its classically Dutch buildings sprawl across rolling hills, with rich details around every corner. Nearby, the Kröller-Müller Museum, located in the middle of Hoge Veluwe National Park, displays a world-class collection of modern art (including rooms full of Van Goghs). It's also a delight to pedal through the park on free loaner bikes.

## PLANNING YOUR TIME

Arnhem, an hour southeast of Amsterdam by train, is doable as a side trip from Amsterdam. Unfortunately, its two museums are far from each other and far from Arnhem's Centraal station. Both are superb and worth the time and effort, but to see both, either spend the night in the town of Otterlo (recommended) or be prepared for a long day of somewhat rushed sightseeing. Note that the Kröller-Müller Museum is closed on Monday.

**By Car:** Drivers can visit both museums within a day...and might have time left to park the car and go for a pedal through the national park. Figure just over an hour's drive from Amsterdam to Arnhem, then about a 20-minute ride into the national park, and an hour back to Amsterdam. For driving directions, see the "Getting There" section for each museum.

**By Public Transportation:** You can day-trip to either museum by taking a train and bus ride; for specifics, see "Getting There" in the individual sight listings and the "Arnhem Area Transportation" map on the next page.

**Arnhem Area Transportation**

To combine both museums in one long day of sightseeing, you must get an early start. Here's a basic outline: From Amsterdam Centraal station, catch the train at about 8:00 for the one-hour ride to Arnhem. In Arnhem, hop a bus to the open-air museum to arrive when it opens at 10:00. Leave the museum by 13:00 and catch a bus via Arnhem to Otterlo, near Hoge Veluwe National Park and the Kröller-Müller Museum. In the park, do the museum first, then the visitors center, then wind down your day by biking around the park. Plan on a late return train to Amsterdam from the Ede-Wageningen station (the station nearest the park).

**For Overnight Visitors:** If you're spending the night in Otterlo, you can get a later start from Amsterdam, linger at the open-air museum (having left your things in a locker at Arnhem station), relax that evening in Otterlo, and tour the art museum and national park at a leisurely pace the next morning.

# Arnhem

Tourists view dreary Arnhem as a transit hub useful only for reaching the open-air museum on its outskirts and the nearby Kröller-Müller Museum and national park. A few hotels line up across from the train station, but I'd rather sleep in charming little Otterlo, near the park entrance (see "Sleeping in Otterlo," later). Arnhem's old town—nowhere near as charming as similar towns in the Netherlands—is just across the busy ring road from the train and bus stations. The train station has a helpful transit-information office. Restaurants with outdoor seating cluster around the square called Korenmarkt and, a few steps deeper into the old town, around Jaansplaats.

**Tourist Information:** Arnhem's TI is about a 15-minute walk from the train station. Easiest for drivers, it sells city guides and a tourist map that includes the national park and Kröller-Müller Museum (Mon-Sat 10:00-17:00, closed Sun, Kerkplein 1, tel. +31 088 540 5805, www.visitarnhem.nl).

**Arrival in Arnhem:** Arnhem's stunning modern **train station** took nearly 20 years to complete; shipbuilding techniques were

used to create an undulating roof with almost no visible supports.

The station has pay WCs and lockers (credit cards only). You'll also find a bike-rental shop in the basement near the front of the station, open long hours daily. A transit-info office (OV Services) in the main hall of the train station has helpful personnel to answer questions and kiosks where you can look up bus connections (Mon-Sat 7:00-21:30, Sun from 8:00, www.ns.nl, +31 30 751 5155).

The **bus station,** with connections to Otterlo, the Netherlands Open-Air Museum, and the Kröller-Müller Museum and national park, is to the right as you exit the train station in a large parking garage along the busy street. Check the sign near the entry to the bus area to find the departure bay for your bus.

**Arnhem Connections:** By train to **Amsterdam** (2/hour, 1 hour, more with transfer in Utrecht), **The Hague** (4/hour, 1.5 hours, transfer in Utrecht; then another 15 minutes if continuing to **Delft**).

# Netherlands Open-Air Museum

Arnhem has the Netherlands' first and biggest open-air folk museum, and it's also one of the best, rated ▲▲. You'll enjoy a huge park of windmills, old farmhouses and other buildings relocated from throughout the Netherlands, traditional crafts in action, and a pleasant education-by-immersion in Dutch culture. It's great for families.

## GETTING THERE

From Arnhem train station to the museum (called "Nederlands Openlucht-museum" in Dutch), take either direct and fast bus #8 (direction: Velp Ziekenhuis) or slower bus #3 (direction: Burgers Zoo/Openluchtmuseum—both

buses run about 2/hour, 10-25 minutes, €2.45, get off at the Openluchtmuseum stop).

From the Arnhem train station, you can also **walk** (45 minutes) or ride a **bike** (strenuous 20-minute uphill ride). A **taxi** from the station costs about €20.

By **car** from Amsterdam, take A-2 south to Utrecht, then A-12 east to Arnhem. Just before Arnhem, take the Arnhem Nord exit (#26) and follow *Openluchtmuseum* signs to the museum (pay parking, buy parking ticket when you buy entrance ticket). If driving from Haarlem, skirt Amsterdam to the south on A-9, take A-2 south to Utrecht, and then follow the previous instructions (via A-12).

## ORIENTATION

**Cost and Hours:** €19.50; daily 10:00-17:00, buildings closed Nov-March.

**Information:** +31 26 357 6111, www.openluchtmuseum.nl.

**Getting Around:** A free, old-fashioned tram does a lazy counterclockwise circle around the museum grounds, making six stops (marked on park maps).

**Eating:** The museum has scattered eateries and covered picnic areas. The **$ café** in the entrance pavilion offers the best variety of lunch options (soups, salads, and sandwiches). The rustic **$ Pancake House** (a.k.a. "De Hanekamp Inn") serves hearty and sweet splittable Dutch flapjacks and more. **$ Brabant Bar–Café Budel**, in the "village" of Budel, resembles an old-fashioned farmhouse café and offers soft drinks and museum-brewed beer.

## ⊙ SELF-GUIDED TOUR

You could spend the whole day exploring this wonderful open-air museum. But to hit a few highlights, follow this tour. Because the layout of the grounds can be confusing, pick up the good free map at the entry—I've used the numbers on that map to help you navigate this tour. Don't hesitate to dip into any buildings that intrigue you, even if they're not on this tour—most have brief English explanations outside, and some have English-speaking docents inside. (Ask them questions...that's their job.) Especially with kids, it would be a shame to do this place in a rush—there's so much to experience.

• *Start in the...*

**Entrance Pavilion:** Consider buying the in-depth English guidebook, and ask about special events and activities, especially for kids. To hit the park, exit the entrance pavilion and cross the tram tracks to walk up the path. You're likely to see animals in the pasture on your right—if so, take a closer look: They're rare Dutch breeds, not the high-yield animals used in modern farms. No longer cost-effective, these special animals are raised by the museum as part of its mission to preserve a piece of Dutch history.

• *After a few buildings on the left, step inside the one-story...*

**Straphorst Farmhouse** (#1.17, just before the pond): The cows lived on one side of this house from 1750 and the people on the other (notice the claustrophobic cupboard-beds). Along the cow stalls, see the patterns the farmwife would make with fresh sand and seashells each summer to show off family status.

• *Nearby, cross the...*

**Yellow Drawbridge** (#2.13): This 19th-century double drawbridge takes you to perhaps the most scenic part of the park: a
pond surrounded by windmills and cabins (inspired by the Waterland area around the town of Marken). Pause on the bridge to look toward the sawmill. You might see kids playing with a small rope-pulled ferryboat.

Continue across the drawbridge into the little **village.** Along the way are some tempting shops where you can pick up a sweet snack, including a bakery and a Venetian gelato parlor from 1930s Utrecht.

• *At the center is the...*

**Village Square:** Here's your chance to play with toys from the 1800s. See if you can make the "flying Dutchman" fly, or try to ride an original "high-wheeled velocipede" without falling off. On the square is a restaurant (#2.8) specializing in *poffertjes* (puffy mini pancakes dusted with powdered sugar).

• *Behind the poffertje shop, cross the little bridge toward the windmills, pass the boat workshop, and enter the...*

**Fisherman's Cottage** (#2.6): The black-tarred exterior hides a bright and colorful interior. Notice it has a rope-controlled smoke hatch, rather than a chimney. Wooden cottages like these were nicknamed "smokehouses." In front of the cottage is the boatyard, where vessels could be pulled out of the water to scrape off the barnacles.

• *Backtrack through the village square, then continue on to the...*

**Laundry** (#2.23, on the right): Inside, an industrial-strength agitator furiously pounds stubborn stains to smithereens. (There was no "delicate cycle" back then.) On nice days, the clean sheets are spread out on the lawn to dry.

• *For an optional detour (best for train buffs), hook around through the little cottages across the street, then turn right to reach the...*

**Tram Depot** (#2.31): Inside, you can actually walk underneath a tram to check out its undercarriage. The adjacent **goods shed** (#2.30) holds a virtual-reality postal carriage.

• *Head back past the laundry, then through the village square to reach the small yellow windmill. At the Deventer **urinal** (#2.19), turn left and walk up the path, watching for the low-profile brown building through the trees on your right, near the bridge.*

**Paper Mill** (#6.13): At this building, dating from around 1850, you'll learn that farmers often made paper in their spare time to help make ends meet. Inside, you might see a demonstration of linen rags being turned into pulp and then into paper. Peek upstairs at the finished paper hanging to dry.

• *Leaving the mill the way you came, walk straight ahead on the brick path, passing various buildings on your right until you reach the...*

**Herb Garden** (#4.7): This tranquil, hedge-lined garden is worth exploring. The map at the entry explains the various parts of the garden, each growing herbs for different purposes: dyes, food, medicine, and so on. Listen for the squeals of lively children from the playground behind the garden.

• *Continue past the garden and cross the tram tracks to the...*

**Freia Steam-Dairy Factory** (at #3.1, with the big smoke-stack): Named after Freia, the Norse goddess of agriculture, this was the Netherlands' first privately owned cheese-and-butter factory. Learn all about the cheese-making process, from the farmer's milk drop-off to the home delivery—by bike, of course. Rooms of equipment and artifacts are well described in English, and a smattering of videos helps you envision the operation in action.

Leaving the factory, loop around to the right—past the little black-and-green windmill—then turn right again, down the path just before the brick-and-thatch woodland cottage (#3.7).

• *On the right, look for the...*

**Peat Hut** (#3.9): As late as the early 20th century, humble little huts like these were used by day laborers and covered with the same turf that those laborers were paid so poorly to gather.

• *Continue to a big, thatched-roof...*

**Farmhouse** (#3.10): Step into the vast and rough 1700s interior, listen to recorded animal noises, and scope out the layout: grain stored up above, cows along the main room, and at the far end, a (no doubt smelly) residential zone for people.

• *Cross the tram tracks in front of the farmhouse to reach the tiny...*

**Village School** (#4.10): Aside from its brick construction (most were made of clay), this is typical of village schoolhouses from around 1750. Only kids from 6 to 12 years old, mostly boys, attended school, with an emphasis on reading and writing, with summers off to help on the farm. Imagine the schoolhouse back then, fragrant with smoke from the peat fire. Notice the slates used to follow along with lessons (stored in the wooden "lockers" on the walls). An underperforming student would have to wear the donkey picture around his neck.

Just beyond the schoolhouse is the **Pancake House** (#B; good for a snack or meal), with an adjacent playground.

• *Go back toward the school and cross the tram tracks. If it's not crowded, cut through the playground; otherwise follow the path past a **farmhouse** (#3.10) and turn right to find the...*

**Dutch Reformed Chapel** (#5.1): In the typical Dutch style, the church has an austere white interior, a central pulpit, and wooden pews. Men sat in the pews along the side, while women used the chairs in the center section.

• *Then continue along the tracks through the village, past the **Brabant Bar–Café Budel** (#5.5), and follow the smell of hops to the modern, working **brewery** (#5.8, on the left; you can buy the brew at eateries around the museum).*

*Just beyond, on the left, look for the...*

**Four Laborers' Houses** (#5.9): These houses offer a fascinating glimpse into the lifestyles of four generations of workers: from 1860, 1910, 1954, and 1970. See how home fashion and amenities—most interestingly, bathrooms—progressed from the rustic 1860s to the garish 1970s.

Continuing through the village, the 1954 **health center** on the left (#5.13) really does smell like a hospital. Follow the sound of a man singing in the shower: There's a bathhouse inside where those who didn't have a bath or shower at home could wash themselves once a week. Just beyond the long building with temporary exhibits is a formal hedge garden (#5.17).

• *Finally, cross the tram tracks and walk to the big, white...*

**Platform Windmill** (#6.11): Hike up the steep steps of the park's centerpiece for an aerial view over the museum. From this perch, the flour miller who worked inside could keep an eye on the weather and adjust the mill's sails.

• *Our tour is over. Head back to the entrance or continue exploring to your heart's content.*

# Kröller-Müller Museum

This memorable museum of top-notch modern art shows off the collection of Helene Kröller-Müller (1869-1939), a wealthy fan of avant-garde art. The ▲▲

museum seamlessly blends artistic beauty and its own peaceful park setting. Stroll through the delightfully landscaped sculpture garden and spend some time with virtually all the top artists of the late 19th and early 20th centuries.

The highlight is the outstanding collection of Van Goghs. But because it's difficult to get to, the Kröller-Müller Museum doesn't suffer from the hordes that descend on the Van Gogh Museum in Amsterdam. This is your best chance to get up close and personal with Vincent.

The museum is located within **Hoge Veluwe National Park,** the Netherlands' largest at 13,000 acres (also rated ▲▲). To visit the museum, you must also buy a ticket for the park. With limited time, a short pedal on one of the loaner bikes and a visit to the museum are enough; with more time, also swing by the park visitors center and cruise around some more.

## GETTING THERE
### By Train

Visitors coming from Amsterdam can take the train to either Arnhem or the Ede-Wageningen station near Otterlo (2/hour, 1 hour, more with transfer in Utrecht). If you're combining your visit here with the open-air museum, head to Arnhem first. If you're not visiting the open-air museum, the Ede-Wageningen station is the better choice.

Either way you'll need to go through the town of Otterlo, near the northwest entrance of the park, just over a mile from the museum. Its Rotonde bus stop is at a roundabout on the edge of town; its Centrum stop is in the center. Buses #105 from Arnhem and #106 to the park make both stops. Bus #108 from the Ede-Wageningen station stops only at the Rotonde stop. See specifics below and the map on page 439.

**Getting Between Ede-Wageningen Station and the Museum:** Exit the station toward signs marked *Centrum* to find the bus stops, where you can catch **bus** #108 to Otterlo (bus marked *Apeldoorn*, runs hourly about :40 past the hour, 20 minutes, €4.90, www.9292.nl). Hop off the bus at the Otterlo Rotonde roundabout,

about a five-minute walk from the center (buses return from Rotonde to Ede-Wageningen station at the top of the hour). The #106
bus, which goes to the museum, usually meets the #108 at this stop.
When the #106 enters the park, the driver will stop at the ticket
booth so that you can buy tickets for the park and the museum. Ask
the driver to let you off at the museum; turn right at the giant blue
trowel and follow the road for a few minutes past the parking lot
with all the white bikes; the museum entrance is on the left.

If you miss the #106, **walk** five minutes into the town center
and then hang a left to the park entrance (about 20 minutes total),
where you can buy your combo-ticket and hop on a free white bike
to ride to the Kröller-Müller Museum or the park's visitors center. A **taxi** from the Ede-Wageningen station to the museum costs
about €45 one-way.

**Getting Between Arnhem Centraal Station and the Muse-
um:** There's no direct bus to the museum, so you'll go via Otterlo.
From Arnhem's bus station (right next to the train station), take
**bus** #105 marked *Barneveld/Syntus* and get off at Otterlo Centrum
(1-2/hour, 30 minutes, €5). Once in Otterlo, you can take bus #106
or **walk** to the park (both options described above). A **taxi** from
Arnhem's station costs about €50.

## By Car

From Amsterdam, take A-1 southeast, then exit on N-310 to Otterlo. From Arnhem, follow A-12 north, then pick up N-310 to
Otterlo. Parking inside the park costs about €8, or you can pay €4
to park at the entrance (then bike or walk in).

## GETTING AROUND HOGE VELUWE NATIONAL PARK

Once at Hoge Veluwe, you have various options for connecting
the attractions. My favorite plan: Bus from Otterlo directly to the
Kröller-Müller Museum and view the collection, then pick up a
free white bike to pedal to the park's visitors center, then bike back
to the park entrance (or, with more time, bike around the park).

**By Bike:** The park has 1,700 loaner bikes—an endearing rem-
nant of Holland's hippie past. The one-speed bikes with no hand
brakes (just pedal brakes) are good enough to get around on, but
not good enough to get stolen. Pick up or drop off wherever you see
a bike rack, including at park entrances, the visitors center, or at
any attraction. While riding through the vast green woods, make a
point of getting off your bike to climb an inland sand dune.

**By Bus:** For a convenient circuit around the park, hop on **bus
#106,** which links the Otterlo Rotonde stop (at the edge of town),
the Otterlo Centrum stop (in the town center), the Otterlo entrance to the park, a stop 200 yards from the Kröller-Müller Muse-

um, and the park's visitors center (1-2/hour, last bus around 20:00 May-Aug, earlier in off-season). It can be a handy way to connect the dots if you're tired or in a hurry.

## ORIENTATION

**Cost:** €12 for timed-entry museum ticket. Since the museum is within Hoge Veluwe National Park, you must also pay a separate €11.30 park fee.

**Hours:** Museum open Tue-Sun 10:00-17:00 (sculpture garden until 16:30), closed Mon. Park open daily 8:00-20:00 (later in summer), shorter hours Oct-April, last entry one hour before closing. Park visitors center open daily 9:30-17:30.

**Information:** Museum—+31 31 859 1241, www.krollermuller.nl. Park—+31 55 378 8100, www.hogeveluwe.nl/en.

**Tours:** A €2.50 museum audioguide is available at the entry.

**Visitor Information:** Maps and brochures are available at the park entrances or at the visitors center.

**Eating:** The museum has restaurants indoors and outside in the sculpture garden. They're both called **Monsieur Jacques,** but the outdoor one serves a more extensive menu (soups, sandwiches, salads). The good **$$ Parkrestaurant** at the park visitors center has surprisingly tasty self-service cafeteria food, with indoor or outdoor seating.

## VISITING THE MUSEUM AND PARK

The south end of the park is just outside Arnhem, while the opposite end is near the town of Otterlo. Start at the museum, buried deep in the forest close to the Otterlo side.

### The Museum

A stern-looking statue of Monsieur Jacques (the museum's mascot) greets you on the entry path. Once inside, pick up the informative booklet-guide, drop your bag at the mandatory bag check, and rent an audioguide if you wish.

There are two parts to the museum: the outside sculpture garden and the interior art collection. Since the garden closes earlier, head here first if you're arriving later in the day.

**MUSEUMS NEAR ARNHEM**

**Sculpture Garden:** More than 150 sculptures are displayed on 60 rolling acres of lawn. Appreciate works by Auguste Rodin, Barbara Hepworth, Christo, and many others—or just enjoy this excuse for a walk in a pretty park with something fun to look at. Look for Jean Dubuffet's beloved *Garden of Enamel (Jardin d'émail)*, a giant, psychedelic, black-and-white roller rink you can climb around on.

**Art Collection:** Inside is like a *Who's Who* of modern art. The works are displayed chronologically and grouped by movement, in keeping with Helene Kröller-Müller's wishes to foster understanding and appreciation of new art styles. You'll go from the hazy landscapes of the Impressionists (Monet,  Manet, Renoir), to the intricate compositions of the Pointillists (Seurat, Pissarro), to the bold innovations of the Post-Impressionists (Gauguin, Van Gogh), to the slinky scenes of Art Nouveau (Toulouse-Lautrec), to the shattered-glass canvases of the Cubists (Picasso, Braque, Gris), and, finally, to the colorful grids of Dutchman Piet Mondrian. All artwork labels and descriptions have good English translations.

The museum's highlight is its Vincent van Gogh collection, the second largest in the world (after Amsterdam's Van Gogh Museum; Kröller-Müller usually displays about 50 of their 87 Vincent canvases). The collection boasts some famous pieces, including various self-portraits, some *Sunflowers,* and *Café de Nuit,* the famous scene of an al fresco café on a floodlit Arles square. Notice how thickly the paint is caked on to create the almost-3-D lamp, the work's focal point.

## The Park

Once you're done touring the museum, head out into the park and explore it on one of the free bikes. The visitors center is a good first stop. You can also visit the hunting lodge, the former residence of the Kröller-Müller family. If you head deeper into the park, you'll find a surprising diversity of terrain, from inland sand dunes to lakes to peat bogs to moorland. Combining the Kröller-Müller Museum, the visitors center, and the lodge makes for a fun 6.5-mile biking loop.

**Visitors Center** (Bezoekerscentrum): This is a good place to get your bearings in the park, with a helpful information desk, a nature exhibit, WCs, a playground, and a restaurant.

The **nature exhibit** features interactive, kid-oriented exhibits, well explained in English. It's divided into two parts: An above-ground section focuses on the parks' various landscapes and the animals that live here; then you'll go through a tunnel to reach the second section, called the "Museonder," which shows life underground (animals, fossils, the water table), with conservation-themed displays. Ask for an English showing of the nature films when you enter (a favorite is the 30-minute movie about park deer).

**St. Hubertus Lodge:** This dramatic hunting lodge at the north end of the park is another popular excuse for a bike ride. Once the countryside residence of the modern art-collecting Kröller-Müller family, it's perched on the edge of a lake with a tower looming overhead. Designed to resemble the antlers of a stag, this structure evokes the story of St. Hubert, who supposedly discovered a crucifix miraculously dangling between a deer's antlers (English audio tour available). The 45-minute walk around the adjacent lake is dotted with sculptures (€5, book online in advance, www.hogeveluwe.nl./en).

## NEAR THE MUSEUM: OTTERLO

The tiny village of Otterlo is located just outside the northwest entrance to the park, which is the closest one to the Kröller-Müller Museum. Though not exciting, it's a good place to spend the night near the park. The town has tandem-bike tourists zipping through on their way to the park, cafés, and a meager **TI** (within a variety store in the town center; Mon-Sat 8:00-17:00, closed Sun; Dorpsstraat 9, +31 318 614 444, www.otterlo.nl).

**Sleeping in Otterlo:** Both of these are on the road between Otterlo and the northwest entrance to the park; Sterrenberg is about a half-mile from the park entrance, and Kruller is closer to the town center.

**$$$ Boutique Hotel Sterrenberg** is a Dutch designer's take on a traditional hunting lodge. With woodsy touches and modern flair in its 33 rooms, it's pleasant but pricey (great deals with dinner—check their website, outstanding breakfast extra, elevator, restaurant with terrace, swimming pool, sauna, pay laundry service, rentable bikes for guests, about 1.5 miles to Kröller-Müller Museum, Houtkampweg 1, +31 318 591 228, www.sterrenberg.nl, info@sterrenberg.nl).

**$$ Hotel Kruller** has 17 stylishly simple rooms over a busy restaurant (family rooms, Dorpsstraat 19, +31 318 591 231, www. kruller.nl, info@kruller.nl).

**Eating in Otterlo:** The hotels listed above both offer good-quality food in their restaurants. Another option, **$$$ De Wald-hoorn** is a cozy restaurant with an outside terrace centrally located in a characteristic village inn that's been open since 1812. The changing seasonal menu features classic and regional dishes such as beef stew, grilled salmon, and pork tenderloin (daily 10:00-22:00, Dorpstraat 2, +31 318 591 239).

# NETHERLANDS HISTORY

Born from the mud of a river delta that spills into the North Sea, the Dutch provinces united to become a global force of hardy seafarers, clever merchants, and freethinkers.

## ROMANS AND INVASIONS (AD 1-1300)

When Rome falls (c. 400), the Low Countries shatter into a patchwork of local dukedoms that are ravaged by Viking raids. It's a poor, agricultural, and feudal landscape ruled loosely by the Counts of Holland. Holland's first major city is Utrecht—a former Roman fort that becomes a crossroads of trade and bulwark of Christianity.

Around 1250, fishermen in Amsterdam build a dike (dam) where the Amstel River flows into the North Sea, creating a prime trading port. Soon the town gains independence and trading privileges from the local count and bishop.

### Sights
- Amsterdam: Dam Square and Amsterdam Museum exhibits
- Haarlem: Grote Markt
- The Hague: Ridderzaal and Binnenhof

## BOOMING TRADE TOWNS (1300-1500)

Amsterdam becomes a bustling little port, trading its signature salt-cured herring for German beer, all financed with a budding capitalism: banking, loans, and speculation in stock and futures.

# Netherlands Almanac

**Official Name:** Koninkrijk der Nederlanden (Kingdom of the Netherlands), or simply Nederland.

**Size:** The Netherlands covers 16,000 square miles—about twice the size of New Jersey. Its population is 17 million (1,200 people per square mile; 15 times the population density of the US).

**Geography:** The Netherlands is located at the delta where three major European rivers empty into the North Sea: the Rhine from Germany and Switzerland, the Maas (Meuse) from Belgium and France, and the Waal (a short but mighty distributary of the Rhine). It shares borders with Belgium and Germany. The Dutch have been beating back the North Sea for centuries, forming polders—flat, low-lying reclaimed lands. The Netherlands has a mild marine climate; even hot, clear, and sunny days can come with surprise rain showers.

**Latitude and Longitude:** 52°N and 5°E. The latitude is similar to Alberta, Canada.

**Biggest Cities:** Amsterdam is the largest city, with 1 million people (850,000 in the core), followed by Rotterdam (993,000), The Hague (650,000), and Utrecht (334,000).

**Economy:** The Netherlands is prosperous, with the planet's 28th-largest economy ($912 billion), a per-capita GDP in the world's top 25 ($53,600), and one of Europe's lowest unemployment rates. Its port at Rotterdam is Europe's largest, and the country relies heavily on foreign trade. The nation's highly mechanized farms produce huge quantities of flowers, bulbs, and produce for export. The economy has also benefited from its many natural-

The city attracts religious pilgrims when a communion wafer mysteriously survives a fire, and subsequently causes a rash of miraculous healings. But Amsterdam is only one among several trade towns in this land of businessmen—Haarlem, Delft, Edam. By 1500, it's Leiden that's the region's biggest city.

Politically, the Netherlands is ruled by the cultured empire of the Dukes of Burgundy (centered in the southern provinces—today's Belgium).

Tiny Holland's future changes forever in the year 1492, when Columbus' voyage hints at the potential wealth awaiting hardy seafarers...like the Dutch.

## Sights
- Amsterdam: Old Church (Oude Kerk) and New Church (Nieuwe Kerk)
- Amsterdam: Mint Tower (from the original city wall) and wooden house at Begijnhof 34

gas fields—including the huge Groningen field, one of the world's biggest.

**Government:** The Netherlands is a parliamentary democracy, with its seat of government at The Hague, although the country's official capital is Amsterdam. The ceremonial head of state is King Willem-Alexander, whose ascension to the throne in 2013 is celebrated each spring on King's Day—usually April 27. He is the first Dutch king in 123 years. The Dutch parliament consists of two houses: the 150-member, directly elected Second Chamber (or Lower House); and the 75-member First Chamber (or Upper House), elected by provincial assemblies. The government is led by a prime minister, currently Mark Rutte of the center-right People's Party for Freedom and Democracy (VVD).

**Flag:** The Netherlands' flag is composed of three horizontal bands of red (top), white, and blue.

**The Dutch:** About 80 percent of those in the Netherlands are native Dutch, who are among the world's tallest people—the average height for a man is 6'1" and for a woman, 5'6". The average age for both men and women is around 42 years old, and they'll live to be 81. They ride their bikes about 1.5 miles a day and smoke half as much marijuana as their American friends. Among the 20 percent of the population who were born elsewhere, 5 percent hail from other EU countries, and the rest are mostly Indonesian, Turkish, Surinamese, or Moroccan. Over 40 percent of the Dutch have no religious affiliation; less than a third are Catholic, under 20 percent are Protestant, and 5 percent are Muslim.

- Haarlem: Grote Kerk
- Delft: New Church (Nieuwe Kerk, see photo)

## PROTESTANTS VS. CATHOLICS, FREEDOM FIGHTERS VS. SPANISH RULERS (1500s)

Protestantism spreads through the Low Countries. Thanks to royal marriages, the Low Countries are now ruled from afar by the very Catholic Habsburg family in Spain. In 1566, angry Protestants rise up against Spain and Catholicism, vandalizing Catholic churches ("iconoclasm") and deposing Spanish governors. William of Orange rallies the Dutch, becoming the father of his country and establishing his

# William of Orange (1533-1584)

A wealthy noble who was the confidant of the Holy Roman Emperor, a sensual aristocrat who had four wives and many mistresses, a religious chameleon who was born a Lutheran, became a Catholic, and ended up a Calvinist—William of Orange sounds like the hero of a romantic novel. But to the Dutch, he will always be the George Washington of the Netherlands—the leader of their war of independence against Spain. They call him *De Vader des Vaderlands,* "Father of the Fatherland," and when they sing the Dutch national anthem (the *Wilhelmus,* the oldest national anthem in the world), the text is actual 16th-century propaganda justifying William's stand.

Born into Lutheran German nobility, as a teenager William inherited the French principality of Orange and several domains in the Low Countries. He was invited to serve in the court of Holy Roman Emperor Charles V—provided he become a Catholic, which he did. Mixing with the ruling elite of his era, William was set to live a life of ease. But he embraced religious tolerance in an era when people were often murdered for their beliefs, setting up a clash with Spanish King Philip II, who began a crusade against Protestants after inheriting the Low Countries from his father.

William, a *stadholder* (sort of a governor-general) of two Dutch provinces, became a leader of the resistance against the Spanish. When summoned before the Spanish governor, he fled to Germany, and from 1568 onward, led several military campaigns against Spanish forces in the Low Countries. William eventually became a Calvinist, and in 1576 seven Dutch provinces signed a treaty to become the United Provinces of the Netherlands—the forerunner to the Dutch Republic.

Philip detested William, calling him a religious opportunist, bigamist, and drunkard. To stop the rebellion, he put a price of 25,000 guilders on William's head. In 1582, an assassin almost succeeded in killing William in Antwerp, but he eventually recovered. William's final days were spent in Delft's Prinsenhof. A French assassin managed to sneak in and shoot William at close range with two pistols—the first head of state in the world to be assassinated by handguns.

When he died the rebellion was still in doubt, but fewer than 25 years later, the Dutch provinces had become a thriving republic—with William of Orange as its founding father.

**HISTORY**

family—and their heraldic color—as national institutions; see the sidebar. (The current king is distantly descended from William.) When Spain sends troops to restore order and brutally punish the rebel-heretics, it begins the Eighty Years' War, also known as the Dutch War of Independence (1568-1648).

During the war, the Dutch stand strong in the brave Alamo-like stand in the siege of Haarlem (1572-1573). In 1574, they flood

South Holland and sail flat-bottomed ships against the Spanish to save Leiden. When the thriving (Belgian) city of Antwerp falls to Spanish troops (1585), Antwerp's best and brightest flee to the Netherlands. Other refugees of religious persecution, including Calvinists and Anabaptists, find a home in tolerant Amsterdam. The influx of talented immigrants would spur the coming golden age.

Within a few years, most Spanish troops are driven south into Belgium. Belgium remains under Spanish control while Holland's towns and nobles form a Protestant military alliance (the United Provinces) to keep the Spaniards at bay.

## Sights
- Amsterdam and Delft: "New" churches stripped bare of decoration during the iconoclasm
- Amsterdam: Civic Guard portraits at Amsterdam Museum
- Haarlem: Mementos of the Siege of Haarlem at Grote Kerk
- Delft: Prinsenhof and Tomb of William of Orange

## HOLLAND'S GOLDEN AGE. . . AND FALL (1600s)

By 1600, Holland gains its independence from the Habsburgs (officially in 1648) and emerges stronger and more energized than ever. When England defeats the Spanish Armada (navy, in 1588), Spain's monopoly on overseas trade is broken and Holland is poised to leap in.

Amsterdam invents the global economy, as its hardy sailors ply the open seas, trading in Indonesian spices, South American sugar, and enslaved African people. The government-subsidized Dutch East and West India Companies establish colonies all over the world. (Henry Hudson sails up America's Hudson River to what would become New Amsterdam.) The Dutch people's nautical and capitalist skills combine to make Amsterdam—population 100,000—the world's wealthiest city. It's home to the painter Rembrandt, philosopher René ("I think, therefore I am") Descartes, plus many different religious sects and a bustling Jewish Quarter.

The golden age is not confined to Amsterdam. Delft is a thriving market town of textiles and export beer, and home to painter Vermeer and microscope-maker Van Leeuwenhoek. In Haarlem, Frans Hals paints humanist portraits. Leiden's prestigious university welcomes scholars, and the tolerant town welcomes the persecuted Pilgrims (Protestants from England), who would eventually leave (in 1620) for the New World.

In 1648, the Eighty Years' War officially ends, and the United Provinces (today's Netherlands) are now an independent and prosperous republic.

Even at Holland's golden age peak (c. 1650), forces are at work that would eventually drag it down. In 1637, after several years of insanely lucrative trade in tulip bulbs ("tulip mania"), the market crashes. As the century progresses, the harbors of Edam and Marken begin silting up.

Holland is overtaken by the rise of the new superpowers on the block—England and France. In 1652, Holland goes to war with England over control of the seas, the first of three wars that would sap Holland's wealth. In 1689, Holland's *stadholder*—William III of Orange—is invited by England's Parliament to rule (with his wife Mary) as King William III of England. Meanwhile, Louis XIV of France invades Holland and gets to within 15 miles of Amsterdam before being stopped when the citizens open the Amstel locks and flood the city. By century's end, France and England control the seas and Holland has been drained by costly wars.

## Sights

- Amsterdam: Rijksmuseum (Rembrandt, Hals, Vermeer, Steen)
- Amsterdam: Old townhouses and gables in Jordaan neighborhood and Red Light District
- Amsterdam: Begijnhof, Royal Palace, Westerkerk, and Rembrandt's House
- Haarlem: Frans Hals Museum
- Edam: Grote Kerk
- Hoorn: Period rooms at Westfries Museum
- Leiden: American Pilgrim and Lakenhal museums
- The Hague: Mauritshuis Royal Picture Gallery (Vermeer, Rembrandt, Rubens)

## ELEGANT DECLINE (1700s)

The Dutch survive as bankers, small manufacturers, and craftsmen in luxury goods—but on a small scale fitting their geographical size. They cruise along on exploited wealth from their colonies in the East Indies and Suriname. Delft continues to crank out Delft-ware, but the quality declines.

The Netherlands hits rock bottom in 1795, when French troops occupy the Low Countries (1795-1815) and Napoleon Bonaparte proclaims his brother, Louis Napoleon, to be King of Holland.

## Sights
- Amsterdam: Our Lord in the Attic Museum (hidden church), Willet-Holthuysen House, and Jewish Museum synagogue
- Amsterdam: Royal Palace
- Amsterdam and Haarlem: Indonesian foods from the colonial era
- Delft: Royal Dutch Delftware Manufactory

## REVIVAL (1800s)

After Napoleon's defeat, Europe's nobles decide that the Low Countries should be a monarchy, ruled jointly by a Dutch prince, who becomes King William I. (Today's King Willem-Alexander is descended from him.) When Belgian patriots revolt against the Dutch-born king and form their own nation, the two countries—the Netherlands and Belgium—officially split. The Netherlands soon becomes a constitutional monarchy with a parliament.

Though slow to join the Industrial Revolution, Holland picks up speed by century's end. In 1876, the North Sea Canal opens after 52 years of construction, revital-izing Amsterdam's port. In the next decade, the city builds Centraal sta-tion, the Rijksmuseum, and Concertgebouw, and hosts a World Exhibition  (1883) that attracts three million visitors. Progressive thinkers are questioning the country's repressive colonial tradition in the East Indies.

## Sights
- Amsterdam: Centraal station (see photo), Rijksmuseum, Stadsschouwburg theater, Concertgebouw music hall, and Magna Plaza
- Amsterdam: Van Gogh Museum

## WAVES OF GERMANS, HIPPIES, AND IMMIGRANTS (1900s)

The 20th century starts off badly, with World War I, though neutral Holland was spared the worst of it.

In 1932, the Dutch Zuiderzee dike is completed, creating many square miles of reclaimed land (including today's Flevoland). On the downside, the project closes off access to the North Sea, reducing once-thriving harbor towns like Enkhuizen and Marken to their role as cutesy time-passed villages.

In World War II, Holland suffers a brutal occupation by Nazi Germany. Queen Wilhelmina (1880-1962) flees to England and Anne Frank goes into hiding. Of the 140,000 Jews living in the Netherlands, more than 100,000 are killed. Rotterdam is utterly destroyed by German bombs. After the war, the city is ultimately rebuilt in a modern style and becomes Europe's busiest port.

In Amsterdam, postwar prosperity and a tolerant atmosphere in the 1960s and 1970s make it a global magnet for hippies...and your co-authors.

ANNE FRANK
TAGEBUCH

In the 1970s and 1980s, the city is flooded with immigrants from former colonies (especially Indonesia and Suriname), causing friction and bringing a degree of ethnic diversity to the population.

Holland continues its eternal battle with the sea. Major floods kill almost 2,000 people (in 1953) and a billion dollars in damage (in 1995), prompting more dams and storm barriers. Facing global warming, the "Low Countries"—with much of their territory below sea level—keep a close watch on rising seas.

The Netherlands is an active participant in the international community. In 1957, it helps found the Common Market and joins the Benelux economic union (in 1960). In 1992, the Netherlands—along with 11 other countries—signs the Treaty of Maastricht (in southern Holland), becoming a founding member of the European Union. The Hague is home to the world court.

### Sights

- Amsterdam: Beurs, Tuschinski Theater, and National Monument on Dam Square
- Amsterdam: Anne Frank House, Jewish Museum, and Dutch Resistance Museum
- Amsterdam: Heineken Brewery, rock-and-roll clubs Paradiso and Melkweg, and the Stopera opera house
- Haarlem: Corrie ten Boom House

HISTORY

# Islam and the Netherlands Today

The hottest hot-button issue in the Netherlands today is the culture clash between the secular, multicultural Netherlands and its recent Muslim immigrants. Many Muslims arrived in the last half of the 20th century after Indonesia (a Dutch colony) gained independence. Guest workers from Turkey and Morocco—drawn by economic incentives—swelled the ranks. Today, one in ten Amsterdammers is Muslim. But Muslim cultures have not meshed seamlessly with the Netherlands' Western, secular, and liberal traditions.

Several events have colored the discussion of Islam in the Netherlands:

During the Bosnian War, 400 Dutch soldiers were serving as UN Peacekeepers in Srebrenica when the town was overrun by Bosnian Serbs in July 1995. While the outnumbered Dutch soldiers huddled in their compound, the Serbs massacred 8,000 Muslim men and boys. To this day, many Dutch people are haunted by why the troops didn't do more to help.

In spring 2002, a charismatic Dutch politician named Pim Fortuyn—socially liberal but strongly anti-immigration—campaigned for Parliament on a platform that Islam posed a threat to Dutch tolerance. On May 6, he was gunned down in a parking lot by a man whose motives remain unclear. Dutch people were stunned by the violence, the kind of thing they thought happened only in America.

On November 2, 2004, Theo van Gogh, a well-known filmmaker and the great-grandnephew of Vincent van Gogh, was shot by a Muslim Dutch citizen of Moroccan descent. The assailant, angered by Van Gogh's controversial film about women and Islam, stabbed a letter into the filmmaker's dead body with threats against the film's female screenwriter, Ayaan Hirsi Ali. Ali, a Somali Muslim who served as a member of the Dutch Parliament and is an outspoken critic of Islam and its treatment of women, currently lives (under a 24-hour security watch) and teaches in the US, where she became a citizen in 2013.

Lately, Dutch politician Geert Wilders has taken up Fortuyn's mantle, advocating the banning of the Quran and an end to Muslim immigration. In 2017, a right-wing nationalist party made a strong showing in the polls, gaining seats in the House of Representatives and highlighting the growing nativist sentiment.

The Muslim immigration issue has forced the Dutch to confront a difficult paradox—how to be tolerant of what they perceive to be an intolerant culture.

HISTORY

- Enkhuizen: Zuiderzee Museum
- Flevoland: Schokland Museum
- The Hague: Peace Palace
- Rotterdam: Striking modern architecture (Centraal station, Cube Houses, skyscraper zone)

## THE NETHERLANDS TODAY (2000-present)

In the early 2000s, the assassinations of Pim Fortuyn and Theo van Gogh caused a backlash against immigration and a move to the right (see sidebar). The country is still feeling varied pressures from its growing and diversifying population, including housing shortages.

Overtourism is a concern, especially where sex work and soft drugs are an issue. The mayor of Amsterdam has announced a plan to move sex workers out of the Red Light District and has threatened to ban foreign tourists from cannabis cafés. Maastricht and other southern Dutch cities have restricted marijuana purchases to Dutch citizens only. In an effort to tamp down illicit-drug activity, the national government is experimenting with the legal production and supply of cannabis—just as some US states have.

In 2013, King Willem-Alexander (b. 1967) became ruler of the Netherlands, the first male on the Dutch throne in 123 years. Increasingly, general-election results are revealing a growing nationalist sentiment: The center-right People's Party for Freedom and Democracy (VVD) currently holds the most seats in the House of Representatives. But overall, today the Netherlands is peaceful, prosperous, and forward-thinking—waiting for you to arrive and make your own history.

### Sights

- Amsterdam: Metro, EYE Filmmuseum, and Muziekgebouw performance hall
- Rotterdam: Centraal station and Market Hall

For more on Dutch history, consider *Europe 101: History & Art for the Traveler*, written by Rick Steves and Gene Openshaw (available at www.ricksteves.com).

# PRACTICALITIES

This chapter covers the practical skills of European travel: how to get tourist information, pay for things, sightsee efficiently, find good-value accommodations, eat affordably but well, use technology wisely, and get between destinations smoothly. For more information on these topics, see RickSteves.com/travel-tips.

## Travel Tips

**Travel Advisories:** Before traveling, check updated health and safety conditions, including restrictions for your destination, on the travel pages of the US State Department (www.travel.state. gov) and Centers for Disease Control and Prevention (www.cdc. gov/travel). The US embassy website for the Netherlands is another good source of information (see below).

**Covid Vaccine/Test Requirements:** It's possible you'll need to present proof of vaccination against the coronavirus and/or a negative Covid-19 test result to board a plane to Europe or back to the US. Carefully check requirements for each country you'll visit well before you depart, and again a few days before your trip. See the websites listed above for current requirements.

**PRACTICALITIES**

**ETIAS Registration:** The European Union may soon require US and Canadian citizens to register online with the European Travel Information and Authorization System (ETIAS) before entering the Netherlands and other Schengen Zone countries (quick and easy process). For the latest, check www.etiasvisa.com.

**Tourist Information:** The Netherlands' national tourist office **in the US** can be a wealth of information (www.holland.com). Its website has trip-planning advice, festival schedules, downloadable city maps, and much more. Another useful website is www.iamsterdam.com (Amsterdam Tourism Board).

In the **Netherlands,** a good first stop is generally the tourist information office (abbreviated **TI** in this book; marked **VVV** locally). Amsterdam's main TI (called the "I Amsterdam Store") is inside Centraal station but is often crowded. You'll also find TIs at Schiphol Airport and in the towns of Haarlem and Delft.

TIs are in business to help you spend money in their town—which can color their advice—but I still swing by to pick up a city map and get info on public transit, walking tours, special events, and nightlife. Some TIs have information on the entire country or at least the region, so you can pick up maps and other info for destinations you'll be visiting later in your trip.

**Emergency and Medical Help:** For any emergency service—ambulance, police, or fire—call 112 from a mobile phone or landline (operators typically speak English). If you get sick, do as the Dutch do and go to a pharmacist for advice. Or ask at your hotel for help—they'll know the nearest medical and emergency services.

**Theft or Loss:** To replace a passport, you'll need to go in person to an embassy or consulate (see next). If your credit and debit cards disappear, cancel and replace them (see "Damage Control for Lost Cards," on page 467). File a police report, either on the spot or within a day or two; you'll need it to submit an insurance claim for lost or stolen items, and it can help with replacing your passport or credit and debit cards. For more information, see RickSteves.com/help.

**US Embassies and Consulates:** Amsterdam—dial +31 70 310 2209 (Museumplein 19, https://nl.usembassy.gov). Online appointments are mandatory for all public services.

The Hague—dial +31 70 310 2209, visits by appointment only (John Adams Park 1, in the suburb of Wassenaar, https://nl.usembassy.gov).

**Canadian Embassy:** The Hague—dial +31 70 311 1600 (Sophialaan 7, Mon-Fri 9:00-13:00 & 14:00-17:30, closed Sat-Sun; consular services Mon-Fri 9:30-12:30, closed Sat-Sun; www.canada.nl).

**Time Zones:** The Netherlands, like most of continental Europe, is generally six/nine hours ahead of the East/West Coasts of the US. The exceptions are the beginning and end of Daylight Saving Time: Europe "springs forward" the last Sunday in March (two weeks after most of North America) and "falls back" the last Sunday in October (one week before North America). For a handy time converter, use the world clock app on your phone or download one (see www.timeanddate.com).

**Business Hours:** Most stores throughout the Netherlands are open from about 9:00 until 17:00 (or 18:00) on weekdays. Some open at 12:00 on Mondays and Sundays. Shops may close earlier in small towns and stay open later in big cities, where they sometimes stay open until 21:00 on Thursdays. Some museums and sights are closed on Mondays.

**Watt's Up?** Europe's electrical system is 220 volts, instead of North America's 110 volts. Most electronics (laptops, phones, cameras) and appliances (newer hair dryers, CPAP machines) convert automatically, so you won't need a converter, but you will need an adapter plug with two round prongs, sold inexpensively at travel stores in the US.

**Rip up this book!** Turn chapters into mini guidebooks: Break the book's spine and use a utility knife to slice apart chapters, keeping gummy edges intact. Reinforce the chapter spines with clear wide tape; use a heavy-duty stapler; or make or buy a cheap cover (see the Travel Store at RickSteves.com), swapping out chapters as you travel.

**Discounts:** Discounts for sights are generally not listed in this book. However, seniors (age 65 and over), youths under 18, and students and teachers with proper identification cards (obtain from www.isic.org) can get discounts at many sights—always ask. Some discounts are available only to European citizens.

**Online Translation Tip:** Google's Chrome browser instantly translates websites; Translate.google.com and DeepL.com are also handy. The Google Translate app converts spoken or typed English into most European languages (and vice versa) and can also translate text it "reads" with your phone's camera.

**Going Green:** There's plenty you can do to reduce your environmental footprint when traveling. When practical, take a train instead of a flight within Europe and use public transportation within cities. In hotels, use the "Do Not Disturb" sign to avoid daily linen and towel changes (or hang up your towels to signal you'll reuse them). Bring a reusable shopping tote and refillable water bottle (Europe's tap water is safe to drink). Skip printed brochures, maps, or other materials that you don't plan to keep—get your info online instead. To find out how Rick Steves' Europe is offsetting carbon emissions with a self-imposed carbon tax, see RickSteves.com/about-us/climate-smart.

# Money

Here's my basic strategy for using money wisely in Europe. I pack the following and keep it all safe in my money belt.

**Credit Card:** You'll use your credit card for purchases both big (hotels, advance tickets) and small (little shops, food stands). Many Dutch businesses have gone cashless, making a card your only payment option. A "tap-to-pay" or "contactless" card is the most widely accepted and simplest to use.

**Debit Card:** Use this at ATMs to withdraw a small amount of local cash. Wait until you arrive to get euros (European cities have plenty of ATMs—see "Cash Machines," later). While most transactions are by card these days, cash can help you out of a jam if your card randomly doesn't work and can be useful to pay for things like tips and local guides. But don't take out too much, or you may find you can't use it all.

**Backup Card:** Some travelers carry a third card (debit or credit; ideally from a different bank) in case one gets lost or simply doesn't work.

**Stash of Cash:** I carry $100-200 in US dollars as a cash backup, which comes in handy in an emergency (for example, if your debit card gets eaten by the machine).

## BEFORE YOU GO

**Know your cards.** For credit cards, Visa and MasterCard are universal while American Express and Discover are less common. US debit cards with a Visa or MasterCard logo will work in any European ATM.

**Go "contactless."** Get comfortable using contactless pay options. Check to see if you already have—or can get—a tap-to-pay version of your credit card (look on the card for the tap-to-pay symbol—four curvy lines), and consider setting up your smartphone for contactless payment (see next section for details). Both options are widely used in Europe and are more secure than a physical credit card: Instead of recording your credit-card number, a one-time encrypted "token" enables the purchase and expires shortly afterward.

**Know your PIN.** Make sure you know the numeric, four-digit PIN for each of your cards, both debit and credit. Request it if you don't have one, as it may be required for some purchases. Allow time to receive the information by mail—it's not always possible to obtain your PIN online or by phone.

**Report your travel dates.** Let your bank know that you'll be using your debit and credit cards in Europe, and when and where you're headed.

**Adjust your ATM withdrawal limit.** Find out how much you can withdraw daily and ask for a higher daily limit if you want to

# Sightseeing

Sightseeing can be hard work. Use these tips to make your visits to the Netherlands' finest sights meaningful, fun, efficient, and painless.

In the wake of the pandemic, be prepared for changes to hours or entry procedures; call ahead to confirm details if it seems like a museum's website hasn't been updated recently.

## MAPS AND NAVIGATION TOOLS

A good map is essential for efficient navigation while sightseeing. The maps in this book are concise and simple, designed to help you locate recommended destinations, sights, hotels, and restaurants. In Europe, simple maps are generally free at TIs and hotels.

You can also use a mapping app on your mobile device, which provides turn-by-turn directions for walking, driving, and taking public transit. Google Maps, Apple Maps, and CityMaps2Go allow you to download maps for offline use; ideally, download the areas you'll need before your trip. For certain features, you'll need to be online—either using Wi-Fi or an international data plan.

## PLAN AHEAD

Set up an itinerary that allows you to fit in all your must-see sights. For a one-stop look at opening hours in Amsterdam, see the "Amsterdam at a Glance" sidebar (page 62). Most sights keep stable hours, but you can easily confirm the latest by checking at the TI or on museum websites.

Don't put off visiting a must-see sight—you never know when a place will close unexpectedly for a holiday, strike, or restoration. Many museums are closed or have reduced hours at least a few days a year, especially on holidays such as Christmas and New Year's. A list of holidays is in the appendix; check for possible closures during your trip. In summer, some sights may stay open late. Off-season hours may be shorter.

Going at the right time helps avoid crowds. This book offers tips on the best times to see specific sights. Try visiting popular sights very early or very late. Evening visits (when possible) are usually more peaceful, with fewer crowds. Late morning is usually the worst time to visit a popular sight.

If you plan to hire a local guide, reserve ahead by email. Popular guides can get booked up.

Study up. To get the most out of the self-guided tours and sight descriptions in this book, read them before you visit. The Rijksmuseum is much more entertaining if you've boned up on ruffs and Dutch Masters the night before.

## RESERVATIONS, ADVANCE TICKETS, AND PASSES

**Reservations and Advance Tickets:** Many popular sights in Europe come with long lines—not to get in, but to buy a ticket. Visitors who buy tickets online in advance can skip the line and waltz right in. Advance tickets are generally timed-entry, meaning you're guaranteed admission on a certain date and time.

For some sights, buying ahead is required (tickets aren't sold at the sight and it's the only way to get in). At other sights, buying ahead is recommended to skip the line and save time. And for many sights, advance tickets are available but unnecessary: At these uncrowded sights you can simply arrive, buy a ticket, and go in.

Don't confuse the reservation options: available, recommended, and required. Use my advice in this book as a guide. Note any must-see sights that sell out long in advance and be prepared to buy tickets early. If you do your research, you'll know the smart strategy.

Given how precious your vacation time is, I'd book in advance both where it's required (as soon as your dates are firm) and where it will save time in a long line (in some cases, you can do this even on the day you plan to visit). Amsterdam has three famous sights—visited by every tourist in town—where reservations are required: the **Anne Frank House,** the **Rijksmuseum,** and the **Van Gogh Museum.**

You'll generally be emailed an eticket with a QR or bar code that you'll store on your phone to scan at the entrance (if you prefer, you can print it out). At the sight, look for the ticket-holders line rather than the ticket-buying line; you may still have to wait in a security line.

**Sightseeing Passes:** Some cities offer sightseeing passes that offer free or discounted admission to several sights. Do the math to determine if a sightseeing pass makes sense for your visit. Even with a sightseeing pass, you'll often still need to make reservations for the most popular sights.

## AT SIGHTS

Here's what you can typically expect:

**Entering:** You may not be allowed to enter if you arrive too close to closing time. And guards start ushering people out well before the actual closing time, so don't save the best for last.

Many sights have a security check. Allow extra time for these lines. Some sights require you to check day packs and coats. (If you'd rather not check your day pack, try carrying it tucked under your arm like a purse as you enter.)

At churches—which often offer interesting art (usually free) and a cool, welcome seat—a modest dress code (no bare shoulders or shorts) is encouraged though rarely enforced.

**Photography:** If the museum's photo policy isn't clearly posted, ask a guard. Generally, taking photos without a flash or tripod is allowed. Some sights ban selfie sticks; others ban photos altogether.

**Audioguides and Apps:** I've produced free, downloadable audio tours for my Amsterdam City Walk, Red Light District Walk, and Jordaan Walk; look for the ◯ in this book. For more on my audio tours, see page 28.

Some sights offer audioguides with recorded descriptions in English. In some cases, you'll rent a device to carry around (if you bring your own plug-in earbuds, you'll enjoy better sound). Increasingly, museums and sights instead offer an app you can download with their audioguide (often free; check websites from home and consider downloading in advance as not all sights offer free Wi-Fi).

**Temporary Exhibits:** Museums may show special exhibits in addition to their permanent collection. Some exhibits are included in the entry price, while others come at an extra cost (which you may have to pay even if you don't want to see the exhibit).

**Expect Changes:** Artwork can be on tour, on loan, out sick, or shifted at the whim of the curator. Pick up a floor plan as you enter and ask museum staff if you can't find a particular item.

**Services:** Important sights usually have a reasonably priced on-site café or cafeteria (handy and air-conditioned places to rejuvenate during a long visit). The WCs at sights are free and generally clean.

**Before Leaving:** At the gift shop, scan the postcard rack or thumb through a guidebook to be sure you haven't overlooked something that you'd like to see. Every sight or museum offers more than what is covered in this book. Use the information I provide as an introduction—not the final word.

# Sleeping

Extensive and opinionated listings of good-value rooms are a major feature of this book's Sleeping sections. Rather than list accommodations scattered through-

out a town, I choose hotels in my favorite neighborhoods that are convenient to your sightseeing.

My recommendations run the gamut, from dorm beds to luxurious rooms with all of the comforts. I

PRACTICALITIES

## Sleep Code

Hotels in this book are categorized according to the average price of a standard double room with breakfast in high season.

| | |
|---|---|
| **$$$$** | **Splurge:** Most rooms over €260 |
| **$$$** | **Pricier:** €200-260 |
| **$$** | **Moderate:** €140-200 |
| **$** | **Budget:** €70-140 |
| **¢** | **Backpacker:** Under €70 |
| **RS%** | **Rick Steves discount** |

Unless otherwise noted, credit cards are accepted, hotel staff speak basic English, and free Wi-Fi is available. Comparison-shop by checking prices at several hotels (on each hotel's own website, on a booking site, or by email). For the best deal, *book directly with the hotel.* Ask for a discount if paying in cash; if the listing includes **RS%**, request a Rick Steves discount.

like places that are clean, central, relatively quiet at night, reasonably priced, friendly, small enough to have a hands-on owner or manager, and run with a respect for Dutch traditions. I'm more impressed by a handy location and fun-loving philosophy than oversized TVs and a fancy gym. Most of my recommendations fall short of perfection. But if I can find a place with most of these features, it's a keeper.

Book your accommodations as soon as your itinerary is set, especially if you want to stay at one of my top listings or if you'll be traveling during busy times. See the appendix for a list of major holidays and festivals in the Netherlands.

Some people make reservations a few days ahead as they travel. This approach fosters spontaneity, and booking sites make it easy to find available rooms, but—especially during busy times—you run the risk of settling for lesser-value accommodations.

## RATES AND DEALS

I've categorized my recommended accommodations based on price, indicated with a dollar-sign rating (see sidebar). Room prices can fluctuate significantly with demand and amenities (size, views, room class, and so on), but relative price categories remain constant. City taxes, which can vary from place to place, are generally insignificant (a few dollars per person, per night).

**Booking Direct:** Once your dates are set, compare prices at several hotels. You can do this by checking hotel websites and booking sites such as Hotels.com or Booking.com. After you've zeroed in on your choice, book directly with the hotel itself. This increases the chances that the hotelier will be able to accommodate special needs or requests (such as shifting your reservation). And when you book on the hotel's website, by email, or by phone, the owner avoids the commission paid to booking sites, giving them wiggle room to offer you a discount, a nicer room, or a free breakfast (if it's not already included).

**Getting a Discount:** Some hotels extend a discount to those who pay cash or stay longer than three nights. And some accommodations offer a special discount for Rick Steves readers, indicated in this guidebook by the abbreviation "**RS%**." Discounts vary: Ask for details when you reserve. Generally, to qualify for this discount, you must book direct (not through a booking site), mention this book when you reserve, show this book upon arrival, and sometimes pay cash or stay a certain number of nights. In some cases, you may need to enter a discount code (which I've provided in the listing) in the booking form on the hotel's website. Rick Steves discounts apply to readers with either print or digital books. Understandably, discounts do not apply to promotional rates.

## TYPES OF ACCOMMODATIONS
### Hotels

In this book, the price for a double room ranges from $90 (very simple, toilet and shower down the hall) to $300 (maximum plumbing and more), with most clustering at about $180. You'll pay more at Amsterdam hotels, less at small-town B&Bs.

Some hotels can add an extra bed (for a small charge) to turn a double into a triple; some offer larger rooms for four or more people (I call these "family rooms" in the listings). If there's space for an extra cot, they'll cram it in for you. In general, a triple room is cheaper than the cost of a double and a single. Three or four people can economize by requesting one big room.

**Arrival and Check-In:** Hotels and B&Bs are sometimes located on the higher floors of a multipurpose building with a secured door. In that case, look for your hotel's name on the buttons by the main entrance. When you ring the bell, you'll be buzzed in.

Hotel elevators are common, though small, and some older buildings still lack them. You may have to climb a flight of steep stairs to reach the elevator (if so, you can ask the front desk for help carrying your bags up).

Most European countries require hotels to collect your name, nationality, and passport number. At check-in, the receptionist might ask for your passport and may keep it for several hours. If you're not comfortable leaving your passport at the desk, bring a copy to give them instead.

If you're arriving in the morning, your room probably won't be ready. Check your bag safely at the hotel and dive right into sightseeing.

# Making Hotel Reservations

Reserve your rooms as soon as you've pinned down your travel dates. For busy national holidays, it's wise to reserve far in advance (see the appendix).

**Requesting a Reservation:** For family-run hotels, it's generally best to book your room directly via email or phone. For business-class and chain hotels, or if you'd rather book online, reserve directly through the hotel's official website (not a booking website). Almost all of my recommended hotels take reservations in English.

Here's what the hotelier wants to know:
- Type(s) of room(s) you want and number of guests
- Number of nights you'll stay
- Arrival and departure dates, written European-style as day/month/year (18/06/25 or 18 June 2025)
- Special requests (en suite bathroom, cheapest room, twin beds vs. double bed, quiet room)
- Applicable discounts (such as a Rick Steves discount, cash discount, or promotional rate)

**Confirming a Reservation:** Most places will request a credit-card number to hold your room. If the hotel's website doesn't have a secure form where you can enter the number directly, it's best to share this info via a phone call.

**Canceling a Reservation:** If you must cancel, it's courteous—and smart—to do so with as much notice as possible, especially for smaller family-run places. Cancellation policies can be strict; read

**In Your Room:** Most hotel rooms have a TV and free Wi-Fi, which can vary in strength and quality. Simpler places rarely have a room phone.

**Checking Out:** While it's customary to pay for your room upon departure, it can be a good idea to settle your bill the day before, when you're not in a hurry and while the manager's in.

**Hotelier Help:** Hoteliers can be a good source of advice. Most know their city well and can assist you with everything from public transit and airport connections to finding a good restaurant, the nearest launderette, or a late-night pharmacy.

**Hotel Hassles:** Even at the best places, mechanical breakdowns occur: Sinks leak, hot water turns cold, toilets may gurgle or smell, the Wi-Fi goes out, or the air-conditioning dies when you need it most. Report your concerns clearly and calmly at the front desk.

If you find that night noise is a problem (if, for instance, your room is over a nightclub or facing a busy street), ask for a quieter room in the back or on an upper floor. To guard against theft in

| From: | rick@ricksteves.com |
|---|---|
| Sent: | Today |
| To: | info@hotelcentral.com |
| Subject: | Reservation request for 19-22 July |

Dear Hotel Central,

I would like to stay at your hotel. Please let me know if you have a room available and the price for:
- 2 people
- Double bed and en suite bathroom in a quiet room
- Arriving 19 July, departing 22 July (3 nights)

Thank you!
Rick Steves

the fine print before you book. Many discount deals require pre-payment and can be expensive to change or cancel.

**Reconfirming a Reservation:** Always call or email to reconfirm your room reservation a few days in advance. For B&Bs or very small hotels, I call again on my arrival day to tell my host what time I expect to get there (especially important if arriving late—after 17:00).

**Phoning:** For tips on calling hotels overseas, see page 490.

your room, keep valuables out of sight. Some rooms come with a safe, and other hotels have safes at the front desk. I've never bothered using one and in a lifetime of travel, I've never had anything stolen from my room.

For more complicated problems, don't expect instant results. Above all, keep a positive attitude. Remember, you're on vacation. If your hotel is a disappointment, spend more time out enjoying the place you came to see.

## Bed-and-Breakfasts

B&Bs offer double the cultural intimacy and—often—nicer rooms for a good deal less than most hotel rooms. Hosts usually speak English and are interesting conversationalists.

In the Netherlands, B&Bs are common in well-touristed areas outside the big cities. Amsterdam has very few B&Bs. Local TIs have lists of B&Bs and can book a room for you, but you'll save money by booking directly with the B&Bs listed in this book.

# Using Online Services to Your Advantage

From booking services to user reviews, online businesses play a greater role in travelers' planning than ever before. Take advantage of their pluses—and be wise to their downsides.

## Booking Sites

Booking websites such as Booking.com and Hotels.com offer one-stop shopping for hotels. While convenient for travelers, they're both a blessing and a curse for small, independent, family-run hotels. Without a presence on these sites, small hotels become almost invisible. But to be listed, a hotel must pay a sizable commission...and promise that its own website won't undercut the price on the booking-service site.

Here's the work-around: Use the big sites to research what's out there, then book directly with the hotel by email or phone, in which case hotel owners are free to give you whatever price they like. Ask for a room without the commission mark-up (or ask for a free breakfast, if not included, or a free upgrade). If you do book online, be sure to use the hotel's own website. The price will likely be the same as via a booking site, but your money goes to the hotel, not agency commissions.

As a savvy consumer, remember: When you book with an online service, you're adding a middleman who takes a cut. To support small, family-run hotels whose world is more difficult than ever, book direct.

## Short-Term Rental Sites

Rental juggernaut Airbnb (along with other short-term rental sites) allows travelers to rent rooms and apartments, often providing more value, space, and amenities than a cookie-cutter hotel. Airbnb fans appreciate feeling part of a real neighborhood and getting into a daily routine as "temporary Europeans." Some places are run by thoughtful hosts, allowing you to get to know a local and keep your money in the community; but beware: Others are impersonally managed by large, absentee agencies.

## Short-Term Rentals

A short-term rental—whether an apartment, a house, or a room in a private residence—is a popular alternative, especially if you plan to settle in one location for several nights. For stays longer than a few days, you can usually find a rental that's comparable to—and cheaper than—a hotel room with similar amenities. Plus, you'll get a behind-the-scenes peek into how locals live.

Many places require a minimum stay and have strict cancellation policies. And you're generally on your own: There's no reception desk, breakfast, or daily cleaning service.

**Finding Accommodations:** Websites such as Airbnb, FlipKey, Booking.com, and VRBO let you browse a wide range of

Critics of Airbnb see it as a threat to "traditional Europe." Landlords can make more money renting to short-stay travelers, driving rents up—and local residents out. Traditional businesses are replaced by ones that cater to tourists. And the character and charm that made those neighborhoods desirable to tourists in the first place goes, too. Some cities have cracked down, requiring owners to obtain a license and to occupy rental properties part of the year (and staging disruptive "inspections" that inconvenience guests).

As a lover of Europe, I share the worry of those who see residents nudged aside by tourists. But as an advocate for travelers, I appreciate the value Airbnb can provide in offering the chance to stay in a local building or neighborhood with potentially fewer tourists.

## User Reviews

User-generated review sites and apps such as Yelp and TripAdvisor can give you a consensus of opinions about everything from hotels and restaurants to sights and nightlife. If you scan reviews of a restaurant or hotel and see several complaints about noise or a rotten location, you've gained insight that can help in your decision-making.

As a guidebook writer, my sense is that there is a big difference between the uncurated information on a review site and the vetted listings in a guidebook. A user review is based on the limited experience of one person, who stayed at just one hotel in a given city and ate at a few restaurants there. A guidebook is the work of a trained researcher who forms a well-developed basis for comparison by visiting many restaurants and hotels year after year.

Both types of information have their place, and in many ways, they're complementary. If something is well reviewed in a guidebook and it also gets good online reviews, it's likely a winner.

properties. Alternatively, rental agencies such as InterhomeUSA.com and RentaVilla.com can provide a more personalized service (their curated listings are also more expensive).

Before you commit, be clear on the location. I like to virtually "explore" the neighborhood using Google Street View. Also consider the proximity to public transportation and how well connected the property is with the rest of the city. Ask about amenities (elevator, air-conditioning, laundry, Wi-Fi, parking, etc.). Reviews from previous guests can help identify trouble spots.

Think about the kind of experience you want: Just a key and an affordable bed...or a chance to get to know a local? Some hosts offer

## Keep Cool

If you're visiting the Netherlands in the summer, you'll want an air-conditioned room. Most hotel air-conditioners come with a control stick (like a TV remote; the hotel may require a deposit) that generally has similar symbols and features: fan icon (click to toggle through wind power, from light to gale), louver icon (choose steady airflow or waves), snowflake and sunshine icons (cold air or heat, depending on season), clock ("O" setting: run X hours before turning off; "I" setting: wait X hours to start), and the temperature control (20 degrees Celsius is comfortable). When you leave your room for the day, turning off the air-conditioning is good form.

self-check-in and minimal contact; others enjoy interacting with you. Read the description and reviews to help shape your decision.

**Confirming and Paying:** Many places require payment in full before your trip, usually through the listing site. Be wary of owners who want to take your transaction offline; this gives you no recourse if things go awry. Never agree to wire money (a key indicator of a fraudulent transaction).

**Apartments or Houses:** If you're staying in one place several nights, it's worth considering an apartment or rental house. Apartment or house rentals can be especially cost-effective for groups and families. European apartments, like hotel rooms, tend to be small by US standards. But they often come with laundry facilities and small, equipped kitchens, making it easier and cheaper to dine in. The city of Amsterdam limits the number of nights a property owner can rent out an entire apartment or house, making those harder to come by here than in other destinations.

**Rooms in Private Homes:** Renting a room in someone's home is a good option for those traveling alone, as you're more likely to find true single rooms—with just one single bed, and a price to match. These can range from air-mattress-in-living-room basic to plush-B&B-suite posh. While you can't expect your host to also be your tour guide—or even to provide you with much info—some are interested in getting to know the travelers who pass through their home.

**Other Options:** Swapping homes with a local works for people with an appealing place to offer (don't assume where you live is not interesting to Europeans). Good places to start are HomeExchange.com and LoveHomeSwap.com. To sleep for free, Couchsurfing.com is a vagabond's alternative to Airbnb. It lists millions of outgoing members, who host fellow "surfers" in their homes.

## Hostels

A hostel provides cheap beds in dorms where you sleep alongside strangers for about $40 per night. Travelers of any age are welcome if they don't mind dorm-style accommodations and meeting other travelers. Most hostels offer kitchen facilities, guest computers, Wi-Fi, and a self-service laundry. Hostels almost always provide bedding, but the towel's up to you (though you can usually rent one). Family and private rooms are often available.

**Independent hostels** tend to be easygoing, colorful, and informal (no membership required; www.hostelworld.com). You may pay slightly less by booking directly with the hostel. **Official hostels** are part of Hostelling International (HI) and share an online-booking site (www.hihostels.com). HI hostels typically require that you be a member or else pay a bit more per night.

# Eating

In the Netherlands, lunch and dinner are served at typical American times (roughly 12:00-14:00 and 18:00-21:00). Traditional Dutch food is basic and hearty, with lots of bread, soup, and fish. Dutch treats include cheese, pancakes *(pannenkoeken),* and "syrup waffles" *(stroopwafels).* Popular drinks are light, pilsner-type beer and gin *(jenever).*

Treat your tongue to some new experiences in Holland: Try a pickled herring at an outdoor herring stand, linger over coffee in a "brown café," sample a variety of cheeses at a cheese market, sip an old *jenever* with a new friend, and consume an Indonesian feast—a rijsttafel.

For listings in this guidebook, I look for restaurants that are convenient to your hotel and sightseeing. When restaurant-hunting, choose a spot filled with locals, not the place with the big neon signs boasting, "We Speak English and Accept Credit Cards." Venturing even a block or two off the main drag leads to higher-quality food for a better price.

When ordering drinks in a café or bar, you can just pay as you go (especially if the bar is crowded), or wait until the end to settle up, as many locals do. If you get table service, take the cue from your waiter. Cafés with outdoor tables generally charge the same whether you sit inside or out.

Waiters constantly say, *"Alstublieft"* (AHL-stoo-bleeft). It's a useful, catchall polite word meaning, "please," "here's your order," "enjoy," and "you're welcome." You can respond with a thank you by saying, *"Dank u wel"* (dahnk oo vehl).

If you enjoy your meal, use the Dutch word for "yummy!": *Lekker!* (LEH-ker). When a Dutch person really enjoys the food, he or she waves one hand to the side of their head.

480 Rick Steves Amsterdam & the Netherlands

PRACTICALITIES

---

## Restaurant Code

Eateries in this book are categorized according to the average cost of a typical main course. Drinks, desserts, and splurge items can raise the price considerably.

| | |
|---|---|
| **$$$$** | **Splurge:** Most main courses over €30 |
| **$$$** | **Pricier:** €20-30 |
| **$$** | **Moderate:** €10-20 |
| **$** | **Budget:** Under €10 |

In the Netherlands, a *friets* stand or other takeout spot is **$**; a basic café or sit-down eatery is **$$**; a casual but more upscale restaurant is **$$$**; and a swanky splurge is **$$$$**.

---

**Tipping:** Tipping is an issue only at restaurants that have table service. If you order your food at a counter, don't tip. At Dutch restaurants that have waitstaff, 15 percent service is included in the menu price, although it's common to round up the bill after a good meal (usually 5-10 percent; so, for an €18.50 meal, pay €20). In bars, rounding up to the next euro ("keep the change") is appropriate if you get table service rather than ordering at the bar.

## RESTAURANT PRICING

I've categorized my recommended eateries based on the average price of a typical main course, indicated with a dollar-sign rating (see sidebar). Obviously, expensive specialties, fine wine, appetizers, and dessert can significantly increase your final bill.

The categories also indicate the personality of a place: **Budget** eateries include street food, takeaway, order-at-the-counter shops, basic cafeterias, and bakeries selling sandwiches. **Moderate** eateries are nice (but not fancy) sit-down restaurants, ideal for a pleasant meal with good-quality food. Most of my listings fall in this category—great for a taste of the local cuisine at a reasonable price.

**Pricier** eateries are a notch up, with more attention paid to the setting, presentation, and (often inventive) cuisine. **Splurge** eateries are dress-up-for-a-special-occasion swanky—typically with an elegant setting, polished service, and pricey and refined cuisine.

## DUTCH SPECIALTIES

**Cheeses:** The Dutch are probably better known for their cheese than for any other food. For more on this quintessential Dutch specialty, see the sidebar.

**French Fries:** Commonly served

with mayonnaise (ketchup, curry sauce, hot peanut sauce, and various flavored mayonnaises are often available) on a paper tray or in a newspaper cone. Flemish *(Vlaamse) friets* are made from whole potatoes, not pulp.

*Pannenkoeken:* Dutch pancakes are typically halfway between a fluffy, American-style pancake and a thin French crêpe. They come with either savory or sweet toppings.

*Haring* (herring): Pickled herring, always served with chopped raw onions and sometimes also with pickles. You can eat them straight, or tucked into a thick, soft, white bun. For more on herring, see page 110.

*Hutspot:* Hearty meat stew with mashed potatoes, onions, and carrots, especially popular on winter days.

*Stamppot:* Hearty side dish—a mash of potatoes and other ingredients—originally designed to fortify farm workers for a busy day in the fields. The basic *stamppot* mixes potatoes with stewed meat and cabbage, but you'll also see *andijviestamppot* (with endive and bacon), *zuurkoolstamppot* (with sauerkraut), and *boerenkoolstamppot* (kale and potatoes with smoked sausage).

*Snert:* Thick pea soup.

*Gehaktbal:* Giant meatball. A *slavink* is a meatball wrapped in bacon.

*Balkenbrij:* Meatloaf made with organ meat and blood mixed with grains.

*Kibbeling/Lekkerbekje:* Little chunks/filets of deep-fried fish, dipped into mayonnaise or other flavored sauces (like fish-and-chips, but without the chips).

*Hapjes* (bar snacks): The Dutch enjoy lingering in bars and brown cafés while nibbling a variety of (mostly deep-fried) bar snacks. Popular options include *kroketten* (not quite "croquettes"—log-shaped rolls of meats and vegetables that are breaded and deep-fried, kind of like corn dogs), *bitterballen* (smaller, deep-fried balls of meat ragù—named not for the flavor, but for the "bitters"-based drinks typically consumed with them), *frikandellen* (minced-meat, uncased sausages, usually deep-fried rather than grilled), *lumpia* or *vlammetjes* (spring rolls), and *bamihap* or *bamischijf* (deep-fried, Indonesian-spiced fried rice). Vegetarians can look for *kaassoufflé,* a deep-fried pastry filled with cheese.

## TYPICAL MEALS

**Breakfast:** Breakfasts are big by continental standards: bread, meat, cheese, and maybe an egg or omelet. Hotels generally put out a buffet spread, including juice and cereal. You might find a little box of candy sprinkles at the buffet. Dutch people

## Dutch Cheeses

The Dutch—who eat about 40 pounds of cheese per person each year—are famous for their cheese. In fact, worldwide, some small Dutch towns (like Gouda or Edam) are synonymous with cheese.

Traditionally, the Dutch produced mostly cow's-milk cheeses—including most of the types described below—but recently goat cheese is becoming more popular. Some Dutch goat cheese is fresh and soft, while other types are hard and aged in big Gouda-like rounds. You can tell the difference by color: Cow's-milk cheese is yellow or orange (from the carotene in the roots of the grass), while goat cheese is white (goats only eat the top of the grass).

Young *(jong)* cheeses are mellow: smooth, buttery, and mild. Mature or "old" *(oude)* cheeses are aged—traditionally in wooden warehouses, with hatches that can be opened and closed to adjust the heat and humidity. Aging brings out salty, crumbly, and pungent qualities—the longer, the stronger. Look for the terms *jonge* (1 month old), *jong belegen* (2 months), *belegen* (4 months), *extra belegen* (7 months), *oude* (10 months), and *overjarig* ("over a year"). Old cheese has no more salt content than new cheese—but the salt is more concentrated, so you taste it more. What look like "crystals" (little, white, crunchy specks) are concentrated pockets of protein. Either new or old, cheese may be seasoned with cumin, cloves, pepper, and other spices—even nettles.

Half of all Dutch cheeses are **Gouda** (HOW-dah)—a term that refers not to a particular cheese, but to the way it is produced and packaged: in giant, wax-covered, 30-pound, tire-sized rounds that could be rolled along streets and wharves for easier transport. Gouda (which was traditionally traded—not necessarily made—in the town it's named for) is typically cow's-milk cheese,

(even grown-ups) like to butter a slice of bread, then scatter the top with chocolate sprinkles (De Ruijter brand). They also have little pellets of candied anise called Muisjes ("little mice") that go on thick, crunchy rusk crackers.

**Lunch:** Simple sandwiches are called *broodjes* (most commonly made with cheese and/or ham). An open-face sandwich of ham and cheese topped with two fried eggs is an *uitsmijter* (OUTS-mi-ter). Soup is popular for lunch, including *snert* or *erwtensoep*, a thick, hearty pea soup.

**Snacks and Takeout Food:** Small stands sell *friets* (french fries) and the flavor varies dramatically with how long it ages. *Graskaas* is a special kind of Gouda that's made with the first harvest of milk after the cows return to the pasture each spring.

**Edammer** comes in smaller rounds (like an oversized softball), is covered with red wax, and travels well without refrigeration. Its portability made it popular during the Age of Exploration, when it was widely exported, which explains its worldwide appeal today: It turns up in national specialties as far away as Latin America and Pacific islands. Young Edam is extremely mild, but it gets firmer and more flavorful with age.

Cheeses that are not as well-known—but still worth trying—include the following: **Leidse kaas** ("Leyden cheese") is a hard cow's cheese flavored with cumin. **Boerenkaas** ("farmer cheese") is farm-produced in small batches with raw (unpasteurized) milk. **Limburger** is a famously fragrant, semi-soft cow's cheese. **Leerdammer** and **Maasdammer** resemble what we'd call "Swiss cheese" (with big holes and a pungent bouquet). **Nagelkaas** ("nail cheese," from Friesland in the far north of Holland) is a firm cow's-milk cheese flavored with cumin and cloves. And **Parrano** and **Prima Donna** are Italian-style cheeses—with a Parmesan flavor, but a smoother texture. Blue cheeses are not traditional but are catching on (look for the brand names Delfts Blauw and Bastiaanse Blauw). Other names you may see—such as Beemster, Old Amsterdam, or Reypenaer—are name brands rather than types of cheese.

To sample some Dutch cheese, drop into any cheese shop; tourist-oriented stores in Amsterdam and other Dutch cities are particularly generous with samples. For a better selection at a top-quality cheese shop with a staff that's knowledgeable and passionate about their cheese, visit De Kaaskamer van Amsterdam, in the Nine Little Streets district (see page 247). Or, for the full Dutch cheese experience, hop on a train to Alkmaar on a Friday morning in spring or summer to experience a traditional cheese market in action (see the Alkmaar and Zaanse Schans chapter).

with mayonnaise, pickled herring, falafels (fried chickpea balls in pita bread), *shoarmas* (lamb tucked in pita bread), and *döner kebabs* (Turkish version of a *shoarma*). Delis have deep-fried meat-and-veggie snacks *(kroketten)*. Although less rigid about "teatime" than their British cousins, the Dutch also enjoy an afternoon cup of tea with a snack. Cafés serve a pricey afternoon tea around 16:00.

**Happy Hour:** The Dutch enjoy what they call *borrel*—an impromptu evening gathering with drinks and heavy (often deep-fried) snacks. Some bars use this term to advertise what we'd (loosely) call "happy hour."

**Dinner:** It's the biggest meal of the day, consisting of meat or seafood with boiled potatoes, cooked vegetables, and a salad. Hearty stews are served in winter. These days, many people eat more vegetarian fare.

**Sweets:** The Dutch work hard to satisfy their sweet tooth. The quintessential Dutch treat is a *stroopwafel*—syrup sandwiched between two crispy, thin waffles. Prepackaged stacks of *stroopwafels* are sold in grocery stores, but a fresh, hot *stroopwafel* from a street vendor is a revelation. Pancake variations include *pannenkoeken* (skinny pancakes with fruit and cream), *poffertjes* (bite-sized, powdered-sugared puffy pancakes), and *wentelteefjes* (french toast). A bottle of *stroop* (sweet syrup—but not as flavorful as North American maple syrup) is on the table for drizzling. *Oliebollen* ("oil balls") are deep-fried dough balls dusted with powdered sugar. A *zeeuwse bolus* is like a cinnamon roll. And while we like to say "as American as apple pie," the Dutch are renowned for their *appelgebak* or *appeltaart*. Another favorite dessert is *spekkoek,* a flavorful spice cake (with very thin, alternating layers of strong spice flavors including clove, cinnamon, nutmeg, and anise) that originated in Indonesia. The Dutch also have an appreciation for licorice *(drop),* including salty licorice *(zoute drop)*—usually sold in small pellets (hence the name).

## INTERNATIONAL CUISINE

If you're not in the mood for meat and potatoes, sample some of the Netherlands' abundant international offerings.

**Indonesian** *(Indisch):* The tastiest "Dutch" food is Indonesian, from the former colony. Find any *Indisch* restaurant and experience a rijsttafel (literally, "rice table"). The spread usually includes many spicy dishes (ranging from small sides to entrée-sized plates) and a big bowl of rice (or noodles). A rijsttafel can be split and still fill two hungry tourists. Vegetarian versions are yours for the asking. For a smaller version, order *nasi rames* (several tiny portions on one plate). For more on Indonesian food, see the menu decoder in this chapter. For an Indonesian experience specific to Amsterdam, see the sidebar in the Eating in Amsterdam chapter (page 214).

**Middle Eastern:** Try *shoarma* (roasted lamb with garlic in pita bread, served with bowls of different sauces), falafel, gyros, or a *döner kebab.* Some shops sell a kitchen-sink gut-bomb called a *kapsalon* ("hair salon"): *friets, shoarma* meat, and melted cheese, with salad on top.

**Surinamese** *(Surinaamse):* Surinamese cuisine is a mix of Caribbean and Indonesian influences, featuring *roti* (spiced chicken wrapped in flatbread) and rice (white or fried) served with meats in sauces (curry and spices). Why Surinamese food in the Netherlands? In 1667, Holland traded New York City ("New Amsterdam") to Britain in exchange for the small country of Suriname (which borders Guyana on the northeast coast of South America). For the next three centuries, Suriname (renamed Dutch Guyana) was a Dutch colony, which is why it has indigenous Indians, Creoles, and Indonesian immigrants who all speak Dutch. When Suriname gained independence in 1975, 100,000 Surinamese immigrated to Amsterdam, sparking a rash of Surinamese fast-food outlets.

**More International Cuisine:** In addition to the types listed here, you'll also find plenty of Thai, Greek, Italian, and other foods.

## TYPES OF EATERIES

Any place labeled "restaurant" will serve full sit-down meals for lunch or dinner. But there are other places to chow down.

A *café* or *eetcafé* is a simple restaurant serving basic soups, salads, and sandwiches, as well as traditional meat-and-potatoes meals in a generally comfortable but no-nonsense setting.

A *salon de thé* serves tea and coffee, but also croissants, pastries, and sandwiches for a light brunch, a lunch, or an afternoon snack. *Bruin* cafés ("brown cafés") are named for their nicotine-stained walls—until smoking was banned indoors in 2008, they were filled with tobacco smoke. These places are usually a little more bar-like, with dimmer lighting and wood paneling.

A *proeflokaal* is a bar (with snacks) offering wine, spirits, or beer.

"Coffeeshop" is the code word for an establishment where marijuana is sold and consumed, though most offer drinks and munchies, too (see the Smoking chapter).

There's no shortage of stand-up, takeout places serving fast food, sandwiches, and all kinds of quick ethnic fare.

No matter what type of establishment you choose, expect it to be *gezellig*—a much-prized Dutch virtue, meaning an atmosphere of relaxed coziness.

## DUTCH DRINKS

**Beer:** Order "a beer," and you'll get a *pils,* a light lager/pilsner-type beer in a 10-ounce glass with a thick head leveled off with a stick. Typical brands are Heineken, Grolsch, Oranjeboom, Amstel, and the misnamed Bavaria (brewed in Holland). Another common tap beer is Palm Speciale, an amber ale served in a stemmed, wide-mouth glass. *Witte* (white) beer is light-colored and summery, sometimes served with a lemon slice

PRACTICALITIES

# Indonesian Menu Decoder

Indonesian food is spicy, flavorful, and satisfying. Rice (nasi), or sometimes noodles (bami), are the base upon which is layered a wide variety of beef, chicken, lamb, fish, shrimp, and vegetable dishes, often simmered in powerful sauces. Spicy pastes called sambal are used to add kick and other hits of flavor. The classic Indonesian dining experience is the rijsttafel—a "rice table" featuring a dizzying array of dishes shared family-style. (For a more detailed description of the rijsttafel, and some places to try it in Amsterdam, see page 214.) But that's a huge amount of food; if you prefer to order à la carte, use this menu decoder. Here's a tip: For a plate with a few samples of several dishes, look for nasi rames or nasi campur.

ayam: chicken

asam: tamarind (sour)

bakar: baked

blado (or balado): spicy sauce

bumbu: spice mixture

bami (or mie): noodles

bami goreng: fried noodles

campur: mix

daging: beef

domba: lamb

gado-gado: steamed veggies with peanut sauce

goreng: fried

ikan: fish

kacang: peanut

kecap: dark soy sauce

krupuk: deep-fried chips (usually shrimp)

kuning: yellow (usually with turmeric)

lodeh: coconut (or veggies in coconut milk)

lumpia: spring rolls

nasi: rice

nasi goreng: fried rice

nasi kuning: turmeric rice

nasi putih: steamed rice

nasi rames or nasi campur: "mixed rice" sampler plate

nasi uduk: sweet coconut rice

pangang: sweet and sour

perkedel: potato fritters

peteh: giant beans

pisang goreng: battered-and-fried bananas

rendang: rich, slow-simmered meat dish

sambal: hot paste, comes in many varieties

sambal goreng: stir-fried veggies with a spicy sauce

sate: grilled meat on a skewer

sayur: vegetables

sayur lodeh: veggies in spicy coconut milk

sayur asem: vegetable tamarind soup

spekkoek: spiced layer cake

tempeh: soybean cake (like fried tofu)

tahu: tofu

udang: shrimp

urap: steamed vegetable salad

Some other terms you might see—including **Bali, Padang,** and **Jakarta**—refer to regions within Indonesia. For example, Padang-style dishes tend to use lots of spice and coconut milk.

(it's like Hefeweizen, but yeastier). *Bruin* ("brown," or dark) beers are also available; one popular brew is Imperator, made by the Brand brewery. Belgian beers—which, most aficionados would insist, are superior to Dutch beers—are quite popular; because many Belgian specialty beers are bottle-fermented, some of the best come in bottles, though others may be available on tap.

**Jenever** (yah-NAY-ver): Try this Dutch gin made from juniper berries. *Jong* (young) is sharper; *oude* (old) is mellow. These terms refer not to how long the *jenever* ages (although some are aged), but to whether they use an older or newer distilling technique. I prefer *oude jenever*, which is smooth and soft, with a more mature flavor—like a good whiskey. It's served at room temperature, while *jonge jenever* is served chilled. *Jenever* is meant to be chugged with a *pils* chaser (this combination is called a *kopstoot*—head-butt). Typically, bartenders will fill your small, tulip-shaped *jenever* glass to the very brim. Wasting *jenever* is frowned upon, so lean over to sip a bit off the top before picking it up.

**Liqueur:** You'll find a variety of local fruit brandies *(brandewijn)* and cognacs. If you have a sweet tooth, try *advocaat*—a super-rich, eggnog-like cocktail of brandy, eggs, and sugar.

**Wine:** Dutch people drink a lot of fine wine, but it's almost all imported.

**Coffee:** The Dutch love their coffee, enjoying many of the same drinks (espresso, cappuccino) served in American or Italian coffee shops. Coffee usually comes with a small spice cookie. A *koffie verkeerd* (KOH-fee fer-KEERT, "coffee wrong") is an espresso with a lot of steamed milk—the closest thing to our latte (but you could also just ask for a latte).

**Soft Drinks:** You'll find the full array.

**Orange Juice:** Many cafés/bars have a juicer for making fresh-squeezed orange juice.

**Water:** The Dutch drink tap water and are proud of how good it tastes. They often promote drinking tap water as a way to reduce plastic-bottle waste. At restaurants, you can get tap water—*kraanwater* (KRAHN-vah-ter)—free for the asking.

## Staying Connected

One of the most common questions I hear from travelers is, "How can I stay connected in Europe?" The short answer? More easily and affordably than you might think.

The simplest solution is to bring your own device—phone, tablet, or laptop—and use it much as you would at home, following the money-saving tips later, such as getting an international plan

PRACTICALITIES

## What Language Barrier?

People speak Dutch in Amsterdam. But you'll find almost no language barrier in the Netherlands, as all well-educated folks, nearly all young people, and almost everyone in the tourist trade also speak English. (When asked if they speak English, the Dutch reply, *"Natuurlijk"*—"naturally.") Regardless, it's polite to use some Dutch pleasantries (see the Dutch survival phrases in the appendix).

or connecting to free Wi-Fi whenever possible. Another option is to buy a European SIM card for your mobile phone. Or you can use European landlines and computers to connect. More details are at RickSteves.com/phoning.

## USING YOUR PHONE IN EUROPE

Here are some budget tips and options.

**Sign up for an international plan.** To stay connected at a lower cost, sign up for an international-service plan through your carrier. Most providers offer a simple bundle that includes calling, messaging, and data. Your normal plan may already include international coverage (for example, T-Mobile's covers data and text, but not voice calls).

Before your trip, research your provider's international rates. Activate the plan a day or two before you leave, then remember to cancel it when your trip's over.

**Use free Wi-Fi whenever possible.** Unless you have an unlimited-data plan, save most of your online tasks for Wi-Fi. Most accommodations in Europe offer free Wi-Fi. Many cafés (including Starbucks and McDonald's) offer hotspots for customers; ask for the password when you buy something. You may also find Wi-Fi at TIs, city squares, major museums, public-transit hubs, airports, and aboard trains and buses.

**Minimize the use of your cellular network.** The best way to make sure you're not accidentally burning through data is to put your device in "airplane" mode (which also disables phone calls and texts) and connect to Wi-Fi as needed. When you need to get online but can't find Wi-Fi, simply turn on your cellular network (or turn off airplane mode) just long enough for the task at hand.

Even with an international data plan, wait until you're on Wi-Fi to Skype or FaceTime, download apps, stream videos, or do other megabyte-greedy tasks. Using a navigation app such as Google Maps over a cellular network can require lots of data, so download maps when you're on Wi-Fi, then use the app offline.

Limit automatic updates. By default, your device constantly

checks for a data connection and updates app content. Check your device's settings menu for ways to turn this off, and change your email settings from "auto-retrieve" to "manual" (or from "push" to "fetch").

**Use Wi-Fi calling and messaging apps.** Skype, WhatsApp, FaceTime, and Google Meet are great for making free or low-cost calls or sending texts over Wi-Fi worldwide. Just log on to a Wi-Fi network, then connect with friends, family members, or local contacts who use the same service.

**Buy a European SIM card.** If you anticipate making a lot of local calls, need a local phone number, or your provider's international data rates are expensive, consider buying a SIM card in Europe to replace the one in your (unlocked) US phone or tablet.

In the Netherlands, SIM cards are sold mostly at vending machines and convenience stores (you may need to show your passport), though there are several phone shops at Schiphol Airport and one at Amsterdam's Centraal station. If you need help setting it up, buy the SIM card at a mobile-phone shop.

There are generally no roaming charges when using a European SIM card in other EU countries, but confirm when you buy.

## WITHOUT A MOBILE PHONE

It's less convenient but possible to travel in Europe without a mobile device. You can make calls from your hotel and check email or get online using public computers.

Most **hotels** charge a fee for placing calls. You can use a prepaid international phone card (usually available at newsstands, tobacco shops, and train stations) to call out from your hotel.

Some hotels have **public computers** in their lobbies for guests to use; otherwise, you may find them at public libraries (ask your hotelier or the TI for the nearest location). On a European keyboard, use the "Alt Gr" key to the right of the space bar to insert the extra symbol that appears on some keys. If you can't locate a special character (such as @), simply copy and paste it from a web page.

## MAIL

You can mail one package per day to yourself worth up to $200 duty-free from Europe to the US (mark it "personal purchases"). If you're sending a gift to someone, mark it "unsolicited gift." For details, visit www.cbp.gov, select "Travel," and search for "Know Before You Go."

The Netherlands has privatized its postal service, which is operated by PostNL. In addition to *Postkantoor* (full-service post offices), a variety of smaller private shops act as shipping agents (look for *PostNL Pakketpunt*). Either one is marked with the orange-triangle PostNL logo. If you're shipping a package overseas, fill out

PRACTICALITIES

# How to Dial

Here's how to dial from anywhere in the US or Europe, using the phone number of one of my recommended Haarlem hotels as an example (023 532 4530). If a number starts with 0, drop it when dialing internationally (except when calling Italy).

## From a US Mobile Phone

Phone numbers in this book are presented exactly as you would dial them from a US mobile phone. For international access, press and hold 0 (zero) to get a + sign, then dial the country code (31 for the Netherlands) and phone number.

▶ To call the Haarlem hotel from any location, dial +31 23 532 4530.

## From a US Landline

Replace + with 011 (US/Canada access code), then dial the country code (31 for the Netherlands) and phone number.

▶ To call the Haarlem hotel from your home landline, dial 011 31 23 532 4530.

## From a European Landline

Replace + with 00 (Europe access code), then dial the country code (31 for the Netherlands, 1 for the US) and phone number.

▶ To call the Haarlem hotel from a French landline, dial 00 31 23 532 4530.
▶ To call my US office from a Dutch landline, dial 00 1 425 771 8303.

## From One Dutch Phone to Another

To place a domestic call (from a Dutch landline or mobile), drop +31 and dial the phone number (including the initial 0).

▶ To call the Haarlem hotel from Amsterdam, dial 023 532 4530.

## More Dialing Tips

**Local Numbers:** European phone numbers and area codes can vary in length and spacing, even within the same country. Mobile phones use separate prefixes (for instance, in the Netherlands, mobile numbers begin with 06).

**Toll and Toll-Free Calls:** It's generally not possible to dial European toll or toll-free numbers from a US mobile or landline (although you can sometimes get through using Skype). Look for a direct-dial number instead.

**Calling the US from a US Mobile Phone, While Abroad:** Dial +1, area code, and number.

**More Phoning Help:** See HowToCallAbroad.com.

all the paperwork online in advance at www.postnl.nl (you'll need to know the approximate weight), then take the package to a *Pakketpunt* or *Postkantoor*, give them your confirmation code, and drop off the box. (These shops typically also sell boxes in various sizes, stamps, and tape and other packing materials.) You can also buy stamps at some newsstands, bookstores, or grocery stores.

For quick transatlantic delivery (in either direction), consider services such as DHL (DHL.com).

PRACTICALITIES

---

## Tips on Internet Security

Make sure that your device is running the latest versions of its operating system, security software, and apps. Next, ensure that your device and key programs (like email) are password-protected. On the road, use only secure, password-protected Wi-Fi. Ask the hotel or café staff for the specific name of their network, and make sure you log on to that exact one.

If you must access your financial info online, use a banking app rather than accessing your account via a browser, and use a cellular connection, not Wi-Fi. Never log on to personal-finance sites on a public computer. If you're very concerned, consider subscribing to a VPN (virtual private network).

---

# Transportation

Figuring out how to get around in Europe is one of your biggest trip decisions. **Cars** work well for two or more traveling together (especially families with small kids), those packing heavy, and those delving into the countryside. **Trains** and **buses** are best for solo travelers, blitz tourists, city-to-city travelers, and those who want to leave the driving to others. Short-hop **flights** within Europe can creatively connect the dots. Be aware of the potential downside of each option: A car is an expensive headache in any major city; with trains and buses you're at the mercy of a timetable; flying entails a trek to and from a usually distant airport and leaves a larger carbon footprint.

Because of the short distances and excellent public-transportation systems in the Netherlands, I recommend traveling by **train.** Trains connect Amsterdam, Haarlem, Delft, and most day-trip destinations faster and easier than you could by driving. A **car** is necessary to visit Flevoland and can be an efficient way to visit Enkhuizen's Zuiderzee Museum or the Kröller-Müller Museum near Arnhem.

For more detailed information on transportation throughout Europe, see RickSteves.com/transportation.

## TRAINS

The easiest way to reach nearly any Dutch destination is by train. Connections are fast and frequent. The Dutch train system—Nederlandse Spoorwegen—is usually identified by its initials, NS. InterCity (IC) trains are speedy for connecting big cities, and the high-speed Thalys is the fastest (the speed comes at a price; see "Seat Reservations for Rail-Pass Holders," later). InterRegio (IR) and *sneltreins* connect smaller towns, *stoptreins* are pokey milk-run

PRACTICALITIES

**Train Lines in the Netherlands**

trains that stop at every station, and the Netherlands' misnamed "Sprinter" trains are actually slow *stoptreins*. Throughout the Netherlands, smoking is prohibited in trains and train stations.

## Schedules

To get train schedules in advance, use the Dutch Rail website (www.ns.nl for domestic trains, www.nsinternational.nl for international trains) or the NS app (available in both domestic and international versions). If you'll be riding the rails beyond Amsterdam, download the NS app before your trip and use it as you travel. Another good resource is the German Rail (Deutsche Bahn) website, which has comprehensive schedules for almost anywhere in Europe (www.bahn.com). Yet another website, www.9292.nl, combines information on Dutch trains, buses, and trams, which can help fill in some gaps. For train information by phone in the Netherlands, dial +31 30 751 5155 (and press 5 for English).

To find schedules at train stations, check the yellow schedule posters, or look for screens listing upcoming departures. The direction of the train is identified by its final station. If you can't find

PRACTICALITIES

your train, or are unclear on departure details, visit an information booth or enlist the help of any official-looking employee.

## Buying Tickets

Dutch train tickets are issued either electronically (with a QR code, through the NS app or website), or on paper "chipcards."

It's best to download and use the **NS app,** which allows you to check schedules and buy tickets with your credit card. When you buy a ticket through the app, you'll get an eticket (with a QR code to get through the turnstile). You can also buy tickets **online** at www.ns.nl; your QR code will be emailed to you.

If you prefer to get tickets at the station, you can buy a **single ticket** at NS ticket machines (or, for a €0.50 service fee, at a ticket desk). This will be issued on a "single-use chipcard"—a paper ticket that contains a chip, which you can scan at the turnstile. Note that single tickets purchased at the station are subject to a €1 surcharge.

If you'll be taking many rides within the Netherlands, you could get a reloadable transit card called an **OV-chipkaart.** Designed mainly for locals, these are not worthwhile for most tourists: You'll pay a nonrefundable €7.50 fee, and you must load it with credit at a store, ticket office, or NS ticket machine; to take an intercity train, you must have at least €20 of credit loaded onto the card (www.ov-chipkaart.nl).

Ticketing is more complicated for **international trains,** including those to Belgium. For example, to buy electronic tickets, you'll need to use a separate app (NS International) or website (www.nsinternational.nl), rather than the domestic Dutch options.

## At the Station

At most Dutch stations—especially in cities and larger towns—you'll need to go through turnstiles to access the platforms. Some services (often a few shops, plus ticket windows and machines) are outside of the turnstiles, while others (more shops, luggage lockers, if the station has them) are inside the turnstile-controlled area.

To **go through the turnstiles,** scan your ticket/QR code. You'll do the same to exit the turnstiles at the other end. Rail passes have a bar code that can be scanned.

## Bikes on Trains

If you're traveling with a bike, you'll pay extra to bring it on the train. In the Netherlands, bikes are only allowed during off-peak hours (9:00-16:00 & 18:30-6:30) plus all day on weekends, holidays, and during July and August. A "Bicycle Day Travel Card" is required (€7.50, no matter the destination).

## Rail Passes

All rail passes that cover the Netherlands also cover Belgium and Luxembourg. Collectively, they're called "Benelux" and count as one country as far as rail passes are concerned. Most visits to the Netherlands don't cover enough miles to justify a rail pass, but if your itinerary extends beyond this relatively small region, a multicountry rail pass could make sense. For more detailed advice on figuring out the smartest rail-pass options for your train trip, visit www.ricksteves.com/rail.

**Seat Reservations for Rail-Pass Holders:** For the most part, you can hop on nearly any Dutch train with just your rail pass in hand. But the fast Thalys trains that run between Amsterdam and Brussels (and between Brussels and Cologne and Paris) do require seat reservations—and they're expensive (Thalys point-to-point tickets also cost much more on these routes—see next).

## Trains to and from Belgium: Thalys vs. IC

Two types of trains run between Dutch and Belgian cities: **Thalys** trains are faster but much more expensive (potentially double or even triple the cost); **IC** (InterCity) trains are a better value unless you're in a huge rush. For example, to get from Amsterdam to Antwerp might take 1.75 hours and cost just €20 on an IC train; on Thalys, you can get there in 1.25 hours, but the ticket costs €45, €65, or even €75 (depending on the connection). Thalys requires rail-pass holders to make expensive seat reservations; IC trains don't require them. Before you book, pay careful attention to your options for train types—and the cost implications.

## BUSES

While you'll mostly use trains to travel in this region, a few destinations (for example, the tulip gardens of Keukenhof, the flower auction in Aalsmeer, or the Kröller-Müller Museum near Arnhem) are reachable only by bus.

Confusingly, there's no unified national bus company for the Netherlands—various destinations are served by different companies. Arriva (www.arriva.nl) and Connexxion (www.connexxion.nl) are the main companies. The best public-transit website in the Netherlands for bus schedules is www.9292.nl.

## TAXIS AND RIDE-BOOKING SERVICES

Most European taxis are reliable and cheap. In many cities, two people can travel short distances by cab for little more than the cost of bus or subway tickets. If you like ride-booking services such as Uber, their apps usually work in Europe just like they do in the US: Request a car on your mobile phone, and the fare is automatically charged to your credit card.

# Rail Pass or Point-to-Point Tickets?

Will you be better off buying a rail pass or point-to-point tickets? It pays to know your options and choose what's best for your itinerary.

**Rail Passes**

A Eurail Benelux Pass lets you travel by train in Belgium, the Netherlands, and Luxembourg for three to eight days (consecutively or not) within a one-month period. All three countries are also covered (along with most of Europe) by the classic Eurail Global Pass.

Discounted rates are offered for seniors (age 60 and up) and youths (ages 12-27). Up to two kids (ages 4-11) can travel free with each adult-rate pass (but not with senior rates). All passes offer a choice of first or second class for all ages.

While most rail passes are delivered electronically, it's smart to get your pass sorted before leaving home. For more on rail passes, including current prices and purchasing, visit RickSteves.com/rail.

**Point-to-Point Tickets**

If you're taking just a couple of train rides, buying individual point-to-point tickets may save you money over a pass. Use this map to add up approximate pay-as-you-go fares for your itinerary, and compare that to the price of a rail pass plus reservations. Keep in mind that significant discounts on point-to-point tickets may be available with advance purchase.

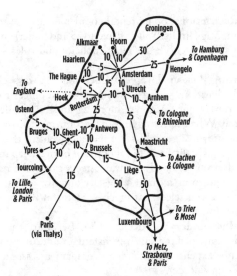

*Map shows approximate costs, in US dollars, for one-way, second-class tickets on faster trains.*

## RENTING A CAR

It's cheaper to arrange most car rentals from the US, so research and compare rates before you go. Most of the major US rental agencies (including Avis, Budget, Enterprise, Hertz, and Thrifty) have offices throughout Europe. Also consider the two major Europe-based agencies, Europcar and Sixt. Consolidators such as Auto Europe (AutoEurope.com—or the sometimes cheaper AutoEurope.eu) compare rates at several companies to get you the best deal.

Wherever you book, always read the fine print. Check for add-on charges—such as one-way drop-off fees, airport surcharges, or mandatory insurance policies—that aren't included in the "total price."

### Rental Costs and Considerations

If you book well in advance, expect to pay $350-500 for a one-week rental for a basic compact car. Allow extra for supplemental insurance, fuel, tolls, and parking. To save money on fuel, request a diesel car.

**Manual vs. Automatic:** Almost all rental cars in Europe are manual by default—and cars with a stick shift are generally cheaper. If you need an automatic, reserve one specifically. When selecting a car, don't be tempted by a larger model, as it won't be as maneuverable on narrow, winding roads or when squeezing into tight parking lots.

**Age Restrictions:** Some rental companies impose minimum and maximum age limits. Young drivers (25 and under) and seniors (69 and up) should check the rental policies and rules section of car-rental websites.

**Choosing Pick-up/Drop-off Locations:** Always check the hours of the locations you choose: Many rental offices close from midday Saturday until Monday morning and, in smaller towns, at lunchtime. When selecting an office, confirm the location on a map. A downtown site might seem more convenient than the airport but could actually be in the suburbs or buried deep in big-city streets. Pedestrianized and one-way streets can make navigation tricky when returning a car at a big-city office or urban train station. Wherever you select, get precise details on the location and allow ample time to find it.

**Crossing Borders in a Rental Car:** Be aware that international trips—say, picking up in Amsterdam and dropping off in Paris—can be expensive if the rental company assesses a drop-off fee for crossing a border.

Always tell your car-rental company exactly which countries you'll be entering. Some companies levy extra insurance fees for trips taken in certain countries with certain types of cars (such as BMWs, Mercedes, and convertibles). Double-check with your rental agent that you have all the documentation you need before you drive off (especially if you're crossing borders into non-Schengen countries, such as Croatia, where you might need to present proof of insurance).

**Picking Up Your Car:** Before driving off in your rental car, check it thoroughly and make sure any damage is noted on your rental agreement. Rental agencies in Europe tend to charge for even minor damage, so be sure to mark everything. Find out how your car's gearshift, lights, turn signals, wipers, radio, and fuel cap function, and know what kind of fuel the car takes (diesel is common in Europe). When you return the car, make sure the agent verifies its condition with you.

## Car Insurance Options

When you rent a car in Europe, the price typically includes liability insurance, which covers harm to other cars or motorists—but not the rental car itself. To limit your financial risk in case of damage to the rental, choose one of these options: Buy a Collision Damage Waiver (CDW; also called "loss damage waiver" or LDW by some firms) with a low or zero deductible from the car-rental company (roughly 30-40 percent extra), get coverage through your credit card (free, but more complicated), or get collision insurance as part of a larger travel-insurance policy.

Basic **CDW** costs $15–30 a day and typically comes with a $1,000-2,000 deductible, reducing but not eliminating your financial responsibility. When you reserve or pick up the car, you'll be offered the chance to "buy down" the deductible to zero (for an additional $10-30/day; this is sometimes called "super CDW" or "zero-deductible coverage").

If you opt for **credit-card coverage,** you must decline all coverage offered by the car-rental company—which means they can place a hold on your card to cover the deductible. In case of damage, it can be time-consuming to resolve the charges. Before relying on this option, quiz your card company about how it works.

If you're already purchasing a **travel-insurance policy** for your trip, adding collision coverage can be an economical option. For example, Travel Guard (TravelGuard.com) sells affordable renter's collision insurance as an add-on to its other policies; it's valid everywhere in Europe except the Republic of Ireland, and some Italian car-rental companies refuse to honor it, as it doesn't cover you in case of theft.

For more on car-rental insurance, see RickSteves.com/cdw.

## Navigation Options

If you'll be navigating using your phone or a GPS unit from home, remember to bring a car charger and device mount.

**Your Mobile Phone:** The mapping app on your phone works fine for navigating Europe's roads. To save on data, most apps allow you to download maps for offline use (do this before you need them, when you have a strong Wi-Fi signal). Some apps—including Google Maps—also have offline route directions, but you'll need mobile-data access for current traffic. For more on using a mapping app without burning through data, see "Using Your Phone in Europe," earlier.

**GPS Devices:** If you want a dedicated GPS unit, consider renting one with your car (about $20/day, or sometimes included—ask). These units offer real-time turn-by-turn directions and traffic without the data requirements of an app. The unit may come loaded only with maps for its home country; if you need additional maps, ask. Make sure you know how to use the device—and that the language is set to English—before you drive off.

**Paper Maps and Atlases:** Even when navigating primarily with a mobile app or GPS, I always have a paper map, ideally a big, detailed regional road map. It's invaluable for getting the big picture, understanding alternate routes, and filling in if my phone runs out of juice. The free maps you get from your car-rental company usually don't have enough detail. It's smart to buy a better map before you go, or pick one up at a local gas station, bookshop, newsstand, or tourist shop.

## Driving

**Road Rules:** Traffic cameras are everywhere in the Netherlands; speeding tickets for even a few kilometers over the limit are common. Kids under age 12 (or less than about 5 feet tall) must ride in an appropriate child-safety seat. Seat belts are mandatory for all, and two beers under those belts are enough to land you in jail. Be aware of typical European road rules; for example, many countries require headlights to be turned on at all times, and nearly all forbid handheld mobile-phone use. In Europe, you're not allowed to turn right on a red light unless a sign or signal specifically authorizes it, and on expressways it's illegal to pass drivers on the right. Ask your car-rental company about these rules, or check the "International Travel" section of the US State Department website (www.travel.state.gov, search for your country in the "Learn About Your Destination" box, then click "Travel and Transportation").

**Fuel:** Gas (*benzine* in Dutch) is expensive—about $7 per gallon. Diesel (*diesel* or *dieselolie* in Dutch) is less—about $5 per gallon—and diesel cars get better mileage, so try to rent a diesel car to save money. Be sure you know what type of fuel your car takes before you fill up. Some pumps are color-coded: Unleaded pumps are green and labeled "E," while diesel pumps (often yellow or black) are labeled "B". Gas is most expensive on freeways and cheapest at big supermarkets. About 30 percent of the filling stations in the Netherlands are unmanned, and your US credit and debit cards may not work at self-service gas pumps unless they have a chip. Look for stations with an attendant or be sure to carry sufficient cash in euros.

**Parking:** Finding a parking place can be a headache in larger cities. Ask your hotelier for ideas, and pay to park at well-patrolled lots (blue *P* signs direct you to parking lots). Parking structures usually require that you take a ticket with you and pay at a machine on your way back to the car. US credit cards may not work in these automated machines, but euro coins (and sometimes bills) will.

## FLIGHTS

To compare flights, begin with an online travel search engine: Kayak is the top site for flights to and within Europe, easy-to-use Google Flights has price alerts, and Skyscanner includes many inexpensive flights within Europe. To avoid unpleasant surprises, before you book be sure to read the small print about refunds, changes, and the costs for "extras" such as reserving a seat, checking a bag, or printing a boarding pass.

**Flights to Europe:** Start looking for international flights at least four to six months before your trip, especially for peak-season travel. Depending on your itinerary, it can be efficient and no more expensive to fly into one city and out of another. If your flight requires a connection in Europe, see my hints on navigating Europe's top hub airports at RickSteves.com/hub-airports.

**Flights within Europe:** Flying between European cities is surprisingly affordable. Before buying a long-distance train or bus ticket, check the cost of a flight on one of Europe's airlines, whether a major carrier or a no-frills outfit like EasyJet or Ryanair, along with Amsterdam-based Transavia (Transavia.com). Be aware that flying with a discount airline can have drawbacks, such as minimal customer service, time-consuming treks to secondary airports, and a larger carbon footprint than a train or bus.

**Flights to the US and Canada:** Because security is extra tight for flights to the US, be sure to give yourself plenty of time at the airport (see www.tsa.gov for the latest rules).

# Resources from Rick Steves

## Begin Your Trip at RickSteves.com

My mobile-friendly **website** is *the* place to explore Europe in preparation for your trip. You'll find thousands of fun articles, videos, and radio interviews; a wealth of money-saving tips for planning your dream trip; travel news dispatches; a video library of travel talks; my travel blog; our latest guidebook updates (RickSteves.

com/update); and the free Rick Steves Audio Europe app. You can also follow me on Facebook, Instagram, and Twitter.

Our **Travel Forum** is a well-groomed collection of message boards where our travel-savvy community answers questions and shares their personal travel experiences—and our well-traveled staff chimes in when they can be helpful (RickSteves.com/forums).

Our **online Travel Store** offers bags and accessories that I've designed to help you travel smarter and lighter. These include my popular carry-on bags (which I live out of four months a year), money belts, totes, toiletries kits, adapters, guidebooks, and planning maps (RickSteves.com/shop).

Our website can also help you find the perfect **rail pass** for your itinerary and your budget, with easy, one-stop shopping for rail passes, seat reservations, and point-to-point tickets (RickSteves.com/rail).

## Rick Steves' Tours, Guidebooks, TV Shows, and More

**Small Group Tours:** Want to travel with greater efficiency and less stress? We offer more than 40 itineraries reaching the best destinations in this book...and beyond. Each year about 30,000 travelers join us on about 1,000 Rick Steves bus tours. You'll enjoy great guides and a fun bunch of travel partners (with small groups of 24 to 28 travelers). You'll find European adventures to fit every vacation length. For all the details, and to get our tour catalog, visit RickSteves.com/tours or call us at +1 425 608 4217.

**Books:** This book is just one of many books in my series on European travel, which includes country and city guidebooks, Snapshots (excerpted chapters from bigger guides), Pocket guides (full-color little books on big cities), "Best Of" guidebooks (condensed, full-color country guides), and my budget-travel skills handbook, *Rick Steves Europe Through the Back Door.* A complete list of my titles—including phrase books, cruising guides, and travelogues on European art, history, and culture—appears near the end of this book.

**TV Shows and Travel Talks:** My public-television series, *Rick Steves' Europe,* covers Europe from top to bottom with over 100 half-hour episodes—and we're working on new shows every year (watch full episodes at my website for free). My free online video library, Rick Steves Classroom Europe, offers a searchable database of short video clips on European history, culture, and geography (Classroom. RickSteves.com). And to raise your travel I.Q., check out the video versions of our popular

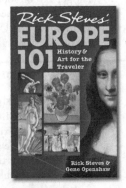

classes (covering most European countries as well as travel skills, packing smart, cruising, tech for travelers, European art, and travel as a political act—RickSteves.com/travel-talks).

**Audio Tours on My Free App:** I've produced dozens of free, self-guided audio tours of the top sights in Europe. For those tours and other audio content, get my free **Rick Steves Audio Europe app,** an extensive online library organized by destination. For more on my app, see page 28.

**Radio:** My weekly public-radio show, *Travel with Rick Steves,* features interviews with travel experts from around the world. It airs on 400 public-radio stations across the US. An archive of programs is available at RickSteves.com/radio.

**Podcasts:** You can enjoy my travel content via several free podcasts. The podcast version of my radio show brings you a weekly, hour-long travel conversation. My other podcasts include a weekly selection of video clips from my public-television show, my audio tours of Europe's top sights, and live recordings of my travel classes (RickSteves. com/watch-read-listen/audio/podcasts).

# APPENDIX

## Holidays and Festivals

This list includes selected festivals in major cities, plus national holidays observed throughout the Netherlands. Many sights and banks close on national holidays—keep this in mind when planning your itinerary. Before planning a trip around a festival, verify the dates with the festival website, the national tourist office (www.holland.com), or my "Upcoming Holidays and Festivals in the Netherlands" web page at RickSteves.com/europe/netherlands/festivals.

| | |
|---|---|
| **Jan 1** | New Year's Day |
| **Feb/March** | Carnival (Mardi Gras) |
| **Mid-March-mid-May** | Keukenhof flower show, Lisse (www.keukenhof.nl) |
| **March/April** | Easter Sunday and Monday: April 9-10 in 2023, March 31-April 1 in 2024 |
| **April** | Bloemencorso Flower Parade, Noordwijk to Haarlem (www.bloemencorso-bollenstreek.nl) |
| **April 27** | King's Day (Koningsdag), Amsterdam (King Willem-Alexander's birthday, party in the streets) |

APPENDIX

| | |
|---|---|
| **May 5** | Liberation Day (Bevrijdingsdag) |
| **May/June** | KunstRAI Art Amsterdam (contemporary-art exhibition, www.kunstrai.nl) |
| **May/June** | Ascension: May 18 in 2023, May 9 in 2024 |
| **May/June** | Pentecost and Whit Monday: May 28-29 in 2023, May 19-20 in 2024 |
| **June** | Holland Arts Festival, Amsterdam (concerts, theater, www.hollandfestival.nl) |
| **June** | Music festivals: Festival Classique (Scheveningen), Parkpop (The Hague), and International Chamber (Utrecht) |
| **Late June** | Grachtenloop, Haarlem (canal run, www.grachtenloop.nl) |
| **Late June/early July** | Amsterdam Roots Festival—Oosterpark (food, music, world culture, www.amsterdamroots.nl) |
| **Mid-July** | North Sea Jazz Festival, Rotterdam (www.northseajazz.nl) |
| **Late July-early Aug** | Amsterdam Gay Pride (www.amsterdamgaypride.nl) |
| **Early-mid-Aug** | Pluk de Nacht, Amsterdam (outdoor film festival, www.plukdenacht.nl) |
| **Aug 15** | Assumption Day |
| **Mid-Aug** | SAIL Amsterdam (every five years, next festival 2025, tall ships and historic boats, www.sail.nl) |
| **Mid-Aug** | Prinsengracht canal concerts on barges, Amsterdam (music and festivities, www.grachtenfestival.nl) |
| **Late Aug** | Haarlem Jazz (free jazz festival on Grote Markt, third weekend of August, www.haarlemjazzstad.nl) |
| **Late Aug** | Jordaan Festival, Amsterdam (neighborhood street party, www.jordaanfestival.nl) |
| **Sept (first week)** | Flower parade on canals, Aalsmeer to Amsterdam |
| **Sept/Oct** | Yom Kippur: Sept 24-25 in 2023, Oct 11-12 in 2024 (Jewish holiday, closures include Anne Frank House and Jewish Museum in Amsterdam) |
| **Nov 1** | All Saints' Day |

| Mid-Nov | Sinterklaas ("Santa Claus") procession, Amsterdam |
|---|---|
| Dec 5 | St. Nicholas' Eve (Sinterklaasavond, when Sinterklaas and Zwarte Piet arrive; procession and presents) |
| Dec 25 | Christmas |
| Dec 26 | "Second Day" of Christmas (Tweede Kerstdag) |

# Books and Films

To learn more about the Netherlands past and present, check out a few of these books or films.

## Nonfiction

*Amsterdam* (Geert Mak, 1999). Academic but engaging, Mak gives a thorough look at centuries of the city's history.

*A Bridge Too Far* (Cornelius Ryan, 1974). Ryan's gripping account of Operation Market Garden recounts the Allies' failed 1944 attempt to sweep through the Netherlands and across the Rhine into Germany (also a 1977 movie).

*Daily Life in Rembrandt's Holland* (Paul Zumthor, 1994). Zumthor's focus on the everyday concerns of Dutch society in the 17th century covers art, history, culture, sports, holidays, and more.

*Dear Theo: The Autobiography of Vincent van Gogh* (edited by Irving Stone, 1995). This collection of letters from Vincent Van Gogh to his brother gives a deeper look into the artist's psyche.

*The Diary of a Young Girl* (Anne Frank, 1952). The remarkable diary of a young Jewish girl details her time spent hiding out from the Nazis in Amsterdam.

*The Embarrassment of Riches: An Interpretation of Dutch Culture in the Golden Age* (Simon Schama, 1997). This detailed overview of Dutch culture paints a portrait of the attitudes of Dutch citizens from their early beginnings to their most famous struggles.

*The Hiding Place* (Corrie ten Boom, 1971). This semiautobiographical book tells the story of a Christian family caught hiding Jews and resistance fighters in Haarlem.

*My 'Dam Life: Three Years in Holland* (Sean Condon, 2003). Australian writer and expat Sean Condon gives a humorous account of his time in the Low Countries.

*Nathaniel's Nutmeg: Or the True and Incredible Adventures of the Spice Trader Who Changed the Course of History* (Giles Milton, 1999). In this lively adventure story, the Netherlands and England struggle to harness the world supply of nutmeg in the 1600s.

*Spice: The History of a Temptation* (Jack Turner, 2005). Turner explores Holland's time at the center of the spice trade, back when a pinch of cinnamon was worth its weight in gold.

*Tales from the Secret Annex* (Anne Frank, 1949). This collection of short stories and other prose was penned by the young Jewish girl who aspired to be a writer while in hiding from the Nazis.

*Tulipmania: The Story of the World's Most Coveted Flower & the Extraordinary Passions It Aroused* (Mike Dash, 2001). This vivid narration brings to life the golden age tulip craze of the 1600s.

*The UnDutchables: An Observation of the Netherlands, Its Culture and Its Inhabitants* (Colin White and Laurie Boucke, 2013). Witty and satirical, this book serves as a modern guide to today's Dutch culture.

*Vermeer's Hat: The Seventeenth Century and the Dawn of the Global World* (Timothy Brook, 2007). Vermeer's paintings serve as points of departure in this exploration of the global context of the Dutch golden age.

*The Wisdom of the Beguines: The Forgotten Story of a Medieval Women's Movement* (Laura Swan, 2016). This book recounts the history of *beguinages,* communities of like-minded women who aided their towns' poor and vulnerable.

## Fiction

*Amsterdam Tales* (translated by Paul Vincent, 2017). This collection of 18 stories explores Amsterdam from the 17th to 21st century via fiction, memoirs, and anecdotes.

*The Black Tulip* (Alexandre Dumas, 1850). A competition to grow the elusive black tulip serves as the heart of this classic swashbuckling tale of fortunes won and lost.

*Confessions of an Ugly Stepsister* (Gregory Maguire, 1999). The Cinderella story takes a twist in Maguire's Haarlem-set retelling.

*Girl in Hyacinth Blue* (Susan Vreeland, 1999). Through eight linked stories, a professor traces the history of a secret, long-lost Vermeer painting he's kept hidden for decades.

*Girl with a Pearl Earring* (Tracy Chevalier, 1999). This historical portrait of artist Johannes Vermeer and his maiden servant in 17th-century Delft was later turned into a fine film.

*Max Havelaar: Or the Coffee Auctions of the Dutch Trading Company* (Multatuli, 1860). A blend of satire and history infuse this novel denouncing the injustices of the Dutch colonial system in the East Indies.

*Tulip Fever* (Deborah Moggach, 1999). Readers follow a love-triangle drama set in 17th-century Amsterdam.

## Films

*Antonia's Line* (1995). Set in the postwar Netherlands, this film paints a portrait of five generations of Dutch women.

*Black Book* (2006). A sexy blond bombshell fights for the Dutch resistance in this thriller.

*The Diary of Anne Frank* (1959). This award-winning film adaptation of Anne's story is both moving and educational.

*Girl with a Pearl Earring* (2003). A fictionalized Vermeer paints—and falls in love with—his servant in Delft.

*Ocean's Twelve* (2004). The heist sequel to *Ocean's Eleven* features scenes set in Amsterdam's Jordaan neighborhood.

*Soldier of Orange* (1977). This epic WWII tale depicts the Dutch resistance to the Nazi occupation.

*Vincent and Theo* (1990). The relationship between the great artist and his brother is captured in this biographical drama.

# Conversions and Climate

## Numbers and Stumblers

- Europeans write a few of their numbers differently than we do. 1 = 1, 4 = 4, 7 = 7.
- In Europe, dates appear as day/month/year, so Christmas 2025 is 25/12/25.
- Commas are decimal points and decimals are commas. A dollar and a half is $1,50, one thousand is 1.000, and there are 5.280 feet in a mile.
- When counting with fingers, start with your thumb. If you hold up your first finger to request one item, you'll probably get two.
- What Americans call the second floor of a building is the first floor in Europe.
- On escalators and moving sidewalks, Europeans keep the left "lane" open for passing. Keep to the right.

APPENDIX

APPENDIX

## Metric Conversions

A **kilogram** equals 1,000 grams (about 2.2 pounds). One hundred **grams** (a common unit at markets) is about a quarter-pound. One **liter** is about a quart, or almost four to a gallon.

A **kilometer** is six-tenths of a mile. To convert kilometers to miles, cut the kilometers in half and add back 10 percent of the original (120 km: 60 + 12 = 72 miles). One **meter** is 39 inches—just over a yard.

| | |
|---|---|
| 1 foot = 0.3 meter | 1 square yard = 0.8 square meter |
| 1 yard = 0.9 meter | 1 square mile = 2.6 square kilometers |
| 1 mile = 1.6 kilometers | 1 ounce = 28 grams |
| 1 centimeter = 0.4 inch | 1 quart = 0.95 liter |
| 1 meter = 39.4 inches | 1 kilogram = 2.2 pounds |
| 1 kilometer = 0.62 mile | 32°F = 0°C |

## Clothing Sizes

When shopping for clothing, use these US-to-European comparisons as general guidelines (but note that no conversion is perfect).

**Women:** For pants and dresses, add 30 in the Netherlands (US 10 = Dutch 40). For blouses and sweaters, add 8 for most of Europe (US 32 = European 40). For shoes, add 30-31 (US 7 = European 37/38).

**Men:** For shirts, multiply by 2 and add about 8 (US 15 = European 38). For jackets and suits, add 10. For shoes, add 32-34.

**Children:** Clothing is sized by height—in centimeters (2.5 cm = 1 inch), so a US size 8 roughly equates to 132-140. For shoes up to size 13 add 16-18, and for sizes 1 and up add 30-32.

## The Netherlands Climate

First line, average daily high; second line, average daily low; third line, average days without rain. For more detailed weather statistics for destinations in this book (as well as the rest of the world), check Wunderground.com.

| J | F | M | A | M | J | J | A | S | O | N | D |
|---|---|---|---|---|---|---|---|---|---|---|---|
| 41° | 42° | 49° | 55° | 64° | 70° | 72° | 71° | 66° | 56° | 48° | 41° |
| 30° | 31° | 35° | 40° | 45° | 52° | 55° | 55° | 51° | 43° | 37° | 33° |
| 8 | 9 | 16 | 14 | 16 | 16 | 14 | 12 | 11 | 11 | 10 | 9 |

# Fahrenheit and Celsius Conversion

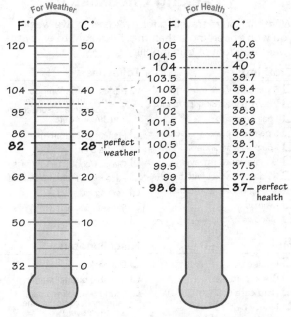

**APPENDIX**

Europe takes its temperature using the Celsius scale, while we opt for Fahrenheit. For a rough conversion from Celsius to Fahrenheit, double the number and add 30. For weather, remember that 28°C is 82°F—perfect. For health, 37°C is just right. At a launderette, 30°C is cold, 40°C is warm (usually the default setting), 60°C is hot, and 95°C is boiling. Your air-conditioner should be set at about 20°C.

# Packing Checklist

Whether you're traveling for five days or five weeks, you won't need more than this. Pack light to enjoy the sweet freedom of true mobility.

## Clothing

- ☐ 5 shirts: long- & short-sleeve
- ☐ 2 pairs pants (or skirts/capris)
- ☐ 1 pair shorts
- ☐ 5 pairs underwear & socks
- ☐ 1 pair walking shoes
- ☐ Sweater or warm layer
- ☐ Rainproof jacket with hood
- ☐ Tie, scarf, belt, and/or hat
- ☐ Swimsuit
- ☐ Sleepwear/loungewear

## Money

- ☐ Debit card(s)
- ☐ Credit card(s)
- ☐ Hard cash (US $100-200)
- ☐ Money belt

## Documents

- ☐ Passport
- ☐ Other required ID: Vaccine card/Covid test, entry visa, etc.
- ☐ Driver's license, student ID, hostel card, etc.
- ☐ Tickets & confirmations: flights, hotels, trains, rail pass, car rental, sight entries
- ☐ Photocopies of important documents
- ☐ Insurance details
- ☐ Guidebooks & maps

## Electronics

- ☐ Mobile phone
- ☐ Camera & related gear
- ☐ Tablet/ebook reader/laptop
- ☐ Headphones/earbuds
- ☐ Chargers & batteries
- ☐ Phone car charger & mount (or GPS device)
- ☐ Plug adapters

## Toiletries

- ☐ Basics: soap, shampoo, toothbrush, toothpaste, floss, deodorant, sunscreen, brush/comb, etc.
- ☐ Medicines & vitamins
- ☐ First-aid kit
- ☐ Glasses/contacts/sunglasses
- ☐ Face masks & hand sanitizer
- ☐ Sewing kit
- ☐ Packet of tissues (for WC)
- ☐ Earplugs

## Miscellaneous

- ☐ Daypack
- ☐ Sealable plastic baggies
- ☐ Laundry supplies: soap, laundry bag, clothesline, spot remover
- ☐ Small umbrella
- ☐ Travel alarm/watch
- ☐ Notepad & pen
- ☐ Journal

## Optional Extras

- ☐ Second pair of shoes (flip-flops, sandals, tennis shoes, boots)
- ☐ Travel hairdryer
- ☐ Picnic supplies
- ☐ Disinfecting wipes
- ☐ Water bottle
- ☐ Fold-up tote bag
- ☐ Small flashlight
- ☐ Mini binoculars
- ☐ Small towel or washcloth
- ☐ Inflatable pillow/neck rest
- ☐ Tiny lock
- ☐ Address list (to mail postcards)
- ☐ Extra passport photos

# Dutch Survival Phrases

Most locals speak English, but if you learn the pleasantries and key phrases, you'll connect better with the Dutch people. To pronounce the guttural Dutch "g" (indicated in phonetics by *h*), make a clear-your-throat sound, similar to the "ch" in the Scottish word "loch."

| | | |
|---|---|---|
| **Hello. (informal)** | Hallo. | **hah**-loh |
| **Good day.** | Dag. | da*h* |
| **Good morning.** | Goedemorgen. | **hoo**-deh-mor-*h*ehn |
| **Good afternoon.** | Goedemiddag. | **hoo**-deh-mid-da*h* |
| **Good evening.** | Goedenavond. | **hoo**-dehn-ah-fohnd |
| **Do you speak English?** | Spreekt u Engels? | shpraykt oo **eng**-ehls |
| **Yes. / No.** | Ja. / Nee. | yah / nay |
| **I (don't) understand.** | Ik begrijp (het niet). | ik beh-*h*ripe (heht neet) |
| **Please. (can also mean "You're welcome")** | Alstublieft. | **ahl**-stoo-bleeft |
| **Thank you.** | Dank u wel. | dahnk oo vehl |
| **I'm sorry.** | Het spijt me. | heht spite meh |
| **Excuse me.** | Pardon. | **par**-dohn |
| **No problem.** | Geen probleem. | *h*ayn **proh**-blaym |
| **Good.** | Goede. | *h*oo-deh |
| **Goodbye.** | Tot ziens. | toht zeens |
| **one / two / three** | een / twee / drie | ayn / t'vay / dree |
| **What does it cost?** | Wat kost het? | vaht kohst heht |
| **Is it free?** | Is het vrij? | is heht fry |
| **Is it included?** | Is het inclusief? | is heht in-**kloo**-seev |
| **Can you please help me?** | Kunt u alstublieft helpen? | koont oo **ahl**-stoo-bleeft **hehl**-pehn |
| **Where can I buy / find...?** | Waar kan ik kopen / vinden...? | var kahn ik **koh**-pehn / **fin**-dehn |
| **I'd like / We'd like...** | Ik wil graag / Wij willen graag... | ik vil *h*rah / vy **vil**-lehn *h*rah |
| **...a room.** | ...een kamer. | ayn **kah**-mer |
| **...a train / bus ticket to \_\_\_\_.** | ...een trein / bus kaartje naar \_\_\_\_. | ayn trayn / boos **kart**-yeh nar \_\_\_\_ |
| **...to rent a bike.** | ...een fiets huren. | ayn feets **hoo**-rehn |
| **Where is...?** | Waar is...? | var is |
| **...the train / bus station** | ...het trein / bus station | heht trayn / boos **staht**-see-ohn |
| **...the tourist info office** | ...de VVV | deh fay fay fay |
| **...the toilet** | ...het toilet | heht **twah**-leht |
| **men / women** | mannen / vrouwen | **mah**-nehn / **frow**-ehn |
| **left / right** | links / rechts | links / re*h*ts |
| **straight ahead** | rechtdoor | re*h*t-dor |
| **What time does this open / close?** | Hoe laat gaat het open / dicht? | hoo laht *h*aht heht **oh**-pehn / di*h*t |
| **now / soon / later** | nu / straks / later | noo / strahks / **lah**-ter |
| **today / tomorrow** | vandaag / morgen | **fahn**-da*h* / **mor**-*h*ehn |

# In a Dutch Restaurant

The all-purpose Dutch word *alstublieft* (**ahl**-stoo-bleeft) means "please," but it can also mean "here you are" (when the server hands you something), "thanks" (when taking payment from you), or "you're welcome" (when handing you change).

| | |
|---|---|
| **I'd like / We'd like...** | Ik will graag / Wij willen graag... <br> ik vil *h*rah / vy **vil**-lehn *h*rah |
| **...a table for one / two.** | ...een tafel voor een / twee. <br> ayn **tah**-fehl for ayn / t'vay |
| **...to reserve a table.** | ...een tafel reserveren.   ayn **tah**-fehl ray-zehr-feh-rehn |
| **...the menu (in English).** | ...het menu (in het Engels). <br> heht meh-**noo** (in heht **eng**-ehls) |
| **Is this table free?** | Is deze tafel vrij?   is **day**-zeh **tah**-fehl fry |
| **to go** | om mee te nemen.   ohm may teh **nay**-mehn |
| **with / without** | met / zonder   meht / **zohn**-der |
| **and / or** | en / of   ehn / of |
| **special of the day** | dagschotel   **dah**s-hoh-tehl |
| **specialty of the house** | huisspecialiteit   **hows**-shpeh-shah-lee-tite |
| **breakfast / lunch / dinner** | ontbijt / middagmaal / avondmaal <br> **ohnt**-bite / **mid**-dah-mahl / **ah**-fohnd-mahl |
| **appetizers** | hapjes   **hahp**-yehs |
| **main courses** | hoofdgerechten   **hohfd**-*h*eh-re*h*-tehn |
| **side dishes** | bijgerechten   **bye**-*h*eh-re*h*-tehn |
| **bread / cheese / sandwich** | brood / kaas / sandwich   brohd / kahs / **sand**-vich |
| **soup / salad** | soep / sla   soop / slah |
| **meat / chicken / fish** | vlees / kip / vis   flays / kip / fis |
| **fruit / vegetables** | vrucht / groenten   fru*h*t / *h*roon-tehn |
| **dessert / pastries** | gebak   *h*eh-**bahk** |
| **mineral water / tap water** | mineraalwater / kraanwater <br> min-eh-rahl-**vah**-ter / **krahn**-vah-ter |
| **milk / (orange) juice** | melk / (sinaasappel) sap <br> mehlk / **see**-nahs-ah-pehl (sahp) |
| **coffee / tea** | koffie / thee   **koh**-fee / tay |
| **wine / beer** | wijn / bier   vine / beer |
| **red / white** | rode / witte   **roh**-deh / **vit**-teh |
| **glass / bottle** | glas / fles   *h*lahs / flehs |
| **Cheers!** | Proost!   prohst |
| **More. / Another.** | Meer. / Nog een.   mayr / no*h* ayn |
| **The same.** | Het zelfde.   heht **zehlf**-deh |
| **The bill, please.** | De rekening, alstublieft. <br> deh **ray**-keh-neeng **ahl**-stoo-bleeft |
| **Do you accept credit cards?** | Accepteert u kredietkaarten? <br> **ahk**-shehp-tayrt oo kray-deet-**kar**-tehn |
| **Is service included?** | Is bediening inbegrepen? <br> is beh-**dee**-neeng in-beh-*h*ray-pehn |
| **tip** | fooi   foy |
| **Tasty.** | Lekker.   **leh**-ker |

# INDEX

# MAP INDEX

# Start your trip at

*Our website enhances this book and turns*

### Explore Europe

At ricksteves.com you can browse through thousands of articles, videos, photos and radio interviews, plus find a wealth of money-saving travel tips for planning your dream trip. And with our mobile-friendly website, you can easily access all this great travel information anywhere you go.

### TV Shows

Preview the places you'll visit by watching entire half-hour episodes of *Rick Steves' Europe* (choose from all 100 shows) on-demand, for free.

*your travel dreams into affordable reality*

### Radio Interviews

Enjoy ready access to Rick's vast library of radio interviews covering travel tips and cultural insights that relate specifically to your Europe travel plans.

### Travel Forums

Learn, ask, share! Our online community of savvy travelers is a great resource for first-time travelers to Europe, as well as seasoned pros.

### Travel News

Subscribe to our free Travel News e-newsletter, and get monthly updates from Rick on what's happening in Europe.

### Classroom Europe®

Check out our free resource for educators with 500 short video clips from the *Rick Steves' Europe* TV show.

## Rick's Free Travel App

Get your FREE **Rick Steves Audio Europe**™ app to enjoy…

- Dozens of self-guided tours of Europe's top museums, sights and historic walks
- Hundreds of tracks filled with cultural insights and sightseeing tips from Rick's radio interviews
- All organized into handy geographic playlists
- For Apple and Android

With Rick whispering in your ear, Europe gets even better.

## Find out more at ricksteves.com

*Gear up for your next adventure at ricksteves.com*

## Light Luggage

Pack light and right with Rick Steves' affordable, custom-designed rolling carry-on bags, backpacks, day packs and shoulder bags.

## Accessories

From packing cubes to moneybelts and beyond, Rick has personally selected the travel goodies that will help your trip go smoother.

**Shop at ricksteves.com**

## Save time and energy

This guidebook is your independent-travel toolkit. But for all it delivers, it's still up to you to devote the time and energy it takes to manage the preparation and logistics that are essential for a happy trip. If that's a hassle, there's a solution.

## Rick Steves Tours

A Rick Steves tour takes you to Europe's most interesting places with great

guides and small groups. We follow Rick's favorite itineraries, ride in comfy buses, stay in family-run hotels, and bring you intimately close to the Europe you've traveled so far to see. Most importantly, we take away the logistical headaches so you can focus on the fun.

## Join the fun

This year we'll take thousands of free-spirited travelers—nearly half of them repeat customers— along with us on 50 different itineraries, from Athens to Istanbul. Is a Rick Steves tour the right fit for your travel dreams?

Find out at ricksteves.com, where you can also check seat availability and sign up. Europe is best experienced with happy travel partners. We hope you can join us.

## BEST OF GUIDES

*Full-color guides in an easy-to-scan format. Focused on top sights and experiences in the most popular European destinations*

Best of England
Best of Europe
Best of France
Best of Germany
Best of Ireland
Best of Italy
Best of Scotland
Best of Spain

## COMPREHENSIVE GUIDES

*City, country, and regional guides printed on Bible-thin paper. Packed with detailed coverage for a multi-week trip exploring iconic sights and venturing off the beaten path*

Amsterdam & the Netherlands
Barcelona
Belgium: Bruges, Brussels,
  Antwerp & Ghent
Berlin
Budapest
Croatia & Slovenia
Eastern Europe
England
Florence & Tuscany
France
Germany
Great Britain
Greece: Athens & the Peloponnese
Iceland
Ireland
Istanbul
Italy
London
Paris
Portugal
Prague & the Czech Republic
Provence & the French Riviera
Rome
Scandinavia
Scotland
Sicily
Spain
Switzerland
Venice
Vienna, Salzburg & Tirol

HE BEST OF ROME

ne, Italy's capital, is studded with
man remnants and floodlit-fountain
ares. From the Vatican to the Colos-
m, with crazy traffic in between, Rome
nderful, huge, and exhausting. The
ds, the heat, and the weighty history

of the Eternal City where Caesars walked
can make tourists wilt. Recharge by taking siestas, gelato breaks, and after-dark
walks, strolling from one atmospheric
square to another in the refreshing evening air.

red *Pantheon*—which
est dome until the
rly 2,000 years old
day over 1,500).

of Athens in the *Vat-
odies the humanistic
nce,

gladiators fought
another, entertaining

is Rome ristoran

Rick Steves books are available from your favorite bookseller.
Many guides are available as ebooks.

## POCKET GUIDES
*Compact color guides for shorter trips*

| | |
|---|---|
| Amsterdam | Paris |
| Athens | Prague |
| Barcelona | Rome |
| Florence | Venice |
| Italy's Cinque Terre | Vienna |
| London | |
| Munich & Salzburg | |

## SNAPSHOT GUIDES
*Focused single-destination coverage*

Basque Country: Spain & France
Copenhagen & the Best of Denmark
Dublin
Dubrovnik
Edinburgh
Hill Towns of Central Italy
Krakow, Warsaw & Gdansk
Lisbon
Loire Valley
Madrid & Toledo
Milan & the Italian Lakes District
Naples & the Amalfi Coast
Nice & the French Riviera
Normandy
Northern Ireland
Norway
Reykjavík
Rothenburg & the Rhine
Sevilla, Granada & Southern Spain
St. Petersburg, Helsinki & Tallinn
Stockholm

## CRUISE PORTS GUIDES
*Reference for cruise ports of call*

Mediterranean Cruise Ports
Scandinavian & Northern European
  Cruise Ports

### Complete your library with...

## TRAVEL SKILLS & CULTURE
*Study up on travel skills and gain
insight on history and culture*

Europe 101
Europe Through the Back Door
Europe's Top 100 Masterpieces
European Christmas
European Easter
European Festivals
For the Love of Europe
Italy for Food Lovers
Travel as a Political Act

## PHRASE BOOKS & DICTIONARIES
French
French, Italian & German
German
Italian
Portuguese
Spanish

## PLANNING MAPS
Britain, Ireland & London
Europe
France & Paris
Germany, Austria & Switzerland
Iceland
Ireland
Italy
Scotland
Spain & Portugal

# Credits

## RESEARCHERS
For help with this edition, Rick and Gene relied on...

### Cameron Hewitt

Cameron Hewitt was born in Denver, grew up in Central Ohio, and moved to Seattle in 2000 to work for Rick Steves' Europe. Since then, he has spent about 100 days each year in Europe—researching and writing guidebooks, blogging, tour guiding, and making travel TV (described in his memoir, *The Temporary European*). Cameron married his high school sweetheart, Shawna, and enjoys taking pictures, trying new restaurants, and planning his next trip.

### Carrie Shepherd

After a childhood spent traipsing around New England, Carrie spent a college semester in London, which spurred her to explore and travel as much as her budget and employers allow. She's spent her career writing and editing arts-and-entertainment content, and now works as a guidebook editor and researcher for Rick Steves' Europe.

## ACKNOWLEDGMENTS
Thank you to Risa Laib for her 25-plus years of dedication to the Rick Steves guidebook series.

# PHOTO CREDITS

Avalon Travel
Hachette Book Group
1700 Fourth Street
Berkeley, CA 94710

Printed in Canada by Friesens.
Fourth Edition. First printing April 2023.

ISBN 978-1-64171-377-1

For the latest on Rick's talks, guidebooks, tours, public television series, and public radio show, contact Rick Steves' Europe, 130 Fourth Avenue North, Edmonds, WA 98020, +1 425 771 8303, RickSteves.com, rick@ricksteves.com.

**Rick Steves' Europe**
**Managing Editor:** Jennifer Madison Davis
**Assistant Managing Editor:** Cathy Lu
**Editors:** Glenn Eriksen, Julie Fanselow, Suzanne Kotz, Rosie Leutzinger, Teresa Nemeth, Jessica Shaw, Carrie Shepherd
**Editorial & Production Assistant:** Megan Simms
**Researchers:** Cameron Hewitt, Carrie Shepherd
**Graphic Content Director:** Sandra Hundacker
**Maps & Graphics:** Orin Dubrow, David C. Hoerlein, Lauren Mills, Mary Rostad, Laura Terrenzio

**Avalon Travel**
**Senior Editor & Series Manager:** Madhu Prasher
**Associate Managing Editor:** Jamie Andrade
**Copy Editor:** Maggie Ryan
**Proofreader:** Elizabeth Jang
**Indexer:** Stephen Callahan
**Production & Typesetting:** Lisi Baldwin, Rue Flaherty, Jane Musser
**Cover Design:** Kimberly Glyder Design
**Maps & Graphics:** Kat Bennett

*Although every effort was made to ensure that the information was correct at the time of going to press, the author and publisher do not assume and hereby disclaim any liability to any party for any loss or damage caused by errors, omissions, bad herring, or any potential travel disruption due to labor or financial difficulty, whether such errors or omissions result from negligence, accident, or any other cause.*

# COLOR MAPS

*Amsterdam • Central Amsterdam •
Amsterdam's Public Transportation • Haarlem •
Western Netherlands • The Netherlands*

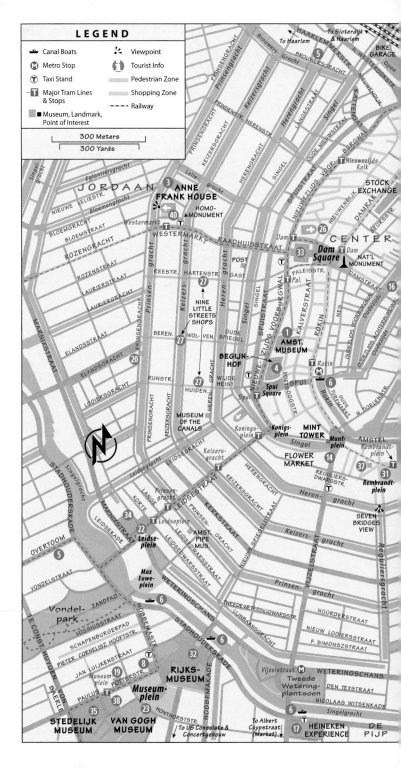

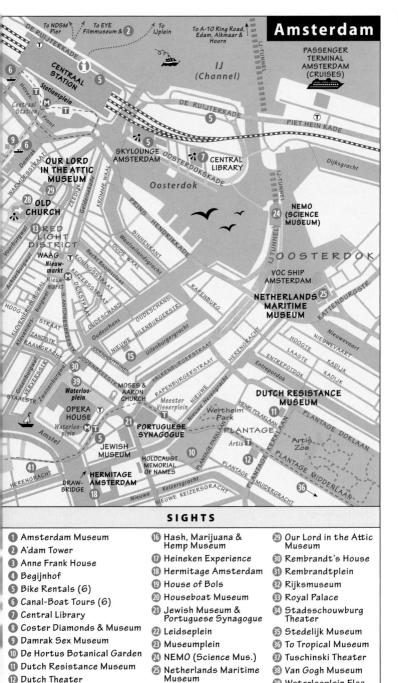

# Amsterdam

To NDSM Pier · To EYE Filmmuseum & 2 · To IJplein · To A-10 Ring Road, Edam, Alkmaar & Hoorn

DE RUIJTERKADE

CENTRAAL STATION

Stationsplein

Centraal Station

IJ (Channel)

PASSENGER TERMINAL AMSTERDAM (CRUISES)

DE RUIJTERKADE

PIET HEIN KADE

Haven Front

Damrak

WARMOESSTRAAT

OUR LORD IN THE ATTIC MUSEUM

OLD CHURCH

RED LIGHT DISTRICT

WAAG

Nieuwmarkt

Nieuwmarkt

Voorburgwal

Achterburgwal

HOOGSTRAAT

KLOVENIERSBURGWAL

ZANDSTR.

RAAMGRACHT

ZEEDIJK

Gelderskade

KROMME WAAL

PRINS HENDRIKKADE

OUDE WAAL

BINNENKANT

Waalseilandsgracht

Recht Boomssloot

KONINGSSTRAAT

DIJKSTRAAT

KEIZERSSTRAAT

S. ANTONIESBREESTR.

OUDESCHANS

Oudeschans

NIEUWE UILENBURGERSTR.

Uilenburgergracht

SKYLOUNGE AMSTERDAM

OOSTERDOKSKADE

Oosterdok

CENTRAL LIBRARY

IJ-TUNNEL

Dijksgracht

NEMO (SCIENCE MUSEUM)

OOSTERDOK

VOC SHIP AMSTERDAM

NETHERLANDS MARITIME MUSEUM

KATTENBURGERSTR.

RAPENBURG

HERENGRACHT

NIEUWEVAART

HOOGTE KADIJK

LAAGTE KADIJK

ENTREPOTDOK

Entrepotdok

DUTCH RESISTANCE MUSEUM

PLANTAGE DOKLAAN

Greenburgwal

Verversstraat

STAALSTR. Zwanenburgwal

Waterlooplein

OPERA HOUSE

Waterlooplein

Amstel

JODENBREESTR.

JODENHOUTTUINEN

NIEUWE HOOGSTR.

MOSES & AARON CHURCH

Meester Visserplein

RAPENBURGERSTRAAT

VALKENBURGERSTRAAT

NIEUWE

Nieuwe Herengracht

HENRI POLAKLAAN

Wertheim Park

PLANTAGE

Artis

ARTIS

PLANTAGE KERKLAAN

Artis Zoo

PLANTAGE MIDDENLAAN

PORTUGUESE SYNAGOGUE

JEWISH MUSEUM

HOLOCAUST MEMORIAL OF NAMES

PLANTAGE PARKLAAN

De Hortus

PLANTAGE MUIDERGRACHT

HERENGRACHT

DRAW-BRIDGE

HERMITAGE AMSTERDAM

Nieuwe Keizersgracht

NIEUWE KEIZERSGRACHT

## SIGHTS

1. Amsterdam Museum
2. A'dam Tower
3. Anne Frank House
4. Begijnhof
5. Bike Rentals (6)
6. Canal-Boat Tours (6)
7. Central Library
8. Coster Diamonds & Museum
9. Damrak Sex Museum
10. De Hortus Botanical Garden
11. Dutch Resistance Museum
12. Dutch Theater
13. Erotic Museum
14. Flower Market
15. Gassan Diamonds

16. Hash, Marijuana & Hemp Museum
17. Heineken Experience
18. Hermitage Amsterdam
19. House of Bols
20. Houseboat Museum
21. Jewish Museum & Portuguese Synagogue
22. Leidseplein
23. Museumplein
24. NEMO (Science Mus.)
25. Netherlands Maritime Museum
26. New Church
27. Nine Little Streets Shopping District
28. Old Church

29. Our Lord in the Attic Museum
30. Rembrandt's House
31. Rembrandtplein
32. Rijksmuseum
33. Royal Palace
34. Stadsschouwburg Theater
35. Stedelijk Museum
36. To Tropical Museum
37. Tuschinski Theater
38. Van Gogh Museum
39. Waterlooplein Flea Market
40. Westerkerk
41. Willet-Holthuysen House

# Central Amsterdam

## LEGEND

- 🚤 Canal Boats
- Ⓜ Metro Stop
- Ⓣ Taxi Stand
- – T – Tram Lines & Stops
- ▪ Museum, Landmark, Point of Interest
- 🖖 Viewpoint
- ⓘ Tourist Info
- ▨ Pedestrian Zone
- ▨ Shopping Zone
- - - - - - Railway

200 meters
200 yards

JORDAAN

**ANNE FRANK HOUSE** ❷

Westermarkt

WESTERKERK

HOMOMONUMENT & PINK POINT INFO CENTER

WEST AMSTERDAM

Prinsengracht

RAADHUISSTRAAT

PART OF "NINE LITTLE STREETS" SHOPPING DISTRICT

REESTRAAT    HARTENSTRAAT    GASTHUIS-MOLENSTEEG

Keizersgracht

Herengracht

Singel

LUTHERSE-KERK

ROOMOLEN-STRAAT

KORSJESPOORT-STEEG

HERENGRACHT

BERG-STRAAT

OUDE LELIESTR.

TORENSLUIS BRIDGE

DRIEKONINGEN-STRAAT

MAGNA PLAZA

NIEUWE NIEUWSTR.

ST. NICOLAASSTR.

BLAEU ERF

GRAVEN.

**NEW CHURCH** ⓰

ZOUT-STEEG

NIEUWEZIJDS VOORBURGWAL

DE BIJEN-KORF DEP'T STORE

**ROYAL PALACE** ㉒

**Dam Square**

NATIONAL MONUMENT

DAM.

HERM.

PALEIS-STR.

JONGE ROELEN-STEEG

PALEISSTRAAT

KEIZERRIJK

VOORBURGWAL

KALVERSTRAAT

GAPER.

WIJDE LOMBARD-STEEG

DE PAPEGAAI HIDDEN CATH. CHURCH

**AMSTER-DAM MUSEUM**

ROSMARIJN-STEEG

SPUISTRAAT

DUIFJES

ENGE KAPEL-STEEG

ROKIN

KUIPERS-STEEG

OUDE LELIESTR.

VLIEGENDE-STEEG

NIEUWEZIJDS VOORBURGWAL

**BEGIJNHOF** ❸

Spui

**Spui Square**

GED. BEG.

WATER-STEEG

TAKST.

SPUI

Rokin Ⓜ

GRIMBURGWAL

**Grimburgwal**

TURFDRAAGS.

ALLARD-PIERSON MUSEUM

OUDE TURFMARKT

ROKIN

HANDBOOGS.

VOETBOOGS.

MUSEUM OF THE CANALS

BERLING STRAAT

DE KRIJTBERG

**Konigs-plein**

KALVERTOREN MALL

HELIGEWEG

KALVERSTRAAT

NIEUWE

KONINGSPLEIN

Koningsplein

**FLOWER MARKET** ⓾

SINGEL

SINGEL

SINGEL

ST. LUCIIE-STRAAT

OPEN-HART-STEEG

SOUTHERN

LEIDSE-STRAAT

To 14

WIJDE HEISTE

Keizersgracht

To Leidseplein

CANAL

Keizersgracht

HERENGRACHT

"GOLDEN CURVE"

Herengracht

BELT

To Rijksmuseum, Museumplein, Van Gogh Museum & Stedelijk Museum

**Muntplein**
**MINT TOWER**

Muntplein

TUSCHINSKI THEATER

REGULIERS

**Tuschinski Theater** ㉓

DWARSSTR.

VIJZELSTRAAT

HERENGRACHT

To Heineken Experience

## SIGHTS

1. Amsterdam Museum
2. Anne Frank House
3. Begijnhof
4. Bike Rentals (4)
5. Canal Boat Tours (3)
6. Central Library
7. Damrak Sex Museum
8. De Hortus Botanical Garden
9. Erotic Museum
10. Flower Market
11. Gassan Diamonds
12. Hash, Marijuana & Hemp Museum
13. Hermitage Amsterdam
14. Houseboat Museum
15. Jewish Museum
16. New Church
17. Old Church
18. Our Lord in the Attic Mus.
19. Portuguese Synagogue
20. Rembrandt's House
21. Rembrandtplein
22. Royal Palace
23. Tuschinski Theater
24. Waterlooplein Flea Market
25. Westerkerk
26. Willet-Holthuysen House

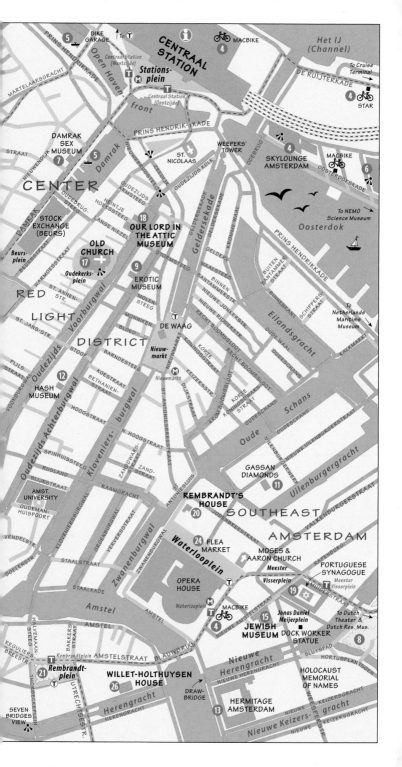

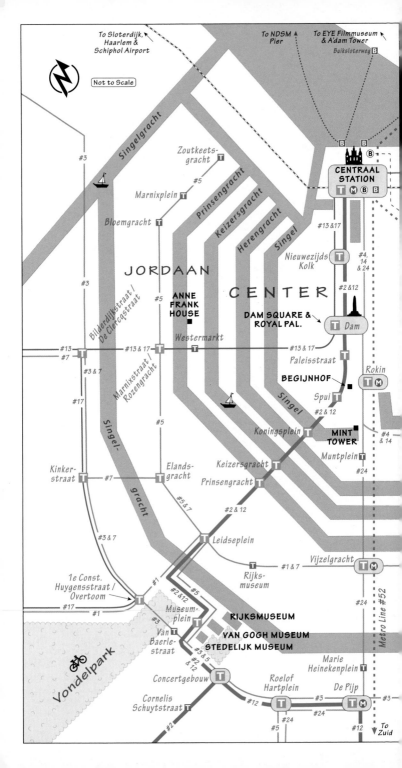

# Amsterdam's Public Transportation

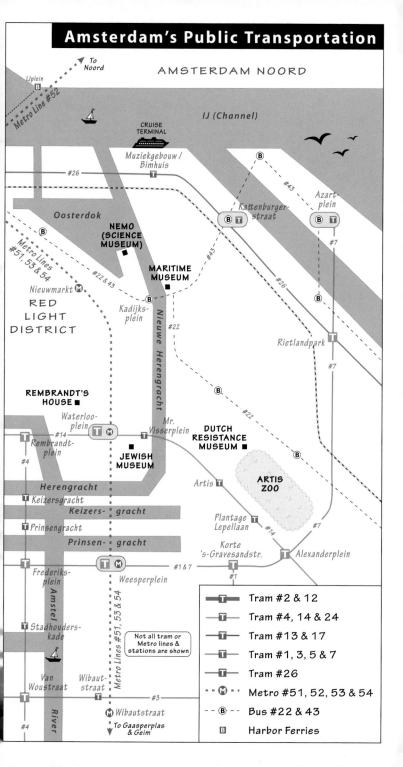

To Noord

IJplein
B

Metro Line #52

AMSTERDAM NOORD

IJ (Channel)

CRUISE
TERMINAL

Muziekgebouw /
Bimhuis
T

#26

B

#43

Azart-
plein
B T

Oosterdok

Kattenburger-
straat
B T

B

Metro Lines
#51, 53 & 54

NEMO
(SCIENCE
MUSEUM)

#22 & 43

#45

MARITIME
MUSEUM

Nieuwmarkt M

RED
LIGHT
DISTRICT

Kadijks-
plein
B

Nieuwe Herengracht

#26

B

#22

Rietlandpark
T

#7

REMBRANDT'S
HOUSE

Waterloo-
plein
T M

#14

Rembrandt-
plein
T

#4

Mr.
Visserplein
T

JEWISH
MUSEUM

B

#22

DUTCH
RESISTANCE
MUSEUM

ARTIS
ZOO

B

Herengracht

Keizersgracht
T

Keizers- gracht

Prinsengracht
T

Prinsen- gracht

T

Frederiks-
plein
T

Amstel

T Stadhouders-
kade

Van
Woustraat
T

#4

Artis T

Plantage
Lepellaan
T

#14

Korte
's-Gravesandstr.
T

T M

#1 & 7

Weesperplein

Not all tram or
Metro lines &
stations are shown

Metro Lines #51, 53 & 54

Wibaut-
straat
T

#3

M Wibautstraat

To Gaasperplas
& Geim

River

#1

#7

Alexanderplein
T

## Legend

| | |
|---|---|
| T━ | Tram #2 & 12 |
| T━ | Tram #4, 14 & 24 |
| T━ | Tram #13 & 17 |
| T━ | Tram #1, 3, 5 & 7 |
| T━ | Tram #26 |
| ··M·· | Metro #51, 52, 53 & 54 |
| --B-- | Bus #22 & 43 |
| B | Harbor Ferries |

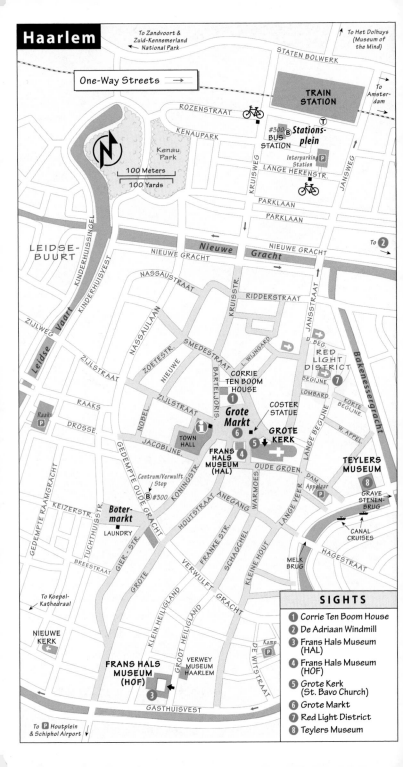

# Haarlem

To Zandvoort &
Zuid-Kennemerland
National Park

To Het Dolhuys
(Museum of
the Mind)

STATEN BOLWERK

One-Way Streets ⟶

TRAIN
STATION

To
Amster-
dam

ROZENSTRAAT

#300
BUS
STATION

Stations-
plein

KENAUPARK

Kenau
Park

KRUISWEG

LANGE HERENSTR.

Interparking
Station

JANSWEG

100 Meters
100 Yards

PARKLAAN

PARKLAAN

LEIDSE-
BUURT

KINDERHUISSINGEL

Nieuwe Gracht

NIEUWE GRACHT

NIEUWE GRACHT

To ②

ZIJLWEG

Leidse Vaart

KINDERHUISVEST

NASSAUSTRAAT

KRUISSTR.

RIDDERSTRAAT

JANSSTRAAT

ZIJLSTRAAT

NASSAULAAN

NIEUWE

ZOETESTR.

SMEDESTRAAT

L. WIJNGARD.

D. BEG.

RED
LIGHT
DISTRICT

⑦

BEGIJNE.

LOMBARD.

KORTE
BEGIJNE.

RAAKS

NOBEL

ZIJLSTRAAT

BARTELJORIS.

CORRIE
TEN BOOM
HOUSE

①

COSTER
STATUE

LANGE BEGIJNE.

W. APPEL.

Bakenessergracht

Raaks
P

DROSSE

JACOBIJNE.

TOWN
HALL

i

Grote
Markt

⑥

⑤

GROTE
KERK

④

TEYLERS
MUSEUM

⑧

GEDEMPTE OUDE GRACHT

FRANS
HALS
MUSEUM
(HAL)

OUDE GROEN.

DAM

GRAVE
STENEN-
BRUG

Boter-
markt

LAUNDRY

Centrum/Verwulft
Stop

B #300

KONINGSTR.

HOUTSTRAAT

ANEGANG

WARMOES.

LANGE VEER

APPELAAR
P

CANAL
CRUISES

GEDEMPTE RAAMGRACHT

KEIZERSTR.

TUCHTHUISSTR.

GIER. STR.

BREESTRAAT

FRANKE STR.

SCHAGCHEL

VERWULFT GRACHT

KLEINE HOUT

HAGESTRAAT

MELK
BRUG

DE WITSTRAAT

Kamp.
P

To Koepel-
Kathedraal

NIEUWE
KERK

GROTE

KLEIN HEILIGLAND

GROOT HEILIGLAND

VERWEY
MUSEUM
HAARLEM

FRANS HALS
MUSEUM
(HOF)

③

GASTHUISVEST

To P Houtplein
& Schiphol Airport

## SIGHTS

① Corrie Ten Boom House
② De Adriaan Windmill
③ Frans Hals Museum (HAL)
④ Frans Hals Museum (HOF)
⑤ Grote Kerk (St. Bavo Church)
⑥ Grote Markt
⑦ Red Light District
⑧ Teylers Museum

# Western Netherlands

## LEGEND

- A-7 — Freeway
- Other Roads
- Major Rail Line
- Ferry Lines
- ✈ Airport
- ■ Museum/Landmark/Other Point of Interest

10 Kilometers
10 Miles

**N**

**Wadden Islands**

Ameland

Terschelling

Vlieland

Waddenzee

**North Sea**

Leeuwarden

Harlingen

A-31

**FRIESLAND**

A-32

A-7

Heerenveen

Texel

t'Horntje

Den Helder

AFSLUITDIJK

A-7

IJsselmeer

Hindeloopen

Medemblik

Stavoren

A-6

**NORTH HOLLAND**

N-9

A-7

N-242

**ZUIDERZEE MUSEUM**

**HISTORIC TRIANGLE**

Enkhuizen

HOUTRIBDIJK

Emmeloord

N-352

**SCHOKLAND MUSEUM**

To Newcastle, England

Alkmaar

A-9

Hoorn

N-307

**Markermeer**

Lelystad

**FLEVO-LAND**

**ZAANSE SCHANS**

A-7

Edam

Volendam

Marken

A-6

Z.Z. Schans Stn.

A-8

N-247

N-302

IJmuiden

**Haarlem**

Sloterdijk

**Amsterdam**

Almere

A-28

Zandvoort

N-206

A-9

Harderwijk

**KEUKENHOF**

A-4

A-9

Schiphol

Aalsmeer

A-1

A-27

Hilversum

To Berlin

Scheveningen

**PEACE PALACE**

A-44

**Leiden**

A-2

Amersfoort

A-1

**KRÖLLER-MÜLLER MUS.**

**The Hague**

A-4

A-28

Barneveld

Otterlo

N-304

Utrecht

A-30

A-50

**Delft**

A-12

Woerden

Hoge Veluwe Nat'l Park

To Hoek

Rotterdam The Hague

A-207

Gouda

Nieuwegein

A-27

A-12

**NETH. OPEN-AIR MUSEUM**

**Rhine (Lek)**

**SOUTH HOLLAND**

**Nederrijn**

**Arnhem**

A-4

A-16

**Rotterdam**

**DELFS-HAVEN**

A-15

Tiel

A-50

**MAESLANT BARRIER**

A-15

A-15

A-50

A-29

A-16

Gorinchem

**Rhine (Waal)**

Nijmegen

Dordrecht

A-27

A-2

A-73

To Antwerp & Brussels

N-59

A-59

**Maas**

A-59

s-Hertogenbosch

# The Netherlands

See Western Netherlands detail map

Wadden Islands

Waddenzee

AFSLUITDIJK

North
Sea

Texel
t'Horntje
Den Helder

Hinde-
loopen

Stavoren

A-7

NORTH
HOLLAND

Medemblik

IJsselmeer

ZUIDERZEE
MUSEUM

Enkhuizen

HOUTRIB-
DIJK
(N-307)

Alkmaar

Hoorn

Marker-
meer

Lelystad

To Newcastle, England

ZAANSE
SCHANS

Edam
Volendam

FLEVO

IJmuiden

Amsterdam

Marken

Haarlem

A-6

Zandvoort

KEUKENHOF

Schiphol

A-4

Leiden

Aalsmeer

A-2

Amers-
foort

Scheveningen

SOUTH
HOLLAND

Utrecht

The Hague

A-12

To Harwich,
England

Hoek van
Holland

Neder-
rijn

Delft

Gouda   Rhine
(Lek)

MAESLANT
BARRIER

Rotterdam

A-15

Rhine
(Waal)

A-16   A-27

Maas

s-Hertogen-
bosch

Zierikzee

Roosendaal

Breda

A-2

ZEELAND

Middelburg

A-58

Eindhoven

Vlissingen

Zeebrugge

Bruges

FLANDERS

Antwerp

BELGIUM

E-313

Ghent

Brussels

Hasselt

Kortrijk

E-17

Brussels

E-40

Leuven

WATERLOO

FRANCE

WALLONIA

Lille

Tournai

To
Paris

# Let's Keep on Travelin'

Your trip doesn't need to end.

Follow Rick on social media!